■ THE RESOURCE FOR THE INDEPENDENT TRAVELER

"The guides are aimed not only at young budget travelers but at the indepedent traveler; a sort of streetwise cookbook for traveling alone."

—The New York Times

"Unbeatable; good sight-seeing advice; up-to-date info on restaurants, hotels, and inns; a commitment to money-saving travel; and a wry style that brightens nearly every page."

—The Washington Post

"Lighthearted and sophisticated, informative and fun to read. [Let's Go] helps the novice traveler navigate like a knowledgeable old hand."

—Atlanta Journal-Constitution

"A world-wise traveling companion—always ready with friendly advice and helpful hints, all sprinkled with a bit of wit."

—The Philadelphia Inquirer

■ THE BEST TRAVEL BARGAINS IN YOUR PRICE RANGE

"All the dirt, dirt cheap."

—People

"Anything you need to know about budget traveling is detailed in this book."

—The Chicago Sun-Times

"Let's Go follows the creed that you don't have to toss your life's savings to the wind to travel—unless you want to."

—The Salt Lake Tribune

■ REAL ADVICE FOR REAL EXPERIENCES

"The writers seem to have experienced every rooster-packed bus and lunar-surfaced mattress about which they write."

—The New York Times

"A guide should tell you what to expect from a destination. Here Let's Go shines."

—The Chicago Tribune

LET'S GO PUBLICATIONS

TRAVEL GUIDES

Alaska & the Pacific Northwest 2003
Australia 2003
Austria & Switzerland 2003
Britain & Ireland 2003
California 2003
Central America 8th edition
Chile 1st edition **NEW TITLE**
China 4th edition
Costa Rica 1st edition **NEW TITLE**
Eastern Europe 2003
Egypt 2nd edition
Europe 2003
France 2003
Germany 2003
Greece 2003
Hawaii 2003 **NEW TITLE**
India & Nepal 7th edition
Ireland 2003
Israel 4th edition
Italy 2003
Mexico 19th edition
Middle East 4th edition
New Zealand 6th edition
Peru, Ecuador & Bolivia 3rd edition
South Africa 5th edition
Southeast Asia 8th edition
Southwest USA 2003
Spain & Portugal 2003
Thailand 1st edition **NEW TITLE**
Turkey 5th edition
USA 2003
Western Europe 2003

CITY GUIDES

Amsterdam 2003
Barcelona 2003
Boston 2003
London 2003
New York City 2003
Paris 2003
Rome 2003
San Francisco 2003
Washington, D.C. 2003

MAP GUIDES

Amsterdam
Berlin
Boston
Chicago
Dublin
Florence
Hong Kong
London
Los Angeles
Madrid
New Orleans
New York City
Paris
Prague
Rome
San Francisco
Seattle
Sydney
Venice
Washington, D.C.

LET'S GO

HAWAII
2003

ERZULIE D. COQUILLON EDITOR
ALLISON MELIA ASSOCIATE EDITOR
MOLLIE H. CHEN ASSOCIATE EDITOR

RESEARCHER-WRITERS
ANGIE CHEN
SARAH ROTMAN
ERIC SHEARER
BRYDEN SWEENEY-TAYLOR
MARC WALLENSTEIN

BRIAN R. WALSH MANAGING EDITOR
ARIEL BENJAMIN ERGAS SHWAYDER MAP EDITOR
MELISSA RUDOLPH TYPESETTER

MACMILLAN

HELPING LET'S GO
If you want to share your discoveries, suggestions, or corrections, please drop us a line. We read every piece of correspondence, whether a postcard, a 10-page email, or a coconut. Please note that mail received after May 2003 may be too late for the 2004 book, but will be kept for future editions. **Address mail to:**

Let's Go: Hawaii
67 Mount Auburn Street
Cambridge, MA 02138
USA

Visit Let's Go at **http://www.letsgo.com,** or send email to:

feedback@letsgo.com
Subject: "Let's Go: Hawaii"

In addition to the invaluable travel advice our readers share with us, many are kind enough to offer their services as researchers or editors. Unfortunately, our charter enables us to employ only currently enrolled Harvard students.

Published in Great Britain 2003 by Macmillan, an imprint of Pan Macmillan Ltd.
20 New Wharf Road, London N1 9RR
Basingstoke and Oxford
Associated companies throughout the world
www.panmacmillan.com

Maps by David Lindroth copyright © 2003 by St. Martin's Press.

Published in the United States of America by St. Martin's Press.

ISBN: 1-4050-0057 0
First edition
10 9 8 7 6 5 4 3 2 1

Let's Go: Hawaii is written by Let's Go Publications, 67 Mount Auburn Street, Cambridge, MA 02138, USA.

Let's Go® and the LG logo are trademarks of Let's Go, Inc.
Printed in the USA on recycled paper with soy ink.

WHO WE ARE

A NEW LET'S GO FOR 2003

With a sleeker look and innovative new content, we have revamped the entire series to reflect more than ever the needs and interests of the independent traveler. Here are just some of the improvements you will notice when traveling with the new *Let's Go*.

MORE PRICE OPTIONS

Still the best resource for budget travelers, *Let's Go* recognizes that everyone needs the occassional indulgence. Our "Big Splurges" indicate establishments that are actually worth those extra pennies (pulas, pesos, or pounds), and price-level symbols (❶ ❷ ❸ ❹ ❺) allow you to quickly determine whether an accommodation or restaurant will break the bank. We may have diversified, but we'll never lose our budget focus—"Hidden Deals" reveal the best-kept travel secrets.

BEYOND THE TOURIST EXPERIENCE

Our Alternatives to Tourism chapter offers ideas on immersing yourself in a new community through study, work, or volunteering.

AN INSIDER'S PERSPECTIVE

As always, every item is written and researched by our on-site writers. This year we have highlighted more viewpoints to help you gain an even more thorough understanding of the places you are visiting.

IN RECENT NEWS. *Let's Go* correspondents around the globe report back on current regional issues that may affect you as a traveler.

CONTRIBUTING WRITERS. Respected scholars and former *Let's Go* writers discuss topics on society and culture, going into greater depth than the usual guidebook summary.

THE LOCAL STORY. From the Parisian monk toting a cell phone to the Russian *babushka* confronting capitalism, *Let's Go* shares its revealing conversations with local personalities—a unique glimpse of what matters to real people.

FROM THE ROAD. Always helpful and sometimes downright hilarious, our researchers share useful insights on the typical (and atypical) travel experience.

SLIMMER SIZE

Don't be fooled by our new, smaller size. *Let's Go* is still packed with invaluable travel advice, but now it's easier to carry with a more compact design.

FORTY-THREE YEARS OF WISDOM

For over four decades *Let's Go* has provided the most up-to-date information on the hippest cafes, the most pristine beaches, and the best routes from border to border. It all started in 1960 when a few well-traveled students at Harvard University handed out a 20-page mimeographed pamphlet of their tips on budget travel to passengers on student charter flights to Europe. From humble beginnings, *Let's Go* has grown to cover six continents and *Let's Go: Europe* still reigns as the world's best-selling travel guide. This year we've beefed up our coverage of Latin America with *Let's Go: Costa Rica* and *Let's Go: Chile;* on the other side of the globe, we've added *Let's Go: Thailand* and *Let's Go: Hawaii.* Our new guides bring the total number of titles to 61, each infused with the spirit of adventure that travelers around the world have come to count on.

CONTENTS

LIST OF MAPS

ACKNOWLEDGMENTS

Mahalo and plenty of love to the RWs, and a special shout out to erstwhile locals Damien and Braddah Joe for extra aloha spirit. Thanks to Brian, Prod for answering every *last* question, Finance for funding trips to Paradise (and by that, we mean Bertucci's), Ari, and Alex Ewing. Mattie G.—buena suerte, comrade. OZ, parting is such sweet sorrow—like a shot through the heart, really. To our readers: good luck, enjoy, *hele on* (let's go)!

ERZ THANKS Mom, Naomi, GM and GP, for the love and support; Team Hawaii for hard work and dedication. To Mollie and Allison, a world of thanks for a summer of laughs. Many mahalos and best of luck to friends, roommates, and all the rest.

MOLLIE THANKS Erz for being our fearless leader and working twice as hard as anyone else. Allie for constant amusement and reality checks. Love to Mom and Dad for Maine getaways, coffee money, and everything else. Stinky, I love you. Mahalo to PP, GG, and the Loui's for research help and a wonderful vacation. Benita, Claudine, Alisha, Shweta, Molly, and Christina for all-around fabulousness. Love to Kristen, Tam, Danny, Casey, and other uber-amazing friends—thanks for being there.

ALLISON THANKS Erz for vision, guidance, and daily laughs. Mollie for sugar & spice & everything nice. Mom and Dad for love, support, and life itself. Annie for wild rides and being my party pal. Amy, Amanda, Ashley, Abby, and Alex for always being ready for fun. Sophie, Sabrina, and Natalie for girl talk. The newly-legal SFC and Bellagio buds Ace, Vegas, and Flippy, for rowdiness and hilarity. Bottoms up to the rest of the 10.

ARI THANKS First and foremost, mapland. Especially Julie for putting up with my constant barrage of questions. The Hawaii girls, who were blazingly fast, making life easier. Cheers to BBC, test match cricket, and NPR for getting me through long days. Salutations to my roomies with our unfathomable obsession with the trials and tribulations of the Griffins. All my love to Abigail.

Editor
Erzulie D. Coquillon
Associate Editors
Allison Melia, Mollie H. Chen
Managing Editor
Brian R. Walsh
Map Editor
Ariel Benjamin Ergas Shwayder

Publishing Director
Matthew Gibson
Editor-in-Chief
Brian R. Walsh
Production Manager
C. Winslow Clayton
Cartography Manager
Julie Stephens
Design Manager
Amy Cain
Editorial Managers
Christopher Blazejewski,
Abigail Burger, D. Cody Dydek,
Harriett Green, Angela Mi Young Hur,
Marla Kaplan, Celeste Ng
Financial Manager
Noah Askin
Marketing & Publicity Managers
Michelle Bowman, Adam M. Grant
New Media Managers
Jesse Tov, Kevin Yip
Online Manager
Amélie Cherlin
Personnel Managers
Alex Leichtman, Owen Robinson
Production Associates
Caleb Epps, David Muehlke
Network Administrators
Steven Aponte, Eduardo Montoya
Design Associate
Juice Fong
Financial Assistant
Suzanne Siu
Office Coordinators
Alex Ewing, Adam Kline,
Efrat Kussell

Director of Advertising Sales
Erik Patton
Senior Advertising Associates
Patrick Donovan, Barbara Eghan,
Fernanda Winthrop
Advertising Artwork Editor
Leif Holtzman
Cover Photo Research
Laura Wyss

President
Bradley J. Olson
General Manager
Robert B. Rombauer
Assistant General Manager
Anne E. Chisholm

RESEARCHER-WRITERS

Angie Chen
Kauai

A researcher for *Let's Go: Mexico 2001*, and editor of both *Let's Go: Mexico 2002* and *2003*, Angie was more than a little qualified. Her past trips to Hawaii and academic background in Environmental Science and Public Policy were just gravy. Despite an untimely ankle injury, Angie blazed through Kauai's rainforests and consumer jungles with efficiency and aplomb. With Hawaii conquered, Angie is ready for her next adventure. Costa Rica, here she comes.

Sarah Rotman
Maui and Oahu's North Shore

Having visited each of the Hawaiian Islands on previous occasions, Sarah arrived in Maui armed with a mountain of experience at Let's Go—among the many positions she's held, Sarah edited brand-new *Let's Go: Boston* in 2001, and served as Publishing Director for the 2002 series. This student of the visual environment added researching to her resume in 2003, cranking out flawless copy before returning to Boston to work at a consulting firm and as a TA at Harvard.

Eric Shearer
Oahu

Eric approached his first Let's Go route equipped with a dog-eared copy of James Michener's *Hawaii*, a love of the islands, and more than a little enthusiasm. Charming his way from coast to coast, Eric unearthed the best that paradise has to offer, and chalked up quite a few adventures in the meantime. Hawaii has yet to relinquish its hold on Eric; he is on an extended vacation in Oahu and plans to freelance write or teach to finance his island-boy lifestyle.

Bryden Sweeney-Taylor
The Big Island

Two semesters on the road for *Let's Go* as a researcher for *Let's Go: Southwest USA 2002* and *Let's Go: South Africa 2003*, a summer's worth of work experience at an organic food cooperative near Ka Lae, and an academic background in Folklore and Mythology served Bryden well as he illuminated Big Island life and culture and dug up local legends for Team Hawaii. He returned to Boston for a brief stint as a soccer coach before delving into his thesis.

Marc Wallenstein
Molokai, Lanai, Southeastern Oahu

Marc tackled his itinerary with all the self-assurance and competence one would expect from a two-time veteran of Let's Go (he researched for *Let's Go: Italy 2000* and edited *Let's Go: Italy 2001*). Whether befriending surly military men or living it up at a local luau, this Texan philosopher acquired a newfound appreciation for the aloha spirit. Next stop: Down Under, as Marc embarks on a year-long photography project in Australia.

CONTRIBUTING WRITERS

Maren Lau was a Researcher-Writer in Hawaii for *Let's Go: California & Hawaii 1997*. She now lives in Maui and attends business school.

Michael Seltzer is the Director of Business Enterprises for Sustainable Travel.

Stephanie L. Smith is a former Let's Go Research-Writer and has worked as a freelance writer for Citysearch Los Angeles. She is currently the features writer/editor for the online division of Channel One News.

HOW TO USE THIS BOOK

INTRODUCTORY MATERIAL. The first chapter, **Discover Hawaii,** will introduce you to the Hawaiian islands and get you primed for an unforgettable adventure. If you grow so anxious to get going that you can barely think straight, fear not! Our **Suggested Itineraries** have a little something for everyone, and make planning the perfect trip a no-brainer.

ESSENTIALS. All the practical information involved in traveling can get downright pesky. Flip to this section to get the quick and easy guide to Hawaii, including getting there, getting around, finding a place to stay, and staying safe.

LIFE AND TIMES. This chapter holds the answers to all your burning questions about Hawaii. Why do so many Hawaiian words sound the same? Who was Kamehameha the Great? What's the deal with Spam? History, culture, music—you name it. It's all here.

COVERAGE. There is a chapter is dedicated to each one of the major Hawaiian islands—Oahu, Maui, Molokai, Lanai, Big Island, and Kauai. The Northwestern Hawaiian Islands, Kahoolawe, and Niihau also have their own, shorter chapters. The **black tabs** in the margins will help you navigate the book quickly and easily.

GLOSSARY. Once in Hawaii, you'll find that although the islands are technically a part of the US, they have a language all their own. In our Hawaiian and pidgin glossaries, we've included many commonly used words and phrases to help you avoid looking (and sounding) like a tourist.

PRICE RANGES AND RANKINGS. Our researchers list establishments in order of value from best to worst. Our absolute favorites are denoted by the Let's Go thumbs-up (🚫). Since the best value does not always mean the cheapest price, we have incorporated a system of price ranges into the guide. The table below lists how prices fall within each bracket.

HAWAII	❶	❷	❸	❹	❺
ACCOMMODATIONS	$0-25	$25-65	$65-110	$110-150	$150+
FOOD	under $7	$7-10	$10-15	$15-20	$20+

GRAYBOXES AND ICONBOXES. Grayboxes provide a wealth of information, including facts about historical events and information on Hawaiian culture. **White boxes,** on the other hand, contain important practical information, such as warnings, helpful hints, and further resources.

PHONE CODES AND TELEPHONE NUMBERS. The area code for phone numbers is 808, unless noted otherwise. Phone numbers are preceded by the ☎ icon.

A NOTE TO OUR READERS The information for this book was gathered by *Let's Go* researchers from May through August of 2002. Each listing is based on one researcher's opinion, formed during his or her visit at a particular time. Those traveling at other times may have different experiences since prices, dates, hours, and conditions are always subject to change. You are urged to check the facts presented in this book beforehand to avoid inconvenience and surprises.

Hawaii

PACIFIC OCEAN

Kauai
- Princeville
- Kilauea
- Haena
- Kapaa
- Wailua
- Mana
- Lihu'e
- Waimea
- Koloa
- Eleele

Kaulakahi Channel

Kii Landing
- Puuwai

Niihau

Kauai Channel

Waho Shelf

Oahu
- Kahuku
- Waialua
- Haleiwa
- Kaaawa
- Wahiawa
- Kaneohe Bay
- Kaneohe
- Kailua
- Waianae
- Waimanalo
- Pearl Harbor
- Ewa Beach
- Kapolei
- Maunalua Bay

Honolulu

Penguin Bank

Kaiwi Channel

RUSSIA
CHINA
Hong Kong
Tokyo
JAPAN
3853mi
5549mi
INDONESIA
5079mi
AUSTRALIA
Sydney
PACIFIC OCEAN

Anchorage
2782mi
Vancouver
2708mi
CANADA
New York
4960mi
San Francisco
UNITED STATES
Miami
2394mi
Los Angeles
2561mi
4857mi
Mexico City
3784mi
MEXICO
Honolulu, HI

World Air Travel
equidistant projection

XII

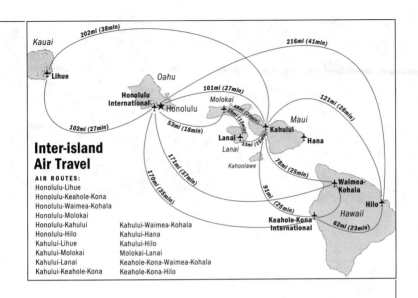

Inter-island Air Travel

AIR ROUTES:
Honolulu-Lihue
Honolulu-Keahole-Kona
Honolulu-Waimea-Kohala
Honolulu-Molokai
Honolulu-Kahului
Honolulu-Hilo
Kahului-Lihue
Kahului-Molokai
Kahului-Lanai
Kahului-Keahole-Kona

Kahului-Waimea-Kohala
Kahului-Hana
Kahului-Hilo
Molokai-Lanai
Keahole-Kona-Waimea-Kohala
Keahole-Kona-Hilo

DISCOVER
HAWAII

The most remote island group in the world, the Hawaiian islands are separated from the mainland US by over 2000 miles and a less quantifiable disparity in culture. Hawaii is composed of 8 major islands—Big Island, Maui, Molokai, Lanai, Oahu, Kauai, and Niihau—and over 120 other small islands and atolls. The so-called "crossroads of the Pacific," the islands have developed into a unique environment of tropical enticements and melting pot of cultures. Hawaii is a geological wonder, encompassing within its shores a wide variety of climates and ecosystems. The awe-inspiring landscape—including rainforests brimming with tropical fruit and desolate remnants of lava flows, all backed by the thundering Pacific—is alive, in every sense of the word, with the forces of creation. The heartbeat of the Earth is so strong here that it is almost palpable, a sense that perhaps explains the strong ties that Hawaiians feel to their land. The allure of the land has enticed voyagers from Polynesia, Europe, Asia, and beyond; and today Hawaii is the most ethnically diverse state in the US. Residents of radically different backgrounds are united under the affectionate term *kama'aina*, and in turn, they add to the brilliant mosaic of the islands. The culture of the islands is an amalgamation of native Hawaiian tradition, laid-back surfer lifestyle, the influence of an on-going military presence, waves of international tourists, and more, all united by the aloha spirit. Generalizations are few and far between in this dynamic, colorful state, however. Along every beach there is yet another more secluded stretch of sand to call your own, and beyond every stunning vista there is an even more breathtaking sight. The diversity of land, people, cultures, and experiences is what makes Hawaii both unique and utterly intoxicating. In Hawaii, the journey never ends.

FACTS AND FIGURES

CAPITAL: Honolulu.	**STATE SPAM CONSUMPTION RATE:** 1100 cans per day.
STATE POPULATION: 1,211,537.	
STATE MOTTO: *Ua mau ke ea o ka 'aina i ka pono* (The life of the land is perpetuated in righteousness).	**NUMBER OF LETTERS IN THE HAWAIIAN ALPHABET:** 12.
	PERCENTAGE OF THE WORLD'S REEFS IN HAWAIIAN WATERS: 70%.

WHEN TO GO

How soon can you leave? With year-round temperatures rarely straying far from 80 degrees Fahrenheit, Hawaii's climate is always welcoming. Even the hotter summer months are kept in check by cooling trade winds, and the ocean averages a pleasant 75 degrees Fahrenheit. Though wind and rainstorms are more common in the winter, they usually pass through the islands quickly and without incident.

DISCOVER

Hawaii's mountainous regions and valleys are often rainy and damp. Weather is often localized, however, and beach-goers are almost always able to find sunny patches on the drier, leeward sides of the islands.

Depending on the focus of your vacation, there may be specific times when you should travel. Winter is surf season, when hard-core boardriders and their groupies pilgrimage to Oahu's North Shore for the biggest waves of the year. Families with young children should consider a summer vacation, when swimming conditions are generally safer than at other times of year, and there are guaranteed to be plenty of other tykes cavorting in the waves. December through April is considered high season in Hawaii; accommodation prices generally drop a bit at other times of year, but flights are consistently expensive.

THINGS TO DO

Hawaii is a veritable smorgasbord of activities, sights, and experiences. Outdoorsy types will be pleasantly overwhelmed by the sheer number of hikes to tackle and mountains to tame. Hedonists will find more than enough sand and surf to occupy the days, and ample frozen concoctions to fill the nights. If one too many mai tais isn't slowing you down, Hawaii's cultural and historical sights provide a contrast to the seemingly endless parade of white-, black-, and red-sand beaches. Throughout this adventure, Hawaii's local culture provides a vivid backdrop, wooing travelers with colorful tales of Old Hawaii, tasty island treats, and a genuinely welcoming attitude.

HIKING. In Hawaii, it is not only the journey that is the reward. Though the diversity of the landscape ensures that any outing—from a short hike to a multi-day trek—is rich with plant species and sights, many trails lead to stunning overlooks, otherworldly lava flows, hidden beaches, and magnificent waterfalls. Hikers can look forward to uncovering all the things one would expect from a passage through paradise.

Oahu is not known as a haven for the hard-core hiker, but it does offer a few trails of varied difficulty in and around Honolulu. The **Mauka system** of trails (p. 114) is suitable for families and those looking for a brief escape from city life. A hike at **Diamond Head** (p. 130) is easy enough for just about anyone (baby steps of the Hawaii hiking experience, if you will) and provides an uninterrupted view of both the city and the sea. The **Maunawili Trails** (p. 161) on the eastern side of Oahu are slightly longer and tougher than the Mauka system, and offer a few good views.

Maui holds the **Haleakala National Park** (p. 225), an island highlight for everyone from the casual walker to the avid outdoorsman. Backcountry camping is available in the park, and trails of various levels lead past cinder cones and rare flora to the summit. Hit the Silversword loop of the Halemau'u trail to see the rare *ahinahina* (silversword) plant that grows only on the slopes of Haleakala. **Ahini-Kinau Natural Area Reserve** (p. 198) near Wailea in South Maui, offers another opportunity to hike through lava fields. The field is the remainder of a lava flow created during Haleakala's last eruption in 1790. The **Twin Falls Hike** and **Waikamoi Ridge Walk** that branch out from the Road to Hana (p. 219), are both attractive and manageable. South of Hana, the **Kipahulu Valley** and **Ohe'o Gulch** (p. 223), technically a portion of Haleakala National Park, have several picturesque waterfall trails. A remote forest in Upcountry Maui, **Polipoli State Park** (p. 233) has several trails good for hiking and mountain biking.

Molokai has plenty to offer those looking to get far enough off the beaten path to forge their own trails. The **Kamakou Preserve** (p. 251) is a rugged area of unique flora and fauna, much of which is unique to Hawaii. Guided tours run by the Nature Conservancy are available to help you tame the wild land, although getting to and hiking through the preserve on your own can be a thrilling, muddy adventure. The **Kalaupapa Peninsula** (p. 248), the site of a former leper colony, draws the most tourists to the island. The steep hike down to the peninsula is a rewarding way to reach the poignant site. East of Kaunakakai, the highlight of **Halawa Valley** is the stunning **Moa'ula Falls** (p. 260), at the end of a moderately challenging trek.

Big Island is well-known for housing **Hawaii Volcanoes National Park** (p. 292), a must-see for outdoor enthusiasts. The volcano Kilauea, within the park, has been continuously erupting since 1983, providing visitors with a glimpse of nature's raw power. Choose your own adventure in the park—there are a number of hikes, which pass through varied terrain of lava flows, lava tubes, and steam vents, or up Mauna Loa. The trails on **Mauna Kea** (p. 303), on Saddle Road near Volcanoes National Park, present another opportunity to view the amazing topography of the region. **Waipi'o Valley** (p. 336), once the religious and political center of ancient Hawaii, has since been reclaimed by the rainforest. The valley is a primal jungle, and a unique hiking experience. Be sure to check out **Hi'ilawe Falls** while you're there—it's the highest single-drop waterfall in Hawaii. An easy path leads to **Akaka Falls** (p. 291), a highlight of the Hamakua Coast.

The lush rainforest trails of **Kauai** create a paradise for the hard-core hiker. The island's true mecca is the famed **Kalalau Trail** (p. 386), the last remaining path cut by ancient Hawaiian traders as they traveled across the **Na Pali Coast.** The coast is now accessible solely by foot or by boat. The jagged cliffs of Na Pali are only the beginning—Waimea Canyon's colorful red cliffs rise from the center of **Waimea Canyon State Park** (p. 402). Beyond it, the 40 miles of breathtaking trails in **Koke'e State Park** (p. 403) offer a little something for everyone. Canyon trail is Koke'e park's most popular hike, and traces the edges of Waimea Canyon, opening out into spectacular views. For those in need of a little guidance, **Kauai Nature Tours** (p. 390) in Po'ipu leads adventures through the island's many natural wonders.

ADVENTURE SPORTS. Hawaii takes sports to a new level. Across the islands, there are athletes and travelers toeing the edge, pushing the limits, and expanding the scope of what is possible. At the same time, adventure sports aren't necessarily just for the most gung-ho of them all—for every grueling hike, there's an equally pleasant one and for every big surf beach, there's a handful of innocuous "learning" beaches. Whatever your level of expertise, Hawaii has you covered.

On **Oahu**, surfing reigns supreme. Every year, countless people catch their first waves at **Baby Queen's** (p. 136) in Waikiki, and many others perfect their techniques on Oahu's innumerable beaches. The winter months bring mammoth waves to the **North Shore** (p. 161) and the Leeward Coast's **Makaha Beach** (p. 178), as well as the surf junkies who roam the globe in search of the perfect wave. The rest of the island is not without appeal; **Kailua Beach** (p. 159), with its seemingly constant breeze, is a windsurfer's paradise and on the eastern coast, **Sandy Beach** (p. 144) and **Makapu'u** (p. 144) are to boogie-boarding what the North Shore is to surfing.

The **Big Island** offers opportunities for on-land adventures, with mountain bike and ski tours on **Mauna Kea** (p. 305) as well as biking, horseback riding, and ATV-ing in **Waipi'o Valley** (p. 337). Snorkelers will delight in the underwater treats of **Kealakekua Bay** (p. 324) and **Lapakahi State Historical Park** (p. 346). Big Island is also the site of the most extreme event of them all—the **Ironman Triathlon** (p. 317) held annually in October.

Maui beckons adventurers with its many charms. Helicopter tours run out of **Kahului** (p. 183), dolphin- and whale-watching cruises leave from **Ma'alea** (p. 189) and snorkel trips to **Molokini** (p. 189) are popular in **Kihei** (p. 189). **Pa'ia** beaches (p. 214) are prime surfing and windsurfing spots and within **Haleakala National Park** (p. 225), several companies offer bike tours. The surf spot **Jaws** is known for its immense waves that are too big to paddle over—extreme surfers have jet-skis tow them in.

Over on Kauai, beginners can get an easy introduction to the art of wave-riding on **Hanalei's** (p. 382) gentle waves. Advanced kayakers flex their muscles as they navigate the **Na Pali Coast** (p. 383) and snorkelers drift happily among the native fish at **Tunnels Beach** (p. 385).

ROPE 'EM AND RIDE 'EM. While Stetsons and spurs may not figure into your vision of a typical Hawaiian holiday, **cowboy** (*paniolo*) culture is alive and well in America's westernmost state. Since John Palmer Parker established the Parker Ranch on the Big Island in the early 19th century and hired Mexican cattlemen (*paniolos*) to help him run it, a number of other ranches have sprung up on the islands, creating an interesting facet of Hawaiian life. If you're looking to break from the monotony of sun, sand, and surf, spend a day or two visiting one of Hawaii's **working cattle ranches.** At Molokai Ranch (p. 261) you can play cowboy and still enjoy all the amenities of a luxury resort. The **Kualoa Ranch** (p. 158) on Oahu allows visitors to explore its grounds on **horseback** (or, for equi-phobes, on ATV). Big Island is Hawaii's veritable cow-country. Here, you can tour the stunning **Waipi'o Valley** (p. 337) on **horseback** or in a **mule-drawn covered wagon.** The historic and still somewhat authentic **Parker Ranch** (p. 342) merits a visit by any wannabe cowpoke. Check out the **Parker Ranch Museum** and tour the property in a **covered wagon.** If you'd rather just watch, swing by Parker Ranch's annual **July 4th Horse Races and Rodeo** for a taste of a real Hawaiian showdown. The **Makawao Rodeo** (p. 234) on Maui takes place the first weekend in July and features favorites such as **steer roping, barrel racing,** and **bareback riding,** all done with classic *paniolo* flair.

◪ LET'S GO PICKS

BEST NATURAL SAUNA: Steam vents near Pahoa on the Big Island (p. 310).

BEST WAY TO SEND ALOHA LOVE: Send a coconut—husk and all—to your loved ones back home from the **Post-a-Nut** post office on Molokai (p. 253).

BEST PLACE TO LOOK BEYOND THE BEACHES: The impressive **Bishop Museum** in Honolulu (p. 107) holds an extensive collection of Hawaiian art and artifacts.

MOST UNIQUE ISLAND FLAVOR: Pineapple-sweetened wine—taste it for free on a tour of **Tedeschi Vineyards,** south of Kula on Maui (p. 234).

BEST PLACE TO FEEL ATHLETICALLY INFERIOR: The **Ironman Triathlon,** a three-part test of true grit, held annually in Kailua-Kona on the Big Island (p. 317).

BEST PLACE FOR A CAFFEINE BUZZ: Get your fix at **Kauai Coffee,** a working coffee farm and museum on Kauai (p. 398), with a conveniently well-stocked gift shop of coffee-related products.

BEST WAY TO PLAY INDIANA JONES: Cross **Hanapepe's swinging footbridge** over the Menehune Ditch, yet another feat of the little guys' skill, on Kauai (p. 398).

BEST PLACE TO ACHIEVE NIRVANA: The Buddhist temple and retreat of **Nechung Dorje Drayang Ling** on the Big Island (p. 330).

BEST PLACE TO WITNESS THE FURY OF PELE: The lava flows of **Kilauea,** the Big Island's active volcano, in Hawaii Volcanoes National Park (p. 292).

BEST PLACE TO GO NUTS: Purdy's Macadamia Nut Farm, a working farm offering tours, hospitality, and all the macadamia nuts you can crack (p. 254).

SWEETEST TESTAMENT TO A FRUIT: Guava Kai, a planation and agronomical engineering center dedicated to the guava fruit, on Kauai (p. 375). The **Dole Plantation Gardens** and gift shop, near Wahiawa on Oahu (p. 140), pays homage to that famed island fruit, the pineapple.

BEST SUNSETS: Ala Moana Beach Park and **Magic Island** near Honolulu (p. 113), **Polihale State Park** (p. 407) on Kauai, and just about any expanse of **open sky** on the islands.

SUGGESTED ITINERARIES

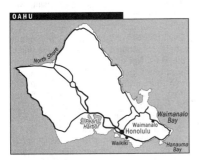

OAHU (1 WEEK). From the Honolulu International Airport, get your bearings by driving around the perimeter of the island—with the windows wide open, of course. Spend a day or two indulging in the whirlwind of **Waikiki** (p. 117). Sip a frosty drink or three, buy a $4 t-shirt, catch a free concert, and enjoy tourism at its best. Next, take a day to explore the historical sights in **Downtown Honolulu** (p. 102), popping into **Chinatown** (p. 98) for a quick bite and a stroll through the markets. Throw on your best surf bum outfit and road trip up the **North Shore** (p. 161). Soak up sun at Sunset Beach, Pipeline, or Waimea Bay (jump off the cliff!). Keep an eye out if you're there in the winter (Dec.-Apr.)—you may spy professional wave riders. Stay overnight in bohemian **Haleiwa** (p. 164), and use the next morning to poke around the various shops and galleries of the area, before getting back on the road. Head toward **Pearl Harbor** (p. 140), stopping at a fruit stand or two along the way. Even if you're not a history buff, an afternoon visit to the Pearl Harbor memorial and museum is certainly worth your while. For the next day or two, pack a beach bag and drive along the eastern coast. Snorkel with the fish at **Hanauma Bay** (p. 142), catch a few waves at **Sandy Beach** (p. 144), and enjoy the spectacular drive. End up in **Waimanalo** (p. 145), where you can pick up an authentic plate lunch and shave ice before returning to Honolulu for your flight home.

WHIRLWIND TOUR (2 WEEKS). Start your trip with a condensed version of our **Oahu** itinerary (see above). Spend one day driving around the island and hit the beaches on the **North Shore** (p. 161). After a night of the club scene in **Waikiki** (p. 123), take it down a notch and wander the historical and cultural sights of **Downtown Honolulu** (p. 93) and **Pearl Harbor** (p. 155). On day 3, steer east to **Hanauma Bay** (p. 142), **Sandy Beach** (p. 144) and **Waimanalo** (p. 145). Camp under the stars, grab a plate lunch or shave ice, and return to Honolulu for your flight to **Big Island**. Be sure to invest in a **7-day island-hopper flight pass** before you leave (p. 56). Drop your bags in **Hilo** (p. 282) and meander through the town's colorful streets, taking in a museum or two and refueling at the Hilo Farmers' Market (p. 286). The next day, set out for **Hawaii Volcanoes National Park** (p. 292). Tour the natural wonders of the park along **Crater Rim Dr.** and **Chain of Craters Rd.** (p. 295). The next day, put your snorkel to good use at **Kealakekua Bay** (p. 324). Take a boat cruise or explore the protected reef on your own. Keep an eye out for spinner dolphins! On your final day, do your best John Wayne impersonation in **Waimea** (p. 338) and **Parker Ranch** (p. 338), then brush the dust off and hop on the next plane—Maui is calling your name. Centrally-located **Pa'ia** (p. 214), with its budget-friendly prices and laid-back attitude, is a perfect base for this leg of the tour. Use the afternoon to scout out the town and wander over to one of the

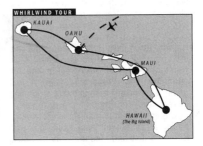

DISCOVER

area beaches for an afternoon swim. View the varied sights of **Haleakala National Park** (p. 225) in a day by driving up the switchback road to the summit, then take the next couple of days to explore—marvel at the sights on the **Road to Hana** (p. 219), soak up the sun at the pristine beaches near **Kihei** (p. 189), and catch a dolphin or whale-watching tour out of **Ma'alaea** (p. 189). With one island to go, bid Maui *adieu* and skip over to **Kauai**. After a brief stop in **Lihu'e** (p. 355) to find a hotel, follow the sounds of Hawaiian music to **Smith's Tropical Paradise** (p. 367). Enjoy the leisurely boat tour to **Fern Grotto** (p. 367), then return to Smith's to gorge yourself at their authentic Hawaiian **luau.** The next morning, roll out of bed and find your way to **Secret Beach** (p. 376) for a full day of sunbathing and swimming. Return to Lihu'e and pack your bags—it's time to go home.

OFF THE BEATEN PATH (2 WEEKS). Invest in a **2-week island-hopper flight pass** (p. 56) when you arrive in Honolulu, then shake off the tourist trappings as you head for a 5-day stay on **Molokai.** You can hang your hat in **Kaunakakai** (p. 243), the island's major town, before hiking down to the **Kalaupapa Peninsula** (p. 248), a former leper colony and one of the most awe-inspiring spots on the island. Rub elbows with locals at a Little League game back in Kaunakakai, and get the inside scoop on **Wailau Valley** (p. 261), a rugged locale where Molokians go for *their* vacations. If your vacation-within-a-vacation has you looking for some excitement, spend a night in **One Ali'l Beach park** (p. 245), and party local-style at the Hotel Molokai's **weekly jam** (p. 248). The next day, get closer to native Hawaiian history and culture at the **'Ili'ili'opae Heiau** (p. 257), the second-largest Hawaiian temple in the islands. Three days in the islands and not yet a day dedicated to sun and sand? Pack your bathing suit and hiking boots, and set off for **Moomomi Preserve** (p. 255). A hike through the preserve encounters a number of rare and endangered plant species, before unfolding into a series of white sand beaches. Last but not least, spend a day at **Halawa Valley** and **Moa'ula Falls** (p. 260). Next, fly out for a 3-day stay on Maui. You can head to **Haiku** (p. 238), a lush and sleepy town near the North Shore and on the Road to Hana. Be sure to stay in a local B&B for real Hawaiian hospitality. Four miles north of Hana, **Waianapanapa State Park** (p. 222) merits a day's excursion, with a number of unique sights including a heiau, lava tube caves, lava arches, and a small black-sand beach. Overlook the tourist glut of **Lahaina,** and instead take one of the **Maui Nei** organization's historical-cultural tours (p. 205) of the city. Equipped with your newfound knowledge, hop a ferry from Lahaina to **Lanai.** Go for an off-road adventure along the **Munro Trail** (p. 272), then park yourself at a local campground to spend a night under the stars. Step into the otherworldly **Garden of the Gods** (p. 274), an area of red earth and rock formations, before sailing back to Maui. From Maui, fly out for the last leg of your journey—a 4-day stint on the **Big Island.** Touch down in **Hilo** (p. 282), the island's low-key metropolis, and make a stop at the **Pacific Tsunami Museum** (p. 288) to learn more about how these natural disasters have affected the city. From there, drive north through the unspoiled **Hamakua Coast** (p. 332) to North Kohala. Explore the abandoned ancient village at **Lapakahi State Historical Park** (p. 346), and snorkel from its coral beach. Next you can pilgrimage to **Mo'okini Heiau** (p. 346), the birthplace of Kamehameha I. Continue east along the coast and down to South Kona. Make a stop at the 15-acre **Amy Greenwell Ethnobotanical Garden** (p. 326) to learn more about the relationship native Hawaiians had with the land, then seek the spirit of the ancients at the extensive **Pu'uhonua o Honaunau National Historical Park** (p. 351). Round out your tour with a jaunt through the diverse **Ka'u** district on your way back to the airport in Hilo.

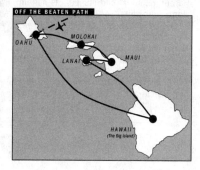

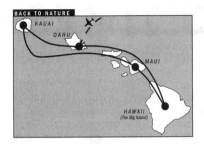

BACK TO NATURE (12 DAYS). Ready to cast off the 9-to-5 drudgery and commune with Mother Nature? From Honolulu, head to **Big Island** for 5 days, stopping first in **Hawaii Volcanoes National Park** (p. 292). During your 3-day stay in the park, be sure to spend at least one night backcountry camping on the world's biggest mountain, **Mauna Loa** (Get a free **permit** at the park **Visitor Center**). Catch a glimpse of how the Hawaiian Islands were formed at **Kilauea,** the world's most active volcano, which has been spewing molten lava continuously for the past 20 years. Stargaze from the slopes of **Mauna Kea** (p. 303), where amateur and professional astronomers alike enjoy some of the best viewing conditions on the planet. In **Akaka Falls State Park** (p. 291), about 4 mi. up Mauna Kea, trek though lush rainforest and check out the park's two spectacular waterfalls. Next, leave the park and head to the northern tip of the island, where you can hike the verdant **Waipi'o Valley** (p. 336) or satisfy your inner equestrian by exploring the valley on horseback. Drive south along the **Hamakua Coast** toward Hilo, being sure to stop at the **Hawaii Tropical Botanical Garden** (p. 291), home to over 2000 different

plant species, along the way. Further so in Puna, the otherworldly forms at **Lav Tree State Park** (p. 309) are a testament to nature's powers of creativity. Head back to **Hilo** (p. 282) to purchase a **7-day island hopper pass** (p. 56) and jet off to **Maui** for 3 days. Stop first at **Kipahulu Valley** and **Ohe'o Gulch** (p. 223), both of which are within the confines of **Haleakala National Park.** Take a hike to the dazzling **Makahiku** and **Waimoku waterfalls** (p. 224), and pass the splendid **Pools of Ohe'o** (p. 224) along the way. Next, travel to **Kihei** (p. 189) and take a snorkeling trip to **Molokini,** where many of the species you will encounter exist nowhere else in the world. From there, head north to the sacred **Iao Valley** (p. 188), the site of countless ancient battles, and the final resting place of *ali'i,* and check out the **Iao Needle.** The last leg of your journey takes you to **Kauai,** where you will spend 4 days in some of Hawaii's most untamed wilderness. Don't miss the world-famous **Kalalau Trail** (p. 386), which runs 11 miles along Kauai's **Na Pali Coast** (p. 386). This strenuous 3-day **hike** affords some incredible **views** as well as stops at a number of picture perfect **beaches** along the way. Apply for a **camping permit** in advance (p. 355). During the final day of your journey, visit the historic **Kilauea lighthouse** at the **Kilauea Point National Wildlife Reserve** (p. 374) in Kilauea. If you're lucky, you'll catch a glimpse of some of the many endangered species that call the reserve home, including **humpback whales, nene geese, monk seals,** and **sea turtles.** Finally, the fragrant blossoms at the **National Tropical Botanical Garden** (p. 391) in Lawa'i will provide you with a last breath of island air before you have to leave for Honolulu and then head for home.

Hawaii is located in the Pacific Ocean, 2400 mi. (3860km) off the coast of the continental US; it is the most isolated populated landmass in the entire world. At approximately the same latitude as central Mexico, it is the southernmost state and the 43rd largest, spanning 6,450 sq. mi. (16,706 sq. km). The average temperature on Hawaii is 85 degrees Fahrenheit (29 degrees Celsius) in summer and 78 degrees Fahrenheit (26 degrees Celsius) in winter. Hawaii stretches 1,523 mi. (world's longest island chain) and contains 132 islands and atolls, all of which are the result of volcanic activity. Only 7 of the islands are inhabited, and with the exception of the large but uninhabited Kahoolawe, most of the rest are too small to make human occupancy viable.

Hawaii (or **Big Island**), the youngest and largest of the Hawaiian islands (4,038 sq. mi.), is home to two active volcanoes, Mauna Loa and Kilauea. Kilauea has been erupting continuously since 1983, and visitors to the Hawaii Volcanoes National Park can observe her lava flows up close. Mauna Kea is the highest point in the state at an altitude of 13,796 ft. (4208m) above sea level. The high cliffs along the northern and southeastern coasts of Big Island make its many waterfalls all the more spectacular. In addition to its spectacular natural wonders, Big Island is known for being the world's leading producer of macadamia nuts and orchids.

Of the two volcanoes on **Maui,** only one, Haleakala, is still considered active, though it hasn't erupted for some time. The remains of the second volcano are known as Halemahina, or the West Maui Mountains. A great deal of sugar cane is cultivated in the fertile valley between Haleakala and Halemahina, while much of eastern Maui is covered by tropical rainforest.

Molokai has three distinct geographical regions: the mountainous east, the arid west, and the verdant central plain. The island also boasts some of the world's tallest sea cliffs, which soar up to 3,000 ft. above the ocean.

Castle & Cooke Co., the makers of Dole pineapple products, owns 98% of the island of **Lanai.** Historically a center for commercial pineapple production, Lanai is aptly nicknamed "the Pineapple Island." Lanai is the only Hawaiian island from which 5 of the other main islands are visible.

Considerable pineapple and sugar production takes place on **Oahu,** in the central valley between the eastern Koolau Mountain Range and the Waianae Range in the west. One of the most famous sights on the island is Diamond Head, an extinct volcanic crater on the southeastern coast. At 760 ft. in height and 3,520 ft. in diameter, it's impressive but all bark and no bite—it hasn't erupted in 150,000 years.

Kauai is home to the rainiest spot on earth, Mount Waialeale, which averages 460 in. (1143cm) of rain per year. Thanks to this heavy rainfall, a number of spectacular canyons have been eroded into the mountains of Kauai. The northernmost and geologically oldest of the Hawaiian islands, Kauai is also the most verdant, earning it the nickname "The Garden Island."

Niihau, "The Forbidden Island," has been privately owned by Kauai's Robinson family since 1864. The semi-arid island functions mainly as a cattle ranch, but is better known for its isolation from the outside world. To prevent the modernization of the island, visitors are not allowed except with express permission from the Robinson family or a resident. Home to the most pure-blood Hawaiians in the world, Niihau is also the only place where Hawaiian is the primary language.

LAVA ME TENDER When Dr. Evil plotted to cover the Earth with "liquid hot magma" in 1999's smash *Austin Powers: The Spy Who Shagged Me,* the would-be world dictator erred in his geological calculations. While the unique volcanic substance made of liquid and solid rock remains below ground, it is known as **magma.** Once magma is exposed, either through a volcanic eruption or a fissure in the earth, it becomes **lava.** How lava behaves once it breaks the surface depends on the amount of **silica** it contains. **Low silica lava,** which is common in Hawaii, flows and can travel for great distances. **High silica lava** (also called pyroclastics), on the other hand, explodes in ash or cinders when it leaves the volcano. The most famous example of this type of lava was the 1980 eruption of Mount Saint Helens in Montana, where the force of the magma being released caused the volcano to self-destruct. In addition to varying chemical compositions, lava also comes in three different forms:

Pahoehoe: This type of lava can be found at almost all volcanoes. Fast-flowing, it hardens into a smooth, ropy solid. The outside of lava channels can solidify before the interior lava, forming lava tubes; lava can flow within these tubes for long distances.

Pillow: A type of Pahoehoe lava, pillow lava is found under water or ice. This form of lava is named for the distinctive way it occurs: newly erupted lava is immediately surrounded by a temporary crust before the next wave of lava breaks through (like toothpaste!), forming another "pillow."

Aʻa: Some attribute the name of this form of lava to an old tale of how Captain Cook walked barefoot across the lava, screaming, "Ah! Ah!" Slow-moving, Aʻa lava is characterized by its rough and jagged appearance. Its flows are much thicker and have been known to pile up (sometimes to heights over 100 feet).

FLORA & FAUNA

None of the plants and animals that exist in Hawaii today originated there, because Hawaii was never part of a larger landmass. The islands of Hawaii were formed from volcanoes on the Pacific floor. Soon after the lava cooled, tides, winds, and birds carried seeds to the islands which grew into dense forests, shrubs and other vegetation. Later, **Polynesian settlers** arrived in canoes, bringing plant and animal species from their native lands. Much of the flora and fauna on Hawaii developed special adaptations to their new home and evolved into brand new species. Today about 90% of the plants and animals on Hawaii are **endemic,** meaning that they exist nowhere else in the world.

Since Hawaii's native plants and animals evolved in the absence of predators or competitors, they did not develop natural defenses such as thorns, poisons, or camouflage. As such, many native species have been pushed to the brink of **extinction** by invasive alien plants and animals that were later introduced to the islands. Hawaii is home to more than half of all of the plants on the US endangered species list, and 70% of species extinctions in the US have occurred in Hawaii alone. In spite of all this, however, Hawaii still boasts an astounding degree of biodiversity.

PLANTS

There are more than 2,500 species of native plants in Hawaii, as well as a considerable number of non-native species. There are 139 different types of **fern** in Hawaii. These lush, green plants were some of the first to arrive on the islands, sprouting up on the cooled lava flows; they form much of the ground cover in Hawaii's forests. Hawaii's most abundant native tree, the **ohia lehua,** is also among the first to spring up on fresh lava flows. Highly distinctive, the ohia lehua can identified by its crooked branches and bright red, pompom-like flowers (which are sacred to the goddess Pele). It is also highly adaptable, and can survive in a multitude of environments, including elevations between 1,000 and 9,000 ft. above sea level.

Hawaii's second most prominent native tree is the **koa**, which, like the ohia lehua, is endemic to the islands. Ancient Hawaiians used the reddish wood of the koa tree to fashion canoes, surfboards, weapons, and other items. The hard wood is highly sought-after today as a material for making household furniture. Cattle and other feral animals have destroyed thousands of acres of Hawaiian koa, but fortunately the tree is fast-growing and highly resilient, and has thrived under recent reforestation programs.

The introduction of **ungulates** such as goats, cattle, horses, pigs and sheep to the islands by Western settlers led to the rapid decline of many native Hawaiian plant species, which never evolved defense mechanisms against these highly destructive aliens. The animals trample vegetation, cause soil erosion, and often introduce more aggressive alien plant species that choke out native growth. The **Haleakala silversword** nearly became extinct in the 1920's due to browsing by goats and cattle. The Haleakala silversword is still very rare due to its limited range; the only place in the world it can be found is on the crater and outer slopes of the Haleakala volcano on Maui. However, protection programs within the Haleakala National Park have saved the species from extinction and its population continues to grow. The silversword is spherical and grows close to the ground. Its thin, spiny leaves are covered with tiny silver hairs, and at the end of its 15- to 50-year life span it produces a tall stalk covered with maroon flowers.

The **ki** (or **ti**) plant was a symbol of power in ancient Hawaii and was also used as a good luck charm. Sacred to the god Lono and the goddess of the hula, Laka, *ki* was introduced to Hawaii by Polynesian settlers. A member of the lily family, the *ki* plant has shiny green leaves, which were used as roof thatching, food wrappers, clothing, and decoration. The leaves are still used in religious ceremonies and in floral arrangements today. **Okolehau,** or **oke,** a clear, potent liquor similar to moonshine is made from the roots of the *ki* plant. *Ki* grows abundantly throughout Hawaii, thriving in areas of low elevation where moisture is plentiful.

Hawaii's state flower is the **yellow hibiscus** (*ma'o hau hele*). Ubiquitous throughout the islands, there are 5 endemic species of hibiscus in Hawaii. These brightly-colored tropical blossoms can measure up to a foot in diameter and have become a popular symbol of the Aloha State. **Orchids, plumeria, bougainvillea,** and **bird of paradise** are also commonly found in Hawaii, though they are not native to the islands.

Sugarcane, pineapples, guavas, mangoes, papayas, coconuts, avocados, bananas, limes, passion fruit, macadamia nuts, taro (*kalo*), breadfruit (*'ulu*), and ginger (*'awapuhi*) are all cultivated on Hawaii. The endangered **sandalwood** tree (*'iliahi*), famous for its aromatic oil, also grows on the islands.

ANIMALS

There are no snakes, crocodiles, or large cats on Hawaii. In fact, Hawaii boasts only two native mammals: the **Hawaiian Monk Seal** and the **hoary bat,** both of which are endemic to the islands. The hoary bat is Hawaii's only native land mammal. Found on the Big Island and in the Koke'e State Park on Kauai, hoary bats feed on insects and, like all bats, they are nocturnal.

Unlike most seals, Hawaiian Monk Seals are solitary animals that are rarely found in groups. They are a very old species; scientists believe that they have remained unchanged by evolution for the past 15 million years. They are primarily found in the remote regions of the Northwestern Hawaiian islands. Like many species native to Hawaii, they evolved in the absence of predators. As such, they did not develop a "fight-or-flight" instinct, and are therefore naturally tame. This spelled disaster for the Monk Seal during the 19th century, as they were killed in large numbers for their oil and pelts. Today they are considered an endangered species, with a population of around 1,500. Because the survival of these gentle creatures remains precarious, it is important that visitors not disturb them— please stay a safe distance away.

Humpback Whales were among the first species to discover the joy of wintering in Hawaii. Each autumn they travel 3,000 mi. (5,000m) from their arctic feeding grounds to the warm, tropical waters of Hawaii to mate and give birth. These baleen whales grow to over 50 ft. in length and weigh 30-50 tons. They are known for their spectacular acrobatics, as well as their complex underwater mating songs. There are now about 20,000 humpbacks world-wide and are an endangered species. Maui is the best island from which to see humpback whales, particularly in the winter, from November to February.

The **mongoose** was introduced to Hawaii in the late 19th century in an attempt to exterminate the rats that were overrunning the islands' sugar plantations. Unfortunately, this solution was highly ineffective, as rats are nocturnal, while mongooses are diurnal. Today mongooses abound on all of the islands except for Kauai, and they are considered pests because they prey on the eggs of ground-nesting birds, many of which are very rare.

Hawaii's state bird, the highly endangered **Nene**, or Hawaiian goose, is the rarest goose in the world—fewer than 900 exist in the wild. Their low numbers are attributable to predation by mongooses, as well as destruction of nests by pigs and other feral animals. Most nene live on the slopes of volcanoes on the Big Island, though they can also be found on Maui and Kauai. Thought to be closely related to the Canadian goose, the nene developed long toes and reduced webbing on their feet for climbing on lava flows.

Kauai has the most varied bird population of any of the Hawaiian islands, possibly because there are no mongooses there to prey upon them. The **honeycreeper, puaiohi,** and **'o'u** are some of the more magnificent. The Big Island is also home to a number of rare birds, including several varieties of honeycreeper and the endangered **Hawaiian hawk** ('io).

There are an estimated 700 different species of fish in Hawaiian waters, many of which exist nowhere else in the world. Impress your friends by telling them about Hawaii's state fish, the **Humuhumunukunukuapua'a** (pronounced HOO-moo-HOO-moo-NEW-coo-NEW-coo-AH-poo-AH-ah), or the **reef triggerfish.** This tiny tropical fish is 8-9 in. long and has a trigger-shaped, blue-and-yellow dorsal fin. There are also about 40 different species of **shark** inhabiting Hawaiian waters. The most commonly seen are **tiger sharks, reef sharks,** and **hammerheads.** Of these, the tiger shark is considered the most dangerous to humans (see **Wilderness Safety,** p. 65).

THE ENDANGERED SPECIES ACT The US Congress
passed the **Endangered Species Act (ESA)** in 1973 to protect plants and animals that are either "threatened" or "endangered." Endangered species are those that are at risk of becoming extinct throughout all or most of their range. Threatened species are those that are likely to become endangered in the near or forseeable future. The ESA makes it illegal not only to kill or capture species that are threatened or endangered, but also to destroy or modify their habitats. Because the law extends even to private property, it has caused a rift between the economically- and the ecologically-minded on numerous occasions, as species are added to the endangered or threatened lists "without reference to possible economic or other impacts of such determination." The ultimate goal of the ESA, however, is to *remove* species from the endangered and threatened lists. Once it is determined that a species is no longer in jeopardy, it is taken off the list and left to fend for itself.

HISTORY

EARLY HISTORY (500-1778 AD)

500-750 AD
Polynesians
arrive from the
Marquesas Islands

The original inhabitants of the Hawaiian islands are believed to have been descendents of Asiatic peoples who migrated over land and water routes, eventually landing in the Central Pacific. **Polynesian voyagers** were probably the first to discover the islands, landing near Ka Lae on the Big Island around 500-750 AD. Archaeological and cultural evidence indicates that these voyagers originated from the Marquesas, an island group north of Tahiti. They navigated the South Pacific seas in double-hulled canoes, using the stars and ocean currents as guides. **Tahitians** were the next wave of peoples to encounter the islands, most likely around 1000 AD. Large numbers of Tahitian immigrants landed on the shores of Hawaii in the 13th and 14th centuries AD; Hawaiian culture reflects this early Tahitian influence. The original Hawaiians had slightly smaller builds than the Tahitian immigrants, and the diminutive size of the natives may have been a basis for the legend of the menehune (see p. 23).

1000 AD
Tahitian settlers
arrive

Around 1175 a Tahitian priest (*kahuna*), known as Pa'ao in ancient oral histories, arrived in Hawaii. He brought with him **Pili**, the first in the royal line which led to Kamehameha. Pa'ao is thought to have founded the *kahuna nui* (high priest) line, initiating the system of division of each island under a ruling king which lasted for the next several hundred years. One *ali'i nui*, the most powerful *ali'i* (chief) of the region, headed each island and distributed land to the chiefs below him (who then allowed the commoners to work on, but not purchase, that land) in a feudal-style system. The *ali'i* were believed to have been chosen by the gods, and served as a link between the people and the deities they worshipped. Below the *ali'i* and the priest class were the *maka'ainana*, or commoners, and a third class of citizens known as *kaua*. The *kaua* were most often those who had broken *kapu* (taboo) and had neither rights nor property. The Hawaiians used little writing, and preserved most of their history in chants, known as *mele*, and legends. Much of Hawaiian history was lost with the deaths of *kahunas* and others whose duty it was to pass on the knowledge of the ancients to later generations.

REDISCOVERY AND WESTERN TRADE (1778-1840)

1778
Captain Cook "dis-
covers" Hawaii and
names it the Sand-
wich Islands

THE BRITISH ARE COMING. The first known European to arrive in the Hawaiian islands was **Captain James Cook,** who happened upon the islands in 1778. He dubbed his new find the Sandwich Isles in honor of the English Earl of Sandwich. Cook's arrival coincided with the Hawaiians' *makahiki* festival, an annual celebration of the god Lono. It is possible that the islanders mistook the white sails of Cooks' ships for Lono's white *kapa* flags, and interpreted his arrival at Kealakekua Bay on the Big Island as the earthly descent of the their god. Whether or not the Hawaiians thought Cook to be an incarnation of the god Lono, Cook and his men were nonetheless welcomed to the islands and allowed to trade with the islanders.

The Captain and his crews departed after two weeks of festivities, only to meet fierce storms which resulted in damage to their vessels. When they returned to Kealakekua Bay, they found the festivities ended and the area deserted. The Hawaiians, upon the Captain's return, began to lose faith in a god on earth who could sustain such sizeable damage in his own domain. With their respect for Cook diminished, the natives helped themselves to metals from one of Cook's ships in exchange for the supplies and gifts which they had given the British sailors upon their arrival. Cook and a small party of his men went ashore to take the island chief, Kalaniopuu, hostage and demand the return of their goods. The plan went awry, however, and Cook and several of his men were killed in a skirmish with the Hawaiians on Valentine's Day, 1779. Some debate has arisen among historians regarding the true manner of Cook's reception; see **Additional Resources** (p. 32) for further readings.

KAMEHAMEHA THE GREAT. At the time of Cook's discovery, the islands were under the rule of a number of warring kings. When Kalaniopuu, king of the Big Island, died in 1782, the chiefs of the island divided into two opposing factions. One faction was that of the chiefs of Kona and Kalaniopuu's nephew, **Kamehameha** (1758-1819). The other faction organized under Kalaniopuu's son, Kiwalao, and his relatives. Although Kamehameha and his forces were victorious in the conflict over the Big Island, it began what would become a decade of civil war throughout the Hawaiian islands. The end of the long struggle came with Kamehameha's **unification** of the islands under his sole rule in 1810.

During Kamehameha's reign, the export of highly-prized **sandalwood** to China increased, facilitating trade with other nations, most notably the United States and Britain. In 1819 the first whaling ships arrived in Kealakekua Bay. The **whaling industry** grew profitable for the Hawaiian economy as Hawaii was established as a stop on New England-based whaling routes through the Pacific. The Westerners brought more with them than tools, provisions and luxury items, however. The introduction of devastating infectious diseases, and the spread of Western ways and culture had a profound impact on the health and habits of the natives.

Under **Kamehameha II, Liholiho** (1796-1824), many changes occurred in the established religion of the islands. Liholiho overthrew the ancient **kapu system** by allowing men and women to eat at the same table at court, and announcing the destruction of *heiaus* along with the old idols. 1820 saw the arrival of the first **Christian missionaries** to the islands from the United States. The missionaries took advantage of the changes that had been occurring in the traditional Hawaiian lifestyle over the previous decades to engender the spread of their Christian

HAWAII

1810
Kamehameha the Great unites the islands into one kingdom

1813
Spanish explorers introduce the pineapple to Hawaii

1819
Kamehameha dies; Prince Liholiho ascends the throne, does away with the *kapu* system

1820
Missionaries arrive from Boston

1825
Kamehameha III
comes to power

teachings. The missionaries established schools, developed the Hawaiian alphabet into the 12-letter form known today, and used this alphabet to translate the Bible into Hawaiian. Religious tolerance was further expanded in 1839 when Kamehameha III issued a declaration of rights known as the **Hawaiian Magna Carta,** and the **Edict of Toleration,** which guaranteed religious freedom.

1835
First sugar plantation started at Koloa on Kauai

SUGAR AND PINEAPPLES (1840-1940)

1839
Declaration of Rights and Edict of Toleration

By the end of the 19th century, sugar and pineapple plantations run by American businessmen had overtaken much of Hawaii's land and the crops were the two most important sources of revenue for the Hawaiian economy. The traditional feudal style of land ownership was abolished in 1848, when Kamehameha II enacted the **Great Mahele** (Division). True to its name, the edict divided land between the *ali'i* and the *maka'aina* (commoners), and provided the first legal basis for private land ownership. The division opened the door for the purchase of land not only by previously disenfranchised native Hawaiians, but also by foreigners *(haoles)* and commercial investors.

1840
First constitution of Hawaii established

1848
The Great Mahele

The freeing up of land in Hawaii coincided with the beginning of the decline of the whaling industry and a subsequent movement toward the development of agriculture. In 1850, the Hawaiian legislature approved the hiring of immigrant laborers from Japan, China, the Phillipines and Portugal to work in the booming **sugar industry.** The ethnic diversity of the inhabitants of today's Hawaii reflects the diversity of these immigrant laborers. Ultimately, the importation of workers and the changes in land ownership laws took land away from many natives, land which was instead bought up for sugar mills. The first sugar plantation in Hawaii, the **Koloa Plantation** on Kauai, was founded in 1835, initiating an explosion in the sugar industry as mills began to appear all over the islands.

The massive Hawaiian **pineapple** industry began as a one-man operation; today, Hawaii produces one-third of the world's commercial supply of pineapples. James D. Dole planted his first pineapple trees near Wahaiwa on Oahu in 1901, and founded the **Hawaiian Pineapple Company.** In 1922, Dole purchased the island of Lanai for the purpose of large-scale production; by 1950 his was the largest pineapple company in the world. Dole was eventually bought out by the **Castle & Cooke** company, which still owns much of Lanai. Pineapples were the state's second-biggest industry until the mid-1940s.

ANNEXATION AND AMERICAN INFLUENCE (1875-1900)

1864
David Kalakaua becomes king

THE END OF THE MONARCHY. David Kalakaua (1836-1891) was elected king in 1874, following a rocky ascent to the crown. The "Merrie Monarch" began his reign with a world tour to meet other heads of state, including an 1881 visit to the United States which marked the first time a Hawaiian king had visited the mainland. Kalakaua was proud of Hawaiian culture, and promoted traditional Hawaiian customs and heritage at home and abroad. The end of his reign was none so joyous, however, but rather, marred by corruption and contention.

Among the controversial acts enacted under Kalakaua's reign was the **Reciprocity Treaty of 1875.** Under the treaty, Hawaiian sugar was admitted tax-free into the US; in return a number of American products could enter Hawaii duty-free. The treaty appeared to give Hawaiian sugar a favorable position in US markets, but it served to consolidate American economic supremacy in Hawaiian trade as well. This influenced the course of events in changes in the power of Hawaiian monarchy by strengthening the influence of American sugar interests in the kingdom.

In 1887, Kalakaua signed the **Bayonet Constitution,** which revised Kamehameha V's Constitution of 1864. The act, so named because it was signed under threat of armed disturbance, undermined the king's authority, transferring much of his power to the cabinet. Stipulations of the Constitution included the election of the nobility rather than their appointment by the king, and a provision allowing foreigners with at least one year of residency in Hawaii the right to vote, if they paid taxes and pledged to honor the constitution. The act enfranchised foreign businessmen, increasing their control over politics in the islands.

Controversy over the constitution and struggles for political power under Kalakaua carried over into the reign of his sister, **Queen Liliuokalani.** Hawaii's last monarch and only reigning queen ascended to the throne in 1891. The 1892 session of the legislature was made up of three political parties: the National Reform Party which supported the Queen; the Reform Party which opposed strengthening the crown; and the Liberal Party. The major concerns of the 1892 session of the Hawaiian legislature were the themes of the Bayonet Constitution—control of the cabinet and changes in the constitution.

Upon gaining power, Lilioukalani appointed members of the National Reform Party to the cabinet; they were promptly voted out of office. Undaunted, Lilioukalani appointed another set of National Reform Party members who met the same unfortunate fate as their predecessors. Working under the third-time's-the-charm hypothesis the Queen then appointed a cabinet of Reform Party members, in order to get the business of the state moving. This plan backfired, however, as frustrated Liberal Party members joined the National Reform Party in a move to overthrow the Reform Party instead. The Queen again appointed members of the National Reform Party to the cabinet right before the legislature adjourned.

Bills to amend the constitution and expand suffrage to the common people were rejected for the second time when the legislature reconvened in 1892. This denial of voting rights elicited widespread protest. Queen Lilioukalani, slowed by ministers who feared a backlash from the white business community, failed to move quickly enough to ratify the proposals. In the meantime, the **Annexationist Club,** a group of white plantation

HAWAII

1875
Hawaii and US enter into the Reciprocity Treaty

1881
Macadamia nuts first introduced to Hawaii

1885
First large group of Japanese immigrant workers arrive to work in sugar plantations

1887
Bayonet Constitution

1889
Father Damien dies on the Kalaupapa leper colony on Molokai (see p. 248)

owners who had banded together earlier that year, held a secret meeting to discuss the proceedings in government. The group formed a Committee of Public Safety, and decided upon a plan to get rid of the monarchy, set up a provisional government, and put forth a bid for US annexation of the islands.

1893
Queen Liliuokalani overthrown; provisional government established, led by Sanford B. Dole

AMERICAN RULE BEGINS. Queen Lilioukalani abdicated and the provisional government gained power in 1893, thanks to the force and manipulations of the Annexationist Club. The Queen stepped down under protest with the belief that the United States would not enforce the annexation. Representatives from the provisional government and Queen Lilioukalani went to Washington to plead their respective cases. Queen Lilioukalani's representatives were delayed, however, as they were denied passage on a plantation-owned ship while the representatives from the annexationists proceeded to Washington, an incident which reflects the relative political power and influence of white planters in Hawaii at the time.

1900
Hawaii made a US territory

US President Grover Cleveland did not immediately ratify the annexation since it appeared that most Hawaiians were opposed to the revolution. President Cleveland sent **James Blount,** a former chairman of the House Foreign Affairs Committee, to investigate the conditions of the overthrow of the monarchy. Blount's report indicated that the majority of Hawaiians had not favored the move, and that American plantation owners had incited the revolt in order to further their own business interests. Blount charged that the uprising had been the result of pressure from revolutionary leaders and United States Minister John L. Stevens.

1912
Duke Kahanamoku participates in the Olympics in Stockholm

1921
Hawaiian Homes Commission Act passed

The annexationists nonetheless succeeded in establishing a provisional government headed by Sanford B. Dole in 1894, despite the US government's subsequent attempts to restore Queen Liliukalani. In 1898, under President Cleveland's successor William McKinley, a joint resolution of the US Congress approved **official annexation** of Hawaii. Native Hawaiians made a silent protest to the action by boycotting the ceremonies. The islands were made a US **territory** in 1900, with Dole serving as governor.

1927
First non-stop flight to Hawaii from the US mainland

WORLD WAR II (1941-1945)

A DAY THAT WILL LIVE IN INFAMY. At 7:55am on the morning of December 7, 1941, Japanese fighter jets swooped through the still air of the military base at **Pearl Harbor** (p. 137), initiating a surprise strike that would prove to be one of the single most destructive attacks in naval history. The Japanese objective was the obliteration of the fighting capacity of the 7 US battleships moored there, and the American military strength in the Pacific as a whole. As air strikes rained on the battleships, Japanese fighter pilots also targeted the American bombers at nearby airfields.

Many on board the ships and on the shore thought the attack was nothing more than another military drill until they saw the marks of the "rising sun" on the sides of the Japanese planes and witnessed the destruction. Of the 7 battleships, the **USS Arizona** suffered the most severe damage, taking 7 bombs and hits from an aerial torpedo. One of the bombs fell through the steel decks, detonating stored ammunition; the twisted hull of the ship lies as a poignant monument to the 1102 men still entombed within. The attack seriously weakened American air strength in the Pacific and took the lives of over 2400 American military personnel and civilians.

On the other side of the world, European nations were caught in the horror of **World War II.** The US had yet to be drawn into the war, although their eventual participation seemed inevitable. For the Japanese, the war provided an opportunity to capitalize on European preoccupation with war to make a bid for supremacy in Southeast Asia through the capture of former European colonial holdings. One of the few obstacles left in their way was the sizeable American fleet that lay within striking distance of the South Pacific—the fleet based at Pearl Harbor. The attack ultimately propelled the United States into World War II, in both the European and Pacific theaters.

Historians and others have questioned how it was that such a massive and well-organized attack could have caught the Americans unawares. The American government had decoded the Japanese secret diplomatic code in 1940, and had suspected Japanese intentions but had discovered no specific plan for an attack at Pearl Harbor. A definitive answer still eludes the general public.

HAWAII'S ROLE IN THE PACIFIC THEATER. As the United States reeled from the attack and began to prepare itself for war, **martial law** ruled in Hawaii. Martial law was declared directly following the attack on Pearl Harbor, and was not lifted until October of 1944. During this time the writ of *habeas corpus* was suspended, and all those considered suspicious—most often those of Japanese descent—were rounded up and placed in custody at immigration stations.

Hawaii nonetheless continued to serve as a base for military operations in the Pacific following the attack at Pearl Harbor. The next notable clash that occurred in the islands was the **Battle of Midway** in June of 1942. The battle—a victory for the US—was a turning point for the American forces in the Pacific and marked Hawaii's movement from a combat zone to a training facility and military base. To this day, Hawaii hosts the largest combined American military presence in the entire world.

Hawaiian citizens stepped up to take part in the war effort. Some civilians participated in domestic defense and administration; island-born Japanese served as language interpreters for the military. Many others took up arms. Among these were a contingent of Americans of Japanese descent (AJAs) who were discharged from the Hawaii Territorial Guard, most likely as a result of paranoia regarding those of Japanese descent. About 1400 of these Hawaiian men banded together to form the **100th battalion,** which fought valiantly in the European theater, earning itself the nickname the "Purple Heart Regiment."

HAWAII

1941
Japanese forces attack the US military base at Pearl Harbor; US enters WWII

1941
Martial law declared in Hawaii; Japanese citizens are held suspect

1942
Battle of Midway

1944
Martial law lifted in Hawaii

1945
V-E Day
V-J Day

War continued to rage in the Pacific for several months after the European theater ended on **V-E Day** (Victory in Europe), May 8, 1945. The Pacific theater closed with the Japanese surrender on September 1, 1945—known as **V-J Day** in the US.

CONSUMER CULTURE TO TOURIST CULTURE (1945-1970)

1946
Devastating tsunami hits Hilo on the Big Island; "Great Sugar Strike" organized by the ILWG

LABOR UNIONS. World War II brought changes in the Hawaiian lifestyle, including military restrictions and shortages, and an influx of *haoles* from the mainland. Following the war, whites employed by the military vacated the islands and locals returned, but still more developments occurred. Immigration restrictions, high wages, and the end of the war reduced the labor force and resulted in an increased reliance on mechanization in the sugar and pineapple industries. The end of martial law—and its **labor freeze**—in 1944 and discontent among workers led the way to a mass **unionization** in Hawaii's major industries, which was headed by the International Warehousemen's and Longshoremen's Union (IWLU). The momentum of the labor movement pushed the National Labor Relations Board to pass the **Hawaii Employment Relations Act** in 1945, which granted the same rights to agricultural workers as those granted to industrial workers. IWLU's regional director, **Jack Hall,** was a prominent figure in Hawaii's labor movement during the postwar years.

Union supporters joined with AJAs and Democrats to shift the political dominance in Hawaii from the Republican party, electing a number of Democrats to political office and expanding the ethnic diversity of the party ticket. In 1956, **Jack Burns,** a force in Hawaiian politics during the last half of the 20th century, became Hawaii's first Democratic Congressman since the 1930s.

1953
First bikinis seen on Waikiki beach

THE QUESTION OF STATEHOOD. In 1937 the first bill promoting Hawaii's conversion to statehood was put forth in the US Congress. It and similar bills like it were defeated for a number of reasons including: the problems of distance; concerns with destruction of traditional Hawaiian ways of life; and the interest of the population in becoming part of the United States. In the islands, the sugar industry and other businesses were concerned with the move to statehood and doubts about the balance in representation between the islands' ethnic groups existed as well.

1959
Hawaii becomes 50th US state

A proposal for Hawaiian statehood was originally presented as part of a combined bill for both Hawaiian and Alaskan statehood. The combination complicated the political processes involved in the plan's debate in Congress, and progress stalled. Hawaiians favored the move to statehood, and in 1954 over 110,000 islanders signed a **petition** urging Congress to act. Hawaii and Alaska were eventually put on separate bills, and in 1959 Hawaii became the **50th US state.**

THE GROWTH OF TOURISM. Advances in air travel and increased investment in the islands during World War II helped to expand the tourism industry in the islands. Once Hawaii became a state, it was marketed as the **"American Paradise"** on the mainland, and tourists flocked to experience it. By the 1970s, tourism had a firm position as the state's **top industry,** surpassing the military.

THE HAWAIIAN RENAISSANCE

HAWAIIAN HOMELANDS. In the early 1920s, **Prince Kuhio,** a member of the nobility and a Republican delegate to Congress, spearheaded the passage of the **Hawaiian Homes Commission Act.** The Act, which became law in 1921, was meant to protect native Hawaiians by releasing public lands for the purposes of agricultural development and homesteading, much of it on the island of Molokai. The Act also set up a Commission to administer the program. The success of the program itself was questionable, as much of the land was leased to corporations. It was, however, a part of the movement that gained particular significance in the wake of the tourism boom during the postwar years.

1969
Hawaii Five-O
debuts on TV

Hawaiian activism in the 1970s focused on love for the land or **aloha'aina.** One of the first markers of the movement was a confrontation over land use in Kalama Valley in 1970. A group of 5,000 Hawaiians near Waimanalo soon formed **The Hawaiians,** and lobbied in protest of the **Department of Hawaiian Homelands'** administration of the Homelands Act. Up to that time, the Department had appropriated only 20% of its 200,000+ acres to native Hawaiians. The group was successful in its bid to obtain more lots for natives. Continuing in the tradition of Prince Kuhio's original conditions in the Hawaiian Homes Commission Act, the **Office of Hawaiian Affairs (OHA)** was founded in 1978 for the protection of the interests of native Hawaiians, using revenue from public lands.

KAHOOLAWE. The tiny island of Kahoolawe has been another focal point of the *aloha'aina* movement. During the 19th century feral goats and sheep roamed the island, devastating plant life and causing massive **erosion.** The **US Navy** seized the island at the start of World War II to use it as a target and training area—for bombing practice. The Navy failed to return the island at the end of the war, and in 1953 an **Executive Order** placed the island under the control of the Secretary of the Navy on the condition that it would be returned in a "habitable condition" once the Navy no longer needed it. The island lay littered with undetonated bombs and other military wreckage for another 20 years until the formation of **Project Kaho'olwae 'Ohana** in 1976. Kaho'olawe 'Ohana challenged the Navy and the government by carrying out a series of occupations which brought national attention to the movement. Kaho'olawe 'Ohana settled a federal suit against the Navy in 1980 with a Consent Decree which allowed access to the island for educational, scientific, and cultural purposes.

1976
Voyage of the outrigger canoe
Hokule'a

1978
Office of Hawaiian
Affairs established

1980
Magnum P.I.
debuts on TV

1983
Kilauea volcano begins erupting on the Big Island. It's still going. Hurricane Iniki hits Kauai

1993
US Congress passes the Apology Resolution

In 1993, the Hawaii State Legislature established the **Kahoolawe Island Reserve,** consisting of the island proper and all the waters around it in a two-mile radius. The area was preserved solely for Native Hawaiian cultural, spiritual, environmental, educational, and historical purposes; commercial usage is strictly prohibited. Congress also passed a law requiring the Navy to both return the island to the state and to conduct a cleanup and environmental restoration of the area. Under the bill, federal funding is allocated to the project through November 2003. Rounding out the list of major legislative events in 1993 is the **"Apology Resolution"** passed in the US Congress, which apologized to native Hawaiians for the overthrow of the monarchy in 1893, and for the deprivation of rights to self-determination.

HOKULE'A. On May 2, 1976 a double-hulled canoe, a replica of the kind that brought the first Polynesians to Hawaii, departed from the islands to begin an overseas voyage recreating the route of those ancient mariners. The vessel, the **Hokule'a** ("star of gladness") was so named in honor of Hawaii's **zenith star,** also known as Arcturus. The 17-man crew traversed the seas using ancient **Polynesian navigational methods,** relying only upon the stars and ocean currents as guides. When they arrived at their destination in Tahiti, there were more than 25,000 spectators waiting to greet them.

The voyage was not only a physical triumph, but a cultural one as well, creating a focal point for native Hawaiian pride. After its successful journey, the vessel was taken to schools throughout Hawaii and used as an educational tool to promote knowledge of Hawaiian heritage. The boat ultimately capsized in a storm off the coast of Molokai in 1978, but not before making a lasting impact on the Hawaiian renaissance movement.

HAWAII TODAY

THE END OF THE TWENTIETH CENTURY. Within the last decade, there have been moves to rectify the injustices of Hawaii's past. Dole's Iwilei pineapple cannery (1992) and the last sugar plantation on the Big Island (1995) closed. There was also national recognition of the role of the US government in the disenfranchisement of native Hawaiian peoples, and in the destruction of Hawaiian land during the 19th century. **Tourism** remained the primary industry of the state, despite a slump in economic and population growth. In 1992, **Hurricane Iniki** hit the island of Kauai and the western shores of Oahu. The storm was the strongest hurricane to hit the islands in a century and caused mass destruction.

1995
The last sugar plantation in Hawaii closes

2000
US Supreme Court decides *Rice v. Cayetano*

THE NEW MILLENNIUM. The US Supreme Court case of **Rice v. Cayetano** (2000) was another seminal event in the series of legislative moves regarding the rights of native Hawaiians. The ruling declared that the restriction of voting in the Office of Hawaiian Affairs to native Hawaiians violates the 15th Amendment. The issue of ethnicity regulations gained another dimension in 2002, when **Kamehameha Schools** admitted a non-Hawaiian school to their Maui campus. Heated debate erupted over the schools' admissions policies, which have traditionally limited the acceptance pool to students of Hawaiian blood. Many critics of the schools' actions claim that they are an attempt to protect the school from claims of discrimination and, in turn, safeguard its tax-free status.

On **September 11, 2001** hijacked planes crashed into the World Trade Center in New York City, the Pentagon in Washington, D.C., and in Pennsylvania, claiming thousands of lives. Air travel was suspended throughout the US following the attacks, and travel by air continued to suffer in the US and abroad in the months that followed. During this time Hawaii saw a significant decline in tourism, as it is primarily accessible by plane. It was estimated that even as of March 2002 the state's tourism was still down 13% from the previous year. However, despite an overall economic slump in the US, tourism in Hawaii has been returning to normal levels throughout 2002.

2001
Terrorist attacks in New York City, Washington, D.C., and Pennsylvania.

2002
Hawaii passes a bill to become the first state to put a cap on gasoline prices. First edition of *Let's Go Hawaii* begins production

PEOPLE

DEMOGRAPHICS

The people of Hawaii are world-famous for their spirit of **aloha.** This attitude of friendly acceptance is characterized by a sense of warmth, kindness, generosity, humility, and patience. And with a population density of about 200 people per square mile, *aloha* becomes practically a necessity in Hawaii.

The secret to Hawaiian harmony may lie in the fact that it is one of the few places in the US, and perhaps the world, where there is no racial or ethnic majority. The state population of 1.2 million (2000) is 24% white (*haole*), 19% Hawaiian, 17% Japanese, 14% Filipino, 5% Chinese, 2% Korean, 2% black, and 20% mixed. Less than 1% of those who identify themselves as Hawaiian are pure Hawaiians, and the high incidence of intermarriage among people of different races and ethnicities makes the population even more diverse.

Among the Hawaiians who have made a name for themselves on the mainland are entertainer **Don Ho;** politician **Hiram L. Fong,** the first Chinese-American senator, elected in 1959; astronaut **Ellison Onizuka,** a member of the ill-fated 1986 Challenger crew; legendary **Duke Paoa Kahanamoku,** Olympic swimmer and gold medalist who introduced surfing to the non-Hawaiian world; and actress **Tia Carrere,** of *Wayne's World* fame.

LANGUAGE

ʻÔleo Hawaiʻi, the Hawaiian language, belongs to a family of Polynesian languages which also includes Tahitian, Maori, Tumotuan, and Rarotongan. Hawaiian's reduplication, apparent in words like *wikiwiki* (fast) and *mahimahi* (dolphin), its application of glottal stops (symbolized by the *ʻokina* (ʻ) and similar to what comes between the "uh" and the "oh" in "uh-oh"), and the prolific use of vowels make it particularly distinctive.

'Ōleo Hawai'i was a strictly oral language until the arrival of Captain James Cook in 1778 and the Protestant missionaries who flocked to the island thereafter. The missionaries' primary goal was to teach the islanders to read the Bible, so they set about giving the Hawaiian language a written form. What emerged was a 12-letter alphabet that became the official **writing system** of the Hawaiian government.

When Hawaii was annexed by the US in 1898, *'Ōleo Hawai'i* was banned from schools and government and English became the state's official language. *'Ōleo Hawai'i* dwindled to near-extinction until the 1970's, when a Hawaiian cultural renaissance (see **History**, p. 19) rekindled interest in the language. In 1978, *'Ōleo Hawai'i* again became an official language of the State of Hawaii (along with English), and it remains the only Native American language that is officially used by a state government. By 1987, public schools were teaching the language, and the number of speakers continues to grow today.

Hawaii's *unofficial* language is **Hawaiian Creole** or **Pidgin.** A by-product of Hawaii's tremendous diversity, Pidgin developed as a means of communication between people who spoke different languages for use in business transactions. It integrates elements from Hawaiian, English, Chinese, and Japanese, among others. Nearly all Hawaiians incorporate some Pidgin into their daily conversation, regardless of education or socio-economic status, though it is primarily used by teenagers. While native Hawaiians often appreciate attempts by visitors to speak *Ōleo Hawai'i*, it is inadvisable for visitors to try to speak Pidgin, as it is usually considered condescending.

RELIGION

Prior to contact with the West, life in Hawaii was governed by the system of **kapu,** or taboo, meaning literally "obey or die." Every aspect of the early Hawaiians' daily life was regulated by this strict set of rules and customs. The *kapu*, while often restrictive and unfair, was largely responsible for the high degree of order in early Hawaiian society. **Kahunas** (priests) wielded considerable power in early Hawaii and were responsible for enforcing the *kapu*. Among their other responsibilities were healing, canoe-building, and leading the islands' chiefs in elaborate religious ceremonies which were carried out in meticulous detail, as the slightest deviation from *aha* (perfection) would incur the wrath of the gods.

Hawaiians believed that all natural phenomena were controlled by the gods, whose aid and protection they sought through offerings and worship. Particularly in times of trouble, sacrifices—sometimes even human sacrifices—would be made in order to appease the gods and encourage them to look upon the people with favor. Idols were a key element of early Hawaiian religion, as it was believed that they represented a link between mankind and the gods. Every home had an altar (*kua'aha*) where families worshipped their guardian deities (*aumakua*). Greater gods (*akua*) were worshipped in more complex ceremonies in heiaus (open-air temples), which were presided over by kahunas. Among the *akua* are: **Kane,** god of creation; **Ku,** god of war; **Lono,** god of peace, prosperity, wind and rain; **Kanaloa,** god of the ocean; and **Pele,** goddess of the volcano.

The **Kumulipo,** an ancient Hawaiian *mele oli*, or chant, tells the Hawaiian version of the story of creation. Handed down from generation to generation in the oral tradition, the kahunas would memorize the poem, which consists of over 2,000 lines, and recite it on special occasions, such as the birth of a first-born child or at festivals honoring the gods. The early Hawaiians believed that the night gave birth to *kumulipo*, the source of all life. Interestingly, it appears that they also believed in some degree of **evolution,** as the *Kumulipo* describes how organisms were created, starting with the simplest and gradually progressing to the complex.

After the death of Kamehameha around 1820, just before the arrival of missionaries from the West, the cult of the ancient Hawaiians dissolved. Heiaus and idols were destroyed, and the *kapu* was abolished, making way for the new religion—Christianity—that was soon to arrive. Elements of this earlier belief system persist in Hawaii today, however, as evidenced by the proliferation of miniature idols. Many people—locals and tourists alike—still make offerings to Pele and other deities in attempts to win their favor.

As one would expect, religion in Hawaii today is as varied as its colorful and diverse population. Protestants, Catholics, Jews, Buddhists, Hindus, and a melange of others exist peacefully alongside one another. Travelers will have no difficulty finding services to meet their spiritual needs, regardless of their faith.

VERTICALLY CHALLENGED The menehune legends are a colorful part of Hawaii's culture. Stories about these fabled "little people" abound—each one more fantastical than the next. The menehune are credited with being superior builders who could construct impressive structures overnight; **Kauai's Alekoko Fishpond** and **Menehune Ditch** are said to be examples of their handywork.

According to scholars, the menehune lore has historical roots. Though the theories vary slightly, most agree that the name "menehune" comes from the Tahitian word for slaves or people of small status, *manahune*. Polynesians from the Marquesas Islands settled Hawaii sometime around the 6th century. 600 or so years later, conquerors from the Tahitian Islands arrived in Hawaii. Before long, they succeeded in subjugating the Marquesans and forcing them north, to Kauai. The Tahitians looked down upon the original settlers, contemptuously calling them *manahune*. Some historians speculate that the menehune legends were born when Western writers heard of the *manahune* and misconstrued the term to mean people of small size. With their active imaginations and a little help from amused Hawaiian contacts (who obligingly revised and expanded their knowledge of the "little people"), the menehune tradition was born.

The more popular accounts of the menehune describe them as elf-like creatures who make their homes in the dense forest or the mountains of Pu'ukapele. They are 2-3 ft. in height, with potbellies, dark eyes, and short noses. Shunning clothes, the menehune grow their hair to their knees and use it to cover themselves.

The menehune make numerous appearances—in many different guises—throughout Hawaiian legends. Sometimes they come across as mischievous practical jokers who enjoy toying with the Hawaiian people. In other tales, they are portrayed as more benevolent creatures—a kind of miniature fairy godmothers for the Hawaiian people. According to lore, the Hawaii state fish got its name when a menehune saw the fish and sneezed, making a noise that sounded like *humuhumunukunukuapua'a*.

CULTURE

FOOD

Hawaiian culture is intricately tied to food. In many ways, the confluence of backgrounds and ethnicities that makes up Hawaii's unique population is most evident in local culinary favorites. Most popular dishes combine elements of several cultures and incorporate unique island ingredients. Much like Hawaii residents, island fare is unpretentious and low-key; anything that isn't beach-friendly is immediately suspect.

The epitome of local cuisine is the **plate lunch.** It's practically sacrilegious to leave the islands without trying this ubiquitous meal. Plate lunches are available almost everywhere, from roadside stands to fast-food chains. The meal is a descendant of the Japanese plantation worker's **bento,** a bucket lunch consisting of rice, meat, and pickled vegetables. A typical plate lunch is a combination of two scoops of white rice, one scoop of macaroni salad, and an entree. For the entree, most places offer an overwhelming array of choices. At the very least, most menus list Japanese teriyaki or *katsu,* Korean short ribs, Filipino *adobo,* Chinese soy-sauce chicken, hamburgers, and chili. Quantity often trumps quality in this island version of comfort food. Most plate lunches (inexpensive at $6-8) can usually feed two people easily.

Many other local favorites have been taken from outside cultures and adapted over the years. **Saimin,** Japanese noodle soup known as Ramen on the mainland, is so common that even McDonalds offers a fast-food version. Locals turn the packaged noodles into more of a stew, adding vegetables, tofu, leftover meat, or dumplings—whatever is handy, really. **Crack seed,** residents' preferred snack, is a generic term that refers to a type of preserved fruit that was brought to Hawaii by Chinese plantation workers. Many generations of kids and teenagers have flocked to neighborhood crack seed shops for afterschool snacks. The little stores are packed with island delicacies—Japanese rice crackers (*arare*), peanuts, coconut candy, dried squid—in addition to the huge glass jars filled with varieties of crack seed. The most popular versions of the treat are **li hing** (a distinct sweet-sour seasoning), plum and mango.

Some other local treats are Hawaiian to the core. **Shave ice** comes from the old days, when islanders would shave blocks of ice into a fine powder and top it with fruit juice. Since then, electricity has taken the grunt work out of the process, but the idea remains the same. Toppings include the basic flavored syrups as well as fancier options such as ice cream, condensed milk, shaved *li hing mui,* and *azuki beans.* **Spam,** the lovable spiced ham in a can, rounds out any true Hawaiian's diet. After being introduced to Spam by the military during World War II, islanders quickly incorporated the food into their cooking. Despite mainland conceptions of Spam as pedestrian and unappealing, islanders are addicted. Hawaii now boasts the highest Spam consumption in the world (11,000 cans daily). **Spam musubi,** sticky rice topped by Spam and wrapped in dried seaweed, is one of the most popular forms of the food's preparation. **Poi** is another unique island dish. Made out of pounded *taro* root, *poi* is a thick, purplish-grey paste. Though it has no strong flavor, *poi's* unfamiliar consistency and appearance make it an acquired taste. However, locals swear by it and some even rave about its semi-magical healing powers.

In recent years, Hawaii-based chefs have developed a style of cooking they call **Hawaii Regional Cuisine.** Led by **Sam Choy, Alan Wong,** and **Roy Yamaguchi,** the chefs have taken advantage of Hawaii's unique ingredients to create a type of cuisine that honors Hawaii's diverse culture while meeting the highest culinary standards.

LUAUS

Under **kanawai,** the ancient Hawaiian system of laws, certain things were **kapu,** or forbidden. Kapu dictated that women eat separate from the men; in addition, they were prohibited from eating many island delicacies. However, in 1819, King Kamehameha II held a huge feast, during which he ate with women. With the event, the ancient religious traditions died and a new tradition, that of the **luau,** was born.

The luau takes its name from the young *taro* leaves that are used in the preparation of many luau dishes. Originally a celebration giving thanks to the gods, the luau has become one of the most well-known aspects of Hawaiian culture. Birthdays, anniversaries, and any other significant events are marked with these traditional feasts. The tourist industry has capitalized on the marketability of the luau; almost every major hotel and restaurant offers some version to tempt visitors.

Historically, luau guests sat on woven mats laid on the floor and used their fingers to devour the feast. Many modern-day luaus are still held on the grass, though bigger celebrations might have tents and picnic tables. There is almost always some form of musical entertainment, whether it is a cousin strumming a guitar or an entire group complete with ukulele, steel guitar, and bass. The main focus of any luau is the traditionally-prepared **kalua pig**. The meat is covered in *ti* or banana leaves and roasted in an **imu** (underground oven). The meat is supplemented by other island dishes, such as **poi, poke** (raw, seasoned sashimi), **lau lau** (meat wrapped in *taro* leaves and coconut milk, then steamed), and **lomi salmon** (salted salmon with tomatoes and Maui onions). The meal is finished with a dessert of **haupia** (coconut pudding), **pineapple,** and **coconut cake.**

HAWAIIAN DRESS

On any given day, locals look beach-ready. The preferred style of dress often incorporates one or more of the following: **slippers** (plastic flip-flops), **boardshorts,** other **surf-inspired clothing,** and anything **aloha-print.** One of the most popular elements of Hawaiian dress, the **aloha shirt,** actually owes its inspiration to both Western and Asian cultures. Supposedly a descendant of the thick "thousand-mile" shirt worn by pioneers and missionaries, the aloha shirt came into its familiar form in the late 1920s at the hands of Waikiki tailor **Ellery J. Chun.** The style only became common, however, after **Herbert Briner** began mass-manufacturing the shirts in the late 1930s. The popularity of the distinctive shirts grew steadily. During the 1950s, the aloha shirt craze spread to the mainland when audiences saw icons like Elvis Presley, John Wayne, and Frank Sinatra wearing them in feature films. In response to the widespread mimicking of the aloha shirt, the Hawaii Chamber of Commerce ruled in the 1960s that a true aloha shirt must be made in Hawaii. Currently, the only company to design and produce shirts entirely in Hawaii is **Reyn Spooner.** Early aloha shirts are auctioned off for as much as $1000.

CUSTOMS & ETIQUETTE

Hawaii residents place so much stock in the **aloha spirit** that there is an actual law in the Hawaii Revised Statutes (section 5-7.5) that requires residents to abide by the spirit of ancient Hawaiians. And, for the most part, locals do. Smiles abound and islanders are quick to wave hello, usually in the form of **shaka,** a greeting made by extending the pinkie and thumb and curling up the middle three fingers of the right hand. It is especially popular with young people in Hawaii; the gesture is a way of saying, "hang loose" or "relax." The word **aloha** is also used extensively throughout the islands. Don't be afraid to use it to say hello; it's not regarded as corny. The **lei,** a garland of flowers, shells, leaves, or even candy, is a traditional Hawaiian symbol of love or friendship. Visitors entering and leaving Hawaii are often gifted with the fragrant necklaces. Leis are also given to mark special occasions like anniversaries, birthdays, and graduations.

While Hawaii is extremely laid-back, there are a few things that travellers should keep in mind. Hawaii is inhabited by an exceptionally diverse group of people. The only people who are referred to as **Hawaiian** are those of Hawaiian blood. Anyone born in the islands, except Caucasians, is a **local.** Whites are called **haoles;** the term is not meant to be offensive. Residents who were born outside of Hawaii but have lived in the state for a considerable amount of time are known as **kamaʻaina.**

Respect is a key word in Hawaiian culture. It is especially important to treat sacred sites, such as *heiaus*, with appropriate consideration. When entering a person's home, it is polite to remove your shoes. Lay off the horn when driving and follow the speed limit. Don't litter.

THE ARTS

ARCHITECTURE. Hawaii's architecture reflects its varied past. **Heiaus** are a remnant of ancient Hawaiian religion. These simple structures were built as temples to the gods and typically consist of altars and taboo houses enclosed by lava or limestone walls. Many, albeit in varying stages of disrepair, still stand today and there have been initiatives to restore them to their original state.

Plantation-style houses are another throwback to Hawaii's past. Built to house immigrant workers from China, Japan, and the Phillipines, the houses were grouped in villages. They stood on lava rock foundations and featured single-wall construction and cedar shingle roofs. The **plantation-style commercial** structures of this era were much more elaborate, often consisting of multiple buildings grouped around a courtyard. The main building would sometimes be modelled in mainland-style, with wide canopies extending over the sidewalk. The **Honolulu Hale** and the **Hawaii State Public Library** are examples of this design.

Along with Christianity, missionaries also brought a more ostentatious style of architecture. Neo-classical edifices such as the **Iolani Palace** and gothic structures like the **Cathedral of St. Andrew's** were built in the late 19th century and strongly reflect Western influences. Most residential houses in Hawaii have been built with regard to the islands' tropical climate. They are typically low, airy structures that make full use of tradewinds.

ARTS. Though it may never rival New York City or Paris, Hawaii has a healthy art community. Along with numerous private galleries, Oahu has two notable art museums. The **Honolulu Academy of the Arts** recently celebrated its 75th birthday. Housed in a historic building in the center of Honolulu, the museum has a permanent stock of over 35,000 pieces, including a celebrated collection of Asian art. The less conventional **Contemporary Museum** has two locations on Oahu. Part of the organization's mission dictates that a significant portion of its exhibitions must focus on art created in Hawaii. Maui too has a strong coalition of artists and art lovers. Each year, the island hosts **Art Maui,** a prestigious exhibition of about 100 new works by Maui County artists.

Hawaii has inspired a number of extraordinary artists. Though prominent oil painter **John Young** died in 1999, he is remembered with a museum within the University of Hawaii. The **John Young Museum of Art** was Young's pet project, fostered out of his belief that all college students should have access to a campus museum. Prior to settling down in Honolulu, Paris-born **Jean Charlot** (1898-1979) worked as Diego Rivera's assistant in Mexico. During his time in Hawaii, Charlot applied the techniques he learned with Rivera to a number of fresco murals that residents can enjoy in various Oahu locations, including the University of Hawaii at Manoa. **Madge Tennent** (1889-1972) concentrated on capturing the beauty she saw in the Hawaiian people. She is best known for her large oil paintings of Hawaiian women, many of which hang prominently in buildings around Honolulu. Other notable Hawaiian artists include: watercolor artist **Hon-Chew Hee;** painter and print-maker **Yvonne Cheng;** and potter and watercolor artist **Charles Higa.**

Art takes on a practical form in the distinctive **Hawaiian quilts.** After learning quilting techniques from New England missionaries, Hawaiian women translated the images from their daily lives onto fabric. The quilts, with their flower, leaf, and vine designs, are still popular today. A full-size quilt can take up to a year to finish.

LITERATURE. Until recently, Hawaiian literature has consisted of tales written by curious outsiders looking in. Early in his career, **Mark Twain** journeyed from San Francisco to Hawaii for a month-long sojourn that became four months. It was Hawaii that helped Twain achieve his mammoth literary stature. Chronicles of his trip were published in the *Sacramento Union* and scholars hold that it was in Hawaii that Twain first began to develop his singular descriptive and interpretive style. Twain later compiled his personal and professional writings from this period into **Roughing It.** Intrigued by the islands and people of the Pacific, **Robert Louis Stevenson** explored the area extensively and lived the last years of his life in Samoa. Much of his writing from that period is compiled in **Travels in Hawaii.** One of the most well-known novels about Hawaii is James Michener's 1,036-page epic titled, simply, **Hawaii.** A combination of fact and fiction, the book begins with the creation of the islands and follows their growth until the year 1955.

Hawaiian authors have begun to assert themselves on the literary scene. Nurtured by local organizations, such as **Bamboo Ridge,** the journal of Hawaii literature and arts, local writers are gaining exposure and (some) critical acclaim. The leader of this generation of authors is Hawaiian-born novelist **Lois-Ann Yamanaka,** who tackles the themes of Asian-American families and local culture in Hawaii. Yamanaka's work addresses the reality of living in paradise; she eschews flowery word painting for authentic pidgin dialogue between her (often dysfunctional) characters. Other authors who are a part of this reinvention of Hawaiian literature include: **Milton Murayama, Darrell Lum, Sylvia Watanabe,** and **Nora Okja Keller.**

MUSIC. Hawaiian music instantly conjures up images of swaying palm trees and crashing waves. Traditional musicians record songs almost entirely in Hawaiian and use the **ukelele, steel guitar** and **slack key guitar** extensively. Legends hold that the ukelele was introduced to Hawaii in 1879 by a Portuguese immigrant named Joao Fernandes. The islanders dubbed Fernandes' braguinha a ukelele (literally, "jumping flea") because of the way the musician's fingers jumped across the strings of the instrument. The ukelele quickly gained popularity; even Hawaiian royalty became proficient. The ukelele became a symbol of Hawaiian beach culture during the 1920s and 30s thanks to a group of men who lived and worked on Waikiki. The **Waikiki Beachboys,** as they were called, serenaded locals and tourists with their ukeleles. The beachboys included such renowned Hawaiian musicians as **Squeeze Kamana** and **Chick Daniels.**

The steel guitar was developed on Oahu by local Joseph Kekuku in the late 19th century. Kekuku's instrument was able to achieve a previously-unthinkable range of sound, and to this day remains a centerpiece of Hawaiian music. Hawaiian musicians round out the distinctive island sound using a guitar technique called slack key, or **ki ho'al.** Literally, "loosen the key," this method of playing consists of relaxing the strings of acoustic guitar and picking them with their fingers. The guitar is reputed to have come to the islands via early 19th-century Spanish and Mexican cowboys. However, Hawaiians developed the unique slack-key sound themselves.

With the Hawaiian renaissance of the 1970s, traditional artists, such as **Israel "IZ" Kamakawiwo'ole,** the **Sons of Hawaii,** and **Keali'I Reichel,** all experienced a boost in their popularity. There remains a large demand for "Island Contemporary" recordings, music that is billed as an "updated Hawaiian sound." Notable artists include: **Teresa Bright, Keola and Kapono Beamer,** and the **Makaha Sons of Ni'ihau.**

DANCE. The **hula** has long been a symbol of Hawaiian culture. Though the precise origins of hula are unknown, the most commonly cited legend holds that the dance began when Pele, the Hawaiian goddess of fire, commanded her younger sister, Laka, to dance. The dances and chants of ancient hula were an integral part of the Hawaiians' oral tradition; through them, elders ensured that their traditions, customs, and history would live on in a younger generation. For a short period in the early 19th century, Christian missionaries convinced the reigning monarchs to outlaw what they regarded as a sinful practice. However, in 1874, **King David Kalakaua** ascended to the throne. The new king, nicknamed the **"Merrie Monarch,"** became hula's greatest patron and during his rule, the dance flourished. The ukelele and the steel guitar were used to accompany dancers, who began wearing *ti* leaf skirts for the first time. Kalakaua is remembered each year in the **Merrie Monarch Festival,** which showcases both ancient hula and the more modern versions that have developed.

FILM. Despite the difficulty of transporting film-making equipment, movie producers have never been able to resist Hawaii's allure. The islands are reputed to have made their onscreen debut as early as 1898, when a film crew stranded by a layover shot footage of the tropical paradise. In the early 1900s, Hawaii was used in numerous silent films, including *Hawaiian Love* (1913) and *The Shark God* (1913).The advent of "talkies" added a new dimension to Hawaiian-set films. In 1937, Bing Crosby starred in **Waikiki Wedding,** playing a crooning press agent for a pineapple cannery. The film's hit song, "Sweet Leilani" garnered an Oscar and earned Crosby his first gold record.

Though World War II put the Hawaii filmmaking on hold for a few years, it also provided the island movie industry with its most enduring subject: war. *From Here to Eternity* (1953) chronicled the days leading up the Pearl Harbor attack but is probably best remembered for the scene of Burt Lancaster and Deborah Kerr's passionate embrace on the sand (and in the water) of Halona Cove. Kauai was used to film the musical *South Pacific* (1958), in which Mitzi Gaynor plays a lovestruck Army nurse who tries, unsuccessfully, to wash a captivating man out of her hair. Elvis Presley fastened the gaze of his adoring fans on Hawaii when he starred in 1961's *Blue Hawaii.* As a lackadaisical island boy back from the war, Presley spends much of the movie strumming the ukelele and wooing beach bunnies with his signature dance moves. The film yielded several musical hits, including "Blue Hawaii" and "Can't Help Falling In Love."

Filmmakers switched gears in 1976, when Hawaii was featured in the blockbuster *King Kong.* Following the movie's release, Hawaii increasingly became the filming site of action-packed crowd-pleasers. In 1980, George Lucas and Steven Spielberg joined forces to produce the first of the Indiana Jones series, *Raiders of the Lost Ark,* filmed partly in Kauai. Spielberg continued his blockbuster trend with *Jurassic Park* (1992), also filmed in Hawaii. The 1997 dino-sequel, *The Lost World,* faltered in the wake of its predecessor's success, though it still featured gorgeous shots of Kauai's lush scenery. Other crowd-pleasers filmed in Hawaii include: *George of the Jungle* (1997), *Mighty Joe Young* (1998), and *6 Days, 7 Nights* (1998).

Hawaii continues to be a popular site for movie-making. In 2001, producer Jerry Bruckheimer let loose his biggest (and longest) film yet, the epic *Pearl Harbor.* Director Tim Burton also used Hawaii for part of his remake of *Planet of the Apes* (2001). Director John Woo, originally of Hong Kong, returned to the World War II theme in *Windtalkers* (2002). In addition to sweeping shots of the Hawaiian islands, the film features Nicholas Cage as U.S. Marine Sergeant who must protect a Navajo codetalker. The Hawaii Visitor's and Convention Bureau joined forces with Disney to market the company's most recent animated feature, *Lilo & Stitch* (2002), which is set in the islands.

Hawaii hosts a few **film festivals** each year. The **Hawaii International Film Festival** began at the University of Hawaii (Manoa) in 1981 as a means of cultural exchange between North America, Asia, and the Pacific. It is now an state-wide event, with screenings on the six major Hawaiian islands. The **Maui Film Festival** is still in its infancy—it began in 2000—but attendance has been strong and it seems like the event is around to stay.

HAWAII

ON LOCATION IN THE ISLANDS Hawaii has had its share of television excitement. From 1968 to 1980, **Hawaii 5-0**, one of the longest-running series on television, was filmed almost exclusively in Hawaii. During the 80s, Tom Selleck charmed viewers across the nation as a dashing Hawaii-based private investigator in **Magnum, P.I.** The **Baywatch** cast packed up its itty-bitty wardrobe and suntan oil in 1999 to relocate from California to Hawaii. The new series, **Baywatch Hawaii**, lasted only two seasons.

RECENT DEVELOPMENTS. In 2000, the Hawaii Television and Development Board was created to facilitate film and TV production in the islands. In a move to encourage the use of Hawaii in film and television, the Hawaii Film Office is working to secure the necessary funds to revamp the Hawaii Film Studio at Diamond Head. The studio was built in 1976 for Hawaii Five-0 and has since been the site for number of projects, including **Final Fantasy** and the yet-to-be-released sequel to **The Matrix.** All plans are currently on hold, as the Hawaii Film Office waits to see whether Governor Ben Cayetano decides to grant them their requested funds. Cayetano, along with other state officials, had hopes of Hawaii building its own film industry. Those wishes all but died with the closure of the Honolulu-based studio **Square USA** after their would-be hit *Final Fantasy* flopped at the box office.

SPORTS & RECREATION

With a myriad of outdoor activities available, Hawaii vacations are more about hopping from activity to activity, than they are about passively soaking up sun. Water sports reign here—some of the **world's best surfing and windsurfing** spots are in Hawaii. **Golf** is the chosen sport of many tourists, and manicured green courses are spread across the islands—most often with luxury resort complexes in tow. Sports in Hawaii run the gamut from the extreme to the tame; other popular activities include paddling, kayaking, snorkeling, surfing, scuba diving, swimming, hiking and biking.

COLLEGE SPORTS AND FOOTBALL. Water polo, volleyball, and sailing are among the most popular high school and college competitive sports in Hawaii. The **University of Hawaii at Manoa** Rainbow Warriors boast a nationally-ranked sailing program, and the 2002 Men's Volleyball team were National Champions. Since 1997, the **Hula Bowl All-Star Football Classic** has been held each year on Maui. Recent negotiations between bowl officials and the **NFL** have resulted in a decision to link the Hula Bowl and the **Pro-Bowl.** The Hula Bowl will move from January to the first weekend in February, the date of the Pro-Bowl. In addition, the newly-created NCAA **Hawaii Bowl** will be played in the Aloha Stadium on Christmas Day.

GOING THE DISTANCE. Laid-back lifestyle aside, Hawaii is home to hundreds of running events and triathlons, from one-mile fun-runs to a 100-mile ultramarathon on the Big Island. Among these is one of the world's most badass multisport events—the **Ironman Triathlon.** Held every fall in Kailua-Kona on the Big Island, the event draws 1500 qualifiers from all 50 US states and over 50 countries to compete in the grueling race. Competitors start with a 2.4-mile ocean swim, followed by a 112-mile bike race, and cap the whole thing off with a full 26.2-mile marathon. The course is open for 17 hours; the current record time is 8:04:08 set by Luc Van Lierde in 1996. Over 50 million viewers world-wide tune in to witness the event each year.

Hawaii also has five official **marathons.** The Honolulu Marathon, held each December, is the 6th-largest marathon in the world. The Maui Marathon, held in

March, was the first of the pack as the oldest continuously-held running event in Hawaii. The other official marathons are the Kilauea Volcano Marathon in July, the Kona Marathon in August, and the Big Island International Marathon in October.

PADDLING. Outrigger canoe paddling is widespread throughout the Hawaii. By all accounts, the phenomenally popular sport originated in the islands. The **outrigger canoe** differs from a regular canoe in that it has a rig, known as an **outrigger**, extending from one or both sides of the vessel. The outrigger acts to balance the hull of the boat. Early Hawaiians used the outrigger canoes extensively in their daily lives, and paddling eventually became a means of recreation.

Encouraged by King Kalakaua, paddling enthusiasts formed the first official outrigger club in 1908. **The Outrigger Canoe Club of Hawaii** was followed shortly after by **Hui Nalu** and, in 1910, canoe racing began. Formal regattas began in the 1940s and there are now over 60 outrigger clubs throughout the islands with 30 on Oahu alone. Paddlers are typically grouped into divisions by age. There is a separate junior season (January-March) to ensure that younger athletes get as much attention as possible. Though paddling had previously been dominated by males, the number of women competing in the sport has increased steadily since the 1980s.

Participants race in six-person canoes in both sprint and distance events. Sprints are held in sheltered water, usually rivers, lakes, or bays, and can range from 250m to 3000m in length (though 250m to 500m is most common). Distance races differ from between age groups. In open divisions, courses can be anywhere from 8km to 60km (the famed Molokai to Oahu race). In extremely long races, some regattas actually allow fresh rowers to switch into the boat in a procedure called a changeover.

The **International Polynesian Canoe Federation** promotes the sport within the Pacific region, though there is no set of official rules. Each state or country develops its own body of regulations. In the Hawaiian islands, the Hawaii Canoe Racing Association (HCRA) is organized by geography into smaller regulatory bodies. At the end of each season, regional events qualify paddlers to the state championships, which rotate between the islands.

Sailing canoes are a variation on the outrigger canoes. Though not nearly as common as paddling, sailing canoe races have been gaining popularity. Each May, participants race the 75 miles between Maui and Oahu in canoe sailing's most well-known competition, the Steinlarger Ho'omana'o Sailing Canoe Race.

SURFING. Surfing was born in Hawaii, and the sport stays true to its homeland. There is no impeding continental shelf surrounding the islands to slow incoming waves, so they arrive huge and powerful on Hawaiian shores in the form of magnificent, world-renown surf. As is the case with weather in Hawaii, there are two seasons for surf—summer and winter. The two seasons constitute the entire year and are differentiated by wind and storm patterns. Storms in the South Pacific generate Hawaii surf in the **summer** (May-August). Summer surf is dominated by northeast trade winds and occurs on the southern shores of the islands. In the **winter** (September-April), storms in the northern Pacific create surf on the northern shores of the islands. The seasons' overlap allows for nearly year-round surfing.

The so-called "sport of kings" began as the ancient sport of **he'e nalu** (wave-sliding) which was perfected by the kings of Hawaii. The revival of interest in surfing in the early 20th century is attributed to Hawaii's **Duke Kahanamoku**. His Highness Duke was a talented swimmer, representing the United States at 4 Olympic Games between 1912 and 1924, winning 3 gold medals and 2 silver to become Hawaii's first Olympic medalist. His first love was surfing, however, and he organized one of the first amateur surfing clubs in 1908. He also invented **windsurfing**—which has become one of Hawaii's most popular sports—and **wakesurfing** (surfing in the wake of a motorboat).

Since then, the evolution of **board design** and material has been a major catalyst in the changes in the face of surfing as an activity and as a culture. The first boards were made of wood; their weight and lack of maneuverability was part of what limited the sport to men. The first big breakthrough in board design came in 1958 when surfboard construction changed to lightweight foam and fiberglass, making surfing accessible to everyone. Surfing had gained popularity in California around the same time as part of the surfing craze of the 1950s and 60s, which included surfing fashion, music, and movies. The lighter boards made surfing more accessible to **women** in particular, and women have been making waves in the surfing world since the 50s. Surfing is the second-fastest growing sport among women, and they are quickly gaining respect and recognition (see **Ride the Wave,** p. 414).

Today, surfers use one of two types of boards: **long boards** (traditional style of board that can range as long as 10-12 ft.) and **short boards.** Short boards are less than 9 ft. in length, are faster, and have better maneuverability. Although beginning surfers generally start off on long boards, most surfers use short boards as well, as they are better for riding larger waves. Surfboards have two to three fins, called a **thruster,** which provide greater maneuverability. The addition of a **leash** improved both the safety of surfing and its style. Before leashes were added, surfers spent a lot of time swimming out to retrieve lost boards after getting knocked off by waves. Lost boards would collide with reefs and rocks as well, resulting in significant board damage. With leashes, surfers can ride waves near rocks and reefs and try radical tricks with greater security.

A SURFING STATE OF MIND For many locals, surfing is not just an activity, but a way of life. Surfers range from the hard-core pro surfers, to local *bruddahs,* to 9-5ers who keep a board in their trunks to catch a post-work wave. While tourists are welcome to pick up a board and try their hand on a curl, don't expect to be inducted into surfer culture fresh off your first wave. Surfers are secretive about the best spots, have their own slang, and abide by their own code. A few tips on **surfer etiquette** for novice wave-riders: never drop-in. The surfer closest to the curl (the breaking part of the wave) has the right of way on that wave, and all other surfers should back up out of it (failure to do so is dropping in). Be careful of body boarders and other surfers—collisions can cause serious injuries.

HOLIDAYS & FESTIVALS

Hawaii celebrates all US national holidays. In addition, the state has several unique days of commemoration:

September 2: Queen Lili'uokalani Day

March 26: Prince Kuhio Day

April 15: Father Damien DeVeusteur Day

May 1: Lei Day

June 11: King Kamehameha Day

Third Friday in August: Statehood Day

HAWAII'S FESTIVALS (2003)

DATE	NAME & LOCATION	DESCRIPTION
Late January	Chinese New Year's Celebration (Chinatown, Oahu)	A lion dance, fireworks, and all the Chinese food you can handle.
Late January	Pacific Islands Arts Festival (Waikiki)	Local culinary favorites, "make n' takes" for kids, and demonstrations by local artists.
Mid-February	Polynesian Festival (Waikiki)	Poi pounding, coconut husking, fire-making, and more! Food, entertainment, and crafts from various Polynesian islands.
Early April	Merrie Monarch Festival (Hilo)	A week of cultural events culminating in Hawaii's most prestigious hula competition.
Late March	Great Hawaiian Rubber Duckie Race and Festival (Oahu)	Family entertainment, food, a duck parade, and, of course, a 20,000 entrant rubber duckie race. All proceeds benefit the United Cerebral Palsy Association of Hawaii.
Mid-June	Maui Film Festival (Wailua)	Film premieres under the stars as well as food and wine events.
Late June	Taste of Honolulu (Honolulu)	An outdoor wine, food, and entertainment festival benefiting Easter Seals Hawaii.
September-October	Aloha Festival (state-wide)	Hawaii's largest cultural festival, spanning two months and featuring events on all the major islands.
Early October	Ironman Triathlon World Championship (Kailua)	Hardcore athletes from around the world flock to the Big Island for this ultimate showing of human endurance.
Late October	Macadamia Nut Festival (Hilo)	Yummy macadamia nut concoctions, local music and entertainment.
November	Hawaiian International Film Festival (state-wide)	Screenings of (mostly) Pacific Rim films in various locations across the state.

ADDITIONAL RESOURCES

HISTORY

A Concise History of the Hawaiian Islands. Phil Barnes (Petroglyph Press Ltd., 1999).

Ancient Hawaii. Herb Kawainui Kane (Kawainui Press, 1998).

The Apotheosis of Captain Cook. Gananath Obeyesekere (Princeton University Press, 1992).

At Dawn We Slept: The Untold Story of Pearl Harbor. Gordon William Prang, et al. (Penguin, 1999).

Day of Infamy: The Classic Account of the Bombing of Pearl Harbor. Walter Lord (Henry Holt & Co., 2001).

How "Natives" Think. Marshall Sahlins (University of Chicago Press, 1995).

In the Shadow of the Pali: A Story of the Hawaiian Leper Colony. Lisa Cindrich (Penguin, 2002).

Niihau: The Last Hawaiian Island. Ruth M. Tabrah (Booklines Hawaii Ltd., 1987).

Paradise Remade: The Politics of Culture and History in Hawaii. Elizabeth Buck (Temple University Press, 1994).

THE GREAT OUTDOORS

A Field Guide to the Birds of Hawaii and the Tropical Pacific. Douglas Pratt (Princeton University Press, 1987).

Hawaii Best Beaches. John R. K. Clark (University of Hawaii Press, 1999).

Hawaii's Best Hiking Trails. Robert Smith and Kevin Chard (Hawaiian Outdoor Adventure, 1999).

Hiking Maui: The Valley Isle. Robert Smith (Hawaiian Outdoor Adventure, 1999).

Kauai Trails: Walks, Strolls and Treks on the Garden Island, Kathy Morey (Wilderness Press, 2002).

Kauai Trailblazer: Where to Hike, Snorkel, Bike, Paddle, Surf. Jerry Sprout (Diamond Valley Co., 2002).

Plants and Flowers of Hawaii. Seymour H. Sohmer (University of Hawaii Press, 1994).

Remains of a Rainbow: Rare Plants and Animals of Hawaii. David Littschwager, et. al. (National Geographic Society, 2001).

SPORTS

The Big Drop: Classic Big Wave Surfing Stories. John Long (ed.) and Hai Van K. Sponholz (ed.) (Falcon Publishing, 1999).

Girl in the Curl: A Century of Women's Surfing. Andrea Gabbard (Seal Press, 2000)

The Hawaiian Canoe. Tommy Holmes (Editions Limited, 1993).

The Next Wave: The World of Surfing. Nick Carroll (Abbeville Publishers, 1991).

Sleeping in the Shorebreak and Other Hairy Surfing Stories. Don Wolf (Waverider Publications, 1999).

The Ultimate Guide to Marathons. Dennis Craythorn and Rich Hanna (Marathon Publishing, 1997).

CULTURE

The Aloha Shirt: Spirit of the Island. Dale Hope and Gregory Tozian (Beyond Words Publishing, 2000).

The Food of Paradise: Exploring Hawaii's Culinary Heritage. Rachel Laudan (University of Hawaii Press, 1996).

The Hawaiian Lei: A Tradition of Aloha. Ronn Ronck (Mutual Publishing Company, 1999).

The Hawaiian Quilt: A Spiritual Experience. Poakalani Serrao and John Serrao (Mutual Publishing Company, 1997).

FICTION AND TRAVEL NARRATIVES

A Hawaii Anthology. Joseph Stanton, ed. (University of Hawaii Press, 1997).

Blu's Hanging. Lois-Ann Yamanaka (Avon Books, 1998).

da word. Lee Tonouchi (Bamboo Ridge Press, 2001).

Growing Up Local: An Anthology of Poetry and Prose from Hawaii. Eric Chock (ed.), et al. (Bamboo Ridge Press, 2000).

Hawaii. James A. Michener (Random House, 1973).

Hawaii One Summer. Maxine Hong Kingston (University of Hawaii Press, 1998).

Hawaii Reflections: Writings of Mark Twain, Jack London, Robert Louis Stevenson, and Charles W. Stoddard. (Mauna Loa Publishing, 1995).

Roughing It. Mark Twain (N A L, 1976).

Travels in Hawaii. Robert Louis Stevenson (University of Hawaii Press, 1991).

FILM

Blue Hawaii (Dir. Norman Tauroq. 20th Century Fox, 1961).

From Here to Eternity (Dir. Fred Zinneman. Columbia TriStar, 1953).

Gidget Goes Hawaiian (Dir. Paul Wendkos. Columbia TriStar, 1961).

Hawaii (Dir. George Roy Hill. MGM, 1966).

Magnum P.I.—Don't Eat the Snow in Hawaii (Dir. Roger Young. Universal Studios, 1980).

Molokai: The Story of Father Damien (Dir. Paul Cox. Unapix, 1999).

Ride the Wild Surf (Dir. Don Taylor. Columbia TriStar, 1964).

Surfing for Life (Dir. David L. Brown and Roy Earnest. 1999).

Tora! Tora! Tora! (Dir. Richard Fleischer. 20th Century Fox, 1970).

HAWAIIAN MYTHS AND LEGENDS

Hawaii Magic and Spirituality. Scott Cunningham (Llewellyn Publications, 2000).

Hawaiian Mythology. Martha Warren Beckwith (University of Hawaii Press, 1977).

The Legends and Myths of Hawaii: The Fables and Folklore of a Strange People. David Kalakaua, R.M. Dagget, ed. (Charles E. Tuttle Co., 1972).

Pele: Goddess of Hawaii's Volcanoes. Herb Kawainui Kane (Kawainui Press, 1996).

The Kulimpo: A Hawaiian Creation Chant. Martha W. Beckwith, ed. (University of Hawaii Press, 1981).

AND MORE...

Hawaiian Dictionary. Mary Kawena Pukui and Samuel H. Elbert (University of Hawaii Press, 1986).

The Kahuna. Likeke R. McBride (Petroglyph Press, 2000).

WHAT'S THE FREQUENCY, KAHUNA?

Tune in, turn on, mellow out. Local radio isn't just about surf conditions anymore—it's a way to get inside info on community happenings—from island politics to farmers' markets to drum circles. Keep an ear open for Jawaiian jams, reggae with a Hawaiian twist as smooth and sweet as a mai tai at sunset. So skip the CDs in the rental car and crank the radio dial to the *real* Hawaii. All frequencies are FM unless otherwise noted.

OAHU

89.3 KIPO Hawaii Public Radio—Need your National Public Radio or BBC fix? Here it is—international news and all the erudite pondering you can stand. (http://www.hawaii-publicradio.org)

90.3 KTUH University of Hawaii Radio—Java jive jazz, far-out funk, and freaky free-form brought to you by the cheeky monkeys at UH. Tune in to "Monday Night Live" for live performances by up and coming local acts, M 9pm-midnight. (http://www.ktuh.org)

100.3 KCCN "FM 100"—Extraordinarily popular island music station that plays *da kine* tracks, *bruddah!* The #1 station in Honolulu, owing in no small part to the morning drive-time stylings of Billy V, Charly, and PP, M-F 5-10am. (http://kccnfm100.com)

102.7 KDDB "Da Bomb"—Hip-hop, rap and urban jams. (http://www.dabombhawaii.com)

105.9 KAHA "Lava Rock"—Molten alternative rock tracks to shred waves by. Tune in Sunday morning for the stacks and stacks of laughing wax from novelty radio's pappy, Dr. Demento. (http://www.lavarock1059.com/)

MAUI

91.5 KEAO Mana'O Radio—Self-proclaimed "Non-commercial, listener-supported radio that doesn't kowtow to corporate America or the record companies!" It's an eclectic, irreverent station established by deadheads and karate black belts. On-air daily 6am-midnight. (http://www.manaoradio.com)

93.5 KPOA Island Music—Ultra-mellow Hawaiian. Think Neil Diamond meets Don Ho. Professes to be the "music you listen to when you clean da house!" Surf reports M-F 7, 9am and 3pm. (http://www.broadcast.com/radio/international/kpoa)

94.3 KDLX Maui's Country—Hey *paniolo*, KDLX ropes in the big ones all the way from Nashville. Grab your cowboy hat and get ready to ride.

95.1 KAOI—Jazz, adult contemporary, and Hawaiian. May the jet-lagged rejoice: jazz great Ramsey Lewis has his own show at the ungodly hours of 6-8am on Sunday.

101.1 KLHI The Point—A fraternity of mainland transplants bring you the alternative rock of Korn, Limp Bizkit, et al. Sponsors bikini contests, battles of the bands and "the island's wildest parties!" Listen responsibly. (http://www.thepointfm101.com)

103.7 KNUQ "The Rhythm of the Islands"—Smooth Jawaiian jams!

BIG ISLAND

94.7 KWXX—Jawaiian and island music, as well as a shot in the arm of mainland pop. Stays true to its roots with *"Alana i Kai Hikina,"* an all-Hawaiian language primetime show purported to be the first of its kind, Su 6-8pm. (http://www.kwxx.com)

99.1 Kona / 100.3 Hilo KAPA—"All Hawaiian, all the time." Many a local declares this their fave rave.

105.1 KINE—All about the traditional island music. For 20+ years, Harry B. Soria, Jr. has hosted the "Territorial Airwaves" show, featuring vintage Hawaiian vinyl, Su 5-6pm. (http://hawaiian105.com)

AM 530—Driving to Hawaii Volcanoes National Park? Tune in for pre-recorded Park and eruption information. Warning: static-laden transmissions are especially eerie when you're driving through cooled lava flows.

KAUAI

90.9 KKCR Kauai Community Radio—The last bastion of free speech in the Hawaiian islands, at least they'll make you think so. Don't miss Manulele's community calendar, M-F 7:30am, or the late-night sociopolitical rock antics of Michele Rundgren and JONES, F 6-10pm. (http://www.kkcr.org)

93.5 KQNG Kong Radio—Top 40 pop rock a la J. Lo, Nickelback and Pink, for those just who are homesick for the mainland. (http://www.kongradio.com)

98.9 KITH "Travelhost Radio"—A siren's song of classic Hawaiian tunes laced with real estate commercials designed to lure unsuspecting mainlanders into staying.

99.9 KTOH "Hits 99.9FM"—Plays a self-described "continuous history of rock 'n' roll."

Former Let's Go Research-Writer Stephanie L. Smith has worked as a freelance writer for Citysearch Los Angeles and is currently the features writer/editor for the online division of Channel One News.

ESSENTIALS

FACTS FOR THE TRAVELER

ENTRANCE REQUIREMENTS
Passport (p. 38). Required for all visitors to the US.
Visa (p. 39). A visa is usually required to visit the US, but can be waived.
Work Permit (p. 78). Required for all foreigners planning to work in the US.
Driving Permit (p. 58). Required for all those planning to drive.

EMBASSIES & CONSULATES

Contact your nearest embassy or consulate for information regarding visas and passports to the United States. The **US State Department** provides contact info for US embassies and consulates abroad at http://usembassy.state.gov. For more detailed info on embassies, consult www.embassyworld.com.

AMERICAN CONSULAR SERVICES ABROAD

US EMBASSIES
   Australia, Moonah Pl., Yarralumla, ACT 2600 (☎02 6214 5600; fax 6214 5970; http:// usembassy-australia.state.gov/embassy).
   Canada, 490 Sussex Dr., Ottawa, ON K1N 1G8 (☎613-238-5335; fax 688-3091; www.usembassycanada.gov).
   Ireland, 42 Elgin Rd., Dublin 4 (☎+668 8777 or 668 7122; fax 668 9946; www.usembassy.ie).
   New Zealand, 29 Fitzherbert Terr., Thorndon, Wellington (☎462 6000; fax 478 1701; http://usembassy.org.nz).
   South Africa, 877 Pretorius St., Pretoria 0083 (☎342 1048; fax 342 2244; http:// usembassy.state.gov/pretoria).
   UK, 24 Grosvenor Sq., London W1A 1AE (☎020 7499 9000; fax 491 2485; www. usembassy.org.uk).

US CONSULATES
   Australia, 553 St. Kilda Rd., Melbourne VIC 3004 (☎03 9526 5900; fax 9510 4646); 16 St. George's Terr., 13th fl., Perth WA 6000 (☎08 9202 1224; fax 9231 9444). MLC Centre, 19-29 Martin Pl., 59th fl., Sydney NSW 2000 (☎02 9373 9200; fax 9373 9125).
   Canada, 615 Macleod Trail S.E., Room 1000, Calgary, AB T2G 4T8 (☎403-266-8962; fax 264-6630); Suite 904, Purdy's Wharf Tower, 1969 Upper Water St., Halifax, NS B3J 3R7 (☎902-429-2480; fax 423-6861); P.O. Box 65, Postal Station Desjardins, Montréal, QC H5B 1G1 (☎514-398-9695; fax 398-9748); 2 Place Terrasse Dufferin, Québec, QC G1R 4T9 (☎418-692-2096; fax 692-4640); 360 University Ave., Toronto, ON M5G 1S4 (☎416-595-1700; fax 595-0051); 1095 West Pender St., Mezzanine, Vancouver, BC V6E 2M6 (☎604-685-4311; fax 685-5285).
   New Zealand, Private Bag 92022, Auckland (☎303 2724; fax 366 0870).

South Africa, 7th fl., Monte Carlo Bldg., Heerengracht, Foreshore, Cape Town (☎021 421 4351; fax 425 3014); 2901 Durban Bay Building, 333 Smith St., Durban 4000 (☎031 304 4737; fax 301 0265); 1 River St., Killarney, Johannesburg (☎011 644 8000; fax 646 6916).

UK, Queen's House, 14 Queen St., Belfast, N. Ireland BT1 6EQ (☎028 9032 8239; fax 9024 8482); 3 Regent Terr., Edinburgh, Scotland EH7 5BW (☎0131 556 8315; fax 557 6023).

DOCUMENTS & FORMALITIES

REQUIREMENTS. All foreign visitors except Canadians need valid passports to enter the United States and to re-enter their own country. Returning home with an expired passport is illegal and may result in a fine. Canadians must demonstrate proof of Canadian citizenship, such as a citizenship card with photo ID. The US does not allow entrance if the holder's passport expires in under six months.

PHOTOCOPIES. Be sure to photocopy the page of your passport with your photo, passport number, and other identifying info, as well as any visas, travel insurance policies, plane tickets, or traveler's check serial numbers. Carry one set of copies in a safe place, apart from the originals, and leave another set at home. Consulates also recommend that you carry an expired passport or an official copy of your birth certificate in a part of your baggage separate from other documents.

LOST PASSPORTS. If you lose your passport, immediately notify the local police and the nearest embassy or consulate of your home government. To expedite the replacement process, you will need to know all info from the previous passport; you must also show ID and proof of citizenship. In some cases, a replacement may take weeks to process, and it may be valid only for a limited time. Any visas stamped in your old passport will be irretrievably lost. In an emergency, ask for immediate temporary traveling papers that will permit you to re-enter your home country. Your passport is a public document belonging to your nation's government. You may have to surrender it to a US government official, but if you don't get it back in a reasonable amount of time, inform your country's nearest mission.

NEW PASSPORTS. File any new passport or renewal applications well in advance of your departure date. Most passport offices offer rush services for a steep fee. Citizens living abroad who need a passport or renewal should contact the nearest consular service of their home country.

Australia: Citizens must apply for a passport in person at a post office, a passport office, or an Australian diplomatic mission overseas. Passport offices are located in Adelaide, Brisbane, Canberra, Darwin, Hobart, Melbourne, Newcastle, Perth, and Sydney. New adult passports cost AUS$144 (for a 32-page passport) or AUS$204 (64-page), and a child's is AUS$68/AUS$102. Adult passports are valid for 10 years and child passports for 5 years. For more info, call toll-free (in Australia) ☎ 13 12 32, or visit www.passports.gov.au.

Canada: Citizens may enter Hawaii with any proof of citizenship.

Ireland: Citizens can apply for a passport by mail to either the Department of Foreign Affairs, Passport Office, Setanta Centre, Molesworth St., Dublin 2 (☎01 671 1633; fax 671 1092; www.irlgov.ie/iveagh), or the Passport Office, Irish Life Building, 1A South Mall, Cork (☎021 27 2525). Obtain an application at a local *Garda* station or post office, or request one from a passport office. 32-page passports cost €57 and are valid for 10 years. 48-page passports cost €69. Citizens under 16 or over 65 can request a 3-year passport (€12).

New Zealand: Application forms for passports are available from any travel agency or Link Centre. Applications may be forwarded to the Passport Office, P.O. Box 10-526, Wellington, New Zealand (☎0800 225 050 or 04 474 8100; fax 474 8010; www.passports.govt.nz). Standard processing time is 10 working days. Adult passports (NZ$80) are valid 10 years; passports for children under 16 (NZ$40) are valid 5 years. Recent proposals would reduce the adult fee to NZ$71 and the children fee to NZ$36.

South Africa: Passports are issued only in Pretoria, but all applications must still be submitted or forwarded to the nearest South African consulate. Processing time is 4 months or more. Adult passports, which cost around ZAR192, are valid for 10 years. Passports for children under 16 (around ZAR136) are valid for 5 years.

United Kingdom: Application forms are available at passport offices, main post offices, travel agencies, and online (www.ukpa.gov.uk/forms/f_app_pack.htm). Apply by mail or in person to one of the passport offices, located in London, Liverpool, Newport, Peterborough, Glasgow, or Belfast. Adult passports (UK£30) are valid for 10 years; under 16 (UK£16) are valid for 5. The process takes about 4 weeks, but the London office offers a 5-day, walk-in rush service for an additional UK£30. The UK Passport Agency can be reached by phone at ☎0870 521 0410. More info is available at www.open.gov.uk/ukpass/ukpass.htm.

VISAS

Citizens of most European countries, Australia, New Zealand, and Ireland can waive US visas through the **Visa Waiver Pilot Program.** Visitors qualify if they are traveling only for business or pleasure (*not* work or study) and are staying for fewer than 90 days. In addition, travelers must provide proof of intent to leave (such as a return plane ticket) and an I-94 form. Citizens of South Africa and some other countries need a visa in addition to a valid passport for entrance to the US. To obtain a visa, contact a US embassy or consulate (see p. 37).

All travelers planning a stay of more than 90 days (180 days for Canadians) need to obtain a visa; contact the closest US embassy or consulate. The **Center for International Business and Travel (CIBT),** 23201 New Mexico Ave. NW, #210, Washington, D.C. 20016 (☎202-244-9500 or 800-929-2428), secures **B-2** (pleasure travel) visas to and from all possible countries for a variable service charge (six month visa around $45). If you lose your I-94 form, you can replace it at the nearest **Immigration and Naturalization Service (INS)** office (☎800-375-5283; www.ins.usdoj.gov), although it's unlikely that the form will be replaced within the time of your stay. **Visa extensions** are sometimes attainable with a completed I-539 form; call the forms request line at ☎800-870-3676. Be sure to double-check on entrance requirements at the nearest US embassy or consulate, or consult the Bureau of Consular Affairs' web site (www.travel.state.gov).

IDENTIFICATION

When you travel, always carry two or more forms of identification on your person, including at least one photo ID; a passport combined with a driver's license or birth certificate is usually adequate. Many establishments, especially banks, may require several IDs in order to cash traveler's checks. Never carry all your forms of ID together; keep them in separate places in case of theft or loss.

STUDENT AND TEACHER IDENTIFICATION. The **International Student Identity Card (ISIC),** the most widely accepted form of student ID, provides discounts on sights, accommodations, food, and transportation. The ISIC is preferable to an institution-specific card (such as a university ID) because it is more likely to be recognized (and honored) abroad. All cardholders have access to a 24-hour emergency helpline for medical, legal, and financial emergencies (in North America call ☎(+44) 208 762 8110). Holders of US-issued cards are also eligible for insurance benefits

ESSENTIALS

(see **Insurance**, p. 44). Many student travel agencies issue ISICs, including STA Travel in Australia and New Zealand; Travel CUTS in Canada; usit in the Republic of Ireland and Northern Ireland; SASTS in South Africa; Campus Travel and STA Travel in the UK; Council Travel and STA Travel in the US (see p. 52). The card is valid from September of one year to December of the following year and costs AUS$13, UK£5, or US$22. Applicants must be degree-seeking students of a secondary or post-secondary school and be at least 12 years of age. Because of the proliferation of fake ISICs, some services (particularly airlines) require additional proof of student identity, such as a school ID. The **International Teacher Identity Card (ITIC)** offers the same insurance coverage but with limited discounts. The fee is AUS$13, UK£5, or US$22. Find more info at www.isic.org.

YOUTH IDENTIFICATION. The International Student Travel Confederation also issues a discount card to travelers who are 25 years old or under, but are not students. This one-year **International Youth Travel Card** (**IYTC**; formerly the **GO 25** Card) offers many of the same benefits as the ISIC. Most organizations that sell the ISIC also sell the IYTC ($22). If you are an ISIC card carrier and want to avoid buying individual calling cards or wish to consolidate all your means of communication during your trip, you can activate your ISIC's ISIConnect service, a powerful new integrated communications service (powered by eKit.com). With ISIConnect, one toll-free access number (☎800-706-1333 in the US, ☎877-635-3575 in Canada) gives you access to several different methods of keeping in touch via the phone and Internet, including: a reduced-rate international calling plan that treats your ISIC card as a universal calling card; a personalized voicemail box accessible from pay phones anywhere in the world or for free over the Internet; faxmail service for sending and receiving faxes via email, fax machines, or pay phones; various email capabilities, including a service that reads your email to you over the phone; an online "travel safe" for storing (and faxing) important documents and numbers; and a 24hr. emergency help line (via phone or email at ISIConnect@ekit.com) offering assistance and medical and legal referrals. To activate your ISIConnect account, visit the service's web site (www.isiconnect.ekit.com) or call the customer service number of your home country: in Australia ☎800 150 812; in Canada ☎800 808 5773; in Ireland ☎800 555 180 or ☎800 577 980; in New Zealand ☎0800 445 108; in the UK ☎0800 731 5664; in the US ☎800-706-1333; and in South Africa ☎0800 997 285.

CUSTOMS

Upon entering Hawaii, you must declare certain items from abroad and pay a duty on the value of those articles that exceed the allowance established by the US Customs Service. Keeping receipts for larger purchases made abroad will help establish values when you return. Upon returning home, you must declare all articles acquired abroad and pay a **duty** on the value of articles that exceed the allowance established by your country's customs service. Goods and gifts purchased at **duty-free** shops abroad are not exempt from duty or sales tax at your point of return; you must declare these items as well. "Duty-free" merely means that you need not pay a tax in the country of purchase. For more specific information on customs requirements, contact the following info centers.

AMERICAN CUSTOMS DECLARATIONS Entering the **US** as a *nonresident*, you are allowed to claim $100 of gifts and merchandise if you will be in the country for 72hr. *Residents* may claim $400 worth of goods. If 21, you may bring in 1L of wine, beer, or liquor. 200 cigarettes, 50 cigars (steer clear of Cubans), or 2kg of smoking tobacco are also permitted.

Australia: Australian Customs National Information Line (in Australia ☎1 300 363 263, from elsewhere ☎+61 (2) 6275 6666; www.customs.gov.au).

Canada: Canadian Customs, 333 Dunsmuir St., Vancouver, BC V6B 5R4 (☎800-461-9999 or 204-983-3500; www.revcan.ca).

Ireland: Customs Information Office, Irish Life Centre, Dublin 1 (☎01 817 1920; fax 878 0836; ceadmin@revenue.ie; www.revenue.ie).

New Zealand: New Zealand Customhouse, 17-21 Whitmore St., Box 2218, Wellington (☎0800 428 786; fax 9359 6730; www.customs.govt.nz).

South Africa: Commissioner for Customs and Excise, Private Bag X47, Pretoria 0001 (☎012 314 9911; fax 328 6478; www.gov.za).

UK: Her Majesty's Customs and Excise, Passenger Enquiry Team, Wayfarer House, Great South West Rd., Feltham, Middlesex TW14 8NP (☎0845 010 9000; fax 8910 3933; www.hmce.gov.uk).

US: US Customs Service, 1330 Pennsylvania Ave. NW, Washington, D.C. 20229 (☎202-354-1000; fax 354-1010; www.customs.gov).

MONEY

No matter how small your budget, if you plan to travel for more than a couple of days, you will need to keep handy a larger amount of cash than usual. Carrying it around with you, even in a money belt, is risky, and personal checks from another country, or even another state, will probably not be accepted no matter how many forms of identification you have (some banks don't even accept checks).

CURRENCY & EXCHANGE

The main unit of currency in the US the **dollar ($),** which is divided into 100 **cents (¢).** Paper money is green in the US; bills come in denominations of $1, $5, $10, $20, $50, and $100. Coins are 1¢ (penny), 5¢ (nickel), 10¢ (dime), 25¢ (quarter), and $1. The chart below is based on rates published in 2002.

DOLLAR ($)		
CDN$1 = US$0.65		US$1 = CDN$1.54
UK£1 = US$1.43		US$1 = UK£0.70
IR£1 = US$1.15		US$1 = IR£0.87
AUS$1= US$0.52		US$1 = AUS$1.91
NZ$1 = US$0.43		US$1 = NZ$2.32
ZAR1= US$0.12		US$1 = ZAR8.29

Banks generally have the best rates. Elsewhere, you can expect steep commission rates. A good rule of thumb is to use banks or money-exchanging centers that have at most a 5% margin between buy and sell prices. Convert in large sums to avoid numerous penalties, but don't exchange more than you'll need. ATM and credit cards (see p. 42) often get very good rates.

If using traveler's checks or bills, carry some in small denominations ($50 or less), especially for times when you are forced to exchange at poor rates. Also carry a range of denominations since charges may be levied per check cashed.

TRAVELER'S CHECKS

Traveler's checks (**American Express** and **Visa** are the most widely recognized) are one of the safest and least troublesome means of carrying funds. Several agencies and banks sell them for a small commission. Each agency provides refunds if your checks are lost or stolen, and many provide additional services, such as toll-free refund hotlines, emergency message services, and stolen credit card assistance.

While traveling, keep check receipts and a record of which checks you've cashed separate from the checks themselves. It also helps to leave a list of check numbers with someone at home. Never countersign checks until you're ready to cash them, and always bring your passport with you to cash them. For lost or stolen checks, immediately contact a refund center of the company that issued your checks to be reimbursed; they may require a police report verifying the loss or theft. Ask about toll-free refund hotlines and the location of refund centers when purchasing checks, and always carry emergency cash.

American Express: In the US and Australia call ☎800-127-333; in Canada ☎905-474-9380; in New Zealand ☎9 367 4567; in the UK ☎1 273 696 933; in South Africa ☎11 359 0200. Elsewhere call the US collect ☎+1 801-964-6665; www.aexp.com. Traveler's checks are available at a 1-4% commission at AmEx offices and banks, or commission-free at AAA offices (see p. 58). *Cheques for Two* can be signed by either of 2 people traveling together.

Citicorp: In the US ☎800-321-2484; in Canada ☎800-387-1616; elsewhere call US collect ☎+1 813-623-1709; www.citibank.com. Traveler's checks (available only in US dollars, British pounds, and German marks) at 1-2% commission. Call 24hr.

Thomas Cook MasterCard: In the US and Canada ☎800-223-7373; in the UK ☎0800 62 21 01; elsewhere call UK collect ☎+44 1733 31 89 50. Checks available in 13 currencies at 2% commission. Thomas Cook offices cash checks commission-free.

Visa: In the US ☎800-227-6811; in the UK ☎0800 89 50 78; elsewhere call UK collect ☎+44 20 7937 8091. Call for the location of their nearest office.

CREDIT CARDS

Credit cards are generally accepted in most of Hawaii. However, establishments in more rural areas are sometimes not equipped for credit card transactions. Major credit cards—**MasterCard** (along with its European counterparts **Euro Card** and **Access**) and **Visa** (with its European counterparts **Carte Bleue** or **Barclaycard**) are the most widely accepted—and can be used to extract cash advances in dollars from associated banks and teller machines throughout both countries. Some places do not accept **American Express,** so make sure to have an alternative method of payment. Credit card companies get the wholesale exchange rate, which is generally 5% better than the retail rate used by banks and other currency exchange establishments. American Express cards also work in some ATMs, as well as at AmEx offices and major airports. All such machines require a **Personal Identification Number (PIN).** You must ask your credit card company for a PIN before you leave; without it, you will be unable to withdraw cash with your credit card outside your home country. If you already have a PIN, check with the company to make sure it will work in Hawaii.

CREDIT CARD COMPANIES. Visa (☎800-336-8472) and MasterCard (☎800-307-7309) are issued in cooperation with banks and other organizations. American Express (☎800-843-2273) has an annual fee of up to $55. AmEx cardholders may cash personal checks at AmEx offices abroad, access a 24hr. emergency medical and legal assistance hotline (in North America call ☎800-554-2639, elsewhere call US collect ☎+1 715-343-7977), and enjoy American Express Travel Service benefits (including plane, hotel, and car rental reservation changes; baggage loss and flight insurance; mailgram and international cable services; and held mail). The Discover Card (in US ☎800-347-2683, elsewhere call US ☎+1 801-902-3100) offers cashback bonuses on most purchases.

CASH CARDS (ATM CARDS)

Cash cards—popularly called **ATM** (Automated Teller Machine) cards—are widely used on most islands. Islands with less of a tourism industry, however, such as Molokai and Lanai, have ATMs in only a few locations. Depending on the system that your home bank uses, you can most likely access your personal bank account from abroad. ATMs get the same wholesale exchange rate as credit cards, but there is often a limit on the amount of money you can withdraw per day (around $300). There is typically also a surcharge of $1-2 per withdrawal. Also, if your PIN is longer than four digits, ask your bank whether you need a new number.

The two major international money networks are **Cirrus** (☎ 800-424-7787) and **VISA/PLUS** (☎ 800-843-7587). To locate ATMs around the world, call the above numbers, or consult www.visa.com or www.mastercard.com. Most ATMs charge a transaction fee that is paid to the bank that owns the ATM.

Visa TravelMoney (☎ 877-394-2247) is a system allowing you to access money with your Visa card from any Visa ATM. You deposit an amount before you travel (plus a small service fee), and you can withdraw up to that sum. These cards give you the same favorable exchange rate for withdrawals as a regular Visa. Obtain a card by visiting a nearby Thomas Cook or Citicorp office, or by checking with your local bank to see if it issues TravelMoney cards.

DEBIT CARDS

Debit cards are a hybrid between credit and cash cards. They bear the logo of a major credit card, but purchases and withdrawals made with them are paid directly out of your bank account. Using a debit card like a credit card often incurs no fee (contact the issuing bank for details), gives you a favorable exchange rate, and frees you from having to carry large sums of money. Be careful, though: debit cards lack the theft protection that credit cards usually have.

GETTING MONEY FROM HOME

AMERICAN EXPRESS. Cardholders can withdraw cash from their checking accounts at any of AmEx's major offices and many representative offices (up to $1000 every 21 days; no service charge, no interest). AmEx "Express Cash" withdrawals from any AmEx ATM in the US and Canada are automatically debited from the cardholder's checking account or line of credit. Green card holders may withdraw up to $1000 in any seven-day period (2% transaction fee; minimum $2.50, maximum $20). To enroll in Express Cash, cardmembers may call ☎ 800-227-4669 in the US; elsewhere call the US collect ☎ +1 336-393-1111.

WESTERN UNION. Travelers from the US, Canada, and the UK can wire money abroad through Western Union's international money transfer services. In the US, call ☎ 800-325-6000; in Canada, ☎ 800-235-0000; in the UK, ☎ 0800 83 38 33. To wire money within the US using a credit card (Visa, MasterCard, Discover), call ☎ 800-CALL-CASH (☎ 225-5227). The rates for sending cash are generally $10-11 cheaper than with a credit card, and the money is usually available at the place you're sending it to within an hour. To locate the nearest Western Union location, consult www.westernunion.com.

FEDERAL EXPRESS. Some people choose to send money abroad in cash via FedEx to avoid transmission fees and taxes. Note that this method is illegal. In the US and Canada, FedEx can be reached by calling ☎ 800-463-3339; in the UK, ☎ 0800 12 38 00; in Ireland, ☎ 800 535 800; in Australia, ☎ 13 26 10; in New Zealand, ☎ 0800 733 339; and in South Africa, ☎ 011 923 8000.

COSTS

The cost of your trip will vary considerably, depending on where you go, how you travel, and where you stay. For foreign travelers, the single biggest cost of the trip will probably be the round-trip **airfare** to Hawaii (see **Getting There: By Plane,** p. 51). A car is necessary for traveling in many parts of Hawaii, and travelers who plan on renting must also figure this expense into account (for information on car rental, see p. 59). It is a good idea to plan a daily **budget** for your trip before leaving.

STAYING ON A BUDGET. On land, **accommodations** start at about $17 per night in a hostel bed, while a basic sit-down meal costs about $8-12 depending on the region. A slightly more comfortable day (sleeping in hostels/guest houses and the occasional budget hotel, eating one meal a day at a restaurant, going out at night) would run $50-65; for a luxurious day, the sky's the limit. Transportation costs will increase these figures. **Gas** prices have risen significantly in the US over the past year. A gallon of gas now costs about $1.60 per gallon (40¢ per L), but prices vary widely according to state gasoline taxes. Finally, don't forget to factor in emergency reserve funds (at least $200) when planning how much money you'll need.

TIPS FOR SAVING MONEY. Considering that saving just a few dollars a day over the course of your trip might pay for days or weeks of additional travel, the art of penny-pinching is well worth learning. Learn to take advantage of freebies: for example, museums will typically be free once a week or once a month, and cities often host free open-air concerts and/or cultural events (especially in the summer). Bring a sleepsack to save on sheet charges in hostels, and do your **laundry** in the sink (unless you're explicitly prohibited from doing so). You can split **accommodation** costs (in hotels and some hostels) with trustworthy fellow travelers; multi-bed rooms almost always work out cheaper per person than singles. The same principle will also work for cutting down on the cost of **restaurant** meals. You can also buy food in supermarkets instead of eating out. These simple tactics make the occasional splurge feel all the more rewarding.

TIPPING AND BARGAINING

In the US, it is customary to tip waitstaff and cab drivers 15-20% (at your discretion). Tips are usually not included in restaurant bills, unless you are in a party of 6 or more. At the airport and in hotels, porters expect at least a $1 per bag tip to carry your bags. Except at flea markets or other informal settings, bargaining is generally frowned upon and fruitless in Hawaii.

TAXES

In Hawaii, the state **sales tax** is 4%. There are often reduced rates for some types of items. Usually these taxes are not included in the prices of items. There is an **accommodations tax** of 11.25%.

INSURANCE

Travel insurance generally covers four basic areas: medical/health problems, property loss, trip cancellation/interruption, and emergency evacuation. Although your regular insurance policies may well extend to travel-related accidents, you may consider purchasing travel insurance if the cost of potential trip cancellation/interruption or emergency medical evacuation is greater than you can absorb. Prices for travel insurance purchased separately generally run about US$50 per week for full coverage, while trip cancellation/interruption may be purchased separately at a rate of about US$5.50 per US$100 of coverage.

Medical insurance (especially university policies) often covers costs incurred abroad; check with your provider. **Canadians** are protected by their home province's health insurance plan for up to 90 days after leaving the country; check with the provincial Ministry of Health or Health Plan Headquarters for details. **Homeowners' insurance** (or your family's coverage) often covers theft during travel and loss of travel documents (passport, plane ticket, railpass, etc.) up to US$500.

ISIC and **ITIC** (see p. 39) provide basic insurance benefits, including US$100 per day of in-hospital sickness for up to 60 days, US$3000 of accident-related medical reimbursement, and US$25,000 for emergency medical transport. Cardholders have access to a toll-free 24hr. helpline (run by the insurance provider **TravelGuard**) for medical, legal, and financial emergencies overseas (US and Canada ☎877-370-4742, elsewhere call US collect ☎+1 715-345-0505). **American Express** (US ☎800-528-4800) grants most cardholders automatic car rental insurance (collision and theft, but not liability) and ground travel accident coverage of US$100,000 on flight purchases made with the card.

INSURANCE PROVIDERS. Council and **STA** (see p. 52) offer a range of plans that can supplement your basic coverage. Other private insurance providers in the US and Canada include: **Access America** (☎800-284-8300); **Berkely Group/Carefree Travel Insurance** (☎800-323-3149; www.berkely.com); **Globalcare Travel Insurance** (☎800-821-2488; www.globalcare-cocco.com); and **Travel Assistance International** (☎800-821-2828; www.europ-assistance.com). Providers in the **UK** include **Columbus Direct** (☎020 7375 0011). In **Australia,** try **AFTA** (☎02 9375 4955).

SAFETY & SECURITY

Hawaii is generally considered a safe place; however, travelers should be sure to exercise the basic precautions described below. For more specific tips and information, see **Specific Concerns** (p. 71) or **Wilderness Safety** (p. 65).

PERSONAL SAFETY

EXPLORING. To avoid unwanted attention, try to blend in as much as possible and familiarize yourself with the area before you set out. The gawking camera-toter is a more obvious target for thieves and con artists than the low-profile traveler. Carry yourself with confidence; if you must check a map on the street, duck into a shop. If you are traveling alone, be sure someone at home knows your itinerary, and *never admit that you're traveling alone.*

Whenever possible, *Let's Go* warns of unsafe neighborhoods and areas, but there are some good general tips to follow. When walking at night, stick to busy, well-lit streets and avoid dark alleyways. Do not attempt to cross through parks, parking lots, or other large, deserted areas. Buildings in disrepair, vacant lots, and unpopulated areas are all bad signs. Keep in mind that a district can change character drastically between blocks and from day to night. Look for children playing, women walking in the open, and other signs of an active community. If you feel uncomfortable, leave as quickly and directly as you can, but don't allow fear of the unknown to turn you into a hermit. Careful, persistent exploration will build confidence and make your stay even more rewarding.

SELF DEFENSE. There is no sure-fire way to avoid all the threatening situations you might encounter when you travel, but a good self-defense course will give you concrete ways to react to different types of aggression. **Impact, Prepare,** and **Model Mugging** can refer you to local self-defense courses in the US (☎800-345-5425) and in Vancouver, BC, Canada (☎604-878-3838). Two- to three-hour workshops start at $50; full courses run $350-500. Both men and women are welcome.

ESSENTIALS

GETTING AROUND. If you are using a **car,** learn local driving signals and wear a seatbelt. Children under 40 lbs. should ride only in a specially-designed carseat, available for a small fee from most car rental agencies. Study route maps before you hit the road. If your car breaks down, wait for the police to assist you. For long drives in desolate areas, invest in a cellular phone and a roadside assistance program (see p. 58). Be sure to park your vehicle in a garage or well-traveled area, and use a steering wheel locking device in larger cities. **Sleeping in your car** is one of the most dangerous (and often illegal) ways to get your rest. When at the beach, never leave valuables in your car, as thieves often target crowded beach parking lots.

Public transportation is generally safe. Occasionally, bus or train stations can be unsafe; *Let's Go* warns of these stations where applicable. Within major US cities, the quality and safety of public transportation vary considerably. It is usually a good idea to avoid buses late at night; if you must use these forms of transportation, try to travel in a large groups. **Taxis** are usually safe. *Let's Go* does not recommend **hitchhiking** under any circumstances, particularly for women—see **Getting Around,** p. 56 for more info.

FINANCIAL SECURITY

PROTECTING YOUR VALUABLES. There are a few steps you can take to minimize the financial risk associated with traveling. First, **bring as little with you as possible.** Second, buy a few combination **padlocks** to secure your belongings either in your pack or in a hostel. Third, **carry as little cash as possible.** Keep your traveler's checks and ATM/credit cards in a **money belt**—not a "fanny pack"—along with your passport and ID cards. Fourth, **keep a small cash reserve separate from your primary stash.** This should be about US$50 sewn into or stored in the depths of your pack, along with your traveler's check numbers and important photocopies.

CON ARTISTS & PICKPOCKETS. In large cities **con artists** often work in groups, and children are among the most effective. Beware of certain classics: sob stories that require money, rolls of bills "found" on the street, mustard spilled (or saliva spit) onto your shoulder to distract you while they snatch your bag. **Don't ever let your passport and your bags out of your sight.** Beware of **pickpockets** in city crowds, especially on public transportation. Also, be alert in public telephone booths: If you must say your calling card number, do so very quietly; if you punch it in, make sure no one can look over your shoulder.

ACCOMMODATIONS & TRANSPORTATION. Never leave your belongings unattended; crime occurs in even the most demure-looking hostel or hotel. Be particularly careful on **buses;** horror stories abound about determined thieves who wait for travelers to fall asleep. Carry your backpack in front of you where you can see it. When traveling with others, sleep in alternate shifts. Do not leave valuables in your car. If you must, however, place them in an area where they are not easily visible.

DRUGS & ALCOHOL

As in the continental US, the drinking age in Hawaii is a strictly-enforced 21. The youthful should expect to be asked to show government-issued identification when purchasing any alcoholic beverage. Most localities restrict where and when alcohol can be sold. Drinking and driving is prohibited everywhere, and it is illegal to have an open container of alcohol inside a car, even if you are not the driver and even if you are not drinking it. Those caught drinking and driving face fines, a suspended license, imprisonment, or all three.

Narcotics such as marijuana, heroin, and cocaine are highly illegal in the US. If you carry prescription drugs while you travel, it is important that you keep a copy of the prescription with you.

HEALTH

Common sense is the simplest prescription for good health. Travelers complain most often about their feet and their gut, so take precautionary measures: drink lots of fluids to prevent dehydration and constipation, wear sturdy, broken-in shoes and clean socks, and use talcum powder to keep your feet dry. To minimize the effects of jet lag, "reset" your body's clock by adopting the time of your destination as soon as you board the plane. It also helps to avoid caffeine and alcohol on the flight; stick to water instead.

BEFORE YOU GO

Preparation can help minimize the likelihood of contracting a disease and maximize the chances of receiving effective health care in the event of an emergency. For minor health problems, bring a compact **first-aid kit** (see p. 50). In your **passport,** write the names of any people you wish to be contacted in case of a medical emergency and list any **allergies** or medical conditions of which you would want doctors to be aware. Allergy sufferers might want to obtain a full supply of any necessary medication before the trip. Matching a prescription to a foreign equivalent is not always easy, safe, or possible. Carry up-to-date, legible prescriptions or a statement from your doctor stating the medication's trade name, manufacturer, chemical name, and dosage. While traveling, be sure to keep all medication with you in your carry-on luggage.

IMMUNIZATIONS & PRECAUTIONS

Travelers over two years old should make sure that the following vaccines are up to date: MMR (for measles, mumps, and rubella); DTaP or Td (for diptheria, tetanus, and pertussis); OPV (for polio); HbCV (for haemophilus influenza B); and HBV (for hepatitis B). For recommendations on immunizations and prophylaxis, consult the CDC (see below) in the US or the equivalent in your home country, and check with a doctor for guidance.

USEFUL ORGANIZATIONS & PUBLICATIONS

The US **Centers for Disease Control and Prevention** (**CDC;** ☎877-FYI-TRIP; toll-free fax 888-232-3299; www.cdc.gov/travel) maintains an international travelers' hotline and an informative website. The CDC's comprehensive booklet *Health Information for International Travel,* an annual run-down of disease, immunization, and general health advice, is free online or available for US$25 via the Public Health Foundation (☎877-252-1200). Consult the appropriate government agency of your home country for consular information sheets on health, entry requirements, and other issues for various countries. For quick information on health and other travel warnings, call the **Overseas Citizens Services** (8:15am-5pm EST ☎202-647-5225; after-hours ☎202-647-4000), or contact a passport agency, embassy, or consulate abroad. US citizens can send a self-addressed, stamped envelope to the Overseas Citizens Services, Bureau of Consular Affairs, #4811, US Department of State, Washington, DC 20520. For information on medical evacuation services and travel insurance firms, see the US government's website at http://travel.state.gov/medical.html or the **British Foreign and Commonwealth Office** (www.fco.gov.uk).

For detailed information on travel health, including a country-by-country overview of diseases and a list of travel clinics in the US, try the **International Travel Health Guide,** by Stuart Rose, MD (US$20; www.travmed.com). For general health info, contact the **American Red Cross** (☎800-564-1234; www.redcross.org).

ESSENTIALS

ESSENTIALS

MEDICAL ASSISTANCE ON THE ROAD

Medical services are available 24hr. at hospitals throughout the islands. Some more rural towns may be driving distance away from the nearest hospital but, for the most part, medical care is readily available. Almost all cities and towns have standard pharmacies.

If you are concerned about obtaining medical assistance while traveling, you may wish to employ special support services. The *MedPass* from **GlobalCare, Inc.,** 2001 Westside Pkwy., #120, Alpharetta, GA 30004, USA (☎800-860-1111; fax 770-677-0455; www.globalems.com), provides 24hr. international medical assistance, support, and medical evacuation resources. The **International Association for Medical Assistance to Travelers (IAMAT;** US ☎716-754-4883, Canada ☎416-652-0137, New Zealand ☎03 352 20 53; www.sentex.net/~iamat) has free membership, lists English-speaking doctors worldwide, and offers detailed info on immunization requirements and sanitation. If your regular **insurance** policy does not cover travel abroad, you may wish to purchase additional coverage (see p. 50).

Those with medical conditions (such as diabetes, allergies to antibiotics, epilepsy, heart conditions) may want to obtain a **Medic Alert** membership (first year US$35, annually US$20 thereafter), which includes a stainless steel ID tag and other benefits, including a 24hr. collect-call number. Contact the Medic Alert Foundation, 2323 Colorado Ave, Turlock, CA 95382, USA (☎888-633-4298; outside US ☎209-668-3333; www.medicalert.org).

ONCE IN HAWAII

ENVIRONMENTAL HAZARDS

SURFING AND SWIMMING PRECAUTIONS Hawaiian waves make for some of the world's best surf, but they can also be deadly. High surf can bring strong currents and rip tides, and each year lives are lost and endangered when surfers and swimmers fail to heed precautions. In Hawaii waters, know your limits and use extra caution whenever you swim or surf. The following are a few simple precautions:

Never swim alone.

Swim and surf only in **lifeguarded** areas.

Do not struggle against a **current** or **riptide;** swim diagonally across it.

Signal for help if you are unable to swim out of a strong current.

Use a **leash** for surf and boogie boards.

Keep your distance from other surfers and swimmers—a loose board can deliver a lethal blow.

Familiarize yourself with **beach and surf conditions,** as well as beach safety signs and symbols before you head out.

If you see **sharks,** get out of the water.

Heat exhaustion can lead to fatigue, headaches, and wooziness. Avoid it and **dehydration** by drinking plenty of fluids, eating salty foods (e.g. crackers), and avoiding dehydrating beverages (e.g. alcohol and caffeinated beverages). Continuous heat stress can eventually lead to heatstroke, characterized by a rising temperature, severe headache, and cessation of sweating. Victims should be cooled off with wet towels and taken to a doctor.

The sunshine of paradise comes at a price if you're not careful. Remember that you can get **sunburned** even on a cloudy day. Be sure to apply sunscreen of SPF 15 or higher before you go out for the day and after swimming. If you do get sunburned, drink more fluids than usual and apply an aloe-based lotion.

In **high altitudes,** allow your body a couple of days to adjust to less oxygen before exerting yourself. Note that alcohol is more potent and UV rays are stronger at high elevations.

INSECT-BORNE DISEASES

Many diseases are transmitted by insects—mainly mosquitoes, fleas, ticks, and lice. Be aware of insects in wet or forested areas, especially while hiking and camping; wear long pants and long sleeves, tuck your pants into your socks, and buy a mosquito net. Use insect repellents such as DEET and soak or spray your gear with permethrin (licensed in the US for use on clothing).

A bacterial infection carried by ticks, **Lyme disease** is marked by a circular bull's-eye rash of 2 in. or more. Later symptoms include fever, headache, fatigue, and aches and pains. Antibiotics are effective if administered early. Left untreated, Lyme can cause problems in joints, the heart, and the nervous system. If you find a tick attached to your skin, grasp the head with tweezers as close to your skin as possible and apply slow, steady traction. Removing a tick within 24 hours greatly reduces the risk of infection. Do not try to remove ticks by burning them or coating them with nail polish remover or petroleum jelly.

FOOD- & WATER-BORNE DISEASES

Travelers in Hawaii experience food and water-related illness much less often than in most parts of the world, thanks to good water-treatment facilities and fairly well-maintained restaurant standards. The tap water in Hawaii is treated to be safe for drinking.

OTHER INFECTIOUS DISEASES

Hepatitis B is a viral infection of the liver transmitted via bodily fluids or needle-sharing. Symptoms may not surface until years after infection. Vaccinations are recommended for health-care workers, sexually active travelers, and anyone planning to seek medical treatment abroad. The 3-shot vaccination series must begin 6 months before traveling.

Hepatitis C is similar to hep B, but the mode of transmission differs. IV drug users, those with occupational exposure to blood, hemodialysis patients, and recipients of blood transfusions are at the highest risk, but the disease can also be spread through sexual contact or sharing items like razors and toothbrushes that may have traces of blood on them.

AIDS, HIV, & STDS

For detailed information on **Acquired Immune Deficiency Syndrome (AIDS)** in Hawaii, call the **US Centers for Disease Control's** 24hr. hotline at ☎800-342-2437, or contact the **Joint United Nations Programme on HIV/AIDS (UNAIDS),** 20, avenue Appia, CH-1211 Geneva 27, Switzerland (☎22 791 3666; fax 22 791 4187). According to US law, HIV positive persons are not permitted to enter the US. However, HIV testing is conducted only for those who are planning to immigrate permanently. Contact the US consulate for information (see p. 37).

Sexually transmitted diseases (STDs) such as gonorrhea, chlamydia, genital warts, syphilis, and herpes are easier to catch than HIV and can be just as deadly. **Hepatitis** B and C can also be transmitted sexually (see above). Though condoms may protect you from some STDs, oral or even tactile contact can lead to transmission. If you think you may have contracted an STD, see a doctor immediately.

ESSENTIALS

WOMEN'S HEALTH

Women traveling in unsanitary conditions are vulnerable to **urinary tract** and **bladder infections,** common and very uncomfortable bacterial conditions that cause a burning sensation and painful (sometimes frequent) urination. Over-the-counter medicines can sometimes alleviate symptoms; if they persist, see a doctor.

Vaginal yeast infections may flare up in hot and humid climates. Wearing loosely fitting trousers or a skirt and cotton underwear will help, as will over-the-counter remedies like Monistat or Gynelotrimin. Bring supplies from home if you are prone to infection, as they may be difficult to find on the road.

PACKING

Pack lightly: lay out only what you absolutely need, then take half the clothes and twice the money. If you plan to do a lot of hiking, also see the section on **Camping & the Outdoors** (p. 64).

LUGGAGE. If you plan to cover most of your itinerary on foot, a sturdy **frame backpack** is unbeatable. (For the basics on buying a pack, see p. 66.) Toting a **suitcase** or **trunk** is fine if you plan to live in one or two cities and explore from there or plan to rent a car, but is a very bad idea if you're moving around a lot. In addition to your main piece of luggage, a **daypack** (a small backpack or courier bag) is a must.

CLOTHING. Dress in Hawaii is like the Hawaiian lifestyle—casual and laid-back. Almost everyone, from grandparents to preschoolers, swears by plastic **flip-flops** ("slippers" or "slippahs" in local speak). If you want to blend in, pick up a pair at any drugstore or supermarket. Otherwise, shorts and light t-shirts or tank tops can suffice for almost any occasion. A light sweater or jacket can come in handy for cooler nights, though during the summer they're almost never needed. No matter when you're traveling, it's always a good idea to bring a **rain jacket** (Gore-Tex® is both waterproof and breathable) and if you're planning on hiking, sturdy shoes or **hiking boots** are a must. Long pants and a light jacket may also come in handy. You may want to add one nicer outfit beyond the jeans and t-shirt uniform. Luckily, women can almost always get away with wearing sundresses and sandals and all men typically need is a pair of khakis and an aloha shirt. If you are planning on splurging on a chi-chi dinner at an exclusive restaurant, you may need to upgrade your wardrobe a smidgen; a nicer sundress for a woman and a jacket for a man.

CONVERTERS & ADAPTERS. In Hawaii, as in the rest of the US, electricity is 110 volts AC. 220/240V electrical appliances don't like 110V current. Visit a hardware store for an **adapter** (which changes the shape of the plug) and a **converter** (which changes the voltage; US$20). Don't make the mistake of using only an adapter (unless appliance instructions explicitly state otherwise).

TOILETRIES. Toothbrushes, towels, soap, talcum powder (to keep feet dry), deodorant, razors, tampons, and condoms are readily available, but it's a good idea to bring extras along. Same goes for **contact lenses.** Bring your glasses and a copy of your prescription in case you need emergency replacements. If you use heat-disinfection, either switch temporarily to a chemical disinfection system (check first to make sure it's safe with your brand of lenses), or buy a converter to 110V.

FIRST-AID KIT. For a basic first-aid kit, pack: bandages, pain reliever, antibiotic cream, a thermometer, a Swiss Army knife, tweezers, moleskin, decongestant, motion-sickness remedy, diarrhea or upset-stomach medication (Pepto Bismol or Imodium), an antihistamine, sunscreen, insect repellent, burn ointment, and a syringe for emergencies (get an explanatory letter from your doctor).

FILM. Less serious photographers may want to bring a **disposable camera** or two rather than an expensive permanent one. Despite disclaimers, airport security X-rays *can* fog film, so buy a lead-lined pouch at a camera store or ask security to hand-inspect it. Always pack film in your carry-on luggage, since higher-intensity X-rays are used on checked luggage.

OTHER USEFUL ITEMS. For safety purposes, you should bring a **money belt** and small **padlock**. Basic **outdoors equipment** (plastic water bottle, compass, waterproof matches, pocketknife, sunglasses, sunscreen, hat) may also prove useful. **Quick repairs** of torn garments can be done on the road with a needle and thread; also consider bringing electrical tape for patching tears. If you want to do laundry by hand, bring detergent, a small rubber ball to stop up the sink, and string for a makeshift clothes line. **Other things** you're liable to forget: an umbrella, sealable **plastic bags** (for damp clothes, soap, food, shampoo, and other spillables), an **alarm clock,** safety pins, rubber bands, a flashlight, earplugs, garbage bags, and a small **calculator.**

IMPORTANT DOCUMENTS. Don't forget your passport, traveler's checks, ATM and/or credit cards, and adequate ID (see p. 39). Also check that you have any of the following that might apply to you: a hosteling membership card (see p. 62); driver's license; travel insurance forms; and rail or bus pass (see p. 56).

ESSENTIALS

GETTING TO HAWAII

Hawaii is primarily accessible by plane and, when it comes to airfare, a little effort can save you a bundle. If your plans are flexible enough to deal with the restrictions, courier fares are the cheapest. Tickets bought from consolidators and standby seating are also good deals, but last-minute specials, airfare wars, and charter flights often beat these fares. The key is to hunt around, to be flexible, and to ask persistently about discounts. Students, seniors, and those under 26 should never pay full price for a ticket.

AIRFARES

Airfares to Hawaii are consistently high throughout the year. Holidays and the winter months are particularly expensive. It is slightly cheaper to travel in the fall and spring. Midweek (M-Th morning) round-trip flights run US$40-50 cheaper than weekend flights, but they are generally more crowded and less likely to permit frequent-flier upgrades. Not fixing a return date ("open return") or arriving in and departing from different cities ("open-jaw") can be pricier than round-trip flights. Patching one-way flights together is the most expensive way to travel. Flights into Oahu are by far more common and, almost always, less expensive than flights into other islands.

If Hawaii is only one stop on a more extensive globe-hop, consider a round-the-world (RTW) ticket. Tickets usually include at least 5 stops and are valid for about a year; prices range US$1200-5000. Try **Northwest Airlines/KLM** (US ☎800-447-4747; www.nwa.com) or **Star Alliance,** a consortium of 22 airlines including United Airlines (US ☎800-241-6522; www.star-alliance.com). **Circle Pacific** fares are another way to incorporate Hawaii into a larger itinerary. One fare allows you to visit various destinations around the Pacific Ocean. The website www.justfares.com helps travelers create a custom itinerary with all their desired destinations and then spits out a quote for that trip. The **World Traveller's Club** (US ☎800-693-0411; www.around-the-world.com) also provides a similar service. Their website lists the most popular Circle Pacific routes but also allows users to design their own trips. The tickets are valid for one year and travellers are (almost always) free to stay in each destination for as long as they desire.

Fares for roundtrip flights to Hawaii from the US or Canadian east coast range from $1000 to $2000, depending on how early you book your flight. From the US or Canadian west coast $500-700; from the UK £800-850; from Australia, AUS$3000-3500; from New Zealand NZ$3000-3500.

BUDGET & STUDENT TRAVEL AGENCIES

While knowledgeable agents specializing in flights to Hawaii can make your life easy and help you save, they may not spend the time to find you the lowest possible fare—they get paid on commission. Travelers holding **ISIC and IYTC cards** (see p. 39) qualify for big discounts from student travel agencies. Most flights from budget agencies are on major airlines, but in peak season some may sell seats on less reliable chartered aircraft.

Council Travel (www.counciltravel.com). Countless US offices, including branches in Atlanta, Boston, Chicago, L.A., New York, San Francisco, Seattle, and Washington, D.C. Check the website or call ☎800-2-COUNCIL (226-8624) for the office nearest you. Also an office at 28A Poland St. (Oxford Circus), **London**, W1V 3DB (☎0207 437 77 67). As of May, Council had declared bankruptcy and was subsumed under STA. However, their offices are still in existence and transacting business.

CTS Travel, 44 Goodge St., **London** W1T 2AD, UK (☎0207 636 0031; fax 0207 637 5328; ctsinfo@ctstravel.co.uk).

STA Travel, 7890 S. Hardy Dr., Ste. 110, Tempe AZ 85284, USA (24hr. reservations and info ☎800-781-4040; www.sta-travel.com). A student and youth travel organization with over 150 offices worldwide (check their website for a listing of all their offices), including US offices in Boston, Chicago, L.A., New York, San Francisco, Seattle, and Washington, D.C. Ticket booking, travel insurance, railpasses, and more. In the UK, walk-in office 11 Goodge St., **London** W1T 2PF or call ☎0207 436 7779. In New Zealand, Shop 2B, 182 Queen St., **Auckland** (☎09 309 0458). In Australia, 366 Lygon St., **Carlton** Vic 3053 (☎03 9349 4344).

Travel CUTS (Canadian Universities Travel Services Limited), 187 College St., **Toronto,** ON M5T 1P7 (☎416-979-2406; fax 979-8167; www.travelcuts.com). 60 offices across Canada. Also in the UK, 295-A Regent St., **London** W1R 7YA (☎0207 255 1944).

usit world (www.usitworld.com). Over 50 **usit campus** branches in the UK, including 52 Grosvenor Gardens, **London** SW1W 0AG (☎0870 240 10 10); **Manchester** (☎0161 273 1880); and **Edinburgh** (☎0131 668 3303). Nearly 20 **usit NOW** offices in Ireland, including 19-21 Aston Quay, O'Connell Bridge, **Dublin** 2 (☎01 602 1600; www.usit-now.ie), and **Belfast** (☎02 890 327 111; www.usitnow.com). Offices also in Athens, Auckland, Brussels, Frankfurt, Johannesburg, Lisbon, Luxembourg, Madrid, Paris, Sofia, and Warsaw.

COMMERCIAL AIRLINES

The commercial airlines' lowest regular offer is the **APEX** (Advance Purchase Excursion) fare, which provides confirmed reservations and allows "open-jaw" tickets. Generally, reservations must be made seven to 21 days ahead of departure, with seven- to 14-day minimum-stay and up to 90-day maximum-stay restrictions. These fares carry hefty cancellation and change penalties (fees rise in summer). Book peak-season APEX fares early; by May you will have a hard time getting your desired departure date. Use **Microsoft Expedia** (msn.expedia.com) or **Travelocity** (www.travelocity.com) to get an idea of the lowest published fares, then use the resources outlined here to try and beat those fares.

ESSENTIALS

 FLIGHT PLANNING ON THE INTERNET.
Many airline sites offer special last-minute deals on the Web. Aloha Airlines (www.alohaair.com) and Hawaiian Airlines (www.hawaiianair.com) often publicize low webfares on their sites. Other sites do the legwork and compile the deals for you—try www.bestfares.com, www.flights.com, www.hotdeals.com, www.onetravel.com, and www.travelzoo.com.

StudentUniverse (www.studentuniverse.com), **STA** (www.sta-travel.com), **Council** (www.counciltravel.com), and **Orbitz.com** provide quotes on student tickets, while **Expedia** (www.expedia.com) and **Travelocity** (www.travelocity.com) offer full travel services. **Priceline** (www.priceline.com) allows you to specify a price, and obligates you to buy any ticket that meets or beats it; be prepared for antisocial hours and odd routes. **Skyauction** (www.skyauction.com) allows you to bid on both last-minute and advance-purchase tickets.

An indispensable resource on the Internet is the *Air Traveler's Handbook* (www.cs.cmu.edu/afs/cs/user/mkant/Public/Travel/airfare.html), a comprehensive listing of links to everything you need to know before you board a plane.

STANDBY FLIGHTS

Traveling standby requires considerable flexibility in arrival and departure dates and cities. Companies dealing in standby flights sell vouchers rather than tickets, along with the promise to get to your destination (or near your destination) within a certain window of time (typically 1-5 days). You call in before your specific window of time to hear your flight options and the probability that you will be able to board each flight. You can then decide which flights you want to try to make, show up at the appropriate airport at the appropriate time, present your voucher, and board if space is available. Vouchers can usually be bought for both one-way and round-trip travel. You may receive a monetary refund only if every available flight within your date range is full; if you opt not to take an available (but perhaps less convenient) flight, you can only get credit toward future travel. Carefully read agreements with any company offering standby flights as tricky fine print can leave you in a lurch. To check on a company's service record in the US, call the Better Business Bureau (☎212-533-6200). It is difficult to receive refunds, and clients' vouchers will not be honored when an airline fails to receive payment in time.

TICKET CONSOLIDATORS

Ticket consolidators, or **"bucket shops,"** buy unsold tickets in bulk from commercial airlines and sell them at discounted rates. The best place to look is in the Sunday travel section of any major newspaper (such as *The New York Times*), where many bucket shops place tiny ads. Call quickly, as availability is typically extremely limited. Not all bucket shops are reliable, so insist on a receipt that gives full details of restrictions, refunds, and tickets, and pay by credit card (in spite of the 2-5% fee) so you can stop payment if you never receive your tickets. For more info, see www.travel-library.com/air-travel/consolidators.html.

TRAVELING FROM THE US & CANADA

Travel Avenue (☎800-333-3335; www.travelavenue.com) finds the best available published fares and then uses several consolidators to attempt to beat that fare. Other consolidators worth trying are **Interworld** (☎305-443-4929; fax 443-0351); **Pennsylvania Travel** (☎800-331-0947); **Rebel** (☎800-227-3235; travel@rebeltours.com; www.rebeltours.com); **Cheap Tickets** (☎800-377-1000; www.cheaptickets.com); and **Travac** (☎800-872-8800; fax 212-714-9063; www.travac.com). Additional consolida-

tors on the web include the **Internet Travel Network** (www.itn.com); **Travel Information Services** (www.tiss.com); **TravelHUB** (www.travelhub.com); and **The Travel Site** (www.thetravelsite.com). Keep in mind that these are just suggestions to get you started in your research; *Let's Go* does not endorse any of these agencies. Be cautious, and research companies before you hand over your credit card number.

TRAVELING FROM THE UK, AUSTRALIA, & NEW ZEALAND

In London, the **Air Travel Advisory Bureau** (☎ 0207 636 5000; www.atab.co.uk) can provide names of reliable consolidators and discount flight specialists. From Australia and New Zealand, look for consolidator ads in the travel section of the *Sydney Morning Herald* and other papers.

CHARTER FLIGHTS

Charters are flights a tour operator contracts with an airline to fly extra loads of passengers during peak season. Charter flights fly less frequently than major airlines, make refunds particularly difficult, and are almost always fully booked. Schedules and itineraries may also change or be cancelled at the last moment (as late as 48hr. before the trip, and without a full refund), and check-in, boarding, and baggage claim are often much slower. However, they can also be cheaper.

 Discount clubs and **fare brokers** offer members savings on last-minute charter and tour deals. Study contracts closely; you don't want to end up with an unwanted overnight layover.

GETTING AROUND HAWAII

BY PLANE

There are three inter-island airlines: Hawaiian Airlines (☎ 800-367-5320), Aloha Airlines (☎ 800-367-5250) and Island Air (☎ 808-833-8817). All three offer competitive rates on inter-island flights. One-way flights from Honolulu to the outer islands start at $50. Aloha Airlines sells a pass for $321 that allows visitors unlimited inter-island air travel for seven days. Hawaiian Airlines has similar deals for five, seven, ten, and fourteen day periods.

BY BUS

Public transportation on **Oahu** is generally safe, clean and relatively convenient. With 86 routes criss-crossing the island and over 4,000 bus stops, it's safe to say that TheBus can get you where you're going. Adult fare is $1.50, student fare is $0.75. Monthly passes ($27 and $13.50, respectively) can be purchased at various supermarkets and drugstores. Contact **TheBus,** 811 Middle St., Honolulu, HI 96819 (☎ 808-848-4500; custserv@thebus.org; www.thebus.org). The county of **Kauai** also maintains a decent bus system. Schedules and other information are available at the **County of Kauai Transportation office,** 3220 Ho'olako St., Lihu'e, Kauai 96766 (☎ 808-241-6410; fax 808-241-6417). The **Big Island** has limited bus service. Contact **County of Hawaii Mass Transit office,** 630 E. Lanikaula St., Hilo, Hawaii 96720 (☎ 808-961-8744; fax 808-961-8745; http://www.hawaii-county.com/mass_transit/transit_main.htm). **Maui** offers only localized shuttle service through Speedishuttle (☎ 808-875-8070; www.speedishuttle.com). **Molokai** and **Lanai** have no form of public transportation.

BY CAR

Though car rental can be expensive, driving is the best and most efficient way to get around in Hawaii. "U.S." (as in "U.S. 1") refers to US highways, and "Rte." (as in "Rte. 7") to state and local highways.

INTERNATIONAL DRIVING PERMIT

If you do not have a license issued by a US state or Canadian province or territory, you might want an **International Driving Permit (IDP)**. While the US allows you to drive with a foreign license for up to a year, it may help with police if your license is written in English. You must be 18 to obtain an IDP, it is valid for a year, and must be issued in the country in which your license originates. You must carry your home license with your IDP at all times. Contact these offices to apply:

Australia: Contact your local Royal Automobile Club (RAC) or the National Royal Motorist Association (NRMA) if in NSW or the ACT (☎08 9421 4444; www.rac.com.au/travel). Permits AUS$15.

Canada: Contact any Canadian Automobile Association (CAA) branch office or write to CAA, 1145 Hunt Club Rd., #200, Ottawa, ON K1V 0Y3 (☎613-247-0117; www.caa.ca/CAAInternet/travelservices/internationaldocumentation/idptravel.htm). Permits CDN$10.

Ireland: Contact the nearest Automobile Association (AA) office or write to the UK address below. Permits €5.08. The Irish Automobile Association, 23 Suffolk St., Rockhill, Blackrock, Dublin (☎01 677 9481), honors most foreign automobile memberships (24hr. breakdown and road service ☎800 667 788; toll-free in Ireland).

New Zealand: Contact your local Automobile Association (AA) or their main office at Auckland Central, 99 Albert St. Auckland City (☎9 377 4660; www.nzaa.co.nz). Permits NZ$10.

South Africa: Contact the Travel Services Department of the Automobile Association of South Africa at P.O. Box 596, 2000 Johannesburg (☎11 799 1400; fax 799 1410; http://aasa.co.za). Permits ZAR28.50.

UK: To visit your local AA Shop, contact the **AA Headquarters** (☎0870 600 0371), or write to: The Automobile Association, International Documents, Fanum House, Erskine, Renfrewshire PA8 6BW. For more info, see www.theaa.co.uk. Permits UK£4.

US: Visit any American Automobile Association (AAA) office or write to AAA Florida, Travel Related Services, 1000 AAA Dr., Heathrow, FL 32746 (☎407-444-7000; fax 444-7380). You don't have to be a member to buy an IDP/IADP. Permits $10. AAA Travel Related Services (☎800-222-4357) provides road maps, travel guides, emergency road services, travel services, and auto insurance.

AUTOMOBILE CLUBS

Most automobile clubs offer free towing, emergency roadside assistance, travel-related discounts, and random goodies in exchange for a modest membership fee. Travelers should strongly consider membership if planning an extended roadtrip.

■ **American Automobile Association** (AAA, emergency road service ☎800-AAA-HELP/800-222-4357; www.aaa.com). Offers free trip-planning services, roadmaps and guidebooks, 24hr. emergency road service anywhere in the US, free towing, and commission-free traveler's checks from American Express with over 1,000 offices scattered across the country. Discounts on Hertz car rental (5-20%), Amtrak tickets (10%), and various motel chains and theme parks. AAA has reciprocal agreements with auto associations in other countries which often provide full benefits while in the US. Membership costs vary depending on which branch you join, but hover between $50-60 for the first year; less for renewals and additional family members. Call ☎800-564-6222 to sign up.

■ **Canadian Automobile Association (CAA),** 1145 Hunt Club Rd., #200, Ottawa, ON K1V OY3 (☎800-CAA-HELP/800-222-4357; www.caa.ca). Affiliated with AAA (see above), the CAA provides the same membership benefits as AAA. Basic membership is CDN $62; CDN $32 for associates.

Mobil Auto Club, 200 N. Martingale Rd., Schaumbourg, IL 60174 (info ☎800-621-558; emergency service ☎800-323-5880). Benefits include locksmith reimbursement, towing (free up to 10 mi.), roadside service, and car-rental discounts. $8 per month covers you and another driver.

ON THE ROAD

Tune up the car before you leave, make sure the tires are in good repair and have enough air, and get good maps. *Rand McNally's Road Atlas,* covering all of the US and Canada, is one of the best (available at bookstores and gas stations, $11).

While driving, be sure to buckle up—seat belts are **required by law** in Hawaii. The **speed limit** in Hawaii varies considerably from region to region. Most of the highways have a limit of 55 mph (89kph), while residential areas can post limits as low as 20 mph (32kph). Heed the limit; not only does it save gas, but most local police forces and state troopers make frequent use of radar to catch speed demons.

Hawaiian drivers are typically polite. Joggers, bikers, and pedestrians have the right-of-way and most drivers respect that rule. Mopeds, which travel at slower speeds than most cars, are common on most roads.

DRIVING PRECAUTIONS. Bring substantial amounts of water (a suggested 5L of **water** per person per day) for drinking and for the radiator. In extremely hot weather, use the air conditioner with restraint; if you see the car's temperature gauge climbing, turn it off. Turning the heater on full blast will help cool the engine. If radiator fluid is steaming, turn the car off for half an hour. *Never pour water over the engine to cool it.* Never lift a searing hot hood. For long drives to unpopulated areas, register with police before beginning the trek, and again upon arrival at the destination. Check with the local automobile club for details. When traveling for long distances, make sure tires are in good repair and have enough air, and get good maps. You might also want to consider renting a **car phone** or purchasing a **cell phone** in case of a breakdown. A **compass** and a **car manual** can also be very useful. You should always carry a **spare tire** and **jack, jumper cables, extra oil, flares,** and a **flashlight.** If you don't know how to **change a tire,** learn before heading out, especially if you are planning on traveling in deserted areas. Blowouts on dirt roads are exceedingly common. If you do have a breakdown, **stay with your car;** if you wander off, there's less likelihood trackers will find you. *Sleeping in a car or van parked in the city is extremely dangerous*—even the most dedicated budget traveler should not consider it.

CAR INSURANCE

Some credit cards cover standard insurance. If you rent, lease, or borrow a car, and you are not from the US or Canada, you will need a **green card,** or **International Insurance Certificate,** to certify that you have liability insurance and that it applies abroad. Green cards can be obtained at car rental agencies, car dealerships (for those leasing cars), some travel agents, and some border crossings.

RENTING A CAR

Car rental agencies fall into two categories: national companies with hundreds of branches, and local agencies that serve only one city or region. National chains usually allow you to pick up a car in one city and drop it off in another (for a hefty charge, sometimes in excess of $1000), and by calling their toll-free numbers, you can reserve a reliable car anywhere in the country. Generally, airport branches have more expensive rates. To rent a car from most establishments in Hawaii, you need to be at least 21 years old and have a major credit card. Some agencies require renters to be 25, and most charge those aged 21-24 an additional insurance fee (around $15-25 a day). Policies and prices vary from agency to agency. Small local operations occasionally rent to people under 21, but be sure to ask about the insurance coverage and deductible, and always check the fine print.

Most rental packages offer **unlimited mileage,** although some allow you a certain number of miles free before the charge of 25-40¢ per mile takes effect. Quoted rates do not include gas or tax, so ask for the total cost before handing over the credit card; many large firms have added airport surcharges not covered by the designated fare. Return the car with a full tank unless you sign up for a fuel option plan that stipulates otherwise. And when dealing with any car rental company, be sure to ask whether the price includes **insurance** against theft and collision. There may be an additional charge for a collision and damage waiver (CDW), which usually comes to about $12-15 per day. Major credit cards (including MasterCard and American Express) will sometimes cover the CDW if you use their card to rent a car; call your credit card company for specifics.

Depending on which island you plan to visit, the business of renting a car varies. **Molokai** and **Lanai** have only a few car rental agencies. In addition, some areas all but demand **4WD** (Lanai in particular). In general, cheaper cars tend to be less reliable and harder to handle on difficult terrain. Less expensive 4WD vehicles in particular tend to be more top heavy, and are more dangerous when navigating particularly bumpy roads.

Alamo (☎800-462-52663; www.alamo.com) rents to ages 21-24 with a major credit card for an additional $25 per day.

Budget (☎800-527-0700; www.budget.com) rents to drivers under 25 with a surcharge that varies by location.

Dollar (☎800-800-4000; www.dollar.com) rents to customers age 21-24 with a variable surcharge.

Enterprise (☎800-736-8222; www.enterprise.com) rents to customers age 21-24 with a variable surcharge.

Hertz (☎800-654-3131; www.hertz.com) policy varies by city.

Rent-A-Wreck (☎800-944-7501; www.rent-a-wreck) specializes in supplying vehicles that are past their prime for lower-than-average prices; a bare-bones compact less than 8 years old rents for around $20-25; cars 3-5 years old average under $30. The only Rent-a-Wreck location in Hawaii is in Lihu'e, Kauai.

Thrifty (☎800-367-2277; www.thrifty.com) locations rent to customers age 21-24 for varying surcharges.

You can generally make reservations before you leave by calling major international offices in your home country. However, occasionally the price and availability information they give doesn't jive with what the local offices in your country will tell you. Try checking with both numbers to make sure you get the best price and accurate information. Local desk numbers are included in town listings; for home-country numbers, call your toll-free directory.

LOCAL AGENCIES

Hawaii also has a number of locally-owned rental services. Be aware that their selection of vehicles may be more limited than that of national chains. Local car rental agencies are listed in the **Transportation** section of towns and cities.

AA Aloha Cars-R-Us (☎800-655-7989; www.hawaiicarrental.com). Researches the lowest rates for cars from major rental agencies. Also offers special Hawaii promotions.

Aloha Rent a Car (☎877-452-5642; www.aloharentacar.com). Maui-based, airport pickup.

Car Rentals in Hawaii (☎888-292-3307; www.carrentalsinhawaii.com). Travelers can search available rentals online.

Harper Car and Truck Rental (☎800-852-9993; www.harpershawaii.com). Kauai and Hawaii locations; rents motorhomes as well.

Kihei Rent a Car (☎800-251-5288; www.kiheirentacar.com). Family-owned business located in Kihei, Maui. Also a certified travel agency.

Paradise Rent a Car (☎808-926-7777; www.paradiserentacar.com). Two Waikiki locations, rents cars as well as motorcycles and mopeds to 18+.

COSTS & INSURANCE
Rental car prices start at around $25-30 a day from national companies, $20-25 from local agencies. Expect to pay more for larger cars and for 4WD. Cars with **automatic transmission** are common.

Many rental packages offer unlimited mileage. Return the car with a full tank of gasoline to avoid high fuel charges at the end. Be sure to ask whether the price includes **insurance** against theft and collision. Remember that if you are driving a conventional vehicle on an **unpaved road** in a rental car, you are almost never covered by insurance; ask about this before leaving the rental agency. Beware that cars rented on an **American Express** or **Visa/Mastercard Gold or Platinum** credit cards in Hawaii might *not* carry the automatic insurance that they would in some other countries; check with your credit card company. Insurance plans almost always come with a **deductible** of around $500 for conventional vehicles. This means you pay for all damages up to that sum, unless they are the fault of another vehicle. The deductible you will be quoted applies to collisions with other vehicles; collisions with non-vehicles ("single-vehicle collisions"), such as trees, will cost you even more. Generally, there is a sliding scale with regard to deductible—the more you pay, the more you're covered. Hawaii is a no-fault state which means that if you don't have collision damage insurance, you have to pay for all the damages before you leave the state (regardless of whether or not you were at fault).

BY MOPED AND BICYCLE

Mopeds are a popular mode of transport in parts of Hawaii, especially Waikiki, although in areas with poor pavement quality or otherwise unsafe road conditions, mopeds are rarely used. A few major rental agencies are listed below.

A&B Moped Rental (☎808-669-0027), 3481 Lower Honoapiilani Highway, Lahaina, Maui 96761.

Adventure Moped Rentals (☎808-941-2222), 1946 Ala Moana Blvd., Honolulu, Oahu 96815.

The Moped Zone (☎808-732-3366), 750-A Kapahulu Ave., Honolulu, Oahu 96815.

BY THUMB

Let's Go never recommends hitchhiking and strongly urges you to consider the significant risks before you choose to do so. On Kauai and the Big Island in particular, hitchhiking is fairly common among locals, but it can take a long time to get from place to place, and comes with the serious risks of riding with strangers.

ESSENTIALS

ACCOMMODATIONS

HOSTELS

Hostels are generally laid out dorm-style, often with large single-sex rooms and bunk beds, although some offer private rooms for families and couples. They sometimes have kitchens and utensils for your use, bike or moped rentals, storage areas, and laundry facilities. There can be drawbacks: some hostels close during certain daytime "lockout" hours, have a curfew, don't accept reservations, impose a maximum stay, or, less frequently, require that you do chores. In Hawaii, a bed in a hostel will average around $15-20.

HOSTELLING INTERNATIONAL

Joining the youth hostel association in your own country (listed below) automatically grants you membership privileges in **Hostelling International (HI),** a federation of national hosteling associations. HI hostels are scattered throughout Hawaii, and are typically less expensive than private hostels. Most accept reservations via the **International Booking Network** (Australia ☎ 02 9261 1111; Canada ☎ 800-663-5777; England and Wales ☎ 1629 58 14 18; Northern Ireland ☎ 1232 32 47 33; Republic of Ireland ☎ 01 830 1766; NZ ☎ 03 379 9808; Scotland ☎ 8701 55 32 55; US ☎ 800-909-4776; www.hostelbooking.com). HI's umbrella organization's web page (www.iyhf.org), which lists the web addresses and phone numbers of all national associations, can be a great place to begin researching hostelling in a specific region. Most student travel agencies (see p. 52) sell HI cards, as do all of the national hosteling organizations listed below. All prices listed below are valid for **one-year memberships** unless otherwise noted.

Australian Youth Hostels Association (AYHA), Level 3, 10 Mallett St., Camperdown NSW 2050 (☎ 02 9565 1699; fax 9565 1325; www.yha.org.au). AUS$52, under 18 AUS$16.

Hostelling International-Canada (HI-C), 400-205 Catherine St., Ottawa, ON K2P 1C3 (☎ 800-663-5777 or 613-237-7884; fax 237-7868; info@hostellingintl.ca; www.hostellingintl.ca). CDN$35, under 18 free.

Youth Hostels Association (England and Wales) Ltd., Trevelyan House, 8 St. Stephen's Hill, St. Albans, Hertfordshire AL1 2DY, UK (☎ 0870 870 8808; fax 01727 84 41 26; www.yha.org.uk). UK£12.50, under 18 UK£6.25, families UK£25.

An Óige (Irish Youth Hostel Association), 61 Mountjoy St., Dublin 7 (☎ 830 4555; fax 830 5808; anoige@iol.ie; www.irelandyha.org). €15, under 18 €7.50.

Hostelling International Northern Ireland (HINI), 22-32 Donegall Rd., Belfast BT12 5JN, Northern Ireland (☎ 02890 31 54 35; fax 43 96 99; info@hini.org.uk; www.hini.org.uk). UK£10, under 18 UK£6.

Youth Hostels Association of New Zealand (YHANZ), P.O. Box 436, 193 Cashel St., 3rd Floor Union House, Christchurch 1 (☎ 03 379 9970; fax 365 4476; info@yha.org.nz; www.yha.org.nz). NZ$40, under 17 free.

Scottish Youth Hostels Association (SYHA), 7 Glebe Crescent, Stirling FK8 2JA (☎ 01786 89 14 00; fax 89 13 33; www.syha.org.uk). UK£6.

Hostels Association of South Africa, 3rd fl. 73 St. George's St. Mall, P.O. Box 4402, Cape Town 8000 (☎ 021 424 2511; fax 424 4119; info@hisa.org.za; www.hisa.org.za). ZAR45.

Hostelling International-American Youth Hostels (HI-AYH), 733 15th St. NW, #840, Washington, D.C. 20005 (☎ 202-783-6161; fax 783-6171; hiayhserv@hiayh.org; www.hiayh.org). US$25, under 18 free.

OTHER TYPES OF ACCOMMODATIONS

YMCAS & YWCAS

Young Men's Christian Association (YMCA) lodgings are usually cheaper than a hotel but more expensive than a hostel. YMCA rates are usually lower than a hotel's but higher than a hostel's and may include TV, air conditioning, pools, gyms, access to public transportation, tourist info, safe deposit boxes, luggage storage, daily housekeeping, multilingual staff and 24hr. security. Many YMCAs accept women and families (group rates often available); some will not lodge those under 18 without parental permission. There are several ways to make a reservation, including via internet (www.travel-ys.com), all of which must be made at least two weeks in advance and paid for in advance with a traveler's check, US money order, certified check, Visa, or Mastercard in US dollars.

YMCA of the USA, 101 North Wacker Drive, Chicago, IL 60606 USA (☎ 888-333-9622 or 800-872-9622; fax 312-977-9063; www.ymca.net). Provides a listing of the nearly 1000 Ys across the US and Canada. Offers info on prices, available services, telephone numbers and addresses, but no reservation service.

YWCA of the USA, Empire State Building, #301, 350 Fifth Ave., New York, NY 10118 USA (☎ 212-273-7800; fax 465-2281; www.ywca.org). Publishes a directory (US$8) on YWCAs across the US.

HOTELS & GUESTHOUSES

Several major hotel chains have multiple locations within Hawaii. **Outrigger** (☎ 800-688-7444; www.outrigger.com) trumps the competition with sheer number of offerings. Between its upscale resorts and the more moderately priced sister chain **Ohana Hotels** (☎ 800-464-6262; www.ohanahotels.com), there are over 30 Outrigger options. The chain offers myriad specials and packages, including discounts for seniors and military personnel. Call to inquire about promotions or see their website. **Hilton** (☎ 800-774-1500; www.hilton.com) has a resort on Oahu and one on the Big Island. **Sheraton** (☎ 888-625-5144; www.sheraton.com), which includes the **Westin** and **W** hotel chains, has locations on each of Hawaii's islands. Sheraton rates range from high to higher, depending on the island and location. **Best Western** (☎ 800-780-7234; www.bestwestern.com) and **Marriott** (☎ 888-236-2427; www.marriott.com) also maintain a number of locations throughout Hawaii.

Hotel singles in Hawaii start around $65-90, depending on the island. Smaller **guesthouses** are often cheaper than hotels. If you decide to make **reservations** in writing, instead of by phone, indicate your night of arrival and how many nights you plan to stay. The hotel will send you a confirmation and may request payment for the first night. Not all hotels take reservations, and few take checks in foreign currency. Enclosing two International Reply Coupons will ensure a prompt reply (each US$1.05; available at any post office).

BED & BREAKFASTS (B&BS)

For a cozy alternative to impersonal hotel rooms, B&Bs (private homes with rooms available to travelers) range from the acceptable to the sublime. Rooms in B&Bs can cost anywhere from $50-150 in Hawaii. For more info on B&Bs, see **Bed & Breakfast Inns Online,** P.O. Box 829, Madison, TN 37116 (☎ 615-868-1946; info@bbonline.com; www.bbonline.com), **InnFinder,** 6200 Gisholt Dr. #100, Madison, WI 53713 (☎ 608-285-6600; fax 285-6601; www.inncrawler.com), or **InnSite** (www.innsite.com). The **Hawaii Island Bed & Breakfast Association**, P.O. Box 1890,

Honokaa, HI 96727 (hibba@stayhawaii.com; www.stayhawaii.com) specializes in accommodations on the Big Island. You can also make reservations at bed & breakfasts throughout the state using **All Islands Bed & Breakfast** (☎ 800-542-0344 or 808-263-2342; fax 808-263-0308; http://home.hawaii.rr.com/allislands).

HOME EXCHANGES

Home exchange offers the traveler various types of homes (houses, apartments, condominiums, even villas), plus the opportunity to live like a native and to cut down on accommodation fees. For more information, contact **HomeExchange.Com** (☎ 800-877-9723; fax 310-798-3865; www.homeexchange.com), **Intervac International Home Exchange** (☎ 800-756-4663; www.intervac.com), or **The Invented City: International Home Exchange,** 41 Sutter St., San Francisco, CA 94404 (US ☎ 800-788-CITY, elsewhere US collect ☎ +1 415-252-1141; www.invented-city.com).

CAMPING & THE OUTDOORS

Camping in Hawaii can be a rewarding way to slash travel costs. Oceanfront campsites afford travelers the opportunity to enjoy a million-dollar view at a fraction of a hotel price. Hawaii's temperate climate only adds to the appeal of camping. Many beach parks have areas set aside for camping, though some are better equipped than others. The number of campsites varies; some parks offer as few as four spots while others can house up to fifty. In addition, Hawaiian state parks are open year-round and issue permits for camping, lodging and group day-use for those who are at least 18 years of age. The fee for camping is generally $5 per campsite per night. Lodging in shelters and cabins is often available, for around $20-55 a night. Contact the **Department of Land and Natural Resources, Division of State Parks,** P.O. Box 621, Honolulu, HI, 96809 (☎ 808-587-0300; www.hawaii.gov/dlnr/dsp/index.html) for permit availability and further information. Guided ecotours are another way to explore Hawaii's natural beauty. Ask the local tourist bureau or look online at www.gohawaii.com/hokeo/activity/tourswd.html#ecotours. An excellent general resource for travelers planning on camping or spending time in the outdoors is the **Great Outdoor Recreation Pages** (www.gorp.com).

USEFUL PUBLICATIONS & RESOURCES

A variety of publishing companies offer hiking guidebooks to meet the educational needs of novice or expert. For information about camping, hiking, and biking, write or call the organizations listed below.

Automobile Association, Contact Centre, Car Ellison House, William Armstrong Drive, Newcastle-upon-Tyne NE4 7YA, UK (general Info ☎ 0870 600 0371; fax 0191 235 5111; www.theaa.co.uk).

Family Campers and RVers/National Campers and Hikers Association, Inc., 4804 Transit Rd., Bldg. #2, Depew, NY 14043, USA (☎/fax 716-668-6242). Membership fee (US$25) includes their publication *Camping Today.*

Hawaii Geographic Society, P.O. Box 1698, Honolulu, HI 96806. Ask for their free brochure. Guided hikes and information sessions for a small fee.

Hawaii Trail and Mountain Club, P.O. Box 2238, Honolulu, HI 96804. Guests are welcome on their hikes (see quarterly schedule online at www.geocities.com/Yosemite/Trails/3660/skednewsl.html). Suggested $2 donation.

The Mountaineers Books, 1001 SW Klickitat Way #201, Seattle, WA 98134 (☎ 800-553-4453 or 206-223-6303; fax 223-6306; www.mountaineersbooks.org). Over 400 titles on hiking, biking, mountaineering, natural history, and conservation.

The Nature Conservancy of Hawaii, 923 Nu'uanu Ave., Honolulu, HI 96817 (☎808-537-4508; fax 545-2019).

Wilderness Press, 1200 Fifth St., Berkeley, CA 94710 (☎800-443-7227 or 510-558-1666; fax 558-1696; www.wildernesspress.com). Over 100 hiking guides/maps.

Woodall Publications Corporation, 2575 Vista Del Mar Dr., Ventura, CA 93001, USA (☎800-323-9076 or 805-667-4100; www.woodalls.com). Woodall publishes the annually updated *Woodall's Campground Directory* (US$22).

WILDERNESS SAFETY

THE GREAT OUTDOORS. Stay warm, stay dry, and stay hydrated. The vast majority of life-threatening wilderness situations can be avoided by following this simple advice. Prepare yourself for an emergency, however, by always packing raingear, a first-aid kit, a reflector, a whistle, high energy food, and extra water for any hike. The sun can be brutal; be sure to take a hat, sunscreen, and sunglasses on any outdoor excursion.

Check **weather forecasts** and pay attention to the skies when hiking, since weather patterns can change suddenly. Whenever possible, let someone know when and where you are going hiking, either a friend, your hostel, a park ranger, or a local hiking organization. Do not attempt a hike beyond your ability—you may be endangering your life. See **Health,** p. 47, for information about outdoor ailments and basic medical concerns.

WILDLIFE. About 40 species of **sharks** inhabit Hawaiian waters, ranging in size from the eight-inch Pigmy Shark to the Whale Shark, which can measure over 50 ft. in length. There are eight species that are commonly sighted near shore, most of which pose little threat to humans. The Tiger Shark, recognizable by its blunt snout and the vertical stripes on its sides, is the most dangerous species of shark found in Hawaiian waters, and is known to attack humans. **Shark attacks** in Hawaii are actually quite rare—only 2-3 occur each year and few of these prove fatal. Surfers and spearfishers are at greatest risk of attack, and swimmers are advised to stay out of the water at dawn and dusk, when sharks move inshore to feed. Experts also advise against wearing high-contrast clothing or shiny jewelry and to avoid excessive splashing, all of which can attract sharks.

Transparent **Box Jellyfish** swarm to Hawaii's leeward shores 9-10 days after the full moon. The Box Jellyfish, which measures 1-3 in. with tentacles of up to 2 ft. long, administers a painful sting, which, in some cases, can cause anaphylactic shock. If you are stung by a box jellyfish, apply vinegar to the sting, pluck any tentacles out of the affected area using a towel or cloth (avoid using your hands), and apply a hot or cold pack. While not technically a jellyfish, the **Portuguese Man-of-War** is also endemic to Hawaiian waters. Purplish-blue in color with tentacles up to 30 ft. long, the Portuguese Man-of-War also has a painful and potentially dangerous sting, which has been know to cause anaphylactic shock, interference with heart and lung function, and even death. Unlike jellyfish stings, do not apply vinegar to a sting from a Portuguese Man-of-War. Instead, rinse the sting with salt or fresh water and apply a cold compress to the affected area. If pain persists or if breathing difficulty develops, consult a medical professional.

For more information on **Hawaiian wildlife,** consult *Pests of Paradise*, by Susan Scott and Craig Thomas, M.D. (University of Hawaii Press, $20). *How to Stay Alive in the Woods*, by Bradford Angier (Macmillan Press, $9) also provides valuable wilderness tips.

CAMPING AND HIKING EQUIPMENT

WHAT TO BUY...

Good camping equipment is both sturdy and light. Camping equipment is generally more expensive in Australia, New Zealand, and the UK than in North America.

ESSENTIALS

Sleeping Bag: Most sleeping bags are rated by season ("summer" means 30-40°F at night; "four-season" or "winter" often means below 0°F). They are made either of **down** (warmer and lighter, but more expensive, and miserable when wet) or of **synthetic** material (heavier, more durable, and warmer when wet). Prices range US$80-210 for a summer synthetic to US$250-300 for a good down winter bag. **Sleeping bag pads** include foam pads (US$10-20), air mattresses (US$15-50), and Therm-A-Rest self-inflating pads (US$45-80). Bring a **stuff sack** to store your bag and keep it dry.

Tent: The best tents are free-standing (with their own frames and suspension systems), set up quickly, and only require staking in high winds. Low-profile dome tents are the best all-around. Good 2-person tents start at US$90, 4-person at US$300. Seal the seams of your tent with waterproofer, and make sure it has a rain fly. Other tent accessories include a **battery-operated lantern**, a **plastic groundcloth**, and a **nylon tarp**.

Backpack: Internal-frame packs mold better to your back, keep a lower center of gravity, and flex adequately to allow you to hike difficult trails. **External-frame packs** are more comfortable for long hikes over even terrain, as they keep weight higher and distribute it more evenly. Make sure your pack has a strong, padded hip-belt to transfer weight to your legs. Any serious backpacking requires a pack of at least 4000 in^3 (16,000cc), plus 500 in^3 for sleeping bags in internal-frame packs. Sturdy backpacks cost anywhere from US$125-420—this is one area in which it doesn't pay to economize. Fill up any pack with something heavy and walk around the store with it to get a sense of how it distributes weight before buying it. Either buy a **waterproof backpack cover,** or store all of your belongings in plastic bags inside your pack.

Boots: Be sure to wear hiking boots with good **ankle support.** They should fit snugly and comfortably over 1-2 pairs of wool socks and thin liner socks. Break in boots over several weeks first in order to spare yourself painful and debilitating blisters.

Other Necessities: Synthetic layers, like those made of polypropylene, and a **pile jacket** will keep you warm even when wet. A **"space blanket"** will help you to retain your body heat and doubles as a groundcloth (US$5-15). Plastic **water bottles** are virtually shatter- and leak-proof. Bring **water-purification tablets** for when you can't boil water. Although most campgrounds provide campfire sites, you may want to bring a small **metal grate** or **grill** of your own. For those places that forbid fires or the gathering of firewood, you'll need a **camp stove** (the classic Coleman starts at US$40) and a propane-filled **fuel bottle** to operate it. Also don't forget a **first-aid kit, pocketknife, insect repellent, calamine lotion, sunscreen,** and **waterproof matches** or a **lighter**.

...AND WHERE TO BUY IT

The mail-order/online companies listed below offer lower prices than many retail stores, but a visit to a local camping or outdoors store will give you a good sense of the look and weight of certain items.

Campmor, 28 Parkway, P.O. Box 700, Upper Saddle River, NJ 07458. (US ☎888-226-7667; elsewhere ☎+1 201-825-8300; www.campmor.com.)

Discount Camping, 880 Main North Rd., Pooraka, South Australia 5095, Australia (☎08 8262 3399; fax 8260 6240; www.discountcamping.com.au).

Eastern Mountain Sports (EMS), 1 Vose Farm Rd., Peterborough, NH 03458, USA (☎888-463-6367 or 603-924-7231; www.shopems.com).

L.L. Bean, Freeport, ME 04033 (US and Canada ☎800-441-5713; UK ☎0800 891 297; elsewhere, call US ☎+1 207-552-3028; www.llbean.com).

Mountain Designs, 51 Bishop St., Kelvin Grove, Queensland 4059, Australia (☎07 3856 2344; fax 3856 0366; info@mountaindesigns.com; www.mountaindesigns.com).

Recreational Equipment, Inc. (REI), Sumner, WA 98352, USA (☎800-426-4840 or 253-891-2500; www.rei.com).

YHA Adventure Shop, 14 Southampton St., Covent Garden, London, WC2E 7HA, UK (☎020 7836 8541; www.yhaadventure.com) The main branch of one of Britain's largest outdoor equipment suppliers.

CAMPERS AND RVS

Renting an RV will always be more expensive than tenting or hosteling, but it's cheaper than staying in hotels and renting a car (see **Rental Cars,** p. 58), and the convenience of bringing along your own bedroom, bathroom, and kitchen makes it an attractive option, especially for older travelers and families with children. Check out motorhomerentals.com, www.rvrentalnet.com, and www.rvamerica.com for more information on RVing in Hawaii.

ORGANIZED ADVENTURE TOURS

Organized adventure tours offer another way of exploring the wild. Activities include hiking, biking, kayaking, and sailing. Tourism bureaus can often suggest parks, trails, and outfitters; other good sources for info are stores and groups that specialize in camping and outdoor equipment like REI and EMS (see above).

Hawaii Activities, Aloha Tower 5th Floor, 1 Aloha Tower Drive, Honolulu, HI 96813 (☎877-877-1222 or 808-524-0008; info@hawaiiactivities.com; www.hawaiiactivities). Service that books activities for tourists. Searchable website with links to different tour companies offering every kind of adventure/excursion/activity under the sun.

The Real Hawaii (☎877-597-7325; information@therealhawaii.com; www.therealhawaii.com). Eco-cultural excursions led by native Hawaiians.

Specialty Travel Index, 305 San Anselmo Ave., #313, San Anselmo, CA 94960, USA (☎800-442-4922 or 415-459-4900; fax 415-459-9474; info@specialtytravel.com; www.specialtytravel.com). Tours worldwide.

Wild Side Eco-Adventures, 84-664 Upena St., Waianae, HI 96792 (☎808-306-7273; fax 696-0103; WildSide@SailHawaii.com; www.sailhawaii.com). Sailing and kayaking adventures on Oahu.

KEEPING IN TOUCH

BY MAIL

SENDING MAIL HOME FROM HAWAII

Airmail is the best way to send mail home from Hawaii. **Aerogrammes,** printed sheets that fold into envelopes and travel via airmail, are available at post offices. Write "air mail" or "par avion" on the front. Most post offices will charge exorbitant fees or simply refuse to send aerogrammes with enclosures. **Surface mail** is by far the cheapest and slowest way to send mail. It takes one to three months to cross the Atlantic and two to four to cross the Pacific—good for items you won't need to see for a while, such as souvenirs or other articles you've acquired along the way that are weighing down your pack. Standard rates for mail from Hawaii (in US$) are:

ESSENTIALS

Australia: Allow 4-7 days for regular airmail home. Postcards/aerogrammes cost $0.70. Letters up to 1 oz. cost $0.80; packages up to 0.5 lb. $14.50, up to 2 lb. $18.75.

Canada: Allow 4-7 days for regular airmail home. Postcards/aerogrammes cost $0.50. Letters up to 1 oz. cost $0.60; packages up to 0.5 lb. $2.35, up to 2 lb. $6.35.

Ireland: Allow 4-7 days for regular airmail home. Postcards/aerogrammes cost $0.70. Letters up to 1 oz. cost $0.80; packages up to 0.5 lb. $6.40, up to 2 lb. $13.30.

New Zealand: Allow 4-7 days for regular airmail home. Postcards/aerogrammes cost $0.70. Letters up to 1 oz. cost $0.80; packages up to 0.5 lb. $7.10, up to 2 lb. $14.90.

UK: Allow 4-7 days for regular airmail home. Postcards/aerogrammes cost $0.70. Letters up to 1 oz. cost $0.80; packages up to 0.5 lb. $6.40, up to 2 lb. $13.30.

US: Allow 3-7 days for regular airmail home. Postcards/aerogrammes cost $0.23. Letters up to 1 oz. cost $0.37; packages up to 0.5 lb. $3.50, up to 5 lb. $7.70.

SENDING MAIL TO HAWAII

Mark envelopes "air mail," or "par avion," or your letter or postcard will never arrive. In addition to the standard postage system whose rates are listed below, **Federal Express** (www.fedex.com; Australia ☎ 13 26 10; US and Canada ☎ 800-247-4747; New Zealand ☎ 0800 73 33 39; UK ☎ 0800 12 38 00) handles express mail services from most home countries to Hawaii; they can get a letter from New York to Hawaii in 2 days for US$16, and from London to Hawaii in 2 days for UK£26.

Australia: Allow 4-6 days for regular airmail to Hawaii. Postcards and letters up to 20g cost AUS$1; packages up to 0.5kg AUS$12, up to 2kg AUS$39. **EMS** can get a letter to Hawaii in 2-5 days for AUS$30. www.auspost.com.au/pac.

Canada: Allow 4-6 days for regular airmail to Hawaii. Postcards and letters up to 30g cost CDN$0.65; packages up to 0.5kg CDN$4.60, up to 2kg CDN$16. www.canada-post.ca/CPC2/common/rates/ratesgen.html#international.

Ireland: Allow 4-6 days for regular airmail to Hawaii. Postcards and letters up to 25g cost €.41. Add €3.40 for Swiftpost International. www.anpost.ie.

New Zealand: Allow 7 days for regular airmail to Hawaii. Postcards NZ$1.50. Letters up to 20g cost NZ$2-5; small parcels up to 0.5kg NZ$16, up to 2kg NZ$50. www.nzpost.co.nz/nzpost/inrates.

UK: Allow 4 days for airmail to Hawaii. Letters up to 60g cost UK£1.35; packages up to 0.5kg UK£4.55, up to 5kg UK£43. UK Swiftair delivers letters a day faster for UK£3.85 more. www.royalmail.co.uk/calculator.

US: Allow 3-7 days for regular airmail to Hawaii. Postcards/aerogrammes cost US$0.23; letters under 1 oz., US$0.37. Packages under 1 lb. cost US$3.50; larger packages cost a variable amount (around US$10). **US Express Mail** can get it there overnight; 1 lb. parcel $16.25. http://ircalc.usps.gov.

RECEIVING MAIL IN HAWAII

There are several ways to arrange pick-up of letters sent to you by friends and relatives while you are abroad. Mail can be sent via **General Delivery** to almost any city or town in Hawaii with a post office. Address General Delivery letters like so:

Erzulie COQUILLON
General Delivery
City, HI ZIP Code
USA

The mail will go to a special desk in the central post office, unless you specify a post office by street address or postal code. It's best to use the largest post office, since mail may be sent there regardless. It is usually safer and quicker, though more expensive, to send mail express or registered. Bring your passport (or other photo ID) for pick-up; there may be a small fee. If the clerks insist that there is nothing for you, have them check under your first name as well. *Let's Go* lists post offices in the **Practical Information** section for each city and most towns.

   American Express's travel offices throughout the world offer a free **Client Letter Service** (mail held up to 30 days and forwarded upon request) for cardholders who contact them in advance. Address the letter in the same way shown above. Some offices will offer these services to non-cardholders (especially AmEx Travelers Cheque holders), but call ahead to make sure. *Let's Go* lists AmEx office locations for most large cities in **Practical Information** sections; for a complete, free list, call ☎800-528-4800.

BY TELEPHONE

   ☎**AREA CODE** The area code throughout the Hawaiian islands is **808.**

CALLING HOME FROM HAWAII

A **calling card** is probably your cheapest bet. Calls are billed collect to your account. You can frequently call collect without even possessing a company's calling card just by calling their access number and following the instructions. **To obtain a calling card** from your national telecommunications service before leaving home, contact the appropriate company listed below (using the numbers in the first column). To **call home with a calling card,** contact the operator for your service provider in Hawaii by dialing the appropriate toll-free access number (listed below in the second column).

COMPANY	TO OBTAIN A CARD, DIAL:
AT&T (US)	800 361-4470
World Telecom Direct	(0) 870 1010101
Bell Canada	800-668-6878
Ireland Direct	800 580 580
MCI (US)	800-444-3333
New Zealand Direct	0800 00 00 00
Sprint (US)	800 877-4646
Telkom South Africa	10 219
Telstra	800 616 606

You can also usually make **direct international calls** from pay phones, but if you aren't using a calling card, you may end up dropping your coins as quickly as your words. Where available, prepaid phone cards (see below) and occasionally major credit cards can be used for direct international calls, but they are still less cost-efficient. (See the box on **Placing International Calls** (p. 70) for directions on how to place a direct international call.)

   Placing a **collect call** through an international operator is even more expensive, but may be necessary in case of emergency. You can place collect calls through the service providers listed above even if you don't have one of their phone cards.

CALLING WITHIN HAWAII

The simplest way to call within the country is to use a coin-operated phone. **Prepaid phone cards** available at newspaper kiosks and drugstores, which carry a certain amount of phone time depending on the card's denomination, and usually save

ESSENTIALS

 PLACING INTERNATIONAL CALLS. To call to and from Hawaii, dial:

1. The **international dialing prefix.** To dial out of **Australia**, dial 0011; **Canada** or the **US**, 011; the **Republic of Ireland, New Zealand,** or the **UK**, 00; **South Africa**, 09.
2. The **country code** of the country you want to call. To call **Australia,** dial 61; **Canada** or the **US**, 1; the **Republic of Ireland**, 353; **New Zealand**, 64; **South Africa**, 27; the **UK**, 44.
3. The **city/area code.** The city/area code for all of Hawaii is **808**. When calling internationally, if the first digit is a zero (e.g., 020 for London) omit the zero (e.g., dial 20 from Hawaii to reach London).
4. The **local number.**

time and money in the long run. The computerized phone will tell you how much time, in units, you have left on your card. Another kind of prepaid telephone card comes with a Personal Identification Number (PIN) and a toll-free access number. Instead of inserting the card into the phone, you call the access number and follow the directions on the card. These cards can be used to make international as well as domestic calls. Phone rates typically tend to be highest in the morning, lower in the evening, and lowest on Sunday and late at night.

TIME DIFFERENCES

Hawaii has its own time zone—**Hawaii Standard Time (HST).** HST is 10 hours behind **Greenwich Mean Time (GMT).** It is 6 hours behind New York, 2 hours behind Vancouver and San Francisco, 12 hours behind Johannesburg, 3 hours ahead of Sydney, and 2 hours ahead of Auckland (NZ). Some countries ignore **daylight savings time,** and fall and spring switchover times vary. The chart below gives the time in various cities around the world when it is midnight in Honolulu.

12AM	2AM	5AM	10AM	6PM	9PM
Honolulu	Vancouver	Toronto	London	China	Sydney
	Seattle	Ottawa	(GMT)	Hong Kong	Canberra
	San Francisco	New York		Manila	Melbourne
	Los Angeles	Boston		Singapore	

BY EMAIL AND INTERNET

Most medium to large cities in Hawaii have at least one Internet cafe. Otherwise, any one of the Hawaii State Public Libraries offers free Internet access with a library card (three-month passes are available for $10). In addition, copy stores such as Kinko's and Mail Boxes Etc. also have Internet access. Generally, the more rural a town, the less chance that email will be accesible.

Though in some places it's possible to forge a remote link with your home server, in most cases this is a much slower (and thus more expensive) option than taking advantage of free **web-based email accounts** (e.g. www.hotmail.com and www.yahoo.com). Travelers with laptops can call an Internet service provider via a **modem.** Long-distance phone cards specifically intended for such calls can defray normally high phone charges; check with your long-distance phone provider to see if it offers this option. **Internet cafes** and the occasional free Internet terminal at a public library or university are listed in the **Practical Information** sections of major cities. For lists of additional cybercafes in Hawaii, check out www.netcafeguide.com.]

SPECIFIC CONCERNS

WOMEN TRAVELERS

In Hawaii, as everywhere in the US, a woman should expect to be treated just as a man would be; though sexism still exists, it is considered unacceptable behavior. If you are treated unfairly because you are a woman, this is grounds for complaint.

Women exploring on their own inevitably face some additional safety concerns, but it's easy to be adventurous without taking undue risks. Generally, it is safe for women to travel in the US, but common sense still applies; women are targeted for muggings and swindlings, as well as general harassment. Watch out for vendors who may try to take advantage of you. If you are camping in isolated areas or traveling in big cities with which you are unfamiliar, try to travel with partners. Wherever you go, walk purposefully and self-confidently; women who look like they know what they are doing and where they are going are less likely to be harassed. When traveling, always carry extra money for a phone call, bus, or taxi. **Hitching** is never safe for lone women, or even for two women traveling together. Consider approaching older women or couples if you're lost or feel uncomfortable.

Your best answer to verbal harassment is no answer at all; feigning deafness, sitting motionless, and staring straight ahead at nothing in particular will do a world of good that reactions usually don't achieve. The extremely persistent can sometimes be dissuaded by a firm, loud, and very public "Go away!" Don't hesitate to seek out a police officer or a passerby if you are being harassed. *Let's Go: Hawaii* lists emergency numbers (including rape crisis lines) in the **Practical Information** listings of major cities, and you can always dial **911.** An **IMPACT Model Mugging** self-defense course will not only prepare you for a potential attack, but will also raise your level of awareness of your surroundings and your confidence (see **Self Defense,** p. 45).

For general information, contact the **National Organization for Women (NOW),** 733 15th St. NW, Fl. 2, Washington, DC 20005 (☎202-628-8669; www.now.org), which has branches across the US that can refer women travelers to rape crisis centers and counseling services.

TRAVELING ALONE

There are many benefits to traveling alone, including independence and greater interaction with locals. On the other hand, any solo traveler is a more vulnerable target of harassment and street theft. As a lone traveler, try not to stand out as a tourist, look confident, and be especially careful in deserted or very crowded areas. If questioned, never admit that you are traveling alone. Maintain regular contact with someone at home who knows your itinerary. For more tips, pick up *Traveling Solo* by Eleanor Berman (Globe Pequot Press, US$17) or subscribe to **Connecting: Solo Travel Network,** 689 Park Road, Unit 6, Gibsons, BC V0N 1V7, Canada (☎604-886-9099; www.cstn.org; membership US$35). **Travel Companion Exchange,** P.O. Box 833, Amityville, NY 11701, USA (☎631-454-0880, or in the US ☎800-392-1256; www.whytravelalone.com; US$48), will link solo travelers with companions with similar travel habits and interests.

OLDER TRAVELERS

Senior citizens are eligible for a wide range of discounts on transportation, museums, movies, theaters, concerts, restaurants, and accommodations. Almost all of Hawaii's major attractions offer some sort of discount for older tourists. If you don't see a senior citizen price listed, ask, and you may be delightfully surprised. The books *No Problem! Worldwise Tips for Mature Adventurers*, by Janice Kenyon (Orca Book Publishers; US$16) and *Unbelievably Good Deals and Great Adventures That You Absolutely Can't Get Unless You're Over 50*, by Joan Rattner Heilman (NTC/Contemporary Publishing; US$13) are both excellent resources. For more information, contact one of the following organizations:

Elderhostel, 11 Ave. de Lafayette, Boston, MA 02111 (☎877-426-8056; www.elderhostel.org). Organizes 1- to 4-week "educational adventures" in Hawaii on varied subjects for those 55+.

The Mature Traveler, P.O. Box 15791, Sacramento, CA 95852 (☎800-460-6676). Deals, discounts, and travel packages for the 50+ traveler. Subscription $30.

Walking the World, P.O. Box 1186, Fort Collins, CO 80522 (☎800-340-9255; www.walkingtheworld.com), organizes trips for 50+ travelers to Hawaii.

BISEXUAL, GAY, & LESBIAN TRAVELERS

Hawaii is one of the most progressive states when it comes to gay and lesbian travelers, though more so in cities than in rural areas. Listed below are contact organizations, mail-order bookstores, and publishers that offer materials addressing some specific concerns. **Out and About** (www.planetout.com) offers a bi-weekly newsletter addressing travel concerns and a comprehensive site addressing gay travel concerns.

Gay's the Word, 66 Marchmont St., London WC1N 1AB, UK (☎20 7278 7654; www.gaystheword.co.uk). The largest gay and lesbian bookshop in the UK, with both fiction and non-fiction titles. Mail-order service available.

Giovanni's Room, 1145 Pine St., Philadelphia, PA 19107, USA (☎215-923-2960; www.queerbooks.com). An international lesbian/feminist and gay bookstore with mail-order service (carries many of the publications listed below).

International Lesbian and Gay Association (ILGA), 81 rue Marché-au-Charbon, B-1000 Brussels, Belgium (☎+32 2 502 2471; www.ilga.org). Provides political information, such as homosexuality laws of individual countries.

FURTHER READING: BISEXUAL, GAY, & LESBIAN

Spartacus International Gay Guide 2001-2002, Bruno Gmunder Verlag. (US$33).

Damron Men's Guide, Damron Road Atlas, Damron's Accommodations, and *The Women's Traveller*. Damron Travel Guides (US$14-19). For more info, call ☎800-462-6654 or visit www.damron.com.

Ferrari Guides' Gay Travel A to Z, Ferrari Guides' Men's Travel in Your Pocket, and *Ferrari Guides' Inn Places*. Ferrari Publications (US$16-20). Purchase the guides online at www.ferrariguides.com.

The Gay Vacation Guide: The Best Trips and How to Plan Them, Mark Chesnut. Citadel Press (US$15).

Gayellow Pages USA/Canada, Frances Green. Gayellow pages (US$16). They also publish smaller regional editions. Visit Gayellow pages online at www.gayellowpages.com.

TRAVELERS WITH DISABILITIES

In main cities, most hotels and restaurants are wheelchair accessible, though this may not be the case in smaller towns or rural areas. Wheelchair-accessible vans are available to rent in most places, as are wheelchairs. Those with disabilities should inform airlines and hotels of their disabilities when making reservations; some time may be needed to prepare special accommodations. Call ahead to restaurants, museums, and other facilities to find out if they are handicapped-accessible. **Guide dog owners** should inquire as to the quarantine policies of each destination country.

In the US, major airlines will accommodate disabled passengers if notified at least 72 hours in advance. For information on transportation availability in individual US cities, contact the local chapter of the Easter Seals Society.

If you are planning to visit a national park or attraction in the US run by the National Park Service, obtain a free **Golden Access Passport,** which is available at all park entrances and from federal offices whose functions relate to land, forests, or wildlife. The Passport entitles disabled travelers and their families to free park admission and provides a 50% discount on all campsite and parking fees.

E S S E N T I A L S

USEFUL ORGANIZATIONS

Mobility International USA (MIUSA), P.O. Box 10767, Eugene, OR 97440, USA (voice and TDD ☎ 541-343-1284; www.miusa.org). Sells *A World of Options: A Guide to International Educational Exchange, Community Service, and Travel for Persons with Disabilities* (US$35).

Society for the Advancement of Travel for the Handicapped (SATH), 347 Fifth Ave., #610, New York, NY 10016, USA (☎ 212-447-7284; www.sath.org). An advocacy group that publishes free online travel information and the magazine *OPEN WORLD* (US$18, free for members). Annual membership US$45, students and seniors US$30.

TOUR AGENCIES

Directions Unlimited, 123 Green Ln., Bedford Hills, NY 10507, USA (☎ 800-533-5343). Books individual and group vacations for the physically disabled; not an info service.

The Guided Tour Inc., 7900 Old York Rd., #114B, Elkins Park, PA 19027, USA (☎ 800-783-5841; www.guidedtour.com). Organizes travel programs for persons with developmental and physical challenges in the US, Canada, Ireland, Cancun, and Paris.

MINORITY TRAVELERS

Hawaii is such a mixed place that no ethnic group stands out as an obvious minority. Caucasians may be uncomfortable with being called a "haole," but in general, if you treat the island and its inhabitants with respect, the same respect will be afforded to you. While there are relatively few people of African descent on the islands, racial prejudice against blacks is extremely rare, especially in larger cities.

TRAVELERS WITH CHILDREN

Family vacations often require that you slow your pace, and always require that you plan ahead. If you rent a car, make sure the rental company provides a car seat for younger children. **Be sure that your child carries some sort of ID** in case of an emergency or in case he or she gets lost.

Museums, tourist attractions, accommodations, and restaurants often offer discounts for children. Children under two generally fly for 10% of the adult airfare on international flights (this does not necessarily include a seat). International fares are usually discounted 25% for children from ages 2 to 11. For more information, consult one of the following books:

> *Backpacking with Babies and Small Children,* Goldie Silverman. Wilderness Press (US$10).
>
> *How to take Great Trips with Your Kids,* Sanford and Jane Portnoy. Harvard Common Press (US$10).
>
> *Have Kid, Will Travel: 101 Survival Strategies for Vacationing With Babies and Young Children,* Claire and Lucille Tristram. Andrews McMeel Publishing (US$9).
>
> *Adventuring with Children: An Inspirational Guide to World Travel and the Outdoors,* Nan Jeffrey. Avalon House Publishing (US$15).
>
> *Trouble Free Travel with Children,* Vicki Lansky. Book Peddlers (US$9).

DIETARY CONCERNS

With a little extra research, vegetarians should be able to find sufficient food options. Although local food tends to be centered around meat, many dining options are also Asian or Asian-inspired, using noodles, rice, and vegetables as ingredients. **The North American Vegetarian Society,** P.O. Box 72, Dolgeville, NY 13329 (☎518-568-7970; www.navs-online.org), publishes information about vegetarian travel, including *Transformative Adventures, a Guide to Vacations and Retreats* (US$15), and the *Vegetarian Journal's Guide to Natural Food Restaurants in the US and Canada* (US$12). For more information, visit your local bookstore, health food store, or library, or consult *The Vegetarian Traveler: Where to Stay if You're Vegetarian,* by Jed and Susan Civic (Larson Publications; US$16).

Travelers who keep kosher should contact synagogues in larger cities for information on kosher restaurants. Your synagogue or college Hillel should have access to lists of Jewish institutions across the nation. If you are strict in your observance, you may have to prepare your own food on the road. A good resource is the *Jewish Travel Guide,* by Michael Zaidner (Vallentine Mitchell; US$17).

OTHER RESOURCES

Let's Go tries to cover all aspects of budget travel, but we can't put *everything* in our guides. Listed below are books and websites that can serve as jumping off points for your own research.

USEFUL PUBLICATIONS

Aloha from Hawaii (www.aloha-hawaii.com/hawaii_magazine/magazine.shtml). Online magazine including features and a Hawaiian dictionary.

Hawaii Magazine (☎949-855-8822; www.hawaiimagazine.com). Monthly magazine with features on restaurants, events and community happenings.

Honolulu Magazine (☎808-537-9500; www.honolulumagazine.com). Articles on community figures and events.

Islander Magazine (www.islander-magazine.com). A web magazine specializing in the Hawaiian islands. Information on Hawaiian cuisine, books and history.

TRAVEL PUBLISHERS & BOOKSTORES

Hawaii Book Publishers Association, P.O. Box 235736, Honolulu, HI 96823 (☎808-734-7159; fax 808-732-3627; www.hawaiibooks.org). Publishes a free newsletter with information on literary events in Hawaii as well as other general information.

Hippocrene Books, Inc., 171 Madison Ave., New York, NY 10016 (☎718-454-2366; www.hippocrenebooks.com). Publishes foreign language dictionaries and language learning guides.

Hunter Publishing, 470 W. Broadway, Fl. 2, South Boston, MA 02127 USA (☎617-269-0700; www.hunterpublishing.com), has an extensive catalog of travel guides and diving and adventure travel books.

Rand McNally, P.O. Box 7600, Chicago, IL 60680 (☎847-329-8100; www.randmcnally.com), publishes road atlases.

Adventurous Traveler Bookstore, P.O. Box 2221, Williston, VT 05495 (☎800-282-3963; www.adventuroustraveler.com).

Travel Books & Language Center, Inc., 4437 Wisconsin Ave. NW, Washington, D.C. 20016 (☎800-220-2665; www.bookweb.org/bookstore/travelbks). Over 60,000 titles from around the world.

WORLD WIDE WEB

Almost every aspect of budget travel is accessible via the web. In 10 minutes at the keyboard, you can make a reservation at a hostel, get advice on travel hot spots from other travelers who have just returned from (your region), or find out exactly how much a surfboard rental in Kauai costs.

Listed here are some budget travel sites to start off your surfing; other relevant web sites are listed throughout the book. Because website turnover is high, use search engines (such as www.google.com) to strike out on your own.

OUR PERSONAL FAVORITE...

Let's Go: www.letsgo.com. Our constantly expanding website features photos and streaming video, online ordering, info about our books, a travel forum buzzing with stories and tips, and links that will help you find everything you ever wanted to know about Hawaii.

THE ART OF BUDGET TRAVEL

How to See the World: www.artoftravel.com. A compendium of great travel tips, from cheap flights to self defense to interacting with local culture.

Rec. Travel Library: www.travel-library.com. A fantastic set of links for general information and personal travelogues.

Lycos: http://travel.lycos.com. General introductions to cities and regions throughout Hawaii, accompanied by links to applicable histories, news, and local tourism sites.

INFORMATION ON HAWAII

Alternative-Hawaii: www.alternative-hawaii.com. "Your guide to the path less travelled." Self-described ecotourism site with links to accommodations and a section on Hawaii's special places.

Atevo Travel: www.atevo.com/guides/destinations. Detailed introductions, travel tips, and suggested itineraries.

Best Places Hawaii: www.bestplaceshawaii.com. An online travel planner with a virtual island tour and information on attractions.

DaKine: www.dakine.net. The local's guide to Hawaii. Reviews of Oahu plate lunch and shave ice establishments. Local humor!

Foreign Language for Travelers: www.travlang.com. Provides free online translating dictionaries and lists of phrases in Hawaiian.

Hawaii: www.hawaii.gov. Official website of the state of Hawaii.

Hawaii Surf Report: www.surf-news.com. Up to the minute weather and surf information.

MyTravelGuide: www.mytravelguide.com. Country overviews, with everything from history to transportation to live web cam coverage.

PlanetRider: www.planetrider.com. A subjective list of links to the "best" websites covering the culture and tourist attractions of Hawaii.

World Travel Guide: www.travel-guides.com/navigate/world.asp. Helpful practical info.

TravelPage: www.travelpage.com. Links to official tourist office sites in Hawaii.

ALTERNATIVES TO TOURISM

If you are looking for a more rewarding and complete way to see the world than merely traveling from place to place, you may want to consider alternative forms of tourism. Working, volunteering, or studying for an extended period of time offers a better way to understand life in Hawaii. This chapter outlines some of the different ways to see the islands, whether you want to pay your way through or just get the personal satisfaction that comes from studying and volunteering.

VISA INFORMATION. All travelers planning to stay for more than 90 days (180 for Canadians) need a visa. To obtain a visa, contact a US embassy or consulate (see p. 37). The **Center for International Business and Travel (CIBT),** 23201 New Mexico Ave. NW, #210, Washington, D.C. 20016 (☎800-929-2428 or 202-244-9500), secures **B-2** (pleasure travel) visas to and from all possible countries for a variable service charge (six-month visa around $45). **Visa extensions** are sometimes attainable with a completed I-539 form; call the forms request line at ☎800-870-3676. Double-check entrance requirements at the nearest US embassy or consulate, or consult the Bureau of Consular Affairs' web site (www.travel.state.gov). For more information on visas, see p. 39.

STUDYING IN HAWAII

Study abroad programs range from basic language and culture courses to college-level classes, which can often be taken for credit. There are two major **universities** in Hawaii: **The University of Hawaii at Manoa** (www.uhm.hawaii.edu) and **Hawaii Pacific University** (www.hpu.edu). Students wishing to study in Hawaii may find it cheaper to enroll directly one of these universities, although getting college credit may be difficult. A good resource for finding programs that cater to your particular interests is **www.studyabroad.com,** which has links to various semester abroad programs based on a variety of criteria, including desired location and focus of study.

The Institute for Cultural Ecology, 758 Kapahulu Ave. #500, Honolulu, HI (☎933-1991 or 934-9175; fax 733-7808; 758 Kapahulu Ave. #500, Honolulu, HI; www.culturalecology.com/index.cfm), runs 10-week programs during the spring, summer, and fall semesters that provide exposure to Hawaiian culture, geology and volcanology, archaeology, and threats to biodiversity. The program costs ($6945) include inter-island transportation, lodging in hostels and campgrounds, and 12 transferable academic credits. Application fee $55.

Pacific Whale Foundation (☎249-8811 or 879-8811; internships@pacificwhale.org; www.pacificwhale.org) is a non-profit organization on Maui dedicated to marine conservation. Interns pay a fee for room and board, but get to assist marine biologists with research. 18+. Moderate to challenging physical demands. College credit available.

LANGUAGE SCHOOLS

Unlike American universities, language schools are frequently independently-run international or local organizations or divisions of universities that rarely offer transferable college credit. Language schools are a good alternative to university study if you desire a deeper focus on the language or a slightly less-rigorous course load. These programs are also good for younger high school students that might not feel comfortable with older students in a university program. Some suggestions include:

Academia Language School, 1600 Kapiolani Blvd., Suite 1215, Honolulu, HI 96814 (☎946-5599). Offers English and TOEFL prep classes starting every week.

EWA International Inc., 2555 Cartwright Rd., Honolulu, HI 96815 (☎922-1677). A 1-4 week homestay program. Costs include tuition and lodging.

Hawaii English Language Program (HELP), 1395 Lower Campus Rd. MC 13-1, Honolulu, HI (☎956-6636). Offers 10-week programs in English on the University of Hawaii at Manoa campus.

Institute of Intensive English, 2255 Kuhio Ave., Suite 920, Honolulu, HI 96815 (☎924-2117). Offers both intensive and short-term English programs, as well as TOEFL prep courses.

WORKING

There are two main schools of thought regarding working abroad. Some travelers want long-term jobs that will allow them to get to know another part of the world in depth (e.g. teaching English, working in the tourist industry). Other travelers seek out short-term jobs such as employment in the service sector or agriculture, and work for a few weeks at a time to finance the next leg of their journey. This section discusses both short-term and long-term opportunities for working in Hawaii. Make sure you understand the **visa requirements** for working in the US. (See the box on p. 77 for more information.)

For US college students, recent graduates, and young adults, the simplest way to get legal permission to work abroad is through **Council Exchanges Work Abroad Programs.** Fees are from US$300-425. Council Exchanges can help you obtain a three-to six-month work permit/visa and provides assistance finding jobs and housing.

LONG-TERM WORK

If you're planning on spending a substantial amount of time (more than three months) working in Hawaii, search for a job well in advance. **Internships,** usually for college students, often provide a good segue into a more permanent position, although they are often unpaid or poorly paid (many say the experience, however, is well worth it). Be wary of advertisements or companies that claim the ability to get you a job abroad for a fee—often times the same listings are available online or in newspapers, or are out of date. Websites such as **www.jobshawaii.com, www.ehawaiigov.org,** and **www.monster.com** are all excellent resources with which to begin your employment search.

AU PAIR WORK

Au pairs are typically women, ages 18-27, who work as live-in nannies, caring for children and doing light housework in exchange for room, board, and a small spending allowance or stipend. Most former au pairs speak favorably of their experience, and of how it allowed them to really get to know the country without the high expenses of traveling. Drawbacks, however, often include long hours of constantly being on-duty, and the somewhat mediocre pay (in Hawaii, this is usually between $120-200 per week, plus room and board). The quality of the au pair experience often depends on the family with whom you're placed. The agencies below provide a good starting point for looking for employment as an au pair.

Au Pair in America, River Plaza, 9 West Broad St., Stamford, CT 06902 (☎800-928-7247; aupair.info@aifs.com; www.aupairinamerica.com).

InterExchange, 161 Sixth Ave., New York, NY 10013 (☎212-924-0446; fax 924-0575; www.interexchange.org).

SHORT-TERM WORK

Traveling for long periods of time can get expensive; therefore, many travelers try their hand at odd jobs for a few weeks at a time to make some extra cash to carry them through their tour. Short-term work in exchange for room and board can be found at farms and hostels in Hawaii. In highly touristed areas there are often jobs to be had on the maintenance and housekeeping staffs of **hotels** and **resorts,** or as cooks, waiters, and busboys at local **restaurants.** Another possibility is to check with the national **car rental agencies,** which may have jobs on their lots that need to be filled. Most often, these short-term jobs are found by talking to hostel and restaurant owners, and many places are eager for even temporary help, due to the high turnover in the tourism industry. Consult the help wanted sections of local newspapers for more listings—*Honolulu Star Bulletin* and *Hawaii Tribune Herald* on Oahu, *Kauai Garden News* on Kauai, *Maui Today* on Maui, and *West Hawaii Today* on the Big Island are good bets. Check out **www.employmentspot.com/state/ha.htm** for links to Hawaii job banks, as well as the classified sections of the aforementioned publications.

Willing Workers On Organic Farms (WWOOF), (wwoofcan@shaw.ca; www.wwoofusa.com/hawaii) matches visitors with host farms. Program applicants are required to fill out a short form and pay a small fee ($15). They then receive a booklet of all the available hosts in their desired destination; travelers are expected to contact the farms they are interested in working at and arrange a situation with the host. Most volunteers stay at the farms for 1-3 weeks. There are WWOOF farms on 5 of Hawaii's islands: Big Island, Kauai, Maui, Molokai, and Oahu.

Kalani Oceanside Retreat, RR2 Box 4500, Pahoa-Beach Rd. (☎800-800-6886 or 965-7828; info@kalani.com; www.kalani.com), on the Big Island, has an interesting program where visitors can work as a part of their staff for 1- or 3-months. This volunteer staff handles a number of jobs from housekeeping to cooking, in exchange for room, board, and access to the center's activities. $900 for 1 or 3 months.

Margo's Corner, Wakea Ave. (☎929-9614), in Ka'u on the Big Island, is an organic farm which sometimes has work exchange set-ups with travelers. In such an arrangement, visitors spend a few hours each day working in the garden, or on other projects, in return for room, board, and an insiders look at Ka'u. Be sure to contact Margo's well in advance if you are interested in this option.

Evie's Natural Food, 79-7460 Mamalahoa Hwy. (☎322-0739), in Mango Court south of Kainaliu on the Big Island, has a bulletin board listing current short-term work possibilities provided by the nearby Kona coffee industry. There are often farm jobs available that trade room and board for labor.

HOSTELS

The following hostels offer the possibility of trading room and board for part-time work around the establishment, in maintenance and housekeeping.

ALTERNATIVES TO TOURISM

Arnott's Lodge, 98 Apapane Rd. (☎969-7097; info@arnottslodge.com; www.arnottslodge.com), acts as a clearinghouse for travelers looking for temporary jobs around the Big Island, particularly in the Hilo area. Work is generally on organic farms, in exchange for room and board.

Backpackers, 59-788 Kamehameha Hwy. (☎638-7838; www.backpackershawaii.com), in Waimea on Oahu's North Shore, exchanges short-term work for room and board.

Banana Bungalow, 310 N. Market St. (☎800-8HOSTEL or 244-3678; fax 244-3678; info@mauihostel.com; www.mauihostel.com), a few blocks from Central Wailuku in Maui. Short-term work is available; email for more information.

Hostelling International Honolulu, 2323 A Seaview Ave. (☎946-0591; fax 946-5904; www.hiayh.org). Turn onto Seaview Ave. from University Ave. opposite the University of Hawaii campus just 4 blocks north of H-1. The hostel is on the left down a short driveway. Contact Mrs. Aiku.

Patey's Place, 75-195 Ala Ona Ona St. (☎326-7018; fax 326-7640; ipatey@gte.net; www.hawaiian-hostels.com) in Kailua-Kona on the Big Island, sometimes needs folks to help run the hostel.

Pineapple Park, 81-6363 Mamalahoa Hwy. (☎877-865-2266 or 323-2224; park@aloha.net; www.pineapple-park.com), north of downtown Captain Cook on the Big Island, trades a bed in the hostel for a few hours of housekeeping a week, and may be able to work out some other flexible work exchange arrangements.

Pineapple Park Hostel, 11-3489 Pikake St. (☎877-865-2266 or 968-8170) in Mountain View near Hawaii Volcanoes National Park on the Big Island. Often offers a dorm bunk in exchange for a few hours of housekeeping a week. If you're volunteering at the park (see below) and need a place to stay, look no further.

YMCA Camp Erdman, 69-385 Farrington Hwy. (☎637-4615; fax 637-8874; www.camperdan.net), in Waialua on Oahu. Short-term work can be arranged for room and board. For more information, contact Bridget (ext. 30).

VOLUNTEERING

Volunteering in Hawaii is a wonderful way to become integrated into local culture while contributing to the community at the same time. Many volunteer services charge you a fee to participate in the program and to do work. These fees can be surprisingly hefty (although they sometimes cover airfare and most, if not all, living expenses). Try to do research on a program before committing—talk to people who have previously participated and find out exactly what you're getting into, as living and working conditions can vary greatly. Different programs are geared toward different ages and levels of experience, so be sure to make sure that you are not taking on too much or too little. The more informed you are and the more realistic expectations you have, the more enjoyable the program will be.

Most people choose to go through a parent organization that takes care of logistical details, and that frequently provides a group environment and support system. There are two main types of organizations—religious (often Catholic) and secular—although there are rarely restrictions on participation for either.

Aloha United Way, 200 N. Vineyard Blvd., #700, Honolulu, HI 96817 (☎536-1951; www.auw.org/givinghelp/volunteerops.asp). Umbrella organization for a wide variety of community-oriented programs.

American Red Cross, 4155 Diamond Head Rd., Honolulu, HI 96816 (☎734-2101; www.hawaiiredcross.org/volunteer.htm). Volunteer opportunities in disaster relief, health and safety instruction, and first aid, among others.

Catholic Charities, 250 Vineyard St., Honolulu, HI 96813 (☎521-4357; www.catholic-charitieshawaii.org). Provides a range of social services.

Earthwatch, 3 Clocktower Pl., Suite 100, Box 75, Maynard, MA 01754 (☎800-776-0188 or 978-461-0081; www.earthwatch.org). Arranges 1- to 3-week programs in Hawaii to promote conservation of natural resources. Fees vary based on program location and duration; costs average $1700 plus airfare.

Habitat for Humanity International, 121 Habitat St., Americus, GA 31709, USA (☎229-924-6935, ext. 2551; www.habitat.org). Volunteers build houses in over 83 countries for anywhere from 2 weeks to 3 years. Short-term program costs US$1200-4000. **Honolulu Habitat for Humanity,** 98-025 Hekaha St., #214A, Aiea, HI 96701 (☎485-2355; www.honhabitat.org).

Haleakala National Park, P.O. Box 369, Makawao, Maui, HI 96768 (volunteer information 572-4487; www.haleakala.national-park.com). Various volunteer positions available, including the **Student Conservation Association Conservation Crew,** which provides meals and lodgings. Apply for SCA positions at least 1 year in advance.

Hawaii Volcanoes National Park, P.O. Box 52, Hawaii National Park, HI 96718-0052 (☎985-6000; fax 985-6004; www.nps.gov/havo). Various volunteer positions available, some of which provide meals and dorm-style housing.

Malama Hawaii (waiwaiohawaii@hotmail.com; www.malamahawaii.org). Sponsors a number of programs to help the environment and other community-based initiatives.

Sierra Club, Hawaii Chapter, P.O. Box 2577, Honolulu, HI 96803 (☎538-6616; www.hi.sierraclub.org). Seeks to improve natural resource management, clean up pollution, and protect biodiversity in Hawaii.

Volunteer Zone (www.volunteerzone.org). A database of volunteer opportunities in Hawaii in a variety of fields.

FOR FURTHER READING ON ALTERNATIVES TO TOURISM

How to Live Your Dream of Volunteering Overseas, by Collins, DeZerega, and Heckscher. Penguin Books, 2002 (US$17).

International Directory of Voluntary Work, by Whetter and Pybus. Peterson's Guides and Vacation Work, 2000 (US$16).

International Jobs, by Kocher and Segal. Perseus Books, 1999 (US$18).

Overseas Summer Jobs 2002, by Collier and Woodworth. Peterson's Guides and Vacation Work, 2002 (US$18).

Work Abroad: The Complete Guide to Finding a Job Overseas, by Hubbs, Griffith, and Nolting. Transitions Abroad Publishing, 2000 ($16).

Work Your Way Around the World, by Susan Griffith. Worldview Publishing Services, 2001 (US$18).

ALTERNATIVES TO TOURISM

OAHU

As the gateway to the islands, Oahu (O'ahu) is where most visitors catch their first thrilling, captivating glimpse of Hawaii. It's known as "the gathering place" for good reason—Oahu is the seat of the state government, as well as Hawaii's financial and business center. Though it is only the third-largest of the inhabited Hawaiian islands, nearly three-quarters of the state's total population make their home on Oahu. Over half of these residents are concentrated in Honolulu, Hawaii's state capital and premier city. This bustling metropolis is the nexus of Oahu, with all the glitz and glamour of a big-time urban center. Thanks in part to Honolulu's hectic feel and the boisterous Waikiki area, Oahu is often pigeonholed as over-commercialized and artificial. Many purists advise travelers to catch the first flight to a neighboring island.

Despite Oahu's unabashedly touristy nature, the island is worth any visitor's time—if only for the sheer diversity and accessibility of its many charms. Within the island's 593 square miles, there are enough sights to fill a lifetime of vacations. Some of these attractions are readily apparent—visitors need look no further than Waikiki to get their fill of tropical *kitsch* and frenzied nightlife, and Downtown Honolulu offers myriad opportunities to explore Hawaii's historical and cultural past. However, Oahu isn't all souvenir shops and guided tours. With minimal effort, visitors can uncover the island's less obvious treasures. On the Windward side, a pleasant drive passes by rickety fruit stands and acres of pineapple fields to the fabled North Shore, one of the world's best surf spots. Drive ten or so miles up the Leeward Coast and both the scenery and the mood change dramatically; you're in rural Hawaii, where inhabitants e+mbrace a slower, more traditional way of life. The luxuriant Manoa Valley overflows with fragrant blossoms and tropical fruit, and hikers have their pick of countless intertwined trails that lead to pockets of unspoiled Hawaiian rainforest.

On Oahu, visitors can discover the multifaceted appeal of Hawaii. There is a trace of Big Island's hippie culture on the sands of the North Shore, some of Maui's beauty and opulence in the Windward Coast's resorts, a dash of Kauai's natural splendor in the lush interior valleys, and a little bit of rustic Molokai in the streets of Waimanalo. Oahu contains distilled versions of the best her sister islands have to offer. Consider this your crash course in Hawaiian appreciation.

HIGHLIGHTS OF OAHU

PAY YOUR RESPECTS at the Pearl Harbor memorials (p. 140).

RELIVE GLORY DAYS at Nu'uanu Pali lookout, the site of Kamehameha's 1795 victory and turning point in his campaign to unite all the islands (p. 157).

TREAT YOUR TUMMY to a plate lunch and shave ice from the unpretentious eateries of Waimanalo (p. 145).

MARVEL at the acrobatics of extreme windsurfers in famed Kailua Bay (p. 159).

CLIFF JUMP into the crystalline waters of North Shore's Waimea Bay (p. 169).

Oahu

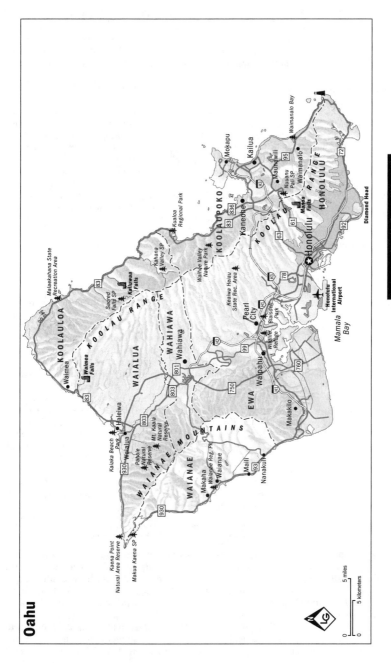

OAHU

5 miles

5 kilometers

⊠ INTERISLAND TRANSPORTATION

Oahu is the major hub for transportation to the Hawaiian islands, as international flights, flights between Hawaii and the mainland, and interisland flights depart from **Honolulu International Airport** in Honolulu (see p. 84). See each city's **Transportation** sections for local transportation.

⊠ CAMPING

In order to camp at any state park on Oahu, you need a **permit.** Camping permits are obtainable from the Department of Parks and Recreation, on the ground floor of the **Honolulu Municipal Building** (650 S. King St., Honolulu, HI 96813-3078; open M-F 7:45am-4pm) or at any **Satellite City Hall** in the county. Camping is allowed from 8am on Friday to 8am on Wednesday, though certain campsites are only open on weekends. Make reservations at least one week in advance, but no more than 2 Fridays prior to camping date. More than 5 days of camping in one month at any single park is prohibited. For more information on camping, call ☎523-4525.

The state of Hawaii's **Division of Forestry and Wildlife** provides all manner of information concerning Oahu trails, including trail maps and descriptions. (1151 Punchbowl St., Rm. 325. ☎587-0058. Open M-F 7:45am-4:30pm.)

HONOLULU

As Hawaii's commanding capital and largest city, Honolulu is the point of entry for most visits to the islands. Although the tourist throngs often pass over Honolulu proper en route to the resorts of its Waikiki district, Waikiki's commercialism is the result of only the most recent wave of newcomers that have changed the face of Hawaii's biggest city. The historical sights in the downtown area and civic center illustrate the complex history of Hawaii's religious and economic modernization at the hands of sometimes benevolent, but frequently heavy-handed, Western influence. Today's Hawaiians inherit a cosmopolitan city of almost 400,000 as their capital—Downtown bustles with aloha-shirt-clad businesspeople every weekday, and Chinatown is crammed to the gills with daytime shoppers in search of its markets, giftshops, and authentic Asian restaurants. The mellow residential areas of Kaimuki and the University of Hawaii at Manoa to the north of the city proper present a marked contrast to the hectic urban lifestyle. Locals in these areas avoid the fast pace of Honolulu by slipping away to Waikiki's beaches or barbecuing *ohana*-style at Ala Moana Beach Park. Honolulu alternates as a beach resort, urban center, commercial hub, international port, and living landmark of Hawaiian history. To the adventure-seeking tourist, it is all of these at once, a capital city paradoxically unlike anywhere else in the state.

⊠ INTERCITY TRANSPORTATION

Honolulu International Airport (☎836-6413; www.honoluluairport.com) is off the Airport exit from H-1, 9 mi. west of Waikiki. The airport is also accessible via Ala Moana Blvd. Take Ala Moana west until it becomes Nimitz Hwy. and continue west. Turn left into the airport just west of the Roger's Blvd. intersection underneath H-1 and follow signs to Arrivals, Departures, or the many opportunistically-placed **lei stands** outside the airport.

Inside the airport, **ATMs** are available in the Interisland Terminal, the central lobby of the main terminal, and near gates 12-13. **Currency exchange** services are available in the central lobby of the main terminal, near gates 12-13 and 24-25. **Lost**

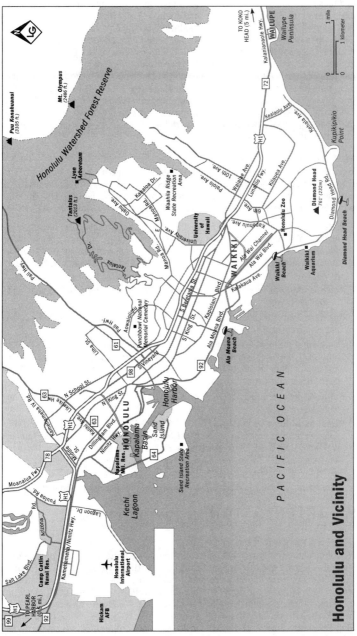

Honolulu and Vicinity

OAHU

and found (☎836-6547) is on the ground level in the parking structure, opposite the Main Terminal. Visitors can make photocopies, buy flight insurance, use postage and mail services, fax, and rent workstations at the **Airport Business Center.** (☎831-3600. Open daily 8am-5pm.) The FAA has shut down all lockers at Honolulu International Airport. **Airport parking** (☎861-1260) costs $1 for the first 30min., $1 each additional hr., $10 per 24hr. and $100 per month, non-prorated. If you leave your car longer than 30 days, it can be towed unless you notify the parking company. Cars may be security-screened. **Reliable Shuttle** (☎924-9292) runs between the airport and hotels in Waikiki and Honolulu (approx. $6), as well as the *USS Arizona* Memorial. Make reservations by phone at least one day in advance. Shuttles run daily 6am-10pm. See **Interisland Transportation** at the start of each chapter for information on flights between the islands.

FLIGHTS

Honolulu International Airport operates the majority of incoming flights to Hawaii, both international and domestic, as well as connecting flights to the other islands. See **Essentials** (p. 51) for further information on flying to Hawaii. The airport serves a number of airlines; the following are a few major US carriers.

Aloha Airlines (☎800-367-5250 or 484-1111; www.alohaair.com) has ticket offices across Oahu. Service from Burbank, Oakland, and Orange County, California; and Vancouver, Canada. Also operates interisland flights from Honolulu to: Hilo and Kona on the Big Island; Lihu'e, Kauai; Lanai City, Lanai; Kapalua and Kahului on Maui; and Hoolehua, Molokai.

American Airlines (☎800-433-7300; www.aa.com) has flights from the continental US via Dallas-Ft. Worth, Los Angeles, and Chicago.

American Trans Air (☎800-435-9282; www.ata.com) provides service from Los Angeles and San Francisco.

Continental Airlines, Ala Moana Center Ste. 2230 (☎800-214-1469 or 946-9786; fax 942-8821; www.continental.com), offers service from Houston, Los Angeles, and Newark, and on partner airlines from Minneapolis/St. Paul, Seattle/Tacoma and San Francisco. Ticket office open M-F 9am-6pm, Sa 9am-5pm.

Delta Airlines (☎800-221-1212; www.delta.com) provides service from Los Angeles and Salt Lake City.

Hawaiian Airlines (☎800-367-5320 or 838-1555; www.hawaiianair.com) has additional ticket offices inside Sears at Ala Moana and Pearlridge Shopping Centers and Windward Mall. Service from: Anchorage, Alaska; Las Vegas; Los Angeles; Phoenix; Portland, Oregon; San Diego; Sacramento; San Francisco; and Seattle. Interisland service to the Big Island, Kauai, Lanai, and Molokai.

United Airlines (☎800-241-6522; www.ual.com) provides service from most US cities.

✷ ORIENTATION

HIGHWAYS AND BYWAYS

Honolulu's main highway, **H-1,** runs east and west along the length of the city from Hawaii Kai, past the airport, and on to Pearl Ridge. Getting onto H-1 can be an ordeal, as some streets only provide access to one direction, either eastbound or westbound. Drivers can avoid the hassle, as well as rush hour traffic Downtown, by using alternate roads. Access is available via: **Ala Moana Blvd.,** which stretches from Waikiki to the airport, and turns into Nimitz Hwy. west of Nu'uanu River; and **King St.,** which leaves H-1 north of Waikiki and splits into two one-way streets between University Ave. and the Aala Park edge of Chinatown. The one-way

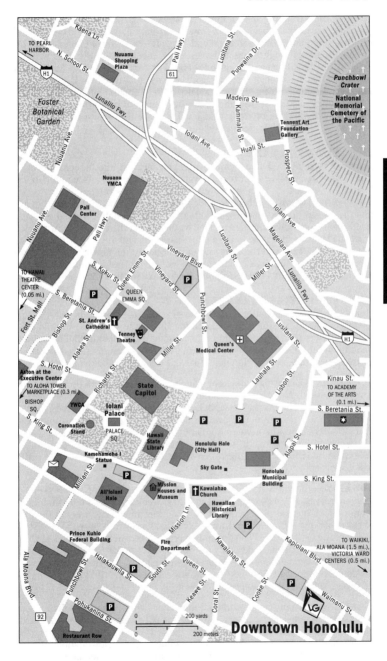

Downtown Honolulu

streets formed from the split of King St., **Beretania St.** (heading west) and King St. (heading east), are the backbone of Downtown and Chinatown, and bear the brunt of intra-Honolulu traffic. Beretania and King streets also front a large portion of greater Honolulu's sights and activities. Most **TheBus routes** ply their way down King St., then head east and back up Beretania St. for the return trip. **Kapiolani Blvd.** is another major thoroughfare, slicing a northeast-southwest passage from Wailae Ave. and H-1, intersecting Waikiki's **Kalakaua Ave.** before plunging westward to the Civic Center at King St. Kapahulu, McCully, and Piikoi northbound one-way, Pensacola southbound one-way, and Ward Ave. are the biggest streets that intersect the east-west usual suspects.

THE LEI OF THE LAND

Honolulu is an abused place-name geographically, and like the local phrase "da kine," it is often used to refer to whatever is presently under discussion. To many, Honolulu means the urban and suburban sprawl that stretches along the south shore of Oahu, from Kokohead at the extreme eastern end of the island to Kalihi and the airport on the western end. Others consider Honolulu to be the comparatively small downtown area surrounded by the diverse districts of **Chinatown** to the west, **Ala Moana** and **Waikiki** to the south, **Kaimuki** and the revitalized **Wailae** area to the east, and **Manoa** and the valley neighborhoods to the north. The **Koolau Mountain Range** creates the city's backdrop, and fixed in the east is **Diamond Head Crater**, which provides a perfect vantage point for some of the best views on Oahu.

HONOLULU NEIGHBORHOODS

Honolulu is an amalgamation of a number of small neighborhoods, but Ala Moana, Downtown and Chinatown, Manoa and the University Area, and Waikiki are the major districts referred to in this guide, although some listings fall near, but not exactly within, the established boundaries of their given districts. **Waikiki** is the nexus of tourist activity in Honolulu. (See p. 117 for all Waikiki information.)

ALA MOANA. Occupying waterfront Honolulu along Ala Moana Blvd. from Downtown to Waikiki, Ala Moana is a shopper's paradise. A number of malls and complexes throw their hats into the capitalist ring, including Aloha Tower Marketplace and Restaurant Row in neighboring Kaka'ako, Ala Moana's sprawling Victoria Ward Centers, and Ala Moana Shopping Center. Ala Moana Shopping Center is also a major bus terminal; if the route you need isn't near some side of the mall (TheBus routes #6, 8, 11, 12, 19, 20, 40, 42, 43, 52-58, 62, 65, 86A, and 88A are), it's just a short connection away.

DOWNTOWN. Downtown Honolulu is Hawaii's financial center, and Bishop Sq. in its center houses Oahu's captains of industry. Weekday work hours find the area teeming with businessfolk, although at any other time of the week it feels more like a ghost town. Downtown draws only a small crowd from with the historical sights of the Civic Center. The downtown area is sandwiched between Ala Moana and Chinatown, and is bordered by the Fort St. Mall, South St., and Kaka'ako. It is notorious for having some of the most expensive parking in the country; avoid the headache of parking woes and one-way streets by taking TheBus #2, 13 or B CityExpress to Hotel St. and exploring on foot.

CHINATOWN. Chinatown assaults all the senses with its pungent fish markets, incense-surrounded shrines, vocal Chinese-speaking bargain-hunters, and sizzling, claustrophobic food markets. Originally the red light district for sailors, Chinatown is now both home to a diverse Asian population and a destination for tourists in search of a cultural experience complete with shopping bargains and inexpensive food. All are readily available in Chinatown, but bargain hunters should come early to beat the crowds. Chinatown itself is a small grid a few blocks square, bordered by Downtown and Aala Triangle Park to the west. Chinatown's shop-lined streets are River St., Maunakea St., Smith St., Nuʻuanu Ave., and Bethel St. before Fort St. Mall. Kukui St. is the northern border of the area, which continues to Nimitz Hwy. on the harbor to the south. Begin pedestrian exploration at the intersection of Hotel and River streets; take TheBus #2, 13 or B CityExpress. Visitors should not travel to Chinatown alone after dark, when most businesses are closed.

MANOA AND THE UNIVERSITY AREA. The University of Hawaii hangs its scholarly hat in the pleasant Manoa valley district, north of central Honolulu. Manoa itself is a peaceful valley overflowing with greenery, lava rock walls, and fruit trees. It seems that the higher up one travels in the valley, away from the city center and toward the **Honolulu Watershed Forest Reserve,** the more cheerful and tranquil the streets become. Two of Honolulu's main arteries, University Ave. and Punahou St., become Oahu Ave. and Manoa Rd. respectively once they hit Manoa. Oahu Ave. and Manoa Rd. continue on to **Lyon Arboreteum** and **Manoa Falls.** A series of strip malls and grocery stores radiates out from the intersection of King St. and University Ave., in the more densely-populated area known as **Moiliili,** at the base of Manoa Valley. West of Manoa, between Punahou School and Punchbowl Crater north of H-1, is the highrise-clogged neighborhood of **Makiki.** Excellent hiking and scenic drives are found at the extreme ends of Makiki Heights Dr., Round Top Dr., and Tantalus Dr., where the latter two loop into the Forest Reserve and the area near Mt. Tantalus, to the west.

TheBus #4 picks up westbound on Kuhio Ave. in Waikiki and continues up University Ave. and on to Downtown. The #5, 6, and 18 all pick up at Ala Moana Shopping Center and head to Manoa. The #80A is an express from Hawaii Kai from 6-7:30am to lower Manoa and Downtown weekdays during school, going as far into Manoa as Dole St. and UH. In the afternoon, the 80A runs from Punahou School at Punahou St. and Wilder Ave. back to Hawaii Kai.

KAPAHULU/WAIALAE. Kapahulu/Waialae and the blocks adjacent to these avenues in the amiable **Kaimuki** area are the cradle of a revitalized neighborhood known for its multitude of diverse dining options, a short walk or Our Neighborhood Trolley ride away from Downtown Honolulu. TheBus #9 from Honolulu travels from S. King St. up Kapiolani Blvd. and on to Waialae and 4th Ave. Alternatively, the #1 goes from west Honolulu to Kahala Mall and Hawaii Kai.

▐ LOCAL TRANSPORTATION

BY BUS. Oahu's public transit system, **TheBus** (☎ 848-4500; www.thebus.org), was recently voted "America's Best Transit System," and offers safe and reliable service across the island. If you are not sure if you are getting on the correct bus or off at the correct stop, the bus drivers are eager to help you find your way. Buses have the same number going in both directions, but the title of the bus changes depending on direction. Throw the driver a friendly signal (*Let's Go* prefers the ▇two-fingered horizontal brow salute) if you wish to board an approaching bus, and push the yellow tape or pull the cord to signal before your stop when riding.

> **Routes and Fares:** One-way fare $1.50; 75¢ for senior citizens, the disabled, and students 18 and under; children under 6 free. Free transfers are good for 2hr., available by request from bus driver. **The Oahu Discovery Passport,** available at ABC Stores, is good for 4 consecutive days of unlimited travel ($15). **Route A,** the CityExpress, goes from Kalihi and Waipahu in the west, down King/Beretania to University Ave. and Manoa.

Route B, the other CityExpress, stops short of University Ave. in Waikiki. **Route C,** the CountryExpress, makes it all the way out from Makaha to Ala Moana Shopping Center. These are just a few of TheBus's many routes; see the website or information lines for details. *Let's Go* lists nearby TheBus stops for sights and towns, where applicable. See **Waikiki Transportation** (p. 117) for Waikiki-based routes.

Information Lines: Call **TheBus Information Service** (☎848-5555) with your location, a time of departure, and destination points, and they will find the best route to get you there. **The 24hr. Recorded Information from Waikiki** (☎296-1818) hotline offers an automated directory of bus routes to sites across the island, on buses that pick up from Kuhio Ave. TheBus also publishes the helpful **Map and Guidebook** ($5 English, $6.50 Japanese), available in convenience stores in the Honolulu area.

BY CAR. Driving is the easiest way to get around Oahu, despite traffic congestion and limited parking. For **parking rates and hours,** call ☎523-4314. Call ☎529-3111 to locate a car **towed** from the street, and ☎529-3231 for **stolen vehicles.** The major **national car rental** chains have branches by the airport (listed below). From within the airport, follow the signs to car rentals. To return the vehicle from Honolulu, take H-1 West to the Airport. Arrivals are on street level, to the extreme left—follow signs that say Car Rental/Car Returns. As the nexus of most tourist activity in Honolulu, Waikiki holds a number of excellent smaller car and moped rental companies (see **Waikiki Transportation, p. 117**). Car rental costs fluctuate by season and availability, even at national chains. Be sure to call well in advance to reserve a vehicle, and to check company websites for online deals and promotions. See **Essentials (p. 58)** for more information on traveling by car in Hawaii.

Alamo (☎800-GO-ALAMO or 833-4585; www.alamo.com), at the airport and in Waikiki. Cars from $40 per day, $160 weekly. CDW $19 per day. Minimum age 21, under-25 surcharge $25 per day. Rentals must be returned to the airport location. All major credit cards. Deposit can also be made with debit card, with proof of departure. Open daily 5am-1am.

Avis (☎800-321-3712 or 834-5536; fax 839-7591; www.avis.com), at the airport. Cars from $38-56 per day, depending on season and availability. Monthly rates around $300 per week. Unlimited mileage. CDW $21 per day unlimited, liability $11 per day. Under-25 surcharge. Returns can be made at Waikiki branch. All major credit cards, no debit cards. Open daily 5am-3am.

Budget (☎800-527-0700 or 836-1700; www.budget.com), at the airport and seven other island locations. Cars from $38 per day, $305 weekly. Unlimited mileage. Minimum age 21, under-25 surcharge $20 per day. Rentals must be returned to the airport location. All major credit cards. Open 24hr.

Dollar (☎800-800-4000 or 944-1544; fax 833-2974; www.dollar.com), at the airport. Branch at 2002 Kalakaua Ave., in Waikiki. Cars from $47 per day, $237 per week. Unlimited mileage. CDW $18 per day. $20 per day under-25 surcharge. Open daily 4:30am-midnight.

Enterprise (☎800-736-8222 or 836-2213, or the Kalihi branch at ☎836-7722; fax 836-7866; www.enterprise.com), at the airport and 16 other island locations. Cars from $30 per day, $150 weekly, $650 monthly. Unlimited mileage. Minimum age 21, no under-25 surcharge. CDW $15. Returns can be made at Salt Lake Kalihi, Waikiki office, and other locations; all usually match airport rates. Open M-F 7am-6pm, Sa 9am-noon.

Hertz (☎800-654-3011 or 831-3500; fax 831-3545; www.hertz.com), at the airport. Cars from $37 per day; no long-term deals. Unlimited mileage. CDW $20 per day. Minimum age 25. Rentals must be returned to the airport location. All major credit cards, no cash deposit. Open daily 5am-2am.

National Car Rental (☎800-CAR-RENT or 831-3800; fax 831-3489; www.national-car.com), at the airport and two other Honolulu locations. Cars from $33 per day, $170 weekly. Unlimited mileage. CDW $19. Minimum age 21, under-25 surcharge $25 per day. Only major credit cards. Returns can be made at other Honolulu locations. Open 5am-midnight.

Thrifty (☎800-367-2277 or 831-2277; fax 831-2263; www.thrifty.com), at the airport. Compact 4-door $30 per day, $160 per week. Unlimited mileage. CDW $19 per day. Minimum age 21, under-25 surcharge $15 per day. Branch at 325 Seaside Ave. in Waikiki; $30 Waikiki drop-off fee. All major credit cards, no cash deposit. Open daily 5:30am-midnight.

⁊ PRACTICAL INFORMATION

The central branches of many of Oahu's services are found in Honolulu. Many tourist services within the city are based in Waikiki, the hub of the city's tourist activity. See also **Waikiki Practical Information** (p. 119).

TOURIST AND FINANCIAL SERVICES

Tourist Office: Hawaii Visitors & Convention Bureau Information Center, at Waikiki Shopping Plaza, 2250 Kalakaua Ave., Ste. 502 (☎924-0266; info@hvcb.org; www.gohawaii.com). The office has statewide tourist information, as well as a number of local brochures and tourist magazines. Open M-F 8am-4:30pm, Sa-Su 8am-noon.

Pleasant Ticket Office, 1601 Kapiolani Blvd., Ste. 940 (☎800-654-4386 or 922-1515), the kiosk in front of 7-11 at the intersection of Kapiolani Blvd. and Kalakaua Ave. The tiny office specializes in air, room, and car packages to the outer islands, and cheaper mainland airfare. Open M-F 8am-5:30pm, Sa-Su 8:30am-5pm. AmEx/MC/V.

Free Tours:

The Mayor's Office (☎841–6442) offers a walking tour of old Waikiki on the 2-mile Waikiki Historic Trail. Look for the Trail Historian at the kiosk in front of the zoo. M-Sa 9-11am.

The Clean Air Team (☎948-3299) volunteers lead a 2-mile, 3-hour pleasant stroll through Kapiolani Park and along the Diamond Head Coast, ending at the Diamond Head Lighthouse. Participants may wish to bring flashlights for caves near the coast. Leaves from the Gandhi statue near the Honolulu Zoo entrance, 151 Kapahulu Ave. Su 9am. Under 18 must be accompanied by an adult; groups of 5 or more must call ahead. Parking available at the Waikiki Shell.

The Diamond Head Story (☎948-3299), a field-trip-like walking tour about the history of Diamond Head that ends at the beginning of a 1-mile hike to the top of the crater. Participants may try the hike, or return to the zoo on their own. Leaves from the Gandhi statue (see above). Sa 9am. Under 18 must be accompanied by an adult; groups of 5 or more must call ahead. Parking available at the Waikiki Shell.

The Program to Preserve Hawaiian Placenames, at the Liliha Public Library, 1515 Liliha St.; take H-1 west to School St. and take N. School St. west to Liliha St. Catch the free "Introduction to Hawaiian Placenames" lecture, the easiest and fastest (1½hr.) way to become acquainted with Hawaiian word structure. The lecture teaches how to pronounce Hawaiian placenames, step by step. First Wednesday of every month, 7pm. No late arrivals.

The Like Hike (☎455-8193; likehike@lava.net), a gay Honolulu hiking club, sponsors a monthly hike, usually on Sundays, to explore the wild outback of Oahu.

Paid Tours:

Hawaii Tours and Travels, 339 Saratoga Rd. Ste. 21 (☎922-4884; www.hawaiitourandtravels.com). See the entire island via a 25-person bus with A/C and big windows on the 120-mile Grand Island Circle Tour (2 per day, 8:20am-4:30pm or 9am-5:30pm, $15; $30 with a 1¼hr. excursion including entrance to Waimea Falls). Four-hour Jungle Rainforest Hiking trip $19, Dr. Livingstone and machete not included. Inexpensive outer-island helicopter rides, swimming with dolphins, and more. Open daily 8am-6pm; orders by phone 7:30am-9pm. MC/V.

Affordable Tours, 334 Seaside Ave., Ste. 102 (☎921-2280), books tours at discounted prices. Circle Island Tour (8:45am-5pm; $17, with entrance to Waimea Falls $35). Exotic Beach Luau with all-you-can-eat dinner buffet and 3 drinks (5-10pm; $30, transportation $4). Open daily 8am-6pm, phone orders 7am-10pm. MC/V.

Equipment Rental: See **Waikiki Practical Information,** p. 119.

Embassies and Consulates: Australia, 1000 Bishop St., Ste. PHOUSE 96813 (☎524-5050). Handles Australian and some **British travel documents.** Open M-F 8am-4pm. **New Zealand,** c/o Hawaiian Electric Industries, Inc. 900 Richards St. #414; P.O. Box 730 96813 (☎547-5117; fax 543-7523; plewis@hei.com). NZ consulate is a one-person operation which mails visa and passport applications. No office hours. See **www.embassyworld.com** for a complete listing of embassies and consulates throughout the US.

Banks and Currency Exchange: American Savings (☎800-272-2566) has offices at 180 S. King St. (☎523-6844; open M-Th 7:30am-3:30pm, F 3:30-5pm) and 1296 S. Beretania (☎591-2255; open M-F 9am-6pm, Sa 9am-1pm). 3% currency exchange fee for non-account holders. **Bank of Hawaii,** 1431 S. Beretania (☎888-643-3888). Open M-Th 7:30am-3pm, F 7:30am-4:30pm. $10 currency exchange fee for non-account holders. **Central Pacific,** 220 S. King St. (☎544-0500). Open M-Th 7:30am-3pm, F 7:30am-4:30pm. $5 currency exchange fee for non-account holders. **First Hawaiian Bank** has offices at 999 Bishop St. (☎525-6340) and 2 N. King St. (☎525-6888). Both are open M-Th 8:30am-4pm, F 8:30am-6pm and charge non-account holders a currency exchange fee of $3 for amounts under $300. **Hawaii National Bank,** 45 N. King St. (☎528-7711), is open M-Th 8am-4pm, F 8am-5pm. $5 currency exchange rate for non-account holders. **Philippine National Bank,** 1145 Bishop (☎521-1493). Open M-Th 8:15am-4pm. No currency exchange. With the exception of the Philippine National Bank, all banks have **ATMs** throughout Honolulu.

LOCAL SERVICES

Libraries: Hawaii State Library, 478 S. King St. (☎586-3500), just east of Iolani Palace, in the civic center—look for the huge white pillars out front. Added to the State and National Register of Historical Places in 1975, the Hawaii State Library anchors the only statewide library system in the United States, with over 500,000 catalogued books and more than a million supporting materials. The children's section is decorated with murals of Hawaiian legends by celebrated artist Juliette May Fraser. Open M, F-Sa 9am-5pm; Tu, Th 9am-8pm; W 10am-5pm. The **McCully-Moiliili Public Library** is at 2211 S. King St. (☎973-1099). Open M-Tu, F-Sa 10am-5pm; W-Th 10am-8pm. Temporary library passes are available at all library branches. Three-month pass $10, non-resident pass (good for one year) $25. **Manoa Public Library,** 2716 Woodlawn Dr. (☎988-0459). Open M, W, F-Sa 10am-5pm; Tu, Th 10am-8pm.

Laundromat: Manoa Laundry, 2855 E. Manoa Rd. (☎988-9015), next to the post office in Manoa. Single load self-service $1, with drop-off service available.

Department of Parks and Recreation, 1000 Uluohia St., Ste. 309 (☎692-5585), in Kapolei. Oahu **camping permits** available at the Main Permits Office, 650 S. King St. Both offices open daily 7:45am-4:30pm.

Hawaii Nature Center, 2131 Makiki Heights Dr. (☎955-0100; www.hawaiinaturecenter.org), in Makiki Valley. Hands-on programs, community events, and guided hikes. Schedule available online. Open daily 8am-4:30pm.

Hawaiian Trail and Mountain Club, 41-023 Pu'uone St. (☎259-5443; www.geocities.com/Yosemite/Trails/3660), in Waimanalo. Hikes a different trail every weekend; visitors are welcome. Quarterly hike schedules available online. All hikes meet at Iolani Palace at 8am. Under 18 must be accompanied by adult. Suggested donation $2.

Sierra Club, Beretania St. (☎ 538-6616), across from the police station. Hikes, outings, and service projects. Visitors and non-members welcome. Schedule available online. Unless otherwise noted, hikes leave at 8am from 2150 Bingham St. Under 18 must be accompanied by adult. $3, Sierra club members and children under 14 $1.

Honolulu Gay and Lesbian Cultural Foundation: ☎ 941-0424.

Weather and Surf Conditions: See **Honolulu and Waikiki Information Lines** (p. 94).

LOCAL MEDIA

Television Stations: ABC (KITV, channel 4/12/13); **CBS** (KGMB, channel 9); **Fox** (KHON, channel 2/7/11); **NBC** (KHNL, channel 13); **PBS** (KHET, channel 11). **KIKU** (channel 20) presents multicultural shows in as many as 8 languages, with over 30 hours of Japanese language shows per week. **KWHE** (channel 14) is primarily family Christian programming, but shows Big 12 football and basketball, as well as Pac 10 Conference collegiate sporting events.

National PublicRadio: 88.1 FM plays classical music and the NPR news; 89.3 FM has news, talk, world music, NPR, and the BBC.

Other Radio Stations: ▨**90.3 FM KTUH Honolulu** (91.3 FM Hawaii Kai, 89.7 FM North Shore), the University of Hawaii's excellent radio station, plays a wide-ranging melange from jazz to jungle, house to Hawaiian. **Urban/Rap/Hip-Hop,** "Da Bomb" KDDB 102.7 FM, KIKI 93.9 FM, KXME 104.3 FM. **Modern Rock,** 97.5 FM KPOI and 101.9 FM KUCD. **Hawaiian music,** KCCN 100.3 FM and KINE 105.1 FM. **Classic Rock,** KAHA 105.9 FM. **Oldies,** KGMZ 107.9 FM for 60s and 70s nostalgia or KQMQ 93.1 for old-school dance and rock hits from the 70s through the 90s. **Adult Contemporary,** KSSK 92.3 FM and KRTR 96.3 FM. **Christian,** K218CH 91.4 FM and KAIM 95.5 FM.

EMERGENCY AND COMMUNICATIONS

Emergency: ☎ 911.

Police: S. Beretania St. (☎ 529-3111). Downtown/Chinatown substation (☎ 527-6990). Airport police (☎ 836-6411).

Crisis Lines: Sex Abuse Treatment Center, ☎ 524-7273. **Crisis Response Team,** ☎ 521-4555. **Poison Center,** ☎ 941-4411. **Missing Child Center,** ☎ 753-9797. **Suicide and Crisis Center,** ☎ 521-4555.

Fire Department: ☎ 831-7771.

Red Cross: Hawaii Chapter ☎ 734-2101.

24-Hour Pharmacies: Long's Drugs at 1330 Pali Hwy. (☎ 536-7302 or 536-5542), on the corner of Pali Hwy. and Vineyard Blvd. Another branch is located at 2220 S. King St. (☎ 949-4781 or 947-2651), across from Honolulu Stadium State Recreation Area.

Hospital: Queen's Medical Center, 1301 Punchbowl St. (☎ 538-9011). An **Emergency Services Department** (☎ 831-4351) provides pre-hospital emergency medical care and ambulance services.

Medical Assistance: Urgent Care Clinic of Hawaii, 2155 Kalakaua Ave., at Beachwalk (☎ 597-2860). **Straub Clinic and Hospital,** 888 S. King St. (☎ 522-4000). See **Waikiki Practical Information,** p. 119.

Planned Parenthood Clinic of Hawaii: ☎ 589-1149.

Internet Access:

etopia, 1363 S. Beretania St. (☎ 593-2050; www.theetopia.com), on the corner of Beretania St. and Keeaumoku St. Non-member Internet access fee $3 per hr. Members get a better rate ($2 per hr.), enjoy a free drink, and go to the front of the waiting lists that sometimes form for the fast, sleek machines. Monthly membership $10. Under 18 not allowed during school hours. Open daily 9am-2am. AmEx/MC/V.

OAHU

Teava Momi, 1726 Kapiolani #101B (☎946-8988), across Kapiolani from the Hawaii Convention Center. Cable access $1.50 per 15min. Snacks include mini ramen, gyoza and Chinese-style pizzas ($1.25-3). Open daily 2:30-11:30pm. No credit cards.

Netstop, 2615 S. King St. (☎955-1020; www.netstopcafe.com), across from Puck's Alley in the University Square strip mall in Manoa. Fast connections and top of the line Intel Pentium computers have Japanese, French, German, Chinese, Korean and other language capabilities. Internet access 7¢ per min. for non-members. Color Inkjet Printing 70¢ per page, B&W laser printing 20¢ per page. Large coffee $1.25. Open M-Sa 9:30am-midnight, Su 11am-11pm.

Post Offices:

Airport branch, 3600 Aolele (☎423-6029). Offers only general delivery (*poste restante*) services on the island. Open M-F 7:30am-8pm, Sa 8am-4pm. **Zip Code:** 96819.

Ala Moana branch, 1450 Ala Moana Blvd., Ste. 1006 (☎532-1987). Open M-F 8am-4:30pm, Sa 8am-noon for package pick-up. **Zip Code:** 96814.

Downtown Honolulu branch, 335 Merchant St. (☎532-1987), west of Ali'Iolani Hale in the civic center. Open M-F 8am-4:30pm. **Zip Code:** 96813.

Kaimuki branch, 1130 Koko Head Ave. (☎737-8937). Open M-F 8am-4:30pm, Sa 9am-1pm. **Zip Code:** 96816.

Makiki branch, 1111 Lunalilo St. (☎532-5689). Open M-F 8am-4:30pm. Package pick-up 6-8am and 2-5pm. **Zip Code:** 96822.

Manoa branch, 2855 E. Manoa Rd. in the mall behind Safeway. Post office boxes, accessible at 10am, $24-68 for six months. Open M-F 8:15am-3:30pm, Sa 8:30am-noon. **Zip Code:** 96822

Moiliili branch, 2700 S. King St., Ste. B (☎532-5689). Open M-F 7:15am-4:15pm. **Zip Code:** 96826.

HONOLULU AND WAIKIKI INFORMATION LINES.

WEATHER AND SURF INFORMATION

National Weather Service Surf Report: (☎973-4381); Oahu beaches surf report (☎973-4383).

Surf News Network: ☎596-SURF.

US Weather Service Recording (☎973-4380) might as well be a broken record saying, "It's 82-86 degrees Farenheit and sunny." For a change of pace, try the **Hurricane Information** recording (☎527-5372) or the Oahu Civil Defense Agency's **Hurricane Preparedness** line (☎523-4121).

Lifeguard Services: ☎922-3888.

HELPFUL SERVICES

Elderly Information and Assistance Services: ☎523-4545. Open M-F 7:30am-4:30pm.

Pacific Gateway Center (Foreign Language Translation Service): ☎845-3918

HandiVan Reservations: ☎454-5050 or 456-5955. Information ☎523-4083. Acquire a pass ☎848-4444; TDD ☎456-5045.

Honolulu Gay and Lesbian Cultural Foundation: ☎941-0424.

Honolulu Job Information: ☎523-5301.

EVENTS AND RECREATION

Mayor's Office of Culture and the Arts (MOCA): ☎523-4674.

Neal Blaisdell Center and Waikiki Shell Calendar of Events: ☎527-5400; Blaisdell Box Office ☎521-2211.

Parks and Recreation Department Information: ☎692-5561.

Camping Permits: ☎523-4527. **Fishing and hunting permits:** ☎587-0072.

PUBLICATIONS

Honolulu Weekly (www.honoluluweekly.com) is a free community paper with incisive articles and reviews, as well as extensive events listings. Pick one up on street corners throughout Honolulu. **This Week Oahu** and **Oahu Gold** are weekly coupon and ad-laden brochure magazines omnipresent in Oahu. A good **map** of Waikiki is never more than a block away, in the pages of the free tourist publications available on every street.

The weekly **Downtown Planet** (www.downtownplanet.com) lists downtown parking locations and their prices, as well as other local information and events. Hawaii Pacific University puts out a monthly award-winning student newspaper, **Kalamalama.** Pick up either paper anywhere in the Fort St. Mall.

The **Honolulu Advertiser** (www.honoluluadvertiser.com) is Honolulu's most esteemed daily paper, covering national and international news, business, technology, entertainment, sports, and island life, as well as the large classified section that gave the paper its name. The *Advertiser* is available in grocery and convenience stores and street vending boxes. (www.honoluluadvertiser.com. M-Sa 50¢, Su $1.75.) The **Honolulu Star Bulletin** (www.starbulletin.com) is a competitive daily broadsheet with travel, sports, editorial, business, and features sections to complement its thorough news coverage. (75¢) **Midweek** is Hawaii's prime source for island entertainment listings and editorials. (50¢)

■ ACCOMMODATIONS

The majority of Honolulu's hotels are crammed together in the tourist jungle of **Waikiki** (see p. 117), where you'll find the best deals. Accommodations in the city's other neighborhoods cater more toward business people, locals, and visitors to the university.

ALA MOANA

Ala Moana Hotel, 410 Atkinson Dr. (☎800-367-6025 or 955-4811; www.alamoanahotel.com), two blocks from Kapiolani Blvd. on Atkinson Dr. The hotel commands what is perhaps the perfect location in Honolulu, within walking distance of the Ala Moana Shopping Center and TheBus routes, Ala Moana Beach Park, and Waikiki, though at enough distance to duck the throngs. It also tops all but the best of Waikiki's hotel's services with a business center, fitness room, pool (including pool bar) and sundeck, as well as **Aaron's** fine continental dining and **Rumours** nightclub all on the premises. 24hr. reception. Check-in 3pm. Check-out noon. Doubles $125-195, Torch Ginger floors 29-35 $215. AmEx/D/MC/V. ❺

Central YMCA, 401 Atkinson Dr. (☎941-3344), across the street from the Ala Moana Hotel. Catering to male-only tourists with a fantastic location just outside of Waikiki and one block from Ala Moana Beach Park. College dorm-style rooms with a smallish single bed, aged desk, chair, and storage closet. No A/C or fan. Pool and fitness room. Limited parking $5 per day. $10 key deposit. Internet access in lobby. No walk-ins; reservations must be made 2 weeks in advance. Must be 18+ and have a valid photo ID. Rooms $30, $149 per week. AmEx/MC/V. ❷

DOWNTOWN AND CHINATOWN

Aston at the Executive Centre Hotel, 1088 Bishop St. (☎800-523-1088 or 539-3000; fax 523-1088; www.astonexecutive.com). Convenient to Bishop Sq.'s banking epicenter, on the corner of Bishop and Hotel streets. From H-1 east take Exit 21A and turn right onto Pali Hwy., which becomes Bishop St. Despite having literally no accommodations competition in the area, Aston keeps this gem of a property gleaming and rewards its customers with well-appointed suites. Full amenities, including same-day laundry

THE BIG SPLURGE

AARON'S

Aaron's pairs continental dining with an incomparable view of Ala Moana's incendiary sunsets for the ultimate in sensory indulgence. Sample the high life cheaply with *escargot* ($10), or indulge decadently with imported Beluga Caviar ($85). Other opulent offerings include *Opakapaka* Gabriella and live Kona cold Maine lobster. Despite the luxurious surroundings and high price tag, Aaron's is nonetheless relaxed, as amicable service and casual resort apparel are the rule rather than the exception. Cocktails go well with the sunset view; catch the Hilton Hawaiian Village's attempts to trump Mother Nature's nightly light extravaganza with its own weekly fireworks display (Friday 8:20pm). Both impressive shows are directly within Aaron's multi-paned view. *(410 Atkinson Dr., atop the Ala Moana Hotel. ☎955-4466. Reservations recommended. Open M-Su 5:30-10:30pm, F-Sa 5-11pm. All major credit cards.)*

and dry cleaning for a fee, complimentary newspaper, 24hr. business center, fitness center, sauna, outdoor whirlpool, and sundeck with a large pool, just to name a few. Breakfast included. 24hr. reception. Check-in 3pm. Check-out noon. Parking $8. Business suite $170, corporate rate $119. 1-bedroom executive suites with full kitchen $220-250, corporate rate $144-154. Ask about weekend discounts. ❺

Nuuanu YMCA, 1441 Pali Hwy. (☎536-3556; fax 521-1181), on the corner of Vineyard Blvd. and Pali Hwy. Bare-bones single rooms for men only, although some female YWCA members come in to use the extensive athletic facilities, including an outdoor lap pool and full cardio room. Hall phones with free local calls. **Tanaka's Tastebuds Cafe** in-house (*loco moco* $4, plate lunch $5-6). Key deposit $5. No A/C. 24hr. reception. Check-in 3pm. Check-out noon. Call ahead for reservations. Rooms $30, $160 per week. All major credit cards. ❷

MANOA AND THE UNIVERSITY AREA

🏨 **Manoa Valley Inn,** 2001 Vancouver Dr. (☎947-6019; fax 946-6168; manoavalleyinn@aloha.net). Take Kapiolani Blvd., S. King St., or H-1 to University Ave. *mauka* and turn left onto Vancouver Dr. Two miles from rainforest hiking and Waikiki, this cozy restored mansion-turned-inn is a perfectly-situated hideaway from hectic Honolulu, boasting a sweeping view of the city and Diamond Head from its breezy veranda. Breakfast included. Rooms $150, guild suite $190. ❹

Hostelling International Honolulu, 2323A Seaview Ave. (☎946-0591; fax 946-5904; www.hiayh.org). Turn onto Seaview Ave. from University Ave.; the hostel is opposite the University of Hawaii campus just 4 blocks north of H-1. The best-kept hostel in Honolulu, situated in a mellow residential neighborhood within walking distance of university nightlife and a short bus ride to Waikiki or Ala Moana. Ask about **short-term work opportunities.** Free lockers. $2 linen/towel deposit. Maid service daily. Communal bath, full kitchen, and TV lounge. Reception 8am-noon and 4pm-midnight. No curfew or lockout. Semester-long dorm-style housing for students available; costs vary depending on length of stay but semester lease is usually around $200. Reservations recommended at least 6 months in advance. 6-bed dorms (single sex) $14 for members, $17 non-members. Private rooms $24 for members, $27 non-members. AmEx/MC/V. ❶

Fernhurst YWCA, 1566 Wilder Ave. (☎941-2231), on the intersection with Punahou St. a few blocks west of University Ave. Rooms for female YWCA members only (membership $30 yearly, $15 for those over age 60). Somewhat decrepit 2-bed accommodations with quad baths for women in transition and visitors, relatively convenient to Ala Moana and Downtown. Breakfast and dinner included M-F. Laundry facilities available. Towel and linen fee $20. Office hours M-F 7:30am-6pm, Sa-Su 7am-2pm. Check-in 1pm. Check-out 11am. Singles $30, doubles $25. Office hours M-F 7:30am-6pm, Sa-Su 7am-2pm. AmEx/MC/V. ❷

GREATER HONOLULU

Pagoda Hotel, 1525 Rycroft St. (☎800-367-6060 or 923-4511). Take Kapiolani Blvd. west from McCully St. and turn right onto Kaheka St., the second right after Kalakaua Ave. From Kaheka St. take the third left or Kanunu St. to the first parking lot on the right. Pagoda has studios, 1-and 2-bedroom suites and its own pool in the same lush garden setting found across Rycroft St. The Terrace rooms have kitchenettes, and all rooms have A/C, TV, and Internet access ($2 per 10min.). 24hr. reception. Check-in 3pm. Check-out noon. Doubles $110, top floors $120. Suites $110-195. ❹

Plumeria Apartment-Hotel and Hostel, 1111 Piikoi St. (☎591-0004; plumeria@usa.com), on the corner of Piikoi and Young streets. The hostel genes in Plumeria's lineage are clearly more dominant than any finer apartment or hotel heritage, as amenities, aesthetics and atmosphere are all sub-standard. Plumeria is predictably cheap, however, and within a block of the many bus routes on King and Beretania Streets. Some rooms have A/C. Linens provided, but no towels. Weekly maid service. Office open daily 9am-9pm. Check-in 3pm. Check-out noon. Shoddy private bedrooms with shared bath and kitchenette $20 and up, depending on length of stay. Renovated doubles with A/C, TV, and mini-fridge $220 per week, longer stays negotiable. MC/V. ❶

Pacific Marina Inn, 2628 Waiwai Loop (☎836-1131; fax 833-0851; pacific_marina_inn_2000@yahoo.com). Take the frontage road from Nimitz Hwy., outside of the airport, east to Lagoon Dr. Take the second left off of Lagoon onto Waiwai Loop, opposite Ualena St. If you have to stay near the **airport,** this is the only place worth the price. Within walking distance to Keehi Lagoon Beach Park, this motel-style inn has a pleasant pool deck accented with ginger and hibiscus plants, cable TV, and an in-house restaurant. Free transportation to Hickam's MAC terminal and the Honolulu airport. 24hr. reception. Check-in 3pm. Check-out noon. Doubles M-F $59, Sa-Su $64. Quad $105, add an economy car rental for $25. $50 deposit required if paying in cash. All major credit cards. Wheelchair accessible. ❸

◨ FOOD

ALA MOANA

Dave and Buster's, 1030 Auahi St. (☎589-2215; www.daveandbusters.com), in the Ward Entertainment Center opposite Ala Moana Beach Park. Much more than an excellent restaurant, this goliath dining and entertainment chain has billiards and shuffleboard tables. The video arcade could make any adolescent's eyes light up, but most patrons are more likely to get lit at the bar. Entrees $8-19. Happy Hour 4:30-7:30pm. Open M-Th 11am-1am, F-Sa 11am-2am, Su 11am-midnight. Under 21 must be accompanied by adult. ❸

Dixie Grill Bar-B-Que and Crab Shack, 404 Ward Ave. (☎596-8359). An open-air beach party shack on a busy street, Dixie's serves up real BBQ that will dirty your hands, mouth, and chin, but leave you grinning. Bust Yo Belly 2lb. cheeseburger is free if you eat it, plus all the other fixins, in 30min.; otherwise it's $20. Jumbo coconut shrimp appetizer $9, Billy Bob's mixed grill with baby back ribs, fresh sausage and BBQ chicken $19. Also a wide selection of meals under $10 (baby back rib basket $10). Open Su-Th 11am-10pm, F-Sa 11am-11pm. AmEx/MC/V. ❸

Kaka'ako Kitchen, 1200 Ala Moana Blvd. (☎596-7488), in shiny new digs at the Ward Center. Kaka'ako Kitchen benefits from the glittering surroundings, with a frequently changing menu. Home-style meat and vegetable specialties ($7.25). Gourmet salads ($5.75-9.25) and sandwiches ($6.50-9.25). Open for breakfast M-F 7-10am, Sa-Su 7-11am; lunch and dinner M-Th 10:30am-9pm, F-Sa 10:30am-11pm, Su 11:30am-5pm. AmEx/MC/V. ❷

California Beach Rock 'n Sushi, 404 Ward Ave. (☎597-8000), next door to Dixie's. A Japanese restaurant and sushi bar with West Coast flare. Lunch specials M-F 11am-2pm ($5.25-9), 5-8pc. California Beach sushi sets ($9-9.50) all day. Open for dinner Su-Th 5-10pm, F-Sa 5-11:30pm. AmEx/V. ❷

DOWNTOWN

The recently renovated **Restaurant Row,** 500 Ala Moana Blvd., between Punchbowl and South streets, provides a number of dining and other entertainment venues. The varied casual and formal environments are competitive amid Honolulu's many other options at Aloha Tower Marketplace, Ala Moana Shopping Center, Victoria Ward Centers and Waikiki. (☎432-4750. From Waikiki on Ala Moana Blvd. headed west, turn right onto South St. and park in the covered garage.)

▨ **Palomino,** 66 Queen St. (☎528-2400), in Harbor Court. To park, drive west on Ala Moana Blvd. one block past Aloha Tower Marketplace. Turn right onto Bethel St.; parking is on the right. Palomino's beautiful facade is just a taste of the sumptuous visual feast that lies within. The plush, color-splashed interior, with beautiful glass chandeliers and bar that oozes class, are worth a trip down Ala Moana Blvd. Affordable thin crust pizzas ($7-10.25), dreamy desserts and nightly specials such as lobster paella ($29). Reservations recommended before 8:30pm. The bar (open M-Th 11:15am-11:30pm, F 11:15am-1am, Sa 5pm-1am, and Su 5-11:30pm) serves the full food menu during restaurant hours. Open for lunch M-F 11:15am-2:30pm; dinner nightly 5-10pm. ❺

Indigo, 1121 Nu'uanu Ave. (☎521-2900), adjacent to the Hawaii Theater Center. Starring Eurasian cuisine in a tastefully understated setting, Indigo's is a show-stopper. Lunch $6-11; grilled shrimp and Thai macadamia nut pesto $21. Its Green Room is also a hopping night spot Tu-Sa. Restaurant open Tu-Th 6am-9:30pm, F-Sa 6-10pm. D/DC/MC/V. ❹

Payao Thai Cuisine, (☎521-3511), in Restaurant Row 500 Ala Moana Blvd. Known as the "home of sticky rice," Payao has affordable, varied vegetarian selections with appetizers $2-7.50 and entrees such as Payao's Evil Tofu ($7.50). Open daily 11am-2pm and 5-9:30pm. AmEx/D/MC/V. ❷

Boomerang's (☎537-5525), in Restaurant Row. A boomerang-bedecked counter-service restaurant, Boomerang's serves entrees (BBQ ham sandwich $5; baby back ribs $6) local-style with rice, coleslaw and macaroni salad. Open daily 10:30am-9pm. MC/V. ❶

Big Island Steak House (☎537-4446), in the Aloha Tower Marketplace. Big Island brings a Hawaiian sensibility to the grill. $2 drafts and half-off pupus (Polynesian Pupu Platter $12) during Happy Hour from 4-7pm. Hearty sandwiches ($7-10.50) and grilled dishes ($9-20) for lunch (served daily until 4pm); Honolulu's best Hawaiian-style baby back ribs ($20) or the baked Mac Nut Mahi Mahi ($23) for dinner. Open 10:30am-10pm. AmEx/D/DC/MC. ❺

CHINATOWN

While this is *the* place to find the best Chinese restaurants, the true thrill of the Chinatown dining experience is in the markets and shops that sell ethnic specialties. This is not a mall, however. Many shops and markets do not accept credit cards, and be prepared to encounter jarringly fresh-cut meats hung about.

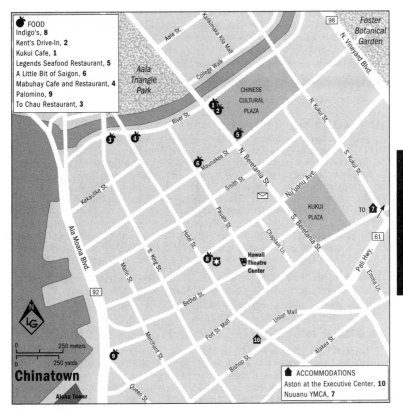

FOOD
Indigo's, **8**
Kent's Drive-In, **2**
Kukui Cafe, **1**
Legends Seafood Restaurant, **5**
A Little Bit of Saigon, **6**
Mabuhay Cafe and Restaurant, **4**
Palomino, **9**
To Chau Restaurant, **3**

Chinatown

ACCOMMODATIONS
Aston at the Executive Center, **10**
Nuuanu YMCA, **7**

🖾 **Legends Seafood Restaurant,** 100 N. Beretania St. #108 (☎532-1868), in the Chinatown Cultural Plaza, directly opposite its sister establishment, Legend Vegetarian Restaurant (open Th-Tu 10:30am-2pm, 5:30-9pm). Legends serves true dim sum, the traditional Chinese brunch where items are selected from a train of circling carts. The succulent dishes are meant to be shared family-style and come in small ($2.15), medium ($2.85), and large ($3.75). Open daily M-F 10:30am-2pm, Sa 8am-2pm and 5:30-10pm, Su 5:30pm-10pm. D/MC/V. ❷

To Chau Restaurant, 1007 River St. (☎533-4549). There's always a line of people out the door, waiting for the unbelievable *pho* noodle soup ($4-6). Open daily 8am-2:30pm. No credit cards. ❶

Mabuhay Cafe and Restaurant, 1049 River St. (☎545-1956), next to Riverside Travel on the corner of N. Hotel and River streets. Top-notch Filipino cuisine in a roomy eatery on the river. Fried pork $8, shrimp *sari sari* $8. Open daily 9:30am-10pm. MC/V. ❷

A Little Bit of Saigon, 1160 Maunakea St. (☎523-3663), near the intersection of Maunakea and Puahi St. Serving Vietnamese entrees as pupus, with vegetables over *bun* (cold soft rice noodles), or as innovative roll-ups wrapped in rice paper and dipped in creative sauces. Try the *Ga Nuong* Chicken (pupu $5.50, roll-ups $8.50, *bun* or rice $6.50). BYOB. Open daily 10am-10pm. ❷

Kent's Drive-In, 100 N. Beretania St. (☎521-3439) shop #176 in the Chinese Cultural Plaza, next to Kukui Cafe. Take-out and phone order local and Chinese plate lunch ($4-5.25; minis $3), breakfast (corned beef and eggs $2.65) and *saimin* ($1.50). Open daily 7am-8pm. No credit cards. ❶

Kukui Cafe, at the corner of N. Kukui and River streets in the Chinese Cultural Plaza. Serves breakfast (Hong Kong-style french toast and milk tea $4.25) a variety of Chinese entrees ($4-6.50) and inexpensive sandwiches ($1.30-2.50). Open M-Sa 7:30am-4:30pm. No credit cards. ❶

MANOA AND THE UNIVERSITY AREA

To get to **Manoa Marketplace,** take University Ave. north from H-1 past UH. Bear right to merge with Oahu Ave. and take a quick right turn onto E. Manoa Rd. The Manoa Marketplace parking lot is after Huapala St., the fourth street on the right. Nearby is a giant **Safeway,** 2855 E. Manoa Rd. (☎988-2058. Open 24hr.) Cheap take-out grinds are a major draw to the market, but most establishments don't take credit cards, so head to the **ATM** in Safeway or at **Bank of Hawaii** (open M-Th 8:30am-4pm, F 8:30am-6pm, Sa 9am-1pm).

Puck's Alley, at the intersection of University Ave. and King St., around the corner from the Moiliili post office, is a strip mall that perfects the collegiate triumvirate of cheap beer, cheap music, and cheap food, all with an appropriately ascetic hipness. The A Express bus stops in front of Puck's, or take TheBus #1, 4, 6, or 18.

Down to Earth, 2525 S. King St. (☎947-7678), is a full-service health food grocery store with wellness center and deli. Open daily 7:30am-10pm. AmEx/D/MC/V.

Kokua Market, 2643 S. King St. (☎941-1922), has natural foods and excellent bulk and vegetable sections. Open daily 8:30am-8:30pm. AmEx/D/MC/V.

Star Market, 2470 S. King St. (☎564-7666). Open daily 5am-2am. D/MC/V.

Maharani Cafe, 2509 S. King St. (☎951-7447), next to Down to Earth grocery. Tasty, authentic Indian cuisine in a casual cafe atmosphere. The house specialty, Shahi Chicken Korma, marinated in yogurt and cooked in a creamy spice sauce, is unique and delicious. Also has a multitude of vegetarian options, including the vegetable jalfrezi masala ($8). Open daily 5-10pm. All major credit cards. ❸

Mamo's All You Can Eat Pizza, 1810 University Ave. (☎955-1649), on the corner of University Ave. and Metcalf St. The only thing better than the quantity is the price ($5). All-you-can-eat salad is also only $5, but due to faulty math, Mamo's will give you all-you-can-eat pizza *and* salad for only $6. Open M-Sa 11am-8:30pm. MC/V. ❶

The Greek Corner, 1025 University Ave. (☎942-5503), in Puck's Alley next to Magoo's. Quality, affordable gyros ($5) and other authentic Greek cuisine in an intimate cafe. Open M-Sa 11am-3pm, 5-10pm; Su noon-3pm, 5-9pm. All major credit cards. ❶

Andy's Sandwiches and Smoothies, 2904 E. Manoa Rd. (☎988-6161), across the street from Manoa Marketplace. This walk-up deli cooks healthy food, a rarity in Honolulu. Known for big sandwiches served on fresh homemade bread (fresh-roasted turkey sandwich $3.50) and plenty of vegetarian options (eggplant melt $5). Open M-F 7:30am-5:30pm, Su 7am-2:30pm. AmEx/MC/V. ❶

Yakiniku Camellia II, 2494 S. Beretania St. (☎946-7595), set back from the street, across from Star Market. Each of Yakiniku Camellia's tables is outfitted with a grill, on which you cook your own all-you-can-eat Korean-style ingredients from the meat and vegetable buffet lines. Lunch $10. Dinner $15.75, including ice cream, a specialty Korean beef, and *sashimi.* Open daily 11am-2:30pm and 3-10pm. AmEx/MC/V. ❸

Kit N' Kitchen, 1010 University Ave. (☎942-7622), next to Varsity Theater. Brightly lit and clean, this modish East meets West fusion diner has a huge menu with diverse selections; try *sake*-drowned prawns ($9) or Crazy Red Seafood (spicy red sauce with shrimp, squid, scallops, and mussels served over pasta $10). Open M-F 11am-2:30pm and 5-10pm, Sa-Su 11am-10pm. MC/V. ❸

O-Bok Korean Restaurant (☎988-7702), in the Manoa Marketplace. A tranquil, simple setting in which to enjoy O-Bok's Kalbi BBQ beef short ribs, champions of the Korean BBQ world, served in heaping portions with rice, *kimchi*, dried cuttlefish and other Korean vegetable dishes ($8). Open Tu-Su 10am-8pm. MC/V. ❷

Ezogiku Noodle Cafe, 1010 University Ave. (☎942-3608), next to Varsity Theater. Ezogiku has been serving enormous portions of traditional Japanese ramen since 1968, prepared with a *miso* ($5.50), *shoyu* ($5.25) or *shio* ($5.50) base. No credit cards. ❶

Bubbies, 1010 University Ave. (☎949-8984), across from Varsity Theater. Heavenly homemade ice cream (1 scoop $2.50-3) and desserts (try a nibble-sized Bite Me $1 each or 12 for $8.50) across from Puck's Alley. Air conditioned and full of college students on weekends during the school year. Open M-Th noon-midnight, F-Sa noon-1am, Su noon-11:30pm. No credit cards. ❶

Coffee Cove, 2600 S. King St. #101 (☎955-2683), in Puck's Alley. A UH haven of wholesome food, Coffee Cove gives Hostelling International members a 15% discount on food and beverage orders. Huge made-to-order sandwiches ($4.25-6) and weekly plate lunch specials. Internet access $1 per 15min., printing 20¢ per page. D/MC/V.

KAPAHULU/WAIALAE

C & C Pasta Company, 3605 Waialae Ave. (☎732-5999). Filled with things that make you go *mmmmm*, C & C Pasta Company is a cleaner, classier cut above its neighbors. Warm up with the *escargot* appetizer ($7.50) or splurge on the stuffed filet of beef with gorgonzola ($24.50), and indulge in desserts like the peach tiramisu ($7). BYOB ($3 glassware fee). Lunch M-Sa 11am-3pm; dinner Su-Th 5-9pm, F-Sa 5-10pm. MC/V. ❺

Eddie's Burgers and Frozen Custard, 3607 Waialae Ave. (☎739-0033). This blue- and white-tiled new kid on the Waialae Ave. block makes its name with budget-friendly black angus 1/3 lb. burgers ($4 and up). The velvety, unbelievably smooth ice cream is technically called frozen custard because of its egg content, but you'll just call it heaven (1 scoop $1.75). Try the ▨Tsunami Shake ($4), king of all disaster-dubbed ice cream treats. Open Su-Th 10:30am-9pm, F-Sa 10:30am-10pm. ❶

Cafe Laufer, 3565 Waialae Ave. (☎735-7717), is a fine pastry and coffee shop that survives admirably in holding its nose up amid the competition. The well-considered menu includes Brie cheese with a mini French baguette and fruit ($7.50). The Chinese chicken salad ($5.50-7.25) will win you over, but the pastries (65¢-$1.50) are what conquer. Open Su-M and W-Th 8am-10pm, F-Sa 8am-11pm. All major credit cards. ❷

Hale Vietnam, 1140 12th Ave. (☎735-7581), less than a block from Waialae Ave. Adding a delightful Vietnamese color to the Kaimuki culinary jigsaw, Hale Vietnam serves up the famous beef noodle soup, *pho* ($5.75-6.25), as well as entrees such as tofu with eggplant ($9) and other vegetarian selections. Open daily 11am-11pm. D/MC/V. ❷

Kaimuki Chop Suey, 3611 Waialae Ave. (☎735-6779). A high-volume Kaimuki budget establishment with quick take-out service. The countless menu options include a wealth of Chinese dishes (chicken chop suey $4, other entrees $3.75-12.50). Open daily 10am-9pm. MC/V. ❸

Kaimuki Inn and Kenji's Bento, 3579 Waialae Ave. (☎735-6555). Popular with Japanese for their *okazu*, authentic a la carte selections (25¢-$4 each) that make a perfect picnic for the beach or park. **Top of the Hill Bar** is open until 2am nightly on the same premises with pool tables, pinball and karaoke (domestic draft $2.50, mixed drinks $4-5). Restaurant open daily 7am-2pm and 5-9pm. ❶

OAHU

Coffee Talk, 3601 Waialae Ave. (☎ 737-7444), on the corner of 12th Ave. and Waialae Ave. A mellow cafe with **Internet access** ($5 per hr.), hot and cold sandwiches ($6-7), and an assortment of coffees. Open Su-Th 5am-11pm, F-Sa 6am-midnight. ❶

GREATER HONOLULU

🍴**Auntie Pasto's,** 1099 S. Beretania St. (☎523-8855), on the corner of Beretania and Pensacola St. Auntie's has affordable pasta dishes ($7-9) big enough to fill a hungry *bruddah* and authentic enough to satisfy any Italian. The eggplant parmesan ($9) is hearty enough for reformed carnivores. Take-out available. Its sister restaurant at 559 Kapahulu Ave. is equally good, and transforms nightly into one of Honolulu's hottest nightlife venues, spinning reggae on Fridays (see **Floating Underground Positivity,** p. 112). Open M-Th 11am-11pm, F-Sa 4pm-midnight. MC/V. ❷

Pagoda Floating Restaurant, 1525 Rycroft St. (☎941-6611). On the grounds of the Pagoda Hotel, the restaurant's dining area is an archipelago of partially paned-in pagodas radiating out from a central island, all "floating" on a canal pond bridged by bamboo-railed walkways. Themed lunch buffets include Seafood Monday (11am-2pm; $11, children $6), *Ohana* Saturday (11am-2pm; $14, children $7), and the celebrated Sunday Brunch Buffet (10am-2pm; $16, children $8). Nightly dinner buffets 4:30-9:30pm ($19-21, children $9-10). Salad bar and dessert table included with all buffets. Reservations required. Open daily 6:30am-2pm and 4:30-10pm. ❺

Mekong Thai Restaurant, 1295 S. Beretania St. (☎591-8841). Eastern-influenced menu includes extensive vegetarian specials ($5-7.50), noodles ($7.25-9), and soups ($6.25-10). Open M-F 11am-2pm and daily 5:30-9:30pm. AmEx/MC/V. ❷

Catch of the Day Sushi, 1718 Kapiolani Blvd. (☎942-8088), one block outside of Waikiki at the intersection with Kalakaua Ave. Quick-service sushi, with popular Shaka sets ($8) such as the *maguro, masago, ebi, unagi* and spicy tuna pack. Open Su-Th 11am-9pm, F-Sa 11am-10pm. All major credit cards. ❷

👁 SIGHTS

DOWNTOWN

🏛**HONOLULU ACADEMY OF ARTS.** This diverse museum contains over 30 galleries, as well as outdoor courtyards and statues. The James A. Michener Collection of Japanese *Ukiyo-e* wood block prints features rotating exhibitions, and the Kress Collection of Italian Renaissance paintings is equally impressive. Pieces by Picasso, Monet, Matisse, Van Gogh, Gaugin, and Cezanne also tour through occasionally. The **modern theater** within the Academy's confines screens experimental, contemporary, and revival films. There's enough here to keep you all day; refuel at the **Pavilion Cafe ❷,** which serves fine fare (feta tapenade and *hau'ula* tomato sandwich $9) on the patio. *(900 S. Beretania St., in front of Thomas Sq. ☎532-8700. www.honoluluacademy.org. Take TheBus #1 or 2 toward town on Beretania. If driving, enter the parking lot on Kinau St. Disabled visitors should call ahead to arrange access. Theater $5; enter on Kinau St. Cafe open Tu-Sa 11:30am-2pm. Gallery open Tu-Sa 10am-4:30pm, Su 1-5pm. $7; seniors, students, and military $4; children under 12 and members free. AmEx/MC/V.)*

THE HAWAII MARITIME CENTER. Despite its small size, the Maritime Center has lots to offer, including one of only two humpback whale skeletons in the world. The center chronicles Hawaii's maritime history, from the outrigger ships of ancient Polynesian explorers to the ocean sports of today. Admission includes passage aboard the storied *Falls of Clyde*, the last four masted, fully-rigged ship in the world. *(On Pier 7 at Honolulu Harbor, across from Aloha Tower Marketplace, off Nimitz Hwy. Open daily 8:30am-8pm. $7.50, ages 4-12 $4.50, under 4 free.)*

LOCAL *KINE* GRINDS Pacific Rim or Hawaii Regional cuisine is fine for the gourmand, but to taste the grinds Hawaiians *mau* every day, there is no substitute for local eats. **Plate lunch** is the general name for a wide variety of meats served with "two scoop" rice and macaroni salad. The typically heaping portions of favorites such as chicken teriyaki, deep-fried mahi mahi, beef stew, and the classic *kalua* pig testify to the titanic appetites of locals (also known for their heart-stopping **Loco Moco** breakfast: two eggs on two scoops of rice with two hamburger patties, all covered in gravy). In Honolulu, the choicest plate lunch is to be found at **Rainbow Drive-In** (see p. 129).

The perfect dessert treat on a hot day in Honolulu, **shave ice** is to snow cones what Hawaii is to Detroit. With none of the gritty, crunchy ice particles or shockingly saccharine syrup, true shave ice has the texture of a machine-made Icee minus the artificiality. Since 1940, **The Waiola Store,** two blocks east of McCully St. and a mile from Waikiki at 2135 Waiola St., has served up the best shave ice in town. They offer an overwhelming 35 flavors and delicious extras such as ice cream, *azuki* beans, and *mochi* balls. (☎949-2269. Open daily 7:30am-6:30pm. Large cone $1.75.)

Spice up your life at the myriad of **Korean BBQ** establishments that serve Asian entrees and side dishes (*kim chee,* long rice, *na mul*) with large portions of rice. Locals rave about the ▓ **kalbi beef** and other Korean BBQ at **O-Bok Korean Restaurant** in Manoa Marketplace (see p. 100). Some islanders will swear that you haven't lived until you try a ▓ **99¢ Spam** *musubi*—a fried slab of the locals' favorite canned meat beached on a hunk of sushi rice and wrapped in *nori,* available 24/7 at 7-11. For more on Hawaii's local cuisine, see **Food** p. 603.

OAHU

CIVIC CENTER

The open, grassy areas surrounding the civic center's government buildings and historical sights are peaceful and sedate in comparison to Downtown's skyscraper-filled business district to the east. Parking can be tight, although there are metered spots in front of the Downtown post office at Richards and Merchant St., and also along King and other sidestreets. Avoid the hassle of parking and navigating street layout by taking TheBus #2, 13 or B CityExpress to S. Beretania and Punchbowl streets, at the corner of the State Capitol's grounds.

▓ **ST. ANDREW'S CATHEDRAL.** This French Gothic cathedral in Queen Emma Sq. is directly behind a 10-foot bronze statue of St. Andrew. The rendering of the fisherman and missionary apostle stands in a fountain, surrounded by ten bronze, water-spouting fish. The cathedral itself is awe-inspiring, with its classical bells rung the old-fashioned way, and the brilliant, stained glass Great West Window. The window is a magnificent 50 ft. high and 20 in. wide, and spans the entire west end of the church. Perhaps the most astonishing part of this cathedral, however, is its enormous Aeolian-Skinner Organ. Organ virtuoso Arlan Sunnarborg coaxes the instrument to emit powerful yet delicate sound every Sunday after the 8am and 10am services. Antsy churchgoers may wish to come in early for the 7am Quick and Quiet Service. (☎524-2822. *On the corner of Beretania and Alakea St., past the State Capitol in Queen Emma Sq. Open M-F 9am-5pm.*)

HAWAII STATE CAPITOL. This unique building replaced Iolani Palace as Hawaii's capitol building in 1969, and is now the place of business for the state's governor, lieutenant governor, and legislators. The capitol's unusual architecture is meant to reflect Hawaiian geography—its conical legislative chambers mimic volcanoes, the surrounding concrete pillars are neo-natural palms, and the pond encircling the structure symbolizes the ocean. Its open-air design is meant to encourage the

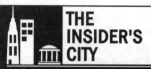

THE INSIDER'S CITY

CHINATOWN GALLERIES

A community of artists and antique collectors thrive in this neighborhood. There is an "official" Downtown Gallery Walk (last Saturday of each month 11am-4pm), but resist the peer pressure and do it on your own, any day you please.

❶ **The ARTS at Mark's Garage,** 1159 Nu'uanu Ave. at Pahani St. (☎521-2903). The 10 artists offer mixed-media art workshops and exhibitions in theatre, dance, sculpture, and painting.

❷ **The Pegge Hopper Gallery,** 1164 Nu'uanu Ave. (☎524-1160). The largest collection of Pegge Hopper's renowned portraits of sensual Polynesian women.

❸ **Lai Fong,** 1118 Nu'uanu Ave. (☎536-6420). Song dynasty-era antiques.

❹ **Pitre Fine Art Gallery,** 1111 Nu'uanu Ave. (☎521-5773). It's a family affair—this gallery features a multimedia display of the work of John Pitre, a master of surrealism, as well as pieces by his wife and daughters.

❺ **Louis Pohl Gallery,** 1056 Fort St. Mall (☎566-6644). Once deemed a "living treasure" by the Hawaii State Legislature, artist Louis Pohl was known for his lava and bird prints.

winds that flow from mountain to sea, and the center lies open to sun, sky, and stars. Fittingly for the dawning of the age, a gorgeous *Aquarius* mosaic graces the floor, but like many things 60s, design flaws have appeared, necessitating costly and extensive maintenance and renovation. *(On the corner of S. Beretania and Punchbowl St. Tours M-F at 1:30pm.)*

IOLANI PALACE. Hawaii's latter monarchs resided in the American Florentine-style Iolani Palace, situated on lovely, coral-fenced grounds. Though you won't hear much about it on the tour, Iolani Palace is an important symbol for Hawaiian sovereigntists who to this day decry the illegal overthrow of Hawaii by self-interested, money-driven Americans. The palace was the official residence of **King Kalakaua** and **Queen Liliuokalani** until American businessmen led a coup d'etat and abolished the monarchy in 1893. It was here that Liliuokalani was tried, convicted and imprisoned for treason, after a failed loyalist retaliation in 1895 (see **History, p. 14**). After falling into disrepair while serving as the capitol of the subsequent Republic, Territorial, and State governments, the palace has been restored and maintained by the Friends of Iolani Palace and it gleams as it did in the monarchy's happier days. The palace is of international as much as Hawaiian interest, with portraits of King Louis Phillippe of France and other French, German, Russian and British leaders, not to mention the Hawaiian monarchs themselves. See one of Hawaii's first telephones, which ran a line down to Honolulu Harbor, where King Kalakaua often held court on his party boat. The **Royal Hawaiian Band** plays free a concert in the Coronation Stand on Fridays at noon.

Across the street from the palace is the old Spanish-style city hall, **Honolulu Hale.** The white-pillared building on the right is the **Hawaii State Library,** recipient of the private book collections of several of the latter monarchs. *(364 King St. ☎538-1471; call ☎522-0832 for tour reservations. Purchase admission to the palace interior at the ticket office inside the Iolani Barracks, the white structure on the Richards St. side of the grounds. Open Tu-Sa 9am-2:15pm. One-hour grand tour $20 (no children under 5). Self-guided gallery tour $10, children 5-17 $5, under 5 free. No cell phones, photos, video cameras or food. MC/V.)*

ALI'IOLANI HALE. Constructed in 1874, Ali'iolani Hale once housed both the legislature and the Supreme Court of the Hawaiian kingdom, and is the current seat of Hawaii's Supreme Court. Its name, Ali'iolani ("chief unto Heavens"), pays homage to King Kamehameha V, who initiated the planning and construction of this symbol of the stability and prosperity of an independent Hawaiian nation. **The**

Judiciary History Center within chronicles 200 years of Hawaiian legal history and is open to the public. You can't miss the complex; it is fronted by one of Hawaii's most recognizable and beautiful landmarks, the golden-caped **King Kamehameha Statue.** Legend holds that Pai'ea Kamehameha (Kamehameha the Great; see **History,** p. 13) was born under Halley's comet in 1758, a clear sign to the kahunas of his greatness. He went on to establish the Hawaiian kingdom from his home island of Hawaii, bringing Maui, Oahu and Kauai under his sway by 1810. The original statue, cast in Paris at the commission of King Kalakaua, was lost in a shipwreck near the Falkland Islands on the way to Honolulu; a second one was cast, shipped, and successfully installed at its present site in 1883. *(417 King St. ☎ 539-4994. Judiciary History Center open for self-guided tours M-F 9am-4pm. Guided tours available by reservation only. Free. Wheelchair access on the Punchbowl St. metered parking lot entrance.)*

KAWAIAHAO CHURCH. Possibly the most impressive feature of this, the first Christian church in Hawaii, is the effort undergone to construct it. Hawaiians dove 10-20 ft. to chisel out the 1000-pound slabs of coral, 14,000 of which were hauled here and used as bricks for the foundation and facade of the impenetrable New England-style structure which was dedicated on July 21, 1842. The church gained its name from to the legendary sacred spring called Kawaiahao ("the water of Ha'o"), where Chieftess Ha'o bathed. *(957 Punchbowl St. ☎ 522-1333. Open M-F 8am-4pm. Services Su 8 and 10:30am, W 6pm; all welcome.)*

MISSION HOUSES AND MUSEUM. This collection of 19th-century buildings once formed the 1820-1863 headquarters of the Sandwich Island Mission. Recreated inside the climate-inappropriate Boston-style houses is the missionaries' printing press, birthplace of the written Hawaiian language. Admission may be purchased from the **Mission Houses Museum,** which leads tours of the mission as well as a Historic Downtown Walking Tour. *(553 S. King St., beyond the old stone church. ☎ 531-0481. 45min. tours of the mission Tu-Sa 10, 11:15am and 1, 2:45pm. Open Tu-Sa 9am-4pm. $10, seniors and military $8, students (all ages) $6, children under 5 free. Historic Downtown Walking Tour an additional $10; call for reservations. Free to all on selected Kama'aina Days. MC/V. Wheelchair-accessible ground floor only.)*

CHINATOWN

KUAN YIN TEMPLE. The beautiful, single-room temple is dedicated to Avalokitesvara, which is Sanskrit for Kuan Yin Boddhisattva. It is the personification of compassion, which is surrounded by a crowd of buddhas. *(170 N. Vineyard Blvd., next to the Foster Botanical Gardens. Drive west on Vineyard from H-1 West to Exit 22 and turn right before Aala St. Free, donations recommended. Open 8:30am-2pm.)*

FOSTER BOTANICAL GARDENS. It's hard to believe you're still in the center of Honolulu as you meander along the winding green walkways of Foster Botanical Gardens' lush 13½ acres. The amazing gardens are home to 26 of Oahu's "exceptional trees," so designated for their outstanding rarity, age, size, aesthetic quality, location, endemic status or historical and cultural significance. Meeting nearly all of these criteria is the garden's great *Bo* tree, which Hindus consider sacred as the abode of Bhavani, and Buddhists honor as the tree under which Buddha attained enlightenment. This tree is an offshoot of the famous Sri Lanka *Bo*, planted there in 288 BC as an offshoot of Buddha's tree. Other worthwhile attractions include the beautiful bronze Dhaibatsu statue and the Mesozoic-era plants in the Prehistoric Glen. *(50 N. Vineyard Blvd. ☎ 522-7060. Take H-1 West or Ward Ave. north from Ala Moana Blvd. to Vineyard Blvd. Turn right into the parking lot after the Kuan Yin Temple, the last drive on the right before the river and Aala St. You can also take TheBus #4 from University to*

Nu'uanu Ave. and Vineyard Blvd. and walk up the block past Zippy's, towards the river. The entrance and visitor parking are on the right past the temple. Free guided tours M-F 1pm or by phone request. $5, ages 6-12 $1, under 5 free. Open daily 9am-4pm. MC/V.)

IZUMO TAISHA. A distinctive peaked roof and pillared entrance mark Izumo Taisha, a Japanese Shinto Shrine. Erected in 1923 and overtaken by the local government during WWII, the shrine is an important remnant of pre-WWII Japanese culture. Today it is once again the site of regular observances, usually on the 10th of the month, for the members of the Izumo Taishakyo Mission next door. Monetary or other offerings are kindly accepted, and instructions for making a prayer and offering are posted at the shrine. In front of the shrine is **The Bell of Peace,** given to Honolulu by the city of Hiroshima in 1985 to celebrate 25 years of sister city affiliation. *(215 Kukui St. Mission ☎ 538-7778.)*

AALA TRIANGLE PARK. Aala Triangle Park has reopened after renovations with a new playground, basketball courts and a sizeable concrete skate park (open 7am-7pm daily). Although unsafe at night, during the day Aala Park is full of kids and skaters enjoying the sun just blocks from Chinatown's throbbing streets. Across S. Beretania St. is a small river mall called College Walk, with a statue dedicated to Dr. Jose Rizal, a Filipino hero, and a few shops. *(N. Beretania and Aala St. There is a small free parking lot for park users. Park closed 9pm-6am.)*

MANOA AND THE UNIVERSITY AREA

UNIVERSITY OF HAWAII (UH) AT MANOA LIBRARIES. University of Hawaii at Manoa is a quiet, suburban campus attended by locals and West Coast mainlanders. **Hamilton** and **Sinclair Libraries,** the main libraries for UH's flagship campus at Manoa and its 17,000 students, hold an impressive 3.1 million volumes in their collection. The libraries are open to anyone who wishes to use them, although certain resources are restricted to University students, faculty and staff. *(2550 McCarthy Mall. Hamilton ☎ 956-7205. Sinclair ☎ 956-8308, ext. 12. Both libraries open M-Th 8am-6pm, F 8am-5pm, Su noon-6pm; limited hours in summer. Children under 13 must be accompanied by an adult. Parking entrance at the Dole St. and East-West Rd. entrance, accessible via University Ave. Alternatively, take the #4 from Kuhio Ave. to UH Manoa.)*

LYON ARBORETUM. The University of Hawaii's impressive 194-acre refuge in the Koolau Mountains holds a wealth of tropical plant species, some of which are extinct in their native habitat. Formerly Manoa Arboretum, the botanical sanctuary begin in 1918 as a forest restoration project. Founder Harold L. Lyon rejuvenated the land—stripped bare by free-ranging cattle—with over 2000 tree species. The arboretum was renamed in 1957, when Lyon passed away. Today, in addition to being a beautiful spot to visit, the facility is highly regarded within the fields of Horticulture, Conservation Biology and Ethnobotany. *(3860 Manoa Rd. Leaving Waikiki on McCully St., take the first right after the Ala Wai Canal onto Kapiolani Blvd. From Kapiolani Blvd., turn right onto Kalakaua Ave., then right on King St. Take the first left onto Puou St. After Punahou St., Puou becomes Manoa Rd. Go left at the fork in the road, just after Kamehameha Ave. Or take TheBus #5 to the last stop, and walk the remaining ½ mi. up Manoa Rd. ☎ 988-0456. Guided tours $2.50 suggested donation. Open M-Sa 9am-3pm.)*

JAPANESE TEA GARDEN PARK. Designed by Japanese landscape architect Kenso Ogata, the garden was a 1963 gift from Japanese businessmen who felt that Hawaii needed a glimpse into Japanese culture. A stream shaped in the form of the chinese character *Kokor* ("heart and spirit") curves through the garden of fragrant gardenia, *yeddo* hawthorne, and mistletoe fig. An authentic Japanese tea house overlooks the gardens. *(Located in the East-West Center adjacent to the University of Hawaii, behind the Imin Center. ☎ 956-7235. Open during daylight hours. Occasional tours. Free.)*

THE CONTEMPORARY MUSEUM. Set at the base of Makiki Heights, the museum overlooks Honolulu, and terraced sculpture gardens cover much of its 3½ acres. Exhibitions address significant contemporary (1940-present) art, with a portion of the museum focusing on Hawaii. The pleasant Contemporary Cafe is a popular spot to grab a scenic lunch. *(2411 Makiki Heights Dr. Take Punahou St. past the YWCA at Vineyard toward Manoa Valley. Turn left on Nehoa St. and right on Mott Smith Dr. Drive until you see the signs for the museum's driveway. Or take TheBus #15 to Makiki Heights Dr. Cafe open Tu-Sa 11:30am-2:30pm, Su noon-2:30pm. Reservations essential. Museum open Tu-Sa 10am-4pm, Su noon-4pm. $5, seniors and students $3, under 12 free. All major credit cards.)*

GREATER HONOLULU

PUNCHBOWL NATIONAL MEMORIAL CEMETERY. The cemetery lies within the the Punchbowl crater north of town, which possesses one of the best views of Honolulu. From outside, the crater appears like a mountain in miniature; within, sweeping stairs pass through a grassy, tree-encircled mall down to the monument where more than 5 million visitors pay their respects each year. The cemetery is the final resting place of over 33,000 veterans, from the Spanish-American War to the present. The memorial building is especially interesting for its mosaics of World War II battle scenes. It is a pleasant 15-minute stroll down to the cemetery and the memorial; the best view is from the path to the left of the memorial building. *(2177 Puowaina Dr. ☎ 566-1430. From Kuhio Ave., take the #2, 13, or B CityExpress away from Diamond Head to Beretania and Alapai streets, in front of the Honolulu Police Headquarters. Walk mauka one block to the bus stop on Alapai St. and transfer to the #15 Pacific Heights, which continues to the cemetery entrance. Open daily 8am-6:30pm. Free.)*

BISHOP MUSEUM. Designated the Hawaii State Museum on National and Cultural History in 1988, the Bishop Museum is the best source of information about indigenous Hawaiian history and practices in the state. Its unparalleled collection of nearly 25 million works of art and artifacts includes historical publications, photographs, films, audio recordings, manuscripts, and millions of specimens of plant and animal life, many of which are extinct. Hawaii's schoolchildren visit each year to participate in hands-on science exhibits, and the museum also sponsors regular outreach programs in local communities. Daily activities include planetarium shows, Hawaiian dance performances, and garden tours. *(1525 Bernice St. ☎ 847-3511; fax 841-8968. From Kuhio Ave., heading away from Diamond Head, take the #2 School St./Middle St. bus to School St. and Kapalama Ave. Walk toward the ocean on Kapalama Ave. to Bernice St. $15, seniors and children ages 4-12 $12. Free with $30 membership.)*

HAWAII NATURE CENTER. The Hawaii Nature Center leads weekly programs for families and adults, and knowledgeable guides can answer your every question during the informative guided hikes. Pick up a free trail map or inexpensive printed trail guides ($1.50-2) with flora info and location. *(2131 Makiki Heights Dr. Drive away from Ala Moana Shopping Center on Keeaumoku St. at Kapiolani Blvd. ☎ 955-0100. Continue beyond H-1 until Nehoa St., then turn right. Take the first left onto Makiki St. and bear left at the fork in the road onto Makiki Heights Dr. At the first hairpin turn, where there is a row of five mailboxes, continue straight ahead onto the narrow one-lane road. Park anywhere on the side of the paved street. Alternately take TheBus #15 to Makiki Heights Dr. Continue along Makiki Heights Dr.; turn left up the one-lane road at the five mailboxes and walk through a green gate, continuing approximately ¼ mi.; the center is on the right. Open daily 8am-4:30pm. Free.)*

THE MADGE TENNENT FOUNDATION GALLERY. This charming gallery, one of Hawaii's registered historic sites, is dedicated to the artist Madge Tennent. Tennent grew up in England and was considered a child prodigy. She studied art in Paris and later moved to Hawaii in 1923. Some of her pieces are on permanent loan to the National Museum of Women in Washington D.C. and hang alongside works by Georgia O'Keefe and Marie Cassatt. She is still considered one of the state's greatest artists. The gallery has a series of Tennent's drawings starting from age 11, as well a number of graceful oils and sketches of Hawaiian women, who Tennet considered to be the ideal subject. *(202 Prospect St. ☎531-1987. Take Ward Ave. away from Ala Moana Blvd. to the base of Punchbowl Crater and turn left onto Prospect St. Bear right at the intersection, hugging the crater on the left between Huali St. and Madeira St. Open Tu-Sa 10am-noon, Su 2-4pm. Donations accepted.)*

🎭 ARTS AND ENTERTAINMENT

THEATER, MUSIC AND DANCE

THE KENNEDY THEATRE. University of Hawaii at Manoa's theater opened in December 1963 and has the dual distinction of being beautifully designed by architectural phenom I.M. Pei (the man behind the John F. Kennedy Library in Massachusetts and the Meyerson Symphony Center in Dallas) and of being the first building named after the late president. The theater is acclaimed for its multicultural approach to the study of theater and dance. Here, Eastern and Western influences are synthesized in both venue and performance. The versatile facility hosts a number of productions each year, many of which are through UH's Department of Theatre and Dance. *(1770 East-West Rd. ☎956-7677; fax 956-4234. Take H-1 to University Ave. From University Ave. turn right onto Dole St. and follow it to the corner of East-West Rd. See www.hawaii.edu/theatre for calendar of events. Box office ☎956-7655; open M-F 10am-3pm. Visit www.ticketplushawaii.com for on-line ticket purchases.)*

HAWAII THEATRE CENTER. Thanks to the relentless campaigning of chairman Bob Midkiff, the Hawaii Theatre Center is in the homestretch of a fund-raising drive to give the dilapidated marquee a face-lift. As head of Honolulu's Downtown Improvement Association, Midkiff brought the State Capitol to the city center and established the Financial Plaza of the Pacific at the heart of Downtown. His efforts at the Theatre Center are the last in a three-part plan to revitalize the Downtown area. The Center is the spearhead of the Honolulu Culture and Arts District, which sponsors a weekly gallery open house (Sa 11am-4pm). It also has an award-winning, volunteer-run gift shop selling ever-changing theater-related merchandise. *(1130 Bethel St. ☎528-0506; http://hawaiitheatre.com. Open Tu-Sa 9am-5pm and 2hr. prior to performances. 1hr. guided tours illuminating the theatre's history, art and architecture Tu 11am, show schedule permitting. Tours $5, reservations recommended. $2 service charge on all tickets purchased. AmEx/D/MC/V.)*

ISLAND FLAVA Because of Hawaii's isolated geography and local pride, Hawaiian music enjoys a great deal of success on the islands, and covers of Jamaican songs (and their originals) get airplay aplenty. The resultant hybrid of island styles, sometimes called **Jawaian** music, borrows the backbeat emphasis of Jamaican ska, rocksteady, and reggae. Hawaiians inject this upbeat rhythm with even more sunshine happiness—the chorus to one great local song goes "I love/ L-O-V-E love you and/ I want/ to K-I-S-S kiss you, girl." It's hard to fault loving exuberance in Paradise, though. To hear the island styles of great local bands such as Natural Vibrations, Three Plus, Fiji, Ten Feet and others, tune in to **Island Rhythm 98.5 FM, 105 FM** or **KCCN 100 FM.** KCCN's Birthday Bash, held at the Waikiki Shell each July, is a two-day event that draws the best local bands. Tickets are available from Ticket Plus Hawaii in Kapiolani Park and the Ala Moana Shopping Center. *(Call ☎526-4400 for tickets; on-line sales at www.ticketplushawaii.com. $18-32. D/MC/V.)*

HONOLULU SYMPHONY. Founded in 1900, the symphony is the oldest orchestra west of the Rocky Mountains. Performances are held at the Neil S. Blaisdell Hall. *(777 Ward Ave., in Ala Moana. ☎ 792-2000; www.honolulusymphony.com. Box office open M-F 9am-5pm. Performances every other week Mar.-May and Sept.-Jan. $15-57. AmEx/MC/V.)*

IONA PEAR DANCE THEATER. The toast of Honolulu's artistic community, Iona Pear Dance Theater presents captivating Japanese *Butoh* dance with dazzling costumes and inspiring performances. The company tours statewide twice annually; if there is a performance you can make, it is worth seeing. *(P.O. Box 61633, Honolulu, HI 96839. ☎ 262-0110.)*

FILM

MOVIE MUSEUM. The "museum" screens classic, modern, and foreign films as they should be seen—on the big screen, from the comfort of one of the intimate theater's 19 leather recliners. You can bring your own concessions; alcohol condoned but not encouraged. *(3566 Harding Ave. In Kaimuki, one block from Waialae's restaurants on 12th Ave. Take the Our Neighborhood Trolley or TheBus #1 or 3. Showtimes vary depending on film length, but generally conform to M, Th, F 5:30 and 8pm; Sa 3, 5:30, and 8pm; Su 2, 4:30, and 7pm. $5; members, seniors, and children under 13 $4. MC/V.)*

VARSITY THEATER. The arthouse theater shows independent, foreign and second-run movies. *(1106 University Ave., across from Puck's Alley in Manoa. ☎ 593-3000 or 973-5835. $7.75, seniors and children ages 2-12 $4.50. Matinee screenings before 4pm $5.)*

THE ARTHOUSE AT RESTAURANT ROW. The theater shows Wallace Theaters' independent foreign and previously released films. *(500 Ala Moana Blvd., in Restaurant Row downtown. ☎ 536-4171; www.hollywood.com. $7 before 6pm, $4.50 on Tu.)*

CONSOLIDATED THEATERS. Consolidated screens mainstream first-run movies in the highest-quality film venue in town, **Ward Stadium 16 Theaters,** in the Ward Entertainment Center (see p. 110). All of the comforts you've come to expect from goliath suburban multiplexes, including the hair-raising prices. Get discounts at many of the Victoria Ward Centers' establishments with a movie ticket stub. *(1044 Auahi St. ☎ 593-300; www.victoriaward.com. $8, military $6, seniors and children $4.50. MC/V.)*

◖ SHOPPING

PEOPLE'S OPEN MARKETS. The markets are a unique chance to buy inexpensive produce from local farmers, fishermen and their representatives, who offer Asian and local products not found in retail stores. The POM holds markets in **Queen Kapiolani Park** (in Waikiki, see p. 109, W 10-11am), **Makiki District Park** (1527 Keeaumoku Ave., next to the Makiki Public Library one block north of H-1, take TheBus #17, 18 or 83; M 8:30-9:30am), **City Hall Parking Lot Deck** at Alapai and Beretania Streets (M 11:45am-12:30pm), **Manoa Valley District Park** (2721 Kaaipu Ave., two blocks down Lowrey Ave. from the 5-way intersection of Manoa Rd. and Oahu Ave.; M 6:45-7:45am) and **McCully District Park** (831 Pumehana St., turn left on Citron, the fifth street after crossing the Ala Wai Canal on McCully St. W 8:15-9:15am). The program is overseen by the City and County of Honolulu. *(☎ 527-5167; www.co.honolulu.hi.us/parks/programs/pom/sked.htm.)*

ALA MOANA SHOPPING CENTER. A 50-acre temple to commerce, Ala Moana is the US's largest open-air shopping center. Over 200 of the most famous purveyors on the globe intersect with over 56 million of the world's most sophisticated shoppers here each year. Rub elbows with the multitude of Japanese and American tourists in the sunny walkways and frigidly air-conditioned stores, or drop a dime to wish for more in one of the center's fountains. Many of the glitziest names in

OAHU

IN RECENT NEWS

ALOHA UP IN SMOKE

A bill passed in mid-June of 2002 prohibited smoking in all restaurants on the island of Oahu as of July 1. Restaurants are required to display a sign reading "Welcome to Smoke-free Dining. Smoking Prohibited by Law," or face fines and loss of operating license. Restaurants that are also classified as bars will have until the same date in 2003 to comply, although bars or clubs that make less than 1/3 of their overall income from food will be exempt indefinitely.

Fearing that the ban would scare off Japanese tourists, restaurant owners campaigned loudly against the bill. A series of advertisements portrayed the ban as "anti-aloha" and predicted devastating consequences for the state's economy, despite the fact that only 27% of Japanese are smokers, and smoking has been on the decline in Japan for nine years running. One zealous group encouraged all tourists to email city council members and threaten never to visit Oahu again. Local newspapers have satirized the new laws as instruments of fascism, and poster-sized political cartoons depicting swastika-clad Tobacco Enforcement Gestapo line telephone polls throughout the city.

Most of those who oppose the ban cite concern about infringing on the rights of smokers. Interestingly, restaurant employees, even those who smoke, tend to favor the bill. A popular bill up for vote in Maui County in October of 2002 proposes nearly identical restrictions, and the US Dept. of Health has made a national smoking ban one of its primary goals.

fashion make the roll call with their national or international flagship stores, including Banana Republic, Diesel, DKNY, Emporio Armani, Gianni Versace, Guess, Polo/Ralph Lauren, Bernini, Prada Sport, Ann Taylor, agnes b, bebe, Chanel, Chistian Dior, and Laura Ashley and dozens more.

Honolulu Satellite City Hall, on the first level, provides city job information, picnic and camping permits, TheBus pass sales, and more info. (Open M-F 9am-5:45pm, Sa 8am-4:45pm.) There's also a small **post office** inside the mall. (1450 Ala Moana Blvd. Suite 1006. Honolulu, HI 96814. Open M-F 8:30am-5pm, Sa 8:30am-4:15pm. Last collection M-F 5:30pm, Sa 5pm.) **Makai Market,** the mother of all mall food courts, is the largest international food court in Hawaii and among the largest in the US, with 20 international restaurants and seating for 1300. *(Between Ala Moana Blvd. and Kapiolani St. TheBus sends over 2100 buses to the center each day; from Waikiki, take the #8, 19 or 20. The shopping center's private shuttle service runs every 15min. M-Sa 9:30am-9:30pm and Su 10am-7:30pm through various stops, including many in Waikiki. For shuttle wheelchair information, call ☎ 831-1555. The Customer Service Center (☎ 955-9517), near the main escalator on the ground floor, has maps and guides, rents free wheelchairs, and sells shuttle bus tickets, international and domestic phone cards, and Ala Moana Gift Certificates. Open M-Sa 9:30am-9pm, Su 10am-7pm.)*

VICTORIA WARD CENTERS. This complex of shops, services and markets aims to package and sell the true island experience to locals and visitors alike. On the corner of Ward Ave. and Auahi St., **Ward Warehouse** is a bi-level open-air mall peddling the latest island apparel from Hurley, Billabong, Quiksilver, and Roxy, among other offerings. **Ward Farmer's Market,** across Auahi St. from Ward Warehouse, is an indoor market where savvy shoppers can save by buying fresh produce, seafood and groceries from local vendors. (Markets generally open M-Sa 7am-5pm, Su 7am-1pm.) **Ward Gateway Center,** west of the Marukai Market Place end of Ward Farmer's Market, has a Ross Dress for Less and the Sports Authority for all your budget clothing and sporting goods needs. **Ward Entertainment Centers,** a block and a half from Ala Moana Park's western exit, holds both cinemas and upscale shops. Inside the theater lobby is the Concierge Services at Ward, where the friendly staff can make your restaurant reservations, call a taxi, and answer all of your eternal, petty questions. (☎ 597-1243. Open W-Su noon-9pm.) **The Ward Village Shops,** on the corner of Kamakee St. and Auahi St., has recognizable shops such as Pier One Imports, edgy apparel with European flare at Sonia Daniel

House of Style, and skate, snowboard, and urban fashions at Massive. (☎593-2374; *www.victoriaward.com. Between Queen St. and Ward Ave. From Auahi St. to Ala Moana Blvd., one block west of Ala Moana Shopping Center. Free parking in the lots and garages on Auahi and Kamakee Streets and Ward Ave. TheBus #19, 20, or 42 from Kuhio Ave. in Waikiki, or the #6 from the University area. Shopping hours M-Sa 10am-9pm, Su 10am-5pm, with restaurants open later. Village Shops open M-Sa 10am-8pm, Su 10am-7pm. Information Center (☎593-2376) in Ward Warehouse has free brochures with maps. Lost and Found ☎597-1172.)*

■ NIGHTLIFE

Ephemerality is the word in late-night Honolulu; the city boasts a variety of night-life archetypes including the laid-back budget dive, sports bars with dreamy island waitresses, ultra-swanky glamour courts, and booty-shaking hot spots. Crowds of fickle Honolulu look-at-me social brahmins and the ever-changing tourist hordes ebb and flow from nightspots on a daily basis, and a thriving, semi-underground floating club scene of island and touring mainland DJs also attracts a youthful and intriguing set in search of more authentic nightlife experiences. Most bars close at 2am, although a few popular establishments stay open until 4am.

To keep up with the ever-evolving scene, visit **http://dj808.com** and **http:// quadmag.com** for up-to-date event and venue listings, or pick up a copy of the monthly **Hype Hawaii,** filled with nightlife news, discounts, and events, free in stores throughout Honolulu. **DaKine magazine,** "the voice of Hawaii's Out Community," and **Odyssey** magazine frequently list gay-friendly events and nightlife. Both magazines are available in stores throughout Waikiki and Honolulu.

ALA MOANA

Compadres Bar and Grill, 1200 Ala Moana Blvd. (☎591-8307), on the second floor of the Ward Center. Compadres is normally a calm cantina perfect for enjoying a $2 draft beer, mai tai or margarita, but *Dios mio!* it gets crowded for the $1 beef or chicken tacos Tu 4-7pm. "Tappy Hours" nightly 10pm-midnight, when crowds of college students come for $2 draft beers and drinks, and half-price pupus. Open M-Th 11am-11pm, F-Sa 11am-midnight, Su 11am-10pm.

Pipeline Cafe, 805 Pohukaina (☎589-1999). Crowded with locals—especially on Bomb Ass Tic Tuesdays (cover $6), when Pipeline breaks out $1 drinks, $1 Jell-O shots and $2 pupus. Get your groove on with the beauties and hunks who cram the dance floor until 4am. Ladies forego cover charge on Foreplay Fridaze (champagne $1). Pool tables, dart machines, foosball, and megatouch video in the sports bar. Cover Th-Sa $5. 21+. AmEx/D/MC/V.

Venus, 1349 Kapiolani Blvd. (☎951-8671), next to the Ala Moana Shopping Center. Venus indulges the sexy touch of aloha that nearby scantily-clad, suntan lotion-lubed Waikiki only hints at. DJs spin hip-hop, R&B, and house on Wednesday Wicked Liquid Import Nights (beer $2 before midnight, shots $2, Corona and Bacardi Limon $3 all night). Sunday's Playhouse event features Wild and Crazy Sex Games (with cash and prizes) and a $2 price tag for a Sex on the Beach or sexy shot. Venus hosts Honolulu's best all-male review and the fantabulous fellas (and bachelorettes) who follow it (F 9pm and Sa 10pm). Sa and Th are predominantly gay nights, though it's always a mixed, open-minded crowd. No shorts or slippers, no tank tops for men. Cover: 18+ $10; 21+ $5. Open Su-Th 10pm-4am, F 9pm-4am, Sa 8pm-4am. MC/V.

Mai Tai Bar, 1450 Ala Moana Blvd. (☎947-2900), on the third floor of the Ala Moana Shopping Center. Mai Tai brings herds of energetic young bargoers in with their late-night Happy Hour (M-Sa 8-11pm, Su 4-11pm; pitchers of Bud Light $5, well drinks $3, Icy Mai Tai $3). Neighboring Bubba Gumps shuttles in appetizers. 21+. No cover. Open daily 11am-1am. AmEx/D/DC/MC/V.

FLOATING UNDERGROUND POSITIVITY

A socially elite clique of artists, DJs, promoters, and their fun-loving friends populate a vibrant, positive club scene in late-night Honolulu. The legendary underground Treehouse near Downtown was long a staple for this hard-working, hard-partying set, and new contenders lease out space in restaurants during off-business hours, and promote actual clubs in attempts to fill the vacuum created by Treehouse's untimely demise. Leader of the pack of new venues is **Auntie Pasto's** (559 Kapahulu Ave.), thanks especially to their **isis** event held the last Saturday of every month from 10pm-2am. Promoted and headlined by the talented all-*womyn* DJ collective **Sisters in Sound** (sistersinsound@yahoo.com), isis exemplifies the best of Honolulu's open-minded underground community. 21+. Cover $10 after 11pm.

Brew Moon, 1200 Ala Moana Blvd. (☎593-0088). This chain microbrewery features a nightly Happy Hour (4-7pm, brews $2-6) and a Salsa night (W, cover $5 after 9pm). Things really get hopping on Su nights for Dark Side of the Moon (cover $5 after 9pm). Food served until 10pm; pupu menu until 1am. Open 11:30am-1am. AmEx/MC/V.

DOWNTOWN

Kapono's, 1 Aloha Tower Dr. (☎536-2161), in the Aloha Tower Marketplace. Named after Hawaiian music legend Henry Kapono (who plays regularly W and F 5:30-7:30pm), Kapono's features excellent live Hawaiian contemporary music every night with no cover. On *Pau Hana* Friday Kapono's rocks with pre-partyers in search of its multiple Happy Hours: from 11am on ($2 drafts), from 4-8pm (add 25% off wells and pupus $4-8, or *poke* for $10), and from 8pm-midnight. No cover. Open daily 11am-2am, bands start around 5:30-7pm. All major credit cards.

The Green Room and Opium Den & Champagne Bar at Indigo's, 1121 Nu'uanu Ave. (☎521-2900). Indigo at night suffers none of the social malaise of the neighborhoods (Downtown and Chinatown) that host it. Busy Tu-Sa, especially during Martini Madness (M-F 4-7pm, free mini-buffet of pupus and $2.75 Martinis). Food served 4pm-midnight. Live entertainment at least once a day, usually adult contemporary. Open nightly 4pm-2am. D/DC/MC/V.

Ocean Club (☎526-9888), inside Restaurant Row at 500 Ala Moana Blvd. Bluntly reminding its guests "Appropriate look overall necessary" and regulating with a pretentious 23+ entrance age most nights, Ocean Club attracts a self-consciously cool throng hoping to see and be seen. Wildly popular Thursday 21+ night. Ultimate Cocktail Hour Tu-F 4:30-8pm with $1.75 Ocean Ritas and Miller Lite drafts, and half-priced pupus. Fashionably casual attire (no shorts, torn or ripped jeans, or athletic attire for men; no beach wear, rubber slippers, or athletic attire for women). Cover $4-5 after 8pm. Open Tu-Th 4:30pm-2am, F 4:30pm-3am, Sa 6pm-3am.

Ground Level, 1154 Fort St. Mall (☎546-9998). A good-times Hawaii Pacific University (HPU) crowd lends an international and communal atmosphere to this local-style college hang-out. Equipped with a Happy Hour (M-F 4-7pm; 48-oz. pitcher $5, wells $3) and all other necessary tools for constructing bar fun including billiards, darts, karaoke, satellite sporting events, and cheap pupus ($4-5). Open M-Sa 10am-2am. MC/V.

Sansei, 500 Ala Moana Blvd., at Restaurant Row. A Japanese-based Pacific Rim restaurant, Sansei is known for affordable sushi ($3-9.50) and sashimi ($6-17). Though there's a Happy Hour M-F from 5-7pm, the real fun starts when Sansei gets caught up in the dance club racket with its busier neighbor, Ocean Club, and throws on the party kimono and karaoke machine (Tu-Sa 10pm-2am). Live DJs spin disco, house and trip hop for the Martini Lounge event on Saturday nights (martinis $3 and up; pupus and sushi half-price). Casual dress; pants, shoes and a collared shirt recommended. 21+. Cover $5. Open Su-M 5-10pm, Tu-Sa 5pm-2am.

Che Pasta, 1001 Bishop St. (☎524-0004), in Bishop Sq. Hosts the Black Garter Cafe, a lesbian-oriented event every Friday night.

MANOA AND THE UNIVERSITY AREA

Anna Banana's, 2440 S. Beretania St. (☎946-5190). A Manoa and UH institution, this dim, love-worn bar has been rocking live music for 33 years. Outstanding Happy Hour daily 11:30am-8pm (beer $1.75). Live music upstairs 5 nights a week, reggae on F. Extremely busy F and Sa after 10:30pm, especially during school year. Cover only for special events $5. 21+. Open daily 11:30am-2pm.

Bedroq Bar and Grill, 2535 Coyne St. (☎942-8822), two blocks up from University Ave. Inexpensive drinks and beer in a laid-back atmosphere with a typical Honolulu mix of college, military, and local crowds. Half-price pupus 3-8pm (*poke* $3, draft beer $1-2). Drinks $1 after 9pm on Monday. 18oz. draft beer 25¢ on Th. Live music F and Sa nights. Cover $5-10 for those under 21. 18+. Open daily 2pm-2am. MC/V.

Eastside Grill, 1035 University Ave. (☎955-6555), across the street from the Varsity Theater; get a discount at the grill with a ticket stub. A sports bar serving grill food with local flavors. Happy Hour daily 11am-6pm (beer $2, margaritas $2.50). Try the extravagant crab dip ($9.25, $6 on Sa) or fish taco with fresh veggies and honey *wasabi* sauce ($6). Lunch specials from $5. All major credit cards.

Magoo's, 1015 University Ave. (☎946-8830), plays Pied Piper to hard-working UH students with the sweet song of ▨ $6 pitchers of Newcastle Ale. Don't let the wall of patio plants out front deter you; the entrance is in the middle by the host's podium. Open-air Magoo's also bakes a mean pizza ($5.50-30) to justify another pitcher ($5 and up). 21+ after 9pm. Open daily 11am-1:30am. AmEx/MC/V.

Cheapo Music, 1009 University Ave. (☎943-0500), next door to Magoo's, sells no food but can fund it—pawn off those Backstreet Boys albums you bought "just to find out" and earn enough for another pitcher. Cheapo buys used CDs (up to $4) and DVDs (up to $6) for resale (95¢ for singles to $11 for CDs). **Cheapo Books** around the corner on 200 S. King St. (☎943-0501) does the same, only with ▨ **books.** Check out the flyers near the door for **nightlife** information around Honolulu. Open daily 9am-midnight.

◪ BEACHES

The most popular sandy beaches in Honolulu are located near Waikiki (see p. 134).

ALA MOANA BEACH PARK. Ala Moana means "path to the sea," and the banyan and palm tree-dotted park does the name justice. The circuits, popular among joggers and roller bladers, connect to the calm bay which is perfect for an easy swim. Jutting out slightly into Mamala Bay, **Magic Island** is actually a peninsula, connected to Ala Moana Park Dr. by a large parking lot that is free to the public. Magic Island is the best spot in the city to watch the sun dissolve into the sea and sky, throwing awe-inspiring color over the hulking clouds that frequently roll over the Koolau Mountains. (*Park located in front of Ala Moana Shopping Center, on Ala Moana Park Dr. Access driveways are at the western end of the park just past Kamakee St., opposite Ward Entertainment Center. Alternately, take TheBus #8, 19, 20, 42 or 58 to the Ala Moana Center.*)

▨ HIKING

The connected rainforest trails that comprise the **Honolulu Mauka System** are typically damp, slippery, and filled with hidden roots, rocks and underbrush that can trip up unwary hikers. At times, the bugs can be aggravating; pack **insect repellent**

OAHU

along with the standard **water** and **sunscreen.** Before setting off on any hike, be sure you know what you are getting into. Allow enough time to return with daylight to spare, never hike alone, and always **stay on the trail**—unmarked offshoots and access roads may be private and are not maintained as public recreation routes. Lastly, respect the land: remember to take out everything you took in. For more information, check out **www.hawaiitrails.org.**

MANOA FALLS TRAIL. (0.8 mi. one-way. Trailhead: Manoa Falls parking area. Elevation change: 800 ft. Level: easy.) This is one of Oahu's most popular trails for good reason. Hikers can take in luxuriant Hawaiian rainforest while traversing the well-marked path that leads through eucalyptus groves, over bubbling streams, and by age-worn guava and mountain apple trees. Manoa Falls cascades down a vertical stone face into a rock-strewn pool at the end of the trail. On any weekend, you're sure to find groups of smiling tourists posing for pictures atop the boulders, as well as a few brave souls testing the chilly waters. Small fissures in the rock wall contain stacks of rocks left by locals in respect for the *mana* of the area. Obey the posted signs at the falls viewing area, as landslides have been known to occur. (*Leaving Waikiki on McCully St., take the first right after the Ala Wai Canal onto Kapiolani Blvd. From Kapiolani Blvd., turn right onto Kalakaua Ave., then right on King St. Take the first left onto Puou St. After Punahou St., Puou becomes Manoa Rd. Proceed straight ahead to the parking area and trailhead. Do not leave valuables in your car.*)

AIHUALAMA TRAIL. (1.3 mi. one-way. Trailhead: From Manoa Falls trail. Elevation change: 1200 ft. Level: moderate.) This trail beckons more experienced hikers approximately 150 ft. before the end of the Manoa Falls Trail. Continuing up the western ridge of Manoa Valley, Aihualama features bamboo forests as well as spectacular vistas of Honolulu and the valley below. The trail also serves as a link between the Manoa Valley hikes and the Tantalus area hikes. To access these trails, keep going 1 mi. after the viewpoint to **Pauoa Flats** and the **Pu'u Ohia Trail.** Otherwise, turn back and return the way you came. Hikers should be especially cautious of wet footing and the occasional landslide. (*Follow the directions through the Manoa Falls Trail to the marker for Aihualama, directly before a chain-link fence on the left.*)

MAKIKI VALLEY LOOP. (2½ mi. round-trip. Trailhead: Hawaii Nature Center. Level: moderate.) Combining three Tantalus area hikes—**Maunalaha, Kanealole,** and **Makiki Valley**—the trail offers a spectacular adventure through varied terrain. The trailhead for Maunalaha is clearly marked behind the **Hawaii Nature Center** (see p. 107) and the path immediately sets off across a bridge before continuing alongside *taro* patches and immense Norfolk pines and eucalyptus trees. This section of the loop is fairly straightforward and covers only 0.7 mi. before reaching a four-way intersection. To continue onto **Makiki Valley Trail,** take the left fork. The middle *mauka* trail is the **Moleka Trail** (see below) and the right path is the **Ualakaa Trail,** an easy ½ mi. loop under canopied forest that ends at Round Top Dr. Makiki travels a brief 0.7 mi. through trees heavy with tropical fruit and flowers before uniting with Kaneaole Trail, just after the **Kaneaole Stream.** On its journey, the trail passes by a field of Job's tears, a tall, thick grass that can grow up to 5 ft. tall. The gray seeds of this plant are often used to make unique leis. Kaneaole ends at the trailhead for Maunalaha after ¾ mi. of muddy trekking under the shade of *kukui* trees. (*Hawaii Nature Center, 2131 Makiki Heights Dr. ☎ 955-0100. Drive away from Ala Moana Shopping Center on Keeaumoku St. Continue beyond H-1 until Nehoa St., then turn right. Take your first left onto Makiki St. and bear left at the fork in the road onto Makiki Heights Dr. At the first hairpin turn, where there is a row of five mailboxes, continue straight ahead onto the narrow one-lane road. Park anywhere on the side of the paved street. Alternately, take TheBus #15 to Makiki Heights Dr. Continue along Makiki Heights Dr. and turn left up the one-lane road at the five mailboxes and walk through a green gate, continuing approximately ¼ mi.; the center is on the right.*)

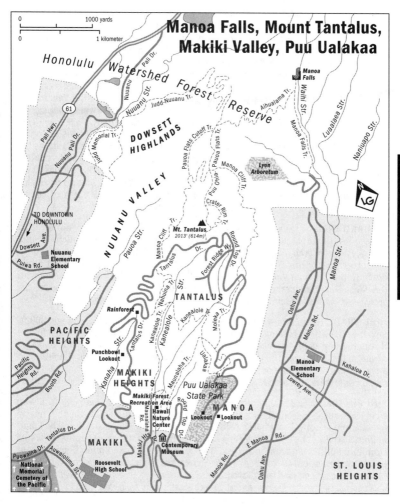

Manoa Falls, Mount Tantalus, Makiki Valley, Puu Ualakaa

OAHU

MOLEKA TRAIL. (¾ mi. one-way. Trailhead: Round Top Dr. or Makiki Valley Trail. Elevation change: 300 ft. Level: easy.) A short jaunt along the upper east edge of Makiki Valley, Moleka Trail ends at the Makiki Valley Trail. On the way, the path plunges through thick forest and passes by expansive vistas of Honolulu's sky-scrapers and Tantalus. *(To reach the trailhead, take Keeaumoku St. past the Makiki Public Library. Turn right on Wilder Ave. and take the first left onto Makiki St., keeping right at the Makiki Heights Dr. Y-intersection. Continue left at the next split in the road, up Round Top Dr. There will be a trailhead sign and small parking lot on the left; actual trailhead is makai. The trail can also be reached via the Makiki Valley Trail.)*

MANOA CLIFF TRAIL. (2.3 mi. one-way. Trailhead: Tantalus Dr. Elevation change: 500 ft. Level: easy.) This fairly painless trail is distinctive because of its predominately native flora as well as its intersection with Tantalus area hikes. After gradually climbing through dense forest, the path emerges at amazing vistas of Manoa Valley. Approximately halfway through the hike, Manoa Cliff leads to the **Pu'uohia Trail.** The unchallenging hike, located off to the left, leads ¾ mi. to the highest point on Tantalus Crater and a **Nu'uanu Valley viewpoint.** Along the way, Pu'uohia features night-blooming jasmine, wild ginger, Christmas berry, and avocado trees as well as awe-inspiring views of Honolulu and Diamond Head. Continuing on Manoa Cliff past the Pu'uohia fork, there is another junction on the right to the **Pauoa Flats Trail.** Leading inland, ¾ mile-long Pauoa Flats traverses through swamp mahogany, wild ginger, and eucalyptus trees before eventually connecting with **Nu'uanu Trail** (see below). If you stick to Manoa Cliff, you will find that the trail ends at a third junction, this time with **Kalawahine Trail.** This final trail delivers you to Tantalus Dr. via an enjoyable 1.1 mi. trek through koa and banana trees, as well as other native and introduced vegetation. *(Follow directions to Moleka trailhead. The parking lot for Manoa Cliff is makai, adjacent to the Moleka trailhead. The trail is across the street from the parking lot. To reach the Kalawahine trailhead, drive mauka on Tantalus Dr. There will be a sign for the trailhead on the left, adjacent to a private road that goes straight up the hill.)*

NU'UANU TRAIL. (1½ mi. one-way. Trailhead: via Kalawahine or Manoa Cliff trails. Elevation change: 600 ft. Level: moderate.) Climbing up the side of Pauoa Valley, Nu'uanu Trail features periodic vistas of Honolulu proper as well as Oahu's western region. After reaching its peak elevation atop the ridge, the trail drops down to the Nu'uanu Valley Floor. Before this, however, the path intersects with the **Pauoa Flats Trail** on the valley side and the **Judd Trail** on the cliff side. *(The trail can be accessed via the Kalawahine Trail or the Manoa Cliff Trail; see above for directions.)*

JUDD TRAIL. (¾ mi. one-way. Trailhead: Nu'uanu Trail. Elevation change: 200 ft. Level: easy.) After crossing a stream, Judd Trail becomes a loop that takes hikers through damp valley vegetation. The rocks can be slick, so mind your balance. About midway through the path, the trail connects with **Nu'uanu Trail.** *(Take Pali Hwy. away from town and turn right on Nu'uanu Pali Dr. Continue until you reach a concrete bridge. The trailhead is to the right, in the clearing. You can park here but be aware that it is a high theft area.)*

PUU PIA TRAIL. (1.2 mi. Trailhead: See below. Elevation change: 400 ft. Level: easy.) Featuring a gradual ascent through dense vegetation and beneath a nearly opaque tree canopy, Puu Pia is a painless hike suited for almost anyone. The climb begins at the heel of Manoa Valley and eventually features sweeping views of Honolulu and the surrounding area. Wet conditions demand a modicum of caution. *(Drive past Manoa Marketplace on E. Manoa Rd., heading mauka. Turn left on Alani Dr. and continue ¾ mi. until the road takes a sharp right. From here, Alani Ln. continues straight. Park and walk down Alani Ln., past the houses and through a cable gate. A dirt road leads to the Forestry and Wildlife picnic shelter; the trailhead is to the left.)*

WAAHILA RIDGE TRAIL. (2.4 mi. one-way. Trailhead: Waahila State Recreation Area. Elevation change: 500 ft. Level: moderate.) Skirting the Waahila Ridge above Manoa and Palolo Valleys, the trail offers amazing views at every turn. This hike is more demanding than others, as it sometimes tiptoes near the edge of the ridge and rises fairly quickly. However, adventurers will enjoy beautiful scenery along the way, including many native plants such as koa and 'ohi'a lehua. At the end of the path, there is a junction with the **Kolowalu Trail,** which is one of the area's most difficult hikes, rising 1100 ft. in a mere mile. *(Take Kapahulu Ave. away from Waikiki and turn right on Waialae. Take the first left, St. Louis Dr., following it up the St. Louis Heights residential area before turning right on Peter Pl. near the top. After the cul de sac, turn left on Ruth Pl. into Waahila Ridge State Recreation Area. The trailhead is at the rear of the park. The trailhead for Kolowalu is near the Puu Pia Trail, on the right side of the Forestry and Wildlife picnic shelter.)*

WAIKIKI

Tourists experience the paradise that they imagined in Waikiki at sunset, although there is always something going down at any time of day. People-watching is the best way to experience Hawaii's under-appreciated diversity amid the hectic, touristy commercialism of Waikiki. European sunbathers flaunt their hard-earned bodies and tans, Japanese tourists mill around in huge groups spending their hard-earned yen, and local Hawaiians talk story and cruise on the beach, laughing at all the hard-earning going on. You can start your day as a wide-eyed and camera-toting tour group junkie on the Kalakaua Ave. strip, take up surf lessons and nihilism in search of the perfect wave on Kuhio Beach in the afternoon, and recreate yourself with a mai tai and a romantic encounter at nightfall. Idyllic sunsets, perfect weather, and plenty to do—this is paradise, and Waikiki is yours to perfect.

⎓ LOCAL TRANSPORTATION

Bus: TheBus's (p. 89) 24hr. Waikiki information hotline (☎296-1818) offers an automated directory of bus routes to sites across the island on buses that leave from Kuhio Ave. Listed below are a few convenient routes that leave from Waikiki. Consult a bus schedule or TheBus's website (www.thebus.org) for more information.

#2 goes up Kuhio and Kalakaua Ave. through the heart of town and Chinatown and back through Waikiki to Kapiolani Park.

#4 goes by the University of Hawaii in Manoa west through Makiki and up Nu'uanu Ave. into Nu'uanu Valley via Downtown Honolulu.

#13 goes from the intersection at Kapahulu Ave. and Campbell Ave. up Kuhio and Kalakaua Ave., through Downtown, and up Liliha St.

#8 begins its island voyage at Kalakaua Ave. and Monsarrat Ave., and exits Waikiki at Kuhio Ave., finishing at the Ala Moana Shopping Center.

#19 leaves Monsarrat Ave. and Kalakaua Ave. for Kapahulu Ave., Waikiki and the Ala Moana Shopping Center, Downtown and finally the airport and Hickam AFB.

#20 follows the route of #19 to the airport, heading to Pearlridge Shopping Center, near the Pearl Harbor memorials and Aloha Stadium.

#22, known as the **Beachbus,** starts at the northwest end of Waikiki at Pau St. and Ala Wai Blvd., turns around at Niu St. onto Kalakaua Ave. and then Kuhio Ave. The Beachbus continues on to the intersection of Kapahulu and Paki Ave., up Diamond Head Rd. and by Kahala Mall. It then jumps on the Kalanianaole Hwy. (designated H-1 West in the other direction) to Hanauma Bay, Sandy Beach, Makapu Beach, ending at Sea Life Park.

#42 leaves Waikiki via Ala Moana Blvd. and heads west through Downtown to Waipahu and Ewa.

#58 leaves Ala Moana and goes through Waikiki east to Hawaii Kai and Sealife Park.

Trolley: Our Neighborhood Trolley, the system's newest line, is the one sensible exception to the over-priced $20-per day **Waikiki Trolleys.** It serves 25 stops in Waikiki, Kapahulu and Kaimuki, from the Waikiki Trade Center at Seaside and Kuhio to Liliuokalani Elementary up Waialae Ave., and is the cheapest ride to the dining and shopping options in Kapahulu ($2 for an all-day pass). There is a $1 one-way fare, but once you alight, you can't re-board unless you pay another $1.

Taxis: Waikiki is small—a ride across the district is around $6. Taxis to the airport are expensive ($25-30); arrange transportation through your hotel or hostel, or via the myriad airport shuttle services ($7). **Charley's Taxi and Tour** (☎955-2211) has 24hr. service to most of Oahu for $2 per mile, $2.25 per drop off. **TheCab** (☎422-2222) offers 24hr. island-wide service, metered at $2.25 per mile, $2.40 per drop-off.

OAHU

Car Rentals:

VIP Car Rental, 2463 Kuhio Ave. (☎924-6500). Other locations all over Waikiki, including 234 Beachwalk (☎922-4605) and 1944 Kalakaua Ave. (☎946-7733). VIP competes with the titans of corporate car rental by renting out older cars for the budget-minded, and exotic cars for the trendy. Mid-90s Nissan or Toyota coupe $13 per day, $99 per week. 3-day minimum rental. Insurance not included. Ask about bike, moped rentals, and airport shuttle. Open daily 7am-5pm.

Ferrari Rentals, 2025 Kalakaua Ave. (☎942-8725). Rents expensive exotic cars, such as the Ferrari F-355 Spyder ($650 per 24hr.), to customers over 21 years of age. Those 18+ can rent sporty Geo Trackers or Pontiac Sunfires for $55 per day. Discounts on longer rentals, free Waikiki pick-up. Open daily 8am-6pm.

Paradise Rent-a-Car, 1879 Kalakaua Ave. (☎946-7777), 355 Royal Hawaiian Ave. (☎924-7777), and 151 Uluniu Ave. (☎926-7777). Paradise offers a wide selection of cars, including Jeeps, sedans, convertibles, and motorcycles. Bicycle and moped rental as well. Compacts $29 per day, mid-size $39 per day, Jeeps $79 per day. Three-day minimum. $20 surcharge for drivers under the age of 25. Open daily 8am-5pm.

Hertz, 1956 Ala Moana Blvd. (☎800-527-0700; www.hertz.com), with locations in the Hyatt Regency at 2424 Kalakaua Ave. and the Hilton Hawaiian Village at 2005 Kalia Rd. Economy cars from $36 a day. Minimum age 25. Credit card required.

Dollar, 1765 Ala Moana Blvd. (☎800-800-4000; www.dollar.com), at the Ilikai Marina, with locations at: Coral Seas Hotel, 250 Lewers St.; Hawaiian Regent Hotel, 2552 Kalakaua Ave.; the Hale Koa Hotel, 2055 Kalia Dr.; and elsewhere. Compact $70; $20 under-25 surcharge, insurance not included.

Moped and Motorcycle Rentals:

The Moped Connection, 750A Kapahulu Ave. (☎732-3366), just outside of Waikiki past the Ala Wai Golf Course on Kapahulu Ave. Generally has the lowest rates and loans customers free helmets. Mopeds $15-35 daily. Open M-F 9am-6pm, Sa-Su 9am-5pm.

Interisland Rentals, 234 Beachwalk (☎926-3356). Rents mopeds to customers 18+, and provides free maps, instruction, and helmet rental. $45 per day, $80 deposit required. Open daily 8am-5pm.

Hawaiian Peddler, 2139 Kuhio Ave. (☎877-HAV-N-FUN or 926-5099). Offers personal service and a wide selection of Jeeps ($59 per day, insurance not included). The pride and joy are the Harley Davidsons ($170 from 8am-4:30pm, $185 until 7pm; overnight not recommended), which are an odd contrast to the mopeds ($32 per day). Ask about bicycle and water activity equipment rentals. Open daily 8:30am-4:30pm.

Blue Sky Rentals, 1920 Ala Moana Blvd. (☎947-0101). $20 deposit required. Mopeds $23 per 8hr., credit card required. Bike $10 per 4hr., $20 per day. Open daily 8am-5pm.

Pineapple Cruzers, 305 Royal Hawaiian Ave. (☎924-0556) rents bicycles, mopeds, and motorcycles. Bicycle rental $15 for 8am-6pm. Open daily 8am-6pm. All major credit cards, no deposit required.

■ ORIENTATION

Waikiki is bordered on the north and west by the Ala Wai Canal, on the south by its famed beaches, and on the east by Diamond Head Crater. Three main thoroughfares run Waikiki's two-mile length from east to west: **Ala Wai Blvd.** parallels the canal with one-way traffic going west; **Kalakaua Ave.** fronts the ritziest hotels and beaches and carries one-way traffic east; **Kuhio Ave.** splits off from Kalakaua Ave. at the western end of Waikiki and bears the brunt of traffic all the way to Kapahulu Ave. on the east end of town. The three main east-west streets intersect numerous one-way sidestreets, necessitating many trips around the block for lost drivers.

The **Ala Wai Canal** is a scenic area, popular with joggers and walkers, although its distance from the action makes it the least safe part of Waikiki at night. Safety, mostly in the form of the hilarious, agile Kushman police buggy, increases closer to Kuhio Ave., which is noisy with unending bus traffic during the day, and the occasional pack of mopeds at night. Kalakaua Ave. is for show, with no bus traffic, lots of pedestrians, and all manner of street performers and vendors. Farther down Kalakaua, toward Diamond Head, the parks and beaches are decidedly less safe after dark. Waikiki police response is impressively quick and thorough, however, and the area is considered safe even at night.

Driving directions to H-1 West: From Kalakaua Ave. or Kuhio Ave., make a left onto Kapahulu Ave. Take Kapahulu past Kaimuki, under the H-1 overpass and left on Waialae Ave., following the signs to merge onto H-1. A more direct route is to take Ala Wai Blvd. and turn right on McCully St. over the bridge. Stay on McCully (you'll drive over H-1), turn left on Dole St., and left on Alexander St. Yield and merge left onto the highway. **To H-1 East:** Take Ala Moana Blvd. over the canal, leaving Waikiki, and turn right on Atkinson Dr. Turn right on Kapiolani Blvd. toward H-1. Or take McCully St. over the canal and make a right on Kapiolani Blvd. The H-1 East on-ramp from Kapiolani Blvd. is a two-lane left turn before the overpass.

⁊ PRACTICAL INFORMATION

TOURIST AND FINANCIAL SERVICES

Tourist Office: Hawaii Visitors and Convention Bureau Information Office at Waikiki Shopping Plaza, 2250 Kalakaua Ave., Ste. 502 (☎800-GoHawaii or 924-0266; fax 924-0290; www.gohawaii.com; info@hvcb.org). A friendly office that directs most visitors to two official tourist magazines—*Connections* and *Islands of Aloha Official Vacation Planner*—to go with the innumerable, apparently unofficial tourist magazines that litter Waikiki. Open M-F 8am-4:30pm, Sa-Su 8am-noon. Hale Aloha tourist information kiosks in front of the Royal Hawaiian Shopping Center, on Kalakaua Ave.; in front of the Sheraton Princess Kaiulani Hotel, at 120 Kaiulani Ave.; and in front of the First Hawaiian Bank at Lewers St. and Kalakaua St.

Tours: See Honolulu Practical Information, p. 91.

Equipment Rental: Most rental agencies on the beach are fairly expensive, and don't take credit cards.

Koa Board Sports, 2420 Koa Ave. (☎923-0189). Surfboards $20 per day or $75 per week.

Wave Riding Vehicles, 1888 Kalakaua Ave. (☎979-4978). Sells surfboards and rents used boards for cheap, depending on availability. Used surfboards $10 per day. Open M-Sa 10am-8pm, Su noon-5pm. MC/V.

Aloha Beach Services (call the Sheraton Moana Surfrider Hotel ☎922-3111, ext. 2341). Go straight onto the beach from Duke's Canoe Club, 2335 Kalakaua Ave. and turn left. For $25, aspiring groms and grommettes get an instructor and surfboard for an hour, and the guarantee that they'll be able to stand up. $8 per hr. for just the surfboard, $12 for 2hr. Body boards $5 per hr. Open daily from 8am, go early for lessons to avoid the crowds.

Outrigger Beach Services (☎926-9889), in front of Duke's under the blue umbrellas, rents surf boards at $10 for the first hr., $5 each additional hr. $30 per hr. for an instructor and board. Body boards $7 per hr. and $3 each additional hr. Open daily 7am-4pm; go before 11am to avoid a long wait for lessons.

Hans Hedemann Surf School, 2586 Kalakaua Ave. (☎924-7778), at the Park Shore Beach Hotel. Other locations at Sheraton Waikiki (booth on beach) or Outrigger Reef (sign says HH Surf School). The premier surf school in Waikiki, founded by famous surfer Hans Hedemann. Sign up for a 2-hour group surfing lesson, $75 per person, including lesson and board. Surfboard rentals are $25 per 24hr., body boards $15 per day. Their booths carry rentals at typical on-the-beach, tourist-gouging prices: surfboards $32 per hr. $25 per 24hr. in store; body boards $15 per day; snorkel $7.50 per day; bikes $15 per day. Open daily 8am-5pm. AmEx/MC/V.

Banks and ATMS:

Currency exchange is available for 20 different currencies at the foreign exchange ATM on the first floor of Hibiscus Court in the Royal Hawaiian Shopping Center, on Royal Hawaiian Ave. Open daily 11am-10pm.

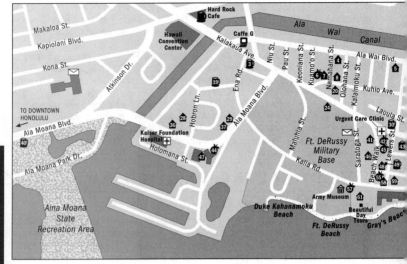

Waikiki

🏠 **ACCOMMODATIONS**

Ambassador Hotel of Waikiki, **7**
Aqua Bamboo, **33**
Aqua Marina, **28**
Aston Aloha Surf Hotel, **14**
Aston Coconut Plaza Hotel, **5**
Aston Hawaii Polo Inn, **36**
Aston Honolulu Prince, **13**
Aston Waikiki Grand Hotel, **56**
Aston Waikiki Parkside Hotel, **29**
The Breakers, **41**
Hale Pua Nui, **46**
Hawaiian Hostel, **9**
Holiday Inn, **37**
Ilima, **10**
The Imperial of Waikiki, **59**
Leisure Resorts, **12**
Miramar Hotel Waikiki, **27**
Ohana Maile Sky Court, **8**
Ohana Waikiki Malia Hotel, **21**
Ohana Waikiki Surf, **11**
Ohana Waikiki Tower, **58**
Ohana Waikiki Village Hotel, **48**
Outrigger Waikiki Shore, **61**

Pat Winston's Waikiki Condos, **17**
Polynesian Beach Club Hostel, **53**
Queen Kapiolani Hotel, **54**
Renaissance Ilikai Waikiki Hotel, **47**
Royal Garden at Waikiki, **4**
Royal Grove Hotel, **34**
Sheraton Waikiki, **60**
Waikiki Beachcomber, **39**
Waikiki Beachside Hostel, **52**
Waikiki Gateway, **20**
Waikiki Sand Villa, **15**
Waikiki Terrace Hotel, **24**

🛏 **NIGHTLIFE**

Duke's Canoe Club, **50**
Fox and Hounds English Pub and Grub, **40**
The Maze, **22**
Michelangelo, **19**
Moose McGillycuddy's Pub and Cafe, **30**
Nashville Waikiki, **18**
The Red Lion, **49**
Wave Waikiki, **3**
Zanzabar, **23**

🍎 **FOOD**

Arancino, **45**
Cha Cha Cha, **26**
Cheeseburger in Paradise, **51**
China Buffet, **44**
Chuck's Cellar, **32**
Keo's, **6**
The Patisserie, **55**
Pyramids, **1**
Rainbow Drive-In, **2**
Ray's Famous Pizza, **16**
Shore Bird Beach Broiler, **57**
Teddy's Bigger Burgers, **35**
Top of Waikiki, **38**
Yasoba, **42**

🛍 **SHOPPING**

DFS Galleria, **25**
The International Market Place, **31**
Royal Hawaiian Shopping Center, **43**

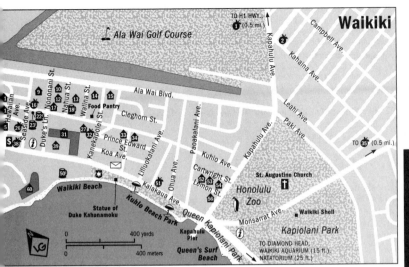

American Savings Bank, 321 Seaside Ave. (☎923-1102; 24hr. service ☎834-4100; fax 971-2944). Currency exchange. Open M-Th 9am-4:40pm, F 9am-5pm.

Bank of Hawaii 2228 Kalakaua Ave. (☎800-643-3888). Currency exchange fee $10. Open M-Th 8:30am-4:30pm, F 8:30am-6pm.

First Hawaiian Bank 2181 Kalakaua Ave. (☎943-4670; fax 943-4952). Currency exchange fee $3 for amounts under $300, $5 for under $500. Open M-Th 8:30am-4pm, F 8:30am-6pm.

Central Pacific Bank 105 Uluniu Ave. (☎971-3277; fax 971-2450). Open M-Th 8:30am-4pm, F 8:30am-6pm.

American Express, 2424 Kalakaua Ave. (☎926-5443; fax 922-3715), in the Hyatt Regency. Open daily 7am-5pm.

LOCAL SERVICES

Laundromats: Waikiki Laundromats (☎923-2057) operates numerous self-serve, coin-operated laundromats in Waikiki which are on hotel premises, but open to the public.

Weather/Surf Conditions: See Honolulu and Waikiki Information Lines (p. 94).

EMERGENCY AND COMMUNICATIONS

Emergency: ☎911.

Police: Substation at **Duke Paoa Kahanamoku Building,** 2405 Kalakaua Ave. (☎529-3801), on Waikiki beach opposite the Hyatt Regency.

Crisis Lines: Sex Abuse Treatment Center (☎524-7273). Crisis Response Team (☎521-4555).

Red Cross: American Red Cross, Hawaii Chapter (☎734-2101).

Medical Services: Urgent Care Clinic of Hawaii, 2155 Kalakaua Ave. (☎597-2860), at beachwalk. Straub Doctors on Call Waikiki (☎971-6000). Planned Parenthood Clinic of Hawaii (☎589-1149).

Internet Access:

Caffe G, 1888 Kalakaua Ave. C106 (☎979-2299; fax 979-7889), across the street from the Wave. A comfortably hip Internet and sandwich joint. High Speed Internet at $1 per min., $1 minimum. B/W printing 50¢ per page; color $1 per page. Domestic fax $2 per page; international fax $3 per page. Fax hours M-F 8am-4pm. 12 oz. cup of joe $1.50.

Beautiful Day Tours, 2161 Kalia Rd., Ste. 110. (☎926-4700; fax 800-926-4701), on the second floor landing facing the beach. High speed $3 per 20min., 96¢ each additional 10min. Copies and printing 24¢ per page, color print 96¢ per page. Local and domestic fax 96¢ per page, no international. Open M-F 9am-8pm, Sa-Su 10am-4:30pm.

Surfside Internet, 159 Kaiulani Ave., #207. Walk down Kaiulani Ave. from Kuhio Ave. and take the first left to the mini mall on the right. In the savory company of a head shop, Smokey's, and Affordable Tattoos of Waikiki (#207-A, ☎923-SKIN), this haphazard Internet *sans* cafe fits in well with its surroundings. $3 per 30min.; first hr. $5, $1 per 10min. thereafter. Backpackers, hostel guests, and senior citizens $4 per hr. Printing or copies 25¢ per page. CD Burning $5 per CD.

Post Office: Waikiki Station, 330 Saratoga Rd. (☎973-7515). Open M-F 8am-4:30pm, Sa 9am-1pm.

Zip Code: 96815.

⌂ ACCOMMODATIONS

Hotels dominate the Waikiki skyline, choking up space along the beach and toward the Ala Wai Canal. Ironically, each hotel manages to obstruct the view of another. In most cases, the impenetrable maze of edifices eliminates any real view, stealing the scene with industrial back-side views as often as with brightly-painted lanais. Wise travelers should ask to see the room before paying extra for any claims to a view, be it city, mountain or ocean. Most hotels offer rotating promotions and discounts that can add up to a significant savings. The prices listed below are standard (rack) rates, but be sure to ask about current deals at all establishments. Unless otherwise noted, all accommodations have A/C and 24hr. reception, 3pm check-in and noon check-out.

HOSTELS

Waikiki Beachside Hostel, 2556 Lemon Rd. (☎923-9566; fax 923-7525; www.hokondo.com). Follow Kalakaua Ave. east toward Diamond Head. Turn left on Kapahulu Ave., take your first left onto Lemon Rd. Whether it's wanderlust or just plain lust that drives them, the young international traveler set that populates the cheerily-painted Waikiki Beachside Hostel are passionate about their destination. Guests share animated nighttime conversations on the open patios, overlooking a parking lot-turned-courtyard (with big screen cable TV and *Tekken 2*) and a lounge. Breakfast included. Internet access ($1 per min., $6 per hr.). A/C in some rooms. Two-week advance reservations recommended in summer. 8-bed dorms $17. D/MC/V. ❶

Polynesian Beach Club Hostel, 2584 Lemon Rd. (☎877-504-2924 or 922-1340; fax 262-2817; reservation@hawaiihostels.com). See directions for Waikiki Beachside Hostel, above. The Polynesian Beach Club is probably the quietest hostel in Honolulu, as testy neighbors have mandated post-10pm quiet hours. Show them a neon flyer from the airport to get $3 off first night's stay and free pick-up with a 2-night stay. Continental breakfast included. Daily kayak tours $10-20. Guests enjoy free use of boogie boards, snorkel gear, safety deposit boxes, and storage at the desk. Checkout 10am. No curfew or lockout. Dorms $19; semi-private double $44; private studio with kitchenette $55. Seventh consecutive night's stay free. MC/V. ❶

Hale Pua Nui, 228 Beachwalk Ave. (☎923-9693; fax 923-9678). Walk with the traffic down Beachwalk from Kalakaua Ave. past the Breakers and the parking lot with moped rentals on the right. The dimly-lit, heavily-worn rooms are reminiscent of a World War II-era exhibit. The spartan aesthetics do afford their benefits, however, which are not overlooked by the many visitors who return for well-priced accommodations so close to the beaches and the Kalakaua strip. All four walk-up floors have clean rooms with one double and one full bed, a tidy bath, and cable TV. Free local calls, no long distance. Reception M-Sa 7am-noon and 2-4pm and 6-7:30pm; Su 7am-noon, 2-4pm. Call ahead for after-hours arrival. Standard room (fits 3) $57; $349 weekly. Roll-away bed $10. MC/V. ❷

Hawaiian Hostel, 419 Seaside Ave. (☎924-3303; fax 923-2111; www.hawaiianhostel.com). Turn left onto Seaside Ave. from Kalakaua Ave. Take Seaside past Kuhio Ave. and turn right down the alley just before Manukai St. on the left. Turn left at the end of the alley; the Hawaiian Hostel is 50 ft. back. This hostel manages to survive among giants by offering cheap, basic accommodations to youth travelers. Communal kitchen, breakfast included. Snorkel and surf equipment rental $5-15 per day. Parking $5 per day. Visitors should be prepared to show both their passports and their tickets off the island. 6-bed dorms with full bath $15; 4-bed dorms $17. Private double (3-night minimum) $40, each additional person $10. MC/V. ❶

HOTELS

■ **Aqua Bamboo,** 2425 Kuhio Ave. (☎922-7777 or 922-9473; http://castleresorts.com/BAM; bamboo1@lava.net). The lobby has pristine bamboo everything, and each corner is filled with the soothing sound of a trickling or chiming bamboo piece. The pool deck is under the constant surveillance of a large stone Buddha—not to be confused with the large, stoned buddhas wandering the streets of Waikiki. The management hosts a complimentary cocktail reception every Wednesday at 6pm. Doubles $135; studio with kitchenette $145. See website for discounts and promotional rates. ❹

Aqua Marina Hotel, 1700 Ala Moana Blvd. (☎942-7722; fax 942-7272; www.castleresorts.com). Take Kalakaua Ave. and turn right onto Ala Moana Blvd. A hidden jewel on the Ala Moana end of Waikiki, the Aqua Marina's sleek rooms are cast in the hotel's namesake light during the day, when the sun illuminates expansive ocean views. It is a true steal if you can get a room with a view, and even the lower floors are worth every penny. Tennis court and swimming pool with sauna and whirlpool (9am-9pm daily). Doubles $59, upper floors $69. One bedroom suite with kitchen $99. Discounts available based on occupancy and availability. AmEx/MC/V. ❷

The Imperial of Waikiki Hotel, 205 Lewers St. (☎923-1827; fax 923-7848; www.imperialofwaikiki.com). Take Lewers St. toward the beach from Kalakaua Ave. The antithesis of a chain, the Imperial is part timeshare and part hotel, with a community feel and approachable management and staff. All of the Imperial's suites will be renovated by 2005, and the additions already made are stunning. Rooftop sundeck with pool, captivating ocean view above the 20th floor. Spacious and modern Ohia Suites have microwave, mini-fridge, coffeemaker, and toaster. Suites for up to two with a double bed and a queen-sized sofa bed, $140. Banyan suites add a bedroom with a queen-sized bed, $165. Seasonal $10 discount Apr.-June and Sept.-Dec. 19. All major credit cards. ❹

Pat Winston's Waikiki Condos, 417 Nohonani St. (☎800-545-1948 or 922-3894; fax 922-3894; www.winstonwaikikicondos.com). Drive down Ala Wai Blvd., turn left on Nohonani. Whatever benefits are gained from being a condominium hotel rather than just a hotel or a hostel, the Hawaiian King passes them on to its guests in its inexpensive accommodations, which are an even greater value during promotions. All rooms have a kitchenette, full-sized refrigerator with freezer, and a fold-out couch. The astroturf pool deck and small pool are lorded over by an angry, 3-foot-tall tiki statue. Deluxe rooms also available. Laundry facilities. Four-night minimum stay. $25 one-time condominium cleaning fee. Budget room (fits 2-4), $79-115, each additional guest $10. AmEx/D/MC/V. One wheelchair-accessible room. ❷

Waikiki Gateway Hotel, 2070 Kalakaua Ave. (☎955-3741; fax 955-1313; www.waikikihotel.com). On Kalakaua Ave. just after the Kuhio Ave. split, before Olohana St. With a park at its feet and a sprawl of skyscrapers at its back, the Waikiki Gateway Hotel offers Waikiki's best. Nick's Fish Market serves excellent seafood onsite, 5:30-10:30pm. Pool with sheet-style waterfall and pleasant view. Breakfast included. Doubles $97-129. All major credit cards. One wheelchair-accessible room. ❸

THE LOCAL STORY

BEYOND WAIKIKI

Nani Loui, 19, was born and raised on Oahu. In 2002, the summer before her sophomore year at Vassar College, she had a brief stint as a hostess at popular Waikiki restaurant Cheeseburger in Paradise.

Q: Waikiki: Tourist trap or Hawaiian haven?
A: Waikiki has a lot to offer. It's well-kept, fun, and there's always tons of interesting (and/or weird) people around. I'm just saying, don't spend your whole vacation here. My favorite times in Waikiki are when I've gone night-surfing. No one's around and the shore looks just like a postcard.

Q: What does the rest of the island have to offer?
A: Everything in Waikiki tends to be more commercialized and stereotyped than anywhere else. It just isn't a good representation of Hawaii as a whole. Tourists will come in and ask if there are any good restaurants in the area, and I'll just tell them to get out of the area. Little holes-in-the-wall, mom-and-pop restaurants—they're a better representation of our culture and the importance of food in Hawaii. Rather than sitting on Waikiki beach, drive 20 or 30 min. away and you'll find your own private beach. The hiking here is amazing, but I don't see tourists flocking to that. It seems like visitors are concentrated in Waikiki. It's like its own little Disneyland.

Ilima Hotel, 445 Nohonani St. (☎923-1877; fax 924-2617; www.ilima.com). The Ilima is centrally located but off Waikiki, one block from the Ala Wai down Nohonani Pl. The facade reads Ilima in pink, and this well-kept hotel keeps it real with pink hallways, doors, and mirrors. Good-sized private lanais and unobstructed Ala Wai views outside of some rooms, and nothing but cleanliness within. Airport shuttle $6. Internet access available. Singles $129-165, doubles $139-175. Save $10 in the low season, Apr.-Dec. 14; ask about promotional rates. D/DC/MC/V. Wheelchair accessible. ❹

Waikiki Beachcomber Hotel, 2300 Kalakaua Ave. (☎922-4646; fax 926-9973; beach@dps.net; www.waikikibeachcomber.com). Sandwiched between the International Marketplace and Duke's Lane, the Waikiki Beachcomber Hotel is across the street from the Royal Hawaiian shopping center and Waikiki Beach. Location like this is pricey, but the Beachcomber rewards its guests with unique rooms and an attentive staff. Singles and doubles $220. Third person or roll-away bed $25 per day. Ask for the value rate, which can go as low as $97, depending on occupancy. AmEx/DC/MC/V. ❺

Holiday Inn Waikiki, 1830 Ala Moana Blvd. (☎924-5454; fax 947-1799; www.holiday-inn.com). Turn right onto Ala Moana Blvd. from Kalakaua Ave. The Holiday Inn steps into the hotel chain ring with a regal lobby, sunny pool deck, and standard rooms. Fitness center. Doubles $120-130. ❹

Leisure Resorts at Honolulu, 431 Nohonani Pl. (☎923-7336; fax 923-1622; www.leisureindustries.com). Take Kalakaua Ave. to Kuhio Ave., and turn left on Nahua St. Drive around the block, taking a left on Ala Wai Blvd., and left on Nohonani Pl. These timeshare suites are frequently available to non-members for short stays, and are good options for small groups. Private lanai, full bath, and electric kitchenette with mini-oven, stove, mini-fridge, microwave, and coffee pot in every suite. Check-in 4pm. Check-out 11am. Suite (fits 4) $110, one-bedroom suite (fits 6) $150. ❹

Waikiki Sand Villa, 2375 Ala Wai Blvd. (☎922-4744; fax 923-2541; www.waikiki-hotel.com). Take Kalakaua Ave. to Kanekapolei St. and turn left. Wrap-around lanais with a 70-foot pool gigantic enough to make guests almost forget the distance to the ocean. Friendly staff, on-site bar. Rental computers $7 per day, free Internet access. Doubles $97, airport rate $54 (call from the airport; based on availability). AmEx/D/MC/V. One wheelchair-accessible room. ❸

Aston Waikiki Parkside Hotel, 1850 Ala Moana Blvd. (☎955-1567 or 955-6010; aloha@waikikiparkside.com). Turn right on Ala Moana from Kalakaua

Ave., it's on the right before the Holiday Inn. With newly renovated pool and lobby, the Waikiki Parkside looks to be the shiny new boat in Aston's fleet. Fitness center, travel desk, nearby 24hr. coffeehouse. 24hr. parking pass $3. Doubles $129, with mountain view and balcony $139. Suites $160-225. ❹

Waikiki Terrace Hotel, 2045 Kalakaua Ave. (☎955-6000; fax 943-8555; www.castleresorts.com). On Kalakaua Ave. just after the Kuhio Ave. split. A gleaming white, sunny lobby greets the guests of this busy park-side hotel. Fitness room, pool with jacuzzi. All rooms have private balconies. Double occupancy $155. Ask about discounts. Wheelchair accessible. ❺

Ohana Maile Sky Court, 2058 Kuhio Ave. (☎947-2828; fax 943-0504; ohanahotels.com). Turn left down Kuhio Ave. when it splits from Kalakaua Ave. The Ohana Maile Sky Court is on the second block on the left, between Namahana and Olohana St. Atop a TGI Friday's, this Ohana hotel is known to locals for its 5th floor outdoor pool and jacuzzi complete with an obstructed mountain view and pool bar (daily 11am-2am; mai tai $1.75). Doubles $109, with kitchenette $119. Simple Saver Rate ($69) available based on occupancy. All major credit cards. ❸

Aston Aloha Surf Hotel, 444 Kanekapolei St. (☎922-2700; fax 922-8785; alohasurfhotel.com). Turn left from Ala Wai Blvd. onto Kanekapolei St. The Aloha Surf is a healthy distance from Waikiki's noisier districts. Thick carpets, gentle peach tones and a staff with *aloha* break the chain hotel mold. Internet access $10 per day. Breakfast included. Doubles $120, $15 discount Apr.-June and Sept.-Dec. 22. All major credit cards. ❹

Miramar Hotel Waikiki, 2345 Kuhio Ave. (☎922-2077; fax 926-3217; miramarwaikiki.com). You can't miss the Miramar's three-story Buddhist mural on busy Kuhio Ave. Combining chain hotel amenities with a touch of personality, the Miramar's rooms are tidy, and the well-designed bathrooms are spacious. The sound of drunken karaoke drifts into the lobby from the Banana Patch Lounge's Happy Hour (6-8pm; beer $2.50) on until the 1am close time. In-room Internet $2 per 10min. Standard room $125. All major credit cards. Wheelchair accessible. ❹

Queen Kapiolani Hotel, 150 Kapahulu Ave. (☎800-367-2317 or 922-1941; fax 924-1982; www.queenkapiolani.com). Drive up Lemon St. from Kapahulu Ave.; it's the first right. The Queen Kapiolani Hotel reaches out majestically from the Waikiki sprawl to the open areas across the street at the adjacent Honolulu Zoo. Singles $125, doubles $155. Check website or call central reservations for discounts. AmEx/D/MC/V. Wheelchair accessible. ❹

Q: What advice do you have for someone vacationing on Oahu?

A: Hawaii is an active place. Maybe spend a couple hours looking for souvenirs, but don't waste all your time shopping. The high-end hotels really aren't worth the money because you shouldn't be spending any time in your room! You can go to a spa or a mall anywhere. Hawaii is unique. Take surfing lessons. Get past the cheeseburgers—go for the $3.50 plate lunch or Spam musubi. Drive to the North Shore and stop at all the *kahuku* corn shacks and fruit stands. Get out of the city. Real Hawaii is white sand beaches, mountains, rainforest hikes, laid-back towns, plate-lunch stands. The most important thing: try and do things that you can't do anywhere else. Get in your rental car and just GO.

Aston Waikiki Grand Hotel, 134 Kapahulu Ave. (☎923-1511; fax 923-4708; http://waikikigrand.com). Turn left on Kapahulu from Kalakaua Ave.; the Waikiki Grand is on the left before Lemon St. The hotel offers well-lit, clean rooms at an affordable price, close to the Zoo and Kapiolani parks and only a stumble from Kuhio and Queen's Surf beaches. Doubles $110, with ocean view $130; studio with kitchenette $150. $20 discount Apr.-June and Sept.-Dec. 22. Ask about other discount rates. AmEx/D/MC/V. ❹

Ohana Waikiki Tower, 200 Lewers St. (☎923-6424; fax 923-7437; http://ohanahotels.com). This chain hotel is a tower of typical. The on-site Waikiki Broiler serves up food 6am-10pm and drop-your-surfboard cheap drink specials (mai tais 95¢ 6-9pm). Coin laundry. Doubles $139. Simple Saver Rate ($89) based on occupancy. All major credit cards. ❹

Ohana Waikiki Village Hotel, 240 Lewers St. (☎923-3881; fax 922-2330; ovg@outrger.com). From Kalakaua Ave., turn south toward the beach on Lewers St. A chain hotel with recently renovated rooms worth bragging about, pool bar and game room. Two restaurants on-site. Charley's Tavern, open 6am-noon, offers an all-you-can-eat pancake breakfast for $3. The Red Lion, a colorful dive bar, is open 11am-4am. Doubles $139, with kitchenette $149. ❹

Ohana Waikiki Malia Hotel, 2211 Kuhio Ave. (☎923-7621; fax 921-4804; http://ohanahotels.com). On the south side of noisy Kuhio Ave., between cacophonous Lewers St. and Royal Hawaiian Ave. The Waikiki Malia, a standard chain hotel, suffers by comparison to the beautiful dining establishment it houses. The East Ocean Seafood Restaurant. Pool access at the Ohana Waikiki Surf; the Malia compensates for its aridity with a rooftop tennis court and stark sundeck. Doubles $129. Simple Saver Rate ($69) availability based on restrictions. All major credit cards. ❹

Ohana Waikiki Surf, 2200 Kuhio Ave. (☎923-7671; fax 921-4959; http://ohanahotels.com). Simple chain hotel with a flora-ringed pool and hot tub shared by refugees from the Ohana Waikiki Malia, across bustling Kuhio Ave. The standard rooms are somewhat cramped, although the suites with kitchenette ($129) are 50% bigger. Doubles $109. Simple Saver Rate ($69) availability based on restrictions. ❸

Aston Hawaii Polo Inn, 1696 Ala Moana Blvd. (☎949-0061; fax 949-4906; http://hawaiipolo.com). Take Kalakaua Ave. and turn right onto Ala Moana Blvd. The Hawaii Polo Inn is on the right after the Aqua Marina Hotel. The Hawaii Polo Inn's inexpensive prices and proximity to Ala Moana make up for the absence of horses, polo grounds and Ralph Lauren. Simple chain rooms on the Western end of Waikiki. Pool, full bath, laundry facilities. Internet access $1 per 5min. Doubles $98, suites $119. Frequent discounts as low as $59 per night. AmEx/D/MC/V. ❸

Aston Coconut Plaza Hotel, 450 Lewers St. (☎923-8828; fax 923-3473; http://astonhotels.com). Drive down the Ala Wai and make an immediate left up the driveway after Lewers St. The clean Coconut Plaza is a complete corporate chain hotel on the Ala Wai Canal with affordable rates, thanks to its distance from the hustle and bustle of central Waikiki. Standard rooms have a city view with private lanais, microwave, cable TV, and dataport. Pool, valet parking ($9 per day). Breakfast included. Doubles $95, $10 discount Apr.-June and Sept.-Dec. 22. Studio (fits 3) $115, with mountain view $140. $15 and $20 discounts respectively during above dates. All major credit cards. One wheelchair-accessible room. ❸

Ambassador Hotel of Waikiki, 2040 Kuhio Ave. (☎941-7777; fax 951-3939; www.ambassadorwaikiki.com). Turn left onto Kuhio Ave. from Kalakaua Ave. and make a quick left on the first street, Namahana. The Ambassador's parking lot is on the left, underneath the hotel. Rooms and units with kitchenettes (stove, oven, full refrigerator) show minor cosmetic disrepair. Pool and Keo's Thai cuisine on premises. Doubles $115, Apr.-Dec. 24 $105; with kitchenette $140, Apr.-Dec. 24 $120. AmEx/MC/V. Wheelchair accessible. ❹

Royal Grove Hotel, 151 Uluniu Ave. (☎923-7691; fax 922-7508; rghawaii@get.net; www.royalgrovehotel.com). Two blocks up Uluniu from glitzy Kalakaua, on the right before unglitzy Kuhio Ave. Like the vintage furniture and second-hand clothing that thrive within, the Royal Grove combines style and affordability for those who can resist pretensions. All rooms have kitchenettes, full bath, cable TV. Maid service twice weekly. Coin laundry. Check-in 2pm. Doubles $59 per night, $360 per week. 1-bedroom suites $75 per night, $450 per week. Weekly rates available Apr.-Nov.; monthly rates available Mar.-Dec. D/DC/MC/V. ❸

The Breakers, 250 Beachwalk Ave. (☎923-3181; fax 923-7174; breakers@aloha.net; www.breakers-hawaii.com). There is something about The Breakers' look that is tropically retro-cool, though less romantic visitors might find the pool recliners to be merely worn out and the layout dated. All rooms have pay safes and an electric kitchenette with mini-fridge, stove, toaster and sink. The 16 Garden Suites, with a queen-sized bed in the master bedroom and two twin beds in the larger common area are a real steal, with the per-person price dropping as you cram in up to five people. Check-in and -out noon. Singles $91-98; doubles $94-100; Garden Suite $125-151, depending on occupancy; each additional person $8. AmEx/D/MC/V. ❸

Aston Honolulu Prince, 415 Nahua St. (☎922-1616; fax 922-6223; http://astonhotels.com). Take Ala Wai Blvd. to Walina St., make right on Kuhio Ave. and another right on Nahua St. A budget hotel at the bottom of the corporate chain ladder. Standard rooms with older mini-fridges and room safes, big closets, and full baths. Standard rooms $75, $90 June-Sept. and Dec. 23-Mar. 30. Each additional person $20. Group and promotional rates based on availability. ❸

OAHU

RESORT HOTELS

Sheraton Waikiki Beach Resort, 2255 Kalakaua Ave. (☎922-4422; fax 923-0308; www.starwood.com/hawaii). Turn right onto Royal Hawaiian Ave. from Kalakaua Ave., into the bowels of the avenue-spanning Royal Hawaiian Shopping Center. Make a right and an immediate left for parking, or continue on Royal Hawaiian Ave. to the hotel driveway. 80% of the rooms in the unique architectural layout have enthralling ocean views and 95% have private lanais. Every facility your heart could desire—and wallet can afford—all on the famed sands of Waikiki. Two pools. 24hr. room service. Yoga, tai chi, aerobics and fitness center. Excellent children's program. Three restaurants. City view $280, mountain view $330, partial ocean view $380, ocean front $490. ❺

Renaissance Ilikai Waikiki Hotel, 1777 Ala Moana Blvd. (☎949-3811; fax 947-4523; www.ilikaihotel.com). Take a right from Kalakaua onto Ala Moana Blvd., going toward the mall from Waikiki, and turn left on Hobron. The parking garage ($12 daily for guests, $16 valet) is the last turn on the left before the stop sign. The hotel front is on Ala Moana Blvd., on the eastbound side of the road. Due to its almost-but-not-quite Waikiki location, on the harbor and a stone's throw away from the tourist-clogged beaches, the Ilikai offers competitive prices that make it the best value among upper echelon hotels. Torch-lighting ceremony daily at sunset. Kawika and Friends Hawaiian Hula Show Th-Sa 6-8pm; fireworks F 6-8pm, in the Chinn Ho Tree Courtyard. Canoes Restaurant on premises (open daily 6:30am-11pm; Bow Thai Pasta $20). Standard rooms $210-290. ❺

Outrigger Waikiki Shore Resort, 2161 Kalia Rd. (☎971-4500; fax 971-4580; www.outrigger.com). A resort condominium directly on the beach, with an amazing lanai sunset view of the Pacific and the Ala Wai Yacht Harbor's forest of masts. With full access to the pool, three dining establishments, and other amenities of the neighboring Outrigger Reef, the Outrigger Waikiki Shore combines the at-home, non-touristed feel of a beach condominium with the service perks of a large chain hotel. Full kitchens in all rooms. Studio deluxe ocean view $245. ❻

Royal Garden at Waikiki Hotel, 440 Olohana St. (☎943-0202; fax 945-7407; www.royalgardens.com). Take Kalakaua Ave. to Kalaimoku St., turn left onto Ala Wai Blvd. and

THE BIG SPLURGE

TODAI

Waikiki's installment of the all-you-can eat Japanese seafood chain, shiny Todai spreads an unbelievable assortment of tasty foods from land and sea across its buffet. The smorgasbord includes crab legs, lobster tail, various preparations of shrimp and salmon, over 40 varieties of fresh sushi, a made-to-order sushi bar, BBQ ribs, beef and chicken teriyaki, soups, salads, fresh fruits, cheesecake, and a made-to-order crepe bar. *(1910 Ala Moana Blvd. ☎ 947-1000. Turn onto Ala Moana Blvd. from Kalakaua Ave.—Todai is at the end of the block on the right before Ena Rd., at Canterbury Place. Turn right on Ena Rd. and park in the garage directly behind the building. Reservations recommended 5:30-6:30pm and for parties of 6 or more. Open for lunch M-F 11:30am-2pm $15, Sa-Su 11am-2pm $17. Dinner M-Th 5:30-9:30pm $36; F-Sa 5-10pm, Su and holidays 5-9pm, $27. Drinks not included. AmEx/MC/V.)*

left on Olohana St. Away from the central Waikiki hubbub, the Royal Garden greets its guests with lusciously appointed, chandeliered hallways. Two pools, each with its own whirlpool and sauna, as well as a palatial marble lobby and an adjoining bar. Doubles $91-130, suites from $237. Each additional person $25. All major credit cards. ❸

🗂 FOOD

Excellent dining options abound in Waikiki, as entrepreneurs rush to meet the demands of the area's many tourists. For those on a budget, stocking up at grocery stores and cooking in hotel kitchenettes provides a relatively inexpensive way to keep oneself fortified and beach-ready.

GROCERY STORES AND MARKETS

Food Pantry, 2370 Kuhio Ave., is relatively inexpensive. Open daily 6am-1am.

Daiei, 801 Kaheka St. (☎ 973-4800), is a cavernous Japanese grocery store stocking exotic Asian foods, is an even better deal for those looking to try out local cuisine. Cross the Ala Wai on Kalakaua Ave., take the second left on Makaloa, and then the second right onto Kaheka St. Open 24hr.

The People's Open Market Program (☎ 527-5167), in Kapiolani Park at Monsarrat and Paki St. Overseen by the City and County of Honolulu, the market sells fresh produce from local farmers and fishermen, as well as many ethnic ingredients not found in retail stores. Wednesdays 10-11am.

RESTAURANTS

▧ **Cha Cha Cha,** 342 Seaside Ave. (☎ 923-7797). Turn left down Seaside Ave. from Kalakaua Ave. and look for the tiki torches on the left. Culinary thrill seekers rejoice at the two Happy Hours (4-6pm and 9-11pm; lime margaritas $2.50) and the variety of hot sauces including the *Cholula, lump up and Kiss Me,* and *Wrong Number Chipotle Habanero Sauce.* Ay yay yay. Authentic Caribbean-Mexican cuisine (grilled Jamaican jerk chicken $12, mahi mahi fish tacos $9.75). Show a copy of *Let's Go: Hawaii* for a free basket of chips and salsa. Open daily 11:30am-1am. Prices subject to change. ❷

Pyramids, 758B Kapahulu Ave. (☎ 737-2900). Take the Our Neighborhood Trolley from Waikiki to the Date St./Kapahulu Ave. stop and walk toward the mountains on Kapahulu. Authentic right down to its bazaar-inspired lanterns and dazzling belly dancer, Pyramids is a tempting dining option. Huge bowl of hummus $6. *Shawarma* with beef, lamb, chicken and rice $16. Open M-Sa 11am-2pm and 5:30-10pm, Su 5-9pm. ❸

Arancino, 255 Beachwalk (☎923-5557), down Beachwalk from Kalakaua Ave., next to the ABC convenience store. Romantic (read: close) seating and traditional Italian music create an intimate atmosphere inside; the lines outside attest to the quality of the flavorful food. Fettuccine alla Crema with asparagus and ham $10. Pizzas $8-15. Reservations recommended 6-8:30pm. Open daily 11:30am-2:30pm and 5-10pm. ❸

Yasoba, 255 Beachwalk (☎926-5303), next to Arancino. Don't be alarmed when the entire staff turns and addresses you with "*irasshai*" (welcome), as you enter their authentic-as-*sake* ($6-10) Japanese restaurant. The *Tenmori Gozen* ($15) features both of the restaurant's specialties, assorted tempura and handmade soba noodles, as well as rice and dessert. Open daily 11:30am-2:30pm and 5:30-9:30pm. ❸

Keo's, 2028 Kuhio Ave. (☎951-9355). Go west on Kuhio Ave. and take a right before the Kalakaua Ave. junction on Kuamoo St. Amazing Thai food, including a wide selection of curries. Panang Curry $11-14 with chicken, shrimp or seafood. Mango sorbet $5. Open daily 7:30am-2pm, dinner Su-Th 5-10:30pm and F-Sa 5-11pm. ❸

Shore Bird Beach Broiler, 2169 Kalia Rd. (☎922-2887), in the Outrigger Reef Hotel at the end of Beachwalk. Elevating beach BBQ to unprecedented heights, the Shorebird sets up their huge grills and provides a 10oz. Kalua Pork Chop ($15), Pulehu Pork Ribs with guava BBQ sauce ($16), or some other hunk of meat to cook yourself. All-you-can-eat salad bar $9. The Shore Bird is all-inclusive, with an on-site beach bar, live Hawaiian entertainment 4pm-midnight, and the Waikiki sunset just over the top of your tropical drink umbrella. Open M-F 7am-2am. ❸

Chuck's Cellar, 150 Kaiulani Ave. (☎923-4488), in the Ohana East hotel. Chuck's packs them in with live jazz from 6-10pm, an Early Bird special from 5:30-6:30pm ($9, includes all-you-can-eat soup and salad bar) and the big kabosh—a prime rib and lobster dinner for $34. Mai tai drink specials $4. Open nightly 5:30-10pm. ❹

Ray's Famous Pizza, 2260 Kuhio Ave. (☎922-9221). Like the Tahitians, the Mormons, and the Japanese, Ray visited Oahu, fell in love with it, and decided to stay, bringing his successful New York-style pizza with him. All pizzas are made to order with fresh toppings. Thin crust pizzas $10-23. Sicilian-style pies $22.50-28.50. Su-Th one extra-large pizza and 25 wings $30. Open Su-Th 11am-11pm, F-Sa 11am-midnight. Take-out available. ❹

Top of Waikiki, 2250 Kalakaua Ave. (☎923-3877), on the 21st fl. of the Waikiki Business Plaza Building, in the flying-saucer-esque restaurant at the top. Boasting a 360° view of Waikiki, upscale food (Maine lobster $39; Hawaiian-style mahi mahi $20), and a romantic atmosphere, the Top of Waikiki is a favorite among tourists. Reservations recommended on F-Su. Closed for renovations summer 2002. Open daily 5-10pm. ❺

Rainbow Drive-In, 3308 Kanaina Ave. (☎737-0177). The Rainbow's walk-up window is the gateway to one of Hawaii's tastiest local dishes, plate lunch ($4-6). The meal is a favorite among locals who jam the parking lot, waiting patiently for their 2 scoops of rice, 1 scoop of macaroni salad or slaw, and entree. Mahi mahi $5.25. Spam and Eggs $5. Try the Mix Plate ($5.60), with steak, mahi mahi and chicken. Open daily 7:30am-9pm. ❶

The Patisserie, 2168 Kalia Rd. (☎922-4974). Take Kalakaua Ave. to Beachwalk; the Patisserie is on the Ohana Edgewater Hotel premises. This unassuming little shop has been serving fresh-baked breads, cakes and pastries for over 30 years. Try a tasty sandwich ($2.50-6) or a smoothie ($3.50). Great for a Waikiki Beach birthday or other celebration, cakes ($10-14) must be ordered by 3pm the day before they are to be filled. Open daily 6:30am-8:30pm. ❶

Teddy's Bigger Burgers, 3114 Monsarrat Ave. (☎735-9411), a ½-mile stroll toward Diamond Head from Kapiolani Park on Monsarrat Ave. Take bus #13 or 22. Juicy 100% chuck burgers with basic fixings in Big (5oz., $4), Bigger (7oz., $5) and Biggest (9oz., $6) sizes. Cheese 35¢, pineapple or avocado 75¢ extra. Guests who tackle the Colossal Combo, with Biggest burger, a heaping load of fries and a large soda ($8), abandon

OAHU

all aspirations of surmounting Diamond Head afterward. The heart-stopping (-ly good) peanut butter shakes are a favorite. Open daily 10:30am-9pm. No credit cards. ❶

Cheeseburger in Paradise, 2500 Kalakaua Ave. (☎923-3731), on the corner of Kalakaua Ave. and Kealohilani Ave. Loveable for its unabashed kitschy-ness, the restaurant is a tourist trap with worthwhile bait: a laid-back beach burger and view of the strip. Heaping basket of famous seasoned french fries $3.75. The namesake Cheeseburger in Paradise ($7.50) comes in beef or gardenburger varieties. Live acoustic rock and Hawaiian music 4-11pm. Open daily 7am-11pm. ❶

China Buffet, 1830 Ala Moana Blvd. (☎955-8817), in front of the Holiday Inn Waikiki, on Ala Moana Blvd. Chinese, Japanese, and American all-you-can-eat buffets for breakfast ($5), lunch ($7), and dinner ($10). Open daily 7:30-10:30am, 11:30am-4:30pm and 5:30-10:30pm. ❷

◎ SIGHTS

■**DIAMOND HEAD.** The 350-acre Diamond Head crater was created about 300,000 years ago during a single, brief eruption that spewed ash and fine particles into the air. These particles eventually cemented together into a rock called **tuff;** geologists consider Diamond Head one of the world's best examples of a tuff cone.

Nicknamed *Le'ahi*, Diamond Head's 760-foot summit resembles the forehead (*lae*) of the *'ahi* (tuna) when viewed from the west. The word can also be translated as "fire headland," referring to navigational fires built to guide canoes traveling along the shoreline. **Diamond Head Light** replaced the fires in 1917. The site finally earned the name "Diamond Head" when explorers from the West mistook calcite crystals in the rocks on the slope for diamonds in the late 1700s.

In 1904, Diamond Head was purchased by the federal government for defense purposes, due to the vast expanse of terrain visible from the top. The military built a fire control station at the summit in 1908, to aim mortar fire by triangulating from batteries at Fort DeRussy in Waikiki and Fort Ruger on the outer slopes of the crater. In 1915, long-range guns were installed, though they have never been fired.

At the park entrance, you'll find picnic tables, restrooms, a pay phone, and drinking water. The 30-minute hike to the 560-foot summit is relatively easy, but strenuous enough to give hikers of all ages a feeling of accomplishment once they've reached the top. Be certain to bring **water** and wear **sturdy shoes.** Toward the end of the trail, after a set of 74 concrete steps, there is a dark, 225-foot tunnel that is difficult to navigate without a **flashlight.** After the tunnel and another set of 99 steps, there is an equally poorly-lit spiral staircase, but the journey soon becomes worthwhile—the view at the top is simply spectacular. *(By bus, take the #22 or #58 from Waikiki (15min., every 30min.). It will let you off across from the entrance road, which leads through a tunnel to the park entrance. Be sure to walk against traffic in the tunnel— there is no sidewalk. By car from Waikiki, take Monsarrat Ave. to Diamond Head Rd. The park comes up quickly on the right and has an easy-to-spot sign. Open 6am-6pm. Entrance fee $1.)*

WAIKIKI AQUARIUM. The aquarium specializes in coral reef exhibits and houses an impressive array of tropical fish, reef sharks and endangered Hawaiian monk seals. Hordes of schoolchildren mob the place on weekdays, contending with the aquatic wildlife for communication in high-pitched frequencies. *(2777 Kalakaua Ave. ☎923-9741. #2 bus stops directly out front every 10min. Limited free parking on the Aquarium side of Kalakaua Ave. Open daily 9am-5pm. $7; students, seniors and military $5; ages 13-17 $3.50; 12 and under free.)*

HONOLULU ZOO. The zoo is divided into exhibits of animals from the African Savanna, Tropical Forest, and Pacific Islands. The latter portion features birds and reptiles unique to the Hawaiian islands. The Children's Zoo allows children to get up close and personal with the zoo's llama and their monitor lizard, Abbey. Family programs offer a more in-depth exploration of the zoo's exhibits, via Moonlight Tours and camping programs, among others (call for info). The zoo is fronted by a small park that stretches to Kalakaua Ave., and houses a statue of Gandhi and a concrete structure filled with lava rocks that is topped by an ironically-unlit eternal flame. (☎971-7171. 151 Kapahulu Ave., on the corner of Kapahulu and Kalakaua Ave. Parking lot entrance on Kapahulu Ave., 25¢ per hr. Zoo open daily 9am-4:30pm except Christmas and New Year's Day. $6, ages 6-12 $1, under 5 free. Family Pass $25.)

ST. AUGUSTINE CHURCH. Staffed by the Congregation of the Sacred Hearts of Jesus and Mary, St. Augustine's beautiful interior is a Waikiki rarity worth seeing. The Father Damien Museum, behind St. Augustine Church, tells the story of one of Hawaii's most inspiring figures. (130 Ohua Ave., at Kalakaua and Ohua Ave. Church ☎923-7024. Museum ☎923-2690.)

🄴 ENTERTAINMENT

HULA SHOWS. In Waikiki, watching beautiful island girls shake their hips, and surf-chiseled local men flex and posture is not only completely civilized, it's also free. The **Kuhio Beach Torch Lighting and Hula Show** has Hawaiian music and performance at the Kuhio Beach Hula Mound, near the Duke Kahanamoku statue at Uluniu and Kalakaua Ave. (Hula show nightly 6:30-7:30pm. Waikiki-style show with hula lesson M-Th. Hawaiian music and hula pageant by celebrated halau (hula troupes) F-Su. Free.) Formerly the Kodak Hula Show, the **Pleasant Hawaiian Hula Show** has been continually enticing tourists with the sounds and sights of traditional Hawaiian music and dance performances since 1937. (Blaisdell Center in Kapiolani Park. Tu-Th 10-11am. Free.) Several **hotels** offer free hula performances open to guests and non-guests alike; earlier arrival ensures better viewing and more time to get another mai tai at the bar. The Hilton Hawaiian Village's popular hula show, near their **Tapa Bar,** occurs every Friday and is highlighted with a fireworks display visible from nearby beaches and roofs. (☎949-4321. M-F 8-11pm.) The Halekulani's **House Without a Key** restaurant has live Hawaiian music starting nightly at 5pm with a hula dancer. (☎923-2311. Hula nightly 6:15-8:15pm.) The Renaissance Ilikai Waikiki's **Paddles Bar** is the place to go for their traditional sunset conch blowing and torch lighting ceremony. (☎949-3811. Th-Sa 6-8pm.) Farther from the beach is the **Sheraton Princess Kaiulani Hotel's** pool-side show. (☎922-5811. Tu and Th-Su 6:15-9:30pm.)

FREE OUTDOOR FILMS. On weekends, The Kuhio Beach Torch Lighting and Hula Show (see Hula Shows, above) is followed by **Sunset on the Beach.** The Honolulu Mayor's Office sets up a tall movie screen on the beach for a double feature of recent or classic family films. (☎523-2489. Kuhio Beach Park. Sa-Su at sunset.) Before the show, a wide variety of area restaurants set up portable booths just east of the Kapahulu Pier to sell mouth-watering (and not surprisingly, overpriced) concessions to the first-come, first-seated beach blanket crowd. (Sa-Su 4-9pm.)

BLAISDELL CENTER AND WAIKIKI SHELL. The Waikiki Shell in Kapiolani Park, operated in conjunction with the Neal Blaisdell Center, hosts concerts throughout the year. The **Kapiolani Bandstand,** next to the Waikiki Shell, hosts weekly concerts of mainly jazz and rock alternated with Hawaiian music every other week. (F 5:30pm. Free.) Full Moon Concerts are also held at the bandstand around 6pm on the evening of the full moon each month. (Call ☎523-CITY for information. At sunset, around 6pm. Free.) The Blaisdell Center hosts the Pleasant Hawaiian Hula Show (see **Hula Shows,** above) as well as concerts and events. (Blaisdell Center, 77 Ward Ave., between King St. and Kapiolani Blvd. King St. gate open M-Sa 5:30am-6pm, Su and holiday

THE MEANING OF ALOHA

Waikiki, the center of tourism in Hawaii's biggest city, is composed of equal parts genuine charm and manufactured gimmick. The tourist ephemerality that soaks modern Waikiki was assured in 1922 when the waters that flowed into what was a marsh at Waikiki were diverted into the then-new Ala Wai Canal. Waikiki beach was built by permanently removing source waters and importing sand onto the Waikiki wetlands, which were formerly a native Hawaiian gathering place. With the completion of the beach, tourism gained an early foothold here, and as a result, a significant portion of today's residents of Waikiki are only temporary visitors.

Tourism is the lifeblood of the economy, and the impact of this is varied and striking. Some friendly locals who would otherwise never miss the chance to offer aloha might raise an eyebrow and give the *stink eye* to the mere mention of Waikiki. However, anyone who gets beyond a service, transactional relationship with the many locals living, working, and playing in Waikiki can attest to the ready warmth and familiarity of local demeanor. Many locals earn their livelihoods in industries that contradict their Hawaiian cultural inheritance. If aloha is the "universal spirit of free hospitality and love," tourism is the practice of buying and selling hospitality. The commercialization of aloha brings with it a cultural ambiguity that robs it of its meaning. Many tourists in Waikiki understand aloha as little more than "a Hawaiian greeting," or worse, "good service."

When locals do extend aloha, the proper response is to do likewise, but that does not make aloha merely a social greeting. Waikiki brags about its world-class shopping, its world-famous beaches, its world-record tourist revenue, but what sets the tourist capital of Paradise apart from Cancun or Disneyland is that the aloha spirit dwells in commercial Waikiki as well. It is a central part of the attraction for millions of tourists, but real aloha cannot be bought or sold in Waikiki. It comes freely, but not easily, from locals genuinely happy to have you as a guest on their island. Waikiki has the most guests of the islands and, if you've noticed, the most accommodations, restaurants, bars, tours, buses, trolleys, ABC convenience stores, and shave ice stands. Aloha thrives not on the number of occasions for hospitality, but on the attitude of everyone— tourists and locals—involved. The spirit of aloha can transform the tenor of an interaction—such as a tourist paying for a lei, consuming a piece of Hawaiian culture—into an exchange of aloha. Because of the aloha spirit, Hawaii is more than a tourist destination—it is a paradise.

hours determined by events. Show information line and Box Office ☎591-2211; open M-F 10am-6pm and Sa 9am-5pm. Event pass $3, daily non-event $4. Waikiki Shell, 2805 Monsarrat Ave., at the Diamond Head end of Waikiki. Call Blaisdell Center or see visitor section of www.co.honolulu.hi.us for more information. Free.)

⬛ SHOPPING

Shopping in Waikiki has a dual nature, including in its scope 4-for-$1 Hawaiiana and knick-knacks in the International Market and chic, top-of-the-line designer items in the Royal Hawaiian Shopping Center or the proliferation of shops that populate the ground floors of Waikiki's myriad hotels.

ART ON THE ZOO FENCE. Art on the Zoo fence is a mellow Waikiki tradition wherein artists display works for sale on the chain-link fence of the Honolulu Zoo, facing the Pacific. (2355 Ala Wai. ☎946-7282; bambumoon@hawaii.rr.com. Open Sa-Su 10am-4pm and Tu 9am-noon.)

THE INTERNATIONAL MARKET PLACE. The market is a maze of kiosk-like stands that hock the summer vacation trends you'll find in every kitschy tourist district around the world—imitation designer sunglasses, "tobacco" pipes, T-shirts, and shot glasses. It's also a prime place to get cheap aloha wear and Hawaiian souvenirs, such as carvings, macadamia nut leis, puka body ornaments, and jade Buddha statues and jewelry. There's even an Internet access booth. Prices are not set and bargaining is recommended. Remember to shop around—many booths sell the same things, so there is always the possibility of a better bargain elsewhere. *(At Kalakaua Ave. and Duke's Ln.)*

ROYAL HAWAIIAN SHOPPING CENTER. The Royal Hawaiian presides over 3 buildings along Royal Hawaiian Ave., holding court with the nobility of the fashion world—names such as Armani, Cartier, Fendi and Chanel. Its East Asian-inspired interior is interesting if only for the impressive display of wealth and fashion it houses. *(On Royal Hawaiian Ave. Visitor Center on the first floor. Shopping Center open daily 11am-10pm.)*

KALAKAUA AVENUE. The avenue hosts many of the same glitzy, high-end offerings of the Royal Hawaiian shopping center, only with more crowds. At the crux of the avenue and the Royal Hawaiian is the **DFS Galleria,** a behemoth mall *cum* Duty Free Shop, which puts on free Hawaiian entertainment and features a cool walk-through aquarium. *(☎ 931-2655; www.dfsgalleria.com. On the corner of Kalakaua and Royal Hawaiian Avenues. Open daily 11am-11pm.)* Twin towers scrape the sky over the little resort-spawned mall in the **Hyatt.** Check out the super-cool and popular Wyland Galleries, as well as the usual suspects, Gucci et. al. *(Most Kalakaua Ave. stores open daily 10am-10pm.)*

▨ NIGHTLIFE

CLUBS

The Maze, 2255 Kuhio Ave. (☎ 921-5800), on the second floor of the Waikiki Trade Center. Get lost in the cavernous dance club's three rooms: the audio-excellent Maze Arena, spinning house, hard house and trance; bumping Red Room dropping hip-hop and crowd-pleasing Top 40; and Paradox Lounge with live instrumental, funk, disco and house. Dress "absolutely fabulous," especially on bumping Friday nights. Many discount and no-cover promotions before midnight. 21+. Open nightly 9pm-4am. MC/V.

Zanzabar, 2255 Kuhio Ave. (☎ 479-9152), on the first floor of the Waikiki Trade Center. Rich and sultry Zanzabar hosts a hotter-than-thou local set *en masse* on F and Sa. $2 drinks all night on M. Free salsa lessons Tu 8-9pm. Live DJs nightly. 18+ Th-Su, 21+ M-W. Cover $5. Open nightly 8pm-4am. AmEx/D/MC/V.

Wave Waikiki, 1877 Kalakaua Ave. (☎ 941-0424; http://wavewaikiki.com), on the right of Kalakaua Ave. from the Ala Wai Canal, before Ena Rd. Wave is Waikiki in microcosm—some consider it the most happening night spot around, others equate it with the worst of MTV's Spring Break. Tourist hordes and locals alike come to shake their action to hip-hop (Su-Th), or live DJs and bands (F-Sa). Happy Hour 9-10pm ($2.75 wells and domestics), but the action doesn't really get started until after midnight. Cover $5 after 10pm. Open nightly 9pm-4am.

Fusion Waikiki, 2260 Kuhio Ave. 2nd fl., across from the Waikiki Trade Plaza. Live DJs spinning house and hip-hop keep the dance floor of this gay bar throbbing, Su-Th starting at 9pm and F-Sa from midnight on. Female impersonator show (F at 11pm, cover $5). All-male strip show on Saturday (11pm, cover $5; if you're feeling ballsy, contact Pat a night in advance for an audition). Fusion opens up for the 18+ crowd on the 1st and 3rd Sunday of the month for the mixed gay and straight Kid's Klub (cover $5). Beer $3.50. 21+. Open M-Th 9pm-4am, F-Sa 8pm-4am, Su 10pm-4am. No credit cards.

Angles Waikiki, 2258 Kuhio Ave. 2nd fl. (☎942-2422), next door to Fusion. A rollicking gay bar equipped with a pool table and a day-long Happy Hour 10am-8pm (10am-8pm; rotating drink specials, drafts $2.25 from 1:30-8pm). DJs on the 1s and 2s W-Su starting around 9pm. All-male strippers Th 11pm. 21+. No cover. Open nightly 10pm-2am. No credit cards.

BARS

Duke's Canoe Club, 2355 Kalakaua Ave. (☎922-2268), inside the Outrigger Waikiki, on the beach. Parking at the hotel $2 per hr., or validate parking at the Ohana East Hotel on Kuhio Ave. A Waikiki institution, Duke's is a casual bar that mixes drinks with live contemporary Hawaiian music (F-Su 4-6pm on the lower lanai, nightly 10pm-midnight). Beachside seating is perfect for that sunset mai tai ($5). Duke's is also a thriving restaurant—try the Thai Chicken Pizza. Open daily 7am-midnight, bar open until 1am.

Moose McGillycuddy's Pub and Cafe, 310 Lewers St. (☎923-0751; www.moosem-cgillycuddywaikiki.com). Moose's serves breakfast, lunch and dinner to slow the inebriation of the crowds that come for the ever-changing theme nights, listed on the webpage. One staple is the bikini contest, webcast every Sunday. Happy Hour stretches from 4-8pm with half-price well drinks to wash down the half-price appetizers (served from 4-7:30pm). Restaurant downstairs, 21+ in the bar upstairs. Cover $3-5. Open daily 7:30am-4am, food served until 10pm. Not wheelchair accessible.

Nashville Waikiki, 2330 Kuhio Ave. (☎926-7911). Basement of the Waikiki West Hotel, on Kuhio Ave. between Walina and Nahua St. The Nashville Waikiki considers itself an authentic Texas-style bar—as authentic as one can get several thousand miles from the real deal, perhaps. Line dancing and "real" cowboys complete the theme. Open daily 4pm-4am. Wheelchair accessible.

Michelangelo, 444 Hobron Ln. (☎951-0008), on the ground floor of Eaton Sq., next to the post office. A mellow gay bar that avoids the nightclub dance floor hoopla, opting instead to serve inexpensive food (shrimp and fries $5.75, 2 chili dog meal $2.50). Happy Hour 10am-6pm, all beer and well drinks $2. Pool table, darts, and video games. Open daily 10am-2am. MC/V.

Fox and Hounds English Pub and Grub, 1778 Ala Moana Blvd. Unit LL (☎947-3776). Fox and Hounds is a little bit of everything, with a pubby dark wood bar, lounge, pool room, and dance floor. 35 brews on tap, food served all day (fish and chips $6.50). Happy Hour 2-6pm (domestic beer $2.50, margaritas $4). DJs on Th, local and Hawaiian music Su nights. 21+ after 9pm. Open daily 7am-2am, food served until midnight. Wheelchair accessible.

The Red Lion, 240 Lewers St. (☎922-1027), in the Ohana Waikiki Village basement. mai tais and well drinks ($1.50) during Happy Hour—and by "hour" they mean "day"—11am-9pm. Everyone, from angry sailors to curious Japanese tourists to broke college students, comes through the doors and ends up at its pool tables and dart boards. Write your name on a Washington and they'll stick it to the ceiling forever and ever. Low ceilings and big crowds on promotional nights (F, Sa, Tu) lead to cramped, hot conditions. Cover $2-5 after 9pm. Open daily 11am-4am.

☢ BEACHES

Waikiki Beach is the general name that refers to any and all of the beaches on the south shore of Oahu. It begins on the Waikiki side of the Hilton Lagoon in the west, continues along the coastline of Waikiki's premier beach hotels, and stretches all the way to the fringes of Diamond Head Crater. Although the beach reaches moments of absolute saturation on busy weekends, the perpetual daytime crowds on Waikiki Beach can be enlivening—the throng of visitors excites a contagious stir and tangible buzz of enthusiasm. During the day, the Waikiki beaches are awash in aquatic activities as surfers paddle between catamarans, canoes paddle around snorkelers, and swimmers jostle into each other in the waves. Quieter, romantic moments occur on the bookends of the frenetic day, at dawn and sunset when the crowds have dispersed and calmed, and the expectant plumeria breeze soothes sun-dried and burned skin.

 BEACH SERVICES. Lifeguards are asked to watch over huge numbers of beachgoers, and caution and common sense goes a long way to ensure your safety in the water. Never swim alone, always check with the lifeguard before entering unfamiliar water, and never dive into breaking surf. For those in need of wheelchairs, **Landeez All-Terrain Wheelchairs** (☎522-7034) can surmount the sturdiest of sand castles and are available free of charge from the Department of Parks and Recreation at Sans Souci Beach Park, 2863 Kalakaua Ave. (☎921-0110; open daily 9am-4pm) and Fort DeRussy Beach, off Kalia Rd. (☎949-8952).

DUKE KAHANAMOKU BEACH PARK. Duke Kahanamoku is the westernmost Waikiki beach, at the edge of the Hilton Lagoon. It houses several canoes that spend their days plying the waves, and experienced surfers can be seen in the distance, surfing the breaks out from the beach. On the fringes of the action, Duke Kahanamoku Beach is usually subdued and relatively quiet, making it a good place to escape the multitudes farther down.

Commemorative efforts in honor of Duke continue at the section of beach between the Sheraton Moana and Kuhio Beach's two seawall-enclosed swimming pools on Kalakaua Ave. The towering **Duke Kahanamoku Statue** of the Hawaiian hero *cum* sheriff, Olympic champion, surfing popularizer, movie star and Ambassador of Aloha resides here, next door to the Honolulu Police's Waikiki Substation in the **Duke Paoa Kahanamoku Building.** The frequently lei-adorned, bronze Duke faces unnaturally away from the Pacific, his board between him and the water as a tourist might pose for a picture on the beach. The position is considered improbable by many surfers and locals who adore his memory. Also nearby are the monuments to four ancient Tahitian soothsayers who visited Oahu and proved themselves to be healers and possessors of wisdom. The boulders—known as the **Wizard Stones**—were recently elevated to pop Hawaiian religious consciousness with their unearthing and by their current conspicuous replacement atop the sand. According to myth, the stones were to be a tangible reminder of the ministrations made and the suffering eased by the soothsayers. Kapaemahu, the leader, had his stone eponymously named, transferring his powers to it via incantations and the sacrifice of a lovely island chieftess. *(There is limited free parking for the beach near the Hilton Lagoon; take Ala Moana Blvd. west to Hobron Lane and turn left after the Renaissance Ilikai Hotel. At the stop sign, turn left and follow the road past the yacht harbor to the lot on the left.)*

DIAMOND HEAD BEACH. Populated primarily by surfers and windsurfers, Diamond Head Beach is a narrow strip of sand below the highway. Most visitors come for the waves, not the sun, and few are beginners. This beach is better for experienced boarders and enthusiasts than for families, since the surf can be dangerous at times and there are better vistas at other beaches. *(By car, take Kalakaua Ave from*

IN RECENT NEWS

THE KAMEHAMEHA ONE

Outrage swept the Native Hawaiian community after the trustees of Kamehameha Schools announced their decision to admit a non-Hawaiian student to their Maui campus. The schools were established in 1884 by Princess Bernice Pauahi Bishop's will, which expressed her wish for a school to meet the needs of Native Hawaiians. Today, the $6 billion private trust sponsors Kamehameha campuses on Maui, Big Island, and Oahu and, until now, enrollment has been limited to blood-Hawaiians. Trustees claim that the non-Hawaiian student was only accepted after all eligible Native Hawaiians had been admitted. However, some contend that the trustees' actions are in response to recent Supreme Court decisions that have redrawn the line between race and ethnicity and, in turn, placed Kamehameha School's policies under intense scrutiny. In 1983, the high court ruled in *Bob Jones University v. US* that schools whose admissions policies violate federal guidelines against racial discrimination can lose their tax-exempt status. If this were to occur, Kamehameha Schools would have upwards of $1 million in back taxes to pay, as well as the loss of 40% of its future income. Others protest that denying sub-par Hawaiian students takes the help away from those who need it most. Despite the trustees' assurance that this decision does not reflect a change in admissions policy, the controversy has already sparked heated debates, protests, and calls for reform.

Waikiki to Diamond Head Road. Park just past the lighthouse and walk down to the beach on the trail beyond the lot. By bus, take the #14 from Waikiki, which stops near the lighthouse. Or, from the Diamond Head park entrance (see above), turn right as you exit and take Diamond Head Road all the way around the crater to the beach.)

GRAY'S BEACH. East of the US Army Museum, stretching from the Outrigger Waikiki Shore to the jetty in front of the pink Sheraton Royal Hawaiian, is an area known as **Gray's Beach,** named after an inn that hosted some of Waikiki's earliest tourists. There's good surfing a long paddle out from the shore, and big daytime crowds begin there.

WAIKIKI BEACH. Tourists happily cram themselves together on the resort beachfront in between the two Sheraton Hotels, the Royal Hawaiian and the Moana Surfrider. This stretch of sand, at the Waikiki Beach Center, is often called **Royal Moana Beach,** or simply **Waikiki Beach,** and it sees almost as many tourists cavorting in its waters as lounging on its soft shores. Swimmers, surfers, catamarans, canoes, and all manner of pushed, pulled and wind-propelled potential water hazards dot the gently rolling Pacific all the way out to the surfers on the breakers.

BABY QUEEN'S. A 50- to 100-yard paddle out from the next stretch of beach, between the Sheraton Moana and Kuhio Beach's two seawall-enclosed swimming pools, is an area favored by some locals as the safest spot to learn to surf. Hawaiians use the area, known as **Baby Queen's,** to teach their children how to ride the waves, as it is less dangerous and crowded than many of the sites favored by professional instructors. Always consult the lifeguard, but a good rule of thumb for water safety is that if novice locals are there, chances are it's safe.

KUHIO BEACH. Kuhio Beach extends beyond the recently-improved Kapahulu Pier (formerly known as Kapahulu Wall). Additions to the Kuhio Beach Park area in recent years have spruced up Waikiki, with grassy outcroppings trimmed in lava rocks and meandering flagstone walkways bordered by Hawaiian flora. From the overlooking pier, beachgoers watch the surfers and boogie boarders tempt fate in waters that often conceal shallow coral. Swimming within the deep pools formed by the seawalls is enjoyable and safe, but inexperienced and unfamiliar boarders should not test the waves on the other side (to the right of the Kapahulu Pier), lest they be caught between the strong current and the slippery rock wall. **Queen's Surf Beach** is beyond the wall and across Kalakaua Ave. from Kapiolani Park.

SANS SOUCI BEACH. Beyond the Waikiki Aquarium (p. 132), on the beach, is the **Natatorium,** a WWI monument and former Olympic training pool. The Natatorium perpetually awaits further renovation before reopening, despite a recent phase of refurbishment to improve its appearance. It does house the nicest public bathrooms on Waikiki's beaches, however. Next to the Natatorium is **Sans Souci Beach** an adjacent grassy area toward the park. It's a favorite spot among local families for its proximity to beach and park recreation, and for its distance from the more urban part of Waikiki. Locals tell different stories about why Sans Souci beach is so named. Many link it to a no-longer extant hotel that formerly occupied the site where the Kaimana Beach Hotel currently resides. Others say it is because of the high proportion of beauties and studs who flock to its sands to flaunt their looks. Regardless, Sans Souci affords a calm view of the divine Waikiki sunset at a distance from the cluster of hotels that provides relative privacy. Beyond Sans Souci is the **Outrigger Canoe Club Beach,** on the edge of Waikiki, which extends all the way to the beaches at Diamond Head's feet.

FORT DERUSSY BEACH PARK. Adjacent to Duke Kahanamoku Beach, in front of the Hale Koa military hotel and Fort DeRussy, is **Fort DeRussy Beach Park.** A wide stretch of sand littered with shells and coral near the shore, Fort DeRussy Beach is less than ideal for wading and swimming, but the neighboring park has shaded lawns for those fleeing the sun.

NEAR HONOLULU

PEARL HARBOR

At 7:55am on that infamous December morning, a wave of Japanese fighter planes wrenched the US out of its steadfast neutrality and into the thick of WWII. Pearl Harbor, about 40min. outside of Honolulu, held the whole of the US Pacific Fleet in 1941, and was the target of Japan's brutally swift surprise attack. The destruction was devastating; during the 2hr. onslaught, over 2400 military personnel and civilians were killed, 188 planes were demolished, and 8 battleships were either damaged or destroyed. For more information, see **History,** p. 16.

ARIZONA MEMORIAL. Solemn and graceful, the *USS Arizona* Memorial is a fitting tribute to the 1177 crewmen who died aboard the ship. The 184-foot memorial spans the partially sunken battleship's midsection, affording visitors a close, poignant view of the ship that still entombs 1100 men. Plans for the memorial began in 1943, but it wasn't until 1958 that President Eisenhower approved its creation. Alfred Preis designed the final structure, and it was dedicated in 1962. The structure features a unique concave middle section that symbolizes America's great tragedy and the country's subsequent rise above it. There are three main sections: an entry room; a central area where visitors can observe the ship; and the shrine room, which has a marble wall engraved with the names of those who died on the *Arizona.* The on-shore **Visitor Center** has a historical museum and leads tours that include a documentary film and boat ride to the memorial itself. The tour is free, but every visitor must pick up his or her ticket in person on a first-come, first-served basis. Come early, as wait times can reach 2hr. and most tickets are gone by 1pm. (☎ *422-0561. From Honolulu, take H-1 West to the Arizona Memorial/Stadium exit which will deposit you on Kamehameha Hwy. Follow the signs to the Battleship Missouri Memorial and USS Bowfin Park, turning left after ½ mi. TheBus #20, 42 or CityExpress A will also get you there; the bus stop is across the street from the Battleship Missouri trolley pick-up at Bowfin Park. Open daily 7:30am-5pm. 1¼hr. tours every 15min. 8am-3pm (Jul. 1-Aug. 31 tours start at 7:45am). No bags, purses, backpacks or strollers with pockets and compartments. Free.)*

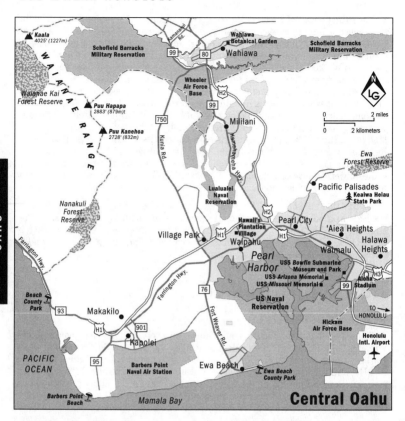

Central Oahu

BOWFIN PARK. One of 15 remaining WWII submarines, the *USS Bowfin* is the centerpiece of its own historical park. Called the "Pearl Harbor Avenger," the sub was set into action one year after the 1941 attack. In 1981, the *Bowfin* was pulled out of commission and given educational duty instead. In addition to the submarine, visitors can explore outdoor exhibits, such as a waterfront memorial, as well as indoor exhibits of submarine-related paraphernalia, including paintings, photographs, battle flags, and models. *(The park is adjacent to the USS Arizona Visitor Center. See directions to USS Arizona above. ☎ 423-1341. Open 8am-5pm, last tour of sub 4:30pm. Submarine and museum admission $8; military, senior citizens, Hawaii residents $6, ages 4-12 $3. Museum only $4, ages 4-12 $2.)*

BATTLESHIP MISSOURI MEMORIAL. After 5 decades of military service, the battleship *Missouri* was finally retired in 1999. The ship (nicknamed "Mighty Mo") was relaunched as a tourist attraction and has already attracted 1 million visitors in the past 2½ years. The 887-foot *Missouri* is a veteran of World War II, the Korean War and, after modernization in the mid-1980s, the Persian Gulf War. Marvelously refurbished and preserved, the ship illustrates to visitors the claustrophobic monotony of the sailors' daily lives. There is a feeling of patriotism aboard the ship—among other historic spots, guests can visit the famed Signature Deck, where the Japanese signed and General Douglas MacArthur accepted the Instrument of Surrender on September 2, 1945, ending WWII. The entertaining **Chief's Guided Tour** ($6), in Japanese or English, takes visitors through the Combat Engagement Center for a real look at the room where all the drama occurred. The **Captain's Tour** (1½hr.; $35, children $25) gives visitors an inside look at the Captain's Cabin and combat centers of the ship as well as a detailed, formerly top-secret debriefing on the Desert Storm mission. Light refreshments are served on the commanding officer's authentic china. The newest attraction, the **Explorer's Tour** (1½hr.; $35, children $25), outfits patrons with hard hats and flashlights so that they can delve into the previously closed and off-limits lower decks, viewing the circa-1943 mechanical analog super-computers. *(From Honolulu, take H-1 West to the Arizona Memorial/Stadium exit which will deposit you on Kamehameha Hwy. Follow the signs to the Battleship Missouri Memorial and USS Bowfin Park, turning left after ½ mi. Or take TheBus #20, 42 or CityExpress A. From the USS Bowfin, take the free trolley. ☎973-2494; www.ussmissouri.com. Bags and backpacks are prohibited. Call for tour reservations. Open daily 9am-5pm. Admission, not included with the tours, $14; ages 4-12 $7; under 4 free. All major credit cards.)*

WAIPAHU

HAWAII'S PLANTATION VILLAGE. Located in suburban Waipahu, Hawaii's Plantation Village documents the life of workers on sugar plantations throughout Hawaii in the early 1900s. The site is composed of several authentic residential buildings relocated from various plantations, each representative of a particular ethnic group. Plantation owners recruited over 400,000 workers from nearly a dozen different nations between 1848 and 1946, after diseases brought by foreigners had ravaged the local population and diminished the workforce. The owners segregated the workers by race in order to prevent organized collective bargaining for wages. Most workers were paid around $3 per month for ten hours of work each day, and nearly all lived communally, with little or no privacy. Much to the owners' chagrin, the different groups began sharing food, competing in athletic events, and intermarrying. From these initial exchanges arose the multi-racial **International Longshore and Warehouse Union** (see p. 18), which successfully challenged the landowners and raised wages and quality of life for workers. Today, Chinese, Portuguese, Japanese, Puerto Ricans, Okinawans, Koreans, Filipinos, Caucasians, and indigenous Hawaiians co-exist in a peaceful, multi-racial society.

Some sites of interest in the village include a 1930s-era barber shop, a public bathhouse, a 1940s-era RC Cola general store, and the last active Inari (a minor Shinto sect) shrine in the world. The free, 1½-hour **tour** of the village is worthwhile, but a good deal of information can be gathered just by meandering through the place on your own, which takes about 30min. There's also a small **museum** that showcases artifacts from plantations and explains some of the historical information in greater detail. The Plantation Village is a good way to spend part of a non-beach afternoon, especially for travelers with children. *(94-695 Waipahu St. By car, take H-1 west to Exit 7. Turn left onto Paiwa St., then right on Waipahu St. The village is on the left about 1½ mi. from the highway. By bus, take the #43 from the Ala Moana Shopping Center to the front gate (1hr., every 30min., 7:03am-5:15pm). ☎677-0110; fax 676-6727. Both the village and the museum are open M-F 9am-3pm, Sa 10am-3pm. Tours run every hour on the hour 10am-3pm. $7, seniors $4, groups of 20 or more $4, ages 5-12 $3.)*

OAHU SUGAR MILL. Looming over the village is the Oahu Sugar Mill, the original mill that processed all the sugarcane on the island during the early 1900s. The mill has been closed since 1979, but it still serves as a rusted reminder that the economy of the island has not always been pineapple-based. *(About a 5-minute walk down Waipahu St. toward Paiwa St., at 94428 Mokuola St. ☎841-1879. Open daily 8:30am-5pm.)*

FILIPINO CULTURAL CENTER. In the lot adjoining the mill is the brand-new $14 million Filipino Cultural Center. Though it serves primarily as a resource for the local Filipino community, there are cultural dance exhibitions throughout the year, as well as festivals celebrating Filipino Independence Day during the second week of June and the Miss Filipino Hawaii pageant during the last weekend in July. *(Intersection of Waipahu St. and Mokuola St.)*

⚡ DAYTRIPS FROM HONOLULU

KEAIWA HEIAU STATE PARK

By car, take Hwy. 78 west from Honolulu to the Stadium/'Aiea exit and continue onto Moanalua Rd. At the second light, make a right onto 'Aiea Heights Dr., which twists and turns its way to the park, about three miles up. By bus, take #11 from the Ala Moana Shopping Center hub (35min., every hr. 6:48am-9:10pm). Ask the driver to let you off at Kaamilo St. The park is a pleasant 25-minute walk up 'Aiea Heights Dr. The Ala Moana Shopping Center is accessible via the #8 bus from Waikiki, or the #19 or #20 from elsewhere in Honolulu, all of which run frequently. The park is open 7am-7:45pm in summer, 7am-6:45pm in winter. Permits $5 per group, good for up to five consecutive days of camping.

Located above 'Aiea Heights, a quiet residential neighborhood north of Pearl Harbor, Keaiwa Heiau State Park is an excellent choice for those in search of a peaceful place to camp far from Waikiki's throngs, but close enough to the city for easy daytrips. Tall ironwood trees, pockets of eucalyptus, and its high elevation (880 ft.) give the place an impressive sense of scale. Splendid views of Honolulu and Pearl Harbor abound within the park's 350-odd acres of lush vegetation.

Although its natural beauty and tranquil atmosphere are the real attractions, the park's namesake gives it at least a marginal degree of historical credibility. In the late 15th century, *kahuna lapa'au*, or herbal healers, practiced their craft in the *keaiwa heiau*, a squat stone structure, harnessing the natural energy of the site as well as the medicinal properties of nearby plants. Today, all that remains of the heiau are foot-high lines of rocks, placed where archaeologists believe walls once stood. The site is considered sacred by the Hawaiian people, and it is disrespectful (and illegal) to move stones or leave offerings of any kind.

The park has four good **campsites**, each of which can accommodate 10-20 people (though you'll rarely find more than five people at any given site). All campsites have restrooms and shower facilities. Those which have been recently renovated are spotless and modern; those which have not are a bit rusty.

All the campsites are accessible via a one-mile road that encircles the ridge near the entrance. The **'Aiea Loop Trail,** an easy 4½-mile hike through the forest, meanders between the restrooms at the park entrance and the second campsite, about a half-mile down the road. In addition to striking views of the mountains and Pearl Harbor, the trail is home to hundreds of species of indigenous plants. Toward the end of the trail, the 1943 wreckage of a C-47 cargo plane is visible through the trees. The trail takes 2-3hr. to complete, and while shoes or lightweight hiking boots are suggested, sturdy sandals are adequate.

WAHIAWA

To reach Wahiawa by car from Honolulu, take H-1 west, then take H-2, which runs through the middle of town. Wahiawa is also on the #52 and #62 bus lines, just over an hour from the Ala Moana Shopping Center hub in Honolulu. Ala Moana is accessible via buses #19 and #20 from Honolulu, or #8 from Waikiki.

Wahiawa is a military town near the **Schofield Barracks.** It is of interest only for its nearby sights; the town itself is full of pawn shops, tattoo parlors, and bars, and is best seen from the inside of an air-conditioned car.

A half-mile north of Wahiawa on **Kamehameha Hwy.** at Whitmore Ave. are a set of *Kukaniloko*, or **royal birthstones,** on which Hawaiian queens laid while giving birth, in order to secure blessings for their children. The stones are fairly plain and not particularly impressive.

About ¼ mi. farther down the highway, in the triangular intersection with Kaukonahua Rd., and Kamananui Rd., the **Del Monte Pineapple Garden** displays pineapples in different stages of growth and explains how commercial pineapple farming works. Another ¼ mi. along the highway from the garden, about a mile from Wahiawa, the **Dole Plantation** gift shop serves fresh pineapples, dried pineapples, chocolate-covered pineapples, pineapple cake, and various pineapple-themed sorbets and beverages. (☎621-8408. Open daily 9:30am-5:30pm. Various pineapple foodstuffs $2-6.) The complex is also home to the world's largest **maze,** according to the *Guinness Book of World Records.* The maze is made out of local plants, and the goal is to reach each of six stations and exit in as short a time as possible; a hall of fame is posted at the entrance. (Open daily 9:30am-5:30pm. Entrance $4.50.) The **Pineapple Express,** a small train to ferry visitors on a tour of the pineapple fields, is scheduled to open in October of 2002.

By January 2003, the **Dole Plantation Gardens** should also be fully operational. Located next to the maze, the gardens include displays about the various stages of pineapple growth, different species of pineapples from all over the world, and information about bromeliads (air plants). Activities for children, such as lei-making and Hawaiian crafts, will also be available. All of the above sights are on the **#52 bus** line, accessible from the Ala Moana Shopping Center in Honolulu.

Back in town, a short mile east of the highway, the 27-acre **Wahiawa Botanical Garden,** 1396 California Ave., makes for a pleasant afternoon stroll, but isn't worth a special trip. If you do stop by, be sure to take one of the free brochures, which has a good map and provides interesting information about the trees and plants in the garden. (☎621-7321. Open daily 9am-4pm. Free.) A mile west of the highway, on the same road, inside a cell-like shrine next to a Methodist Church, reside several plain-looking **healing stones** that are considered holy by the Hawaiian people. They once attracted visitors from all over the islands, but their popularity has faded in recent years.

Fast food establishments of all varieties abound in Wahiawa. To avoid them, head three blocks east from Kamehameha Hwy. on Kiliani Ave. to N. Cane St., where **Sunnyside ❶** serves super-cheap local eats. The teriyaki burger ($2) is a good deal, and people come from all over central Oahu for the famous **cream and fruit pies** ($5-6), which tend to sell out by noon. (☎621-7188. Open M-F 6am-6pm, Sa 6am-4pm.)

SOUTHEAST OAHU

KOKO HEAD REGIONAL PARK AND ENVIRONS

The entire area west of Honolulu along Kalanianaole Hwy. (Hwy. 72) from Koko Head to Sandy Beach is a county park that includes **Hanauma Bay,** the **Halona Blowhole and Cove,** and the **Koko Crater.** All these sites are easily accessible by car from the highway, and two major bus routes serve the area. Bus #22, affectionately referred to as the "Beach Bus," runs along the highway from Waikiki to **Sea Life Park,** and has stops at each of the destinations mentioned above, as well as Makapu'u point and beach. (Departs Waikiki 8:15, 9:15am, every hr. at five minutes before the hour. Last return from Sea Life Park 5:30pm.) Bus #58 serves a similar area, but it leaves the highway and runs through **Hawaii Kai,** a suburban residential community. Bus #58 serves the same destinations with the exception of Hanauma Bay and Sandy Beach (every 30min., 6:50am-7:15pm).

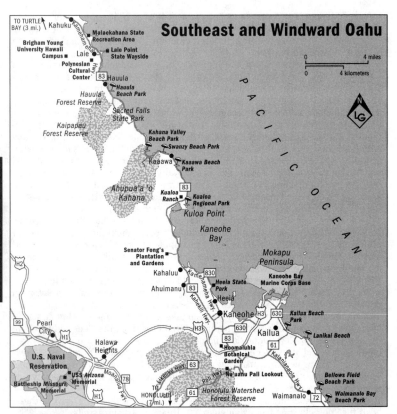

Southeast and Windward Oahu

HANAUMA BAY MARINE LIFE CONSERVATION DISTRICT. Hanauma Bay is like Disneyland: a fun time, but the crowds are maddening. Nearly 10,000 people flock to this picturesque beach every day (over 1 million visitors annually), and while the **snorkeling** is among the best on the island, the legions of tourists and children can detract from the experience. Arrive as early as possible to avoid the crowds.

Hanauma means "Curved Bay." The wide, sandy beach is at the base of a ring of volcanic rock below **Koko Head,** and its waters are teeming with hundreds of species of brightly-colored fish. The concave bay is mirrored by an arc of rocky reef about 100 yards into the ocean; the space between the reef and the shore is shallow and encloses a beautiful latticework of coral.

Once a favorite local fishing spot, the bay has been a conservation area since 1967. In the past, overfishing was a big problem. These days, however, the problem is **overfeeding.** The local fish population has become dependent on human handouts, and aggressive species foreign to the area, such as the Hawaiian Whitespotted Toby, have started to migrate in and take over. Respect the bay (and the law) by not feeding the fish.

In the spring of 2003, a **Visitor Center** is scheduled to open where park goers will be required to watch a video about the fragile ecosystem of the bay area. Until then, be aware of the fact that standing on or touching the reef kills the living coral. Hundreds of years of growth can be destroyed in an instant, and much of the reef has already been badly damaged by years of dense tourism. Be sure to read the **bulletin board** at the entrance to get the latest info on surf conditions, and to learn which parts of the bay are safe for swimming each day. Hanauma Bay has more serious injuries and deaths each year than any other beach on the island (admittedly, it also has the most visitors, which inflates the statistic somewhat).

The largest of the open areas in the rock, **Keyhole,** is in the center of the bay. It is quite shallow and calm, which makes it a good spot for novice snorkelers, though it often has poor visibility due to kicked-up sand. Snorkeling is better outside the reef, but the current is strong, and a surprise wave can throw even an experienced swimmer against the rocks. Be careful not to swim too far from the reef either; an infamous rip current called the **Molokai Express** has washed many a snorkeler deep into the ocean (few manage to make it all the way to Molokai). *Let's Go* does not recommend swimming beyond the reef.

The two most dangerous areas of the bay are Toilet Bowl and Witches Brew, both of which are closed to public access by chain-link fences and signs threatening fines and imprisonment for trespassing. Serious injury and death occur at both sites every year, so heed the warnings. Toilet Bowl is a natural pool about a 10-minute walk along the left bank of the bay. It is connected to the sea by a submerged tunnel through the rock, and the water level rises with the surf and then drops 4-8 ft. almost instantly as the waves "flush" out. It is difficult to exit the water once in the pool, even with help from above, so avoid temptation, especially if you're alone. Witches Brew is a turbulent area on the right side of the bay near its mouth, with a notoriously strong rip current and powerful waves that have swept many unsuspecting beachgoers into the sea. Do not enter the water at either location.

The park has showers, restroom facilities, changing rooms, pontoon wheelchairs for the disabled, a picnic area, and various food cart vendors selling expensive eats. *(By car, take Kalanianaole Hwy. east from Honolulu. The entrance to the parking lot is on the right on top of the hill just past the Foodland shopping center. Parking costs $1, and the lot is usually full by midday. Bus #22 runs between Waikiki and Sea Life Park, and stops right in Hanauma Bay (30min.; every hr.; first departure 8:15am, last return 5:20pm). Most departures throughout the day occur 5min. before the hour, and most returns depart 20min. before the hour. If you can't walk down the steep slope to the beach, you can take a trolley for $1. The park is open and lifeguards are on duty 7am-7pm in summer, 7am-6pm in winter every day except Tu. Admission $3, 12 and under free. A set of mask, fins, and snorkel are available for rent. Rental $6 per day, plus car keys or credit card and a $30 refundable deposit.)*

KOKO HEAD. Koko Head is the mountainous area to the southwest of Hanauma Bay, and should not be confused with Koko Crater (p. 144) several miles down the highway. The 642-foot summit was accessible to hikers via a trail at the top of the entrance road for the Hanauma Bay parking lot until 1998, but the hike is now closed to the public. Determined hikers frequently disobey the signs in order to visit the two craters that make up Koko Head, and to catch a glimpse of the ocean view and radar facilities on the summit.

HALONA BLOWHOLE. About two miles past Hanauma Bay is the Halona Blowhole, a lava tube submerged in the ocean. Passing waves push through the tube and create a geyser-like explosion of sea and sound. The quality of the spectacle depends on surf conditions; some days the water barely bubbles out of the blowhole, other days it shoots high into the sky. Be careful not to lean over it; people have been killed by falling in.

OAHU

To the right of the parking lot is the small, secluded **Halona Cove,** a quiet spot to sunbathe unmolested by the beach-going crowd. There is no easy path down, so be careful as you scramble through the rocks. Just before the blowhole is a stone wall and monument erected by the Honolulu Japanese Casting Club to please the Japanese god of protection, and to honor fishermen who have passed away at sea. *(Located along Kalanianaole Hwy. and the #22 bus route.)*

KOKO CRATER. Koko Crater contains a 60-acre **Botanical Garden** and a **stable** that offers morning horseback-riding lessons as well as pony rides. A two-mile **loop trail** leads visitors through collections of plants from various regions of the world, including the Americas, Hawaii, Madagascar, and Africa. The gardens are a worthwhile stop if you're in the area for the afternoon.

According to Hawaiian legend, the goddess Pele's sister, Kapo, had a detachable flying vagina. Kapo sent the vagina to lure Kamapua'a, the pig god, away from Big Island, because he intended to rape Pele. The ruse was successful, and the crater is allegedly the imprint left by the mystical vagina. *(408 Kealahou St. By car, take Kalanianaole Hwy. east from Honolulu until you reach a stoplight just past Sandy Beach at Kealahou St. Turn left, and then left again onto a dirt road after about a mile at the sign for the Koko Crater. The road leads directly to the stables and garden. The #58 bus runs along Kealahou St. and stops near the dirt road every half hour. Buses to Waikiki run to the left, away from the ocean; buses to Sea Life Park run to the right. ☎ 395-2628. Horseback-riding lessons $40; pony rides $25. Gardens and stables open daily 9am-4pm. Free.)*

SANDY BEACH PARK. The best beach for **bodysurfing** on Oahu, Sandy Beach is a good spot to spend an afternoon whether you're an experienced boarder, or just a fan of watching experienced boarders. The consistently large waves break close to the shore all year long and are better for bodyboards than for surfboards. The beach itself is wide enough to accommodate the sunbathing crowd, and has a reputation for being a lively social center for the island's youth.

Sandy Beach is also among the most dangerous beaches on the island, however. Hanauma Bay may have more drownings, but Sandy has more broken necks and backs by far. Check with the lifeguards at either of the two stations for up-to-date surf information, and be sure to keep an eye out for **red flags,** which indicate dangerous water conditions.

The large grassy area to the left of the park entrance is a popular kite-flying destination, and is sometimes used as a landing strip for hangliders. There are usually a few food stands in the area, and the park has restrooms and showers. *(Sandy Beach is on the #22 bus route on Kalanianaole Hwy., just past the Halona Blowhole.)*

MAKAPU'U POINT. The lighthouse that sits atop the 647-foot Makapu'u Point marks the easternmost point of Oahu and has been in operation for nearly 100 years. From the lighthouse, it is possible (but difficult) to scramble down to the beach below. Such a feat should only be undertaken at low tide, when there is actually something to scramble down to.

A bit farther down the highway on the right is a lookout stop. Both the lookout and the lighthouse have fantastic views of **Manana and Kaohikaipu Islands.** Manana, the larger of the two, means "rabbit," and the island bears the name because it both resembles and is inhabited by rabbits. Kaohikaipu, the smaller island, was declared a bird sanctuary by the state in 1972. *(Makapu'u Point is located about 1½ mi. past Sandy Beach, just before Sea Life Park, on a mile-long dirt road on the right.)*

MAKAPU'U BEACH PARK. Located below Sea Life Park, Makapu'u Beach Park is a favorite hangout of hangliders and surfers. The beach itself is surrounded by dark volcanic rock which contrasts pleasingly with the white sand. Makapu'u isn't all about vistas and pretty surroundings, however. Though the area is usually flat in the summer, in winter the waves range from 6-12 ft., attracting surfers and body-boarders alike. Makapu'u is nearly as infamous as Sandy Beach for broken bones—be on the lookout for **red flags,** which indicate dangerous surf.

SEA LIFE PARK. A pretty standard aquatic-themed amusement park, **Sea Life Park** is expensive and full of children dragging their parents from tank to tank. It makes a good diversion if you're looking for something non-beach-oriented to do with the family—it has enough different parts to keep the kids amused for hours. If you aren't looking to spend your day (and your cash) feeding sea lions and watching dolphins jump through hoops at the **Hawaii Ocean Theater Show,** however, then consider heading elsewhere.

The main attraction of the park is a 300,000-gallon tank full of thousands of species of fish, moray eels, stingrays, and other indigenous reef life in a captive version of the natural habitat you can find just down the beach. A spiral walkway surrounds the tank, providing views of the mock-reef from different depths. The **Stingray Ballet** is among the more palatable of the free events, and the **Hawaiian Monk Seal Center** does good work—the facility houses injured pups who have been rescued by the Coast Guard until they are well enough to be released back into the sea. There are also a slew of additional activities that aren't included with regular admission, including **Sea Trek,** an underwater photo safari in the big reef tank, and **Dolphin Adventures,** a pricey way to play with dolphins in person. *(41-202 Kalanianaole Hwy. ☎ 259-7933; www.sealifeparkhawaii.com. By car, take Kalanianaole Hwy. east from Honolulu (approx. 35min.). The park is on the left just above Makapu'u Beach. Both the #22 and #58 buses run from Waikiki to Sea Life Park (just under an hour, every 30min.). The park also runs an infrequent shuttle service to major Waikiki hotels for $5; ask your concierge if you'd like to arrange one. Sea Trek $89; Dolphin Adventures $129. Park open daily 9:30am-3pm. $24, ages 4-12 $12.)*

WAIMANALO

Waimanalo is quintessentially Hawaiian. The residents of this small town are ethnically and economically diverse, and they go about their daily lives in a characteristically slow-paced fashion. Some keep chickens, others quietly promote Hawaiian independence, and almost everyone is laid-back and relaxed. The rougher neighborhoods add to the town's character, but valuables are best not left unattended here. Waimanalo's main attraction is its stunning ▧**beach,** the longest (and perhaps the best) on Oahu. Backed by the Koolau mountains, Waimanalo Beach stretches nearly five miles in an arc of white sand against the green-azure waters of the Pacific.

■▨ **ORIENTATION AND PRACTICAL INFORMATION.** Waimanalo is located along the **Kalanianaole Hwy.** (Hwy. 72), about 50min. by car or 1hr. on the #57 bus from Honolulu. The town itself sits just beyond the last of the three beach parks listed below, and is spread thinly along the highway for about 2½ mi. There's a **Waimanalo Laundry** next door to KimoZ. (25¢ per 5min. of wash or dry, 65¢ per lb. drop-off service. Open M-Sa 6am-10pm, Su 6am-5pm.)

▨ **ACCOMMODATIONS. Nalo Winds Bed and Breakfast ❸** is located just off Kalanianaole Hwy. in the heart of Waimanalo. If the red VW bus parked out front doesn't clue you in, the organic garden surely will. The friendly owners, Kini and Ana, have a positive outlook on life that's contagious. Some suites have kitchens and screened patios for cooking or socializing. Beach chairs, boogie boards, masks, fins, and snorkels are loaned for free. No A/C. No walk-ins accepted, so call ahead. (☎866-625-6946 or 808-224-6213; www.nalowinds.com. Suites $85-145 per

IN RECENT NEWS

VIVE LA RESISTANCE!

Waimanalo may be a small highway town, but it has a lot of in-your-face local pride. Waimanalo is the epicenter of the Hawaiian Independence Movement on Oahu; many residents fly Hawaiian flags upside down to protest annexation by the US, and each month, a community gathering to celebrate local pride is held in one of the beach parks. The push for secession from the Union is not taken seriously by most locals (nor by their representatives), due to the devastating economic consequences of such a move, but talking about secession is a way for many locals to vent their frustrations with disrespectful tourists and the cultural imperialism of the mainland US. The general sentiment among locals is that the West is the reason that the islands are no longer pristine, and the reason that there are so few ethnic Hawaiians left.

night, $525-1075 per week for 2-6 people.) Appealing to a more mature crowd, **Kom A'ona Inn B&B ❹**, 41-926 Laumilo St., is classier and a bit less funky than Nalo Winds. The gated lawn and garden are lush and well-kept, and the place has a genuine Hawaiian feel. Most of the seven units are located in a clean, upscale house with a shared kitchen and pool table. All have handicapped bathroom access. (☎866-TRIP2HI, 259-8108 or 225-3708; inkeep@aloha.net. Units $110-175.)

🍴 **FOOD.** Locals and tourists alike flock to the window of ◪**Keneke's ❶**, 41-857 Kalanianaole Hwy., a drive-up plate-lunch mecca to sample the divine *kalua* pig and other authentic local eats. The mixed plate ($6.50) could satisfy even the biggest of appetites; the plate lunch ($5.50) and the mini plate ($4.50) are a bit more manageable. Sandwiches are a steal at $3 or less. Keneke proudly supports the local Fear God Power Lifting Team, whose stickers adorn the walls. (☎259-5266. Open daily 9am-5:30pm, but hours vary.) **KimoZ ❷**, 41-1537 Kalanianaole Hwy., is a bit pricier than Keneke's, but the cuisine is also slightly more refined. The Hawaiian Plate ($9) is a good deal, and includes *kalua* pig, beef stew, local *poke* (tuna), lomi salmon, and *poi;* most other entrees around $12. (☎259-8800; fax 259-8192. Open M-Th 8:30am-9pm, F 8:30am-10pm, Sa 7:30am-10pm, Su 10:30am-9pm.)

Mel's Market, 31-1029 Kalanianaole Hwy., is a one-stop market with a wide array of sundries. (☎259-7550. Open M-Sa 8am-8pm, Su 8am-6:30pm.) **Bobby's,** 41-867 Kalanianaole Hwy., is a small grocery store with no sign and the coldest beer in Hawaii, located four doors down from Keneke's. (☎259-5044. Open M-Sa 7am-8:45pm, Su 7am-7:15pm.)

🏖️ **BEACHES AND CAMPING.** Waimanalo Beach is very long, and some parts of it are better than others. The first beach on the right heading into town from Honolulu is **Waimanalo Beach County Park**, easily identifiable by the city of tents alongside the highway. Manana Island peeks around the southern portion of the beach, and the tall ironwood trees complement the beautiful mountains that stand tall on the inland side of the highway. **Camping** here requires a state permit (see p. 84). The snorkeling is decent and the bathroom and shower facilities are adequate, though the area is not as beautiful as other parts of the beach.

Five minutes down the highway toward Waimanalo, the gorgeous ◪**Waimanalo Bay State Recreation Area** is less developed and more secluded than Waimanalo Beach County Park. The beach is wider, and the view more striking, than elsewhere along the bay. Helicopters from the nearby **Bellows Air Force Base** do maneuvers along the beach, sometimes to sunbathers' chagrin. The parking lot is nicknamed "Sherwoods" by the locals, and while there are fewer Robin Hoods frequenting the area today than there were in days past, you should still keep your valuables on your person rather than in your car. The bathroom and shower facilities are clean, and camping requires a state permit. The water is considered the bunny slopes of bodysurfing in the summer, but it picks up significantly in winter, so be careful. The park is open and lifeguards are on duty daily 7:45am-6pm.

Bellows Field Beach County Park, a beach park within the Bellows Air Force Base, sits another 2min. along the highway toward Waimanalo. The beach and campgrounds are open to the general public from noon on Friday until 8am on Monday morning only, and, again, camping requires a state permit. Picnic, restroom, and shower facilities are spartan but neat. The water is relatively calm and safe for swimming all year, and lifeguards are on duty Sa-Su 7:45am-6pm.

WINDWARD OAHU

As its wind-swept name implies, the Windward Coast of Oahu is rough country—rural land along the highway is punctuated by towns and scattered with upturned barrels that house fighting roosters. Winding along Kamehameha Hwy. to the base of the Koolau Mountains, a trip through Windward Oahu provides a scenic cruise from Honolulu to the North Shore through towns such as Lanikai and Laie, and by the well-known Polynesian Cultural Center. **Kailua,** the major tourist destination on the Windward coast, draws visitors with its famous turquoise bay and world-class windsurfing. Close enough to Honolulu to make it a convenient base for exploration, Kailua is an unspoiled community—Paradise without having to prove it. **Kaneohe,** Honolulu's largest suburb on Kailua Bay, is the starting point for sightseeing tours of the Windward and North Shores from Honolulu. The smaller settlements along the Kamehameha Hwy. beckon with isolated charms, from sunny beach to rainy valley, barren oceanscape to rugged mountain vista.

◪ ORIENTATION

Driving directions along the Windward Coast are confusing, to say the least. The first town is **Kailua,** north of Waimanalo. Kailua is just south of **Kaneohe** and the military's Mokapu Peninsula, and is bordered on the east by the windswept Kailua Bay. Three highways zip through here, over the Koolau Mountain Range which separates the Windward Coast from the south shore. These are **H-3, Likelike Hwy.** (Hwy. 63), and scenic **Pali Hwy.** (Hwy. 61). Pali Hwy. is the most direct route from Waikiki, just 15 miles away.

To reach Kailua from the Honolulu Airport, take H-1 West to Exit 1D, H-3 East/Kaneohe. Exit at Mokapu Blvd. and make the third right onto Oneawa St. The street becomes Kailua Rd. after the Kailua town center, eight blocks down from Oneawa St.

From eastbound H-1, take Exit 21A, Pali Hwy., and turn left; from H-1 West take Exit 21B Pali Hwy. and bear right until you merge with the mountain-bound Pali Hwy. (Hwy. 61). After the mountains, Hwy. 61 intersects Hwy. 83, Kamehameha Hwy. (or simply "Kam. Hwy."), which continues west to Kaneohe. Continuing beyond this intersection, Hwy. 61 is called the Kalanianaole Hwy. for 2 mi. until the right-hand junction with Hwy. 72, opposite the Castle Medical Center. Hwy. 72, which heads southeast to Waimanalo, is called the **Kalanianaole Hwy.** from here on.

Continue straight ahead on Hwy. 61, now called **Kailua Rd.** Three miles farther is a complex intersection which marks the center of Kailua town. Left is **Oneawa St.**, and if you drive straight you will be on Kuulei Rd., which ends shortly at Kalaheo Ave. To stay on Kailua Rd., you must turn right at the Kailua town center intersection, and then left at the next intersection ½ mi. away. From the Wanaao Rd. intersection at the blinking yellow traffic light, Kailua Rd. heads straight for the western end of **Kailua Beach Park,** or over the canal on Kawailoa Rd. if you turn right at S. Kalaheo St.

Turning left at Kailua's main intersection onto **N. Kalaheo Ave.** will take you past **Kalama Beach Park** to Kaneohe Marine Corps Base and **Kaneohe Bay Dr.** The right turn onto S. Kalaheo St. will take you to the drainage canal bisecting Kailua Beach Park, with Kawailoa Rd. bridging it.

The **H-3** highway links Pearl Harbor to the **Kaneohe Marine Corps Base** (KMCB), which dominates the Mokapu Peninsula north of Kaneohe town. The **Likelike Hwy.** (Hwy. 63) travels from Honolulu over the Koolau Mts. and through southern Kaneohe, becoming **Rte. 630 (Kaneohe Bay Dr.).** Kaneohe Bay Dr. veers north to KMCB before changing names to **N. Kalaheo Ave.** and heading south into Kailua. Kaneohe's main artery, the **Kamehameha Hwy.** (Hwy. 83), runs north-south through the heart of Kaneohe to Castle Junction, where the Pali Hwy. becomes the Kalanianaole Hwy. The **Kaheliki Hwy.** parallels the Kamehameha Hwy. up the west side of Kaneohe, and is known as Hwy. 83 until its junction with Kamehameha Hwy. north of town. The Kamehameha Hwy. becomes Hwy. 830 through town, reverting to 83 when it absorbs the Kaheliki Hwy. near Kahaluu park. This unified Kamehameha Hwy. contours the winding, scenic Windward coast.

⌐ TRANSPORTATION

Buses: From Ala Moana Shopping Center in Honolulu, #56 and 57 run to **Kailua.** The #55 Circle Island and #65 go to **Kaneohe.** The Circle Island route runs up the Windward Coast's Kamehameha Hwy. and returns to Ala Moana as the #52 via Wahiawa and central Oahu. $1.50, students 75¢.

Car Rental:

Enterprise Kailua, 345 Hahani St. (☎261-4282; fax 261-0037). From Hwy. 61 heading toward Kailua, turn right at the Kailua Center intersection, and turn right at Hahani St. The only car rental in town gives off-season spring and fall weekend specials. Compact $32 per day, CDW $15 per day. Minimum age 21. Under 25 must have full insurance coverage and a major credit card. All cars must be returned to Kailua. Open M-F 8am-6pm, Sa 9am-noon. AmEx/MC/V.

Enterprise Kaneohe, 46-003 Alaloa St. (☎247-2909). Take the Kamehameha Hwy. northbound to Kahuhipa St., and turn right at the light, onto Alaloa St. Compact $33 per day. CDW $18 per day, full coverage $26. Minimum age 21; must have a major credit card. Open M-F 8am-6pm, Sa 9am-noon. AmEx/MC/V.

⃗ PRACTICAL INFORMATION

TOURIST AND FINANCIAL SERVICES

City Halls: Kailua Satellite, 1090 Keolu Dr. (☎261-8575). **Kaneohe Satellite,** 46-024 Kamehameha Hwy. (☎235-4571). **Laie Satellite** mobile bus at 55-510 Kamehameha Hwy. Open Tu 9:30am-2:45pm.

Banks: First Hawaiian Bank Kailua, 705 Kailua Rd. (☎261-3371). Open M-Th 8:30am-4pm, F 8:30am-6pm, Sa 9am-1pm. **City Bank Kaneohe,** 45-1054 Kamehameha Hwy. (☎233-4750). Open M-Th 9am-5:30pm, F 9am-6pm, Sa 9am-noon.

LOCAL SERVICES

Libraries: Kailua Public Library, 239 Kuulei Rd. (☎266-9911), 2 blocks from Kailua town center, next to the police and fire stations. **Internet access** available with a visitor's card ($10). Open M, W, F-Sa 10am-5pm; Tu, Th 1-8pm. **Kaneohe Public Library,** 45-829 Kamehameha Hwy. (☎233-5676), in front of the police station ½ mi. north of Likelike Hwy. Open M, W 10am-8pm; Tu, Th, Sa 10am-5pm; F, Su 1-5pm.

Laundromats: U-Wash and Dry Center Kailua, on Hoolai St. off Kailua Rd. The paradise of the self-service laundromat world—clean and spacious. **Kaneohe Laundromat,** 46-020 Alaloa Rd. (☎247-2360), behind the Windward Mall.

Equipment Rental:

Kailua Sailboards and Kayaks Inc., 130 Kailua Rd. (☎262-2555). Rents kayaks (single $32, double $42 per day), surfboards ($25 per day), sailboards (starting at $39 per day), kiteboards ($25 per day), and bicycles ($25 per day). Lessons also available: private windsurfing lessons $35 per hr. ($49 for 3hr. group lesson, including gear), kitesurfing group introductory lesson $79, private lesson $99. Ask about hiking tours as well. Weekly and half-day rates also available; the $225 Funpak allows you to use any of Kailua Sailboards' water toys for a full week. Open daily 9am-5pm. All major credit cards.

Naish Hawaii, 155a Hamakua Dr. (☎262-6068), is the destination of choice for experienced windsurfers in Kailua. Though they operate as a B&B and vacation rental booking agency, their main business is renting equipment. Beginner boards from $20 for 2hr. rental; boards for beginner through advanced $30-45 per day. Windsurfing lessons for beginners and intermediate-level surfers $55 for 1 person, $75 for 2 including 2hr. equipment rental. Kite board rental $20 per day, beginner lesson $100. Open 9am-5:30pm. All major credit cards.

Aaron's Dive Shop, 307 Hahani St. (☎888-84SCUBA or 262-2333). From Kailua Rd., turn right at the town center intersection and then take the second right onto Hahani St. Aaron's will set you up with scuba gear for $30 per 24hr. plus $8 per tank, or bring you along on one of their daily dive trips ($125 for a 2-tank dive including equipment rental). Open M-F 7am-7pm, Sa 7am-6pm, Su 7am-5pm. All major credit cards.

EMERGENCY AND COMMUNICATIONS

Emergency: ☎911.

Police: Kailua Substation, 219 Kuulei Rd. (☎262-6555). **Kaneohe Substation,** 45-270 Waikalua Rd. (☎247-2166). **Kahuku Substation,** 56-470 Kamehameha Hwy. (☎293-8565).

Medical Services: Braun Urgent Care Kailua, 130 Kailua Rd. Ste. 111 (☎261-4411), in the Kailua Beach shops. Walk-in patients welcome. Open daily 8am-8pm. **Castle Medical Center,** 640 Ulukahiki St. (☎263-5500; emergency services ☎263-5164), at the junction of Hwy. 61 and 72, 1½ mi. south of Kailua. **Straub Kaneohe Family Health Center,** 46-056 Kamehameha Hwy. (☎233-6200), inside the Windward Mall. Walk-in hours daily noon-7:30pm.

Fax Office: Island Printing Centers Kailua, 305 Hahani St. (☎261-8515). Fax and copy rates vary; mailboxes also available ($42 for 3 months).

Internet Access: Kailua Recreation Center, 21 S. Kainalu Dr. (☎266-7652) around the corner from the Kailua Public Library and the police station. Internet access free with registration. Available M, W 2-5pm; Th 11am-2pm; Sa 1-5pm.

Post Offices: Kailua Main Office, 335 Hahani St. (☎266-3996). Last collection M-F 5pm, Sa 4pm. Open M-F 8am-4:30pm, Sa 8am-noon. **Zip Code:** 96734. **Kaneohe Main Office,** 46-036 Kamehameha Hwy. (☎235-1055). Last collection M-F 5:30pm, Sa 4:30pm. Open M-F 8am-4:30pm, Sa 8am-noon. **Zip Code:** 96744. **Kaawa Main Office,** 51-480 Kamehameha Hwy. (☎237-8372). Open M-F 8am-noon and 1-3:45pm, Sa 9:30-11:30am. **Zip Code:** 96730. **Laie Main Office,** 55-510 Kamehameha Hwy. Suite 20 (☎293-0337). Open M-F 9am-3:30pm, Sa 9:30-11:30am. **Zip Code:** 96762.

OAHU

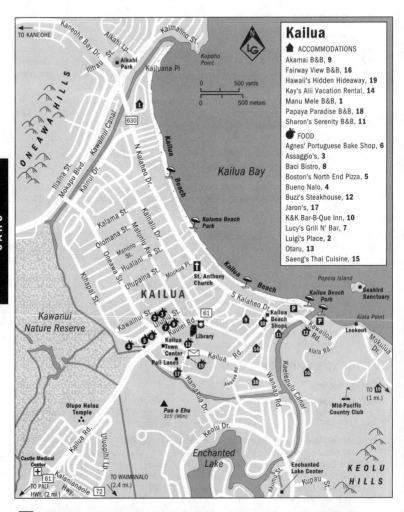

Kailua

🏠 **ACCOMMODATIONS**
Akamai B&B, **9**
Fairway View B&B, **16**
Hawaii's Hidden Hideaway, **19**
Kay's Alii Vacation Rental, **14**
Manu Mele B&B, **1**
Papaya Paradise B&B, **18**
Sharon's Serenity B&B, **11**

🍴 **FOOD**
Agnes' Portuguese Bake Shop, **6**
Assaggio's, **3**
Baci Bistro, **8**
Boston's North End Pizza, **5**
Bueno Nalo, **4**
Buzz's Steakhouse, **12**
Jaron's, **17**
K&K Bar-B-Que Inn, **10**
Lucy's Grill N' Bar, **7**
Luigi's Place, **2**
Otaru, **13**
Saeng's Thai Cuisine, **15**

🔏 ACCOMMODATIONS AND CAMPING

In general, the bed and breakfasts in Kailua fill up weeks or months in advance; it is essential to make reservations as early as possible to ensure availability. Check-in times tend to be as fluid as owners' schedules, and travelers should make arrangements for arrival and departure ahead of time.

BOOKING SERVICES

Many more B&Bs can be found in Kailua and Lanikai, as well as in Kaneohe and the rest of the Windward coast, through booking agencies.

All Islands Bed and Breakfast (☎ 800-542-0344 or 263-2342; fax 263-0308; www.all-Islands.com), takes customized preferences for location, lodging type and travel dates, and matches them with available B&B clients. Their list of clients numbers over 700 from across the islands, including 95 establishments in Kailua alone. Reservations require a 20% deposit for the room and a 3% deposit fee for the booking service, payable by credit card. The room balance must be paid to the B&B where you're staying via whatever payment method they accept. Reserve online or by phone. Open M-F 8am-5pm. AmEx/D/MC/V.

Hawaiian Islands Bed and Breakfast (☎800-258-7895 or 261-7895; fax 262-2181; www.lanikaibb.com) is run by Rick and Nini Maxey, owners of the lovely **Lanikai Bed and Breakfast.** The pair reserves B&B and vacation rentals throughout the islands.

KAILUA

▨ **Hawaii's Hidden Hideaway,** 1369 Mokolea Dr. (☎877-HIDE-AWAY or 262-6560; www.ahawaiibnb.com). Take Kawailoa Rd. and make a left on Alala Rd. at the stop sign. Follow Alala as it changes its name to Aalapapa Dr. Drive 1 mi. on Aalapapa Dr. and turn right onto Mokolea Dr. A basket of fruit and a plate of cookies welcome guests to this dreamy hideaway; Japanese kimonos in the closets, carefully landscaped rock gardens, outdoor beach shower, and an aromatic plumeria tree complete the idyllic aesthetic. Private entrance, bath, lanai, cable TV, telephone, and kitchenette in each unit—all just a block and a half from Lanikai Beach's soft sands. Check-in 3pm. Check-out 10am. 3-night minimum stay. Suites $95-175. No credit cards. ❹

▨ **Akamai Bed and Breakfast,** 172 Kuumele Pl. (☎800-642-5366 or 261-2227; www.akamaibnb.com). Take Kuulei Rd. and turn right after the library onto Kainalu Dr. Make the third left onto Kuukama St., and another left onto Kuumele Pl. Two roomy units with pleasing Hawaiian decor. Each studio has a king-sized bed, private entrance, spotless bathroom, cable TV, radio, phone, full-sized fridge stocked with continental breakfast, and kitchenette with microwave. Take a dip in the large pool on the brick patio behind the units. 3-night minimum stay. No children. Check-in 2pm. Check-out 10am. $85 per couple. No credit cards. ❸

Manu Mele Bed and Breakfast, 153 Kailuana Pl. (☎/fax 262-0016; www.pixi.com/~manumele). Units are immaculate and self-sufficient, each with its own private entrance to the pool and patio, as well as a bath, mini-fridge, microwave, coffee maker, cable TV, ceiling fans, and A/C. Assorted baked goods and fruit comprise the first morning's continental breakfast. Beach access is a 3min. walk down a path that flanks the property. 5min. from Safeway and a few blocks from the #85, 86 and 70 bus stop. 2-night minimum stay. Check-out 11am. Rooms $70-80. No credit cards. ❸

Papaya Paradise Bed and Breakfast, 395 Auwinala Rd. (☎/fax 261-0316; www.kailu-aoahuhawaii.com). From Kailua Rd. continue straight onto Wanaao Rd. Turn right onto Awakea Rd. and make a quick left onto Auwinala Rd. Bob and Jeanette have lovely units furnished in tropical rattan and wicker, each with a private entrance, private bath, A/C, cable TV, and telephone. Guests share a kitchenette with refrigerator and microwave, as well as a pool-side lanai with an amazing view of Olomana and the Koolau Mts. The knowledgeable hosts can tell you all there is to know about Kailua. Boogie boards, snorkels, masks, and beach gear available for loan to guests free of charge. Check-in 3pm. Check-out 11am. 3-night minimum stay. Doubles $85, each additional person $15. No credit cards. ❸

Sharon's Serenity Bed and Breakfast, 127 Kakahiaka St. (☎263-3634; www.sharons-serenity.com). Take Kailua Rd. to Wanaao Rd. and turn left at the blinking yellow light at the canal onto Kakahiaka St. Sharon's relaxed nature is evident in her home, where she prepares a delicious continental breakfast in her own kitchen, in true bed and breakfast fashion. All 3 rooms have full private baths, ceiling fans, TV, and mini-fridge. No children under 8. 3-night minimum stay. Check-in 1pm. Check-out 11am. Varied rooms $70-80. No credit cards. ❸

FROM THE ROAD

A PAT ON THE BACK

In the midst of busting my hump researching Honolulu, I scraped $25 out of my budget by subsisting solely on spam *musubi* and Christy's 99¢ breakfast for 2 days. Money in hand, I hopped on the #57 bus and snagged a window seat (the better to see Olomana and the two turquoise bays that peek from behind him). I alighted 40min. later at Kailua Rd. and Hamakua Dr. and transferred onto the #70 at the same bus stop.

Today I would right the wrongs done by uncomfortable beds in overcrowded Waikiki hotels—I lounged on the secluded sands of Lanikai before busing back to Kailua town for a **$30, 1-hour backrub** from the apprentices at **Massage Professionals.** (407 Uluniu St. ☎266-2468. Open M-F 9am-9pm, Sa-Su 9am-5pm. No credit cards.) Students at the American Institute of Massage Therapy in Kailua, the apprentices are getting their pre-certification training at this richly appointed clinic. Those seeking the pinnacle of massage experiences with a healthy dose of incense can make an appointment with acupuncturist and all-around healer Dr. M. Gloria Martin at **The Wellness Center.** (44-C Kainehe St. ☎261-8036).

For an inexpensive finish to my day, I picked up some fruit at **The Source** (p. 153) and transferred once again, onto the #86, jumping ship at Camp Kokokahi to relive the lonesome glory of summer camp like an aristocrat, with a fully soothed body and a little **Room Service in Paradise** (see p. 153).

—Eric Shearer

Kay's Alii Vacation Rental, 232 Awakea Rd. (☎262-9545; fax 262-6932; www.kaysvacation.com). Heading toward town on Kailua Rd., continue onto Wanaao Rd., then turn left onto Awakea St. Kay's properties are across the street from each other, at 232 and 237 Awakea St., before Aumoe Rd. Rooming options include a bedroom with shared bath and mini kitchenette; a studio with a king-sized bed and trundle, kitchenette, and private bath; a 1-bedroom cottage and 1-bedroom apartment that each sleep up to 4, each with full bath; the 8-person, 4BR house with 2 full baths (one with jacuzzi), full kitchen, and dining and living rooms. All rooms have cable TV, as well as access to BBQ grill and coin-op washer and dryer. A/C in some rooms. 3-night minimum stay. Check-in 4pm (call ahead). Check-out 11am. Bedroom $45, studio $70, cottage $80, house $215. Rates based on double occupancy; each additional person $10. AmEx. ❷/❸

Fairway View Bed and Breakfast, 515 Paumakua Pl. (☎263-6439; www.fairwayviewbnb.com). Take Kawailoa Rd. past Kailua Beach Park toward Lanikai and turn right onto Alala Rd. at the stop sign. From Alala Rd. turn right onto Paumakua Rd. True to its name, you can see the Mid-Pacific Country Club's second fairway from the large windows in the living room of this well-maintained B&B. 2 rooms, 1 with a queen-sized bed and small TV and the other with 2 double beds. Each have a mini-fridge and share a full bathroom. 3-night minimum stay. 2 guests maximum. Check-in 2pm. Check-out 11am. Singles $50, doubles $55. High season singles $60, doubles $65. No credit cards. ❸

KANEOHE AND THE WINDWARD COAST

■ **Camp Kokokahi YWCA,** 45-035 Kaneohe Bay Dr. (☎247-2124; fax 247-2125). The simple single and multi-bunked cabins and communal baths and showers inspire a summer camp feel. A common kitchen, heated lap pool, and full indoor gym with basketball court, ping-pong, foosball, and an outdoor volleyball net satisfy the whole troop. Daily guided hiking tours and kayak rentals ($10) to round out your merit badge, Scout. Check-in Su-M 2:30pm, Tu-Sa 4:30pm. Check-out 11am. Office open Su-M 10am-3pm and Tu-Sa 8:30am-5pm. Reservations recommended at least 1 week in advance. Dorm-style bunk $15. Private single cabin $25, private double $36. MC/V. ❶

Alii Bluffs Windward Bed and Breakfast, 46-251 Ikiiki St. (☎235-1124; fax 236-4877). Take Kamehameha Hwy. through Kaneohe, turn right onto Ipuka St. after King Intermediate School, then take the immediate left onto Ikiiki St. The influences of the house's owners (an artist and a real estate agent) are apparent in the beautiful artwork which graces the interior, as well as the home's choice bay view location. Victorian- ($70, $75 Dec. 15-Jan. 1) and Circus- ($60) themed rooms. Private bath for Victorian room. Bath across the hall for the Circus Room. Breakfast included. Laundry available. All are welcome at this gay-owned and gay-friendly establishment. MC/V. ❸

CAMPING

Permits for camping at the many beach and regional parks along Kamehameha Hwy. in Windward Oahu are available from the state **Department of Parks and Recreation** in Honolulu (see Camping and Outdoors, p. 84), or from a **Satellite City Hall** in the area (see Windward Oahu Practical Information, p. 148). The campsites below are along Kamehameha Hwy.

Malaekahana State Recreation Area, 1 mi. north of the Mormon Temple on the coastal side of Kamehameha Hwy. This popular, isolated camping area features indoor and outdoor shower facilities, picnic areas, and a swimming beach on Laie Bay. See **Beaches,** p. 159, for more information. Reserve permits two Fridays in advance. $5. ❶

Kualoa Regional Park, on Kaneohe Bay off Kamehameha Hwy. Camping Th-Tu. Free. ❶

Ahupua'a 'O Kahana, on Kamehameha Hwy., north of Kaneohe. 10 beach campsites available. See **Hiking,** p. 160, for more information. $5. ❶

Swanzy Beach Park, north of Kualoa on Kamehameha Hwy., beyond Kaaawa Point and beach park. Swanzy beach is not great for swimming, but it is popular among snorkelers. Conveniently located across the highway are the **Kaaawa Main Post Office** and a **7-11.** Camping Th-Tu; make reservations 2 Fridays in advance. Free. ❶

Hauula Beach Park, north of Kaneohe, beyond Kahana Bay on Kamehameha Hwy. The park has restrooms, picnic facilities, and the occasional volleyball game, beach attendance permitting. Camping Th-Tu. Free. ❶

▟ FOOD

Kailua holds a wealth of dining options; compared to it, the trip up the Windward coast from Kaneohe to Turtle Bay is nearly devoid of good restaurants. Nonetheless, Kaneohe has a few gems, and there are a couple of worthwhile stops on a leisurely day's cruise through the rest of the Windward coast.

GROCERY STORES AND MARKETS

The Source, 32 Kainehe St. (☎262-5604), ½ block west of Kailua Rd. A small natural foods store in Kailua. Open M-F 9am-9pm, Sa 9am-6pm, Su 10am-5pm. D/MC/V.

Kalapawai Market, 306 S. Kalaheo Dr. (☎262-4359), at the intersection of Kalaheo Dr. and Kailua Rd., is a convenience store with the closest **ATM** to Kailua Beach Park. Open daily 6am-9pm. MC/V.

Safeway, 200 Hamakua Dr. (☎266-5222). From Kailua at Castle Junction, turn right 1 block before the Kailua center intersection, onto Hamakua Dr. You can't miss the supermarket on the right, at the corner of Hahani St. Open 24hr. AmEx/MC/V. Another **Safeway** is located north of Kailua at 25 Kaneohe Bay Dr., 2 mi. up N. Kalaheo Dr. from the Kuulei St. intersection. As you cross the Kawainui Canal, where N. Kalaheo St. becomes Kaneohe Bay Dr., turn right on Mokapu Blvd. and make an immediate left into the Safeway shopping center parking lot.

Foodland, 108 Hekili St. (☎261-3211), in the Windward City Shopping Center in Kaneohe. Open 24hr.

Room Service in Paradise, 2639 S. King Suite 201 (☎941-3463; fax 942-5494). These saviors of Oahu's hungry, immobile masses charge $4-5 to deliver orders from partici-

IN RECENT NEWS

THE ROAD TO NOWHERE

How are there interstate highways on an island, you ask? Because in addition to interstate transit, the US Interstate Highway System's lesser-known function is defense access. For example, H-3 links Pearl Harbor to Kaneohe Marine Corps Base. It also stands as the most expensive public works project in Hawaii's history.

Envisioned in 1960 as a $250 million, six-lane highway through Moanalua Valley, H-3 was rerouted several times, finally opening 37 years later through Halawa Valley, at a total cost of $1.3 billion for 16.1 mi. of four-lane highway. Many of the delays had to do with environmental concerns, and H-3 was the first public project in Hawaii to file an Environmental Impact Statement. Native Hawaiians considered the project damaging to culturally significant and sacred grounds, pointing to the many accidents and complications during construction as proof that the route was cursed.

Following a series of legal battles which went all the way to the US Supreme Court, the highway was opened on December 12, 1997 with an ancient Hawaiian cleansing ceremony, or *Oli*, performed by the same group of native Hawaiians who had fought the project for years. They wanted to make peace with the highway and cleanse it of curses that might harm Hawaiians who drove on it. Popular among motorists for its impressive views of Kaneohe Bay, H-3 now hosts 30% of the trans-Koolau traffic, a level not expected until 2008. For once, it appears as if H-3 is ahead of schedule.

pating area restaurants in Honolulu and Kailua town. If you're isolated on an idyllic beach far from civilization, fear not—they deliver island-wide for a $10 out-of-area fee and 15% gratuity (mandatory on all in-area orders over $70). Delivery time varies, but is generally up to 1hr. Phone and fax orders daily 9am-10pm. Pick up a menu at restaurants around Honolulu and Kailua town. AmEx/D/MC/V.

KAILUA

Luigi's Place, 442 Ulunui St. (☎263-5678). Heading into Kailua on the Kailua Rd., turn left onto Oneawa St. then right on Ulunui. Semi-hidden Luigi's is across from TCBY, set back from the street. This unassuming restaurant features one outdoor table and an intimate interior in which to savor the masterful Italian-influenced cuisine. Vegetarian and seafood options only; tofu meatballs ($13) and lobster ravioli ($16) are both delicious and come with soup or salad. Appetizers $6.50-7.50. BYOB, $4 corkage fee. Reservations recommended F-Sa. Open Tu-Sa 5:30-9:30pm. MC/V. ❸

Buzz's Steakhouse, 413 Kawailoa Rd. Take Kailua Rd. all the way to Kailua Beach Park and turn right onto S. Kalaheo; Buzz's parking lot is on the right after the bridge. People *still* buzz about the Clintons' unexpected drop-in visit in 1994; a plaque on the lanai commemorates the event. Locals flock to the all-you-can-eat salad bar that includes pickled Maui onions, avocados, pineapple, spinach, bacon, tofu, pickled watermelon, and fresh-baked bread ($9). Salad bar and 10 oz. top sirloin $18. $9 minimum order. Reservations recommended. Open daily 11am-4pm and 5-10pm. No credit cards. ❸

Agnes' Portuguese Bake Shop, 46 Hoolai St. (☎262-5367), across the street from Boston's North End Pizza. Specialty baked goods and desserts served in an elegant cafe. Call 15min. ahead for fresh *malasadas*—divine, Portuguese-style doughnuts (55¢ each, $5.40 per dozen). Open Tu-Su 6am-6pm. ❶

Lucy's Grill N' Bar, 33 Aulike St. (☎230-8188). Aulike is the first left past the town center, approaching Kailua from the south. Lucy's serves gourmet pupus (blackened *ahi sashimi* with sweet and spicy mustard $9), inexpensive pizzas ($8-11), and grill favorites with gumption (*kiawe*-broiled baby back ribs with Mongolian BBQ sauce $16). All entrees come with a starch and vegetable. Reservations recommended 6-7:30pm. Open nightly 5-10pm. MC/V. ❷/❸

Baci Bistro, 30 Aulike St. (☎262-7555), across the street from Lucy's. Emphasizing Old World know-how with authentic ingredients, Baci Bistro has earned its reputation as Kailua's best Italian restaurant. Fettuccine *al quattro formaggio* with parmesan, pecorino, mozzarella and emmenthal cheeses, $8.50. *Saltimbocca di vitello,* layers of veal, mozzarella, and prosciutto sauteed in a wine and demi-glace, $19. Panini sandwiches start at $5.50. Wine by the glass $5.50-8.50. Reservations strongly recommended. Open M-F 11am-2pm and 5:30-10:30pm. AmEx/MC/V. ❸

Otaru, 572 Kailua Rd. (☎263-4482). Otaru is known for its excellent Pacific Rim and Japanese-style cuisine. Sample the teriyaki and tempura with *tsukemono, miso* soup, and salad ($16) or the live Maine lobster and *sashimi* ($32). A la carte sushi $5-7. Sake $4-13. Open M-F 11am-2pm and 5-9:30pm. All major credit cards. ❺

Jaron's, 201A Hamakua Dr. (☎261-4600). Hamakua Dr. is the last right from the Kailua town intersection, heading north on Kailua Rd. An excellent restaurant and popular Kailua nightlife spot, Jaron's tweaks typical local seafood offerings (blackened *ahi* Caesar salad $12). The down-home bacon cheeseburger and his perky cousin, the pepper jack avocado burger, both ring in at $10. Live Hawaiian Contemporary music soothes a local crowd 8:30pm-midnight, and everything from reggae to hip hop plays F and Sa 10pm-1:30am. Happy Hour daily 4-6pm (drinks $5.50). 21+ after 10pm. Open M-Sa 11am-10pm, Su 9am-2pm and 4-10pm. D/MC/V. ❸

Assaggio's, 354 Uluniu St. (☎261-2772). A premier establishment among Kailua's many Italian eateries, Assaggio's boasts an eager staff and a menu full of typical and unexpected Italian dishes. The restaurant is well-known for its caesar salad, prepared table-side ($6), and huge martinis ($4.50). Seafood prices can be high ($10-19), but the average entree is $14-15. Hot homemade bread, free in a bottomless basket, is reason enough to head to Assaggio. Wine $5-6.50 by glass. AmEx/D/DC/MC/V. ❸

Saeng's Thai Cuisine, 315 Hahani St. (☎263-9727). Head toward the beach on Kailua Rd. from the Kailua town center intersection and turn right onto Hahani St. Fine Thai selections at budget prices. Spicy Evil Prince (beef, chicken or pork) $7.50. Seafood curry $10. Plenty of vegetarian options as well (Masman tofu, sauteed in Thai curry with peanuts, potatoes, onion, and coconut milk $7). Open M-F 11am-2pm and 5-9:30pm, Sa-Su 5-9:30pm. AmEx/MC/V. ❷

Boston's North End Pizza, 29 Hoolai St. (☎263-7757). Hoolai St. is the last left on Kailua-bound Kailua Rd. before Oneawa St. The huge 19-inch pizza pies weigh 3 lb., and that's just the plain variety ($13.25). Add a few toppings (including anchovy, green peppers, pepperoni, ham, and, of course, pineapple) and you have a fold-it-in-half-or-die slice of pizza paradise, which maximizes the value-volume curve at $3.25+ per huge slice. Open Su-Th 11am-8pm, F-Sa 11am-9pm. No credit cards. ❶

Bueno Nalo, 20 Kainehe St. (☎263-1999). As you come into Kailua from the south, turn left onto Kainehe St. after the Kawainui Channel, two blocks before the Kailua town center. Owner Andy and his family have a taste for waves as well as good Mexican food, and the midday meal runs on a laid-back schedule dictated by the quality of the day's wave action. They're always available for a post-surf dinner, however (6-9pm). Their signature Best Chimichanga Ever, $10. Live music has the joint absolutely rocking on Taco Tuesdays 8pm-1am, with 50¢ mini-tacos, $2 tequila shots, and Coronas ($6). Live rock bands Sa 8pm-1am. Open roughly Su-M 6-9pm, Tu 6pm-2am, W-F 6am-9pm (or until the crowd leaves), Sa 6pm-2am. ❷

K & K Bar-B-Que Inn, 130 Kailua Rd. #102A (☎262-2272), in the Kailua Beach Shops. Fast local-style grinds, with breakfast 9-11am ($3.15-4), affordable sandwiches all day (BBQ cheeseburger $1.65), and the obligatory plate lunch in mini ($3.75-4.25) and regular ($5-6.15) sizes. Excellent Chinese specialties and spicy fried chicken wings (12 for $5.50). Open M-Sa 9am-9pm, Su 9am-4pm. No credit cards. ❶

KANEOHE AND THE WINDWARD COAST

⬛ Taco 1, at the intersection of Kamehameha Hwy. and Wailehua Rd., beyond where Kaheliki Hwy. joins Kamehameha Hwy. Taco 1's small kitchen does a brisk breakfast business with locals who start the day with satiating breakfast burritos, flour tortillas wrapped around egg, potato, cheese, salsa, and choice of ham, spam, or bacon ($2.40). Tacos are $1 until 11am. ❶

Pah Ke's, 46-018 Kamehameha Hwy. (☎235-4505). Recently renovated, Pah Ke's richly detailed dragon decor is the perfect setting for their superb Chinese food. The extensive menu includes black pepper steak sizzling platter ($9), braised black mushrooms with vegetables ($7), and Hong Kong-style fried chicken ($6). $3.50 plate lunch special M-F 10:30am-3pm. Open daily 10:30am-9pm. MC/V. ❷

Masa and Joyce, 45-582 Kamehameha Hwy. (☎235-6129), in Kaneohe. Kaneohe locals crowd this haven of Hawaiian favorites. Send your taste buds on an island marathon with the Hawaiian Plate's *poi* or rice, chicken or pork *lau lau, kalua* pork, chicken long rice, *lomi lomi* salmon, and *shoyu poke* for only $7.50. Plate lunch $5.50 (locals favor the *kalua* pig and cabbage). Everything is made to order, so allow 15min. or call ahead. Open M, W-F 9am-6pm; Sa 9am-4pm; Su 9am-2pm. MC/V. ❶

Crouching Lion Inn, 51-666 Kamehameha Hwy. (☎237-8511). The classiest place to eat on the Windward side before Kaneohe, the Lion feeds famished road trippers with a gourmet bacon cheeseburger or mahi mahi melt (both $8.50) for lunch. Dinner brings out the superior house specialty: *kalua* pork with sweet steamed cabbage and *poi* bread pudding ($15). Craving mainland cuisine? You can't go wrong with the New York steak and lobster ($25). Open daily 11am-4pm and 5-9pm. AmEx/D/DC/MC/V. ❹

Kim Chee, #1 46-010 Kamehameha Hwy. (☎235-5560), next to Pah Ke's. Kim Chee's Korean BBQ has it all—*kalbi* beef ($14), fish *jun* ($8.50), and BBQ chicken ($7). Adventurers can try a combination plate ($6.75-7.75). Open daily 7am-9pm. MC/V. ❷

Kin Wah Chop Suey, 45-588 Kamehameha Hwy. (☎247-4812), on northbound Kamehameha Hwy. in Kaneohe; turn left onto Hualukini Pl. just before the Windward City Shopping Mall. A casual sit-down Chinese restaurant specializing in chow mein (*gon* lo mein $4.75, chicken and lobster chow mein $8.75). The best bargains are the special plates (beef with broccoli, *gon* lo mein, lemon chicken, crispy won ton, and rice $5). Open daily 10am-9pm. AmEx/D/DC/MC/V. ❶

⊙ SIGHTS

HOOMALUHIA BOTANICAL GARDEN. This botanical garden encompasses 400 acres of plants, trees, and flowers, all organized by world geography—there are plants from the Philippines, Hawaii, Africa, Sri Lanka and India, Polynesia, Melanesia, Malaysia, and South America. Visitors to the gardens can hike and horseback ride along the many trails, or **camp** in designated areas. Camping permits are available at the Satellite City Halls throughout the Windward Coast (see **Practical Information,** p. 148). Restrooms and showers are spread throughout the park, as are fire pits, picnic tables and parking. Keep in mind that this is the Windward side, and campers should expect moist to extremely wet conditions in the rainforest-like setting. (*Driving northbound on Kamehameha Hwy., turn left onto Kualukini Pl. at the Aloha Gas Station just before Kaneohe's Windward City Shopping Mall. Alternatively, take TheBus #55 or 56 to this junction. Continue on Kualukini Pl., following the frequent signs. The garden is 1 mi. from Kamehameha Hwy.; the entrance is by the security shack. Gates open 9am-4pm, after which all cars staying in the park must be registered. The Visitor Center is just beyond the entrance. ☎233-7323. Open M-Sa 9am-4pm. Free.*)

VALLEY OF THE TEMPLES. A Christian church and a Buddhist temple on the grounds honor the followers of both religions who are buried in this unique, beautiful cemetery. Byodo-In, the Buddhist temple, is a perfect replica of the 900-year-old temple in Uji, Japan, which is built around an enormous statue of the Buddha. The ring of the temple's 3-ton brass bell echoes over the *koi*-filled pools and tranquil groves of the grounds, which are home to a number of peacocks. *(North of Kaneohe on Kahekili Hwy.; turn left on Valley of the Temples Dr. Open daily 8am-4:30pm. Entrance fee $2.)*

QUEEN EMMA SUMMER PALACE. Victorian treasures and memorabilia of the Hawaiian monarchy are housed here, in the former retreat of Kamehameha IV's cosmopolitan Queen. *(2913 Pali Hwy. ☎ 595-3167. Open daily 9am-4pm. $5, children free.)*

NU'UANU PALI LOOKOUT. As you creep up the Nu'uanu side of the Koolau Mt., imagine King Kamehameha's onslaught of Big Island warriors, aided by two Western canons, savagely driving Oahu's warriors up the *pali* ("cliffs"), finally forcing them over the 980-foot drop. The moment was a decisive victory in Kamehameha's campaign to unite the islands, completed 15 years later in 1810. This is the site of the Battle of the Nu'uanu Pali's dramatic finish, and where rural legend claims the wind is strong enough to knock a man from the cliffs and then blow him right back up. Apparently, the latter did not hold true for the unfortunate warriors from Oahu. The vista spans the Windward coast, beginning at the Koolau Mountain crater, the eroded remains of which now lie under Kailua, Kaneohe, and the Pacific.

Early improvements to the passage over the Nu'uanu Pali were made around 1825, so that wood for the Kawaiahao Church in distant Honolulu could be brought over from Kaneohe. During the 1830s and 40s, missionaries constructed steep stairs, and it is believed that the opening line to Liliuokalani's song *Aloha 'Oe (Ha'aheo ka ua i na pali*, or "proudly by the rain of the cliff") was composed as she descended the path on horseback. The first carriage road was built in 1898 after the overthrow of the monarchy. Jack London wrote of it in 1917, "we coasted the intricate curves of the road that is railed and reinforced with masonry, fairly hanging to a stark wall for the best part of two miles." The passage is easier now, thanks to the completion of tunnels bored through the mountain, the first of which was completed in 1957.

The tunnels exit immediately below the Pali Lookout, affording drivers the same sweeping bay view; if you're heading back to Honolulu from the Windward side, there is a roadside scenic overlook on the right as the highway begins to curve to the left to enter the tunnels. Coming from Honolulu to Kailua, there is a marked scenic overlook with excellent photographic opportunities, as well as parking for the **Maunawili Trail** (see p. 161), just after the hairpin turn. The Pali lookout has informative placards and plenty of parking. *(North of Honolulu on the Pali Hwy. Open daily 9am-4pm. Don't leave valuables in your car.)*

THE POLYNESIAN CULTURAL CENTER. Equal parts cultural exhibit and amusement park, this mammoth tourist attraction employs an army of native and Polynesian performers, artisans, cooks and other cultural conservators to display the rich traditions of Polynesian cultures. The islands of Tonga, Fiji, Tahiti, Samoa, Aotearoa (New Zealand), Marquesas, and Hawaii all have villages with surprisingly authentic and intriguing performances—see real Tahitian hula, or learn how Samoans start a fire with sticks, open coconuts with their bare hands, and climb palm trees of dizzying heights. There's an IMAX screen, canoe rides, free tram tours of Laie town, a nighttime spectacular, and much more, all accessible depending on the variety of high-priced tickets purchased. *(55-370 Kamehameha Hwy. in Laie; you can't miss the 12-foot wooden tiki statues that frown over the roadside just before the parking lot. ☎ 877-722-1411; www.polynesia.com. Transportation can be arranged from around the island by calling ☎ 800-367-7060. Open M-Sa 12:30-9pm; island villages open 1pm. $54-165, children ages 5-11 $37-115. All major credit cards.)*

THE MORMON TEMPLE. Truly a sight to behold, this was the first Mormon temple built outside the continental US. The temple, built of crushed volcanic rock and coral, was dedicated on November 27, 1919 and sits on the 6000-acre plantation

IN RECENT NEWS

IDENTITY CRISIS

Announcements in the summer of 2002 that The Rock (über-popular wrestler-turned-actor) would play Hawaii's adored King Kamehameha in an upcoming Hollywood film made headlines and caused state-wide out-cries among native Hawaiians. The Rock (a.k.a. Dwayne Johnson) was born in California to a Samoan mother and African-Canadian father, and was a high school and college football star before joining the pro wrestling circuit.

The protests against The Rock's potential portrayal of King Kame-hameha have been voiced most loudly by native Hawaiian political and cultural organizations. These opponents have expressed fears that the conspicuously flamboyant star will deliver a shallow, inaccurate portrayal of the king. More important, however, are the questions which have arisen regarding the propriety of having Hawaiian Kamehameha played by a man of Samoan descent. The controversy sheds light on the complex definition of what it means to be Hawaiian in Hawaii. Living in the state does not necessarily make one a Hawaiian, but neither does being born there of Polynesian ancestry.

The term "local" tends to mean someone who knows the islands through living there, though they are not necessarily current residents (there are many locals living on the mainland, for instance). However, having lived in Hawaii for some time does not necessarily make one a local, but simply a resident.

purchased in 1865 by The Church of Jesus Christ of Latter-day Saints. Beyond the temple, the 11-acre site is comprised of well-manicured formal gardens and a Visitor Center with a 10-foot marble replica of Thorvaldsen's *Christus.* The Center's guided tours explain the saints' beliefs with obvious but unobtrusive missionary overtones. *(55-645 Naniloa Loop. ☎ 293-9297. A tram line runs here from The Polynesian Cultural Center, through historic Laie (every 20min. 1-7pm, free). By car, turn left onto Hale La'a Blvd., the second street after the Laie Shopping Center. Open daily 9am-8pm. Free.)*

KUALOA RANCH AND REGIONAL PARK. The **Kualoa Ranch,** a privately owned 4000-acre working cattle ranch-turned-tourist attraction, stretches up Ka'awa Valley. The establishment gives visitors the chance to play cowboy with horseback riding ($42); those not so fond of animals can hop on an iron steed and cruise around Kualoa's many off-road trails in an ATV ($42). Package deals include transportation from Waikiki, lunch, and access to Kualoa's private Secret Island Beach (where you can kayak, canoe or jet ski), as well as one adventure activity (e.g. horseback or ATV riding) for $69. Nearby **Kualoa Regional Park,** on the coastal side of the highway south of the ranch entrance, is a peaceful grassy flat leading to a narrow beach. From here you can see Chinaman's Hat, an offshore island and Windward landmark named for its tapering, peaked shape. **Kualoa Point,** at the extreme end of the park, marks the northern edge of Kaneohe Bay. *(49-560 Kamehameha Hwy. ☎ 237-7321.The main entrance to the ranch is on the mauka side of Kamehameha Hwy., north of Kualoa Regional Park. Open M-F 9:45am-3:15pm. MC/V. For information on camping at Kualoa Regional Park, see Camping, p. 150.)*

GARDENS. The serene tropical garden of **The Gallery and Gardens** includes six rooms of excellent Hawaiian art and rare flowers such as Queen Emma lilies and the Chinese cinnamon tree. The gallery is located on an affluent hillside a short drive up Wailehua Rd., which stands in stark contrast to the rougher highway side areas nearer to the coast. *(47-754 Lamaula Rd. Turn left on Lamaula Rd. from Kamehameha Hwy. northbound and look for the signs on the left. ☎ 239-8146; www.galleryandgardens.com. Open Sa-M 10am-5pm or by appointment. Free.)* Turn left onto Pulama Rd., another 0.8 mi. up Kamehameha Hwy., and follow the signs to **Senator Fong's Plantation and Gardens.** A popular site for local weddings, receptions, and celebratory luaus, the gardens also run a narrated tram-line tour across the 725 acres of lush valleys and plateaus. *(47-285 Pulama Rd. ☎ 239-6775. Open daily 10am-4pm. Tours depart 10:30, 11:30am, 1, 2, and 3pm.*

$10, seniors 65+ $8, children ages 5-12 $6. Hawaiian lei class $6.50. AmEx/MC/V.)

ULUPO HEIAU. This sacred heiau is set on a peaceful plateau of lava rocks beside a shady grove with benches and a few placards. Heiaus were traditionally built at the orders of kahunas to ensure success in war and agricultural and aqua cultural fertility; from this heiau the *ali'i* of the political and religious center in Kailua could survey his holdings at Kawainui. The holdings became a *taro* patch following the abolition of the native religion in 1819. Chinese buyers converted the same land into a rice paddy in the late 1800s, but it had been abandoned as marshland by 1920. Thick growth conceals the bottom of the morass, which is home to numerous endangered native waterfowl. *(Near Kailua. Turn right onto Uluoa St., from Kailua toward Pali Hwy., and take the first right onto Manu Aloha and drive to the end of the block. Park behind the Windward YMCA and then walk around it to the heiau. Call the Oahu District division of the Department of Parks and Recreation for more info, ☎ 587-0300.)*

☑ BEACHES

KAILUA BEACH. Though proclaiming a particular beach the nation's best is as subjective as naming its most beautiful woman, the delicately curving neck of white sands around Kailua Bay's splendid waters pleads a strong case. The winds in Kailua Bay harken from nearly all directions, making the bay the best **windsport** area on Oahu, especially during the winter. Spectators gather to gape at the expert **windsurfers** and **kiteboarders** who careen over the whipped-up waves. **Kayakers** also brave the surf, frequently crossing to the State Bird Sanctuary on **Mokulua Islands** offshore. There are parking lots (which fill up early on weekends), bathrooms, showers, a small craft storage building, and, on the eastern end, a boat ramp in **Kailua Beach Park.** On the secluded northern half of Kailua Beach lies the grassy marsh of **Kalama Beach Park.** The virgin sand here has fewer visitors than the beach park, and the choppier waves are free of the watersport traffic farther south. Kalama is a good learning spot for novice **boogie boarders** and **body surfers.** Beach facilities include a restroom, showers, and picnic tables. *(Take the Lanikai-bound bus #70 from Kailua town center. By car, stay on Kailua Rd. through Kailua town to S. Kalaheo Dr., and turn right. S. Kalaheo will become Kawailoa Rd. to cross the drainage canal, and one of the parking lots is on the left immediately before the drainage canal. To reach Kalama Beach park, turn left on N. Kalaheo Dr. from Kuulei Rd.; the parking lot is on the right, before Kapaa St.)*

"Local," as opposed to *haole*, means Hawaiian (i.e. native Hawaiian). Hawaiian can mean "born in the state of Hawaii," but locally it indicates "of native Hawaiian racial descent." The latter requires a more precise clarification of Polynesian racial and Hawaiian historical descent. Yet another phrase, *kama'aina* (meaning "child of the soil") can indicate someone who is either native born, or a long-time resident of the islands. The issue of Hawaiian identity made headlines once again in the summer of 2002 when Kamehameha Schools admitted a student of non-Hawaiian racial lineage, to the dismay of many native Hawaiians. (See **The Kamehameha One,** p. 101.)

LANIKAI BEACH. Residential **Lanikai** is just around Alala Pt. from Kailua Beach Park, on the utterly romantic Lanikai Beach. You can live out your beachside cottage fantasies here in a warm, wealthy community comfortably crowded between the siren song of the beach and the Keolu Hills, which crown Lanikai's own little side of Oahu. Public beach access to these secluded sands is on Mokulua Dr. You may park streetside, but do not obstruct the bus stops (bus #70 makes a loop around Lanikai) or the bike path. *(See directions for Kailua Beach, above.)*

MALAEKAHANA STATE RECREATION AREA. This popular, isolated **camping** area (see p. 153) features indoor and outdoor shower facilities, picnic areas, and a **beach** on Laie Bay that is safe for swimming. Studded with shady ironwood trees, the narrow beach is perfect for a leisurely stroll, and the mellow waves make good training grounds for novice bodysurfers. **Goat Island** is a state bird sanctuary just offshore beyond Kalanai Point. Kamehameha Hwy. leaves the coast north of Malaekahana, passing through the faded environs of Kahuku, with its dilapidated sugar mill, the last stop before Turtle Bay and the North Shore. *(Entrance to the park 1 mi. north of the Mormon Temple on the coastal side of Kamehameha Hwy.)*

CROUCHING LION, HIDDEN DEITY
A mile north of Swanzy Beach Park on Kamehameha Hwy., before Ahupua'a 'O Kahaha (see below), is the **Crouching Lion Inn** (see **Food**, p. 156), named for the big, cat-shaped rock formation that towers above it. According to Hawaiian legend, the rock is Kauhi, a watchman from distant Kahiki, who was sent here to be the "Watchtower of Heaven."

◨ HIKING

AHUPUA'A 'O KAHANA. Formerly Kahana Valley State Park, Ahupua'a 'O Kahana is around the corner from Kahana Bay as you drive northward on Kamehameha Hwy. It is Hawaii's only publicly owned *ahupua'a*, an ancient Hawaiian land access system designed to fully share all available resources from sea to beach, valley to *pali*. The intention of reclaiming the *ahupua'a* is to foster native Hawaiian cultural traditions, but the piles of rubbish speak more of the passerby than any particular cultural initiative. The **Kapaeleele Koa and Keaniani Lookout Trail** (1 mi. round-trip. Trailhead: Orientation Center. Level: easy.) loops around the front flank of the park through two cultural sites to stunning views of the bay. The **Nakoa Trail** (5 mi. round-trip. Trailhead: Orientation Center, or follow the main road up the valley to the trailhead sign. Level: easy.) meanders into the valley's rainforest through koa trees (hence the name), passing Kahana Stream twice (mountain stream swimming enthusiasts take note). Hungry hikers can pick fruit, including plenty of guava, when it's in season. Wet conditions are treacherous regardless of the difficulty of the terrain, and precaution is necessary. Also, be aware that the lands immediately adjacent to the park are hunting grounds; consult the Orientation Center (☎237-7766), on the right by the second parking area on the main road. *(On Kamehameha Hwy., north of Kaneohe. There are 10 beach campsites available at the park; $5 permits are available from the State Parks office ☎587-0300.)*

HAUULA. The **Maakua Ridge Trail** and **Hauula Loop Trail** (2½ mi. Trailhead: Hauula Homestead Rd., across from **Hauula Beach Park** (see **Camping**, p. 153). Level: easy.) The trail comes to a fork initially; take the right fork, climbing up the ridge to cross Waipilopilo Gulch. This path then turns back toward the ocean, overlooking Kipapau Valley, and loops to rejoin the beginning part of the trail. The initial trail is easy, and well-suited for families. The Maakua Ridge Trail begins in a *hau* forest on the left side of the access road, beyond the Hauula Loop Trailhead. After a stream crossing, there is a switchback to a ridge-top shelter with benches overlooking seaside Hauula. The loop begins here, and you may proceed in either direction to rise 800 ft. in moderate to difficult terrain. Both trails are accessible for mountain bikers, so use caution when heading out on foot. *(By car from Kamehameha Hwy. northbound, take Hauula Homestead Rd., which curves sharply to the left. Continue straight on the access road, and park roadside before the cable gate. Hauula Loop Trail begins on the right, just beyond the hunter/hiker check-in station.)*

KAIWA RIDGE TRAIL. (2 mi. round-trip. Trailhead: Kaelepulu Dr. near Lanikai. Level: moderate.) Also known to locals as "Pillboxes," this moderately difficult hike climbs up the ridge behind Lanikai (see **Beaches**, p. 159) to WWII army bunkers overlooking the beach. From the top, 600 ft. up, you can see Molokai, Lanai and, on a superbly clear day, Maui. Despite its popularity, the trail receives minimal maintenance, and hikers are advised to use caution and not to climb the bunkers. You may either return the way you came up, or continue along the trail to loop back around to Mokolea Dr. *(Take Aalapapa Dr. into Lanikai and then take a right on Kaelepulu Dr. At the Mid-Pacific Country Club, park in the turnout on the right side of the street. The dirt trailhead is across the street, to the left of the chainlink fence.)*

MAUNAWILI DITCH TRAIL. (2¾ mi. Trailhead: Waikaupanaha St. Level: easy.) This equestrian, bike, and hiking trail rises an easy 200 ft. and ends at the Waimanalo side of the **Maunawili Trail.** *(Driving north from Waimanalo on the Kalanianaole Hwy., turn left onto Kumuhau St. about 0.6 mi north of the Waimanalo Shopping Center. Turn right on Waikaupanaha St. and park near the fence and gate on the right, after Mahiku Pl. at the bend in the road. Proceed through the fence, mauka along the dirt road.)*

MAUNAWILI TRAIL. (10 mi. round-trip. Trailhead: Pali Hwy. Elevation change: 500 ft. Level: moderate.) The terrain of the Maunawili ("twisted mountain") Trail varies from wet, overgrown gulches to open forest canopies as it traverses the Windward base of the Koolau Mountain Range. The voyage among koa, lobelia, 'ohia, naupaka, ti, mountain apple trees and other vegetation ends with transcendent views of Olomana, the Koolaupoko watershed and, at the south end, Waimanalo. *(Driving on Pali Hwy. to Kailua from Honolulu, as you come out of the tunnels, turn into the parking area marked "Scenic Overlook," just after the hairpin turn on the right. The trailhead is adjacent to this parking area.)*

MAUNAWILI FALLS TRAIL. (1¼ mi. Trailhead: Maunawili Rd. Level: moderate.) The wet and muddy falls trail crosses the Maunawili stream frequently, passing through mountain apple and coffee trees. There is a stair descent at the last stream crossing to reach the payoff: a cool, deep pool and a short cascading waterfall. Look but don't drink—the water carries biological impurities. Bring your own. *(Driving toward Kailua on the Pali Hwy., continue through Castle Junction and past Kapa'a Quarry Rd. The next intersection on the right is Auloa Rd.; the road splits almost immediately, so be sure to take the left fork, Maunawili Rd. Follow this road until it ends in a residential neighborhood, and look for the trailhead signs. Make sure to park on the right. Do not leave valuables in your car.)*

NORTH SHORE

With only 18,000 residents, the North Shore is relatively quiet, and remains rural and undeveloped in places. The area has long been a place for city dwellers to escape urban life, though the surf industry certainly attracts its share of visitors and traffic these days. **Haleiwa** (p. 164) is the center of life on the North Shore, with first-rate eateries, shops, and galleries, as well as plenty of places to stock up on surf gear. There is one spectacular beach after another northwest of Haleiwa, from **Waimea** to **Sunset Beach**; while some are quite popular for surfing and sunning, others are

THE BIG SPLURGE

TURTLE BAY RESORT

A jewel of a resort on the northern-most shore of Oahu, Turtle Bay boasts a garland of emerald golf courses. The resort commands a mesmerizing view of bayside sunsets, as it rests along the rural coastline between two tranquil beaches. Its first-class amenities include a recently renovated pool, horseback riding, golf, and tennis. Fine dining at The Cove restaurant completes the package; the helipad sends it into excess. Though the resort is secluded on the North Shore of Oahu, Honolulu is only an hour's drive away. Specialty tropical drinks ($6) at the Hang Ten Bar (well drinks $5.75, beer $4-5.50; open daily 11am-11pm) go down well with the sun. *(57-091 Kamehameha Hwy. ☎ 800-203-3650 or 293-8811; fax 293-9147; www.turtlebayhotel.com. Check-in 3pm. Check-out 11am. 24hr. reception. Standard rooms for 2-4 $139-179; suites $500+. All major credit cards.)*

astonishingly empty. Past Sunset Beach, the hotel and golf course at **Turtle Bay** (see p. 162) is the area's sole resort, and is situated amid the corn fields and shrimp farms of **Kahuku,** the shore's northernmost village.

To reach the North Shore by car, take H-1 from Honolulu to the end of H-2, then follow Rte. 803 or Hwy. 99. Kamehameha Hwy. (Hwy. 83) is the main road that runs along the coast through each town from Haleiwa to Kahuku, and down the Windward Coast. The North Shore is also served by TheBus #52, which runs from Honolulu via Wahiawa to Haleiwa, and then up the coast on Kamehameha Hwy. to Turtle Bay. TheBus #76 runs between Haleiwa and Waialua along Farrington Hwy.

WAIALUA AND MOKULE'IA

Located at the base of the Waianae Range on the western stretch of the North Shore, Waialua was originally a port for the sandalwood trade. Until recently, Waialua's economy was fueled by the sugar cane industry, but the town has lacked stable agricultural production since the mill closed in 1997. Currently, the town is trying its hand at banana and asparagus production. Primarily a residential and agricultural community, Waialua is of little interest to travelers. The unpopulated beaches of Mokule'ia to the west, however, have a few campsites and promise hours of thrills for kitesurfers (see **Kiteboarding to Extremes,** p. 166).

◧▱ ORIENTATION AND PRACTICAL INFO. The small commercial center of **Waialua** sits at the crossroads of **Kealohanui** and **Goodale Rd.** To reach **Mokule'ia** from Waialua, drive *mauka* on Goodale Rd. and turn right onto **Farrington Hwy.,** which ends just before Ka'ena Point. TheBus **#76** connects Haleiwa and Waialua.

The Waialua **library** is located at 67-068 Kealohanui St. (☎637-8286. Open Tu-Th 9am-6pm, F 9am-5pm, Sa 9am-2pm.) The town also has a gas station, and a small shopping center with a Bikram yoga studio, Chinese take-out, and a convenience store. The Waialua **post office,** 67-079 Nauahi St., is open M-F 9am-4pm and Sa 9-11am. **Zip Code:** 96791.

▛ ACCOMMODATIONS AND CAMPING. There are no hotels or substantial development of any kind in the area—in fact, Mokule'ia's beaches may be the last undeveloped beaches on Oahu. There are only two choices in Mokule'ia for camping and budget accommodations. The first, and least expensive, option is **Camp Mokule'ia ❶,** 68-729 Farrington Hwy. The site, owned by an Episcopal Church, is frequently booked by groups for conferences, but it's

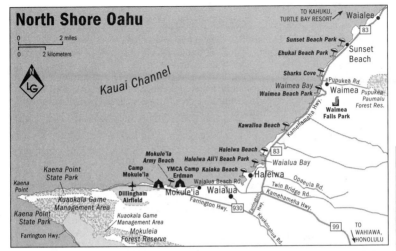

North Shore Oahu

TO KAHUKU, TURTLE BAY RESORT
Waialee
83
Sunset Beach Park
Ehukai Beach Park
Sunset Beach
Kauai Channel
Sharks Cove
Pupukea Rd.
Waimea Bay
Waimea Beach Park
Waimea
Pupukea-Paumalu Forest Res.
Waimea Falls Park
Kawailoa Beach
Haleiwa Beach
83
Mokule'ia Army Beach
Haleiwa Ali'i Beach Park
Waialua Bay
Camp Mokule'ia
YMCA Camp Erdman
Kaiaka Beach
Haleiwa
Kaena Point State Park
Waialua Beach Rd.
Opaeula Rd.
Kaena Point
Dillingham Airfield
Mokule'ia
Waialua
Twin Bridge Rd.
Kamehameha Hwy.
Kuaokala Game Management Area
Farrington Hwy.
930
Farrington Hwy.
Kaukonahua Rd.
Kaena Point State Park
Kuaokala Game Management Area
99
TO WAHIAWA, HONOLULU
Farrington Hwy.
Mokuleia Forest Reserve

0   2 miles
0   2 kilometers

N

OAHU

open to the public at all other times. Its small, windswept beach is too rough for swimming any time of year, but it's ideal for **kitesurfing** (see p. 166). The tent area is in a wooded grove near the beach and has hot water showers and toilet facilities. There are cabins that contain 14-22 beds with two shared bathrooms in each. Large groups can reserve the kitchen. (☎637-6241; fax 637-8808; www.campmokuleia.com. Check-in 4pm. Check-out 1pm. Reservations required. Tent camping $6 with own tent; dorms $51-56 or $175 for a 14-person cabin. AmEx/D/MC/V.)

The other option is **YMCA Camp Erdman ❷**, 69-385 Farrington Hwy., which sits a bit farther down the road, on a nicer (though still rough) beach. The camp is frequently rented to large groups, especially in the summer and on weekends; call for availability. Facilities on the property include a ropes course, swimming pool, climbing wall, basketball and tennis courts. No independent tent camping is allowed. There are tent sites available for a maximum of 10 people, as well as 8-person cabins with kitchens. Individuals can stay in shared cabins. (☎637-4615; fax 637-8874; www.camperdman.net. Tent site $50; cabin $160; shared cabin $51, including meals. **Short-term work** can be arranged for room and board; contact Bridget (ext. 30) for details. Reserve tent sites 7 days in advance and cabins 24hr. in advance. AmEx/MC/V.)

🄐 **BEACHES.** Mokule'ia's empty beaches are not great for swimming, as the water is usually quite rough. Even though they are relatively empty, the beaches don't feel secluded because they are close to the road. **Mokule'ia Army Beach,** across from the airfield, has restrooms and showers but a reef, rather than a sandy bottom (other stretches to the left and right have sandy areas).

🄐 **ACTIVITIES.** Two companies operate out of **Dillingham Airfield,** on the inland side of Farrington Hwy. **Sailplane Ride Adventures** (☎637-3147; www.soarhawaii.com) offers flying lessons, scenic and acrobatic rides; call for rates and free hotel pick-up. **Mr. Bill's** (☎677-3404) offers shorter 20-40min. glider and sailplane rides from $45.

Where Farrington Hwy. ends, you can continue on foot or mountain bike to **Ka'ena Point** (see p. 176), tracing the former sugar cane railroad route. For **mountain bike rentals,** check out **Island Bike Rentals,** 66-199 Kamehameha Hwy., in Haleiwa. (☎637-9991. $30-40 per day, $100-150 per week. Open Tu-Su 9am-5pm.)

HALEIWA

It's easy to see how folks can come to Haleiwa for a weekend and end up staying awhile. For surfers and locals, the town is a place to refuel on tasty grinds and talk story; for vacationers, it's an opportunity to trade the chaos of the city for the leisurely tempo of the country. Many visitors make the trip up from Honolulu simply to peruse Haleiwa's distinctive galleries and shops, and to grab a rainbow-hued shave ice. Haleiwa is the undisputed center of life on the North Shore, and the double-arched Anahulu River bridge on the edge of town is the gateway to the world-famous beaches that are strung like pearls along the coast.

■ ORIENTATION

Haleiwa center is located along **Kamehameha Hwy. (Rte. 83),** just north of the traffic circle where **Hwy. 99** meets Rte. 83. **Haleiwa Rd.** runs along the harbor toward Waialua, intersecting Kamehameha Hwy. by the **Anahulu Bridge.** Haleiwa is served by TheBus **#52,** which runs from Honolulu via Wahiawa up Kamehameha Hwy. to Turtle Bay, and **#76,** which shuttles between Haleiwa and Waialua.

■ PRACTICAL INFORMATION

Banks: American Savings Bank and **First Hawaiian** are both located on Kamehameha Hwy., between Haleiwa Super Market and Aoki's Shave Ice. There are **ATMs** in both banks, as well as in both supermarkets and the Coffee Gallery.

Copy/fax services: In the North Shore News office behind the post office (copies 10¢).

Internet Access: The **Coffee Gallery,** in the North Shore Marketplace, has 3 finicky terminals. $1 per 10min. Open daily 7am-8pm.

Post office: 66-437 Kamehameha Hwy. (☎ 637-1711), in the buildings next to Celestial Foods on the southeastern edge of town. Open M-F 9am-4pm, Sa 9am-noon.

Zip Code: 96712.

■ ACCOMMODATIONS

There are numerous properties on the beaches near Haleiwa that are available as **vacation rentals.** Houses on the beach range from surfer shacks to luxurious homes. You can expect to pay $100 per bedroom per night for a moderate house, with a price break for weekly and monthly rentals. **Sterman Real Estate** (☎ 877-637-6200; www.sterman.com) and **Team Real Estate** (☎ 800-982-8602; www.teamreal-estate.com) are both based in Haleiwa and handle vacation rentals all over the North Shore. Neither company charges a user's fee but they do require a deposit and one-time cleaning fee, in addition to the rent. For high season (Nov. 15-Feb. 15), reserve at least four months in advance.

The only accommodation in Haleiwa is the **Surfhouse ❶,** 62-202 Lokoea Pl., about a 5min. walk from the bus station at the Chevron, and a 10min. walk to the center of town. The Surfhouse is a good choice if you want to pitch a **tent** in the midst of their citrus grove, or if you want to be within walking distance of town (other budget accommodations near **Waimea** are more comfortable and nearer to the big surf spots). Mostly European backpackers stay here, although there are several people that stay semi-permanently while looking for employment and housing elsewhere. There is one private tin-roof cabin and a six-bed dorm; neither have doors that lock but there is a safe in the office. All guests share an outdoor kitchen and one toilet, sink, and shower in a separate outbuilding. (☎ 637-7146; surfhouse@aol.com. Dorms $16; tent site $9; cabin for one person $32, for two people $36.50.)

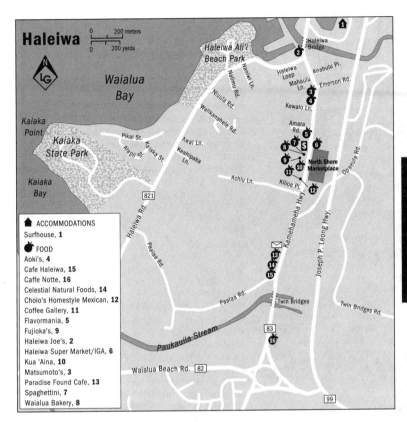

Haleiwa

0 ─── 200 meters
0 ─── 200 yards

ACCOMMODATIONS
Surfhouse, **1**

FOOD
Aoki's, **4**
Cafe Haleiwa, **15**
Caffe Notte, **16**
Celestial Natural Foods, **14**
Cholo's Homestyle Mexican, **12**
Coffee Gallery, **11**
Flavormania, **5**
Fujioka's, **9**
Haleiwa Joe's, **2**
Haleiwa Super Market/IGA, **6**
Kua 'Aina, **10**
Matsumoto's, **3**
Paradise Found Cafe, **13**
Spaghettini, **7**
Waialua Bakery, **8**

OAHU

FOOD

Haleiwa has plenty of burger grills and take-out joints, as well as a few excellent sit-down restaurants. Vegetarians will have no problem—surfer food tends toward the healthy and filling (and cheap), which means burritos, brown rice, and tofu galore. And, as Haleiwa is on the water, the fish is reliably good wherever you go.

There are also a number of markets in and around Haleiwa. **Fujioka's,** right in the center of town, sells liquor, basic staples, and decent vegetables. (Open M-Sa 8am-8pm, Su 8am-5pm.) Across the street, **Haleiwa Super Market/IGA** has similar offerings. (Open M-Sa 8am-8pm, Su 8:30am-5:30pm.) **Foodland,** in Waimea (p. 170), has a better selection but outrageous prices. You'd be better off buying fruit at the produce stands northwest of town. **Celestial Natural Foods,** 66-443 Kamehameha Hwy., next to the post office and across from Cafe Haleiwa, has a limited selection of organic produce and packaged foods. (Open M-Sa 9am-6pm, Su 10am-6pm.)

RESTAURANTS AND CAFES

Haleiwa Joe's, 66-001 Kamehameha Hwy. (☎637-8005). Formerly a Chart House restaurant, Haleiwa Joe's kept the tiki torches but has added its own local style. There may be a wait for sunset dining, but you can just join the crowd at the bar for pupus and

THE BIG SPLURGE

KITEBOARDING TO EXTREMES

So you've stayed in a surf shack for a month and have a bit of cash jangling around in your pockets. If you're looking for something fun and worthwhile to splurge on, look no further than KiteHigh, above the Coffee Gallery in Haleiwa. They rent kayaks, surfboards, and snorkeling gear, but specialize in kiteboarding, the fastest growing watersport on the planet. What other sport lets you jump 30 feet in the air with a butter-soft landing? Better yet, kitesurfing lessons leave you with an actual skill that you can do anywhere once you have the gear. If you've never tried it before, this is a great place to learn, as KiteHigh is the only kitesurfing school on the North Shore. The beaches they use for lessons are absolutely empty, making for much safer conditions than crowded Kailua. Basic lessons with instructors certified in CPR, first aid, and kitesurfing instruction cost $97, but a more substantial lesson that will take you from zero to kitesurfer in an afternoon runs around $250 (mention *Let's Go* for a discount). KiteHigh provides free snorkel gear and cold drinks for friends and family who want to watch you fly. Advanced lessons available too. (☎250-5483; andy@kitehigh.com; www.kitehigh.com.)

drink concoctions. Save room for the substantial entrees—the prime rib is about 2 in. thick and requires a team effort. The fish is fresh and well-prepared—notable creations include the baked *ono* with mango chutney and green curry, and the guava glazed salmon. The wine selection is both excellent and reasonably priced. Entrees $13-24. Happy Hour 4:30-6:30pm. Open daily 11:30am-2pm, 5:30-9:30pm. AmEx/MC/V. ❸

🍴 **Caffe Notte,** 66-560 Kamehameha Hwy. (☎636-2285). Recently opened by the owners of Cholo's (see below), this new Italian restaurant has a comfortable and classy atmosphere. They've already gotten off on the right foot—the pasta sauces are fresh and flavorful, with plenty of garlic and some real heat in the spicy marinara. The tomato and broccoli pasta goes well with a side of the Italian sausage, and the seafood specials are perfect with a glass of white wine. Entrees $9-16. Open daily 5-10pm. AmEx/MC/V. ❸

🍴 **Kua 'Aina,** 66-214 Kamehameha Hwy. (☎637-6067). This jam-packed sandwich and burger joint has become so popular over the years that there are now satellites in Honolulu and Tokyo. The mahi mahi burgers are legendary, and are perfectly accompanied by the crispy homemade fries. Burgers $5-6. Open 11am-8pm. ❶

🍴 **Coffee Gallery,** 66-250 Kamehameha Hwy. (☎637-5355), in the North Shore Marketplace. It seems as though everyone in Haleiwa comes here for their daily caffeine fix. They don't come for the food (the fruit in the granola-fruit bowl is frozen and the muffins are from CostCo)—so the draw is more likely the winning combination of good conversation and top-quality beans roasted daily on the premises. **Internet access** $1 per 10min. Open daily 7am-8pm. ❶

Cholo's Homestyle Mexican, 66-250 Kamehameha Hwy. (☎637-3059), in the North Shore Marketplace. Cholo's is always packed, and for good reason—the fish tacos are chock-full of well-seasoned *ahi,* the tamales are moist and tender, and the chips and salsa are always fresh. Nothing on the menu is over $8, and many dishes come a la carte for the meager of appetite or budget. Open daily 8am-9pm. AmEx/MC/V. ❷

Cafe Haleiwa, 66-460 Kamehameha Hwy. (☎637-5516). A Haleiwa institution for 2 decades, Cafe Haleiwa serves hearty breakfasts and lunches substantial enough to fuel a day of surf and sun. Contemplate the psychedelic surf paintings on the walls as you take on Breakfast in a Barrel (what less surf-minded folks might call a breakfast burrito) or plunge Off the Lip (an egg and veggie scramble). Nothing is over $7. Open for breakfast M-Sa 7am-12:30pm and Su 7am-2pm, lunch (burgers and Mex plates) served M-Sa 11am-2pm. No credit cards. ❶

Paradise Found Cafe, 66-443 Kamehameha Hwy. (☎637-4540), in the back of the Celestial Natural Foods Store. The wisdom of the hippie poetry on the walls is questionable, but there are no doubts as to the quality of the made-to-order vegetarian food. Salads are layered with creamy avocado, heirloom tomatoes and tangy feta, and the tofu curry scramble is big on flavor. Everything is $5-6. Open M-Sa 9am-5pm, Su 10am-5pm. No credit cards. ❶

Spaghettini, 66-200 Kamehameha Hwy. (☎637-0104). Don't be fooled by the modest facade—Spaghettini doesn't scrimp on quality ingredients in their homemade pizzas and pasta sauces, and everything is cooked to order. The pizza crust is crisp and chewy and just thick enough—*much* better than overpriced Pizza Bob's across the street. Slices $2-2.70, large pizza $12.70, plus $1.50 for each topping; pastas $6-9. Open daily 11am-8pm. ❶

Waialua Bakery, 66-200 Kamehameha Hwy. (☎637-9079). The fresh loaves of baked bread are soft and savory (best unsliced), and make tasty sandwiches ($5). Add a refreshing smoothie ($3-4) and you're good to go. Open M-Sa 8am-4pm. ❶

SHAVE ICE AND ICE CREAM

Shave ice is to Haleiwa what gelato is to Venice—you're doing yourself a disservice if you pass up these colorful treats.

▨ **Matsumoto's,** 66-087 Kamehameha Hwy. (☎637-4827), is by far the most famous (tour buses now stop directly outside), as evidenced by the huge lines. There is a strict protocol for ordering: state how many small or large cones you want, whether you want ice cream and/or sweet *azuki* beans (try them!), and only when they *ask* do you state your flavors. Plain with 3 flavors $1.20, with ice cream and beans $1.80. Shave ice can get pretty drippy, so consider shelling out an extra quarter for a reusable plastic shave ice catcher. Open noon-5:30pm. ❶

▨ **Aoki's** (☎637-70-17), next door to Matsumoto's, is just as good and also makes its own syrups. The only difference is that Matsumoto's has a few more flavors and a much longer line. Follow the same ordering rules (see above). Plain with 3 flavors $1.20, with ice cream and beans $1.80. Open noon-5:30pm. ❶

▨ **Flavormania,** 66-145 Kamehameha Hwy. (☎637-9362). If you're craving a little sweetness, Flavormania has superior ice cream. All the flavors—from Kona Koffee to Bonzai Banana—are made on the premises. Single scoop $1.80. Open daily 11am-8pm. ❶

⌂ SHOPPING

In addition to plenty of surf boutiques and Patagonia and Quiksilver chain stores, Haleiwa has a number of unique shops worth perusing.

JEWELRY AND APPAREL

▨ **Black Pearl Source,** 66-220 Kamehameha Hwy. (☎637-7776). The store and everything in it was designed and built by architect and jeweler Ben Thompson. Many of Thompson's rings, pendants, and earrings are designed to cradle the high quality, natural-color Tahitian black pearls (which are not black but green, blue, golden, apricot, and even purple) without drilling them, retaining the integrity of the pearl. The pearls are rarer and more expensive than white *akoya* pearls, but the store carries pieces to fit any budget. Open daily 10am-6:30pm.

▨ **Silver Moon Emporium,** 66-250 Kamehameha Hwy. (☎637-7710), in the North Shore Marketplace. Moms and daughters alike will swoon at the rows of dresses and casual wear by Betsy Johnson, Custo Barcelona, and other fabulous designers. The sale rack offers some generous bargains. Open daily 10am-6pm.

North Shore Swimwear, 66-250 Kamehameha Hwy. (☎637-6859; www.northshore-swimwear.com), in the North Shore Marketplace. In addition to the stylish bikinis and sporty one-pieces sold ready-made in the store, custom suits can be ordered in person or on the website. Mix and match designs and fabrics for tops and bottoms, specify your measurements, and voila! You've got yourself a custom bikini guaranteed to turn heads. Open daily 10am-6pm.

Haleiwa Surf & Sea, 62-595 Kamehameha Hwy. (☎637-9887; www.surfnsea.com), just past the Anahulu Bridge. Of the town's several surf shops, Haleiwa Surf & Sea is the most well-known. Since 1965, they've supplied the North Shore surf community with affordable boards and accessories, as well as men and women's clothing. Open daily 9am-7pm.

GIFTS AND SOUVENIRS

Sea Shell Man (☎637-2716), on Kamehameha Hwy. next to KFC. Mixed in with the cheesy shell chandeliers are exquisite rare seashells that you won't find at the beach (but you can tell your friends at home you did). Open daily 10am-6pm.

Coffee Gallery, 66-250 Kamehameha Hwy. (☎637-5355; www.roastmaster.com). First-rate Hawaii coffee doesn't come any fresher than at the Gallery, where beans are roasted on-site daily. For online orders, the beans are roasted the day they are shipped. Local Waialua french roast and Molokai blend are well-rounded and affordable at $14 per lb., while 100% pure Kona sells for $30 per lb. Open daily 7am-8pm.

◪ BEACHES

Although the most famous beaches and surf spots are near **Waimea** and **Sunset Beach** (p. 169), there are a few decent spots right in Haleiwa, and northwest between Haleiwa and Waimea. The beaches east of Haleiwa off Waialua Beach Rd. are known spots for shark breeding, but there is excellent **kiteboarding** (see sidebar on p. 166) farther east in Mokule'ia.

HALEIWA ALI'I BEACH PARK. Haleiwa Ali'i Beach Park is placid during the summer, but the winter brings three good surf breaks offshore to the left. The one farthest east (left, if facing the water) is known as **Walls,** to the right of Walls is **Avalanche,** and **Haleiwa** is directly out from the beach park. The latter is a good place for beginners when the waves are small, but for experts only when they get big. The beach has restrooms, showers, and picnic tables. (*Off Haleiwa Rd.*)

HALEIWA BEACH PARK. Although the beach is unremarkable, Haleiwa Beach Park is a local gathering place in the summer. **Haleiwa Surf & Sea,** 62-595 Kamehameha Hwy., launches **canoes** from this harbor, and arranges **scuba dives** and lessons, **sport fishing trips, surf lessons,** as well as **snorkel** tours and gear rental. (☎637-9887; www.surfnsea.com.) There are two surf breaks off the point to the right: **Pua'ena** and the experts-only **Pua'ena Point** on the outside. The beach has restrooms, showers, and picnic tables. (*Just past Anahulu Bridge.*)

KAWAILOA BEACH. Kawailoa Beach is the general name for this stretch of sometimes sandy, sometimes rocky coastline edged by private homes. **Chun's Reef** is the most popular surf break in this stretch, and has beachfront parking across from it, at the intersection of Plantation Rd. and Kamehameha Hwy. One of the largest pull-outs for cars (about 2 mi. southeast of Waimea Beach) is opposite a moss-covered rocky formation popularly known as **Alligator Rock.** If you park at Alligator Rock, there is a surf spot directly in front of you and, if you walk south (left) over the rock to the sandy beach, you'll come to two more surf spots: **Left Overs** and **Right Overs.** The swimming here is decent in the summer (the beach is rarely crowded), although there can be a bit of a riptide between the two surf breaks. Large **sea turtles** are commonly spotted swimming close to shore; look, but don't touch lest you incur a fine of $1000 from the turtle protectors who patrol the beach. *(Kawailoa stretches from Pua'ena Pt. to Waimea.)*

WAIMEA AND SUNSET BEACH

Along the coast northwest of Haleiwa, Kamehameha Hwy. meanders through the communities of **Waimea** and **Sunset Beach.** Though there are no real town centers, both have clusters of roadside food stands, surf shacks and hostels, as well as miles and miles of beaches. This is *the* place to stay if you're serious about winter surfing, but it's also worthwhile during the calmer summer months, when there is great snorkeling, swimming, and hiking up Pupukea.

One thing worth noting is the **walking path** that stretches for several miles between Waimea and Sunset Beach; rollerbladers, bikers, and strollers alike enjoy the path separated from the road and the houses by thick trees and shrubbery.

■ 🛈 ORIENTATION AND PRACTICAL INFORMATION. Kamehameha Hwy. is the main road from Haleiwa through Waimea and Sunset Beach. There is an **ATM** and a **Starbucks** inside **Foodland.** (Open daily until 11pm.) There is a **convenience store** and a **laundromat** next to Sunset Pizza. (Laundromat open daily 7am-9pm.) The nearest **post office** is in Haleiwa (see p. 164). Another option is the **Kahuku post office,** 56-565 Kamehameha Hwy., past Sunset Beach. (☎ 293-0485. Open M-F 8:30am-4:30pm, Sa 8:30am-11:30am.) **Zip Code:** 96731.

🛏 ACCOMMODATIONS. There are numerous **vacation rentals** available along the beaches near Waimea; call the real estate agents listed in Haleiwa (p. 164) for more information. The **Ke Iki Beach Bungalows ❸** have an unbeatable location directly on a long, sandy (and almost always empty) beach. The waves are only big during the winter but the view is spectacular year-round. The studio and 1- and 2-bedroom bungalows are newly renovated and landscaped, with patios and hammocks on the beach side. They are reasonably good values, but have high cleaning fees. (☎ 638-8829; keikibeachbungalows@hawaii.rr.com. Cleaning $45-85. Street-side bungalows $65-130, beachside $130-199.)

Waimea also has a couple of budget accommodations. Both are right across from a beach and a #52 bus stop, and are within walking distance of Foodland. **🏠Sharks Cove Rentals ❷,** 59-672 Kamehameha Hwy., across from Sharks Cove snorkel and dive spot and Log Cabins surf spot. The owners live on the premises and keep everything in ship-shape, even providing homey touches such as towels and soap in the rooms. There are three houses, each with its own living room, kitchen, and bath. All rooms have bunk beds, and some also have a double-sized bottom bunk. BBQ, pay phone, and coin-op laundry are located in the central courtyard. There is also free snorkel equipment for guests. (☎ 888-883-0001 or 638-7980; info@sharkscoverentals.com; www.sharkscoverentals.com. 3-day minimum stay. Linen and key deposit $20. Shared doubles $25, private doubles $60. An entire house can be rented for groups.) **Backpackers ❶,** 59-788 Kamehameha Hwy., across from Three Tables beach, has 120 beds for surfers looking for the cheapest digs in town. There are a variety of accommodations, from 2- to 6-bed dorms to private beachfront cottages, but all are very basic. Dorms and some private rooms share kitchen and bath; cottages have their own. Perks include free daily airport shuttle (with reservations), nightly meals ($6), free snorkel equipment and boogie boards, discounts on activities, **Internet access** ($7 per hr.), and equipment storage. **Short term work** can be arranged in exchange for room and board. (☎ 638-7838; www.backpackers-hawaii.com. Reception 8am-7pm. Check-in noon. Check-out 10am. Reserve dorms a day or so in advance in high season. Dorms $15-18, private doubles $45-55, cabins $80-200. MC/V.)

OAHU

◘ FOOD. The **Foodland** by the traffic light in Waimea has the largest selection of groceries on the North Shore, but the prices (1 lb. of tomatoes $7) will shock you. (Open daily until 11pm.) Within Waimea and Sunset Beach, there are quite a few roadside food stands and take-out establishments that have earned solid reputations. **⬛Ted's Bakery ❶**, 59-024 Kamehameha Hwy., has been a North Shore favorite for 15 years. The experts whip up donuts that make Krispy Kremes taste like hockey pucks by comparison, as well as cakes and pies made with real butter, eggs, and cream. Ted's opens at 7am, and the fresh, warm donuts are long-gone soon after. **⬛Taste of Paradise ❷**, 59-256 Kamehameha Hwy., near Sunset Beach, is another winner. They serve up Brazilian-style plates ($7-12) made with fresh, high-quality ingredients from a food truck in the back of a giant rainbow tent. Eggplant, fish, shrimp, chicken, or beef come with brown or white rice, and are topped with grilled onions and pineapple, garlic toast, and organic greens. (☎348-5886. Open daily noon-9:30pm. Live music on weekends.) **Sunset Pizza ❶**, next to the laundromat and market, is known for their pizza but also makes a tasty mahi mahi burger. Take-out only with some outdoor seating. (☎638-7660. Open daily 7am-9pm.)

◪ ◪ SIGHTS AND HIKING. The biggest tourist attraction in the area is **Waimea Falls Park,** 59-864 Kamehameha Hwy. (☎638-8511), which is a total rip-off at $25 per person. The only way it might be worth going is after 4pm, when admission drops to $10 ($14 after 3pm). The park includes pleasant botanical gardens, a few Hawaiian cultural displays, and a very anticlimactic waterfall that lies at the end of ¾ mi. of paved path. Cliff diving shows are performed five times daily, but you can't jump yourself. Horseback riding, mountain biking, and kayaking are also available within the park, but can be done for cheaper elsewhere.

A more direct communion with nature can be reached hiking the trails of **Pupukea,** which begin at the end of Pupukea Rd. From the Boy Scout Camp, there are two excellent trails, the six-mile **Kaunala Loop** and the nine-mile **Pupukea Summit Trail.** Conditions are frequently rainy and always muddy, so rain gear and sturdy hiking boots (and mosquito repellent!) are strongly recommended. The Kaunala loop trail winds through several gulches through *ti* plants, sandalwood and koa trees, with wild orchids sprouting up occasionally. To reach the trailhead, follow the dirt road past the camp, around the locked gate, and sign in on the sheets inside the mailbox on the left. Continue down the road, keeping to the left; just past the fork, there's a marked trailhead on the left side. Follow the arrows on the signs whenever there is an intersection or ambiguous fork. The trail connects with a dirt road; turn right onto it and follow the ridge along several ups and downs. On clear days, there are views of the shore along this leg. The road eventually loops back to the original dirt road you started on (turn right at the intersection and continue down the hill to return to the parking area). The Pupukea summit hike requires permission from the US Army, as they maintain the trail and train here. For information and permission, write to: Commander, U.S. Army Garrison, Schofield Barracks, HI 96857 (attn: APVG-GWY-O).

◪ BEACHES. If the beach is your thing, you're in luck—from Waimea to Sunset Beach, it's sand, sand, and more sand. One of the most spectacular sites is **Waimea Beach Park,** a deep crescent of sand visible from the road above as it curves into the gulch toward Waimea Falls. Though Waimea Bay is impossibly flat during the summer, it morphs into an experts-only surf spot come winter. There's good snorkeling and cliff jumping off to the left when it's calm, but these can be dangerous when conditions are bad. The parking lot fills up quickly, and you may be ticketed if you park on the road above. Between Waimea and Foodland, **Three Tables Beach** is named for the three plateaus of reef that emerge from the water at low tide. The reef makes for great snorkeling in summer and world-class surfing in winter. Just after Foodland, **Pupukea Beach Park** and **Shark's Cove** offer some of the best snorkeling on Oahu (masks can be rented at several kiosks and homes across the street). Past Shark's Cove on the other side of Kalalua Point, there is a long stretch of sandy beach that is practically empty all the time. The undertow can be strong in summer and during the winter it's known as **Log Cabins** surf spot. Farther down is the famous **Bonzai Pipeline.** Shoreline access is marked along the walking path between Kamehameha Hwy. and the private beachfront homes; park wherever there is a pullout on the path. Between **Ehukai Beach Park** and **Sunset Beach Park,** there is one surf spot after another. Ehukai breaks on a sandy bottom while Sunset Beach has a strong riptide, but that doesn't keep the crowds away from this world-famous spot. Both have parking, restrooms, and lifeguards.

LEEWARD COAST

The geography of Oahu's Leeward Coast deviates from the stereotypical picture of idyllic Hawaii. The stark land here is characterized by tangles of undergrowth unlike the lush, green trees that flourish elsewhere on the islands. On calm days, the placid Pacific resembles a mirror, with only the occasional abrupt wave; on rough winter days, the agitated surf can surge up to 20 ft. in height.

OAHU

Oahu Leeward (Western) Coast

OAHU

The Leeward Coast is also home to a large population of native Hawaiians, who have suffered low social and economic standing for centuries. When King Kamehameha surged through Oahu and forced the island's surrender at the Battle of the Nu'uanu Pali (see **Nu'uanu Pali lookout**, p. 157), the inhabitants of Oahu were banished to the barren side of the Waianae mountains, unprotected from the blazing sun. The advent of agricultural advances and successful drilling for water brought powerful business interests, such as the sugar cane industry, to the Leeward Coast. With the help of the state government, they snatched up the majority of the water rights and the best land. Today, the region remains a bucolic wasteland, with native Hawaiians still lacking economic and political clout.

In general, Hawaiians here are wary of outsiders and visitors should be aware of the high incidence of theft in the area. Avoiding trouble requires common courtesy and sensitivity to the attitudes of locals, as well as common sense—don't get caught in the Leeward area alone late at night. While there are plentiful campgrounds, locals joke that if you plan to camp, you'd better bring at least three friends along. It's sometimes impossible to avoid confrontations; the best advice is to attempt to diffuse the situation, offer up your best aloha spirit, and, if that fails, leave the area.

✦ ORIENTATION

The **Leeward Coast** encompasses the land that lies between the Koolau and Waianae Mt. To get there, take H-1 west from Honolulu for 40min.; H-1 will end at **Hwy. 93** (Farrington Hwy.). Traveling west on Hwy. 93 past Ewa, the road goes by **Kapolei,** just north of **Campbell Industrial Park,** an industrial community in the shadow of Honolulu that has a few spruced-up amenities. From here, the two-lane highway marches directly up the sun-baked Leeward Coast, past the rural communities of **Nanakuli, Maili, Waianae,** and **Makaha** and finally peters out before the wilderness of the westernmost tip of Oahu, **Kaena Point.**

▐ TRANSPORTATION

Buses: TheBus #51 and the 93 Express both serve the Leeward Coast as far as **Lawaia St.,** a few hundred yards south of Keau Beach park. The 51 starts service at the Ala Moana Shopping Center; the 93 brings commuters from Downtown in the evenings only, running from the Leeward side to Downtown in the morning. $1.50, students 75¢.

▐ PRACTICAL INFORMATION

City Hall: Waianae satellite, 85-670 Farrington Hwy. (☎696-6371), at the Neighborhood Community Center. Just north of where the Kaupuni Channel meets Pokai Bay, before Waianae Intermediate School. Open M-F 7:45am-4:30pm.

Banks: Within the **Waianae Mall Shopping Center,** 86-120 Farrington Hwy., there is a **Bank of Hawaii** (☎696-4227). Open M-Th 4:30am-4pm, F 8:30am-6pm.

Library: Waianae Public Library, 85-625 Farrington Hwy. (☎697-7868). Open M, W 10am-8pm; Tu, Th, Sa 10am-5pm; F 1-5pm.

Equipment rentals:

Hale Nalu, 85-867 Farrington Hwy. (☎696-5897), across from The Waianae Store on the *mauka* side of the highway. Waianae's leader rents everything you need to make the most of your Leeward visit, even **beach chairs** and **umbrellas** ($4 and $6 per day, respectively). **Snorkeling** gear ($6 per 24hr., $20 per week), **body boards** ($11, $36 per week), **short boards** ($18, $66 per week), **long boards** ($21, $75 per week), **bicycles** ($21, $70 per week), and **fins** ($4, $12 per week). Open daily 10am-7pm. AmEx/D/MC/V.

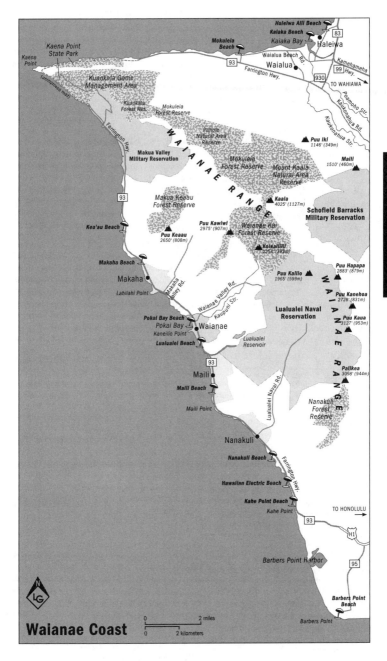

OAHU

Waianae Coast

LUAUS Modern-day luaus are typically sunset feasts that celebrate auspicious occasions with food, music, dancing, and games. The tradition stems from the ancient Hawaiians' ritualistic food offerings to the gods. It was *kapu*, or taboo, for women to eat with men until 1819, when Kamehameha II abolished the system by holding a grand feast and sitting alongside women. From then on, luaus became an integral part of Hawaiian culture. The 19th century was the great era of the luau, when Hawaiian royalty lavished guests with feasts of epic grandeur. King David Kalakaua, the "Merrie Monarch," was especially fond of large parties and reportedly invited 1500 people to his 50th birthday luau.

The luau takes its name from the young *taro* leaves that are used in the preparation of many feast dishes. These leaves were used to wrap the food that went into the *imu*, or underground earthen oven. Other luau cuisine includes *poi*, chicken long rice, *lomi lomi* salmon, *haupia* (coconut pudding), sweet potato, *kalua* pig, fish, and rice.

On Oahu, the **Polynesian Cultural Center's** (p. 118) Ali'i Luau is considered the most authentic. The Leeward, southwestern corner of Oahu is home to the other two main luaus on the island, both of which are quite expensive. Look for coupons in tourist publications to save on this must-see Hawaiian tradition. The luau at **Paradise Cove,** in Ko Olina, starts off on the right foot with a mai tai greeting and live Hawaiian music. There is also a Hawaiian village with games, arts and crafts, and an amphitheater to explain just how the *imu* works. Many packages are available, including dinner, drinks, and transportation from Waikiki. (Take Farrington Hwy. to the Ko Olina exit and continue to Ali'inui Dr. Call ☎842-5911 to make reservations, or do so online at www.paradisecove.com. $55, ages 13-18 $45, ages 6-12 $34. AmEx/MC/V.) Watch the Hawaiian court, enjoy dinner, and take in a Polynesian extravaganza at **Germaine's Luau,** at Barber's point in Waianae. Free shuttle transportation from Waikiki included. (Call ☎949-6626 to make reservations. $49, seniors over 60 $40, ages 14-20 $39, ages 6-13 $27. Closed M from the second week of Sept. until June MC/V.) For more information, see **Luaus** p. 24.

Gravity Hawaii (☎942-2582; sky phone ☎381-7696) **Kite boarding** and **paragliding** from island expert Marc "Nalu" Hill, who operates from a mobile office. Boards and gear also available.

Emergency: ☎911.

Police: Waianae Station, 85-939 Farrington Hwy. (☎696-4221), is currently closed for renovation. Otherwise, for police assistance contact the **Kapolei Station,** 1100 Kamokila Blvd. (☎692-4620).

Medical Services: Waianae Coast Comprehensive Health Center, 86-260 Farrington Hwy. 24hr. Emergency Department (☎696-7081).

Post Offices: Nanakuli Station, 87-2070 Farrington Hwy. (☎696-0161). Last collection M-F 4pm, Sa 2:30pm. Open M-F 10am-noon, 1pm-4:15pm. **Waianae Main Office,** 86-014 Farrington Hwy. (☎696-0161). Last collection M-F 5pm, Sa 4:30pm. Open M-F 8am-4:30pm, Sa 9am-noon.

Zip Code: 96792.

❚ ACCOMMODATIONS

There are very few accommodations on the Leeward side of Oahu. Of the paltry bunch, only a few are feasible for travelers. All of the Leeward Coast's county beach parks allow **camping** with a permit; however, the fact that these are predominately local spots makes it unwise for tourists to intrude. *Let's Go* does not recommend camping at any Leeward beaches. For information on acquiring a permit, see **Camping** p. 84.

OAHU

JW Marriot Ihilani Resort and Spa, 92-1001 Olani St. (☎679-0079; fax 679-0080; www.ihilani.com). Take H-1 West and exit at Ko Olina onto Aliinu Dr. Continue through 2 security stations and turn right onto Olani. The white facade of the imposing Ihilani Resort is visible from afar and, nestled on the circuitous fairways of Ko Olina Golf Club, the resort is everything the Leeward Coast isn't—green, lush, well-populated, and opulent. The lobby's ceiling rises all 17 floors to skylights at the pinnacle of the hotel and the sounds of footfalls on marble and the trickle of fountains filled with *koi* fish echo through the open space. Guests rave about the award-winning spa's full arsenal of treatments and other top-shelf amenities, which include swimming and lap pools, fine and casual dining, pool side bar, excellent tennis courts, and premier golfing. The rooms are tastefully appointed in beige and white, with deep European tubs in the grandiose bathrooms. 24hr. reception. Check-in 3pm. Check-out noon. Rooms $354-434. AmEx/D/DC/MC/V. ❺

Makaha Resort and Golf Club, 84-626 Makaha Valley Rd. (☎695-9544; fax 695-7558). At the southern end of Makaha Beach Park, take Kili Dr. (on the right as you drive north on the Farrington Hwy.). Turn right on Huipu St. and continue along this road to the resort. All of the sparkling rooms have 2 doubles or 1 king-sized bed. Full bath, TV, A/C, and mini-fridge in every room, and a much-appreciated pool. And of course, there's a golf course. Makaha also boasts the **Peacock Restaurant,** which serves the best food on this side of Oahu (see **Food,** below). 24hr. reception. Check in 3pm. Check-out noon. Rooms $95. All major credit cards. ❸

Makaha Surfside Condos, 85-175 Farrington Hwy., 1 mi. south of Makaha Beach Park. This 4-story cinder-block condominium sits on the beach and has 1-bedroom, 1-bath condos in addition to 2 pools and a covered parking garage. Various owners of the different units rent them to visitors; however, as they are not centrally organized under one owner, conditions, rates, and taxes may vary. 2 coin-operated laundry facilities, private phone. One owner you may contact is Vicky (☎841-0871) who charges $60-65 per night for her units, which can sleep 4. She also charges a cleaning fee of $65. ❸

Sun Estates, 85-786 Farrington Hwy. (☎696-6500), in Waianae. Vacation rentals ranging from 1-bedroom, 1-bath condos to bare beachside cabanas. Be sure to inquire about A/C, as the Leeward side can get pretty toasty, and beware of hidden add-ons such as cleaning fees, taxes, and parking. Prices are higher and advance reservations become essential during high season (Dec. 14 to mid-Apr.). $55-95. AmEx/MC/V. ❷

◘ FOOD

Most of the dining options on the Leeward side are in Waianae, as business does not support a great deal of eateries in this sparsely populated area of Oahu. The **Waianae Store,** 85-863 Farrington Hwy., is a basic market. (☎696-3131. Open M-F 7am-9pm, Sa-Su 7am-8pm. D/MC/V.) There is a **Sack N' Save,** 87-2070 Farrington Hwy., in **Nanakuli.** (☎668-1277. Open daily 5am-11pm. AmEx/D/MC/V.)

Within the Makaha Resort and Golf Club (see **Accommodations,** above), the **Peacock Restaurant ❹** is one of the best the Leeward Coast has to offer. Lunch is moderately priced, with plate lunches from $6-8. Dinner is simply divine and the amazing desserts such as the Kahala Delight ($4-6) end things with a bang. (☎695-9544. Open for lunch 10:30am-2pm; dinner Su-Th 5:30-9pm, F-Sa 5:30-11pm.) **The Red Baron ❷,** 85-915 Farrington Hwy., is a cozy restaurant known for its pizza ($7-26), mini-pizza ($3-7) and "authentic" spaghetti plate lunch ($6.50, served until 5pm). They also serve beer and wine. (☎697-1383. Open M-Th 11am-9pm, F-Sa 11am-10pm. AmEx/MC/V.)

A trio of drive-in eateries offer similar plate lunch, sandwich, and burger fare at the intersection of Waianae Valley Rd. and Farrington Hwy. **Purple Masago's Drive-In ❶** caters to the early morning Waianae work community and features a tasty garlic chicken plate with soft drink for $5. (☎696-7833. Open M-F 4:30am-3pm, Sa 5:30am-3pm, Su 6am-5pm. No credit cards.) **Barbecue Kai ❶** has a mean BBQ Mix Plate ($5) that comes with chicken, teriyaki and BBQ short ribs. (☎696-7122. Open daily 8am-11pm. No credit cards.) **L and L Drive-In ❶** has found its way to the Leeward Coast and locals flock to $1.50 cheeseburgers and $5.15 chicken *katsu* plates. (☎696-7989. Open daily 6:30am-11pm. D/MC/V only on orders $10+.) Two mi. north of this fast-food mecca, just past the intersection of Makaha Valley Rd., **Makaha Drive-In ❶**, 84-1150 Farrington Hwy., has comparable offerings (plate lunches $4-6) at competitive prices. (☎696-4811. Open M-Th 6am-8pm, F 6am-10pm, Sa-Su 8am-10pm.)

◉ SIGHTS

KAENA POINT STATE PARK. The northwestern most point on Oahu, Kaena Point lies within the 853-acre Kaena Point State Park. *Kaena* translates to "the heat" and the point truly is one of the hottest and driest spots on Oahu. The park itself is almost completely undeveloped, though home to beautiful **Keawaula Bay** (see p. 178). In 1983, Kaena Point and its surroundings were designated the **Kaena Point Natural Area Reserve,** due to the region's exemplary coastal lowland dune ecosystem. Among the animals that frequent Kaena Point are laysan albatross, Hawaiian monk seals, green sea turtles, and various seabirds.

Within the park, the **Kaena Point Trail** (2½ mi. one-way. Trailhead: the northern end of Farrington Hwy. Level: easy.) is a great family hike. The trail was originally built for the Oahu Railroad and Land, and runs between the ocean and the Waianae Mountains. Tip-toeing along the water's edge, the trail allows hikers to get intimate views of the ocean, tide pools, and natural stone formations. Although the footing can be unsteady, the path is generally undemanding and you'll be able to take plenty of time to enjoy the tremendous scenery. This hike can be made more difficult by beginning from the north, in Mokoleia. *(At the end of Farrington Hwy.)*

KANEAKI HEIAU. Though it is located within a ritzy residential district, this 17th-century sacred site is Oahu's most authentically restored heiau. Here, visitors can catch a glimpse of ancient Hawaii, embodied in traditional prayer towers and altars. *(Take H-1 west to Farrington Hwy. Take the highway to Makaha Valley Rd. and turn right. Follow the signs to the heiau, which is located on private property, within the Mauna Olu Estates. Open Tu-Su 10am-2pm. Free.)*

KANEANA CAVE. This 100-yard deep grotto, also known as **Makua Cave,** was carved out many years ago when the seas were higher. The cave is the subject of a colorful legend involving **Nanue,** the shark man (see **Lady Killer,** p. 177). Many centuries ago, the cave was regarded as sacred and kahunas performed religious ceremonies there. Nowadays, the cavern's visitors tend to be teenagers, and broken glass and graffiti decorate the interior. *(Off Farrington Hwy., about 2 mi. south of Kaena State Park. The cave is marked by a concrete barrier in front; park across the street.)*

LADY KILLER A number of legends
revolve around the Leeward Coast's **Kaneana Cave.** The shark god and notorious shape-shifter **Kamahoalii** is a regular feature in most of the tales, with the most popular myth alleging that he sired a son with a Hawaiian woman. The resulting half-man, half-shark was christened **Nanaue** and supposedly lived in the vicinity of what is now Kaneana Cave. Nanaue was a bloodthirsty soul and would catch unsuspecting victims, bring them to the cave, and eventually eat them. Some legends elaborate that Nanaue was lovers with a beautiful girl whose parents turned her into a *mo'o* (lizard) to keep her away from him. However, the girl-lizard traveled down Kalena Stream, through Ko'iahi Gulch, to meet her love near his cave.

MAKUA VALLEY. Though it looks beautiful from the highway, Makua Valley has seen much violence in its life span. As one of the three valleys that make up the **Makua Military Reservation,** Makua was the site of tactical maneuvers and ammunitions practice during WWII. Undetonated training munitions supposedly remain in the valley and the area is closed to the public. A contract (set to expire in 2029) between the US Army and the state of Hawaii gives the Army control of 4190 acres of land in the area. *(Off Farrington Hwy., south of Kaena Point State Park.)*

◪ BEACHES

There are a number of beaches on the Leeward Coast, all located off of Farrington Hwy. The following beaches are listed from south to north, along the highway.

KAHE POINT BEACH PARK. More rocky ground extending into the water than an actual beach, the park is located a few hundred yards up the highway, opposite the rusted Hawaiian Electric Kahe Power Plant. The beach does have one outstanding feature:

Almost as remarkable as the technology itself is the fact that it was discovered in Hawaii, a state not generally known for cutting-edge weapons defense research.

A prototype should be ready for testing in the next four years or so and the most likely testing site is a military facility located on Kauai. A portion of the grant has been earmarked for exploring alternate uses of the technology, such as screening baggage or cargo for nuclear, radioactive, and biological hazards. With the right programming, the laser is capable of detecting many other chemicals, and could make US borders and airways safer.

the view. Don't forget to tear your eyes away from the horizon every so often to make sure your car is still there. Camping is allowed with a permit. *(Kahe Point is the first beach north of Ko Olina on Farrington Hwy.)*

HAWAIIAN ELECTRIC BEACH PARK. More popularly known as "Tracks," for the old railroad tracks that run through it, Hawaiian Electric Beach has little to brag about. However, it is safe for swimming during the summer and there are picnic tables, a pavilion, and restrooms. The beach is best known for its gentle waves that are perfect for beginning **bodysurfing**. *(Off Farrington Hwy., north of Kahe Point.)*

NANAKULI BEACH COUNTY PARK. This popular local beach is located within the native Hawaiian stronghold of Nanakuli. The park is actually divided into northern and southern sections by a housing community. There are basketball courts, a baseball diamond, and a playground. The southern part of the beach is known for its clear snorkeling conditions. Although the northern section (also known as **Kalanianaole**) tends to be less agitated than the southern part, visitors should avoid swimming in the heavier winter surf. *(86-269 Farrington Hwy.)*

MAILI BEACH COUNTY PARK. Maili's long stretch of sand has been sectioned off into three parts by housing developments. **Snorkeling** is decent here and locals advise swimmers that the best spot is near the lifeguard stands. There are picnic tables and restrooms and, across Farrington Hwy. at the northern edge of the park, the **Maili Market** has a snack bar and tackle shop. *(87-021 Farrington Hwy., at the southern end of the town of Maili.)*

LUALUALEI BEACH COUNTY PARK. With a rocky shoreline and tempestuous waters, this park isn't good for much other than horizon-gazing and fishing. There are picnic facilities and restrooms, however. *(86-221 Farrington Hwy., in Waianae.)*

POKAI BAY BEACH PARK. Named after famed Hawaiian chief Pokai, this is reputed to be the safest swimming on the Leeward Coast, thanks to its protective coral reef. Locals do warn that the boat traffic here can leave the water oily and unpleasant, however. The southern end of the bay, which has picnic tables, restrooms, and lifeguard stands also has the ruins of **Kuilioloa Heiau.** The once-sacred site was damaged by army training during WWII and has since been eroded by the sea. *(85-037 Waianae Valley Rd., off Farrington Hwy. in Waianae.)*

MAKAHA BEACH PARK. Makaha is famous for its ferocious winter surf that averages 15 ft. in height, as well as the annual **Makaha International Surfing Competition**. Visitors are cautioned that swimming is extremely dangerous when the surf is up. However, the beach is popular even during waveless days, when the flat waters make for superior **diving** in the myriad coral caves offshore, where white-tipped reef sharks and turtles have been spotted. The view from the wide, white beach south to **Mauna Lahilahi**, a small mountain that sits right on the water, is one of the coast's most picturesque. Grab a **shave ice** from the Granny Goose ice cream trucks that are often parked in the lot during the day and enjoy the view. The beach has picnic tables, restrooms, showers, and lifeguard towers. *(84-369 Farrington Hwy.)*

KEA'AU BEACH PARK. Though Kea'au isn't particularly good for swimming, the beach is known as a choice snorkeling and offshore diving spot. The park has very little sand and is edged by rocks that make entry difficult. *(Off Farrington Hwy., north of Makaha Beach Park around Kepuhi Point.)*

KEAWAULA BAY. Located within **Kaena State Park** (see p. 177), this area is nicknamed **Yokahama Bay,** after a group of Japanese fishermen who used to frequent the spot. The area is much better for fishing and snorkeling than for swimming, as the surf can be rough. There are lifeguards on duty during the summer, but there is little in the way of other amenities. *(At the end of Farrington Hwy.)*

MAUI

The second oldest, second largest, and second most developed island in the Hawaiian chain, Maui is far from second best. Maui strikes an appealing balance between a vacation paradise and a real place, complete with a thriving culture and economy. Not nearly as developed as Oahu, and with plenty more to do and see than Kauai, Maui makes a solid claim for the motto that locals hold to be true: *Maui no ka `oi!* (Maui is the best!). Visiting families delight in the activities available on the buzzing beaches of Ka`anapali and Kihei and honeymooning couples discover romance on secluded coasts and waterfall hikes. This is only the beginning, however, and travelers will be surprised at how much Maui has to offer.

Most visitors first become familiar with the dry, leeward side of the island where the resorts have turned *kiawe* deserts into golf courses. However, Maui's landscape is incredibly diverse. The less-developed windward side of the West Maui mountains has acres of dense rainforest alive with native ferns and ripe fruits. At the high altitudes of Haleakala Crater, rainforest gives way to forests of towering pines, redwoods, and eucalyptus. The central valley, located in the narrow isthmus between Haleakala and the West Maui mountains, is carpeted from end to end with stalks of sugarcane. Fringed with pineapple fields, this area forms the heart of Maui's agricultural economy. Maui is the only island that maintains a significant sugarcane crop (43,000 acres), which staves off residential and commercial development in the valley.

Offshore, Maui's waters are teeming with marine life, including hundreds of species endemic to the island's reef—a veritable paradise for divers and snorkelers. Winter is Maui's high season. December through April, humpback whales gather off the southern coast and their antics are visible from any beach. Big wave surfing on the North Shore coincides with whale watching and attracts its own onlookers. Surfing, bodyboarding, windsurfing, and kitesurfing are popular sports year-round and form the center of both tourism and island life. Countless young people move to Maui to work and surf, cultivating a connection between their bodies and the natural environment. It's easy to see why the land remains such an integral part of native Hawaiian culture, as well as a highly relevant topic as Maui's land is increasingly threatened by over development.

As commercialized as Maui seems to have become, the Hawaiian community's sense of identity remains strong and is constantly evolving to face contemporary challenges. Grassroots movements have sprung up to reclaim sacred lands, to educate visitors about Hawaiian history and culture, and to deal with internal community issues. The lively debates in the editorial pages of *Maui News* provide a glimpse of the most current concerns, and there a growing number of opportunities for visitors to learn actively from locals about native traditions. Maui's rich local culture is the essence of what makes the island so special—a fusion of ethnic groups whose love of the island is contagious.

◪ INTERISLAND TRANSPORTATION

Flights to Maui from the neighboring islands start at around $100 round-trip, although some cost as much as $175 round-trip. Maui's major airport is **Kahului International Airport (OGG),** in Kahului on the northern coast of Central Maui. It is served by international and national airlines, as well as interisland carriers.

HIGHLIGHTS OF MAUI

BE THE FIRST TO SEE DAY BREAK as the rising sun illuminates the horizon on Haleakala (p. 225).

SHED YOUR INHIBITIONS at clothing-optional Little Beach in Makena (p. 197).

ADMIRE the majestic grace of hundreds of humpback whales as they frolic off of Maui's shores from December to April (p. 196).

SNORKEL IN A SECRET COVE in the Ahihi-Kinau Natural Area Reserve (p. 198).

Aloha Air (☎800-367-5250; www.alohaair.com) flies to: **Honolulu,** Oahu (30min., 19-23 per day 6:24am-8:34pm); **Hilo,** Big Island (1¼hr.; daily 8:30am, F-Sa 6:55pm); **Kona,** Big Island (1½hr.; daily 8:30am, 12:30pm, 1:55pm); and **Lihu'e,** Kauai (1¾hr., 13-15 per day 6:24am-6:05pm). **Hawaiian Airlines** (☎800-367-5320; www.hawaiianair.com) flies to: **Honolulu,** Oahu (1½hr., 27-29 per day 6:15am-8:45pm); **Hilo,** Big Island (30min., 11 per day 6:15am-5:30pm); **Kona,** Big Island (2hr., 19 per day 6:15am-6pm); and **Lihu'e,** Kauai (40min., 27-35 per day 6:15am-6pm). **Pacific Wings** (☎888-575-4546 or 873-0877; www.pacificwings.com) offers daily service to: **Hana,** Maui; **Kamuela-Waimea,** Big Island; **Kaunakakai,** Molokai; and **Lanai City,** Lanai. In addition, they have scheduled flights to the **Kalaupapa Peninsula** on Molokai. There are two other airports on Maui: **Hana Airport (HNM),** on Maui's east coast, which sees mostly commuter flights and unscheduled air traffic; and **Kapalua Airport (JHM),** which facilitates only propeller airlines and commuter flights.

Speedishuttle runs from the airport to various locations on the island. (☎875-8070; www.speedishuttle.com. Make reservations one day prior to arrival. As you add people to your party, the fares get progressively cheaper.) **Akina Aloha Tours** runs shuttles between South and West Maui. For schedule and rates, see www.akinatours.com/maui_shuttle.htm. (☎879-2828; fax 879-0524; info@akinatours.com.)

The **Molokai Princess** (☎800-275-6969 or 667-6165; www.molokaiferry.com) makes daily trips between Maui, Molokai and Lanai. It leaves from Lahaina Harbor (1½hr; daily 5:15pm; M, W, F-Sa 6:30am. One-way $40, children $20).

The easiest and most convenient way to get around Maui is to rent a car. For **inter-city** and **local transportation,** consult the **Transportation** section for each town.

⌐ ACCOMMODATIONS

In Maui, travelers can stay in budget hostels in Wailuku, Paia, or Lahaina for less than $20 per night, in condominiums in Kihei for $65 per night and up, in bed & breakfasts anywhere for $55-150 per night, or in hotels for $100 and up. For **long-term** accommodations, check the *Maui News,* in print or online at www.mauinews.com, for notices advertising rooms and cottages for rent. A studio cottage, depending on the location, costs $500-1000 per month.

Whatever your accommodations, make reservations as soon as you know the dates of your trip. High season generally runs December 15-April 15, and rates are even higher during December and January. During high season, accommodations are booked 3-4 months in advance (even longer for some popular B&Bs). Most charge higher rates during the high and peak seasons; the low season (Apr. 15-Dec.15) is a good time to visit if you're looking to save some cash. The tourist industry has been in a slump since September 11, 2001 however, and many Maui hotels may have vacant rooms available on relatively short notice.

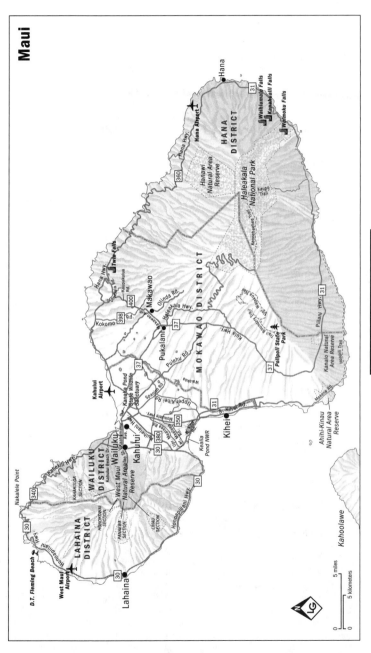

Maui

MAUI

CAMPING

Camping in Maui is possible with a little advance planning. Beaches and parks where you can pitch a **tent** all require permits, and some have maximum stays. There are a few **cabins** in state and national parks that are cozy, but they book months in advance (see individual site coverage for details). If you plan on camping in Maui, make sure you rent a **car** with a lockable compartment (not a Jeep) for your gear. Prepare for mosquitoes, sun, rain, and if you are camping on Haleakala, extreme cold and wind. Building a fire, where permitted, can be difficult due to lack of wood, so bring a **stove** for cooking and boiling water. Each type of park— county, state, and national—issues its own **permits:**

County parks (☎270-7389; www.countyofmaui.com), including Kanaha Beach and Papalaloa near Lahaina, require a permit ($3 per person per night; 50¢ per child), good for a maximum of 3 consecutive nights. Mail a money order in the appropriate denomination to: **Dept. of Parks and Recreation,** 1580-C Ka'ahumanu Ave., Wailuku, HI 96793. Permits can be picked up at the War Memorial Gym next to Baldwin High School on Rte. 32 in Wailuku.

State parks (☎984-9109), including Polipoli (free for tents; $45 for cabins) and Waianapanapa ($5 per person for tents; $45 for cabins), require permits, good for a maximum of five days. Write to: **Division of State Parks,** 54 South High St., Rm. 101, Wailuku, HI 96793.

Haleakala National Park issues its own permits at the Park Headquarters. They are free and available on a first-come, first-served basis. Apply three months in advance for the cabin lottery; see park coverage (p. 225) for details.

CENTRAL MAUI

Central Maui refers to the valley that stretches between the West Maui mountains on one side and the Haleakala volcano on the other. Aside from the county seat **Wailuku** and the commercial center of **Kahului** along the northern coast, there isn't much in the valley but vast fields of sugar cane. **Ka'ahumanu Ave.** and **Rte. 32/Main Street** run along the northern part of the valley all the way to the spectacular **Iao Valley** (p. 188) in the West Maui mountains. **Routes 36** and **37** connect the valley with the North Shore and Upcountry towns in the east (p. 225), and **Rte. 350/311** (Pu'unene Ave./Mokulele Hwy.) cuts through the cane fields to Lahaina (p. 200) and the towns and beaches of South Maui (p. 188).

WISE WORDS When immersed in a bilingual culture, visitors can learn much about local values and beliefs by taking note of the words that are never translated. In Hawaiian newspapers, which are written primarily in American English, you'll often see the word "ohana" used to refer to anything from a lost-and-found classified ad ("Dogs lost—they are *ohana*—please return") to a story on political favoritism ("Pols take care of *ohana* first"). Although the word can be translated easily enough into "family," the concept of *ohana* has no counterpart in Anglo-American culture. Family means something to Hawaiians that cannot be explained in words other than their own. Similarly, when driving in rural places, you may see a sign marked "kapu," or forbidden. The word *kapu* carries the connotation of being cursed, and implies a respect for the power of the land that "forbidden" does not. So if you want to understand how to think like the *kama'aina,* there's no better way than learning the language of the land.

MAUI

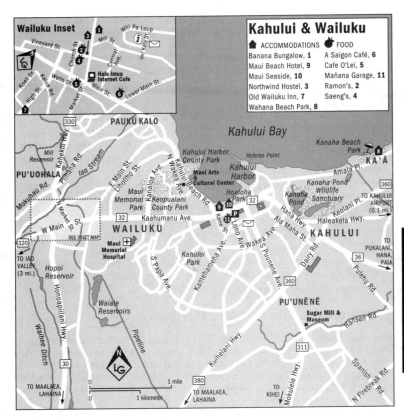

KAHULUI AND WAILUKU

On the northern coast of the central Maui valley, these two towns merit little notice for their charms, but both offer several options for budget accommodations, including two dirt cheap hostels. Kahului, the major airport gateway to Maui, is not a town so much as a sprawling chain of shopping centers along the main road, **Ka'ahumanu Ave.**, and **Dairy Rd.**, which runs from Ka'ahumanu Ave. south to Lahaina and Kihei. Aside from the sugar cane fields, Kahului doesn't look all that different from anywhere else in America--this is where locals come to do their shopping at Costco and Walmart. West of Kahului, Wailuku has a more cohesive town center than Kahului, centered around **West Main St.**, the continuation of Ka'ahumanu Ave. There are no attractions of note in Wailuku itself, but it is the gateway to the **Iao Valley.**

🖅 TRANSPORTATION

Flights: Kahului International Airport (OGG), on the northern coast of Central Maui, in Kahului. Kahului is the main airport for Maui, served by international carriers as well as **Hawaiian Airlines** (☎800-367-5320; www.hawaiianair.com; flights from HNL approx. every 50min. 5:20am-7:35pm; $115 round-trip + tax), **Aloha Air** (☎800-367-5250;

www.alohaair.com; flights from HNL approx. every 30 min.), **Pacific Wings** (☎888-575-4546; www.pacificwings.com; daily flights from HNL), and **Trans Air** (☎800-435-9282; www.ata.com).

Buses: From the airport, **Speedishuttle** (☎875-8070; www.speedishuttle.com) will take you where you need to go. Reserve a day in advance. As you add people to your party, the fares get progressively cheaper.

PRACTICAL INFORMATION

Tourist Office: Maui Visitors Bureau, 1727 Wili Pa Loop (☎244-3530; www.visit-maui.com), off Imi Kala St., across from the Post Office. While the obscure location makes visiting the office a futile exercise; call with questions. Open M-F 8am-4:30pm.

Emergency: ☎911.

Internet Access: Hale Imua Internet Cafe, 1980 Main St., Wailuku (☎242-1896; www.haleimua.com), on the corner of Market St. Full cafe menu of sandwiches ($6.50), salads ($4.25), espresso, and frozen drinks in addition to fast DSL connections ($2 for first 2min., and 10¢ per min. after; weekly rates available). Laptop connections, scanning, fax, and printing services also available. Open M 9am-9pm, Tu-F 9am-7pm, Sa 9am-5pm, Su 9am-4pm.

Post Office: 138 S. Pu'unene Ave., Kahului or 250 Imi Kala St., Wailuku, off Mill St. Both open M-F 8:30am-5pm, Sa 9am-noon.

Zip Code: Kahului 96732; Wailuku 96793.

ACCOMMODATIONS AND CAMPING

Accommodations in Kahului and Wailuku lean toward the budget end of the spectrum. Wailuku's hostels attract backpackers, windsurfers, and hangabouts, while Kahului's functional hotels draw business travelers and over-nighters looking for a bed near the airport. Lodgings in these towns provide a convenient base for exploring the natural beauty of the Iao Valley, but are a bit of a drive to Lahaina nightlife or Upcountry vistas.

■ **Banana Bungalow,** 310 N. Market St. (☎800-8HOSTEL or 244-5090; fax 244-3678; info@mauihostel.com; www.mauihostel.com), a few blocks from central Wailuku. The free tours offered by this well-maintained private hostel take you places no other tour does. Inside the communal hostel, the receptionist's surfboard art decorates every wall, the hallways are newly carpeted, and the dorms are freshly painted. Linens, luggage storage, and safe available. Free Internet. Laundry and communal kitchen. 2-day min. stay. **Short-term work** opportunities available; email for information. Reception 8am-11pm. Quiet time after 10pm. Check-out 10am. Reservations recommended. 4- and 6-bed dorms $17.50; singles $32, doubles $45, triples $55. MC/V. ❶

■ **Old Wailuku Inn at Ulupono,** 2199 Kaho'okele St. (☎244-5897; fax 242-9600; MauiBandB@aol.com; www.mauiinn.com). Follow Main St. (Rte. 32W) through central Wailuku and turn left on High St. (Rte. 30). The third left (after the county offices) is Kaho'okele. Each of the seven rooms in this B&B is lovingly decorated with native woods and locally handmade quilts. Owner Janice cooks gourmet breakfasts each morning. All rooms have their own bathrooms, some with whirlpool tubs. 2-night minimum. stay. Reception 9am-5pm. Check-in 2pm. Check-out 11:30am. Reserve at least 3 months in advance with a $50 non-refundable deposit. Rooms $120-180 for double occupancy; each additional person $20. AAA and seniors 10% discount. MC/V. ❷

Maui Seaside, 100 Ka'ahumanu Ave. (☎800-560-5552; fax 877-4618; info@sand-seaside.com; www.mauiseasidehotel.com), between Lono and Kane, near the Kahului airport. Although it's nothing fancy, this family-owned hotel on Kahului Bay is more cheerful and better kept than other budget hotels nearby. All rooms have A/C, cable, and fridge, and the bathrooms have a real shower and tub. Breakfast included with some rooms. No airport shuttle, but you can rent cars through the hotel for $29-54/day. Reception 24hr. Check-in 3pm. Check-out noon. Reservations with credit card recommended. Standard ground floor $98; with pool view and breakfast $110; with bay view and breakfast $140. AAA discount 10%. AMEX/MC/V. Wheelchair accessible. ❷

Maui Beach Hotel, 170 Ka'ahumanu Ave. (☎877-0052; fax 871-5797; mbhfrontdesk@aol.com), between Lono and Kane, near the Kahului airport. There's no beach at this hotel, although some rooms do overlook Kahului Bay. Convenience and price are what attract travelers here—most stay only a night on their way to or from the airport. All have TVs, refrigerators, and A/C. The restaurant on the second floor offers a breakfast buffet ($6-8) and dinner menu. Free shuttle to and from airport runs hourly 7am-10pm. Reception 24hr. Check-in 3pm. Check-out noon. One-night deposit required for reservations; 72hr. notice required for cancellation refund. Singles $98; doubles $120-135; triples (king with pull-out couch) $145-185. MC/V. Wheelchair accessible. ❷

Northwind Hostel, 2080 Vineyard St. (☎244-9991), down an alley between Market St. and Church St. in downtown Wailuku. Formerly the Northshore Inn, this laid-back private hostel is not the tidiest, but the price is right for the surfers and backpackers who stay here. The breezy private rooms have a bed, a fridge, and not much else. Free Internet. Shared kitchen. No lockers or luggage storage. Laundry $1.75. Reception open until 10pm. Reservations accepted, but not required. Credit card surcharge. Weekly rates available. Dorms $18; singles $32; doubles $45. Not wheelchair accessible. ❶

Wahana Beach Park, off Amala Pl. From Kahului Airport, follow the road past the car rental agencies to the gravel lot. You can camp in the lot or on the beach (restrooms and outdoor showers on-site). Permits required; see **Camping,** p. 182. Campsite closed Tu-W for maintenance. Permits $3 per adult per night, 50¢ per child. ❶

📷 FOOD

While neither town offers any restaurants worth writing home about, there are a few surprisingly good choices should you happen to be nearby. In Kahului, food options and supermarkets are located in the shopping centers along **Ka'ahumanu Ave.** In Wailuku, **Vineyard St.** offers the most variety, although there are a few cafes and lunch counters along **W. Main St.** On **Market St.,** there is an **open market** that sells fresh local produce and homemade baked goods (open M-F 7am-7pm).

📷 Mañana Garage, 33 Lono St. (☎873-0220), off Ka'ahumanu Ave. Sandwiched between car dealerships and gas stations, the Manana Garage is a pleasant surprise. Purple walls and the namesake metal garage door in the back create an inviting atmosphere to savor the creative Latin American cuisine. The entrees are a bit pricey (*paella* $24; guava tamarind salmon $17.25), but on Mondays they come at half-price! Tempting desserts (chocolate *dulce de leche* cake; $5) round out the menu, while *caipirinhas* and *sangria* complement everything nicely (cocktails $5-7; sangria $18 per pitcher). Live music Tu-Sa, ranging from Brazilian lounge to homegrown rock. Dancing after dinner Sa. Open M-Tu 11am-9pm, W-F 11am-10:30pm, Sa 5-10:30pm, Su 5-9pm. ❷

A Saigon Cafe, 1793 Main St. (☎243-9560). From Wailuku, bear right where Main St. meets Ka'ahumanu Ave., then take a left under the bridge. The no-frills tables of this unassuming Vietnamese restaurant are constantly filled with hungry tourists and locals. The house specialty *banh hoi* (vegetables, meat, and noodles that you roll yourself in rice paper; $9.25-10) is especially popular. The crispy noodles are an excellent choice as well, served steaming hot with shrimp, squid, and vegetables in a garlic sauce ($9.25).

MAUI

THE BIG SPLURGE

MAUI BY AIR

It doesn't come cheap, but you won't soon forget the rush of a helicopter ride past Maui's dramatic waterfalls and craters. Several companies book trips—all leave from **Kahului Airport** or the nearby heliport—and all sell video recordings of the journey. For discount coupons, see *Maui Magazine Vacation Guide*, a free publication available at most tourist kiosks. Prices listed are per person.

Blue Hawaiian Helicopters, Kahului Heliport #105 (☎871-8844; www.bluehawaiian.com). Standard and luxury 'copters fly to: West Maui mountains (30min., $125-150); Hana and Haleakala (45min., $180-215); West Maui and Molokai or East Maui (1hr., $230-275).

Hawaii Helicopters, Kahului Heliport #106 (☎877-3900; www.hawaiihelicopters.com). Twin-engine jet helicopters fly to: Hana and Haleakala (45min., $150); Haleakala, Hana, North Shore and West Maui coast (50-55min., $175); Haleakala, Lanai, Molokai, and West Maui (2hr. with stop, $250).

Sunshine Helicopters, Kahului Heliport #107 (☎871-0722; www.sunshinehelicopters.com). "Black Beauties" fly to: West Maui (30min., $125); Hana and Haleakala (45-50min., $185); West Maui, Haleakala and Hana (50-55min., $205).

Pacific Wings (☎873-0877; www.pacificwings.com) offers a lesson on the basics of flying and navigations, and then lets you fly a twin-engine Cessna for a 2½-hour flight. (Total 4hr., $309 + tax. Price includes pilot and two additional guests.)

Complement your meal with fresh-squeezed juices or iced coffee drip-brewed at your table ($2.35). Open M-Sa 10am-9:30pm, Su 10am-8:30pm. MC/V. ❷

Cafe O'Lei, 2051 Main St. (☎244-6816), in downtown Wailuku. A gourmet bargain, this mostly take-out lunch counter showcases fresh local ingredients. Daily specials (blackened mahi mahi with fresh papaya salsa and rice $6) complement the stand-by menu of salads (ginger chicken $7) and sandwiches (prosciutto baguette $6). Open M-F 10:30am-3:30pm. MC/V. ❶

Saeng's, 2119 Vineyard St. (☎244-1567), at N. Church St. in downtown Wailuku. Among a cluster of restaurants that have seen better days, Saeng's stands out for its elegant atmosphere, both in the upscale dining room and the open-air, garden lanai. The extensive Thai menu highlights local seafood (mahi mahi ginger $12) and creative vegetarian options (Evil Prince Tofu $7.50). Lunch served M-F 11am-2:30pm; dinner nightly 5-9:30pm. MC/V. ❷

Ramon's, 2102 Vineyard St. (☎244-7243), across the street from Saeng's. During the day, Ramon's draws a casual crowd for Hawaiian plate lunches (*kalua* pig with cabbage $7), burgers ($6), and burritos ($7-10). At night, the bar, pool tables, and live entertainment become the main attractions. M-W karaoke, Th DJ and $2 drinks, F-Su live music. F $2 drafts, $9 pitchers, and sushi specials. Lunch served until 2:30pm. Open daily until 1:30am. ❷

🎵 ENTERTAINMENT

For evening entertainment, some of the restaurants listed above offer **live music.** The **Iao Theater** on Market St. in Wailuku (☎242-6969) and the **Maui Arts and Cultural Center (MACC)** off Kahului Beach Rd. (☎242-7469) both hold live performances, the latter attracting international stars as well as local artists. There are two **movie theaters** in Kahului, the **Maui Mall Megaplex** (☎249-2222) and the **Ka'ahumanu 6** (☎878-3456), both off Ka'ahumanu Ave. The ✦**Maui Film Festival** (www.mauifilmfestival.com) screens art films every Wednesday at the MACC, with live music and food served before and after the first screening.

🛍 SHOPPING

In addition to the shopping centers in Kahului, N. Main St. and Market St. in Wailuku are lined with antique stores, galleries, and bookstores. On Saturday mornings (7am-noon), the **swap meet,** on Pu'unene Ave. next to the post office, is *the* place to get amazing local produce, as well as peruse the giant junk sale.

For music lovers, **It's a Beautiful Day,** 10 Market St., is worth a trip. This second-hand music store has an impressive selection of CDs ($9 and up), from hard-to-find indie labels to rows and rows of reggae. The vinyl is mostly pop and rock. Downstairs, **Malice and Wonderland** sells second-hand and vintage clothes (polyester shirts $15; leather jackets $35). Both open M-Sa 10am-6pm.

⊙ SIGHTS

While there is little to do in the towns proper, Kahului serves as a springboard for **adventure tours** and **helicopter rides,** and Wailuku is the gateway to **Iao Valley.**

KANAHA BEACH PARK. The best time to visit Kanaha is late afternoon, when the kite surfers are out in full force. The beach itself is narrow, and the murky water and choppy waves make swimming unappealing. However, it's a great place to watch the colored sails jump through the surf as the adventurous catch air. *(Off Amala Pl., behind the airport.)* If spectating isn't enough for you, **Action Sports** offers **kite surfing lessons** and will deliver the equipment to the beach. *(☎871-5857. $210 for 3hr. group lesson; $280 for 3hr. private lesson.)*

SUGAR MILL AND MUSEUM. Across the street from the still-operating sugar mill in Pu'unene (just south of Kahului), the **Alexander & Baldwin Sugar Museum** offers a sampling of the sights, sounds, and tastes of the Maui sugar industry. Photographs, clothing, models, and artifacts document the history of the industry, with a focus on both the white plantation owners and the immigrants who worked the fields and mills. Sounds of old Hawaii accompany the different exhibits; you can hear the chants of the Polynesians who introduced sugar cane to Hawaii 1000 years ago, the sound of water running through the irrigation ditches when Europeans began cultivating the plant for sugar, and other audio aspects of sugar cane's history. The museum invites visitors to sample raw Maui sugar on the way out. *(3957 Hansen Rd., at Pu'unene Ave. From Kahului, take Pu'unene Ave. south; there will be signs for the sugar museum before Hansen meets Pu'unene. ☎871-8058; www.sugarmuseum.com. Open M-Sa 9:30am-4:30pm. $5, ages 6-17 $2.*

BAILEY HOUSE MUSEUM. This 1833 mission house, now run by the Maui Historical Society, contains a small museum with artifacts that chronicle early Hawaiian history up to, and following, European contact. The placards don't say much, allowing visitors to imagine for themselves how the objects were used by their original owners. The front room displays portraits of the Baileys, the family of sugar moguls who constructed the house and operated a female seminary here. Two rooms to the left display the tools and ornaments of the early Hawaiians, and the two rooms on the opposite side use hats, clothing, and other artifacts to illustrate the style that resulted from the fusion of European and Hawaiian culture. The upstairs bedrooms hold period furniture, handmade quilts, and items that belonged to Hawaiian royalty. *(2375 Main St., just outside Wailuku center on the road to Iao Valley. ☎244-3326; www.mauimuseum.org. Open M-Sa 10am-4pm. $5, ages 7-12 $1.)*

TROPICAL GARDENS OF MAUI. If you're on the way to Iao, you might consider stopping here for a picnic and a stroll. Orchids, hibiscus, and the rare *nanu* (Hawaiian gardenia), are just some of the blossoms that line the garden paths. In the adjacent greenhouse, travel-safe plants are for sale. *(200 Iao Valley Rd. ☎244-3085; www.tropicalgardensofmaui.com. Open M-Sa 9am-5pm; last entrance at 4pm. Ages 8 and up $3, under 8 free.)*

KEPANIWAI PARK AND HAWAII NATURE CENTER. Farther up the road to Iao, **Kepaniwai Park** commemorates the various immigrant groups that have settled in Hawaii. The park is of minimal interest for adults, but it's free and if you're on the

SUGAR'S LABOUR LOST

During the century between the US Civil War and the 1960s, sugar ruled supreme in Hawaii. While harvest months still bring the acrid smell of burning sugar to Maui's central valley, the Hawaiian sugar industry has shrunk considerably. Both the industry's development and decline are linked to the larger economic trend to move labor-intensive industries to places where labor is cheap, assuring industry leaders of higher profit margins.

In 1863, the end of slavery in the US spelled disaster for the South's sugar growers. The industry that had previously flourished in the deep South suddenly faced fierce competition from Hawaii's climate, soil, and relatively cheap labor supply. With the US-Hawaii Free Trade Agreement in 1875, the tariffs on Hawaiian sugar were removed, and Hawaii became the leader in sugar production for US consumption. The sugar industry built much of the infrastructure on the islands, and the immigrant laborers from Japan, the Philippines, Portugal, and elsewhere helped create the rich syncretic culture that exists today.

With the incorporation of Hawaii as a state in 1959 and the subsequent enforcement of US labor laws, Big Sugar (for the most part) abandoned Hawaii for cheaper labor in the Philippines and Indonesia. Today, sugar is still a $400 million industry in Hawaii and the state's leading agricultural export, but tourism has far surpassed sugar to become Hawaii's main source of income. (See **History**, p. 14.)

way to Iao, you may as well stop and marvel at the volcanic walls that surround you. Next to the park, **Hawaii Nature Center** offers pricey guided tours of the rainforest valley ($25, ages 8-12 $23; 1½hr. tours daily at 1:30pm; call ☎ 244-6500 for reservations), and houses an all-ages interactive nature museum. (Iao Valley Rd. Park open daily until 7pm; free. Museum open daily 10am-3:15pm; $6, children $4.)

IAO VALLEY AND THE IAO NEEDLE. The result of thousands of years of water pressure eroding the volcanic rock, the Iao Needle rises 2250 ft. above the Iao Valley. The Hawaiians affectionately called the structure *Kuku'emoku*, meaning the phallus of the sea god Kanaloa. They considered the valley a sacred space, burying their *ali'i* here and using the valley to fight their most important battles. In 1790, this was the site of the bloody victory of Kamehameha over the rival chief of Oahu, which led to his coronation as the first king of Hawaii. Today, with the proliferation of camera-wielding tourists, it's hard to get a sense of the sacredness of the place, but the beauty of the natural forms is still awe-inspiring. Walk up the 133 steps to the top of the path for a more intimate view of the formation. The paved path meanders down to the fast-moving Iao Stream, where native kids blatantly ignore the "no swimming" signs, frolicking in the water that once irrigated the *taro* crops cultivated on the lush valley floor. (Take Main St. through Wailuku and continue for 3 mi. The road ends at Iao Valley Park. There is **no off-trail hiking** in Iao Valley; allow 30-35min. to see the entire park via the paved paths and steps. Open daily until 7pm. Free.)

SOUTH MAUI

Stretching from the port of Ma'alaea on the southern coast to Kihei, Wailea, and Makena on the southwestern shores of the Haleakala volcano, South Maui encompasses a vastly varied region. Kihei is the Miami Beach of Maui, a six-mile strip of condos, honky tonk bars, and touristy restaurants. Past Kihei, the swanky resorts of Wailea occupy the best beachfront property. Farther down, less developed Makena boasts the most impressive beaches of all, with dramatic cliffs, wide sandy shores, and views of Kaho'olawe and Molokini across the water. Beyond Makena, the paved road becomes an ancient path, winding past lava fields and bays teeming with fish. South Maui is hotter and drier than the rest of the island—December through April is the best time to visit. In addition to the pleasant weather, this is the only time to view the hundreds of **humpback whales** that migrate to Hawaii's coastal waters each year to breed.

MA'ALAEA

Ma'alaea isn't much of a town—what there is to see is concentrated in the commercial complex of **Ma'alaea Harbor Center**, off **Rte. 30** between Lahaina and Kihei. Tour companies use the harbor as the setting off point for many boating trips.

◻ FOOD. There is a **restaurant** and **snack bar** in the Ocean Center, as well as several dining options in the Ma'alaea Harbor Center. The **Ma'alaea Grill ❹** matches upscale seafood cuisine, such as sauteed mahi mahi in ginger butter with papaya salsa ($16), with an equally posh location overlooking the ocean. (☎243-2200. Open M lunch only, Tu-Su 10:30am-9pm.) Sate your sweet-tooth with a snack from **Hula Homemade Cookies and Ice Cream ❶.** (Chocolate chip macadamia cookie $1.20. Open daily 10am-5pm.)

▨ ACTIVITIES. In the port behind the Harbor Center there are a number of boats that run **snorkel** trips to Molokini, **sunset cruises,** and seasonal **dolphin- and whale-watching trips.** Several different companies run boats, all of which are represented in the **activities kiosk** in the Ma'alaea Harbor Center. Prices vary based on the length of the trip, number of passengers on the boat, and the food and drink served. Note that boats with an open bar tend to adopt a frat-party feel; if you don't intend to drink, your money may be better spent elsewhere. Known for their eco-friendly and educational tours, the ▨**Pacific Whale Foundation** (☎249-8811; www.pacificwhale.org), a non-profit organization dedicated to marine research and conservation, runs several kinds of trips, all led by certified naturalists. They also offer internships and volunteer programs; for more information, see **Alternatives to Tourism,** p. 77.

The other main attraction in Ma'alaea is the ▨**Maui Ocean Center,** an indoor/outdoor aquarium that showcases the mind-boggling diversity of Hawaii's marine life. The admission price is a bit steep, but the fish don't disappoint—many of the beautiful and bizarre species displayed can only be found in local waters, and even experienced snorkelers and scuba divers will be impressed by the range of creatures here. Tactile displays such as the Touch Pool will entertain small children, while the placards beside the visual displays aim to educate visitors of all ages. (192 Ma'alaea Rd., off Hwy. 30 in the Ma'alaea Harbor Center. ☎270-7000; www.mauioceancenter.com. Open daily 9am-5pm; July-Aug. daily until 6pm. $19, seniors $17, ages 3-12 $13. Wheelchair accessible.)

◪ BEACHES. A narrow strip of sandy beach lines Rte. 30, but the current here is quite rough, and better swimming can be found farther south beyond Kihei. When the surf is up, experienced surfers and bodyboarders rip the southern swells that roll unobstructed into Ma'alaea Harbor; you can watch them from the seawall next to Buzz's Wharf restaurant, behind the Harbor Center. Public restrooms are located to the right of the restaurant.

KIHEI

Kihei was just a small town on an unpaved road fifty years ago. In the last few decades, however, development has exploded, and for several years, Kihei was ranked among the fastest-growing towns in America. Today, it must strike a balance between the consequences of overbuilding and the continued local demands for more affordable housing. While some consider Kihei, with its traffic and noise,

MAUI

the least attractive of Maui's charms, others enjoy an affordable vacation in the town's condos, take-out tacos, and Happy Hours. If you do choose to stay in Kihei, make sure you find time to leave the strip—the best South Maui beaches lie beyond Kihei in Wailea and Makena.

■*■ ? ORIENTATION AND PRACTICAL INFORMATION

Kihei sprawls along the southwestern shore of the Haleakala volcano, which gradually rises above the condos and hotels on the *mauka*, or inland, side. **South Kihei Rd.** runs along the coast, and is studded with traffic lights and shopping centers. Cars move slowly here any time of day; the inland **Pi'ilani Hwy. (Rte. 31)** that runs above Kihei all the way to Makena is a good alternate route.

Tourist Information and Services: Activity World books activities such as snorkel trips and helicopter rides at wholesale prices. Several Kihei locations include Kihei-Kalama Village (☎874-7400) and 2531 S. Kihei Rd. (☎874-9507). The **Maui Information and Visitors Center** (☎874-4919) offers a personalized concierge service, making reservations for car rental, accommodations, activities, etc. free of charge.

Library: Across from the Kukui Mall, next to the Fire Station on Waimahaihai (☎875-6833). Open Tu noon-8pm, W and F 10am-6pm, Th and Sa 10am-5pm.

Pharmacy: There is no 24hr. pharmacy in Kihei. **Long's Drugs,** 1215 S. Kihei Rd. (☎879-2259), in Azeka Plaza, is open M-F 8am-10pm and Sa-Su 8am-9pm.

Emergency: ☎911.

Police: Non-emergency ☎244-6400. The station is next to the Foodland in the Kihei Town Center.

Fax Services: Mail Boxes Etc., 1215 S. Kihei Rd. (☎874-5556), in Azeka Plaza.

Internet Access: Cyber Surf Lounge (☎879-1090), in Azeka Plaza, charges 10¢ per min. $3 minimum. Open daily 8:30am-8pm.

Post Office: 1254 S. Kihei Rd. (☎879-1987). Open M-F 8:30am-4:30pm, Sa 9am-1pm.

Zip Code: 96753.

▐ ACCOMMODATIONS

The majority of Kihei accommodations are unremarkable, though reasonably priced, condominiums. Many places have a 3- or 4-day minimum stay, and a price break for stays of more than 7 days. A stay at a **bed & breakfast** (see p. 192) is a good alternative to the condo scene. B&Bs are generally located in quiet residential neighborhoods with proximity to Kihei restaurants and beaches, but a world away from the noisy strip. The ones listed below are some of the few **licensed B&Bs** in Kihei; if these are booked, the hosts may be able to recommend one of many unlicensed B&Bs nearby.

CONDOS

Several companies specialize in Kihei condo and vacation rentals, including **Affordable Accommodations Maui** (☎888-333-9747; books properties starting at $55 per night; no fee); **Condominium Rentals Hawaii** (☎879-2778; properties start at $71 per night; reservation fee $25); **Maui Condominium and Home** (☎879-5445; reservation fee $25); and **Kihei Maui Vacations** (☎879-7581; properties start at $64 per night; 10% commission charge). In addition to the rates quoted below, be prepared to pay an 11.25% accommodations tax, a reservation fee or commission charged by the reservation services (see above), and around $50 for a **cleaning fee** when you check out. If you are booking a condo through a service without seeing the place first, keep in mind that the beaches get progressively nicer as you head south along Kihei Rd. Condos with addresses in the mid- to high-2000s along S. Kihei Rd. typically have the best access to one of the Kamaole parks or Keawakapu Beach. Those listed here are only a few of the dozens of condos available, but they are all on or across from the nicest Kihei beaches.

Mana Kai Maui, 2960 S. Kihei Rd. (available through Condominium Rentals Hawaii, see above). This high-rise on Keawakapu Beach offers hotel rooms with A/C as well as 1- and 2-bedroom condo units with and without A/C. All units have ceiling fans, cable TV, and access to the pool; condos have full kitchens and private lanais. Daily cleaning service included. No minimum stay. Check-in 3pm. Check-out 11am. Reserve with $250 deposit. Full pre-payment due 30 days before arrival or Sept. 1 for any booking Dec. 15-Jan. 5. Car and condo packages available. Peak season (Dec. 16-Jan. 5 and Feb. 1-28) $125-280. High season (Jan. 6-Jan. 31 and Mar. 1-Apr. 15) $116-247. Low season (Apr. 1-Dec. 15) $95-217. AmEx/MC/V. ❹

Maui Kamaole, 2777 S. Kihei Rd. (available through Maui Condominium and Home, see above), next to the Hale Kamaole and across from Kamaole Park III. Features a heated pool, jacuzzi, two tennis courts, BBQ, and an activities desk. The 1- and 2-bedroom units are newer and more spacious than those next door. All units have two bathrooms, A/C, cable TV and VCR, washer/dryer, and full kitchen. Check-out cleaning included. 4-night minimum stay. Check-in 2pm. Check-out 10am. Reserve with 3 nights deposit. Full pre-payment due 30 days before arrival, or Sept. 1 for any booking Dec. 15-Jan. 5. For more than 7 nights, rates are $15-20 less per night. High season $170-250. Low season $135-200. MC/V. ❺

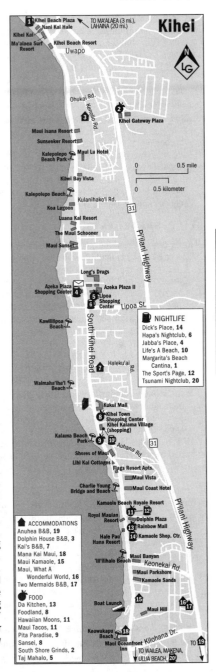

Kihei

TO MA'ALAEA (3 mi.), LAHAINA (20 mi.)

Kihei Beach Plaza
Nani Kai Hale
Kihei Kai
Ma'alaea Surf Resort
Kihei Beach Resort
Uwapo

Ohukai Rd.
Kenolio Rd.

Kihei Gateway Plaza

Maui Isana Resort
Sunseeker Resort
Kalepolepo Beach Park
Maui Lu Hotel

0   0.5 mile
0   0.5 kilometer

Kihei Bay Vista
Kalepolepo Beach
Kulanihako'i Rd.
Koa Lagoon

Luana Kai Resort

The Maui Schooner

Maui Sunset

Piilani Highway

Long's Drugs

Azeka Plaza Shopping Center
Azeka Plaza II
Lipoa Shopping Center
Lipoa St.

Kawililipoa Beach

South Kihei Road

Haleku'ai Rd.

Waimaha'iha'i Beach

NIGHTLIFE
Dick's Place, 14
Hapa's Nightclub, 6
Jabba's Place, 4
Life's A Beach, 10
Margarita's Beach Cantina, 1
The Sport's Page, 12
Tsunami Nightclub, 20

Kukui Mall
Kihei Town Shopping Center
Kihei Kalama Village (shopping)
Kalama Beach Park
Auhana Rd.

Shores of Maui
Lihi Kai Cottages
Flags Resort Apts.
Maui Vista
Charlie Young Bridge and Beach
Maui Coast Hotel
Kamaole Beach Royale Resort
Royal Mauian Resort
Dolphin Plaza
Rainbow Mall
Hale Pau Hana Resort
Kamaole Shop. Ctr.
Maui Banyan
'lil'ilihalo Beach
Keonekai Rd.
Maui Parkshore
Kamaole Sands

ACCOMMODATIONS
Anuhea B&B, 19
Dolphin House B&B, 3
Kai's B&B, 7
Mana Kai Maui, 18
Maui Kamaole, 15
Maui, What A Wonderful World, 16
Two Mermaids B&B, 17

FOOD
Da Kitchen, 13
Foodland, 8
Hawaiian Moons, 11
Maui Tacos, 11
Pita Paradise, 9
Sansei, 8
South Shore Grinds, 2
Taj Mahalo, 5

Boat Launch
Maui Hill
Keawakapu Beach
Maui Oceanfront Inn
Kilohana Dr.
TO WAILEA, MAKENA, ULUA BEACH
TO 19

Piilani Highway

MAUI

Hale Kamaole, 2737 S. Kihei Rd. (available through Condominium Rentals Hawaii, see above), next to the Maui Kamaole and across from Kamaole Park III. 1- and 2-bedroom condos each have a private lanai, A/C, cable TV, full kitchen, and access to two pools, tennis courts, BBQ, and on-site laundry. 4-night minimum stay. Check-in 3pm. Check-out 11am. Reserve with $250 deposit; full pre-payment due 30 days before arrival or Nov. 1 for any booking Dec. 15-Jan. 5. $250 security deposit at check-in. Discounts for stays longer than 7 nights. Peak season (Feb. 1-28) $145-167. High season (Jan. 6-31 and Mar. 1-Apr. 15) $137-175. Low season (Apr. 16-Dec. 15) $115-141. MC/V. ❹

Kihei Akahi, 2531 S. Kihei Rd. (available through Maui Condominium and Home, see above), across the street from Kamaole Park II. Studio, 1- and 2-bedroom units are not air-conditioned but all have a ceiling fan, lanai, cable TV, washer/dryer, full kitchen, and access to two pools, tennis, and BBQ. 4-night minimum stay. Check-in 2pm. Check-out 10am. Check-out cleaning included. Reserve with 3 nights deposit; full pre-payment due 30 days before arrival or Sept. 1 for any booking Dec. 15-Jan. 5. For more than 7 nights, rates are $10-15 less per night. High season (Dec. 15-Apr. 15) $115-165. Low season (Apr. 16-Dec. 14) $85-130. ❹

BED & BREAKFASTS

▨ **Kai's Bed & Breakfast/Vacation Rentals,** 80 Welakahao Rd. (☎800-905-8424, ext. 24 or 874-6431; mauibb@kihei.net; www.mauibb.com). Welakahao Rd. is off S. Kihei Rd. between the Foodland and Star Market; #80 is about 2 blocks from the beach. Owners Patty and Rob go out of their way to ensure that their guests have privacy and relaxation. Each room has a different arrangement and theme, and all feature elegant stone floors, microwave, and fridge. Continental breakfast with seasonal fruit from the garden. Beach towels, coolers, boogie boards, snorkels, bicycles, garden jacuzzi, and washer/dryer are available for guests to use. 4-night minimum stay, negotiable depending on season. Check-in 2pm. Check-out 10am. Reserve with 50% deposit at least 2 months ahead in low season (Apr. 15-Dec. 15), earlier for high season (Dec. 15-Apr. 15); balance due 30 days prior to arrival. $60-100 per night, $400-700 per week; slightly less in low season. MC/V. Not wheelchair accessible. ❸

Maui, What a Wonderful World B&B, 2828 Umalu Pl. (☎800-943-5804 or 879-9103; amauibnb@maui.net; http://amauibedandbreakfast.com), a 10-minute walk from the beach. From S. Kihei Rd., turn left at the Haleakala Shores sign. Go up the hill and turn right on Ohina. Go over 3 speed bumps, turn left, and then right onto Umalu Pl. Each of the four suites in this welcoming B&B has been freshly painted and thoughtfully decorated by hosts Eva and Jim Tantillo. All have private entrances and bathrooms, TV, and A/C; two have kitchenettes and one has a full kitchen. Extended continental breakfast served on the breezy lanai. Free laundry. No minimum stay. Check-in 4pm. Check-out noon. Reserve 2-3 months ahead with 50% deposit; balance due 60 days before arrival. Studios $75-89, 1-bedroom $99. AmEx/MC/V. Not wheelchair accessible. ❸

Dolphin House B&B, 69 Kalola Pl. (☎800-419-2521 or 874-0126; fax 875-1799; ray@dolphinhouse.com; www.dolphinhouse.com). From S. Kihei Rd., turn onto Ohukai, then right on Kenolio Rd., and right on Kalola Pl. Its central location, spacious and comfortable accommodations, and reasonable rates make Dolphin House a great deal. The spacious garden rooms have king-sized beds, private lanais, and bathrooms; some have A/C. Non-garden rooms are smaller but still very comfortable. A studio cottage, separate from the house, has a kitchenette and luxurious blue-tiled bathroom. Continental breakfast with fruit straight from the garden. 2- to 3-night minimum stay. Check-in 2pm. Check-out 11am. Reserve with $100 deposit; 30-day cancellation policy. Rooms $55-90; studio cottage a steal at $90. MC/V. Not wheelchair accessible. ❷

Two Mermaids on the Sunny Side of Maui Bed & Breakfast, 2840 Umalu Pl. (☎800-598-9550 or 874-8687; kawaiola@maui.net; www.twomermaids.com). Follow directions for Wonderful World, above. Located in a quiet residential neighborhood, this B&B is still close to the action. The mermaid hosts, Juddee and Miranda, advise visitors on the best scuba diving spots and other local secrets. The two suites are colorful and homey, both with kitchens, cable TV, private bathrooms, and access to a well-kept pool. Continental breakfast features fresh fruit and local breads. No minimum stay. Reserve at least 3 months in advance with 50% deposit; balance due 60 days prior to arrival. Suites $95-175. Not wheelchair accessible. ❸

Anuhea Bed & Breakfast, 3164 Mapu Pl. (☎800-206-4441 or 874-1490; anu-hea@maui.net), in the Maui Meadows neighborhood off Pi'ilani Hwy., just before Wailea. Host Cherie Kolbo greets her guests with a warm *aloha,* welcoming them to her peaceful B&B and health spa. The secluded location of the house—a drive from the nearest beach—allows guests to enjoy a quiet escape, especially on the elevated lanai bedecked with flowers and fountains. 3 rooms have A/C. Full sit-down breakfast. 3-night minimum stay negotiable depending on availability. Reserve with 50% deposit; balance paid on arrival. Check-in 2pm. Check-out 10am. All rooms low season $95, high season $115. AmEx/MC/V. Not wheelchair accessible. ❹

HOTELS

There are only two hotels in Kihei, both of which offer an alternative to the minimum stay and cleaning fees that condominiums require.

Maui Oceanfront Inn, 2980 S. Kihei Rd. (☎800-263-3387 or 879-7744; fax 874-0145; www.mauioceanfrontinn.com), on Keawakapu Beach. With the best beach location in Kihei and reasonable prices, the Maui Oceanfront Inn is a great value. Each unit has a queen-sized bed, A/C, TV, microwave, fridge, and telephone with data port. Reception 24hr. Check-in 3pm. Check-out noon. Reserve with credit card; 3-day cancellation policy. High season (Feb.-Mar. and June 20-Aug. 22) $189-399. Low season (Apr.1-June 19 and Aug. 23-Dec. 19) $159-379. Internet special 20% discount, AARP 25%, AAA 50%. AmEx/D/DC/MC/V. Not wheelchair accessible. ❺

Maui Coast Hotel, 2259 S. Kihei Rd. (☎800-895-6284 or 874-6284; fax 875-4731; www.westcoasthotels.com/mauicoast), across the street from Kamaole Park I. This newly renovated hotel has little charm and unimpressive views, but offers good value for standard hotel comfort. Fitness center, pool, tennis courts. Free laundry on-site. No min. stay. Reception 24hr. Check-in 3pm. Check-out noon. Reserve with one-night deposit; 72hr. cancellation policy. Standard double $165-350. Discount for seniors and AAA members. AmEx/D/DC/MC/V. Wheelchair accessible. ❺

◪ FOOD

Kihei restaurants run the gamut from fast food to fine cuisine. Practically every place on the strip caters to tourists, so it can be hard to find a good value. For do-it-yourself cuisine, there are several supermarkets in the shopping centers on S. Kihei Rd., including **Foodland,** in the Kihei Town Center, and **Safeway,** off Pi'ilani Hwy. in the Pi'ilani Village Center. The hot bar at **Hawaiian Moons Natural Foods** store, 2411 S. Kihei Rd., has healthy take-out meals that you can enjoy at the beach across the street. (Open M-Sa 8am-8pm, Su 8am-7pm. AmEx/DC/MC/V.)

South Shore Grinds, 362 Huku Li'i Pl. (☎875-8472), in the Kihei Gateway Plaza off Pi'ilani Hwy. Take Ohukai up from S. Kihei Rd. and keep going. Counter service by day, table service and take-out by night, this casually sleek eatery serves "killer grinds with huge aloha." Kula greens, tropical fruit, and locally caught fish come together in healthy harmony in the Fresh Catch Salad ($9.50), while plate lunches and burgers ($6-8) provide some stick-to-yer-ribs grinds. Delicious homemade desserts change daily. Open M-F 11am-3pm and 5:30-8pm, Sa 11am-5pm. No credit cards. ❷

$$$

THE BIG SPLURGE

SUSHI AT SANSEI

Much to the delight of South Shore seafood lovers, the success of Sansei's Kapalua location has led to a second Sansei opening in Kihei. Sansei's popularity is well deserved—the ambience is swank and the sushi is first-rate. The *nigiri* is made with fresh, sweet fish and just the right amount of seasoned rice. The stars of the menu, though, are the *maki* rolls, creatively assembled into caterpillars and pink cadillacs. The sushi doesn't come cheap (*nigiri* $4.25-9.50, rolls $4-16), but early-bird and late-night specials make things slightly more affordable. The menu also includes cooked entrees and noodle dishes ($16-24) that infuse local produce with a Japanese flair. The descriptive *saki* and wine list will help you pair your meal with the perfect cool or dry beverage. *(1881 S. Kihei Rd. (☎879-0004), in the Kihei Town Center near Foodland. Open Su-W 5:30-10pm, Th-Sa 5:30pm-2am. 25% off all food Tu-Sa 5:30-6pm; 50% off all food and free karaoke until closing (21+ only) Th-Sa 10pm-1am. AmEx/MC/V.)*

Da Kitchen, 2439 S. Kihei Rd. (☎875-7782), in the Rainbow Mall. This no-frills, counter-service restaurant sells cheap, freshly prepared local and Hawaiian-style food. For a smattering of everything, try the Hawaiian Plate (pork *lau lau*, *kalua* pork, chicken long rice, and *lomi* salmon, $8.50). Breakfast (served 9-11am) features hearty omelettes ($5.75), plate lunches, and Maui-style sweetbread french toast ($5.25). Open daily 9am-9pm. No credit cards. ❶

Taj Mahalo, 41 E. Lipoa St. (☎874-1911), next to Hapa's nightclub. If you're eating in at this Indian curry shop, the vegetarian buffet ($8) is a great deal for rice, vegetables, and all-you-can-eat curry. For take-out, the aromatic Biryani (medium spicy curry with raisins, pineapple, and almonds) or the mild and creamy Korma are good choices. Tandoori chicken ($2.50) or lamb ($3.50) can be added to any dish. Open daily 10:30am-3:30pm and 4:45-9pm. No credit cards. ❷

Maui Tacos, 2411 S. Kihei Rd., next to Hawaiian Moons. The fish tacos at this counter-service Mexican joint are a favorite of surfers and tourists alike. Burritos $4.50-7, tacos $3.50. Breakfast (*huevos rancheros* with rice and beans, $5) served daily 9-11am. Open daily 9am-9pm. AmEx/DC/MC/V. ❶

Pita Paradise, 1913 S. Kihei Rd. (☎875-7679), in the Kihei Kalama Village across from Kalama Park. Reasonably priced Mediterranean food ranges from $10-19. Authentic Mediterranean salad is heaped with cucumbers, tomatoes, olives, and feta ($8). Take-out available. Open M-Sa 11am-9:30pm. MC/V. ❸

🎵 NIGHTLIFE

Hapa's Nightclub 41 E. Lipoa St. (☎879-9001). The best known nightspot in Kihei, Hapa's draws a sizeable crowd every night. Hapa's Monday, when the legendary Uncle Willie K. plays, is a local favorite; Wednesday is Aloha Nite with $2 drinks 'til midnight; Fridays feature local bands, and Saturday "Flava Zone" means drink specials all night. No dress code. 21+ every night except Sundays, when doors open at 6:30pm for an all-ages dance party. Cover $5-10. Open every night until 1:30am.

Tsunami Nightclub, in the Grands Wailea Hotel. Take the second entrance to park. This 10,000 sq. ft., $4 million club draws a flashy crowd for hot DJs and dancing on weekends. Dress to impress: no tank tops, flip-flops, or beachwear; no worn or torn clothing. 21+. Cover $10.

Life's A Beach, 1913 S. Kihei Rd. (☎891-8010), next to Foodland, is the home of the eternal $2 mai tai, as well as karaoke and the occasional live band.

Margarita's Beach Cantina (☎879-5275). Toward Ma'alaea on N. Kihei Rd. The tequila flows like water at this Mexican-inspired bar on the Kihei strip. $2 mai tai and $2 margarita on the rocks from 2:30-5pm daily. Double shot of alcohol at any time of day for $1 more. Open nightly until midnight or thereabouts.

Dick's Place, Kamaole Beach Center (☎874-8869), next to Denny's, is a relaxed bar and billiards hall, as well as a restaurant. Billiards free with purchase before 7pm; $4 per person per hr. after. $2 drafts 11am-5pm. 21+ after 10pm. Food served until 2am.

The Sports Page, 2411 S. Kihei Rd. (☎879-0602), next to Maui Tacos. The ultimate sports bar, with 2 satellite dishes, 17 TVs, and a daily Happy Hour ($2 drafts; 2-6pm and 10pm-1:30am). Free pool 2-6pm with purchase; W-Sa live music and dancing.

Jabba's Place (☎891-0989), in the Azeka Plaza I, is a lively spot for gay nightlife. A restaurant/bar/club, Jabba's serves New Orleans-style food and features Tu karaoke; W, F, Sa DJ; Th drag show; Su shirtless tea dance.

BEACHES AND ACTIVITIES

BEACHES. The expanse from Ma'alaea to Makena is basically one long beach broken up by lava formations. The North Kihei beaches are popular for windsurfing and sailing; the beaches farther south are better-suited for swimming. Many of the beach parks have recreational facilities. **Kalama Park** is popular with skaters, and features tennis courts and sports fields. Just south of Kalama, **Charlie Young Bridge and Beach** is full of sunbathers. All the **Kamaole Parks (I, II, and II)** have showers; Kamaole II and III are set back farther from the road than Kam I and have some nice shady spots in addition to plenty of sun. **Keawakapu Beach,** past Kam III, is usually uncrowded, so it may be worth the walk to check it out (parking is past Sarrento's Restaurant, in a lot at the entrance of Wailea on the left). For more beaches farther south, see **Wailea** (p. 196) and **Makena** (p. 197).

SNORKELING. With over 450 different species of fish, 25% of which are found only in Hawaii (and 20% of those only in Molokini!), snorkeling in Maui is a can't-miss experience. Mornings are generally best for snorkeling, as the water is relatively calm and flat. Nearly every beach has a formation of lava rocks jutting into the sea where fish congregate. **Kamaole I, II, and III** are great for novices. In Wailea, **Ulua Beach,** just past the Renaissance Wailea Hotel, has a rocky point that divides it from Mokapu Beach, and a reef that extends farther out. **Ahihi Bay,** two miles past the Maui Prince Hotel in Makena (see p. 197), is a marine life preserve where fishing is prohibited, making it a spectacular spot for snorkeling. Two miles past Ahihi Bay, the fish preserve at **La Perouse Bay** is suited for advanced snorkelers who can handle the difficult entrances and exits along the rocky coast. Several companies run snorkel trips to **Molokini** and **Turtle Arches,** including the eco-friendly **Pacific Whale Foundation** (see p. 189), and the **Maui Dive Shop** (see below), both of which include gear in the cost of excursions. Kihei has plenty of purveyors of snorkel gear to rent daily or weekly; two of the most visible are **Boss Frog's,** 2395 S. Kihei Rd. (☎875-4477; $1.50-8 per day; weekly rates available) and **Snorkel Bob's,** 2411 S. Kihei Rd. (☎879-7449; $2.50-8.50 per day; weekly rates available).

SCUBA DIVING. As sea conditions change daily, so do the best diving spots. The several diving shops on Kihei Rd. are more than happy to give advice on where to go; most shops that offer excursions plan their itineraries that day. Many companies rent gear, offer certification classes, and lead guided trips. **Dive and Sea Maui,** 1975 S. Kihei Rd. (☎874-1952; www.diveandseamaui.com), offers a 4-day basic open water certification class (private $350, group $250) as well as advanced classes. They also charter boats (gear included), and rent gear separately for

MAUI

FROM THE ROAD

DOUBLE FEATURE

Golf courses usually don't do much for me. Tonight, however, I make an exception, as the Wailea Gold and Emerald Golf Course has been transformed into the "Celestial Cinema," an outdoor theater with state-of-the-art sound and projection that serves as the centerpiece performance venue for the annual Maui Film Festival. A local band plays as the crowd mingles about, setting up beach chairs and donning sweaters. Behind us, a spectacular show is just ending—a Wailea sunset that sets the standard of drama for the evening. Dusk falls, and with a few *mahalos* and opening remarks, the festival begins, Maui-style. First, a kahuna chants a blessing for the festival. He is followed by half a dozen young Hawaiian girls who perform a hula ceremony, welcoming the guests and praising the splendor of the volcano Haleakala, on whose rolling slopes the festival takes place. Then, an astronomer takes the stage, pointing out which constellations and planets are visible in the dazzling night sky above. Just as I'm thinking, "I bet this doesn't happen in Cannes," the film starts rolling, and the double feature begins.

—*Sarah Rotman*

The Maui Film Festival occurs annually in mid-June. For information, see www.mauifilmfestival.com, or call ☎ 579-9244.

those with certification ($20 per day). **Maui Dive Shop** (☎ 879-3388; www.mauidiveshop.com) has 3 locations in Kihei, and offers basic certification (private $450, group $300) and advanced classes, combination packages for gear and charters, and other discounted activities (helicopter, Haleakala bike rides, etc.).

SURFING AND BODYBOARDING. Summer is the season for south shore surfing. Even in summer, however, the big waves don't come every day—ask a local surfer when the next big set is coming in, or call **High Tech Surf Report** (☎ 877-3611) for daily surf conditions. Various places along the strip rent **surf boards** (approx. $25 per day) and **boogie boards** (approx. $10 per week). Most **surf schools** operate out of Lahaina (see p. 200).

KAYAKING. These lightweight craft are becoming an increasingly popular way to see some of Maui's more secluded coves. The **Ahihi Bay** fish preserve, between Makena and La Perouse Bay, is a popular kayak/snorkel destination. **Kayak Eco-Adventures** (☎ 891-2223) rents single kayaks for $25 per day, double kayaks for $40 per day, and gives guided tours starting at $49. **South Pacific Kayaks and Outfitters** (☎ 875-4848) leads tours starting at $59 per person and rents kayaks from $30.

WHALE WATCHING. From December to April, anywhere you can see the ocean in South Maui, you can see whales, and anywhere you stick your head underwater, you can hear them. This unparalleled natural spectacle is truly incredible. The **Ocean Center** in Ma'alaea, the **Whale Observatory** near Kaleolepo Park off S. Kihei Rd. (just south of Ohukai), and any of the hotels in Wailea make especially good whale watching perches. To get up close, **whale watching cruises** can be fun and educational (see **Pacific Whale Foundation** for our eco-friendly favorite, p. 189).

WAILEA

"Affordable paradise" is not the first phrase that comes to mind as one drives along the impeccably landscaped Wailea Alanui Drive, Wailea's main drag, which is edged on one side with world-class golf courses and on the other with five-star resorts. Even if you can't afford the $200+ pricetag, don't be shy about taking advantage of Wailea's beautiful beaches. All Maui beaches are public, and those who own beachfront property are required to provide public access to the shore.

◘ FOOD. If you want to splurge on a gourmet beach picnic, head to **Cafe Ciao ❷,** behind the pool in the Fairmont Kea Lani hotel. This boutique grocer sells sandwiches ($8.50), as well as high-end wine, cheeses, pastries, and other sundry items. (Open daily 6:30am-10pm. AmEx/MC/V or charge it to the room, dahling.) **Harry's Sushi Bar,** 100 Wailea Ike Dr., sells pricey but amazing sushi. Don't miss the melt-in-your-mouth Baked California Roll for Two. (☎ 879-7677. Open daily 5:30pm-midnight.)

BEACHES. There are five main beaches in Wailea, each occupying a crescent of soft sand bordered with outcroppings of volcanic rock. The first beach, **Keawakapu,** stretches for a ½ mi. along the border between Kihei and Wailea. Less of a "scene" than other Kihei beach parks, Keawakapu offers great swimming and snorkeling on its artificial reef about 400 yards offshore, which was installed in 1962 by sinking old cars 80 ft. down. Parking is available in the lot at the entrance to Wailea, on the *mauka* side of S. Kihei Rd. **Mokapu** and **Ulua** are both pretty, but they are generally crowded with resort guests from the nearby Renaissance Wailea Hotel. The rocky point between the beaches makes for excellent snorkeling, however. **Wailea Beach** is the widest of the Wailea beaches, backed by the Four Seasons Hotel. A landscaped trail leads from Wailea to **Polo Beach,** a narrower beach fringed by an immaculate park with picnic tables, showers, and restrooms. (Parking for Polo Beach is down a marked road just past the entrance of the Kea Lani, about ½ mi. south of the Shops at Wailea).

MAKENA AND BEYOND

Until very recently, the area south of Wailea, Makena, was entirely undeveloped. There is still only one hotel in Makena, the Maui Prince Resort, but the golf courses and tennis clubs on the *mauka* side of **Makena Alanui** (the main and only road) stretch ever farther south. After you pass the Maui Prince and the last golf course, the kiawe desert resumes, and dirt roads on the *makai* side lead to the best (and still gloriously undeveloped) beaches in Maui. Past the last sandy beach, a number of mansions have sprouted up in recent years, but even big houses don't detract from the rugged natural beauty at the end of the road.

BEACHES

PO'OLENALENA BEACH. After you pass the Fairmont Kea Lani, but before you reach the Maui Prince Hotel, about 1.7 mi. south of the Shops at Wailea, there is a small sign for Po'olenalena Beach. A small parking lot marks the entrance to the beach. Also known as Chang's or Paipu Beach—the names of two of the coves encompassed by the larger Po'olenalena Beach—this is the least crowded of Makena's beaches, and a real find at any time of day. The reddish sand of this isolated coastline can be a bit windswept and the currents are often very strong, but it is still a favorite among locals. You can see the Maui Prince down at the far southern end, but otherwise, the beach is undeveloped. There is some illegal camping under the shade trees, but if police see cars in the lot they will come inspect the beach, confiscate your tent, and possibly arrest you.

MAKENA LANDING. Heading south, the next cove is **Makena Landing,** which was Maui's busiest port for sugar and cattle throughout the 1920s. Next to Makena Landing, **Keawalai Church** (built in 1832 from offshore reef coral) still holds Hawaiian-Anglo church services on Sundays.

MALUAKA BEACH. If you continue, you'll reach golden Maluaka Beach at the Maui Prince Hotel, the best all-around beach for swimming and a favorite with families. Past the Maui Prince, the road winds beneath 360 ft. Pu'u Olai, the visual landmark for Makena. Due to erosion and steep slopes, hiking is discouraged.

MAUI

SHOREBREAK WARNING. Although the clear aqua water at Big Beach may look tempting, the calm is deceptive; powerful waves break right on the shore, sweeping swimmers and bodysurfers off their feet and slamming them on the sand at forces strong enough to break necks and backs. Swimming and bodysurfing is not recommended at Big Beach. The surf at adjacent Little Beach may look choppier but is generally safer for swimming and bodysurfing, as the waves break farther out on the reef. Still, the riptide and currents are incredibly strong—make sure someone is watching you and signal if you feel yourself being pulled out. If you can't get back to shore, don't panic; swim parallel to the shore and head in once you're out of the current.

BIG BEACH. Depending on time of day and the whim of proprietors, you might see a few **roadside food stands** selling burgers, fish tacos, and cold drinks outside the three entrances for **Big Beach.** Big Beach, also called **Oneloa,** is part of **Makena State Park,** and the entrance signs are marked as such. There are portable restrooms and picnic tables by the first (northernmost) entrance. There is no sanctioned **camping** on the beach—the area attracts some unsavory characters after dark, making camping unsafe as well as illegal. The last sandy beach for 43 mi., Big Beach stretches stunningly along the coast for a half-mile. There is no development on the beach, save for a graffiti-covered concrete bunker left over from World War II when the Allies used the beach for training exercises. Surfer lore has it that far below the sand is a stretch of poured concrete used during the war for landing amphibious vehicles on the beach.

LITTLE BEACH. Along the northern end of Big Beach, beneath Pu'u Olai, an outcropping of volcanic rock hides a short, steep trail that leads to Little Beach on the other side. From its sandy shores, there are unobstructed views of Kaho'olawe, Molokini, and Lanai offshore. A lingering hippie hangout, Little Beach is unofficially **"clothing optional."** If you're used to the discretion exercised on most nude beaches, be prepared for the somewhat hormone-laden (gay and straight) scene of Little Beach. On Sunday afternoons, the hippie contingent holds a drum and dance circle that can be quite a spectacle for the uninitiated observer. Over the rocks on the northern end of Little Beach lies **Oneuli Beach,** a cozy black sand beach with similar views of the offshore islands.

🔵 🏔 SIGHTS AND OUTDOORS

AHIHI-KINAU NATURAL AREA RESERVE. Past the last entrance to Big Beach, the road narrows down to one lane and winds through the **Ahihi-Kinau Natural Area Reserve,** a 2000-acre conservation area. As you enter the reserve, several protected coves of **Ahihi Bay** are visible from the road. Since there is no fishing allowed in the reserve, any calm spot along the coast makes for excellent **snorkeling.** Most of the coves require entering and exiting on the rocks, so exercise caution. Continuing past Ahihi Cove, the road winds inland through a lava field—the path of the lava flow during the last eruption of Haleakala volcano around 1790. The area formed by the lava path is **Cape Kina'u,** and all the waters surrounding it are part of a protected natural reserve. No longer a well-kept secret, but still an adventure off the beaten path, a 45-minute **hike** through the lava field ends in a more secluded spot for snorkeling. If you plan to hike, bring your snorkel gear and wear sturdy shoes. Clear mornings are best, as the water in the pool will be flat with good visibility. To find the trailhead, look at the numbers posted on the telephone poles. Around pole #18, there is a pull-out for cars where you can park (don't leave valuables in

your car). On the *makai* side, there is a spray-painted marking on the r(
metal pipe (it may have a blue cloth tied on as well). This marks the begin(
the trail, which is in surprisingly good shape. False starts to the left and righ
to huge precipices; the actual trail is a continuous path. With views of the (
ahead and the rolling pastures of Haleakala behind, the walk is worthwhile for the
unusual surroundings alone. The path terminates in a protected cove, and the narrow black sand and pebble beach on the left is the easiest entrance for snorkeling.
Underwater growth has accumulated on the volcanic rock, and the area is populated by a diverse array of colorful fish.

KING'S TRAIL. In ancient times, *ali'i* would travel this trail between Makena and
Hana to collect taxes from villagers. The southernmost portion of the King's Trail
was obliterated by lava around 1790. The fishing villages documented in 1786 by
the French explorer Jean Francois de La Perouse (the first Westerner to visit
Maui) have been destroyed as well. In 1824, Governor Hoapili rebuilt the first four
miles of the trail, but beyond that, the path is in extremely poor condition. To hike
this first leg of the trail (with sturdy shoes and lots of water), park in the small lot
at the northwest end of **La Perouse Bay.** *Do not leave valuables in your car;* this
is a known spot for break-ins, and it's pretty hard to run back across the lava to
chase away a thief. From the lot, follow the rough, unpaved road around the bay
(not the path that leads to the sea). About ½ mi. down, you'll reach a small beach,
past which the trail forks. Take the right fork south, look for the opening in the
stone wall, and turn inland; the trailhead is about 30 yards in. The trail continues
another mile or so over loosely packed lava rock to **Kanaio,** a shady stretch of
coast where there's a campsite and clearing. The trail continues on, but conditions
worsen, so you might want to turn back after resting at Kanaio.

WEST MAUI

West Maui's mountains are older than Haleakala, and have been scarred over the
years with deep rifts from stream erosion. Driving south through the central isthmus of the island with the mountains on the right, the huge forms rise out of the
cane fields in velvety folds before disappearing into the cloud cover. Unlike the
valleys northwest of Wailuku (Iao and Waihee), which get almost 400 in. of rainfall
per year, the *pali* on the leeward side are extremely arid.

It's a wonder how the region—especially the bustling port city of Lahaina—has
managed to thrive without rain. Lahaina's burgeoning population has surely put a
strain on the fresh water resources that once flowed freely down the mountains
since its early days as the home of the Hawaiian kings, to its heyday as a whaling
port, and in its current status as the busiest tourist town on Maui. Despite the
apparent lack of hydration, West Maui has continued to grow, and the resorts now
stretch for ten miles north of Lahaina from Ka'anapali to Kapalua. The popularity
of the area's real estate is well warranted, for the western coast is lined with gorgeous beaches and few sunbathers would trade the leeward coast's dry heat for
the windward side's rain showers.

There is only one road in and out of West Maui, **Hwy. 30,** or **Honoapi'ilani Hwy.,**
which becomes **Rte. 340 (Kahekili Hwy.)** north of Kapalua. Hwy. 30 is a two-lane
road that hugs the scenic coastline from Ma'alaea north. Near Ma'alaea, Hwy. 30
intersects with **Rte. 380** (Dairy Rd.), which goes northeast to Kahului and **Rte.
310/31,** which heads southeast to Kihei. Although on maps it may appear that the
northern route around the mountains (Rte. 340) is the shortest distance between
Kapalua and Wailuku, it isn't. The road narrows down to one lane, which in many
places is barely the width of a car, and hugs the cliffs with no guardrail protection

from the water below. This route can be done as a **scenic drive** at a leisurely pace, but for everyday travel, stick to Hwy. 30. Also note that accidents occur frequently on Hwy. 30, and when they do, the road is closed for as long as it takes to investigate and document the accident. Rte. 340 is closed as well, so no one will be tempted to take the hazardous back route. If this happens, just be prepared to sit and wait for a few hours, or turn around and go to the beach!

LAHAINA

Lahaina means "cruel" or "merciless sun" and visitors will quickly find that the city is aptly named—in any season, Lahaina is *hot*. Though it may be difficult to visualize, Lahaina was once prized by the Hawaiian royalty for its abundance of fresh water—streams used to flow freely down the mountains to the harbor. Fresh water, good food, and local hospitality also attracted commoners—Lahaina became a great whaling center of the Pacific during the first half of the 19th century. Whalers who came searching for humpbacks would often wreak havoc on the town, starting drunken riots and fighting each other with clubs and stones. The missionaries who set up homes to care for the unwanted progeny of sailors and local women were constantly at odds with the rowdy crews—they were even the target of cannonfire after laws were passed prohibiting women (naked and willing) from swimming out to meet the ships.

Remnants of Lahaina's colorful history are still visible in the restored buildings and sites of the downtown historic district, although they are overpowered in many places by t-shirt shops, activities booths, and theme restaurants. Lahaina has become a tourist trap, but that doesn't keep people from enjoying it. Sitting on the seawall on Front St. provides never-ending people-watching entertainment (and the sunset over the water is pretty sweet too). Just keep in mind that if you tire of mai tais and timeshare proposals, there *is* another Lahaina to discover.

✈ ORIENTATION

Lahaina is half-way up Maui's western coast, to the left of the West Maui mountains. **Honoapi'ilani Hwy. (Hwy. 30)** is the current two-lane bypass highway (another is reputed to be in the works), running inland of the town center all the way north past Ka'anapali and Napili. In light traffic, it takes about 15min. to drive the 10 miles from Lahaina north to Kapalua. Lahaina's main drag, **Front St.,** parallels the highway along the waterfront and is connected to it by five cross streets (from south to north: **Shaw St., Dickenson St., Lahainaluna Rd., Papalaua St.,** and **Kenui St.**). **Waine'e St.** runs the length of Lahaina, between the highway and Front St. The **Molokai Princess** makes daily trips to **Molokai.** The ferry leaves from Lahaina Harbor. For more information, call ☎800-275-6969 or 667-6165, or see p. 179.

🔢 PRACTICAL INFORMATION

TOURIST AND FINANCIAL SERVICES

Tourist Office: In the Old Lahaina Courthouse in Banyan Tree Sq. (☎667-9193; www.visitlahaina.com). A free walking tour map of historic sites is available, in addition to brochures on activities. A gift shop, one-room museum, and restrooms are also on the premises. Open daily 9am-5pm.

Tours: See **Sights,** below.

Banks: There is a **Bank of Hawaii, American Savings Bank,** and **First Hawaiian Bank** on Papalaua St., and there are **ATMs** in every shopping center.

LOCAL SERVICES

Library: (☎ 662-3950). Across the street from the Baldwin Home on Front St.; entrance is on Wharf St. Open Tu noon-8pm, W-Th 9am-5pm, F-Sa 10:30am-4:30pm.

Laundromats: Kahana Koin-Op Laundromat, 4465 Honoapi'ilani Hwy. (☎ 669-1581), and **One Hour Martinizing Dry Cleaning,** 3350 L. Honoapi'ilani Hwy. (☎ 661-6768).

Public Toilets: There are public toilets in every shopping center along Front St., as well as on the second floor of the Visitor Center in the Old Lahaina Courthouse.

Parking: Every shopping center has 2-4hr. parking for customers with validated tickets. There is some free street parking (pay attention to the time limits because police do ticket here), and a town lot on Dickenson and Front St. with free 3hr. parking.

EMERGENCY AND COMMUNICATIONS

Emergency: ☎ 911.

Police: ☎ 244-6400. Located north of Lahaina above Wahikuli Wayside Park.

Pharmacies: There are no 24hr. pharmacies in Lahaina. **Long's Drugs** (☎ 667-4384), in the Lahaina Cannery Mall, is open M-F 8am-10pm and Sa-Su 8am-9pm. **Lahaina Pharmacy** (☎ 661-3119), in the Lahaina Shopping Center, is open until 5:30pm.

Medical Services: Kaiser Permanente Clinic, 910 Waine'e St. (☎ 661-7400), and **Maui Medical Group,** 130 Prison St. (☎ 661-0051), are both open M-F 8am-5pm, Sa 8am-noon.

Internet Access:

Down to Earth Natural Foods Store, on Lahainaluna St., is a very comfortable place to check your email ($3 per 15min.) with A/C, fresh veggie juices, and a salad bar. Open daily 8am-8pm.

Ali'i Mocha Internet Cafe, 505 Front St. (☎ 661-7800), has 4 DSL terminals and serves teas, coffees, and a few sandwiches. $2 for the first 10min., 20¢ for each additional min. Open daily 7am-1pm and 4-9pm.

Swiss Cafe (☎ 661-6776), on Front St. across from the Banyan Tree, serves Italian espressos and smoothies, and charges 15¢ per min. with a $2 minimum.

Karma Kafe, in Anchor Sq., has vegetarian sandwiches, chai and coffee drinks, and DSL for 20¢ per min. Open M-Th 8am-5pm, F 8am-4pm.

Post Office: 132 Papalaua St. (☎ 661-0904), in the Old Lahaina Center. Open M-F 8am-5pm and Sa 9am-1pm.

Zip Code: 96761.

▟ ACCOMMODATIONS

Staying in Lahaina is possible on any budget, and most of the affordable accommodations have more character than the chain hotels and condos in the resorts farther north. If you plan to partake of Lahaina's limited nightlife, it's a good idea to stay in town so you won't have to drive home. Although everything in town is within walking distance, having a car is useful to access the best beaches, hikes, and sights of the area. Note that some accommodations charge holiday rates for Halloween (when there is a big party in Lahaina) and Christmas.

The nearest **campsite** is at **Camp Pecusa** (☎ 661-4303), a private campground on the coast, 5 mi. south of Lahaina and just east of Olowalu. Tent camping costs $6 per person; no reservations are accepted. There are six-person cabins that can be booked ahead of time. In addition, there is a county-maintained campsite at **Papalaua Wayside Park,** just north of the tunnel on Honoapi'ilani Hwy. This beachfront site is close to the road and frequently crowded with homeless people. For information, call ☎ 270-7389 or check the county website, www.countyofmaui.com.

B&BS AND HOSTELS

Old Lahaina House, 407 'Ilikahi St. (☎800-847-0761 or 667-4663; fax 667-5615; info@oldlahaina.com; www.oldlahaina.com), on the corner of 'Ilikahi and Kaua'ula St., 1 block south of Shaw St. Nestled in the quiet, residential southern end of Lahaina, the house is only 1 block from a sandy beach (good for surfing and sunsets) and a brief walk from the historic district. Owner Sherry Barbier is a gracious hostess who sees that all the rooms are equipped with beach towels and a picnic cooler. Rooms all have A/C, TV, phone, microwave, fridge, coffeemaker, and private bath. Sherry also manages a gorgeous 1-bedroom cottage across the street, complete with custom tiled kitchen and 4-poster bamboo bed, A/C, washer-dryer, and full bath. 3-night minimum stay somewhat flexible. Reserve with 50% deposit; balance due 30 days prior to arrival. Rooms $79-115; cottage $150. AmEx/MC/V. ❸

Bambula Inn, 518 'Ilikahi St. (☎800-544-5524 or 667-6753; www.bambula.com). Down the street from Old Lahaina House, Bambula is another comfortable guesthouse that offers privacy with 2 free-standing cottages and 1 additional room in the main house (with a private entrance). Each cottage has a full kitchen and bath, patio and outdoor shower. The best part is the free sunset sail on host Pierre Chasle's boat, *Bambula*. 3-night minimum stay somewhat flexible. Reserve with 50% deposit. Room $79; cottages $100-110. AmEx/MC/V. ❸

Patey's Place, 761 Waine'e St. (☎268-2259). Patey's Place is a very basic hostel, offering the cheapest beds in West Maui and not much else. It is not as well supervised as other hostels on the island, but the 10pm "quiet time" rule tries to keep the partying to a minimum. Mostly young people stay here, although there are several long-term guests and hangabouts. Guests share a kitchen, coin-op laundry, TV room, and back porch for lounging and ping-pong. 2 of the private rooms have private bathrooms; other guests share 4 bathrooms among themselves. Reception 8:30am-noon and 5-10pm. Checkout 10am. 6-bed dorms $20, singles $45, doubles $60. No credit cards. ❶

HOTELS AND INNS

Makai Inn, 1415 Front St. (☎662-3200), on the quieter northern end of Front St. An allaround excellent value for a budget accommodation. All suites have bedroom, small sitting area, private lanai, full kitchen, and new bathrooms (no TV or phone, though). No A/C, but rooms are comfortable with ceiling fans and the ocean breeze. All suites face the inner courtyard garden, and the pricier rooms have ocean views (the inn is right on the harbor). On-site parking and coin-op laundry. Check-out 11am. Reserve with credit card; no deposit required. Garden view $75; ocean view $90. AmEx/MC/V. ❸

Lahaina Inn, 127 Lahainaluna Rd. (☎800-669-3444 or 667-0577; fax 667-9480; inntown@lahainainn.com; www.lahainainn.com). Perfect for a romantic stay in old Lahaina. Each of the 9 rooms and 3 suites is uniquely decorated with turn-of-the-century period furnishings and oriental carpets. Modern comforts include in-room classical music, A/C, and phones (but no TV). Guests can enjoy people-watching from the rocking chairs on the street-facing lanais. Continental breakfast (delivered to your room) included. Check-in 3pm. Check-out 11am. Reserve with 1-night deposit. Rooms $109-169, depending on size, season, and view. AmEx/MC/V. ❹

Best Western Pioneer Inn, 658 Wharf St. (☎800-457-5457; fax 667-9366; www.pioneerinnmaui.com). In its early days as Lahaina's only hotel (the harbor-facing section was built in 1901), the Pioneer Inn saw some rough n' ready guests—the house rules still posted in the lobby suggest that those who can't stay sober before noon should find a room elsewhere. Since then, it's been cleaned up and fully renovated but its character is largely intact. The standard rooms all have cable TV, A/C and fan, coffeemaker, and lanai overlooking Banyan Sq. or the hotel courtyard and pool. Some rooms smell a bit musty; ask for a non-smoking one if cigarette odor bothers you. Reserve with credit card. Rooms

$115-180; more expensive rooms are slightly larger with fridge and wet bar, and most have an extra bed. AmEx/D/DC/MC/V. ❹

Lahaina Shores Beach Resort, 475 Front St. (☎800-642-6284 or 661-3339; fax 667-1145; info@classicresorts.com; www.lahainashores.com). The reason to stay here is the outside, not the inside—it's the only hotel in Lahaina located on a sandy beach, and it has a well-maintained pool and jacuzzi to boot. Rooms are nothing special, but they all have a full kitchen and bath. The oceanfront rooms feature a very nice beach view; mountainside rooms glimpse the *pali* over the parking lot. Check-in 3pm. Check-out 11am. Reserve with $150 deposit. Studios $160-205; 1-bedroom $200-270. AmEx/MC/V. Not fully wheelchair accessible. ❺

▐ FOOD

It's hard to find a restaurant in Lahaina without a Hollywood theme and logo merchandise—predictable but ever-popular chain restaurants such as Bubba Gump Shrimp, Cheeseburger in Paradise, and the Hard Rock Cafe have hit Front St. full force. Pretty much every place in town caters exclusively to tourists, which means that there's a lot of inflated prices, but also a lot of variety—you can get pretty much anything in Lahaina, from burgers to *bok choy*. With only a few exceptions, Lahaina restaurants stop serving by 9pm, so plan accordingly.

For a do-it-yourself meal, there is a 24hr. **Safeway** at 1221 Honoapi'ilani Hwy. and a **Foodland** in the Lahaina Sq. Marketplace. **Down to Earth Natural Foods Store,** on the corner of Waine'e and Lahainaluna Rd., has organic and local produce and packaged foods as well as a salad and hot bar. (Open daily 8am-8pm.) **Mr. Wine,** across the street from Down to Earth, sells wine, beer, and liquor. (Open M-Sa 11am-7pm.)

MAUI

Lahaina

🏠 ACCOMMODATIONS
Bambula Inn, **5**
Lahaina Inn, **2**
Lahaina Shores, **6**
Makai Inn, **1**
Old Lahaina House, **7**
Patey's Place, **3**
Pioneer Inn, **4**

THE BIG SPLURGE

FIT FOR A KING

Let your inner royalty shine at **The Feast at Lele,** a delight for all the senses. Brought to you by the producers of the Old Lahaina Luau, it's less a traditional luau than a truly phenomenal meal served oceanfront at sunset, with a hula performance. Chef James McDonald, of Pacific'O and I'o (see **Food,** p. 96) fame, has designed a sumptuous 12-course meal that takes your tastebuds on a Polynesian tour. The courses are served in a leisurely manner so that you can enjoy the dance that goes along with each country. Guests begin in Hawaii with steamed *moi* fit for a king, then travel to Tonga for robust flavors and powerful dancing. Most guests claim Tahiti as their favorite, with the sophisticated French influences melding in the creamy scallops or the *poisson cru,* but Samoa makes a strong showing in the fire-dancing finale. In short, the Feast of Lele contradicts everything you've heard about luaus—the food comes first and it's served at your table. For a special occasion, the Feast of Lele is absolutely worth the splurge—it costs about the same as dinner for two with a good bottle of wine at Maui's best restaurants, and it's a truly unique culinary experience. *(Held on the beach behind I'o. 505 Front St. ☎866-244-LELE or 667-LELE; www.feastatlele.com. Tu-Sa evenings. Reserve 2-4 weeks in advance. $89, ages 12 and under $59. Gratuity not included.)*

CAFES AND TAKE-OUT

Cafe O'Lei Lahaina, 839 Front St. (☎661-9491), through the entrance of the Ocean Front Marketplace. In contrast to most of Front St.'s overdone and over-priced options, Cafe O'Lei is a real find. Right on the water, the breeze and the view are delightful. The food emphasizes fresh local ingredients, prepared creatively (*taro* salad with okinawan sweet potatoes $9; sauteed mahi mahi with ginger butter and papaya salsa $16). The lunch menu features salads and foccacia sandwiches in the $7-8 range. BYOB. Open daily for lunch 10:30am-4:30pm and dinner 5-9pm. ❸

Penne Pasta Cafe, 180 Dickenson St. (☎661-6633). Good-sized portions of pasta with homemade sauce (bolognese fettucine $8) are served in a casual but classy atmosphere. Vegetarian options, such as the whole wheat spaghetti with roasted eggplant, tomatoes, oregano, and basil ($9) are big on flavor. Save room for dessert (tiramisu $6). Open M-Th 11am-9:30pm, F 11am-10pm, Sa 5-10pm, Su 5-9pm. Take-out and delivery available. ❷

Maui Tacos (☎661-8883), in Lahaina Sq. Fresh corn tortillas, 5 kinds of homemade salsa, and a more-than-filling meal for under $6: either it's heaven or Maui Tacos. Open for breakfast too (egg burritos or *huevos rancheros* $5). Additional locations in Napili Plaza and Kihei (see p. 194). Take-out only. Open M-Sa 9am-9pm, Su 9am-8pm. ❶

No Ka Oi Deli, 222 Papalaua St. (☎667-2244), in Anchor Sq. A local favorite for take-out lunches, No Ka Oi serves subs ($5-6), salads ($5.25), and plate lunches (teriyaki chicken $4.75). Their specialty is Hop Wo bread, made according to the traditional recipe from the **Hop Wo Store,** a Front St. landmark from the 1920s to the 60s. Open M-F 10am-2pm. ❶

Aloha Mixed Plate, 1285 Front St. (☎661-3322), on the harbor next to the Old Lahaina Luau. A great place to sample Hawaiian food. *Kalua* pig and other traditional Hawaiian meats are served plate lunch-style, with 2 scoop rice, 1 scoop macaroni salad. Everything is served on paper plates (you may have to ask for napkins and utensils), but the ocean view is first-class. During dinner, the drumbeats of the luau next door provide unexpected ambience. Plate lunches $5-13. Outdoor seating only. Cocktails $4. Open daily 10:30am-10pm. ❶

House of Saimin (☎667-7572), in the Old Lahaina Center next to the Lahaina Pharmacy. Steaming bowls of *saimin* (homemade fish broth with noodles and other accompaniments) are served on a red U-shaped counter, beneath photos of the local Little League teams. The only place in town that serves food late at night. Open M 5-10pm, Tu-Th 5pm-2am, F-Sa 5pm-3am. ❶

Sunrise Cafe, 693A Front St. (☎661-8558). A decent breakfast and lunch place with patio seating overlooking the harbor. American breakfasts, Hawaiian-style *loco moco*, and plate lunches will fill you up for less than $10. Open daily 6am-6pm. ❷

RESTAURANTS

Lahaina Coolers, 180 Dickenson St. (☎661-7082). Serves up reliably good food at decent prices in a relaxed, open-air atmosphere. Varied menu with everything from tasty fish tacos marinated in fresh garlic and tomatoes to Evil Jungle Pasta in a Thai-style peanut sauce to burgers and steak. Egg and griddle breakfasts $6-11, lunch $8-11, dinner entrees $9-20. Happy Hour twice daily 3-6pm and 10pm-2am features $3 well drinks and microbrews. Open daily 8am-2am. ❸

Thai Chef (☎667-2814), in the Lahaina Shopping Center, tucked into the strip of stores next to Maui Myth and Magic Theater. This cozy Thai restaurant has a solid reputation, with an extensive menu of curries, seafood dishes, and vegetarian options ($8-13). Open for lunch M-F 11am-2:30pm; dinner nightly 5pm-close. D/DC/MC/V. ❸

UPSCALE DINING

David Paul's Lahaina Grill, 127 Lahainaluna Rd. (☎667-5117), is consistently stellar, serving innovative New American food in a stylish (and air-conditioned) environment. Offerings change frequently, but usually draw inspiration from local ingredients. Entrees $28-38. Reservations required. Open nightly from 6pm.

Pacific'O, 505 Front St. (☎667-4341), on the beach. Executive chef and owner James McDonald serves beautifully presented Pacific Rim cuisine at the more traditional of his two restaurants (the other is I'o, listed below). Open-air with waterfront views. Lunch $12-15, dinner entrees $24-30. Reservations required. Open daily 11am-4pm and 5:30-10pm. ❺

I'o, 505 Front St. (☎661-8422), on the beach. The more contemporary of chef James McDonald's restaurants, I'o has a slightly more adventurous menu; vegetarians especially will appreciate the three well-balanced entrees (no pasta primavera default here). If you want to sample Chef McDonald's cuisine in a sumptuous sunset feast, with the added bonus of hula entertainment, consider the **Feast of Lele** (see **Fit for a King,** p. 204). Entrees $24-30. Reservations necessary. Open daily 5:30-10pm. ❺

🗺 SIGHTS

The **Lahaina Restoration Foundation,** a non-profit agency that manages and maintains many of Lahaina's historic sites, publishes a brochure entitled *Lahaina, A Walking Tour of Historic and Cultural Sites,* available for free at their headquarters in the Masters' Reading Room on Dickenson and Luakini St. It is also published in color with ads, as the *Maui Historical Walking Guide,* and can be obtained for free at the Visitor Center in the Old Lahaina Courthouse. The walking tour describes 31 sites in Lahaina's historic district, reconstructing bits of the town's history through its whaling and missionary days and also detailing the churches and cultural centers of Lahaina's various immigrant groups who were brought in to work the plantations. The sights are rather dry by themselves—what makes them interesting are the stories behind them, which is why a guided tour (see below) is worthwhile.

If you're interested in native Hawaiian culture, especially pre-white settlement, the best money you can spend in Lahaina is the $34 it costs to take a guided tour with ▨**Maui Nei,** a grassroots organization devoted to relating the history of

Lahaina from Hawaiians' point of view. Local guides, working from oral histories and traditional chants as well as original archival research, lead small groups along a 1½hr. walking tour of Lahaina's harbor and backstreets. In addition to breathing life into the historical sites, Maui Nei offers insight into what visitors can't see. The tour ends on what was once the sacred island of **Moku'ula,** the home and burial site of Hawaiian royalty. The island, once surrounded by wetlands used for the royal fish ponds and *taro* patches, now lies buried underneath a baseball field and parking lot—desecrated, but as the tour reveals, not completely hidden. Half of the proceeds of the tour go toward the reclamation and restoration of this holy ground, which will eventually house a cultural center, host educational programs, and accept volunteers for an archaeological excavation. (☎661-9494. Tours are conducted several times per week. Call or see www.mauinei.com for more information and reservations.)

ACTIVITIES

The activity booths that line Front St. offer an overwhelming number of choices. This is a big business—between helicopter rides, biking, and parasailing—companies market thrills from air, land, and sea. Most of these activities can be quite costly, and the brokers take a hefty cut as commission. Sometimes booking with the company directly can be cheaper; if you choose to go through an activity broker for the sake of convenience, be assertive and don't be afraid to walk to the next booth if they are not entirely accommodating. There are also activities (boogie boarding, coastal snorkeling, hiking) that cost little or nothing and don't require a middleman; don't fret if the pricier options are out of your budget.

BIKING. Lahaina is more than manageable on two wheels. Although the coastal scenery may be appealing, biking along Honoapi'ilani Hwy. north or south of Lahaina isn't the safest due to heavy traffic and narrow shoulders in some areas. **West Maui Cycles** (☎661-9005), on Waine'e St. near Maui Tacos, rents road and mountain bikes with daily and weekly rates. Many companies offer bike tours down the volcano. (For more information, see **Haleakala National Park,** p. 225.)

BOOGIE BOARDING. Catching waves on a boogie board is a lot easier than surfing. Driving toward Lahaina from the south, just look for spots with good conditions and other boarders, pull over, and jump in. **Puamana Beach,** just south of Lahaina, is usually a good spot. Some of the beaches in Ka'anapali are also excellent for boogie boarding, especially the south end of **Ka'anapali Beach** and the blissfully deserted **Oneloa Beach** (see p. 198). All the surf shops in Lahaina also rent boogie boards for $5-8 per day or about $20 per week.

HELICOPTERS. While beautiful from the ground, West Maui and Molokai are spectacular from the air. Most companies tour both West Maui and Molokai during a one-hour trip, peeking at the waterfalls hidden in the West Maui mountains, zipping across to the sea cliffs of Molokai, circling Molokai and returning to Iao Valley. This trip is best done as early in the morning as possible, to ensure prime visibility in the West Maui mountains. Most companies list this trip at around $200 per person, but the activity booths cut that price almost in half; there's definitely flexibility for last minute bookings as well. Of all the companies that offer trips, **Alexair** (☎877-4354) is the only one that has two-way headsets so you can talk to the pilots. **Blue Hawaiian** (☎871-8844) also has an excellent reputation, but there are several other companies that charge comparable rates.

PARASAILING. Parasailing definitely looks scarier than it is—the ride is a gentle glide that lasts for about 10 minutes. Companies only operate May-December, so as not to interfere with the whales during their breeding season. **Parasail Ka'anapali**

has the best deal for singles and tandems and leaves from Mala Wharf on the northern end of town. (☎669-6555. $24-40 depending on season.)

SAILING. Lahaina looks even better from offshore. The **Hyatt** in Ka'anapali rents Hobie Cats you can sail yourself for $45 per hour. Many companies have sunset and daytime sailing trips (some include dinner; others just snacks and drinks) on schooners or catamarans. (☎661-1234 ext. 3290.) **Trilogy** is by far the biggest operator, with numerous boats running all kinds of excursions. In addition to its beautiful boats, Trilogy's real advantage is their Lanai excursions—they're the only company that owns property on the island where they can land and do a nice barbeque lunch (or dinner, for sunset sails) overlooking Manele Bay. (☎888-MAUI-800; www.sailtrilogy.com. Rates run $169-199 depending on the trip.)

SCUBA DIVING. The two most popular places for offshore dives are **Lanai** and the **back wall of Molokini.** There are multiple companies competing for boat dive business in Lahaina. **Extended Horizons** (☎667-0611) is known for good service on boat dives; **Maui Dive Shop** (☎661-5388) is larger and more impersonal, though still reliable. For shore dives, **Kahekili Beach Park** is a good place for beginners (most certification classes start here); **Black Rock,** below the Ka'anapali Sheraton, and the right side of **Honolua Bay** (in summer) are also popular West Maui dive spots. For shore dives, **Pacific Dive** (☎667-5331) is reputable and reasonably priced. Numerous companies give introductory classes, starting at around $50.

SNORKELING. Before you splurge on a boat excursion, know that there is excellent snorkeling at beaches all along the West Maui coast. A self-guided adventures will cost you only a few bucks for the mask and fins. Many companies in Lahaina rent equipment for $2-10 per day. **Maui Dive Shop** (☎661-6166) is courteous and professional, with several locations including the Lahaina Cannery Mall.

The best West Maui snorkel spots are north of Lahaina; see **Honolua Bay** (p. 212), **Kapalua Beach** (p. 212), **Kahekili Beach Park** (p. 211), and **Black Rock/Ka'anapali Beach** (p. 211) for details. If you still want to take a boat excursion to the submerged crater fish paradise of **Molokini.** On a good day, visibility at Molokini is over 100 ft. Plan on spending anywhere from $45-95; excursions typically take a few hours, and include equipment (mask, snorkel, fins, and sometimes a wetsuit), demonstration, drinks, and deli or BBQ lunch. When choosing a company, keep in mind the size of the boat (smaller boats take about 25 passengers while bigger boats take over 100) and the time of day (mornings are always clearer and calmer, though afternoons are cheaper). Conditions can be variable at any time of year, and many a snorkeler set on going to Molokini has ended up at "Turtle Town" or "Coral Gardens," less glamorous spots just offshore that have decent snorkeling, but are not measurably better than what you can see from beaches for free.

SURFING. Ah, surfing, the sport of kings and bums alike. Driving into Lahaina from the south, you'll see surfers from the road—**Olowalu** and **Launiopoko** usually have reliable breaks, though conditions change daily so your best bet is to ask the locals. There is a local surf spot about a block south of the Lahaina Shores hotel that is usually uncrowded and good for beginners; watch out for waves breaking in the shallow water over the coral, however. **Honolua Bay** is famous for its winter surf, but beginners should stick to watching from the sand. Board rentals start at about $20 per day with price breaks for weekly rentals. Expect to pay about $55 for a two-hour surf group lesson and twice that for a private lesson.

WHALE-WATCHING. From mid-December to mid-April (peaking in February and March), hundreds of humpback whales come to Maui to breed before continuing up to Alaska for the summer. All along the southern and western coasts, the whales put on quite a show, and you don't need to leave shore to see them breaching and spouting. If you do want a closer look, the best company by far is **Pacific Whale Foundation** (☎879-8811), a non-profit organization that contributes to whale research and conservation. They run a number of different trips; the basic two-hour whale watch runs $24-34.

🔊 HIKES

LAHAINA PALI TRAIL. (5½ mi. Trailhead: Ma'alaea, off Hwy. 30's 5-mile marker. Elevation change: 1600 ft. Level: challenging.) This trail across the mountains is made all the more strenuous by the intense sun at any time of year. It is most rewarding during whale season, when the view from the top can include hundreds of whales frolicking in the channel (bring binoculars!). This hike works best if you have two cars, or can be dropped off in Ma'alaea and picked up in Olowalu. Starting from the eastern trailhead in Ma'alaea allows you to get the steep part over with first and finish at the beach. The path begins with a steep climb up to Kealaloloa Ridge; once there, hikers are treated to views of the central valley, Haleakala, and Kahoolawe, Molokini, and Lanai offshore. The trail descends more gradually from the ridge, and *kiawe* trees provide some shade along the way. The end of the hike is in Olowalu, across the highway from the beach. Hikers should be equipped with sturdy hiking boots, plenty of water, and sunscreen. *(To reach the Ma'alaea trailhead from Lahaina, turn left at the 5-mile marker on Hwy. 30, just south of the junction with Rte. 380. The trailhead and parking lot are clearly marked. Parking is available for a second car or pickup at the lot at the 11-mile marker on Hwy. 30.)*

OLOWALU MASSACRE Though no evidence remains of the encounter, a bloody massacre occurred in the tiny town of Olowalu. In 1790, the US vessel *Eleanora* was moored off shore. Native Hawaiians, curious about the iron ship parts, stole a dinghy from the ship to examine its workings. The *Eleanora*'s captain, Simon Metcalf, retaliated by luring the Hawaiians out to the ship with offers of trade. As they sailed toward him in their canoes, Metcalf fired his cannons at them. Over 100 Hawaiians were killed and numerous others were injured.

OLOWALU PETROGLYPHS. (0.6 mi. Trailhead: Behind the general store. Level: easy.) The tiny village of Olowalu—the site of the worst massacre of Hawaiians in the history of Western contact (see p. 208)—is home to a French restaurant, a general store, and a treasure of centuries-old Hawaiian petroglyphs. Walk behind the store to a water tank on the left and follow the old sugar cane road into the valley. After less than a mile, there is a viewing platform facing a lava rock outcropping on which the petroglyphs are carved. Animals, sailing vessels, chiefs and commoners are identifiable alongside more recent graffiti. *(At the 15-mile marker.)*

🏖 BEACHES

Lahaina itself is not the place for sunbathing and swimming—the few sandy beaches have somewhat murky water, and are really only good for watching the sun set. There is a sandy beach behind the Lahaina Shores hotel and a good local surf spot at the break a block south of the hotel, but other than those, the beaches north and south of town are much more appealing. Heading toward Lahaina from the south, the good surf spots are visible from the road. **Puamana Beach County Park,** the first beach south of Lahaina, is a nice spot for a beachside picnic. **Launiopoko Wayside Park,** a mile farther south, has restrooms and showers and a surf break popular with beginners. Both these parks, however, are unimpressive when compared to the beaches north of Lahaina; for details see **Ka'anapali** (p. 210), **Napili** (p. 212), and **Kapalua** (p. 212).

ENTERTAINMENT

Lahaina has a number of options evening entertainment options, some of which are loosely related to Hawaiian culture. If your visit to Maui won't be complete without a **luau**, Lahaina is definitely the best place to attend one, and other performances can also make for enjoyable entertainment.

LUAUS

Many of the hotels in Ka'anapali and Wailea offer their own versions of this traditional Hawaiian feast, but the most authentic is the **Old Lahaina Luau**, 1251 Front St., held nightly on the waterfront near Mala Wharf, across from the Cannery Mall. Guests are greeted with fresh flower leis (a change from the cheap shell ones other luaus have) and a mai tai from the open bar, and then ushered into the grounds. Along the water, local craftspeople display their wares and demonstrate lei-making and *poi*-pounding. Just before sunset, the *kalua* pig is unearthed from the *imu*, and the feast begins, served buffet-style from thatched huts. Everything is laid out and organized to avoid lines and backups, and the food is very good (much better than any other commercial luau). Guests sit on traditional cushions or in chairs at tables arranged in a large semi-circle around the grassy hula mound. The hula performance takes a historical approach, narrating the Polynesians' arrival to Hawaii and progressing through the missionary and plantation periods to modern times. On the whole, the evening is quite enjoyable, and definitely worth the price for the upgrade in food, service, and atmosphere from the average hotel luau. (☎800-248-5828 or 667-1998; www.oldlahainaluau.com. Reserve 2-4 weeks in advance. $75, ages 12 and under $45.) Another, albeit more expensive, option is **The Feast at Lele** (see **Fit For a King**, p. 204).

SHOWS

Lahaina has two performances that do not include dinner, although both can be arranged with dinner packages at nearby restaurants. **'Ulalena** is a modern interpretation of ancient Hawaiian myths and recent Hawaiian history, communicated through dance, song, chant, and projected text and images. A live percussion group provides a pounding rhythm for the performers on stage. The show is colorful, engaging, and complex, impressing mainland visitors and attracting locals for return performances. This memorable performance is definitely worth the price. (Maui Myth and Magic Theater, 878 Front St. ☎877-688-4800 or 661-9913; www.mauitheatre.com. Shows Tu-Sa. $45-55, ages 3-10 $25-35.)

Entertaining in an entirely different way, **Warren and Annabelle's**, 900 Front St., campy showtunes and astonishing magic tricks have a Vegas-like feel to them. The singing cocktail waitresses who accompany the resident "ghost" Annabelle as she plays the piano fully admit that the show is better when you've had a few drinks. Getting tipsy on $7 tropical cocktails, however, can be an expensive endeavor when you add it to the price of the tickets. Once you leave Annabelle's parlor for the main show in the intimate purpose-built theater, magician host Warren carries the show on his own, entertaining even the most sober straight faces in the crowd. Performing magic and sleight-of-hand card tricks up-close, Warren gives his audience a good show, though his comedy routine is a bit weak at times. The evening begins at 6pm with good but pricey pupus and drinks, and the magic ends after 9pm, so you may prefer to eat early as most restaurants are closed by the end of the show. (☎667-MAGIC; www.warrenandannabelles.com. 21+ only. $40.)

🔲 SHOPPING

In addition to the glut of t-shirt shops, tacky jewelry stands, and galleries hawking "island art," there are a few places in Lahaina actually worth seeking out. For crafts, keepsakes, clothing, and souvenirs that are actually made in Hawaii (as opposed to the Philippines or Taiwan), there's no better place than ▨**Na Mea Hawaii** (☎661-5707), which has two locations in Lahaina. Everything in the store is local and handmade, from the carved fishhooks on woven cord to the belts made of the bright feathers once used for the cloaks of *ali'i*. The Cannery Mall location is larger and has a bigger selection, including clothing; the store in the Masters' Reading Room, a historic landmark on the corner of Dickenson and Front St., has a more limited selection but a cozy armchair for perusing the excellent selection of books and music. For light beach reading, head to the **Old Lahaina Book Emporium,** in the courtyard of 505 Front St. Selling new and used books, the Emporium has an extensive Hawaiiana section as well as fiction, mysteries, poetry and more lining its dusty shelves. There's a very interesting Jim Crow-era collection of rare books and figurines behind the counter. (☎661-1399. Open daily 10am-9pm.)

There are a number of **shopping centers** in Lahaina. Beginning at the southern end of town, the **505 Front St.** complex is one of the nicer ones, with a few shops and cafes tucked into a quiet courtyard. The **Wharf Cinema Center,** 658 Front St., has a first-run movie theater (the three-screen **Lahaina Cinemas**) and three floors of nondescript aloha shirts and trinkets.

🔲 NIGHTLIFE

As active as Lahaina is during the day and early evening, it is disappointingly short on nightlife. Most of the restaurants along Front St. have bars with cheesy live bands. **Moose McGillycuddy's,** 844 Front St., is reliably lively, especially on Tuesday $1 drink nights. (☎667-7758. Open daily 7am-2am, kitchen open until 10pm.) The crowd moves to **Maui Brews,** in the new Lahaina Center, for $1 drinks on Wednesdays. Both bars have live music nightly with dance clubs in the back and can be fun if you go with the right attitude. **Longhi's,** with live music every Friday, is definitely worth checking out for dancing. (888 Front St. ☎667-2288. F Live music 9:30pm-close. 21+ after 9:30pm.)

KA'ANAPALI

Ka'anapali has long been a resort community. Hawaiian chiefs once prized its beaches for surfing; now tourists use them for every kind of beach activity. All the major hotel chains own properties on Ka'anapali Beach, a 3-mile stretch of golden sand punctuated by the volcanic Black Rock that makes for spectacular snorkeling, scuba diving, and (for the brave) cliff jumping. This is one of the most prized places to stay in all of Maui; hotels here run at least $250 per night. Travelers on a budget may have more luck staying in Lahaina or renting a condo in Napili or Honokowai (see p. 212).

🔲🔲 ACCOMMODATIONS AND FOOD. Of the major chain hotels on Ka'anapali Beach, the **Hyatt Regency Maui** ❺ is the biggest and most luxurious. (☎800-233-1234. Rooms $285-525; suites $600-3000.) **The Sheraton Maui** ❺ has the best location, right on the cliff at Black Rock. (☎800-782-9488. Rooms $280-470; suites from $850.) The best deal on the beach is the **Ka'anapali Beach Hotel** ❺, which is definitely less over-the-top than its neighbors, and relatively affordable considering its oceanfront location. (☎800-262-8450. Rooms $185-285; suites

$225-600.) Most of the restaurants in Ka'anapali are located in the hotels, but locals eat at **Jonny's Burger Joint ❶**, downstairs from Luigi's, a hole-in-the-wall that serves the best burgers on the coast and cheap drafts (open daily 11:30am-1am). **Hula Grill ❺**, on the waterfront in Whalers' Village, is a bit overrated and overpriced, but still one of Ka'anapali's more reasonable options, serving salads, sandwiches and pizzas for lunch ($9-16) and seafood specialties ($20-32) for dinner. (☎ 667-6636. Open daily 11am-midnight, dinner served until 9:30pm.)

◪ BEACHES. Ka'anapali's southernmost beach, **Hanake'o'o**, or **Canoe Beach,** is the launch site for canoe races, jet skiing, and other activities (park in the lot between mile-markers 24 and 25). It is technically part of the same stretch of sand as **Ka'anapali Beach,** a popular beach fronted by the major hotels (parking is in the free lot next to the Sheraton). This section the Ka'anapali Beach Hotel and The Whaler is known as **Dig Me Beach,** for obvious reasons. People-watching here is great any time of day, and sunset is particularly beautiful. Ka'anapali Beach is marked by **Pu'u Keka'a** or **Black Rock,** an ideal place for **snorkeling** and beginner **scuba** (max. depths are about 35 ft.). King Kahekili's warriors used to demonstrate their bravery by jumping off the rock; today the brave (or crazy) do it voluntarily.

On the northern end of Ka'anapali, **Kahekili Beach Park** stretches for ½ mi. to Black Rock to the left, and quite a bit farther to the right, where it is much less crowded. This long, narrow stretch of sand is edged by hotels and a grassy park with picnic tables, restrooms, showers, and parking. Its clear, calm waters are popular with families, and are frequently used for introductory scuba classes.

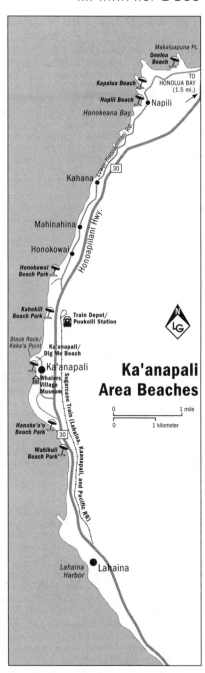

Ka'anapali Area Beaches

MAUI

HONOKOWAI, KAHANA, AND NAPILI

These three communities consist of one condominium development after another built along **Lower Honoapiʻilani Rd.**, and it's difficult to distinguish where one "town" ends and the next begins. **Honokowai** is the first development north of Kaʻanapali, on a sandy beach that can't quite rival Kaʻanapali Beach farther south. The next town, **Kahana**, consists of 1970s-style condos lining its rocky beaches. Finally, **Napili** is wedged between Kahana and Kapalua, with all of its condos either on or across from the sandy crescent of **Napili Bay,** an ever-popular family beach.

ⓚ ACCOMMODATIONS. The condos in this area are, in general, more moderately priced than the Kaʻanapali hotels to the south and the Kapalua resorts to the north. It's a good place to base your vacation for easy access to West Maui beaches and activities. Staying in a condo is especially convenient for families who want more than one bedroom, as well as access to a pool and recreational facilities. *Let's Go* recommends **Accommodations Hawaii,** a vacation rental company based in Lahaina that handles 160 properties in Kaʻanapali, Honokowai, Kahana, and Napili. All units are privately owned, and the prices are reasonable for every category—from beachfront highrises to luxury homes. Pictures, rates, and details of the properties are on the website. (☎800-847-0761; www.accommodations-hawaii.com. Rentals around $75-350 per night, with weekly and monthly rates available.)

ⓕ FOOD. There are grocery stores and several tasty take-out options in the **Honokowai Marketplace,** on Lower Honoapiʻilani Rd., and **Napili Plaza,** on Napilihau Rd. In AAAAA Rent-A-Space mall, just north of Honokowai Beach, ▨**Honokowai Okazuya and Deli ❶,** 3600D L. Honoapiʻilani Rd., is hands-down the best take-out in West Maui. There is literally something for everyone, from deli sandwiches and pasta to spicy Chinese eggplant to chicken *katsu* plates. As if that weren't enough, they also make delicious mahi mahi sauteed with mushrooms and capers, or *panko*-crusted and fried. There are only a few stools inside, so everything is made-to-order and boxed to go. (☎665-0512. Plates $6-9. Open M-Sa 10am-2:30pm and 4:30-9pm. Cash only.) In Napili Plaza, **Maui Tacos ❶** makes their own corn chips and tortillas, 5 kinds of salsa, and serves a filling meal for under $6—you can't beat that. (☎665-0222. Open M-Sa 9am-9pm, Su 9am-8pm.) Also in Napili Plaza, **The Coffee Store** is blissfully air-conditioned and has **Internet access** ($2.50 per 15min.).

ⓑ BEACHES. The best beach in these parts is **Napili Bay,** a crowded crescent of sand. Though the condos that front the beach do not allow public access to their parking lots, there is a limited amount of street parking. Public access to the shoreline is off Hui Dr. and Napili Pl.
   Kahana Beach, in front of the Kahana Sunset condos, has a sandy bottom, but lots of seaweed. Stay away from **Kaʻopala Beach** and **S-Turns Park,** which have been polluted by a dirty creek that empties into the ocean just south of the beaches. **Honokowai Beach Park** is a good place for a picnic (Okuzaya is across the street), but better beaching can be had in Kaʻanapali or Kapalua.

KAPALUA AND BEYOND

Towering Cook pines line the carefully planned roads of Kapalua, the most exclusive resort in Maui. There's none of the glitz of Wailea, just the understated elegance of the **Ritz Carlton Kapalua** and the **Kapalua Bay Hotel,** both of which have rooms from around $350 per night and (way) up. There are a few expensive shops and galleries next to the Ritz Carlton and a ▨**Sansei Seafood Restaurant & Sushi Bar ❺,** which has truly phenomenal sushi, as well as a full menu of creative Pacific Rim entrees. (Open for dinner nightly from 5:30pm. Early bird specials 25% off

5:30-6pm, late night 50% off, free karaoke Th-F 10pm-2am. See **Kihei** location, p. 194 for full review). There is really nothing in Kapalua for the budget traveler except **beaches,** which are free.

■ **BEACHES.** It's definitely worth the effort to navigate through Kapalua's resorts to reach **Kapalua Beach,** a gem of a beach located below the Ritz Carlton. The beach is a perfect crescent, far recessed into the coastline and protected by reef. The water is relatively clear and calm enough for children; the whole family will enjoy the ideal **snorkeling** conditions (equipment available for rent at the booth at the entrance to the beach). Parking is available in the lot beyond the Ritz.

North of Kapalua Beach, **Oneloa Beach** is another great find. It's usually nearly empty, and is perfect for secluded suntanning. It's better suited to boogie boarding than swimming though, as the sand gives way to reef and the waves are rather large. To reach public parking and shoreline access, take Office Rd. (the main road leading from the highway into Kapalua) and turn left at the end, then right on Ironwood Ln. Parking is before the gate, and the access path is opposite the parking lot. North of Oneloa, the better-known **D.T. Fleming Beach Park** has full facilities, shade, and a mighty riptide. Turn left off the highway just after mile-marker 31; the beach is at the end of the road. **Molule'ia Bay** and **Honolua Bay,** between mile-markers 32 and 33, offer some of the best **snorkeling** on the island when it's calm (huge swells roll into Honolua Bay in winter, and only experienced surfers should take them on). Molule'ia Bay, also known as **Slaughterhouse Beach,** has a sandy entrance; Honolua Bay is rocky but has an easy entrance via an old boat ramp in the center of the bay. Parking is available in pull-outs along the road. To Honolua Bay, walk around the gate on the dirt road and continue for 5min. through forest and across a dry riverbed; the road leads you right to the boat ramp.

■ **KAHEKILI HIGHWAY SCENIC DRIVE.** One of the most beautiful, and certainly the most heart-pounding, drive on Maui, **Kahekili Hwy. (Rte. 340)** winds its way along the coast between Kapalua and Wailuku. In many places, the one-lane road narrows to the width of your car (seriously), with a cliff on one side and no guardrail between the road and the ocean a hundred feet below. The road is paved, so no 4WD is necessary, just alertness and a resignation to the 10mph speed limit. You'll be glad you did if you encounter a car coming from the other direction, and have to back up around hairpin turns. This route is never an efficient alternative to the southern route on Honoapi'ilani Hwy.; it's just a very pretty drive.

Traveling from Kapalua to Wailuku, the road continues as part of Hwy. 30 in two lanes past **Honolua Bay** (see **Beaches,** above), which has excellent snorkeling when the water's calm, and legendary surfing when it's not. Between mile-markers 34 and 35, there is a little-known beach called **Punalau.** You can see the beach from the road—look for the dirt road leading down to the left once you round the bay. The road may be blocked with boulders; park at the top and walk down. The beach is edged by cliffs and lava arches, making it truly spectacular for walking or picnicking, but it's too rough for swimming and snorkeling.

There is a large pullout between mile-markers 38 and 39, with a dirt trail leading down to the **Nakalele Blowhole** (about a 30min. walk each way). The height of the spray depends on the tide; it can be the size of a building or nothing at all. Use caution—visitors have been killed when they venture too close and the spray catches them with surprising force.

Past mile-marker 41, the road becomes narrow and is not as well maintained. There are a few stands selling shave ice and banana bread in the tiny village of **Kahakuloa.** Just past Kahakuloa, a rock formation known as **Kahakuloa Head** towers 636 ft. above the water; together with **Kahuli'anapa** behind it, the two hills form a distinctive silhouette identifiable from beaches on the North Shore. There's not much between Kahakuloa and Wailuku besides some breathtaking coastal and valley views. As you near Wailuku, you enter the lush **Waihe'e Valley,** which receives almost 400 in. of rain per year from its nearly constant cloud cover. (To access this drive coming from the other direction, take Market St. straight out of Wailuku, or go along the coast from Kahului Beach Rd. to Waiehu Beach Rd. and turn right at the end onto Rte. 330.)

NORTH SHORE

Hana Highway begins just outside Kahului, but most travelers feel the road to Hana really starts in **Pa'ia,** a former sugar plantation town that now epitomizes Maui's laid-back surfer lifestyle. Past Pa'ia, the sleepy town of **Haiku** lies a few miles inland of the highway, and most Hana-bound travelers don't even realize it's there. The **Twin Falls,** on the eastern end of Haiku near **Huelo,** are just a few of the many waterfalls along Hana Hwy. Unfortunately, most of these falls are on privately-owned land, and hiking them is technically trespassing. Past Huelo, settlements are sparse, and the road winds around hairpin switchbacks, hugging the spectacular coastline all the way to Hana. A few small villages lie between Huelo and Hana, including the *taro* farming village of **Ke'anae,** but for the most part the road is surrounded only by lush tropical forest. **Hana** itself is a beautifully peaceful town with beaches and parks that warrant more than just a harried glance from the car. If time allows, it's worth continuing past Hana to **Ohe'o Gulch,** where you can hike to waterfalls and swim in freshwater pools. Those who haven't promised their rental car companies otherwise can continue around the southern coast of Haleakala on **Hwy. 31,** returning to Kahului via the vast and arid **Kaupo Valley.**

PA'IA

People come to Pa'ia for one of two reasons: either to chill out or to surf, surf, surf. During summer, its beaches are world-famous for windsurfing; winter brings waves of staggering heights and the most daring of surfers. Any time of year, Pa'ia makes for great people-watching—from bikini-clad Maui chicks to aging hippies to Rastas to salt-covered surfer dudes, Pa'ia attracts all kinds.

■✈🛈 ORIENTATION AND PRACTICAL INFORMATION

Pa'ia is essentially a crossroads town, located at the intersection of **Hana Hwy.** (Hwy. 36) and **Baldwin Ave.,** which runs between Pa'ia and **Makawao** (see p. 234). Just west of Pa'ia and *makai* of Hana Hwy., there is a small residential community called **Sprecklesville,** which has a beach of its own but is within easy walking distance of Pa'ia's town center and beaches.

The **Nagata General Store** sells basic necessities (open daily 6am-7pm). There are two **gas stations** in Pa'ia along Hana Hwy. The Pa'ia outpost of the Makawao **post office** is located on Baldwin Ave., just south of town. (Open M-F 8:30am-4:30pm and Sa 9-11am.) **Zip Code:** 96768.

☎ ACCOMMODATIONS

Pa'ia is one of the few places on Maui where good beaches, restaurants, and bars are all within walking distance of one another. It's easy to find a cheap place to stay here; many places even offer long-term rates for windsurfers and others reluctant to leave. For additional budget accommodations nearby, see **Peace of Maui** (p. 217) in Hali'imaile, about a 10min. drive from Pa'ia.

■ **Rainbow's End Surf Hostel,** 221 Baldwin Ave. (☎579-9057; riki@tiki.net; www.mauigateway.com/~riki/). Clean, friendly, and well-run, this privately owned hostel is within walking distance of both Pa'ia town and the beach. Free Internet, a safe for valuables, board and bike storage, laundry, and parking. Linens included. Common living room with TV/VCR. Two kitchens and 3 bathrooms shared among 3 dorms and 3 private doubles. No curfew; quiet time after 10pm. Reserve as far in advance as possible with $50 deposit. Dorms $110 per week, $335 per month. Doubles $200 per week, $675 per month. No credit cards. ❶

Mama's Beachfront Cottages, 799 Poho Pl. (☎800-860-4852 or 579-9764; fax 579-8594; info@mamasfishhouse.com; www.mamasfishhouse.com), 1½ mi. east of Pa'ia off Hana Hwy. Located behind Mama's Fish House restaurant on Kuau Cove, (cottage guests get a discount at the restaurant!), the cottages are not as quiet or private as other vacation rentals in the area. All units are nicely finished, with terra cotta tiled floors and patios, A/C, full kitchen, TV, VCR, stereo, and grill. Daily maid service included. 3-night minimum stay; 7-night minimum stay over Christmas. Check-in 3pm. Reserve a few months in advance with one-night credit card deposit. Cottages $140-350. AmEx/MC/V. ❺

Pa'ia Gardens (☎800-948-2877 or 579-8728). Basic rooms and apartments in a residential neighborhood, 2 blocks from Pa'ia center and the beach. Laundry, parking, and equipment storage on premises. Five-night minimum stay somewhat flexible. Reserve with $50 deposit. Rooms $35-45, apartments $45-75. No credit cards. ❷

YMCA Camp Keanae, 13375 Hana Hwy. (☎248-8355; YMCACampKeanae@aol.com). About halfway between Pa'ia and Hana, on the edge of the Ke'anae Peninsula. Pitch a tent on the property or stay in one of the co-ed dorms. Dorms share toilets and single-sex shower rooms, BBQ pit, industrial-sized kitchen, and gym. There are a few 4-person cabins, each with a queen-sized and 2 twin beds, bathroom, kitchenette, lanai and grill. Coin-op laundry available. Bring bedding for dorms. The entire camp is frequently rented to large groups for weeks in the summer; call ahead for availability. Check-in 3pm. Check-out noon. Camping and dorms $15, cabin $100. ❶

MAUI

🍴🍷 FOOD AND NIGHTLIFE

As befits a town whose inhabitants enjoy life to the fullest, there are plenty of choices for excellent eating in Pa'ia. A mecca for the health-conscious, **Mana Foods** sells bulk whole foods, organic and local produce, and packaged groceries (open daily 8:30am-8:30pm). There are several bakeries in town, including **Moana Bakery and Cafe** (see below) and the exceptional **Cakewalk Pa'ia Bakery** on Baldwin Ave. next to the Pa'ia Fishmarket (open M-Sa 8:30am-5pm and Su 8:30am-2pm). For the best **fish tacos** in town, check out the stand in the alley off Baldwin Ave. (tacos $3; open daily 11am-4pm).

■ **Pa'ia Fishmarket** (☎579-8030), at the corner of Baldwin Ave. and Hana Hwy. Filled with happy people sitting at long wooden tables, eating good food, and sipping their favorite beers (Hefeweizen $4). The mahi mahi burgers ($6.50) are the best on the island. Golden fries, fish tacos, salads, seafood entrees ($12-17), and sushi also available. Counter-service. Open daily 11am-9:30pm. ❷

■ **Cafe des Amis,** 42 Baldwin Ave. (☎579-6323). The scrumptious crepes are just as popular with the morning latte crowd as with the evening diners toting their own Merlot. Savory crepes ($6-9) are substantial enough for a full meal, while sweet crepes ($2-4) finish things off nicely. The curries, served in crepes all day or as dinner specials after 5pm, pack a tasty punch. Huge salads ($8) can easily be shared. Table-service and take-out. BYOB. Open daily 8:30am-8:30pm. ❷

Moana Bakery and Cafe, 71 Baldwin Ave. (☎579-9999). Relax in a deep booth and enjoy the creations of chef Thierry Michelier. Breakfasts are a treat with homemade pastries, Belgian waffles, and hearty omelettes, but dinner is an adventure in artfully-presented, decadent cuisine. Entrees include island pesto pasta with basil, cilantro, macadamia nuts and ginger ($16) and chili-seared *ahi* with mango salsa ($20). Breakfast served daily 8-11am, lunch ($80-13) 11am-3pm, dinner 3-9pm. ❹

Milagros, 3 Baldwin Ave. (☎579-8755). On the corner of Baldwin and Hana Hwy., Milagros' large outdoor seating area makes for the best people-watching in Pa'ia. Hearty breakfasts (macadamia nut pancakes $7) and Mexican-inspired lunch and dinner menus. Open daily 8am-10pm. ❷

Jacques Northshore, 120 Hana Hwy. (☎579-8844), is a windsurfers' hangout with (loud) live local music nightly. Photos of famous surfers bedeck the walls, and brightly colored umbrellas substitute for a roof. The food and prices are decent for lunch (the salads are excellent), but dinner is a bit pricey for hit-or-miss entrees—skip it and head straight for the beer and music. ❸

Charley's Restaurant and Saloon, 142 Hana Hwy. (☎579-9453), has pool tables, live music and dancing, and serves 3 meals a day. Hearty breakfasts feature pancakes so huge they literally spill off the plate ($3.25-6.25) and *ono* eggs benedict ($10). The dinner menu includes everything from burgers and ribs to pastas and pizza. Live music Sa, M, and W 10:30pm-1am. Open daily 7am-1am, food served until midnight. ❸

🗂 SHOPPING

For sassy beachwear, Pa'ia is the place to shop. There are also a number of touristy alohawear and craft stores that are not included here.

SURF SHOPS

▣ **Maui Tropix,** 90 Hana Hwy. (☎579-9816). With locations in Kahului, 261 Dairy Rd., and Lahaina,715 Front St., Maui Tropix is the exclusive purveyor of the Maui Built brand (the surf company whose logo is displayed on every local truck's bumper). Surfboards, t-shirts, stickers and sunglasses all sold here. Open M-Sa 9am-6pm, Su 10am-6pm.

Hi-Tech, 58 Baldwin Ave. (☎579-9297; www.htmaui.com). A smaller version of the Kahului store at 425 Koloa St., this branch carries surfboards, accessories, and clothes, with a good selection of sunglasses. Open daily 9am-6pm.

MIND-BODY MAUI Maui is a mecca for those who seek health and youth through mind-body practices. Makawao and Paia have a number of places where you can get in touch with that inner *om.*

Beyond Heaven, 3660 Baldwin Ave. in Makawao (☎573-8828), offers Kundalini, Iyengar, prenatal, and hatha yoga classes, tai chi, massage therapy, and Nia Dance, in addition to a chemical-free hair salon. Classes $10-12. For schedules and information, call or check www.beyondheaven.com.

Maui Yoga Shala, 120 Hana Hwy. in Paia (☎579-6257), offers some of the best yoga classes on Maui in a light-filled, hardwood-floored, and mirrored studio. Kriya Hatha, Ashtanga, and owner Nadia Toraman's special "Maui Yoga" technique all work your body and release your mind. African dance, *capoeira,* prenatal and kids yoga, tai chi, and Pilates mat classes available as well. Classes $10-15. For schedules and information, call, stop by, or check www.maui-yoga.com.

WOMEN'S CLOTHING

🟦 **Maui Girl,** 12 Baldwin Ave. (☎579-9266). Burn up the beaches in one of Maui Girl's original bikinis. In the center racks are the bikinis you'll lust after, with the silkiest fabrics and funkiest styles (not to mention $100 price tags). Open daily 9am-6pm.

Maui Yoga Shala, 120 Hana Hwy., upstairs from Jacques. In the anteroom of the yoga studio you'll find a small but well-chosen selection of stylish women's clothing—Brazilian-cut bikinis, sleek flared pants, frilly feminine shirts, and print skirts in addition to yoga wear and locally designed "Chicks with Sticks" t-shirts. Open daily 8:30am-6:30pm. Cash or check only.

Nuage Bleu, 76 Hana Hwy. (☎579-9792). Funky, sexy women's clothes. On the expensive side, but with a good sale rack in the back of the store. Fancy kids' clothes sold too. Open daily 10am-6pm.

🌊 BEACHES

Pa'ia is surrounded by first-rate beaches. Walk west (left) of town to **Pa'ia Bay,** which is great for swimming during the summer and is usually not crowded, especially later in the day. To the left, there is a trail that leads to a small, generally unpopulated, unofficial **nude beach.** A half-mile west of town, **H.P. Baldwin Beach Park** is a long, wide, golden sand beach with a playful surf (though it sometimes has a dangerous shorebreak). There are changing rooms and showers, as well as picnic tables and a large recreational field separating the road from the beach. Farther west, Baldwin Beach turns into **Spreckelsville Town Beach (Baby Beach),** which can be accessed separately by heading onto Nonohe Rd. off Hana Hwy. and turning right then left to access the shore. Baby Beach is so named for the protected swimming area to the right of the parking lot whose calm waters are perfect for *keiki.* Both Baby and Baldwin beaches are subject to strong winds that can kick up brutal sandstorms. About 2 mi. east of town along Hana Hwy., **Ho'okipa Beach** is world-famous for windsurfing. In summer, the relatively small waves attract beginners and longboard surfers to the break along the eastern end of the beach, while windsurfers race along the western end. The entrance is fairly rocky, making the beach poorly-suited for swimming. In winter, the entire bay is rocked with giant swells; only experienced surfers should venture out.

NEAR PA'IA: HALI'IMAILE

About halfway between Pa'ia and Makawao on Baldwin Ave., **Hali'imaile Rd.** branches off and runs through the pineapple fields to the tiny plantation town of Hali'imaile. The road continues past Hali'imaile to **Hwy. 37,** meeting it just south of the Pukalani exit. In addition to a cluster of homes, Hali'imaile is home to the **Maui Fresh Fruit Store and Pineapple Museum,** which sells pineapples, mangoes, and other local produce at an adjacent farmers' market (☎573-5129; open M-F 10am-6pm and Sa 9am-5pm). The **Hali'imaile General Store ❺,** 900 Hali'imaile Rd., a highly acclaimed (though decidedly overpriced) restaurant, features the inspired "fusion" cuisine of Cordon Bleu-trained chef Beverly Gannon. On Monday nights, each diner who brings a can of food to donate to the local food pantry receives 50% off his or her entree (regularly $20-32), making the scallop risotto with truffles or the rack of lamb *hunan*-style delightfully affordable. (☎572-2666. Open for lunch M-F 11-2:30pm; dinner served nightly 5-9pm. AmEx/MC/V.)

🏠 **ACCOMMODATIONS.** The very reasonably priced **Peace of Maui ❷,** 1290 Hali'imaile Rd., is surrounded by pineapple fields and boasts great views of Haleakala on clear days. The six hostel-style rooms on the ground floor of the main

1 HO'OKIPA LOOKOUT. About 2 mi. east of Pa'ia on the *makai* side, Ho'okipa Lookout offers a killer view of Ho'okipa Beach. In summer, windsurfers fly over the choppy waves at lightning speed while longboard surfers wait patiently for a sizeable wave. In winter, the surf changes entirely, and swells over 10 ft. high (some over 25 ft.) fill the bay.

2 TWIN FALLS. If you want to make Twin Falls a worthwhile excursion, go at 7am or don't go at all because by 8:15 the parking lot is full and the narrow trail to the falls is packed. Furthermore, as with most waterfall hikes, don't stop at the first fall—keep going! Usually where you see one fall, there is a bigger one above, and another above that—Twin Falls is no exception. Assuming you beat the crowds, you may enjoy a lovely secluded swim beneath the falls, sharing them with nobody but the mosquitoes (don't forget your bugspray!). To get to the falls, most people pull over when they see the fruit stand, ignoring the "Private Property-No Tresspassing" signs. Ten minutes in, the trail forks at a large, flat rock. Visitors then take the left fork and follow the path along the irrigation canals. After 3min., the first fall appears. A (somewhat slippery) path around to the right leads up to the second fall, about 10min. farther.

3 WAIKAMOI RIDGE NATURE WALK. *Makua,* between mile-markers 9 and 10. This is an excellent short hike among native ferns, bamboo, eucalyptus, mango, and strawberry guava. There are picnic tables at the start of the trail just above the parking lot, as well as a more scenic and less crowded picnic area at the top of the trail. Just beyond the first picnic spot, the trail forks into two nested loop trails. To take the longer one (about 1 mi. total), bear left, then left again past the second bench. The trail climbs a bit past strawberry guava and *hala* trees, before leveling out and making a switchback to another bench. To the right, the trail continues through a stand of bamboo. It ends in a clearing with a picnic shelter under mango trees, overlooking the ocean down the cliff below. To loop back down to the parking lot, turn right and walk down the old 4WD road. The end of the road is fenced off, but you can easily cut to the right just before the end and go around the fence.

ROAD TO HANA/HANA HWY.

4 KEʻANAE ARBORETUM. Less than 1 mi. past the YMCA Camp Keʻanae, just before mile-marker 17, the Keʻanae Arboretum offers another chance to stretch your legs. A corridor of impatiens leads to the main park, a well-maintained garden of labelled trees and flowers that includes a section of plants brought over by the Polynesians such as *taro*, breadfruit, and sugar cane. The park is pleasant enough, but extremely damp, and the mosquitoes are worse here than in other areas, which may discourage you from staying long.

Time: 2-4hr.

Distance: 52 mi.

Season: Any

5 KEʻANAE PENINSULA. The *taro*-farming village of **Keʻanae** lies on a wave-thrashed coast, not far past the arboretum. Here you'll find a peaceful Hawaiian town, centered on the **Keʻanae Congregational Church,** built in 1860 at the tip of the peninsula. The floor of the church is covered with mats traditionally woven from *hala* leaves. There is a lovely picnic spot on the seawall overlooking the rocky beach, and a fruit stand just beyond, but not much else—please respect the locals who live here by coming and going quietly.

6 WAILUA. Just past mile-marker 19, the **Wailua Lookout** offers views of the tiny village of Wailua. The pride of the town is the **Our Lady of Fatima Shrine,** built in 1860, and the bougainvillea gardens maintained by many of Wailua's residents.

7 PUAʻA KAʻA. Between mile-markers 22 and 23, the freshwater pools of **Puaʻa Kaʻa State Park** are visible from the road. The two swimmable pools connected by a small waterfall make for a refreshing dip, but because they are less than a 2min. walk from the car, they are frequently crowded. The park also has picnic tables, restrooms, and a pay phone.

8 NAHIKU. Between mile-markers 25 and 26, a road leads seaward to **Nahiku,** a small fishing village that is home to historic Christian church, built in 1867.

HANA HWY. DRIVING TIPS While enjoying the scenery along Hana Hwy., please keep in mind that many residents commute several times a day on this road. Keep an eye on your **rearview mirror,** and use the pull-outs along the road to let cars pass you. **Do not stop on the road** to look at scenery or take pictures; this is very dangerous and inconsiderate. Use designated lookouts or pull over on the shoulder of the road instead. The road to Hana is dotted with **one-lane bridges;** obey the yield signs but do not stop unnecessarily if you can see that the road ahead of you is clear. On steep downhill passages, **switch to a lower gear** rather than riding your breaks. In general, stay alert and use caution, and enjoy a safe ride.

FROM THE ROAD

DINING LOCAL IN HANA

The original plan was to catch some fish ourselves and grill it up for dinner. After several hours of standing on the pier, baiting hook after hook, the fish were eating a lot better than we were. Eventually night fell, and as the rain came misting down, we decided to forage elsewhere. 7:33pm—the general stores had just closed. Hana Ranch Restaurant was closed as well, with nary a person in sight. A cursory glance at the menu at the Hotel Hana-Maui revealed entrees at staggering prices, leading us to give up and head for home, dejectedly settling for peanut butter sandwiches. As we rounded Ha'oli Rd., lights appeared before us, stunning in their artificial brightness. We had discovered nightlife in Hana: the entire town was gathered at the ballpark for a heated softball match between the home team and the Ke'anae Brad-dahs. Spirits were high—everyone knew the players' names and either cheered them on or good-naturedly spit pidgin insults, depending on which team was at bat. Our noses led us to the row of families selling hot food out of giant pots and bowls from the beds of their pickup trucks: *saimin*, steamed rice, various meats, and giant vats of green beans mixed with canned corn. We bought ourselves two sesame chicken plates, and chowed down as the home team got creamed by the visitors, 2-12. Defeat never tasted so good.

-Sarah Rotman

house share two bathrooms, a common living room, and a kitchen. Four rooms have queen-sized beds; two have bunk beds. All have TVs, fans, and access to free Internet and laundry. There is also a cottage that sleeps two to four people, with full bath, kitchen, and lanai. (☎ 888-475-5045 or 572-5045; www.peaceof-maui.com. No minimum stay for rooms; 7-night minimum stay for cottage. Reserve with 50% deposit. Singles $40, doubles $45. Cottage $85 for two people, $5 each additional person. AmEx/MC/V.)

HANA

Since the Hana Hwy. was paved in 1984, the town has undergone a considerable tourist boom. While not exactly "the last of old Hawaii," as it is sometimes called, Hana is relaxed enough to allow visitors to stop and smell the plumerias. There isn't much going on here, which is part of its charm. Activities such as exploring ancient heiaus, watching the sun rise, strolling along secluded beaches, and joining the entire town in cheering on the local ball team are the little things that make time in Hana feel like a vacation from your vacation.

ORIENTATION AND PRACTICAL INFORMATION

Approaching Hana from the north, Hana Hwy. splits at the **police station** (☎ 248-8311), **fire station** (☎ 248-7525), and **Hana Medical Center** (☎ 248-8294). **Hana Hwy.** continues to the right, past the Hotel Hana-Maui (Hana's largest employer). To the left of the police station, **Ua Kea Rd.** leads to **Hana Beach Park** and the accommodations along **Hana Bay**. Ua Kea ends after the community center and **Hana Ball Park**; turn right on Ha'oli St. to return to Hana Hwy. Ha'oli St. crosses Hana Hwy. by the Wananalua Congregational Church, just north of Hana's main business district.

A **Bank of Hawaii** (☎ 248-8015) and the **post office** (☎ 800-275-8777) are located in the center of town. (Bank open M-Th 3-4:30pm, F 3-6pm.) The only **ATM** in Hana is located in the **Hasagawa General Store.** (Open daily 7am-7pm.) **Zip Code:** 96713.

TRANSPORTATION

Hana Airport is located 4 mi. north of town. **Pacific Wings** (☎ 888-575-4546) offers regular nonstop service to and from **Honolulu** and **Kahului**; other airlines run less frequent flights. The only rental car company in Hana is **Dollar Rent-a-Car**, at the airport. (☎ 800-800-4000. Open M-Sa 8am-5pm and Su 9am-5pm.)

There is a **gas station** at the southern end of town on the right-hand side of the street; gas costs about 30¢ more per gallon here than elsewhere in Maui. For **24hr. emergency road service** and repair anywhere between Ke'anae and Kaupo, call **East Maui Mechanics** (☎248-8085 or 264-2446).

ACCOMMODATIONS AND CAMPING

There are a number of accommodations in rural Hana that offer solitude, but the area is humid and thick with mosquitoes. Staying in **Hana town** is peaceful enough, especially if you have views of **Hana Bay** at sunrise. Vacation rentals in **Hamoa Bay,** 2 mi. south of Hana, are also enviably located, along Hana's best beaches.

Hana Bay Hale, 4950 Ua Kea Rd. (☎800-327-8097 or 248-8980; fax 327-8097; twt@maui.net; www.hanamaui.com), across from Hana Beach Park. Spacious 1- and 2-bedroom units overlooking Hana Bay. Hardwood floors, high ceilings, and huge bay windows invite rest and relaxation. Lanai with outdoor furniture and electric grill, full bath, kitchenette (full kitchen in 2-bedroom unit), TV, VCR, stereo, laundry. 2-night minimum stay. Reserve with credit card deposit. Rates $120-195. AmEx/MC/V. ❹

Hana Ali'i Holidays (☎800-548-0478 or 248-7742; www.hanaalii.com). Hana Ali'i manages 16 properties of varying quality, but all with excellent locations. Properties range from older budget studios that face the secluded black sand beach next to Hana Beach Park ($75), to a luxury 3-bedroom house on spectacular Hamoa Bay ($300). Pictures and details of all properties can be seen on the website. ❸/❺

Joe's Place, 4870 Ua Kea Rd. (☎248-7033; joesrentals@aol.com). A very decent budget option. The rooms are simple, with old carpets and bedspreads, but are kept clean. Guests share a common kitchen and recreation room with picnic tables. Check-in 3pm. Check-out 10am. Quiet time after 10pm. Reserve with credit card about 2 months ahead during high season. Rooms with shared bath $45, with private bath $55. ❷

Aloha Cottages (☎248-8420). Retired Mrs. Nakamura keeps her 5 cottages in Hana town very clean. The studio cottages are good value and are within walking distance of Hana Beach Park. $80. ❸

Waianapanapa State Park, 4 mi. north of Hana town, has campsites located only a few steps from the park's lava tube caves and coastal hiking trails. Facilities include restrooms, picnic tables, outdoor showers, and BBQ pits. A limited number of 6-person **cabins** are available ($45 per night for four people, $5 for each additional person), but they are generally booked at least one month in advance. Campsites $5 per night. See **Camping,** p. 180 for permit information. ❶

Hana Kai-Maui Resort, 1533 Ua Kea Rd. (☎800-346-2772 or 248-8426; hana-kai@maui.net; www.hanakaimaui.com). The only AAA-approved accommodation in Maui, Hana Kai's standard condo-style units are not a "resort," but are comfortable nevertheless. The 18 studio and one-bedroom units are located on the black sand beach next to Hana Beach Park, although not all units have ocean views. Full kitchens, private lanais. Reserve with full payment for 1-5 nights or half of the total for 6 or more. Check-in 2-5pm. Check-out 11am. Quiet time after 10pm. Studio $125–195. AmEx/MC/V. ❹

FOOD

Bring groceries with you to Hana. There are two general stores where you can buy some necessities, (**Hasagawa General Store** and **Hana Store,** both downtown) but their selections of fresh produce, meat, and fish are very limited, and the prices of other items are high. There are numerous **fruit stands** on the road north and south of Hana. If you want fresh **fish,** try your luck fishing off the pier in Hana Bay (Hasagawa's sells fishing tackle and Hana Ranch Store sells bait shrimp and frozen

THE BIG SPLURGE

MAMA'S FISH HOUSE

If there is one place on Maui to splurge on an extraordinary dining experience, Mama's is it. Located on its own beach on Ku'au Bay just north of Pa'ia, Mama's setting allows for prime sunset views overlooking the windsurfers at Ho'okipa. Through an arch of *hala* trees, the inside of the restaurant blends seamlessly with the outside. The Hawaiiana decor is elegant without feeling contrived, and the meal itself is exquisite from start to finish. A cadre of waiters attends to your every need. The menu changes nightly, but the focus remains on local seafood. Mama's takes such pride in the freshness of their fish that the name of the fisherman who caught each one is printed on the menu. The head waiter is more than happy to explain each type of fish and preparation, which range from creatively decadent (macadamia nut-crusted mahi mahi stuffed with lobster) to deliciously authentic (*ono* served Hawaiian-style, steamed with mango in *ti* and roasted with bananas and homemade *poi*). Save room for the final course—coffees are handpicked and brewed at the table, and homemade desserts such as the lilikoi *creme brulee* immerse your tongue in luxury. (☎ *579-8488. Located on Hana Hwy., 1½ mi. past Pa'ia town. Entrees range from $32-42. Mama's serves less expensive but equally excellent lunches (daily 11am-2:30pm). Dinner reservations are essential. All major credit cards.)*

squid), or if you see a boat trailer parked at the pier, wait until the fishermen return and ask if they will sell to you.

At Hana Beach Park, **Tutu's Snack Shop** ❶ sells burgers ($4.25), ice cream, and cold drinks. (Open daily 8am-3:45pm.) The **Hana Ranch Restaurant** ❷ (☎248-8255), to the left of Hana Ranch Store, is open for breakfast, lunch, and dinner. The only other option is the astronomically-priced restaurant at the **Hana-Maui Hotel.**

BEACHES AND OUTDOORS

WAIANAPANAPA STATE PARK. Four miles north of Hana, a marked road *makai* leads to Waianapanapa State Park. In addition to the campsite and cabins (see **Accommodations and Camping,** above), the park encompasses several miles of shoreline along the rocky lava coast. There is a well-defined trail that parallels the coast all the way to Hana town, past ancient Hawaiian burial sites and heiaus. Any part of the trail is worth doing; the section from the park headquarters to the **Ohala Heiau** and back is only 1.5 mi., and is surrounded by *hala* tree groves on one side and the violent sea crashing through lava arches and blowholes on the other. To the left of the campsite, there is a short loop trail that leads through the **lava tube caves.** Though the caves are steeped in poetic myth about a murdered princess, the crowds, stagnant water, and mosquitoes make them a rather disappointing sight. Below and to the right of the caves is a **black sand beach.** Depending on the tide and season, there may not be much beach there at all, and most people don't bother to stay. (There is a more substantial black sand beach close to Hana town called **Popolana Beach.** It's in the cove just north of Hana Beach Park.)

DENGUE FEVER WARNING There have been a few confirmed cases of **dengue fever** in Hana in the past year, and although the disease is reported to be under control, the mosquitoes along all of the hikes are copious and hungry. Make sure you wear and bring plenty of **insect repellent.** Dengue fever can only be contracted from a bite from a mosquito who has previously bitten an infected person. Symptoms appear in 3-14 days, and may include headache, fever, and nausea. If you think you may be infected, seek medical help immediately.

HANA BEACH PARK. Just off Ua Kea Rd., past the Hana Cultural Center, Hana Beach Park occupies a stretch of dark sand along **Hana Bay.** The bay is protected and relatively calm, making it a popular place for families with small children. Facilities include picnic tables, restrooms, and a snack bar (see **Food,** p. 221). The beach is set against the red cliffs of **Kauiki Head.** The cliffs served as a fortress and battleground in 1775, when the Kahekili, the king of Maui, attempted to recapture East Maui from the king of Hawaii who had conquered it several years before. Kauiki Head did not fall in battle until Kahekili besieged the fortress, cutting off its water supply. Kahekili brutally dispatched his foes by baking their bodies in *imus,* underground earthen ovens. Because of the steep grade and exotic plant life, hiking on Kauiki Head is not recommended.

KAIHALULU (RED SAND) BEACH. On the other side of Kauiki Head, a crescent of pebbly red sand beach has been carved from the cliffs above. The deep blue water that abuts the beach is incredibly clear, so bring your snorkel mask. Although the lava rocks form a barrier to keep the larger waves out, there is still a surprisingly swift current; exercise caution while swimming. The beach is strikingly beautiful and feels secluded, since most of its visitors don't stay long. Nude bathing is a relatively common practice at this beach. To get there, follow Ua Kea Rd. to the end, and park on the left-hand side before the lot designated for Hotel Hana-Maui guests (parking in the lot or on the other side of the street may get you ticketed or towed). Cut left through the small grassy park; the trailhead is to the right and is marked with signs that warn you of the dangers you may encounter along the way. The trail leads to the left on a narrow ledge on the cliff. The grade is steep and slippery in places and becomes particularly hazardous in the rain; a fall off the cliff to the rocky shore below could result in injury or death. Eventually, the trail bends around the cliff and deposits you on the beach.

KOKI AND HAMOA BEACH. Two miles south of Hana towards Kipahulu, a sign marks the road to Koki Beach and Hamoa Beach, the two best spots for swimming and surfing. **Koki Beach** is the first beach on the left. Red cliffs rise above the soft salt-and-pepper sand to the left, while offshore to the right, lies **'A-lau Island,** looking like a deserted cartoon island with its three little palm trees. The sand stretches far into the water before the ocean gets too deep, making for a dangerous shorebreak. Although the beach is popular for surfing and bodysurfing, visitors should ask locals about currents and underwater hazards. Farther down the road, **Hamoa Beach** is maintained by the Hotel Hana-Maui but is open to the public. Both Koki and Hamoa Beach get crowded in the afternoons but are virtually empty in the mornings and evenings.

NEAR HANA: KIPAHULU AND OHE'O GULCH

Kipahulu is located 10 mi. south of Hana on Hana Hwy. The road to Kipahulu is narrow, but paved and easily negotiated by any vehicle. For practical information on the park, see **Haleakala National Park,** *p. 225. Maps and information about the park can be obtained at the Kipahulu rangers' station (☎ 248-7375), located in the main parking lot. The admission fee of $10 per vehicle is good for 7 days at both entrances to the park. Camping in the park does not require a permit. Campground facilities include chemical toilets, picnic tables, and BBQs, but* **no potable water;** *visitors must bring their own water to the park. Mosquitoes plague the area, so be sure to wear and bring plenty of* **insect repellent.** *Sturdy shoes are recommended footwear for the waterfall hikes.*

Continuing 10 mi. south of Hana on Hana Hwy., a swath of **Haleakala National Park** stretches down to the coast through **Kipahulu Valley** and **Ohe'o Gulch,** home to the famed **Pools of Ohe'o.** This portion of the park is not connected to the crater by trails—beyond the hikes listed here are hundreds of acres of preserved forest that are not open to the public. The park is worth a stop if you have time to spare.

POOLS OF OHE'O. (0.3 mi. Trailhead: northeast edge of parking lot. Level: easy.) *Ohe'o* is the Hawaiian name for what are ironically referred to as the **Seven Sacred Pools,** considering there are many more than seven pools and there is no evidence that they were ever considered sacred. From the bluff above the pools, you can usually get a clear view of the Big Island across the channel. Many choose to swim in the pools, although if you plan to hike to the ■waterfalls, you'll find less crowded pools at **Makahiku Falls.** Under no circumstances should you swim in the ocean beyond the pools; the hazards include sharks that gather around the mouth of the Ohe'o Stream.

MAKAHIKU FALLS. (0.7 mi. Trailhead: across the street from the parking lot. Level: easy.) Climbing through Christmas berry and strawberry guava, the trail approaches the falls from above, skirting the ridge of the gulch. At the top of the falls are two shallow pools where you can swim. A peek over the lip of the second pool reveals the falls thundering 185 ft. to the churning stream below.

WAIMOKU FALLS. (3.7 mi. Trailhead: across the street from the parking lot. Level: moderate.) Those who continue on the trail for another 1½ mi. above Makahiku Falls will enjoy a hike through a guava orchard, under the boughs of a dripping banyan tree, across two bridges, and through a bamboo forest, finally ending at the base of the towering falls. The valley beneath the falls makes for a lovely picnic spot. Many choose to brave the icy water for a photo under the falls. However, keep in mind that this pool is not as deep as those above Makahiku Falls. To shorten the walk on the way down, cut to the right of the trail into the cow pasture and guava orchard, and then rejoin the trail before the gated fence (just above Makahiku Falls). The trail to the upper falls can often be slippery—sneakers or sturdy footwear are recommended.

THE ROAD FROM HANA

The road from Hana along **Pi'ilani Hwy. (Hwy. 31)** from Kipahulu to Kula, couldn't be more different from Hana Hwy. Gone are the lush rainforests and roadside waterfalls. The southern route around Haleakala gives some sense of the vastness of the volcano; its arid plains and valleys are stark and desolate, meeting the sea in spurts of hardened black lava. In many ways, this route is even more spectacular than that of the Hana Hwy., and it is certainly the road less traveled. From mile-marker 38 to 25, the one-lane road is paved in patches, and hugs a cliff with no guardrail. Most car rental companies do not permit their cars to be driven on this route. Four-wheel drive may be helpful in places, but is not essential. Falling rocks and unseen hazards make traveling on the road especially unsafe after dark.

Eight bumpy miles past Kipahulu, the quiet town of **Kaupo** sits at the base of the Kaupo Valley. The **Kaupo Store** sells cold drinks and snacks, and merits a stop merely to peruse its collection of antique cameras, pocket watches, and miscellaneous relics left on the shelves since the early 20th century. The three-day hike from the Haleakala crater (see **Haleakala National Park,** p. 225) ends in Kaupo; the store is a good place to have a car meet you if you plan on doing the hike.

Past Kaupo, there's nothing but ranch land for another twenty miles. As the road winds northward above Makena, the **Ulupalakua Ranch** and **Tedeschi Vineyards** appear as a welcome oasis. If you arrive during business hours, stop in for wine tasting and refreshment (see p. 197 for details). Past Ulupalakua, the road meets **Kula Hwy. (Hwy. 37),** which leads through **Upcountry** to Kahului and central Maui.

MAUI

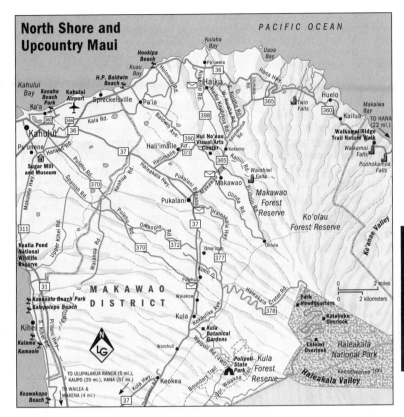

UPCOUNTRY MAUI

Upcountry loosely encompasses the rural townships built on the slopes of the Haleakala volcano. In the heart of it lies **Kula,** where much of the produce for the island is grown. In addition to sweet corn, greens, tomatoes, avocados, papayas, and other foodstuffs, Kula is home to magnificent floral gardens, including the strange and hearty protea flower. South of Kula along **Kula Highway** (Hwy. 37), the tiny hamlet of **Keokea** boasts a coffee shop, general store, gas station, and art gallery, as well as thousands of acres of ranch land grazed by cattle and horses. The ranches' *paniolos* (cowboys) strut their stuff every year at the Fourth of July rodeo in **Makawao,** the only town in Upcountry with a sizeable main street. North of Makawao, **Haiku** connects Upcountry and the North Shore and spills down to the coast from **Kaupakulua Road** (Rte. 365) to **Hana Highway** (Rte. 36/360).

HALEAKALA NATIONAL PARK

The gradually sloping shield volcano of Haleakala ("house of the sun") dominates the island of Maui. Haleakala National Park encompasses the upper slopes of the volcano and stretches down to Kipahulu, on the southeast coast near Hana (see p. 223 for **Kipahulu** coverage). The extreme landscape of Haleakala is an incomparable sight. The "crater" at the summit (it's actually an erosional depression, not a true crater) is so vast that the entire island of Manhattan, skyscrapers included, could fit within it. Sunrise atop the volcano summit (at 10,023 ft.) is a stunning event; above the cloud line, you can see the sun rise out of the ocean, illuminating the horizon with every color in the spectrum. The hikes from the top traverse varied terrain, and can be modified to suit both the casual day-hiker and the camping trekker. The switchback road that runs from the crater moonscapes down through subalpine shrubland, cloud forest, rolling pasturelands, and intensely fragrant eucalyptus groves provides the most spectacular of all scenic drives, and leaves visitors humbled by the lonely majesty of the mountain.

AT A GLANCE: HALEAKALA NATIONAL PARK

AREA: 30,183 acres.

FEATURES: Haleakala Volcano, Kipahulu Valley, Oheo Gulch (p. 223)

HIGHLIGHTS: Hiking to the huge crater at Haleakala's summit; observing endangered wildlife such as the silversword plant and nene goose in their natural habitat.

GATEWAY TOWNS: Kipahulu, p. 223; Kahului, p. 183; Kihei, p. 189.

CAMPING: Camping is free but requires a permit, which are issued at Park Headquarters on a first-come, first-served basis. Permits are good for a maximum of 3 nights per month, with no more than 2 nights at any given site.

FEES: Entrance fee $10 per vehicle, good for 7 days. No reservations required.

ⓐ PRACTICAL INFORMATION

Information: Haleakala National Park, P.O. Box 369, Makawao, HI 96768. ☎572-4400; www.nps.gov/hale.

Open: The park is open 24hr. everyday. The road may be closed in extreme weather.

Fees, Permits, and Regulations: The entrance fee is $10 per vehicle, good for 7 days at both entrances to the park (the other entrance is in Kipahulu, south of Hana). Permits are required for camping, and can be picked up at Park Headquarters. Camping permits, good for a maximum of three nights per month, with no more than two nights at any site, are free and issued on a first-come, first-served basis. Hunting, firearms, in-line skates, and skateboards are prohibited in the park. Pets are not allowed on trails. Do not pick flora or feed fauna in the park. Hikers must stay on marked trails to prevent erosion and so as not to disturb the fragile ecosystem.

Driving: From Kahului, take Rte. 37 to 377 to 378. Allow at least 2hr. from Kihei and 2½hr. from Ka'anapali and Napili. It takes a good 45min.-1hr. to ascend the final 20 mi. once you turn onto Rte. 378. If you want to see the **sunrise,** start driving no later than 3am. Once you enter the park, the road is a series of steep **switchbacks;** take your time and watch for bikers, cattle, and other hazards. On the way down, **switch to a low gear** instead of riding your breaks to prevent break overheating and failure. Slower vehicles must use pull-outs to let cars pass; **do not attempt to pass cars in front of you.**

Weather: Weather and viewing conditions at the summit are extreme and can change rapidly. If you are going for the sunrise, be prepared for cold (30-50°F); wear layers and bring blankets. If you are hiking, prepare for hot, cold, wet, and windy conditions. Sunscreen and water are essential. Call ☎877-5111 for weather, viewing conditions, and time of sunrise and sunset.

Emergency: Visitors are responsible for their own safety in the park. There is a public phone in front of Park Headquarters at 7000 ft. The nearest hospital is 2hr. away, and in bad weather, helicopter rescues can be difficult or impossible.

Haleakala National Park

○ Cinder cones

WAIHO'I VALLEY

Hana Forest Reserve

Ko'olau Forest Reserve

Kapolo Str.

Heleakoloa Str.

KUHIWA VALLEY

Hanawi Natural Area Reserve

Ke'anae Valley

W. Wailaiki Str.

Ko'olau Forest Reserve

Hosmer Grove

Pu'u Nianiau

Park Headquarters / Visitor Center

TO KAHULUI (31 mi.)

Haleakala Crater Rd.

378

Halemau'u Trailhead 7990' (2435m)

Leleiwi Overlook 8840' (2694m)

Kalahaku Overlook 9324' (2841m)

KOOLAU GAP

Holua (cabin & campsite)

Halemauu Tr.

Silversword

Pu'u o Maui

Ka Lu'u o ka Oo

Kamoali'i

Sliding Sands Trailhead

Haleakala Visitor Center 10,008' (3050m)

Pu'u 'ula'ula Summit 10,023' (3055m)

Magnetic Peak 10,008' (3050m)

Haleakala Observatories

TO KULA FOREST RESERVE

Kawilinau

Halali'i

Ka Moa o Pele

Pu'u o Pele

Haupa'akea 9159' (2792m)

Pu'u Kumu

HALEAKALA CRATER DISTRICT

Na Mana o ke Akua

Pu'u Nole

Pu'u Naue

Sliding Sands Tr.

Kapaloa Cabin

KALAPAWILI RIDGE

Hanakauhi 8907' (2715m)

Mauna Hina

Honokahua

Palikea Str.

Pali'ku (cabin & campsite)

La'ulu Tr.

Kaluaiki

Halemauu Tr.

O'ili'pu'u

Pu'u Maile

Haleakala 8201' (2500m)

KAUPO GAP

Kaupo Tr.

Haleakala National Park

KIPAHULU VALLEY

Kaukauai Stream

KIPAHULU VALLEY BIOLOGICAL RESERVE (closed to entry)

Palikea (2234m)

Kipahulu Biological

Waimoku Falls

Alelele Str.

Nuanualoa Gulch

Kipahulu Forest Reserve

TO KAUPO

Underground Aqueduct

Waoala Gulch

Kahahulu Gulch

Kahikinui Forest Reserve

Wailaulau Gulch

Waiopai Gulch

0   1 mile
0   1 kilometer

RECENT NEWS

A LIVING HISTORY OF THE LAND

As the federal government continues efforts to preserve the lands within the boundaries of Haleakala National Park, the people whose ancestors once lived and worked those lands are exploring what their role should be in recounting the history of the land. "We're the ones who know all the names of the places, the stories of the places," local *taro* farmer John Lind told the *Maui News* in a 2002 interview. "We just don't want to be treated like volunteers." Such was the motivation for the formation of the **Kipahulu 'Ohana,** an organization dedicated to creating a living history program to share aspects of native culture with park visitors. A large part of the project includes unearthing and restoring ancient *loi*, or *taro* fields, which were once cultivated on the Hana side of Ohe'o Gulch. The 'Ohana has won the rights to restore the native plants and trees, build traditional structures, and conduct cultural demonstrations in the park reflecting Hawaiian life before Western contact. "Working tours" of the *loi* will actively involve visitors who want to try some *taro* farming for themselves.

The 'Ohana is responding to locals' concerns that visitors to the national park are experiencing the land out of context. "If you take out the culture, the park is just another swimming pool," says 'Ohana president Mike Minn. "It's just 'seven pools: come swim and sun.' Now, it's 'come and learn about the culture.'"

Facilities: There are three **Visitor Centers** in the park. **Park Headquarters** at 7000 ft. issues camping and cabin permits and has phones, restrooms, maps, books, and information on the park. (Open daily 8am-4pm.) The **Haleakala Visitors Center** at 9740 ft. has restrooms, displays, a glassed-in overlook of the crater, and a helpful staff that dispenses hiking maps and information about the park. (Open daily 6:30am-3pm.) **Kipahulu** also has a Visitor Center and public phones. There is **no food or gas** in the park, so come prepared. There is **no water** in Kipahulu, and water from the sources in the Wilderness Area must be boiled or treated before drinking.

Guided hikes and events: 20-minute talks on natural and cultural history are held at the Summit building daily at 9:30, 10:30, and 11:30am. Park rangers lead two guided hikes. The Waikamoi hike meets M and Th at 9am at the Hosmer Grove shelter. The 3hr., 3-mile hike is moderately strenuous, with a 500 ft. ascent/descent. The Sliding Sands hike meets Tu and F at 9am at the trailhead in the Visitor Center parking lot. The 2hr., 2-mile hike is moderately strenuous with a 420 ft. descent/ascent.

Activities: Dozens of independent companies offer activities in the park, including biking down the volcano and horseback-riding in the crater. Rangers in the park report numerous serious injuries associated with the bike tours and do not endorse any of the companies. Bike tours range from about $50-80 per person, depending on the company and the time of day. Companies that run tours include: Cruiser Phil's (☎893-2332); Maui Downhill (☎871-2155); Maui Mountain Cruisers (☎871-6014); Mountain Riders (☎877-4944); and Upcountry Cycles (☎573-2888). Tours generally include hotel pick-up, breakfast, thermal suits, helmets, and equipment.

ALTITUDE SICKNESS The summit of Haleakala is over 10,000 ft. in elevation. Hiking at high altitudes can cause shortness of breath, headaches, dizziness, nausea and dehydration. Take it slow, stay hydrated, and go back if you have serious symptoms. Pregnant women, young children, and those with respiratory and heart conditions should consult with a doctor before traveling to high altitudes.

CAMPING AND CABINS

Overnight facilities in the park include two drive-in campgrounds, two wilderness campgrounds, and three wilderness cabins. The two drive-in campgrounds do not require permits; permits are required at the wilderness campgrounds and are issued on the day of the hike (8am-3pm) at **Park Headquarters.**

Hosmer Grove Campground. Near Park Headquarters at 6800 ft. Accessible to cars. Tables, grills, potable water, and chemical toilets available. Conditions are often cool, windy, and rainy. No permit required.

Kipahulu Campground. A 40-minute drive south of Hana on the coast, Kipahulu is not connected to the rest of the park by hiking trails or roads through the park. Accessible to cars. Tables, grills, and chemical toilets. No water. Conditions are often warm and wet with lots of mosquitoes. No permit required.

Holua Wilderness Campground. Holua is the most accessible of the wilderness sites, a 4-mile hike down the Halemau'u Trail, at the top of Ko'olau Gap. Pit toilets and limited non-potable water (boil or treat before drinking). No open fires. Permit required.

Paliku Wilderness Campground. Located at the base of a rainforest cliff, Paliku is accessible via a strenuous 10-mile hike up either Sliding Sands or Halemau'u Trail. It is the last campsite before the descent into the Kaupo Gap. Pit toilets and limited non-potable water (boil or treat before drinking). No open fires. Permit required.

Wilderness Cabins. There are primitive cabins at Holua and Paliku, as well as at Kapalaoa, 6 miles down the Sliding Sands Trail in the cindercone desert. Each cabin has a wood burning stove, cooking utensils and dishes, 12 padded bunks, pit toilets, limited non-potable water and firewood. No electricity. Cabin reservations are awarded by monthly lottery. Applications must be submitted in writing 3-12 months prior to requested date. No phone or fax requests accepted. A waiting list is not maintained; you will be contacted only if you have been awarded a reservation. Calls regarding vacancies and cancellations are accepted daily from 1-3pm (☎572-9306). Full payment must be received 3 weeks prior to stay or your reservation will be cancelled. Cabins $40 per night for groups of 1-6; $80 per night for groups of 7-12. Mail applications to: Haleakala National Park, P.O. Box 369, Makawao, HI 96768.

◪ HIKES

The drive to the summit, the overlooks along the road, and the summit itself give visitors a sense of the range of landscapes the park has to offer. However, to experience these landscapes more intimately, you must hike them. The park can challenge hikers of any level with trails of various lengths; some can be completed in an hour or two, while others take multiple days. There are two main trails from the summit area—**Halemau'u** and **Sliding Sands**—which connect on the crater floor.

There is also a practical purpose filled by the 'Ohana's project: employing local residents who are excluded from current park employment policies that favor those who already work in the national park system. This aspect of the 'Ohana's mission has helped assuage initial fears among locals that they are "selling out" to the federal government. The project takes an innovative approach to easing the often tense and always complicated relationship between Hawaiians and the federal government. Within the last decade, the park administration has welcomed the 'Ohana's proposals and has helped set its projects in motion.

*To find out more, visit the Kipahulu 'Ohana's website at www.kipahulu.org. The 'Ohana offers guided **tours** of the taro fields and hikes in the surrounding area. Tours meet on the first Tuesday of each month outside the Pools of Ohe'o Visitors Center at 1pm. Specialized group tours can be arranged by calling ☎248-8974.*

UPCOUNTRY SCENIC DRIVE

Discover the sights and smells of lush island growth along the winding roads of Upcountry and the North Shore on this 30-mile loop.

1 PA'IA. Begin in this former plantation town, now the haven of health-conscious New Agers and devoted surfers. **Take Baldwin Ave.** southeast, past the old sugar mill, through the rustling cane fields.

2 MAKAWAO. After 7 mi., Baldwin Ave. ends in the cowboy town of Makawao. At its termination, cross Makawao Ave. (between Polli's and Casanova's restaurants) to **Olinda Rd.** The farther you go on Olinda, the prettier it gets—ranches and country pastures yield to thickening eucalyptus groves (roll down the window and breathe deeply). As the road climbs to 4000 ft. in elevation, the switchbacks get steeper, the shoulder narrows, and the corners become more difficult to see around, so take your time and drive carefully.

3 PI'IHOLO RD. Just before the 12-mile marker, turn left on Pi'iholo Rd. to loop back down. The turns here are tighter still; to save your brakes while riding downhill, switch to a lower gear. A cathedral of eucalyptus trees lines the way as the rural homesteads grow more eccentric—look for the house with the teepee. In the last mile or so before town, the landscape opens up to fields of pineapples growing in rust-red soil. A left takes you back to Makawao, where you can easily backtrack to Paia. You can also continue the scenic drive by turning right at the end of Pi'iholo. This takes you to **Kaupakulua Rd.,** where dramatic cliffs hug the road's twists and turns. Kaupakulua Rd. ends 6 mi. later when it meets Hana Hwy. See **Hana Hwy.** scenic drive, p. 219.

(This drive can also be reversed, starting from Hana Hwy. in Haiku, taking Kaupakalua to the Pi'iholo-Olinda loop, and going back through Makawao on Baldwin Ave. to Paia. The advantage of this direction is that you have an ocean view along Baldwin heading toward Paia; the disadvantage is that it's a bit harder to find the streets. If you have a good map and are attentive, you should have no problem.)

Time: 1-2hr.

Distance: 30 mi.

Season: Any

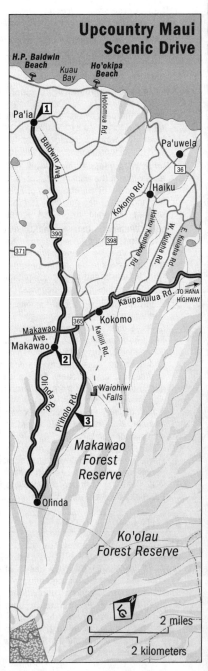

Upcountry Maui Scenic Drive

HALEAKALA FLORA AND FAUNA

The extreme conditions on Haleakala make the diversity of life there even more incredible. The rare **ahinahina,** or silversword plant, is endemic to the volcanic uplands of Maui and the Big Island of Hawaii. Its silvery spines grow for 30-50 years, then blossom once with hundreds of purplish blooms, after which the plants shrivel and die. If you don't want to hike 10 mi. to the **Silversword Loop** on the valley floor, just stop at the **Kalahaku Overlook,** off the main road at 9324 ft., where the plants proliferate near the paved path. Silver geraniums are easy to identify along the Halemau'u Trail, with five-petaled white flowers blossoming in summer and early fall. Not too many creatures live in the summit lava fields, so the inch-long **black wolf spider** is at the top of the food chain. This spider carries its young on its back and hunts for food on the ground instead of building a web. The **nene** (the Hawaiian goose, and State Bird), is nearly extinct, but occasionally makes an appearance in the park. Never feed a wild nene, or any fauna in the park. It is illegal to pick flowers or disturb plants in the park. So look, but don't touch!

HOSMER GROVE NATURE LOOP. (0.5 mi. Trailhead: Hosmer Grove. Elevation change: 240 ft. Level: easy.) To reach this easy loop, which travels through cloud forest and subalpine shrubland, park at Hosmer Grove (6880 ft.), near Park Headquarters. Brochures describing the flora and fauna on this half-mile nature walk are available at the trailhead.

HALEMAU'U TO VALLEY RIM. (2.2 mi. Trailhead: Halemau'u. Elevation change: 800 ft. Level: easy.) The first leg of the Halemau'u trail, to the valley rim and back, is a fairly level short hike. Follow the signs off Haleakala Crater Rd. for the Halemau'u trailhead (8000 ft.), 3½ mi. above Park Headquarters. The trail begins with a clearly defined path paved with rocks and gravel, and winds through an aeolian meadow, before suddenly opening to a mist-filled valley. About one mile in, you reach the rim of the vast crater, with its 300-foot high reddish cindercones looking like mounds of sand. You can turn back here, or continue down the switchbacks to the valley floor (another 2 mi. and 1200 ft. elevation change).

SLIDING SANDS TO THE FIRST CINDERCONE. (5 mi. Trailhead: Visitor Center. Elevation change: 2800 ft. Level: moderate.) Sliding Sands is a steep and windswept descent through the dramatic moonscape of the crater. The trailhead is at the bulletin board in the Visitor Center parking lot (9740 ft.). After the winding descent, the trail forks; the left fork leads to **Ka Lu'u O Ka 'O'O,** the first cindercone. Because of the altitude and steep grade, going out takes twice as long as going in, so pay attention to the time as you hike.

HALEMAU'U TO SILVERSWORD LOOP. (10 mi. Trailhead: Valley Rim. Elevation change: 2800 ft. Level: moderate.) Follow the directions for the first leg of the Halemau'u trail. After reaching the valley rim, continue down the series of switchbacks to the valley floor. About 4½ mi. past the Holua cabin, a spur trail loops around past a field of the rare ahinahina (silversword) plant. Again, plan on spending twice as long ascending the switchback trail as it took on the way down.

SLIDING SANDS TO HALEMAU'U TRAILHEAD. (11 mi. Trailhead: Visitor Center. Elevation change: 6000 ft. Level: moderate.) This combination allows you to experience the radically different terrain that both trails have to offer. The trailheads are 6 miles apart, so before hiking in, stop at Park Headquarters and arrange a car drop or ride with other visitors.

KAUPO GAP. (18 mi. one-way. Trailhead: Visitor Center. Level: challenging.) This 3-day hike traverses the crater floor and descends through the rainforest in the southern valley of the park. To do the Kaupo hike, request a brochure at the Visitor Center or Park Headquarters; you'll need to arrange a ride back unless you want to do the whole trek twice.

KULA

Kula is full of surprises. The countryside is patched with rural pastures and eucalyptus forests traced by the coastline that spreads 4000 ft. below. Driving through Kula is a treat—every side road you venture down reveals something unexpected. Roaming herds of cattle share the roads that spill into vast fields of exotic protea flowers and are shaded by the clouds that hug the rolling slopes of the volcano. And of course, there is **Haleakala** itself (see p. 225), rising to a majestic 10,023 ft. above sea level and occupying an entire range of climate zones from cloud forest to crater moonscape. Expect cooler weather here at any time of year—hikers should dress in layers and bring long-sleeved shirts as well as rain gear.

ORIENTATION

The main road that runs north-south through Kula is **Kula Hwy.** (Rte. 37). Taking Rte. 36 east out of Kahului, you can pick up Rte. 37 at its junction near **Pukalani.** Kula Hwy. runs south through Kula and **Keokea** all the way to the **Ulupalakua Ranch** and **Tedeschi Vineyards** where it becomes Hwy. 31 and runs along the southern coast all the way to Hana (see **The Road From Hana,** p. 224). **Kekaulike Ave.** (Rte. 377) makes a loop detour from Rte. 37, which makes for a very scenic drive past the flowering jacaranda trees; **Haleakala Crater Rd.** (Rte. 378) spurs out from Rte. 377. A good shortcut to Kihei or Kahului from Kula is **Pulehu Rd.** (Rte. 370), which cuts down the hill and west through the sugar cane from Rte. 37 just north of the **post office,** intersecting with Hansen Rd. by the sugar mill in Pu'unene. If you miss the turn, Holopini Rd. to the north also meets up with Pulehu. **Zip Code:** 96790.

ACCOMMODATIONS

There are no big hotels in Kula, but several cottages and B&Bs provide Upcountry peace and solitude. Nights are a bit cooler at these higher altitudes, so pack a few sweaters and long pants. Staying in Kula means that you'll have at least a 30min. drive to get to the beach, but you'll have Haleakala hikes in your backyard.

Star Lookout, 622 Thompson Rd. (☎907-346-8028; www.starlookout.com). Take the left fork immediately after Grandma's Coffee House and the first right after that onto Thompson Rd. The glass front of the cottage looks down onto the cane valley below, framed by the ocean on both sides, with the West Maui mountains looming in front and Haleakala rising behind. The cottage has a full kitchen and sleeps 4-8 in 2 queen-sized beds, a loft, and a bunk room below. Lovingly tended by a retired couple from Alaska, the property features landscaped gardens, a bonfire pit, gas barbecue, and celestial telescope. The cottage has a wrap-around deck, cable, VCR, and a wood-burning stove. Laundry access available. 2-night minimum stay. Reserve 6 months to a year in advance. $150 per night for 4 people, each additional person $15. ❸

Silver Cloud Ranch, 1373 Thompson Rd. (☎800-532-1111 or 878-6101; fax ☎878-2132; slvrcld@maui.net; www.silvercloudranch.com). Follow directions for Star Lookout, above; Silver Cloud is past it on the left. The lawn and gardens sprawl in front of the main house and guest cottages, affording an unobstructed view of the West Maui mountains, the ocean, and the valley between them. The elegant country living room—furnished with an antique piano, writing desk, spinning wheel, and comfortable sofas—opens through glass doors to a lovely patio and garden. Full breakfast served in the sunny dining room. No minimum stay; $15 surcharge for 1-night stays. Studio cottages $110-195 depending on size and season. Plantation house rooms $85-162; all have private bath, 2 have lanais and ocean views. AmEx/MC/V. ❸

Kula Lodge and Restaurant (☎800-233-1535 or 878-1535; fax 878-2518; info@kula-lodge.com; www.kulalodge.com), on Kekaulike (Rte. 377) just before the intersection of Haleakala Crater Rd. (Rte. 378). This chalet-style lodge is as close to Haleakala National Park as you can get without camping there. Popular with older guests, the larger chalets have lofts that could accommodate a group of four, as well as fireplaces and private lanais. On-site restaurant with impressive views (entrees $14-28). No minimum stay. Check-in 3pm. Check-out 11am. Reserve with full payment; cancel 30 days in advance for $25 fee. Chalets $110-165 for 2 people, each additional person $10. AmEx/MC/V. ❹

⚬ FOOD

Kula has surprisingly few eateries, considering the amount of produce grown in the area. **Grandma's Coffee House** ❶, 153 Kula Hwy., in the settlement of Keokea, is an Upcountry institution that serves excellent coffee and decadent cakes and pastries, as well as sandwiches and a daily hot special. (☎878-2140. Open daily 7am-5pm.) **Cafe 808** ❶, just up the road from the Holy Ghost Church on Lower Kula Rd., is a local joint that serves plate lunches (teriyaki chicken $5) in a no-frills, cafeteria-like space.

◉ ❀ SIGHTS AND ACTIVITIES

BOTANICAL GARDENS. Unusual flowers proliferate in Kula's rich soil, and there are several botanical gardens and flower farms that are open to the public. Just off Kula Hwy., the **Enchanting Floral Gardens** mitigates the pleasure of discovering plants from around the world with tacky yellow arrows painted on the paved path, directing visitors in a firm direction. (2505 Kula Hwy. ☎878-2531. Open daily 9am-5pm. $5, children $1.) The sound of birds chirping greets visitors at the **Kula Botanical Garden,** which is removed from the road on a six-acre site. (638 Kekaulike Ave., 0.7 mi. from the intersection of Kula Hwy. and Kekaulike (Rte. 377). ☎878-1715. Open daily 9am-4pm. $5, children $1.) To meander through the exotic protea blossoms which flourish in Kula as readily as in their native African environments, try **Cloud's Rest Protea Farm,** on Upper Kimo Dr. off Rte. 377, or **Sunrise Protea Farm,** not far from the start of Haleakala Crater Rd. (Rte. 378). Both offer free walks through the gardens and ship tropical bouquets.

POLIPOLI STATE PARK. The park's remote location deters many travelers from ever making it to Polipoli, which lies 6200 ft. above sea level on the slopes of Haleakala. The park is a damp forest of non-native trees such as redwoods, ash, cedar, and eucalyptus, and is used by locals for pig-hunting and camping. If you do make the trek, there are three trails worth hiking or mountain biking: the **Redwood Trail** (3 mi., 1½hr., elevation gain 900 ft.); the **Kahua Road** trail (9 mi., 4½hr., elevation gain 1200 ft.); and the **Skyline Trail** that connects Polipoli with the summit of **Haleakala** (13 mi., 6½hr., elevation gain 3700 ft.). **Camping** in the park is recommended because hikes are long and it takes a while to get there in the first place. Camping permits cost $5 per night and can be obtained from the Division of State Parks. Another option is to reserve a rustic **cabin** ❷ far in advance from the Division of State Parks. (☎984-8109. $45 for 4 people, each additional person $5. 10-person max.) There is **no drinking water** in the park. (To reach the park, take Hwy. 37 to the second junction with Rte. 377. Turn onto Rte. 377 and continue 0.3 mi. to Waipoli Rd. Turn right onto

FROM THE ROAD

TALES FROM THE RODEO

For a week before the event, I saw the signs: *Bud Light welcomes YOU to the Makawao Rodeo!* The rodeo promised to be more than just a show for tourists, however. As the day approached, so too came cowboys and cowgirls from throughout the Hawaiian islands, and Maui locals arrived in droves to cheer them on. Mainlanders like myself wore a dazed look as we entered the rodeo grounds, unsure of what to make of the hats, spurs, hoots n' hollers. The show began with rather tame events—steer roping and racing around giant barrels of Bud Light—but the announcer and rodeo clowns kept the crowd warmed up. Even a light rain couldn't dampen the whoops of the crowd when the steer wrestling began (experienced rodeo-goers came prepared with their beach umbrellas). My favorite event was the eight-second bareback ride, where each contestant had to ride his horse bareback with one hand in the air as the horse violently tried to buck him off (or her—one hearty Kula cowgirl gave a good show). If the contestant could last 8 seconds without lowering their arm or falling off, they qualified for the next round. No one ever said riding *paniolo*-style was easy...

The Makawao Rodeo occurs the first weekend in July and is preceded by a week of Fourth of July festivities.

—Sarah Rotman

Waipoli Rd.; you are now 1hr. from the park. Drive uphill on Waipoli; after 6 mi. the road becomes unpaved and hazardous and after 9½ mi. it forks. Bear right and continue ½ mi. to the parking, picnic, and camping area.)

ULUPALAKUA RANCH AND VINEYARDS. The company that once owned most of Upcountry, and still owns a sizeable ranch south of Kula, now operates the ⬛**Tedeschi Vineyards,** which produces Maui's local vintages. The ride down to the ranch is beautiful, with undeveloped pastures on both sides and views of the Kihei coast far below. It's definitely worth the stop for the **free wine tasting** and a stroll around the grounds beneath cyprus trees and towering Norfolk pines. The wines ($8-35) make great gifts—who would expect champagne from Maui? A one-room exhibit on the history of the *paniolo* tradition on Maui provides interesting food for thought as you decide between the Ulupalakua red or pineapple-sweetened Maui blush. There are picnic tables and a deli across the street. (☎878-1266; www.mauiwine.com. *Take Hwy. 37 south from Kula for 5 mi. past Grandma's Coffee in Keokea. The vineyards also make a refreshing stop on the way back from Hana via Hwy. 31. Open daily 9am-5pm. Free guided tours at 10:30am and 1:30pm.)*

MAKAWAO

Makawao is the only real "town" in Upcountry, with shops, restaurants, and a discernible main street. The Western-style storefronts hint at Makawao's *paniolo* past, but aside from the annual Fourth of July rodeo, Makawao spends most of the year catering to tourists. In addition to store after store of "alohawear," you'll find a plethora of galleries displaying locally-made arts and crafts. As one would expect from the heart of cow country, the steak here is prime. Casanova's is the only real nightclub 'round these parts, and features live music and nightly DJs.

✦ ⁊ ORIENTATION AND PRACTICAL INFORMATION

The central district of Makawao is located where **Makawao Ave.** (which runs from **Pukalani** and Hwy. 37) intersects with **Baldwin Ave.** (which continues 7 mi. northwest to **Paia**). **Olinda Rd.** meanders upcountry from the end of Baldwin Ave. **Kaupakulua Rd.** continues north to **Haiku** from the end of Makawao Ave.

The **library** is on Makawao Ave. next to Down to Earth. (☎573-8785. Open M and W noon-8pm; Tu, Th, and Sa 9:30am-5pm.) The **post office** is just south of town at 15 Makawao Ave. (Open M-F 8:30am-4:30pm, Sa 8:30-11am.) **Zip Code:** 96768.

⌐ ACCOMMODATIONS

Makawao makes a convenient base for exploring Upcountry and the North Shore, although the charms of the town itself are limited to a good place to wake up with a cup of coffee, and perhaps an afternoon of shopping. The nearest beach is about a 15min. drive from town. There are no hotels in Makawao, but there are several B&Bs of varying quality just outside of town.

> **Hale Ho'okipa Inn Makawao,** 32 Pakani Pl. (☎572-6698; fax 573-2580; mauibnb@maui.net; www.maui-bed-and-breakfast.com), off Makawao Ave. a few blocks south of town at the end of a residential street. Host Cherie Attix is a 30-year resident of Maui and an expert on local hikes and outdoor adventures. The plantation-era antiques she collects bedeck every room in the house. The bedrooms all have antique beds, painted wood floors, and private bathrooms with shower. Buffet breakfast. No minimum stay, $15 surcharge for 1-night stay. Check-in 3pm. Check-out 11:30am. Reserve with 50% deposit; balance due on arrival. Rooms $85-125; 2-room suite $155. MC/V. ❸

> **Wild Ginger Cottage,** 355 Kaluanui Rd. (☎573-1173). Take Baldwin Ave. a few miles out of town toward Paia. Just before Hali'imaile Rd., Kaluanui Rd. will be on your right, marked with a sign for Maliko Orchid Farms. Turn right and continue 1 mi.; just over the bridge, turn left through the iron gates and drive to the end. Descend into the tropical jungle of Maliko Gulch to find this cozy studio cottage, nestled among banyan trees and kahili ginger. Owners Sunny and Bob keep the cottage as they would their home, paying attention to artistic detail. Queen-sized bed, ceiling fan, TV, VCR, gas grill, private screened-in porch. 2-night minimum stay. Reserve with 50% deposit, balance due on arrival. Check-in 3pm. Check-out noon. $115 per night. No credit cards. ❹

> **Banyan Tree Vacation Rentals,** 3625 Baldwin Ave. (☎572-9021; fax ☎573-5072; banyan@hawaii-mauirentals.com; www.hawaii-mauirentals.com), 0.8 mi. from Makawao town. The grounds of Banyan Tree are lush and luxurious, featuring a swimming pool fringed with banyan trees and tropical flowers. The bungalows may offer "a taste of Old Hawaii," but peeling paint indicates it could be time for a face-lift. Studio cottages $85-110; 3-bedroom, 3-bath plantation house $300. No credit cards. ❸

⌐◪ FOOD AND NIGHTLIFE

Makawao has better shopping than dining options, but there are several good places for a light lunch on Baldwin Ave., in addition to heavier Mexican and steakhouse options. For more culinary selection, **Paia** (p. 214) is only a 10-15min. drive down Baldwin Ave. Natural foods store **Down to Earth,** next to the library on Makawao Ave., is open daily 8am-8pm for healthy groceries and salad. The **Komoda Store and Bakery,** on Baldwin Ave., is famous for their *lilikoi malasadas,* cream puffs, and freshly baked donuts. (Open M-Tu and Th-F 7am-5pm, Sa 7am-2pm.)

CAFES AND RESTAURANTS

> ▨ **Cafe O'lei,** 3669 Baldwin Ave. (☎573-9065), tucked into the Paniolo Courtyard. Locations also on Main St. in Wailuku and in Ma'alaea. Cafe O'lei uses the freshest local ingredients in their focaccia sandwiches ($6-8) and luscious salads (*taro* and Molokai sweet potato on Kula greens, $8). Open for lunch M-Sa 11am-4pm. No credit cards. ❷

> **Duncan's Coffee Company,** 3647 Baldwin Ave. (☎573-9075). Fresh brewed and bulk coffee (Hawaiian and imported), Lappert's ice cream, pastries, and sandwiches (grilled panini $6) available at the counter. Open M-Sa 6:30am-5pm, Su 8:30am-3pm. AmEx/DC/MC/V. ❶

MAUI

THE BIG SPLURGE

OLINDA COUNTRY COTTAGES AND INN

More spectacular locations are hard to find: Past the 12-mile marker on Olinda Rd. (see **Upcountry Scenic Drive**, p. 209), at 4000 ft. elevation in the foothills of Haleakala, the air is crisp and clear, scented with the fragrance of nearby eucalyptus groves. An 8.6-acre protea farm provides a gracious and secluded setting for the two private cottages and B&B inn, which have been lavished with every thoughtful touch by hosts Ellen Unterman and Rupa McLaughlin. The Country Cottage enjoys ocean and mountain views from the lanai, while the Hidden Cottage has a bathtub for two on the private back deck. Both cottages have king-sized beds, full kitchens, washer/dryer, TV, VCR, and a fireplace to keep things cozy on cooler nights. Both cottages, as well as the B&B rooms in the main house, are impeccably furnished with antiques. This is truly a special place, and certainly worth the splurge for a romantic country getaway. (2660 Olinda Rd. (☎572-1453 or 800-932-3435; www.mauibnbcottages.com). From Makawao, take Olinda Rd. (which intersects Makawao Ave. between Polli's and Casanova's) past the 12-mile marker. $120-140 per night for B&B rooms and $195-245 for cottages.)

Polli's, 1202 Makawao Ave. (☎572-7808). A Makawao landmark, Polli's motto is "Come in and eat or we'll both starve." True enough. Polli's serves up heaping portions of Mexican and American dishes, all under $12. Entrees are satisfying, if a bit salty, and home-made chips and salsa come with every meal. Anything on the menu can be modified for vegetarians. The bar in back is a local hangout (Bud $2, margaritas $4.50). Open daily 10am-10pm. MC/V. ❷

Casanova's Deli, 1188 Makawao Ave. (☎572-0220). Casanova's Deli has more reasonable prices than the full Italian restaurant next door, but a similarly funky atmosphere. Mirror mosaics bedeck the walls, and there are a few wooden tables in the rear alcove where you can take your counter-service sandwiches (baked eggplant and smoked mozzarella $5). Open M-Sa 7:30am-6pm, Su 8:30am-6pm. AmEx/MC/V. ❶

Cafe del Sol, 3620 Baldwin Ave. (☎572-4877), tucked in the plaza behind Maui Hands. Creative egg breakfasts (Mediterranean frittata $7), fresh baked muffins and pastries, local greens, and sandwiches are served at the counter. The sandwiches are a bit pricey (chicken salad on a croissant $7), but the atmosphere is relaxed and playful, with high ceilings and brightly painted walls bedecked with fanciful artwork. Breakfast M-Sa 8-11am, Su 8am-1pm; lunch M-Sa 11am-5pm. DC/MC/V. ❶

Kitada's Restaurant (☎572-7241), on Baldwin Ave. across from Maui Hands gallery. Cheap local food for breakfast (M-Sa 6-11am) and lunch (until 1:30pm). *Saimin* $3.25, plates $4.25-5.50. No credit cards. ❶

NIGHTLIFE

Both **Polli's** (see above) and the **Stopwatch Bar and Grill,** 1127 Makawao Ave. (☎572-1380), have bars with cheap drafts that attract a local crowd of devotees, but upscale Italian restaurant **Casanova's,** 1188 Makawao Ave. (☎572-0220), is the real pulse of Upcountry nightlife. Wednesday is ladies' night ("Wild Wahine Wednesday") is packed by 10:30pm, and by 11:30pm, people actually start dancing to the DJ-spun mainstream hip-hop. Fridays and Saturdays also attract a crowd for live bands starting at 10pm. ($5 cover and 21+ after 10pm.)

🎁 SHOPPING

Crafts stores and artists' galleries line Baldwin Ave. Handmade wooden bowls, jewelry, paintings, and prints are well represented in the galleries; although they aren't cheap, you may find that unique souvenir you've been looking for. There are a number of women's clothing stores as well, mostly carrying "aloha wear" and tropical-themed garments.

BOOKS AND ESOTERICA

Miracles Bookery, 3682 Baldwin Ave. (☎572-2317), sells a variety of books, with an excellent Hawaiiana section. Music, crystals, incense, and other New Age knick-knacks round out the offerings of self-discovery. Open daily 10am-8pm.

BATH & BODY

Upcountry Bath & Body, 3619 Baldwin Ave. (☎572-1411). Locally made soaps with names like Monkey Bait and Mango Tango that smell good enough to eat. Soaps $7 or two for $11. Open daily 10am-5pm.

GALLERIES

Maui Hands, 3620 Baldwin Ave. (☎572-5194; www.mauihands.com). Representing over 200 local artists, this gallery displays hand-crafted ceramics, glass, wood, prints, and more for a range of prices. Open M-Sa 10am-6pm, Su 10am-5pm.

Hot Island Glass, 3620 Baldwin Ave. (☎272-4527; www.hotislandglass.com), behind Maui Hands. Visitors come to marvel as artist-owners Chris Lowry and Chris Richards blow their one-of-a-kind glass pieces (glass-blowing most days 10:30am-4pm). The finished pieces are reasonably priced for works of art, with bowls starting at around $60 and their trademark jellyfish for $300. Open daily 9am-5pm.

David Warren Gallery, 3625 Baldwin Ave. (☎572-1288; www.davidwarrengallery.com). This family-owned gallery displays the works of the talented Warrens, including unusual and reasonably priced woodworking (Maui driftwood vase $25) and other crafts. Open daily 10am-6pm. AmEx/D/MC/V.

Hui No'eau Visual Arts Center, 2841 Baldwin Ave. (☎572-6560; www.maui.net/~hui), 1mi. from Makawao. Hosts a gallery that eschews the ubiquitous "island art," offering 6 exhibits per year of challenging work by contemporary local artists. The center also offers classes and workshops in painting, photography, printmaking, ceramics, and other areas, and sponsors visiting artists in residence. The 1917 house and landscaped grounds, once part of the Baldwin estate, are worth a stroll.

TOW-IN SURFING AT JAWS

Every year in late December or early January, there is a grand *Pohai na keiki nalu* ("gathering of the surf kids") to witness one of the greatest spectacles in the islands: tow-in big wave surfing at Jaws. When the waves are breaking just right off of a certain coastline below a pineapple field in Haiku, surfers have jet skis tow them into waves that can reach heights of 100 ft. from crest to trough (the average Jaws wave measures 25-40 ft. high). Surfers are strapped into their boards (a controversial technological shift that has changed the entire sport of surfing), allowing them to rip nasty tricks on their way down the wave—comparable to skiing down a mountain that is about to eat you. After the unbelievable ride, the surfer holds his breath and waits for the jet ski to tow him to safety before the next wave breaks. Surfers train for years to do this, practicing holding onto heavy rocks below the surface to increase their lung capacity, which they'll need to survive the wave breaking above them, creating so much foam in its wake that they can't tell which way is up. Speedcrafts of lifeguards wait just outside the impact zone should they be needed—even though only the best of the best pros surf Jaws, it's still a death-defying act. News of when and where Jaws occurs spreads by word of mouth, so keep your ears open for a chance to see this crazy event. You can monitor the waves yourself at **www.mauiweathertoday.com,** which uses unclassified US Navy charts to monitor ocean activity.

THE HIDDEN DEAL

HAIKULEANA B&B

Set on a two-acre estate, this country inn and health retreat has many quiet areas in which to relax and meditate hidden within its fragrant gardens of fruit trees. The house dates from the 1870s, and was once the home of the doctor on the Haiku pineapple plantation. Today, treasures abound within. Original hardwood floors and tongue-and-groove ceilings provide a historical setting for the owners' collection of unusual 16th-, 17th-, and 18th-century art and artifacts, including Persian, Tibetan, and Navajo tapestries; Norse helmets; rare maps and color lithographs. The walls of one bedroom are covered in original signed glamorshots of MGM studio stars from the 1920s to the 40s. Another bedroom has a nautical theme, with 18th-century chart maps and a ship captain's bureau. Haikuleana's host, Brook Katz, is a massage therapist, reflexologist, and nutritionist, and can arrange any outdoor activity (e.g. hiking, kayaking), health service, or mind-body practice (e.g. yoga, tai chi) his guests desire. He also happens to be a gourmet chef who has published five cookbooks, and uses his homegrown organic garden harvest and original recipes to craft delicious (and healthy) full breakfasts. Guests are certain to leave Haikuleana re-centered, relaxed, and wishing they could stay longer! *(555 Haiku Rd. ☎575-2890; www.haikuleana.com. Suites $115 per night, including breakfast.)*

HAIKU

The sleepy town of Haiku is as poetic as its name, and consists of little more than a few stores and a post office. The sprawling lands around it occupy a sizeable chunk of land on the north side of Upcountry, spilling down to the North Shore along Hana Hwy. Frequent rain showers result in lush land, cool and humid air, and strikingly vivid rainbows. Torch ginger speckles the verdant landscape with flaming color, while plumeria and soft orange *puakinikini* infuse the air with heavy floral perfume. Staying in Haiku is a peaceful experience close to North Shore windsurfing beaches and on the road to Hana.

■ ⁊ ORIENTATION AND PRACTICAL INFORMATION. Hana Hwy. defines the northern boundary of Haiku with Paia to the west and Huelo to the east. **Haiku Rd.** loops inland from Hana Hwy., intersecting with **Kokomo Rd., West Kuiaha,** and **East Kuiaha** before reconnecting with Hana Hwy. Kokomo, W. and E. Kuiaha Rd., and **Ulumalu Rd.,** all run northwest-southeast from Hana Hwy. to **Kaupakulua Rd.,** which is the main road connecting **Makawao** to residential Haiku. Kaupakulua ends at Hana Hwy. just before **Twin Falls.** The town center of Haiku is located at the intersection of Haiku Rd. and Kokomo Rd., where Haiku Rd. turns eastward. The only other orientation you might need to find your way around Haiku is to recognize **Five Corners,** the awkward intersection where Kaupakulua intersects with Ulumalu Rd. and several smaller roads. The **post office** is located on Haiku Rd. in the town center. (Open M-F 8:30am-4:30pm, Sa 9-11am.) **Zip Code:** 96708.

⁊ ACCOMODATIONS. There are a number of private homes that rent out "ohana" or cottages on their property. The cottages vary enormously in price and quality. Two of the finest cottages anywhere are found at ▨**Eagle's Nest ❷**, 2360 Umi Pl., perched at the top of Haiku Hill, with killer views of Ho'okipa and the North Shore below. The cottages themselves are extremely private and impeccably crafted, with terra cotta tiled floors, 18-foot open beam ceilings, and full kitchens with granite countertops. Each has a work of art for a front door, sculpted by the artist-owner. (☎575-9041. 7-night minimum stay or $65 cleaning fee for shorter stays. Reserve with $300 deposit; balance 30 days prior. 2-bedroom cottage $135 per night, $15 each additional person. Studio cottage $75 per night. Monthly rates available. Cash or check only.) In an entirely different, strikingly beautiful rainforest setting near Twin Falls, the ▨**Aloha Maui Bed & Breakfast ❸**, 101 Ulalena Rd., provides a relaxing getaway close to nature and far from crowds. Tropical flowers loom over the three simple cottages of this B&B, all of which use solar energy and run filtered rainwater through their pipes. Continental breakfast includes home-grown fruit and flowers. All cottages have full kitchens; some have indoor and others have outdoor bathrooms. (☎ 572-0298. 3-night minimum stay. Reserve with 50% deposit. Guest room w/ kitchen $65, cottages $75-100; weekly rates available. AmEx/MC/V.) Less dramatic, but a good value, is the **Haiku Getaway Maui ❸**, 1765 Haiku Rd., located at the intersection of Haiku Rd. and W. Kuiaha in the low-lying (wet and humid) area of Haiku. The two studios and the two-bedroom cottage have full baths; the larger studio and the two-bedroom both have a screened-in lanai and washer/dryer. All units have a full kitchen, gas grill, TV, VCR, and ceiling fan. (☎ 575-9362. 3-day minimum stay with cleaning fee for stays shorter than one week. Reserve with credit card. Studios $65-85, 2-bedroom $99.)

❒ FOOD. On the Kokomo Rd. side of the shopping center in Haiku town, ▨**Colleen's Bake Shop and Cannery Pizza ❷**, 810 Haiku Rd., offers flaky pastries, hearty sandwiches ($6.50 with a chocolate chip cookie), salads, and gourmet pizza ($9-19) like the Sweet Pea with ricotta cheese, roasted red peppers, sweet green peas, and pesto. (☎ 575-9211. Open daily 6am-9pm.) Tucked into the building behind the post office (across the street from the main shopping complex), **Veg Out ❶**, 810 Kokomo Rd., caters to vegetarians and vegans with wholesome and tasty stir-frys ($7), sandwiches ($3-5), smoothies, and juices ($3) served at the counter. (Open M-F 10:30am-7:30pm, Sa 11:30am-6pm.) For grocery staples, visit the **Star Market** in the main shopping complex, or **Fukushima General Store** across the street.

MAUI

MOLOKAI

If Oahu is heading toward the future, Molokai (Moloka'i) is happily tied to the past. Amid Hawaii's many resorts and tourist traps, Molokai is the closest you can get to old Hawaii. Fishponds dating from the 17th century, several of which are still operational today, line the southern coast, and some residents choose to spend a portion of the year living in true Hawaiian fashion—at beach campsites. The island's population is over half native Hawaiians, a percentage that is second only to Niihau. Molokai is fighting to preserve its current state of non-modernization; there has been controversy over development plans and private residences that encroach on traditional hunting grounds.

At one time, Molokai was respected and revered for its many powerful kahunas, and visitors from all over made pilgrimages to the island to seek the priests' counsel. For a time, the island was even free from armed conflict because it was considered sacred. Now Molokai retains little of its former influence, however, and the island is struggling. Jobs are scarce and unemployment, sometimes as high as 15%, rivals even the mainland's most depressed counties.

Molokai's laid-back residents nonetheless maintain a positive outlook on life. The birthplace of both the aloha spirit and the hula, Molokai is known as "The Friendly Isle" for a reason. Drivers smile and wave amiably at passersby, and you won't find a single stoplight here. The two-lane highway that stretches from one end of the island to the other is perpetually traffic-free, although the slow pace of some of the island's 7000 inhabitants sometimes causes a bit of a backup. Nobody seems to mind, however, since there's no reason to be in a hurry. A sign that greets visitors at the airport says it all: "Aloha! Slow down: this is Molokai."

HIGHLIGHTS OF MOLOKAI

SET FOOT ON SACRED GROUND at the 'Ili'ili'opae Heiau, the second-largest traditional Hawaiian temple in the islands (p. 257).

GET BACK TO NATURE at the rugged Kamakou Preserve, home to 219 endemic plant and animal species (p. 251).

SOJOURN to the sobering former leper colony at Kalaupapa Peninsula (p. 248).

ROPE A STEER in *paniolo* lessons at the Molokai Ranch in Maunaloa (p. 262).

✈ INTERISLAND TRANSPORTATION

Molokai is most easily accessible by plane, though there is also a ferry service from Maui.

🛩 **Molokai Air Shuttle,** 99 Mokuea Pl. in Honolulu (☎545-4988), along Lagoon Dr., just behind the airport. There is also an office at the Molokai airport (☎567-6847). By far the cheapest way to get to Molokai. From Honolulu, 4-6 flights daily ($40 one-way, $70 round-trip). Also flies to the **Kalaupapa peninsula** ($25 one-way, $50 round-trip from the Molokai Airport; $40 one-way, $70 round-trip from Honolulu). Offices open M-Sa 6am-9pm.

Molokai

MOLOKAI

Halawa
Halawa Bay
Moaula Falls
Murphy's Beach
Kahiwa Falls
450
Wailau Valley
Kamakou 4970' (1515m)
Hina Falls
Kakahaia National Wildlife Refuge
Kamehameha V Hwy.
KALAWAO DISTRICT
Kalaupapa National Historical Park
One Alii Park
Kalaupapa Airfield
Kaunakakai
One Alii Beach
450
Kalaupapa
Pala'au State Park
470 Hwy.
Kualapu'u
Kaunakakai Harbor
Manunui Rd.
Kualae
Kala St.
Maunaloa Hwy.
Puupeelua Ave.
Farrington Ave.
Moomomi Ave.
Hoolehua
465
Moomomi Beach
460
Kalani Beach
Maunaloa Hwy.
Kamakana Rd.
Kolo Beach
Molokai Ranch Wildlife Park
460
Maunaloa
Halena Beach
Kawakiu Beach
Make Horse Beach
Kaluakoi Rd.
Papohaku Beach
Dixie Maru Beach
Pohakuloa Rd.
Hale O Lono Harbor

0   4 miles
0   4 kilometers

N

Pacific Wings (☎ 888-575-4546 or 873-0877; fax 873-7920). Hawaii's most scenic airline. 3 flights daily from Honolulu and 1 from Kahului ($64 one-way, $128 roundtrip). Also flies to the **Kalaupapa peninsula** ($65 one-way, $130 round-trip).

Island Air, 99 Kapalulu Pl., on Lagoon Drive behind the airport in Honolulu (☎ 800-323-3345 or 484-2222; fax 833-5498; www.islandair.com). From Honolulu (11 flights daily) or Maui (4 flights daily) $80-85 one-way, $160-170 round-trip. 5% discount for Internet bookings.

Paragon Air (☎ 800-428-1231 or 244-3356), a charter-only company that flies to **Molokai** and **Kalaupapa** from Honolulu and Maui ($50-70 one-way, $89-110 round-trip), and also offers **air tours** of Molokai. Rates vary, depending on duration of flight.

The Molokai Princess (☎ 661-8397 or 667-6165; www.Molokaiferry.com) runs between the **Molokai Wharf** and **Lahaina,** Maui. (90 min.; departs Maui 5:15pm daily, and 6:30am M, W, F, and Sa. Departs Molokai M-Sa 5:45am; Su 3:30pm; M, W, F, and Sa 2:30pm. $40 one-way, children $20.)

▐ LOCAL TRANSPORTATION

Once on the island, renting a car is an absolute necessity, as there is no public transportation. There is a single highway that stretches east-west from one side of the island to the other, making Molokai easy to navigate.

Budget has an office in the Molokai Airport (☎ 800-527-0700 or 567-6877; www.budget.com), as does **Dollar** (☎ 567-6156). Both offices are open 6am-7pm daily. Check the web for Internet specials. **Island Kine Auto Rental** (☎ 553-5242; fax 553-3880; www.Molokai-car-rental.com), a local outfit if ever there was one, rents cars, trucks, vans, and 4x4s from their lot on Ala Malama Ave., east of town. Telephone and web rentals $40-66 per day. **Molokai Rentals and Tours** (☎ 800-553-9071 or 553-5663) rents cars, jeeps, and 4x4s ($30-150). All rental agencies accept AmEx, D, M, and V. Also try **Molokai Outdoors** for car and moped rentals, as well as **shuttle** service from the airport (☎ 553-4477, see p. 243). **Taxis** are astronomically expensive but available any time flights are running—usually early morning to 9pm—from **Molokai Off-Road Tours & Taxi** (☎ 553-3369), just outside of Kaunakakai.

No rental cars, including 4x4s, are technically permitted off paved roads by any of rental car companies, but the rule is rarely enforced (or announced, for that matter). Even in a 4x4, be absolutely certain never to drive off-road in the **rain,** as you will inevitably get stuck and be forced to call for help, an embarrassing (and usually quite expensive) predicament.

Gas prices in Molokai are often substantially higher than on Oahu or Maui. Always drive with your fuel level in mind, as there are only three gas stations on the island, none of which are east of Kaunakakai or near the airport. If you need assistance, call one of the full-service stations in Kaunakakai. Shirley Rawlins' **Chevron,** 20 Maunaola Hwy. (☎ 553-5580), is open daily from 6:30am-8:30pm. **Kalama's Gas Station,** 53 Ala Malama Ave. (☎ 553-5586), is usually a few cents cheaper. Open M-Th 6:30am-8pm, F-Sa 6am-9pm, Su 7am-6pm.

▐ ACCOMMODATIONS AND CAMPING

Molokai isn't an easy place to find budget accommodations, especially if you're traveling solo. There is no hostel, and most of the more reasonably-priced options are condos or beach houses better suited for couples and large groups. But this alone should not deter you. Couples can find fabulous deals at the various **B&Bs** on the island; try them before staying at a hotel or renting a condo. For a comprehensive list of nearly all the accommodations available, including a large number of properties that are leased directly by their owners, pick up an **Accommodations Directory** at the **Molokai Visitors' Association,** 28 Kamoi St. in Kaunakakai.

Also consider paying a visit to the website of **Swenson Real Estate,** located at the intersection of Hwy. 460 and 470, which rents houses, condos, and cottages for $75-600 per night. Most 2- or 3-bedroom houses go for $100-125. (☎800-558-3648; fax 553-3783; www.island-realestate.com. Open M-F 9am-4:30pm. AmEx/MC/V.) **Friendly Island Realty** leases dozens of properties all over the island, from studio apartments ($65-90) to 1-bedroom condos ($75-125) to full beach houses ($75-125). Check website for photos and more information. (☎800-600-4158 or 553-3666; www.Molokairealty.com; www.Molokairesorts.com. Office open M-F 8am-5:30pm, Sa 8am-3pm.)

In addition, Molokai has several excellent campgrounds. **Camping permits** are required, and may be obtained through the **Department of Parks and Recreation,** 90 Aiona St., in the Mitchell Pauole Center in Kaunakakai. (☎553-3204. Office open M-F 8am-4pm.) The **Hawaiian Home Lands Department** (☎567-6296) on Puukapele Ave. in Hoolehua also issues camping permits for some sites for individuals and groups on a first-come, first-served basis.

KAUNAKAKAI

Kaunakakai is a lot like the rest of Molokai—there isn't much there, but with a little patience, you can probably find what you're looking for. It takes less than an hour to walk every paved road of the island's largest town, and the place is almost completely deserted after 5pm and on Sundays. Many local establishments do not accept credit cards, and, like everything else on Molokai, things happen slowly. If you visit the island, you're sure to spend at least a few hours stocking up on groceries or sampling local food along the dusty main drag, Ala Malama Ave.

ORIENTATION

The heart of Kaunakakai is the intersection of **Maunaloa Hwy.** (Rte. 460) and **Ala Malama Ave.** There's a **Chevron** station in the northwest corner of the intersection, and both of the town's banks are located on the northeast side in the **Molokai Center,** a business complex that stretches north along the first block of Ala Malama. At the end of the block, Ala Malama turns east for another 3 blocks, the area where most of the town's businesses are located. The highway continues east about a block below Ala Malama, but its name changes to **Kamehameha V** (Rte. 450) as it leaves town. The easiest way to navigate is by the highway mile markers, which are listed in this chapter as if one is driving away from Kaunakakai center.

PRACTICAL INFORMATION

TOURIST AND FINANCIAL SERVICES

Tourist Office: The **Molokai Visitors' Association,** 28 Kamoi St., in the Kamoi Professional Center, dispenses a very useful **directory** of hundreds of private accommodations, but offers little in the way of firsthand knowledge of the island.

Travel Agencies: Friendly Isle Travel, 64 Ala Malama Ave. (☎553-5357). Open M-F 8am-5pm. **Molokai Outdoors,** across from the front desk at Hotel Molokai (☎553-4477), is the island's best resource for information about anything and everything to do outdoors, including hiking, kayaking, biking, trips to the leper colony on the Kalaupapa Peninsula (see p. 248), and hiking in Halawa Valley and the rainforest. Among the many rentals available are: snorkeling gear ($10 per day), kayaks ($30, $40 for two),

MOLOKAI

surfboards ($20), mopeds ($35), and even cars ($35, $135 for a 4x4). If there's something you want to do that they don't offer, they're certain to send you in the right direction. Open M-F 8am-5pm, Sa 8am-4pm.

Banks and ATMs: Bank of Hawaii, 20B Ala Malama Ave. (☎553-3263), and **Money Express Savings Bank,** 40 Ala Malama Ave. (☎553-8635), in the Molokai Center. Both banks open M-Th 8:30am-4pm, F 8:30am-6pm. **ATMs** are out front.

LOCAL SERVICES

Library: The small **Molokai Public Library,** 15 Ala Malama Ave. (☎553-1765), in the Civic Center has free **Internet access.** M and W 12:30-8pm; Tu, Th, and F 10am-5pm.

Laundromat: Ohana Launderette, on Kamoi St. at the highway intersection. $1 wash, $1.25 dry. Quarters only, no change machine, no detergent dispenser, no love. Open daily 6am-9pm.

Recreation Center: The **Mitchell Pauole Center,** at Ala Malama Ave. and Aiona St. Free access to tennis courts and a swimming pool, which are rarely full during the winter.

EMERGENCY AND COMMUNICATIONS

Emergency: ☎911.

Police: 110 Aiona St. (☎553-5355), in the Mitchell Pauole Center next to the ballpark.

Pharmacy: Molokai Drugs, 28 Kamoi St. #100 (☎553-5790), in the Kamoi Professional Center. **Wheelchair rental** $9 per day. $10-14 to process 35mm **film.** Open M-Sa 8:45am-5:45pm.

Hospital: Molokai General Hospital, 205A Puali St. (☎553-5331). Veer to the left side of the Vietnam Memorial at the end of Ala Malama Ave. and follow the blue signs. Emergency room open 24hr.

Post Office: 120 Ala Malama Ave. Open M-F 9am-4:30pm, Sa 9-11am.

Zip Code: 96748.

▐ ACCOMMODATIONS AND CAMPING

Kapuaiwa Coconut Grove is now administered by the Hawaiian Home Lands Department on Puukapele Ave. in Hoolehua (☎567-6296) which issues a camping permit ($5) to one individual or group each night on a first-come, first-served basis. See **Accommodations and Camping** (p. 242) for further information.

▨ **Ka Hale Mala,** 7 Kamakahana Pl. (☎553-9009; www.Molokai-bnb.com), just before the 5-mile marker east of town on the left. One of Molokai's best accommodations, Ka Hale Mala occupies the first floor of a beautiful private residence. The spacious suite features a master bedroom, a dining room with a full kitchen, a living room that can sleep two, and a patio overlooking a lush garden. Ever-amiable owners Jack and Cheryl Corbiell are knowledgeable about nearly every aspect of the island and will actively help you make the most of your trip. The breakfasts are legendary, and all manner of beach and outdoor equipment are available for guests' use. $70 per night (two guests), each additional person (including children) $15. No credit cards. ❸

Kaona Beach House, 75 Ala Malama Ave., the 6th house on the right after the One Ali'i campgrounds on the highway east of town. Leased through Friendly Island Realty (see above). A large and well-maintained beach house with two bedrooms, two bathrooms, a cavernous living room, full kitchen, carport, and a raised patio—all right on the beach. $125 per night. Friendly Island also leases other properties in the area (see p. 243). ❸

Molokai Shores (☎553-5954; fax 553-3241; www.marcresorts.com), 1½ mi. east of town on Kamehameha Hwy. These roomy condos, most with ocean views, are a decent

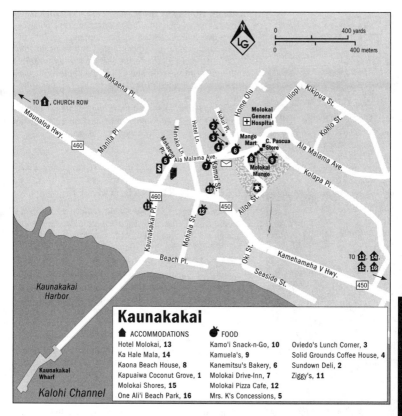

Kaunakakai

🏠 ACCOMMODATIONS
Hotel Molokai, **13**
Ka Hale Mala, **14**
Kaona Beach House, **8**
Kapuaiwa Coconut Grove, **1**
Molokai Shores, **15**
One Ali'i Beach Park, **16**

🍎 FOOD
Kamo'i Snack-n-Go, **10**
Kamuela's, **9**
Kanemitsu's Bakery, **6**
Molokai Drive-Inn, **7**
Molokai Pizza Cafe, **12**
Mrs. K's Concessions, **5**

Oviedo's Lunch Corner, **3**
Solid Grounds Coffee House, **4**
Sundown Deli, **2**
Ziggy's, **11**

value, although they might seem expensive; all have full kitchens, patios, cable TV, pool access, and ceiling fans. No A/C. 20% discount for Internet booking, 25% discount for AAA members. 1-bedroom (1-4 people) $155; 2-bedroom (up to 6) $199. AmEx/D/MC/V. ➎

Hotel Molokai, Box 1020, Kamehameha V Hwy. (☎553-5347; fax 553-5047), just before the 2-mile marker east of town. Hotel Molokai is the least expensive hotel on the island, and a sort of hub for tourism. Nearly every first-time visitor stops at ▨ **Molokai Outdoors,** the hotel's activities desk (see p. 243), and the closest thing to Molokai nightlife is the bar area around the pool, which is open to the public. The hotel **restaurant** ➍ is good but pricey (entrees $14-19). All 45 of the hotel's units have telephones, cable TV, ceiling fans, patios, and laundry access. No A/C. Some units have kitchenettes. Rooms $82-137. AmEx/D/MC/V. ➌

One Ali'i Beach Park, just past the 3-mile marker on the right. A very large but rather spare site located 10min. east of town, One Ali'i (pronounced oh-neh ah-lee-ee) is frequently rented out by locals for large parties, especially on weekends, and kids usually cruise by at night. The beach is small and unappealing for swimming, but there's a concrete pavilion with picnic tables, working lights, and electrical outlets, as well as restrooms and showers in an adjoining building. Camping permits required. $3 per night, 3-night maximum stay. See **Accommodations and Camping** (p. 242). ➊

FROM THE ROAD

A LOCAL LUAU

At the moment, I'm sitting in the passenger seat of a metallic-blue Ford Ranger pickup, avoiding the rain and drinking a Coors Light as I watch a band of local Hawaiian children hula to the sounds of Eminem. Next to my truck is a one-man tent—my home for the next two weeks. I am camping on Molokai, one of the smallest and least-inhabited of the islands.

A large extended family of 20-30 locals has taken over the campground to prepare for a luau tomorrow. They have invited nearly 450 people—myself included. A full kitchen has been set up in the concrete shelter, and a half-dozen elderly women are busy chopping vegetables and peeling potatoes around a table-sized cutting board. The other adults are pitching tents, arranging chairs, and talkin' story in Hawaiian. The children are hula dancing or playing with water guns. They've come prepared—they even have arrow-shaped wooden signposts with "Da Chow Line" and "Da Latrine" in large stenciled letters. Though they asked me to move my tent before the festivities begin, they also invited me to the luau. So far, Molokai seems to be the living up to its reputation as the birthplace of the aloha spirit.

-Marc Wallenstein

Kapuaiwa Coconut Grove, just west of Kaunakakai, across from Church Row. This 11-acre expanse of coconut trees gone wild is the original stomping grounds of King Kamehameha V; he planted the trees in the 1860s to provide shade for visiting royalty as they bathed in the sea. Permits ($5) available from the Hawaiian Homelands Dept. (see p. 242). Though the park is usually used by locals for luaus, there is nothing preventing solo travelers from taking advantage of the prime beach location near town—just be sure not to park your car under any coconut trees. ➊

⬧ FOOD

GROCERY STORES AND MARKETS

Friendly Market, 1919 Ala Malama Ave. (☎ 553-5821 or 553-5595). The largest grocery store on the island, though not the cheapest place to buy produce. Open M-F 8:30am-8:30pm, Sa 8:30am-6:30pm. AmEx/MC/V.

Misaki's (☎ 553-5505), on Ala Malama Ave. near Mohaia St. Slightly smaller than Friendly Market, but has a better selection of wine, as well as specials on beer. Creatively decorated with deer heads and antlers. Open M-Sa 8:30am-8:30pm, Su 9am-12pm. AmEx/MC/V.

Natural Foods Outpost, 70 Makala St. (☎ 553-3377). An organic grocery store with various herbs ($2) growing out front. Hearty vegetables ($1) on sale inside, next to a burrito-and-sandwich shop ($3-5). 100% local produce. Open M-Th 9am-6pm, F 9am-4pm, Su 9am-5pm. Sandwich shop open M-F 10am-3pm.

C. Pascua Store, 109 Ala Malama Ave. (☎ 553-5443). Run by the same family since 1969, this is Molokai's premier junk food store. Open M-F 5:30am-10pm, Sa 6am-10pm, Su 7am-10pm.

Molokai Mango and Mango Mart, 93a and 93d Ala Malama Ave., respectively (☎ 553-3981 or 553-8232). The one on the left sells household/health/beauty items, the one on the right stocks groceries, and runs a basic deli (sandwiches $3). Open M-Sa 9am-7pm, Su 10am-6pm. MC/V.

RESTAURANTS

▦ **Kamuela's** (☎ 553-4286), located on Ala Malama Ave. between the two Mango shops (see above). Marginally more expensive than other eateries in town, but you get what you pay for. The rotating dinner specials ($10-15) are the real reason to dine at Kamuela's, especially if they're serving ribs, which are so tender that you'll devour them in a second ($11.25). Open M-Sa 6:30am-3pm and 5:30-9pm. No credit cards. ➌

▨ **Kanemitsu's Bakery,** in the center of Ala Malama Ave. A buzzing breakfast hang-out for locals who gather to gossip, Kanemitsu's sells Molokai French Bread, famous throughout the islands for its distinctive flavor and texture ($2 per loaf). Omelettes $5-6, 3 large pieces of french toast smothered in butter $5. Kanemitsu's also sells hot bread Tu-Su at 10 or 10:30pm from the kitchen accessible via the alley to the right of the store. The bread is the first batch for the following day, fresh from the oven ($3.50). Breakfast served until 11:30am. Open W-M 5:30am-6:30pm. No credit cards. ❶

▨ **Oviedo's Lunch Corner** (☎553-5014), at the very end of Ala Malama Ave., a few doors down from Solid Grounds Coffee Shop. Unapologetic, authentic Filipino food, such as crunchy roast pork and chicken papaya. Lunch ($7.75) comes with rice and a main dish. Open M-F 10am-4:30pm, Sa-Su 10am-4pm. ❷

Sundown Deli, 145 Puali Pl. (☎553-3713). A good place for a deli sandwich ($5), or a bacon, egg, and cheese sandwich ($4), and the only place in town where you can find a good bagel and lox ($10). Open M-F 7am-4pm, Sa 7am-2pm. MC/V. ❶

Molokai Drive-Inn (☎553-5655), on the north side of the highway at Kamoi St. Fastfood island-style—no franchise, greasy and good. Two eggs, meat, hash browns, and a drink, $4.80; waffles $3; plate lunches $6-7. Open M-Th 6am-10pm, F-Sa 6:30am-10:30pm. No credit cards. ❶

Molokai Pizza Cafe (☎553-3288), on the wharf road at its intersection with the highway. Decent pizza. Medium $12; large with one-topping $14.50. Free delivery to Hotel Molokai and Molokai Shores. Open M-Th 10am-10pm, F-Sa 10am-11pm, Su 11am-10pm. MC/V. ❷

Kamo'i Snack-n-Go, 28 Kamo'i St. #800 (☎553-3742). A convenience store that also sells delicious and inexpensive ice cream (2 scoops $3). Open M-F 9am-5pm, Sa 9am-4pm. AmEx/MC/V. ❶

Mrs. K's Concessions (☎553-3201), in the Molokai Center, across from the library on Ala Malama Ave. A small burger joint that serves plate lunches ($6) and sandwiches ($3). Open M-F 5am-5:30pm, Sa 5am-2pm. No credit cards. ❶

Big Daddy's Shop and Restaurant (☎553-5841), in the middle of Ala Malama Ave. Part convenience store, part plate-lunch dispensary ($6.25 for two choices), Big Daddy's also sells shave ice ($2) and fresh *poke, shoyu,* and *limu ogo* sashimi salads by the pound. Open M-F 8am-6:30pm. No credit cards. ❶

Solid Grounds Coffee House, 125 Puali Pl. (☎553-8433), at the end of Ala Malama Ave., attached to a Christian bookstore. A cool place to sip an iced mocha, the house specialty ($3.50). Five different specialty coffees daily. **Internet access** planned for 2003. Open M-Sa 5:30am-5pm. ❶

Ziggy's, #10 Mohala St. (☎553-8166). A restaurant and sportsbar with pool tables, moderately-priced plate lunches ($6-8), dinner specials ($8-12), and Happy Hour from 3-6pm (free pupus, domestic beer $2.25). Open M-Th 10:30am-9pm, F-Sa 10:30am-10pm. AmEx/MC/V. ❷

Subway, 230 Kamehameha Hwy. (☎553-4432), on the east end of town. The only chain restaurant on the island, notable because it's open late and on Sunday, and has low-fat options (unlike most island fare). Open Su-Th 8am-8pm, F-Sa 8am-9pm. MC/V. ❶

◙ SIGHTS

Kaunakakai itself has few sights of interest, apart from the **coconut grove,** and **Church Row** directly across the street. The **Hawaiian Home Lands Department** grants land along the stretch of highway just west of town to any religious organization that has a sufficient percentage of native Hawaiians in its congregation. The result is a row of over half a dozen places of worship. Some are small, one-room opera-

MOLOKAI

tions, and others are larger and more modern. Locals from all over the island swarm to services on Sunday morning, creating the island's only noticeable traffic.

The **Kaunakakai Wharf,** accessible by turning south at the intersection of the highway and Ala Malama Ave., is a favorite local swimming and fishing spot. Every other Saturday morning, a crowd gathers to watch **outrigger races** and sip cold drinks from concession stands run by local high school students. The **Molokai Ice House,** a mostly-defunct fisherman's cooperative on the east side of the wharf, was established in 1988 and used to sell the freshest fish on the island several times a week. (Open on occasional Friday evenings. Call ☎ 553-3048 for more information.)

Just before the wharf on the right, a raised stone platform is all that remains of King Kamehameha V's old vacation home. The area is designated **Malama Park,** and archaeologists believe that the area was once the site of a heiau.

🎵 ENTERTAINMENT

Witness Molokai nightlife at its finest at the weekly ▨**jam,** held around the pool at Hotel Molokai every Friday and Saturday from 4-6pm. Locals gather to play ukuleles and drums, and there is informal singing and hula dancing as well. A live band usually comes on after the jam session and plays until the bar closes (around 10:30pm). If you're lucky, they might be serving complementary pupus.

Next to the **Mitchell Pauole Center** at the intersection of Ala Malama Ave. and Aiona St. is the **Kaunakakai Ball Park,** where the Molokai Farmers have a substantial home field advantage over all the competition (who must fly in from Maui or Lanai). Since there isn't much else to do on the island, the locals take their little league very seriously, and games can be quite a spectacle.

For the under-21 crowd, **Club Zero,** a youth center on Ala Malama Ave., has pool tables, super couches, a 64-inch TV, video games, and cable. (☎ 553-8169. Open Tu-Th 4-10pm, F-Sa 4pm-midnight.)

It's not unusual for locals to throw spontaneous **beach parties** and **luaus** to celebrate birthdays, graduations, or summer weekends. Popular spots include the One Ali'i campground and the Kapuaiwa Coconut Grove, as well as temporary beachside pavilions between the 8- and 12-mile markers. Though it is never polite to crash somebody else's party, if a gathering is large enough, a discreet request for some chow will most likely be met with friendly approval. Be sure to reply in the negative and run for your car if anybody bigger than you asks if you like beef (it's a fight they're after).

Local youths frequently **drag race** their souped-up trucks at the end of Hwy. 470 in the Pala'au State Park in the evening on weekends. *Let's Go* does not recommend drag racing against local Hawaiians in the dark on the winding roads of Kalae, since it is illegal and extremely dangerous, but there's nothing wrong with observing the spectacle from afar. Just don't get in anybody's way.

CENTRAL MOLOKAI

KALAUPAPA PENINSULA

Kalaupapa is a flat, leaf-shaped land formation on Molokai's northern shore. It is separated from "topside" (the rest of Molokai) by a 1000-foot wall of mountains, and is accessible solely by air or a steep trail. Kalaupapa's beauty is rivaled only by its infamy—the area is home to a former leper colony that ceased operations in 1969. Many ex-patients still inhabit the peninsula. Kalaupapa's story is one of both tragedy and selfless heroism, and a visit to the site is deservedly among the most popular activities on the island.

KALAUPAPA'S STORY

The first documented case of **leprosy** in the Hawaiian Islands was in 1835. At the time little was known about the disease, apart from the fact that it was introduced by westerners. King Kamehameha V, however, knew enough to fear that leprosy could infect his people and tear apart his kingdom. To prevent this, he chose the most isolated spot in all the islands, a cove called Kalawao on the southeastern part of the Kalaupapa peninsula, and starting in 1866, persons with any type of skin condition were banished there. Patients would be "diagnosed," rounded up without notice, put on a ship, and dumped in the water near Kalawao. Some drowned, others succumbed to hunger or exposure, but none returned.

By 1870, the drop-off point had moved to the more hospitable western side of Kalaupapa, and Christian missionaries arrived to tend to the sick. The missionaries built grass huts for themselves, but most patients lived outdoors. Few missionaries remained on the peninsula for more than a few months until **Father Damien,** or Joseph De Veuster, a Catholic priest, arrived in 1873. In the same year, **Gerhard Hansen** isolated the bacteria that causes leprosy, and the disease came to be known as **Hansen's disease.**

Damien was very devoted to improving the lives of the residents; he built houses and dug graves by day, and at night he worked to build an addition to **St. Philomena Church.** Though he never finished the church, he did build nearly 300 box-like houses, and, on average, dug about one grave per day. Until Damien arrived, residents hid themselves from outsiders and were ashamed to enter the church, as many had lost portions of their cheeks or mouth and feared they would desecrate the building with their saliva. Damien cut holes in the floor for these poor souls to discreetly spit through, and welcomed them into the church.

Damien was diagnosed with leprosy in 1883 and died in 1889, at the age of 49. Even without treatment, leprosy is among the least contagious of diseases. Of the over 1000 workers on the peninsula since 1870, Damien is the only documented case of infection. In 1995, Damien was beatified by Pope John Paul II and is now a candidate for sainthood. His native Belgium acquired Damien's remains in 1936, but his right hand was re-interred at St. Philomena Church in 1995.

Mother Marianne Cope, a Franciscan nun from Syracuse, NY, arrived during the last year of Damien's life and remained on the peninsula for nearly 30 more. She managed to acquire more supplies for the residents than any other missionary, and is known as the founder of the hospice movement. **Brother Dutton,** who came in 1886, carried on Damien's work for 44 years, building more homes and working to finish St. Philomena.

M O L O K A I

HULL HOUSE
In the early 1800s, expanded international trade presented the *ali'i* with tantalizing goods imported from lands as far away as Turkey. Merchant salesmen from the West, aware of the great demand for aromatic sandalwood in Asia, tempted the *ali'i* with offers of jewelry, firearms, and alcohol in exchange for the precious trees. The members of Hawaiian royalty couldn't resist, and they forced the *maka'ainana* to cease their work in the taro fields and instead, to uproot the sandalwood forests. In order to measure the amount of wood that could be moved in any one voyage, a pit was dug in the approximate size and shape of the hull of a merchant vessel. The greed of Hawaii's elite pushed the commoners to the point of famine. The blood and sweat of the common folk furnished the royalty with expensive trinkets and toys, and allowed exploitative merchants to reap staggering profits from Asian sales of sandalwood. The *maka'ainana*, in turn, destroyed all new sandalwood saplings to prevent future generations from suffering a similar fate; but the island had already been forever robbed of its beautiful sandalwood trees.

In 1909, a Dr. Gibson used federal funding to build a treatment center in Kalawao called the Federal Experimental Station. Gibson mistakenly believed that diet was the cause of leprosy, and he required that his patients give up all local foods and quarantine themselves. His facility had 60 beds and 16 buildings, but over the course of the four years that it remained open, it attracted only nine patients.

In the 1940s, sulfa antibiotics were discovered to be an effective treatment for leprosy, and by the 1960s the disease was no longer considered contagious. However, the quarantine on Kalaupapa was not lifted until 1969. Until then, children born to residents were taken by the state and put up for adoption. After 1969, no new patients were admitted, and residents were free to leave, but many opted to stay rather than try to reintegrate themselves into families or start a new life.

During its years of operation, over 7000 people were sent to the Kalaupapa colony. From its peak of 1800 residents in 1970, there are fewer than 41 left today, and they range in age from 61-90. Residents get the mail and the newspaper daily; groceries and supplies are airlifted in twice each week, and larger items such as furniture and automobiles are brought in once a year on a barge. All the homes on the peninsula are owned by the state, though they are furnished by the residents themselves. The grounds are maintained by Hawaii Parks Services.

> **!** The only way to travel through the Kalaupapa Peninsula is as part of an organized tour. It is against state law to explore the peninsula on your own, and it is disrespectful to the area's residents.

▐ TRANSPORTATION

There are three ways to get to Kalaupapa. You can hike down a 2.8-mile trail that descends over 1000 ft. in a series of 26 numbered switchbacks, you can fly to an airstrip on the far side of the peninsula, or you can ride a mule down the trail. All three require advance reservations.

BY FOOT. Hiking is by far the cheapest and most rewarding option, though the trail is hard on the knees and may be difficult for those not in decent physical condition. The trail begins just inside the Pala'au State Park. From town, take Hwy. 460 west, then turn right at Hwy. 470. The trail entrance is 15min. down the highway, just past the mule stables, on the right at a metal gate with a sign warning not to enter without a permit. Though the laws requiring permits are now defunct, you must have an advance reservation with Damien Tours (see below), or else you will be turned away at the bottom of the trail.

If you plan to **hike,** be absolutely certain to start out *before* the mules depart at 7:50am to avoid slipping on their excrement on the way up. Bring plenty of **water.** The hike takes about an hour and fifteen minutes, and allows for fabulous views of Kalaupapa. At the base of the trail, walk toward the settlement. You'll pass a black sand beach—one of the island's most dangerous—and as you enter a large open area, notice the bleachers on the right that read, "wait here for tour."

BY AIR. If you prefer to **fly,** you will need to arrange both a flight and a tour reservation with **Damien Tours,** unless your airline explicitly states that they will handle the tour reservation. The prices listed here are for the flight only and do not include the tour. Consider hiking down and flying back, or vice versa, as the hike can be very enjoyable. **Molokai Air Shuttle** is the cheapest option. (☎ 545-4988. $25 one-way, $50 round-trip from the Molokai Airport; $40 one-way, $70 round-trip from Honolulu. Offices open M-Sa 6am-9pm.) Other options include **Pacific Wings,** which flies from Honolulu (☎ 888-575-4546 or 873-0877; fax 873-7920; $65 one-way, $130 round-trip), or **Paragon Air,** a charter-only company that services Kalaupapa from Honolulu and Maui and can combine the trip with a scenic air tour of Molokai for an extra fee. (☎ 800-428-1231 or 244-3356; $50-70 one-way, $89-110 roundtrip.) Someone will pick you up at the airport and take you to the bleachers.

BY MULE. The final option, the **mule ride,** differs from the preceding two in that the **Molokai Mule Ride** company (☎ 800-670-6503 or 567-6088) includes both lunch and a tour in the price ($135 per person). Though many participants enjoy the ride immensely, there are two potential drawbacks to riding the mules: first, mule riders are generally part of a tour led by someone other than Richard Marks (see **Tour** below); second, in the rare cases where Richard includes mule riders on his tour, he affectionately refers to them as the "jackass patrol" just before they board the bus, giving hikers and fliers a sense of camaraderie at the expense of mule-folk.

◥ TOUR

Damien Tours (☎ 567-6171) operates all of the tours of Kalaupapa. You must have advance reservations to visit the settlement, and tours cost $30 (cash or personal check only, payable at the start of the tour) and take place every day except Sunday. Be sure to bring your own lunch, since it is not provided as part of the tour.

Once you arrive at the bleachers near the mule corral, wait for the avuncular and charismatic ◪**Richard Marks** to arrive in his big blue bus, cat food in tow. Richard is both the tour guide and the sheriff of Kalaupapa, as well as a former patient. Nearly 40 years ago, he became the third member of his family to be exiled to Kalaupapa. He's quite a character, and his tours are heartfelt as well as entertaining. The tour begins around 9:45am and ends around 2pm.

The first stop on the tour is the **docks,** where residents gather once a year, as the barge delivers supplies, to gossip about everybody's new cars and furniture. The next stop is **St. Francis Church,** the walls of which are adorned with images of **Father Damien,** followed by a brief pause at the grave of **Mother Marianne.** The **Visitor Center** is next, which is filled with a large array of books about Damien and Kalaupapa. Richard can advise you as to which are worthwhile, but *Yesterday at Kalaupapa* is an excellent choice for its photography, and *Separating Sickness* contains some of the better narratives about residents' lives. The latter portion of the tour takes place around the old Kalawao settlement site. During lunch in Judd Park, Richard will try his best to feed the runt of a litter of wild pigs who come daily to sniff out leftovers. From the park, you can see dome-shaped **Okala Rock,** the only place in the world where the Okala Palm grows wild.

The most poignant part of the tour is the history of Father Damien's life, recounted at **St. Philomena Church.** His grave, though not his body (see above), is located outside. While the tour bus passes through the settlement, no stops are made at places where residents might congregate, such as the post office, the hospital, or the parks services office. This is to protect the privacy of the residents. Also be aware that **photography of residents is strictly prohibited.**

KAMAKOU PRESERVE

The 22,774-acre Kamakou Preserve is like no other place in the islands. The peak of Kamakou, the highest point of the island, is just shy of 5000 ft. above sea level. The preserve itself is home to more than 250 different species of Hawaiian plants, 219 of can only be found in Hawaii. The plants feed indigenous insects, which in turn support the local bird population. Among the rarities of the area are the Molokai thrush and the Molokai creeper, which have not been seen outside the region in nearly a decade. If you camp, you may even catch a glimpse of a *pueo* (Hawaiian owl) in the twilight.

The preserve owes its existence to the generosity of the Molokai Ranch, which sold the land rights to the Nature Conservancy in 1982. The ranch maintains control of the water rights, however, as the area provides 60% of the island's water via a tunnel to the Kualapu'u reservoir (see **Kualapu'u Reservoir**, p. 255).

GETTING THERE To reach the preserve safely, a **4WD vehicle** is essential. Though 2WD trucks with enough clearance have been known to successfully make it as far as the Waikolu Lookout, this is only possible after several rainless days, when the roads are especially dry and mud-free. Keep in mind that the last few miles of the road are at high elevation; they can be rainy even when it is sunny at the bottom. If driving a 2WD vehicle, **turn around at the first sign of rain.** In the event you get stuck, you'll have to hike all the way back down, and you'll suffer the embarrassment (and substantial expense) of car retrieval. Call your rental agency or one of the gas stations in Kaunakakai. When driving to Kamakou, use first gear and go slowly. Be careful to drive around (not over) the manhole covers that appear at odd intervals along the road, as they can damage your axles. Try not to drive in ruts; instead, straddle them with the wheels of your vehicle, or drive up on the shoulder to avoid them. If you lose traction and start to slide, ease up on the gas and turn into the skid. Lastly, avoid stopping if your vehicle is on an upward incline, as many parts of the road are passable only with momentum.

■ ⁊ ORIENTATION AND PRACTICAL INFORMATION. The road that leads to the preserve begins west of Kaunakakai on **Hwy. 460.** Turn right just before the Manawainui Bridge, which precedes the 4-mile marker. The pavement ends almost immediately at the Homelani Cemetery, and the dirt road begins. The first 5 mi. or so of this road are fairly easy-going until you pass the entrance sign for the **Molokai Forestry Reserve** after 5.7 mi. Though the massive silver-barked trees may be beautiful, the road is not. Even a 4WD vehicle may encounter traction problems while trying to climb up the steep grades after this point. If you see a trickle of water running down the ruts of the road, do not continue unless you are in a 4WD; this indicates that the ground is saturated and almost guarantees that you will get stuck.

This part of the island was a popular place to live back in the days of Kamehameha the Great, but the only people you'll see today are hikers, locals checking on remote *pakalolo* gardens, and the resident woodcutter, who sells carvings from his business just past the forest reserve entrance. If you honk loudly enough to get his attention over the noise of his shop, he'll even give you a tour. There's also a restroom just outside his gate.

After around 9 mi. total, you will just be able to make out **Lua Moku 'Iliahi,** or the Sandalwood Measuring Pit, on the left (see **Hull House,** p. 249). After another mile and a bit, you will reach the entrance to the Kamakou Preserve and the **Waikolu Lookout.** Waikolu translates to "three waters," and refers to the many waterfalls that run over the mountains and into the region's streams. At 3700 ft., the lookout has stunning views of the surrounding valleys. Though Waikolu's frequent rain and clouds can obstruct the view, early morning is often clearer. There are squat toilets and a spare **campground,** but no potable water. The lookout makes a great base camp for exploring the preserve, though it can be a bit chilly and wet. Camping permits ($5) are required and can be purchased from the caretaker at the **Pala'au State Park** or the **Department of Land and Natural Resources** (☎ 567-6891), located south of the Post-a-Nut post office on Hwy. 480 in Hoolehua. Both offices are open M-F 9am-4pm. Camping is not permitted anywhere else in the preserve, and fires are prohibited. (See **Accommodations and Camping,** p. 242).

GUIDED TOURS. If you are concerned about getting to and hiking through the preserve yourself, or if you'd simply like to avoid the long walk from the Waikolu Lookout, consider arranging a guided hike with **Molokai Outdoors** (☎ 553-4477. Approx. $95) or the Nature Conservancy. Guided hikes are generally less time-consuming, since you are driven directly to the trailheads, and the tour leaders often have worthwhile background knowledge about the region. The **Nature Conservancy,** 23 Pueo Pl., runs an eight-person trip usually (but not always) on the first Saturday of the month. (☎ 553-5236. Office open M-F 7:30am-3pm. Call far in advance to reserve a spot. Suggested donation $25.)

HIKING. The Nature Conservancy asks that you stay on the roads and marked trails to avoid damaging the surrounding vegetation. From the Waikolu Lookout, the road is impassable in anything but a 4WD, and you'll have trouble even in a 4WD. The safest course of action is to park here and walk to the trailheads, unless you have extensive off-road driving experience—or a bunch of people to help you push. Before you leave the lookout, sign in on the Nature Conservancy's log sheet, which often has information about road conditions. In addition, be sure to bring lots of water, as well as rain gear and sturdy shoes or hiking boots that you won't mind getting (very) muddy.

A few minutes down the road from the lookout, the **Hanahilo Trail** veers off to the left at a tree stump. The trail is quite difficult and very poorly marked. Only those looking for a strenuous hiking experience should take this trail. The trail rises nearly 600 ft. as it runs through a dense forest of ironwoods before ultimately merging with the Pepeopae Trail after 1¾ mi. Turning right leads back to the road, and a left takes you to the Pelekunu Overlook (see below).

To avoid Hanahilo altogether, continue walking down the road from the Waikolu Lookout for about 1½hr. (just under 3 mi.). Stay on the main road; the small side roads lead to private property. Continue straight and to the left at the sign for the **Pepeopae Trail.** You'll see a small 6-inch wide **boardwalk** covered with reinforced chicken wire, which runs for just over a mile through one of Hawaii's wettest regions. The substantial rainfall (over 170 in. annually) has miniaturized the plant population of the area, creating a forest bog. The boardwalk gives hikers a chance to experience the remarkable vegetation and topography of the preserve without jeopardizing the environment. Stay on the boardwalk, lest you kill an endangered plant.

At the end of the boardwalk, the gaping **Pelekunu Valley Overlook** offers truly spectacular views of high grassy cliffs towering over the Pelekunu river, as well as the turquoise waters of the Pacific to the left. On a good day, wispy clouds just barely obscure the tops of the cliffs from view. The 5760-acre valley is under the care of the Nature Conservancy and closed to the public, as it is one of the few remaining spawning grounds for several species of marine life.

If you turn right at the sign for the Pepeopae Trail instead of veering left toward the boardwalk, you'll follow a deeply rutted road about ¾ mi. until it ends. The trail at the bottom leads over a ridge and continues to the left of a small bridge into a long **tunnel** that passes through the mountain. With the help of a flashlight, you'll make it to the other side without much difficulty; be careful not to hit your head where rocks protrude from the top of the tunnel. At the other end of the tunnel is another bridge and **Cymoh Falls,** a small waterfall set in a bubbling creek. The entire trip from the Pepeopae sign is less than two miles long.

KALA'E AND KUALAPU'U

The area toward the end of Hwy. 470 is called **Kala'e,** and is high enough in elevation to get a lot of sun and a little rain on most days. A choice spot for agriculture, the tiny town of **Kualapu'u,** located at Farrington Ave. at Hwy. 470, was once the island headquarters of the Del Monte fruit company. When they closed shop in the 1980s, the town suffered and shrank. In recent years, the coffee bean has replaced the pineapple, and the town's main attraction is now a small coffee plantation.

FOOD

Coffees of Hawaii, Inc. ❶, at the corner of Farrington and Hwy. 470 (☎567-9241), serves local brew any way you like it. Eight ounces of the Malolani Medium Roast, famous for its chocolate aftertaste, will set you back a mere $7. The shop also serves deli sandwiches, as well as other light fare. (**Tours** M-F 9:30 and 11:30am. $7, children $3.50. Call ahead to ensure that a tour will be running. Open M-F 7am-4pm, Sa 8am-4pm, Su 10am-4pm.) **Kamuela's Cookhouse ❶,** a few doors down, is the older sister of the Kamuela's in Kaunakakai and is just as good. This Kamuela's is only open for breakfast and lunch, however. The lemon chicken plate lunch ($7.50) is superb, and the hamburgers ($4.50) are large and juicy, a rarity in the islands. (☎567-9655. Open M-Sa 7am-3pm.) Next door on Farrington is the **Kualapu'u Market,** a grocery store that also rents VHS tapes and DVDs for $2-5. (☎567-6243. Open M-Sa 8:30am-6pm.)

SIGHTS AND CAMPING

PALA'AU STATE PARK. Pala'au is a peaceful state park in an often-clouded forest of ironwood trees that leans over the highway. It would make an ideal camping spot, if not for the frequent drizzles and lack of potable drinking water. If you don't mind getting a little wet, however, bring your own water and pitch a tent on the soft needles that cover the ground—chances are, you'll have the park to yourself. **Camping permits** are an absolute necessity, lest your car be ticketed by the police. Buy one from the caretaker's office, on the left at the mouth of the park. (Office open M-F 9am-4pm. Permits $5 per group, 5-night maximum.) Also be aware that local youths frequently drag race on the highway on weekend nights and can be quite noisy. The park has restrooms and outdoor showers.

The decision to pitch a tent notwithstanding, a visit to **Phallic Rock,** 5min. from the end of the highway by foot, will be rewarding whether you're a woman seeking fertility or just a fan of phalli. A sign declares that the rock is a natural formation, which has only been carved "to some extent" by humans. Judge for yourself. Five minutes in the opposite direction is the **Kalaupapa Lookout,** which has stunning views of the peninsula of the same name. If you don't hike down to the leper colony, you should be certain to at least check out the view, as it is one of Molokai's best. The trail that leads to the left into the forest from the lookout is a pleasant hike that few take, but it peters out after about 20min. *(At the very end of Hwy. 470.)*

■ **PURDY'S MACADAMIA NUT FARM.** Purdy may very well run the most hospitable macadamia nut farm in the world. Visitors are welcomed by the man himself and given a full tour of the working farm. Unlike commercial operations on Oahu, Purdy does not use any irrigation, pesticides, or chemicals of any kind, and visitors have the privilege of wandering freely throughout the property. The trees on his five-acre farm are about 80 years old, and they produce nuts year-round. You'll have the opportunity to crack all the nuts you can eat, as well as sample macadamia honey on slices of fresh coconut. *(On Lihi Pali Ave., ½ mi. from the intersection with Farrington Ave., on the right. From Hwy. 470, turn left on Farrington Ave., then right on Lihi Pali after 1 mi. ☎567-6620. Open Tu-F 9:30am-3:30pm, Sa 10am-2pm, weather permitting. Free.)*

MOLOKAI MUSEUM AND R.W. MEYER SUGAR MILL. The R.W. Meyer Sugar Mill operated from 1878-1889 and was the smallest sugar mill in Hawaii. A 16-year restoration process culminated in a grand dedication and museum opening in 1988. Numbered placards throughout the mill make the various steps in the sugar production process easy to follow, and the small museum has an informative video and historical background information. *(On Hwy. 470 about 4 mi. from the intersection with 460 on the left. ☎ 567-6436. Open M-Sa 10am-2pm. $2.50, children $1.)*

IRONWOOD HILLS GOLF COURSE. A beautiful public golf course, Ironwood Hills is well worth the price, and is run by a good-natured caretaker. *(3.7 mi. from the intersection with Hwy. 460 on Hwy. 470 on the left down a dirt road, just before the sugar mill. ☎ 567-6000. Non-residents $15 for 9 holes, $20 for 18. Cart rental $8 per 9 holes. Club rental $7 for 9 holes, $12 for 18. Open daily 7:30am-5pm.)*

WORLD'S LARGEST RUBBER-LINED RESERVOIR. Easiest to see on the way out of Kualapu'u, the reservoir holds nearly 1.5 billion gallons and supplies most of the western portion of the island with water, which is piped through an eight-foot tunnel from the wet valleys on the eastern side of the island. *(Just below Kualapu.)*

HOOLEHUA

This large, dry area west of Kala'e divides eastern and western Molokai. Most of the land in the area is under the auspices of the department of Hawaiian Home Lands, which provides homesteads to ethnic Hawaiians.

⟁ PRACTICAL INFORMATION. The ▩post office (☎ 567-6144), located on Puupeelua Ave. (Hwy. 480) at its intersection with Farrington Ave., is home to the world's only **Post-A-Nut** service—you can send a genuine Molokai coconut to your friends and family back home for the price of postage (usually $3-7, depending on coconut weight). Peggy, the smiling postmaster, collects and provides the nuts and even keeps a few felt pens around to write on the husks. (Open M-F 7:30-11:30am and 12:30-4:30pm.) **Zip Code:** 96729.

◙ SIGHTS. One of the only coastal sand dune ecosystems left in Hawaii, the ▩**Moomomi Preserve** is home to a half-dozen endangered plant species that cannot be found anywhere else on the planet. Its pristine coast is a breeding ground for green sea turtles, a rarity in the populated portions of the islands, and the terrain is colorful and rugged. The many white-sand beaches located along this portion of the coast are expansive and perpetually empty.

To reach the preserve, take Hwy. 460 from Kaunakakai to Hwy. 480. Turn left at Farrington Ave., and continue straight until the asphalt ends. The dirt road straight ahead leads to the preserve. Though it is smooth most of the way, the few ruts can be monsters and may tilt your vehicle at odd angles. After about 2 mi., the road forks. Veer to the right for another short mile to reach a campground pavilion that has restrooms but is usually locked if it's not being rented out. Unless it is raining or muddy, a car can make the trip without too much trouble, if you drive slowly and pay attention to the road. If you want to play it safe, go with a truck or a 4x4.

The rocky **beach** around the bend to the left of the parking area is not good for swimming nor sunbathing, but the purple volcanic tide pools are worth checking out. Continue to the left along the coast for 10min. or so to reach Moomomi Beach, an idyllic spot to let the hustle and bustle of the populated world soak away into the sands. The surf can be dangerous, so stay alert, as there are no lifeguards on the beach—or anybody else, for that matter. On the last Saturday of each month, the **Nature Conservancy** runs a tour out of Moomomi Beach. (☎ 553-5236. Office open M-F 7:30am-3pm. Call far ahead to reserve a spot. Suggested donation $25.)

MOLOKAI

Beyond Moomomi is **Kawaaloa Bay,** a similar (but slightly longer) stretch of beach. If neither Moomomi nor Kawaaloa suits you, just keep walking to the left along the coast. You'll discover a new beach every 10 or 15min., and the chances that you'll encounter another human being diminish with every step. Be absolutely certain to **stay on the roads and walking trails,** lest you kill an endangered plant or squash a rare sea bird's underground nesting area. Also keep in mind that it is illegal to remove any part of the preserve, be it animal, vegetable, or mineral.

THE FIGHTING COCKS OF KALA'E AND HOOLEHUA. As you drive along the highways of Molokai, keep your eyes open for A-frame huts or wire cages about a foot high, located in front yards or fields. The chickens raised inside are intended neither for eggs nor for food. Rather, these structures are pseudo-barracks where fighting cocks are trained. Originally brought to the islands by Filipinos, cockfighting has become a popular pastime on Molokai. The animals are generally kept close together in order to encourage aggressiveness, but they are tethered far enough apart so that they cannot actually fight one another. Although cockfighting is illegal, raising fighting cocks is not. Despite the grisly end which most of these creatures face, their long feather plumes and bright colors are quite beautiful, and are worth a closer look. The farther reaches of Farrington Ave. are the best place to hunt for fighting cocks, though you might encounter a few along Hwy. 470 east of Kaunakakai, past mile 5.

EAST OF KAUNAKAKAI

The drive east from Kaunakakai becomes progressively more beautiful the further you go, beginning around mile 7 and increasing exponentially in grandeur after mile 20. The "towns" listed here are really nothing more than clusters of houses along the road. Other than the **'Ili'ili'opae Heiau,** few sights are worth more than a sideways glance. Just roll down your windows and enjoy the drive.

ACCOMMODATIONS

Kamalo Plantation Cottage ❸, through the gate next to mailbox 300 on the mountain-side of the hwy., just across from St. Joseph's Church before the 11-mile marker. A stay on the lush 5-acre property of Glen and Akiko Foster is truly an island-style experience. The guest cottage is a lovely and well-furnished studio apartment with a king-sized bed, kitchen, bird-watching deck, indoor and outdoor showers, tons of privacy, and access to the nearby luau hut complete with a gas grill for BBQs. (☎558-8263; fax 558-8263; kamaloplantation@aloha.net; www.molokai.com/kamalo. 2-night minimum stay. $85 single/double occupancy. Traveler's checks, cash, or advance payment with a personal check only.)

The Fosters also rent the A-frame **Moanui Beach House ❹,** at mile 20, near the golden sands of Murphy's Beach. Both the cottage and the beach house are stocked with fruit from the plantation and home-baked bread. The residence has two airy bedrooms with king-sized beds, 1.5 baths, a large kitchen, as well as living and dining rooms. (3-night minimum stay. Single/double occupancy $140, each additional guest $20.)

The **Wavecrest Resort ❸** is located at mile 13. All of its units are leased through Friendly Island Realty (see p. 242) A laid-back condo complex, the resort sits on an attractive lagoon with a good view of Maui. There are two lighted tennis courts, as well as shuffleboard facilities and a putting green. All rooms have a kitchen, patio, TV, and ceiling fans. No A/C or telephones. (Wavecrest management office open M-F 8am-2pm, Sa 11:30am-12:30pm. 1 BR $70-80, plus $40 cleaning fee for stays less than a week; 2 BR $135, plus $50 cleaning fee for stays less than a week.)

FOOD

Just about the only place to grab groceries or some lunch on the east side of the island is the **Neighborhood Store and Counter ❶** (☎558-8498), just beyond mile 16. In addition to the pleasant market, the food order window serves up mahi mahi burgers ($4) and other treats (honey dip chicken plate lunches $7; milkshakes $3.50). Video rental ($3) is available for a rainy day. (Open daily 8am-6pm, food counter closed Wed.)

SIGHTS

'ILI'ILI'OPAE HEIAU

To reach the heiau, watch for the Hawaiian Home Lands marker on the right just after the small Mapulehu bridge, about ½ mi. past mile 15. It is difficult to find a place to park, since all the shoulders are narrow (and privately owned). It is easiest to turn around once you've passed the bridge and park on the mountain-side of the road just west of the bridge, where there is a small expanse of grass to the right of a mailbox and dirt road. Immediately across the street from the Home Lands marker is mailbox #488 and yet another dirt road with a gate that reads, "No Hunting, Private Property, Keep Out, Keep Gate Closed."

Located within the tiny village of Puko'o, the colossal 'Ili'ili'opae Heiau is not to be missed. Fortunately, in recent years, the site has been opened to the public. At one time advance permission was required to access the heiau; however, the property owners became so frustrated by the number of telephone calls requesting access that they now allow visitors to stop by unannounced, provided that they stay on the road and don't make their presence known. Disregard the signs with confidence and walk *around* the gate along the path on the left side (opening the gate is a bad idea, since the gate holds up the fence). Continue walking up the dirt road for 10 or 12 minutes until you see a wall of stones near a house on your right. These stones are a heiau, but they are not *the* heiau. A narrow path leads into the forest just a bit farther up on the left, underneath a handpainted sign that reads "heiau" and has an arrow.

The dappled sunlight that radiates through the leafy canopy of the forest should be the first clue that you've entered an awesome and holy place. As you approach the four-tiered structure, notice the size of the larger stones. Legend has it that this heiau was built in one marathon night by a massive human chain that snaked its way inland over the mountain to the Wailau Valley. To view the entirety of this feat of human engineering, continue walking along the trail to the right, which leads up the hill. You will be able to see the flat surface of the heiau, which rivals a football field in size. The surface is remarkably level; the 20-foot west side is nearly twice as tall as the east side, and it is commonly believed that the heiau was more than twice its present size while it was in use.

'Ili'ili'opae is the second-largest heiau in Hawaii, and was used as a temple for human sacrifice, as well as a training ground for kahunas from all the islands. It is believed that the surface was covered with mounds of sand to make it flat, then layered over with grass mats and wooden huts. The heiau is holy to the Hawaiian people; it is the work of a mighty civilization that has all but disappeared. Treat it with respect by not touching, moving, or climbing on any of the rocks.

MOLOKAI

THE LOCAL STORY

ALOHA'AINA

In June 2002, Let's Go research-writer Marc Wallenstein had the opportunity to spend an illuminating evening with 20-year-old June, a native of Molokai. Speaking from his first-hand experience, June attempts to explain his and some other locals' objections to development and mainland intrusion. Aloha'aina means "love of the land."

Q: You keep using this word, *aina*, to describe the land. What is *aina*?

A: Saying like, the west side, the places up there, it's like a desert...it's open land. And when these white people they come over to the west side, they see a lot of open land not being used, so they go think they just gonna pick up and go buy that, purchase that land, just put up a house...and it's for a vacation home, man...By doing that, they take away our land, they take away our way of life, our work, our way of life. They're destroying the *aina*, the land. There used to be a resting spot or the eating spot, and there we'd go to hunt, but now we cannot hunt there no more because the property is being put up over there. And even the South Shore, you cannot even throw net, you cannot even go fishing. People they call the cops and the game warden be down there as fast as the snap of a finger. Just to get the guys out of m'yard. Just like that. It's our way of life.

Q: Is the game warden Hawaiian?

A: Yeah he is. But see, a lot of people don't dig the same things. The police station, the rangers, the warriors, the security guards—they all Hawaiians.

OTHER SIGHTS

KAWELA. A small residential development between miles 4 and 6, Kawela is notable for its views. Drive up any of the streets on the mountain side of the road for beautiful vistas. At mile 6, the **Kakahai'a Beach Park** sits too close to the highway to make it a worthwhile stop. Just after the beach park, notice the **Kakahai'a National Wildlife Refuge,** the green wetland area on both sides of the road that has been set aside as a seabird sanctuary.

KAMALO. Between miles 10 and 11, Kamalo was once the economic and civic center of the island. The **Kamalo Wharf** can be accessed via the dirt road on the right at the major bend in the highway after mile 10. Once the island's main unloading docks, the wharf is now home to a few shacks and the occasional outrigger race. A ¼ mi. farther down the road is **St. Joseph's Church,** one of two remaining churches built by Father Damien outside the Kalaupapa peninsula. The church is a simple, one-room affair, with a statue of Damien and a small cemetary. Another ½ mi. farther, a poorly-visible sign on the right denotes the **Smith-Bronte Landing Site,** where the first civilian flight from the mainland to Hawaii ended in a safe crash-landing in 1927. The flight took 25 hours, and Honolulu was the original destination.

UALAPUE. Notable mostly for its fishpond, Ualapue is also home to the abandoned **Long Ping Store and Gas Station,** on the left, just past the fishpond. The antiquated pump's gears are visible from the back, and during the 1930s, the central building was a Chinese-owned general store. Though trespassing is prohibited, nobody resides on the property, and the gate is not locked.

KALUA'AHA. A bit past mile 14, you can see the remnants of the **Kalua'aha Church,** built in 1844 by the first missionary to the island. The church is hard to spot because it is set back from the road. Less than ½ mi. farther, **Our Lady of Sorrows Church** is much easier to find. The still-active church is a reconstruction of the original, which was built by Father Damien in 1874.

EAST TO HALAWA BAY

From about mile 20 onward, the road is basically one lane and has a fair number of cliff's-edge hairpin turns. The view is well-earned by braving the ride. Sea cliffs, secluded beach coves, and expansive pastures await in this remote region.

The road is paved and smooth all the way to Halawa Bay, but exercise caution nonetheless, especially the first time you make the trip or in the rain. Don't hesitate to lay on the horn as you approach tight corners, and drive slowly. Be certain your first time driving beyond mile 20 is not at night, both because it would be dangerous to do so, and because you'd miss out on the view, which is half the reason to go to Halawa in the first place.

WAIALUA BEACH. Just before the 19-mile marker, Waialua Beach is popular place among locals who gather here to sunbathe, snorkel, and socialize. The beach is located at the confluence of a small stream and the ocean, and in the summer, children jump from the highway bridge into the stream to rinse off the salt before heading home.

MOANUI SUGAR MILL. If you opt not to stop at Waialua, continue past the several small strips of sand along the highway, keeping a watch for the remains of the chimney of the Moanui Sugar Mill about 20 yards in and on the left, which was operational until it burned down in the late 1800s.

MURPHY'S BEACH. At the 20-mile marker, just after an exceptionally well-preserved fishpond (see p. 260), lies Murphy's Beach, a picturesque sunbathing spot. The water is good for swimming near shore, but rocks encroach on the beach and prevent safe swimming farther out. Like Waialua, Murphy's Beach is distinctly Molokaian: no shower or restroom facilities, but still a fabulous place to relax and enjoy the day, provided you aren't in a hurry to get anywhere.

ROCK POINT. Just past Murphy's beach, around a bend in the road before the 21-mile marker, is a rocky area called (appropriately enough) Rock Point. The area is a good spot for surfing, especially in the winter, but can be dangerous. The rocks are sharp and the water is quite shallow in places, so be sure you know what you're doing before you charge into the spray. Right at the 21-mile marker, at a low point in the road, is a small white-sand beach across from a couple of houses. This unnamed beach has a protected shoreline and makes for good swimming. Another small, unnamed beach cove with similar surf conditions (but a little more sand) can be found ½ mi. farther down the road.

PU'U O HOKU RANCH. After mile 21, the road winds its way upward into the cattle pastures of the Pu'u O Hoku Ranch. Around mile 24, the road levels out and widens a bit, and you should be able to catch a glimpse of **Moku Ho'oniki Island,** recently named a bird sanctuary but originally used for target practice by WWII bombers. Located right at the 25-mile marker, the main offices of the ranch double as the **Last Chance Store,** where you can pick up basic food items and candy.

They need the jobs. Without the jobs, they cannot live. They try to live off the land but they cannot because these new homes, these new properties that have been built, they put in the "No Trespassing" signs. One trespass, one gunshot, they calling the cops. Well, I can't even shoot gun near a *haole* or even a regular hunting spot. They're afraid their house might get shot, or that they might be in danger, but the hunters, they're more smart than that. They wouldn't shoot directly at a house. I mean, that's our way of life, so let us be. This island doesn't have much in government abilities, so a lotta families, they marginal. They welfare guys, they gotta really live more off the land...but it's getting more hard for them to do that.

How much we would like to have our nation back, be a nation, be the Hawaiian nation. We just want our nation back, but they still wouldn't give it to us, they'll always be the elite. They'll always have property ownership because they got the money, the power, and the back—the state power—and no matter who we get, we can't equal them money-wise. The US is the one of the most powerful countries in the world. What thinks the Hawaiians, these little eight lands in the middle of the Pacific Ocean, can take on the big...ahh... [frustrated]. Our whole thing put together I don't even think could take up the smallest state in the United States. It wouldn't even come close to being the same size. Places like [this]...they don't count.

After the 25-mile marker, the road descends into a forested region with trees arcing overhead in a cavernous latticework of green and gray. A grove of sacred *kukui* trees nearby on ranch property marks the **grave of Lanikaula,** one of the most powerful kahuna ever to inhabit Molokai. It is rumored that his spirit haunts the grove even today, and locals refuse to approach the site. Ask at the ranch office for specific directions and permission to visit.

The ranch has two tremendous guest cottages. The **Sunrise Cottage** is a 2-bedroom, 2-bath house with a kitchen and a covered lanai. The ▨**Grove Cottage** ❹ is a 2100 sq. foot, 4-bedroom, 3-bath house with spectacular views of Maui and a sunny master bedroom. Both are set in bucolic pastures, far enough even from the ranch offices to have complete privacy. *(Last Chance Store, ☎ 558-8109; fax 558-8100. Store and offices open daily approximately 9am-4pm. Both guest cottages are $125 per night for one or two people, each additional person $20.)*

▨ **HALAWA VALLEY AND BAY.** About a ½ mi. past the 26-mile marker, there's a mesmerizing **lookout** over Halawa Valley, with views of Moa'ula and Hipuapua Falls, as well as the half-black sand of the beach below. As you descend into the valley, be mindful of the stone wall on the edge of the highway, especially while passing oncoming traffic (that is, if you encounter any).

Believed to be the site of Molokai's first settlement in 700 AD, Halawa Bay epitomizes the essence of Molokai: primal and untouched. Though the area had quite a few residents at one point, tsunamis in 1946 and 1957 left so much salt behind that the farmland went bad and all but a half-dozen of the residents moved out. The bay is a fabulous (and free) place to **camp,** and is popular among locals, who usually pitch semi-permanent tarps and tents on the far side of the bay.

At the bottom of the highway, there's a small **church** on the left and a campground restroom with an outdoor shower on the right. Be careful not to drink the water, as it does not meet health standards. If you plan to camp, consider the area just past the end of the highway. It is close enough to the campground to make use of the facilities, but far enough away to have an ocean view. It is also a considerable distance from the far side of the beach, which is more crowded. Be certain to lock your car and keep a close eye on your valuables.

MORE MULLETS THAN A TRAILER PARK

Molokai is unique in that most of the southern coast is quite shallow because the reef is far from the shore. From the late 13th century on, locals built a vast network of nearly 60 fishponds in the protected coves and bays of the island. The basic design includes a wall of rocks from the sea floor to the surface, constructed with special gates that allow small fish to enter but prevent them from escaping after they became large enough to eat. Placement was crucial as well; the tides had to be strong enough to refresh the water in the pond, but not so strong as to damage the walls. A well-built fishpond could cover hundreds of acres of ocean, and some are rumored to have become so full of fish that one pass with a net could yield two or three large mullet.

Fishponds were the property of the *ali'i* (royalty), but were built and staffed by commoners. Molokai had many fishponds and many chiefs, and was considered a plentiful and wealthy island. Today, Molokai has little economic power and few job opportunities, but a grant from the Hawaiian Homelands Department has provided work for several dozen local youths, who are being paid to rebuild the Ualapu'e fishpond in the traditional manner. The fishpond is operating presently, and is visible a half-mile past the mile-13 marker. Other fishponds worth a visit are Kaloko'eli, just behind Molokai Shores, as well as Kaina'ohe and Keawanui, both located on the bay just past mile 12.

MOA'ULA FALLS. Halawa's real attraction, aside from the overall grandeur of the place, is the hike to the magnificent **Moa'ula Falls.** The hike crosses private property and for some time, was closed to visitors except as part of a guided tour. After a bit of a squabble between local landowners and the state parks department, people have relaxed for the most part—be confident about making the hike, but be respectful; try not to make your presence a nuisance to the people who are allowing you the privilege of crossing their land.

The hike takes about 1½hr., which can vary depending on the weather and the strength of the river near the pool at the base of the waterfall. Since the trek involves a good bit of scrambling over river rocks and through some muddy patches, it might be difficult for those unaccustomed to hiking through the woods. *(As you enter the Halawa Valley from the highway, park your car on the road past the church near the state campground on the right. Walk back to the church, and continue straight and to the right along the dirt road in front of the church until you cross the bridge over Halawa stream. Take the tire-track dirt road with a "no parking" sign on a fencepost on the left just after the bridge. The trail to the falls begins up and to the left of the house about 30 yards down the road, at a plank that crosses a small stream. The trail runs through a taro farm, and then past a privacy fence. It follows a white pipe on the ground for most of its length, so if you're unsure which way to go, just keep your eyes on the pipe. About ¾ of the way there, the trail becomes very difficult to follow; keep the river on your left and walk toward the sound of the falls as best you can. Eventually, you will be forced down to the riverbed by the terrain. The last 250 yards of hopping from rock to rock should be taken slowly. Let's Go recommends wearing sturdy shoes or hiking boots.)*

NEAR HALAWA

NORTH SHORE SEA CLIFFS AND WAILAU VALLEY

Accessible only by boat, the north shore of Molokai is home to the world's largest sea cliffs. The cliffs were formed when the Makanalua Peninsula, a large chunk of the island created by the Kauhako Caldera, fell off and sank into the sea after thousands of years of pounding surf eroded its foundation. The stunning masses of rock and earth are spotted with swaths of bright green grass and the occasional herd of mountain goats. The sea below the cliffs can be quite rough but is a popular spot for advanced sea kayaking. The current flows swiftly away from Halawa, and kayakers must arrange in advance for a boat to retrieve them. The cliffs are also home to the **Kahiwa Falls,** the highest ocean-terminating waterfall in the world.

A good way to see the cliffs is to visit the **Wailau Valley,** just over an hour from Halawa. Like the rest of the north shore, the valley is accessible only by boat. This is where local Molokaians go for *their* vacations, to escape the "hustle and bustle" of Kaunakakai. You'll probably see only one or two tarps, if any at all. The Wailau Valley is hard-core, undeveloped, untouristed jungle.

Whether you want to kayak, snorkel, fish, hunt, whale watch, or just check out the cliffs, call Wally, the owner-operator of **Molokai Action Adventures** (☎558-8184). Depending on what you want to do and how many of you there are, a trip to see the cliffs will cost $50-100 per person, though prices are negotiable.

WESTERN MOLOKAI

Western Molokai is vast and, for the most part, uninhabited. The Molokai Ranch owns most of the land in this region, and apart from the small town of Maunaloa and the condo developments around the now-defunct Kaluakoi Hotel, it is mostly empty pasture land. Dry and dusty, the west gets 12 inches of rain or less each year, and water has to be piped in from the wetter east side to support human habitation. The beaches on this side of Molokai are by far the best on the island and,

IN RECENT NEWS

WEST SIDE STORY

There are few better cases of the problematic nature of development in Hawaii than the Molokai Ranch. In the mid-1800s, Kamehameha V created the Molokai Ranch to manage the majority of the land on the western half of the island. After his death in 1897, a group of private businessmen purchased the ranch from his estate. Del Monte leased much of the property from the investors for pineapple production, but the company pulled out in the late 1970's. The owners of the Molokai Ranch then sold 14,000 acres of its land to developers who envisioned the creation of a legitimate suburb of Honolulu, complete with daily commuter ferries and nearly 30,000 homes. Locals opposed the plan almost unanimously and succeeded in blocking it from fruition. The investors tabled a second proposal, which entailed the building of four hotels, over 1000 condos, and nearly as many homes, that locals accepted.

After constructing 200 condos, one hotel, and a golf course, the operation began to wane. The expense of bringing water from the east side of the island, combined with a lack of tourism, quashed any plans for further development. In 2000, the Kaluakoi Hotel closed, and the area has since begun to feel a bit like a ghost town. Though some of the hotel's rooms have been turned into condos, many of the buildings are showing signs of age. The parking lots have almost as many weeds as the golf course, and the area lays dormant, in the hope that the (very slowly) increasing tourism will attract new investors.

with the area's remoteness, you're certain to find at least one you can have all to yourself, if you so desire.

On your way out west, be sure to stop at the ⚑**Beach Boy Ranch** in Hoolehua, past the back end of the airport on Maunaloa Hwy. (Rte. 460). You can't miss it—it's the only kooky organic produce farm (and the only building) on the highway. The owners live out back in an immobile school bus as they make slow progress constructing their adobe dream house by hand. If you ask, John, the big friendly foreman, will give you a tour of the operation. All produce grown on-site ($1 per lb.).

MAUNALOA

The only real reason to visit Maunaloa, a one-block town dominated by the Molokai Ranch, is buy a kite or see the ranch. The town's 374 residents are nearly all employed by either the ranch or the condo developments down the road, and the newness of most of the buildings is a striking contrast to the older false fronts of the stores in Kaunakakai. The ⚑**Big Wind Kite Factory,** 120 Maunaloa Hwy., is well worth a trip to Maunaloa. Kites of all colors and styles adorn the walls ($25-95). Nearly all are made on the premises, except for a handful that are imported from Bali. The store also has an eclectic mix of knick-knacks from around the globe, as well as an impressive collection of books about Molokai, Hawaiian music CDs, intricate marionettes, and extreme kite-boarding magazines. A line of well-made Hawaiian shirts ($35) rounds out the store's huge selection. (☎ 552-2364. Open M-Sa 8:30am-5pm, Su 10am-2pm.)

The Molokai Ranch runs an **outfitters center** that rents every kind of equipment imaginable and offers dozens of activities for relatively steep prices. Options include hikes of various difficulties ($45-125), sea kayaking ($65), and learn-how-to-lariat-a-steer *paniolo* lessons ($105). Mountain biking ($30-100) is advertised prominently, and the guides at the excellent bike shop are knowledgeable about the surrounding trails.

To reach Maunaloa, take Hwy. 460 west, which becomes the main road of the town. The post office is located across from the general store. (☎ 522-2852. Open M-F 8am-4:30pm. Zip Code: 96770.) Once there, the only place to stay is the **Molokai Ranch ⑤,** a 54,000-acre working ranch with 7000+ head of cattle that moonlights as a first-class luxury resort. The facilities are superb but may stretch the financial resources of those traveling on a budget. Though the ranch is privately owned, Sheraton assumed management duties as of February 2002. Accommodations are split between the ranch's lodge and the Kaupoa campground, located nine miles (by dirt road) from Maunaloa, on a pleasant beach. Three years young, the lodge has a majestic foyer, 22 rooms equipped with footed bathtubs, a zero-horizon pool, a fitness center, and an expensive restaurant. The campground is populated by 40 "tentalows," solar-powered, steel-and-canvas structures that all come with lanai, restroom, shower, fan, and bed. (☎660-2710; fax 552-2908. Lodge rooms $335-850, some sleep up to 4; Tentalows $260-299 for up to 2.) See **Kaluakoi** (p. 263) for more accommodations.

With the recent closing of the Village Grill, the only place to eat other than the ranch's dining room is **KFC Express ❶,** on N. Wai'eli St., next to the cinema (☎552-2625. Open M-F 11am-7:30pm, Sa-Su noon-7:30pm.) There's also some snack food at **Lucky's Gas and Oil** convenience store, next to the general store and across from KFC, which happens to be the only gas station east of Kaunakakai. (☎552-2627. Open M-F 7am-5pm, Sa-Su 10am-4:30pm.) For groceries, try the well-stocked **Maunaola General Store,** 200 Maunaloa Hwy. (☎552-2346. Open M-Sa 8am-6pm.)

KALUAKOI

About a mile and a half before Maunaloa, a turnoff from the highway on the right leads down Kaluakoi Rd. to several condo developments, as well as most of the western side's beaches. A block down Lio Pl., you'll find **Paniolo Hale ❹,** a beautiful 77-unit condominium complex. Eighteen of the units are in the rental pool, and many of the rest are available through Friendly Isle Real Estate or the directory at the Molokai Visitors' Association. Most are well-furnished condos that feel like houses, all with full kitchens and spacious living rooms, and some with screened lanais. This is, by far, the best value on the West End. (☎552-2731; www.paniolohaleresort.com. Low season: studios $95-115, 1-bedroom $115-135, 2-bedroom $145-165. High season: studios $135-155, 1-bedroom $210-230, 2-bedroom $245-265.)

Across the street from the Kaluakoi Villas, on Kepuhi Beach Rd., sits **Ke Nani Kai ❸,** another condo complex with slightly smaller rooms than Paniolo Hale. It's a nice place to stay if you can take advantage of one of the many deals offered online. (☎800-535-0085; fax 922-2421; www.marcresorts.com. 1-bedroom start at $93. Office open M-F 8am-3pm, Sa 8am-1pm. 20% discount for AAA members.)

The Kaluakoi Hotel closed in 2000 due to a lack of investor confidence and a decline in tourism. The units that have not been subsumed by Kaluakoi Villas are in a state of disrepair and give a depressed feeling to the area. The **Kaluakoi Villas ❹** are fairly well-maintained, however. They're a bit pricey for what you get, but frequent Internet specials can save you 20% or more. (☎800-552-2721 or 525-1470; fax 522-2201; www.castleresorts.com. 1-bedroom studio with kitchenette $135-155, 2-bedroom with kitchenette $160-240.)

WEST END BEACHES AND CAMPING

PAPOHAKU BEACH. Approximately 2½ miles long, Papohaku Beach has the most surface area of any beach in Hawaii; it can measure up to 60 yards in width, depending on the time of year and the tide. The beach has so much sand, in fact, that some of it was sent to Oahu during the mid-1950s to create Waikiki Beach. Papohaku is backed by a number of small dunes, and the wind frequently picks up the sand. The water is not good for snorkeling, although it's just right for a quick dip between sunbathing sessions. Although you may see an occasional bodysurfer, the water is known for a strong undertow, and even locals exercise caution.

Papohaku Beach has three main access points from **Kaluakoi Road,** all with showers and signs reading "Beach Access, Public Right of Way" displayed prominently. The first is **Papohaku Beach Park,** which is also the only campground on the

M O L O K A I

HULA BABY The goddess Laka is said to have given birth to the hula in Ka'ana, located in Western Molokai. Some accounts suggest that divine Laka created the dance herself; others claim that Laka was merely a member of a family who had been practicing the dance for five generations in a lush *lehua* forest.

Before the intrusion of the West, the hula was a Hawaiian religious practice. The dance was extremely ritualized, with eight dancers accompanied by the sounds of a sharkskin log drum called a *pahu*. The dancers and the drummer were all devotees of the sacred Laka and made regular offerings to her. However, after Christian missionaries converted local chiefs and acquired a great deal of influence in the early 1800s, the hula was deemed heathen and forced underground.

During the late 1800s, despite the misgivings of missionaries and converted Hawaiians, King David Kalakaua encouraged the teaching and open practice of the hula, calling it the "heartbeat" of the Hawaiian people. This incarnation of the dance, known as *hula ku'i*, used an *ipu* gourd as a drum rather than the *pahu*, out of respect for the holiness of the older ritual. By the mid-1900s, Hollywood had sensationalized the dance. Tourists were more interested in the sexually suggestive moves of coconut bra-clad dancers than the cultural and religious significance of the hula, and the traditional chant was abandoned in favor of a more catchy song-based accompaniment.

Today, a resurgence of interest in the hula has generated a diverse array of schools and techniques. The birth of the hula is celebrated the third weekend in May at Papohaku Beach on Molokai. The festival is called **Ka hula Piko,** and the dancing begins late at night. The dancers are only visible at first as shadows against the stars, and as the sky brightens with the morning sun, a traditional chant begins. The dancing continues throughout the day, and there are workshops every evening by renowned *kumu hula* (teachers) from throughout the islands.

West End. It is usually uninhabited and peaceful. The site has showers, restrooms, picnic tables, and BBQ grills. Camping permits are required and can be purchased at the Department of Parks and Recreation (see p. 242).

The second access point, **Lauhue,** has the most pleasing setting. Located about ½ mi. from Papohaku Beach Park, it's surrounded by taller dunes and sits farther away from the condo developments. It also has more beach area than the third access point, **Papapa.** The site of **Ka hula Piko,** a hula festival held every May (see **Hula Baby,** p. 264), the Papapa Beach is a little rocky. However, it does boast a good view of the entire expanse of Papohaku. The other access points are far too rocky for swimming, and neither has enough sand to satisfy the serious sunbather.

■ **DIXIE MARU.** At the end of Kaluakoi Rd. The beach on the right, Dixie Maru, is a protected cove that is almost circular in shape. The surrounding rocks and vegetation give the place an air of seclusion and the water is calm and good for swimming. Boarders should look elsewhere for surf, however.

KEPUHI BEACH. At the opposite end of Papohaku Beach, this beach is accessible by turning off Kaluakoi Rd. onto Lio Pl. and walking through the Paniolo Hale complex. Kepuhi Beach is the most crowded of all the beaches on the west side due its proximity to the condos.

■ **MAKE HORSE.** For a far better sand and sun experience, walk down the dirt road at the Paniolo Hale parking lot to Make Horse Beach, which may very well be one of the best beaches in Hawaii. The beach is actually a series of three crescent-shaped bays of white sand, separated by high volcanic rock that obscures each from view. If you have too much company at the first beach, just try the others to the right. A favorite fishing spot among locals, the beach is also quite wide, but not so wide that the wind kicks up the sand. To add to its virtues, the surf is good in the winter, although it isn't the best place to snorkel. The beach's unique name is descended from its less-than-pleasant past. "Make" (mah-kay) means "dead," and the beach is so named because during the 1800s, locals would slaughter horses by running them off the high plateau to the right of the beach.

KAWAKIU BEACH. The most isolated of the West End beaches, Kawakiu Beach takes a little work to find. To get there, continue straight instead of turning left towards the Paniolo Hale parking lot. The road ends after about 100 yards. Park here and walk down the red dirt road immediately ahead for about 35min. The road is in poor condition, and even a 4x4 is likely to get stuck. Keep on the main road, as there are several smaller roads that veer off along the way. The hike passes through cattle pastures and ranchland, and the pristine beach that awaits at the end is sure to be devoid of tourists (though there may be a couple of locals camping on the far end).

HALE O LONO HARBOR. The only part of the southern portion of the western shore that is open to the public, the harbor is accessible via a dirt road just beyond the Molokai Ranch Lodge in Maunaloa. It was built to facilitate the moving of sand from Papohaku Beach to Oahu during the 1950s, though it isn't much to look at these days. A quiet beach lies just east of the harbor. If you encounter a locked gate along the dirt road, you can get the key from the Molokai Ranch front desk.

MOLOKAI

LANAI

Though Lanai (Lana'i) is a quiet and slow-paced, with just one small town and only a few paved roads, the island was once home to the world's largest **pineapple plantation.** Its 15,000 acres accounted for over 90% of total US production, and many of the island's older residents are former field laborers. The community is small and close-knit, and people are friendly—it is considered common courtesy to wave at all oncoming drivers and pedestrians, especially outside of town. Prices on Lanai are a bit higher than on other islands, but if you're looking to escape the dense tourism of Oahu and Maui, you'll certainly get what you pay for here.

Lanai has been under the control of nearby **Maui** since before recorded history. It is still part of Maui County, but has too few voters to hold much sway in local politics. For generations, Maui chiefs believed that evil spirits inhabited the island. Prince Kaulula'au, the unruly son of King Kaka'alaeo, is said to have used trickery to rid Lanai of its spirits during his exile there in 1400. As a reward, Kaulula'au was given control of the island and he encouraged immigration from other islands.

In 1802, the island's first foreign resident, a Chinese man, started a small sugarcane plantation near Naha. He left Lanai a few years later, and things remained calm until 1854, when a group of Mormon missionaries, led by **Walter Murray Gibson,** arrived and began to build a holy city in the Palawai Basin. In 1864, it was discovered that Gibson had been using church funds to acquire land for himself, and he was excommunicated. This didn't phase him in the slightest; he befriended King Kalakaua, who eventually appointed him Prime Minister. As such, Gibson effectively controlled the entire kingdom. After his death, Gibson's daughter, Talula, and her husband, Frederick Hayselden, started the Maunalei Sugar Company at Keomuku, but were forced to cease operations in 1901 when their wells turned brackish. In 1910, the couple acquired even more land to form the **Lanai Company,** and tried their hands at cattle ranching. New Zealander George Munro was hired as foreman, and he is credited with planting the tall pine trees that still shade the central portion of the island (see p. 270). In 1917, the Baldwin Brothers bought the Lanai Company and sold it to James Dole in 1922.

Dole had studied Agriculture, with a specialization in canning, at Harvard. He built Kamalapau Harbor and Lanai City and connected them with highways, and is responsible for much of the island's infrastructure. Thanks to his business savvy, the exotic pineapple became a daily household staple for millions of Americans. By the late 1930s, the Great Depression and the availability of cheap land and labor in Southeast Asia had lured Dole overseas, and the **Castle and Cook Company** bought out his interest in the island. Today, Castle & Cook owns 98% of the land on Lanai. David Murdoch is the current CEO of Castle & Cook, and the two world-class luxury resorts that now comprise the island's primary industry are his brainchildren.

HIGHLIGHTS OF LANAI

GO OFF-ROAD on the rugged Munro Trail and experience untamed Lanai (p. 272).

TRAVEL BACK IN TIME in the Garden of the Gods, with its ancient stone formations and mythical history (p. 274).

LET YOUR IMAGINATION WANDER at Shipwreck Beach, where many a doomed sea vessel has run aground (p. 275).

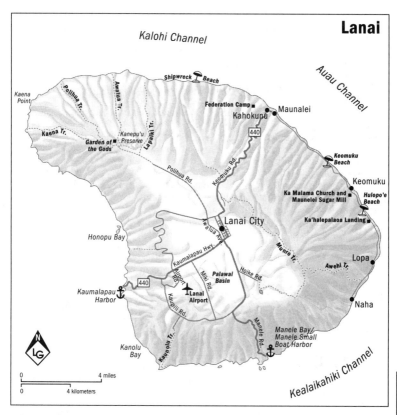

Lanai

Kalohi Channel

Auau Channel

Kaena Point

Pollhua Tr.

Awalua Tr.

Shipwreck Beach

Federation Camp
Kahokupu
Maunalei

Kaena Tr.

Kanepu'u Preserve
Garden of the Gods

Lapaiki Tr.

440

Keomuku Rd.

Pollhua Rd.

Keomuku Beach

Keomuku

Ka Malama Church and
Maunelei Sugar Mill

Hulopo'e Beach

Lanai City

Ka'halepalaoa Landing

Honopu Bay

Iwalua Hwy.

Munro Tr.

Lopa

Kaumalapau Hwy.

Hoike Rd.

Awehi Tr.

Airport Rd.

Miki Rd.

Palawai Basin

440

Kaumalapau Harbor

Kaupili Rd.

Lanai Airport

Naha

Kaunolu Tr.

Manele Rd.

Manele Bay/
Manele Small
Boat Harbor

Kanolu Bay

Kealaikahiki Channel

N

0   4 miles
0   4 kilometers

✈ INTERISLAND TRANSPORTATION

The easiest and least expensive way to reach Lanai is by **ferry**, which runs from **Lahaina, Maui** to the Manele Harbor (5 per day 6:45am-5:45pm; $25 one-way, children $20) and back (5 per day 8am-6:45pm). The ride takes less than 1hr. To make a reservation, call **Expeditions** (☎ 800-695-2624 or 661-3756), or just show up at the pier; there are usually seats available.

If you aren't coming from Maui, you'll have to fly. **Hawaiian Air** (☎ 800-367-5320 or 838-1555 on Oahu; 800-882-8811 on neighboring islands) flies from **Honolulu** (30min., 2 per day 6:30am-4:10pm, $66.50 one-way). **Island Air** (☎ 800-323-3345; Oahu ☎ 484-2222, neighbor islands 800-652-6541) flies from: **Honolulu** (30min., 6-8 per day, approx. $80 one-way) and **Kahului, Maui** (15min., 2 per day 10am-5pm, approx. $80 one-way). **Pacific Wings** (☎ 888-575-4548 or 873-0877; fax 873-7920), flies from: **Honolulu** (30min., 3 per day 9:30am-5:30pm, approx. $70 one-way) and **Kahului, Maui** (15min., 2 per day 8:15am-4:20pm, approx. $70 one-way).

⬛ LOCAL TRANSPORTATION

Once on the island, you'll need to rent an automobile, as there is no local transportation other than **Rabacca's Limousine Service.** (☎ 565-6670. Open 24hr. $5 per person between town and the airport, $10 to Manele Bay. 2-person minimum.) The island has less than 30 miles of paved surface, and the dirt roads are suitable only for 4WD—a necessary luxury if you want to get anywhere on the island. No supplemental auto insurance is available from any company on Lanai. The island is covered in loose red dirt, so be sensible—get a hard top unless you want to end up covered in dust and mud when you drive.

■**Adventure Lanai Ecocentre,** 338 8th St., is a laid-back operation run by John, an amiably sarcastic hippie, and Lilinoe, a no-nonsense young local. They rent safari-style 4WD Jeep Wranglers with big off-road mud tires, roof racks, A/C, snorkel gear, boogie boards, and an ice chest for $104 per day. Unlike the competition, they let you take their vehicles anywhere. Reservations suggested. Free laundry machines for customers. Adventure Lanai also rents rooms (see **Accommodations and Camping,** p. 269) and every kind of outdoors equipment you can imagine. They run several **tours,** including a 4x4 adventure along the Munro Trail, the Garden of the Gods, and Shipwreck Beach ($79), a kayak/snorkel trip ($79), a downhill road bike trek ($79), and surfing and diving trips ($79, 129). (☎565-7373; www.adventurelanai.com. Open M-Sa 8am-5:30pm.)

If you prefer to rent from a national company, **Dollar,** 1035 Lanai Ave., south of Dole Park, has a fleet of Jeep Wranglers ($129 per day) and Jeep Cherokees ($145 per day) that are usually available without a reservation. Cars, which are restricted to paved roads by both the rental agreement and the terrain, range from $60-129 per day, depending on size and make. Reserve well in advance. Dollar has useful daily updates on road conditions, and the only safe way to travel off-road is to be informed. (☎800-JEEP-808 or 565-7227. Open daily 7am-7pm.)

The only **gas station** on the island is located at the **Lanai Plantation Store,** on the Dollar property. Gas costs an arm and a leg, frequently pushing $2.50 per gallon of regular. (Open daily 7am-7pm.)

LANAI CITY

Built by Jim Dole in 1922 to house plantation workers and their families, Lanai City was the first planned community in the islands. Almost all of Lanai's inhabitants live in the brightly painted houses of this quiet town, with the exception of a scattering of homes along the southeast coast. At an elevation of nearly 1600 ft., Lanai City is usually cool and misty, and clouds frequently obscure the tops of Munro's pines. The tall trees appear throughout the town, giving it the feel of a forest park.

✈ ORIENTATION

Lanai City surrounds **Dole Park,** a large, rectangular grassy area that runs basically east-west. Its longer borders are **7th St.** to the north and **8th St.** to the south. Most of the town's stores and eateries are located along these streets. The town is bordered by the two largest streets—**Fraser Ave.** to the west, and **Lanai Ave.** to the east. All streets are at right angles, and those running east-west are numbered 3rd-13th, with 3rd St. the farthest north. Those running north-south have first letters that follow each other in the alphabet, starting with Fraser on the western side and ending with Nani in the east.

⁊ PRACTICAL INFORMATION

Banks: Bank of Hawaii, 460 8th St., at Lanai Ave. (☎656-6246). **First Hawaiian Bank,** 644 Lanai Ave. at 7th St. (☎565-6969). Both are open M-Th 8:30am-4pm, F 8:30am-6pm and have **ATMs** in front.

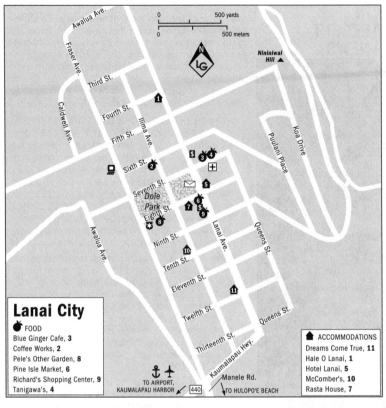

Lanai City

🍎 FOOD

Blue Ginger Cafe, **3**
Coffee Works, **2**
Pele's Other Garden, **8**
Pine Isle Market, **6**
Richard's Shopping Center, **9**
Tanigawa's, **4**

TO AIRPORT,
KAUMALAPAU HARBOR

Manele Rd.
TO HULOPO'E BEACH

♠ ACCOMMODATIONS

Dreams Come True, **11**
Hale O Lanai, **1**
Hotel Lanai, **5**
McComber's, **10**
Rasta House, **7**

Laundromat: Launderette Lanai, on 7th St. and Jacarinda. $1.50 wash, 75¢ dry. Detergent 75¢. No change machine. Open daily 5am-8:30pm.

Emergency: ☎911.

Police: 312 8th St., at Fraser Ave. (☎565-6428). Open 24hr.

Hospital: 628 7th St., east of Lanai Ave. (☎565-6411). **Emergency room open 24hr.,** administrative office open M-F 8am-4:30pm.

Internet Access: At the **public library,** 555 Fraser Ave., (☎565-7920). $10 temporary library membership required. Open W 1-8pm, Tu and Th-F 8am-4pm, Sa 11am-4pm.

Video Rental: Lanai Family Store, 443 7th St. (☎565-6485). Wide selection of VHS tapes ($3 per day). Open M-Sa 10am-noon and 3-7pm, Su 4-7pm.

Post Office: 620 Jacarinda, north of Dole Park (☎565-6517). Open M-F 9am-4pm, Sa 10am-noon.

Zip Code: 96763.

🏠 ACCOMMODATIONS AND CAMPING

Lanai is famous for its five-star luxury resorts, due in large part to the **Lodge At Koele** (☎800-565-3868), located just north of town. Though a room at the legendary

LANAI

IN RECENT NEWS

TOPPLING OLD MYTHS

The Lanai Pines aren't just the local little league team; they're the trademark trees of Lanai City and a source of controversy. It is commonly believed that the tall pine trees that are spread throughout Lanai City and along the Munro Trail are Norfolk Pines, but holders of such a conviction are sorely mistaken. George Munro, a New Zealander hired by the Lanai Company as ranch foreman, was responsible for planting the pines. A naturalist at heart, Munro wanted to do away with the scrubby vegetation of arid Central Lanai and coax the land into a lusher, greener state. For this to happen, he also had to make the place wetter. Though mist and fog were quite common on the island, rain was not, and the land was dusty and dry. Back then, Munro's residence was located below the giant Norfolk Pine in front of the present-day Lodge at Koele. Fog would condense on the tree's needles and drip onto the corrugated steel roof of the residence, keeping him awake at night. It dawned on Munro that he could bring water to the Central Lanai with acres of pine trees and he promptly brought clippings and seeds from his native New Zealand for the task. Munro had intended to plant Norfolk Pines, in honor of the tree that gave him the idea and, to this day, the literature at the lodge, as well as the testimony of many locals, holds that he followed through with this intention. Recent botanical research, however, has proven that Monroe made a mistake, and instead of sowing Norfolk pines, he planted ones of the Cook variety.

lodge ($325-2200) will almost certainly break the bank, a walk through the grounds is free. The Internet terminal hidden under the stairs to the left of the main entrance is for hotel guests only. **Okamoto Realty,** 730 Lanai Ave. (☎565-7519; www.lanairealestate.com), has several vacation rentals, mostly upscale 3-bedroom cottages ($150-175). Check online for details and photos. Several **B&Bs** in town offer a range of good, affordable options.

Dreams Come True, 1168 Lana'i Ave., at 12th St. (☎800-566-6961 or 565-6961; fax 565-7056; www.dreamscometruelanai.com). Each room in this bright, cheery 3-bedroom B&B has private marble bath, whirlpool tub, and bathroom skylight. Rooms share access to a full kitchen and backyard garden deck. Jeep Cherokees available to rent for guests ($100 per day). Also ask about massage therapy ($50). Singles/doubles $98.50, additional person $25. Entire house (fits 10) $380. Check the website for constantly-changing information about vacation rentals. AmEx/MC/V. ❸

Rasta House, 338 8th St. Rented through Adventure Lanai Ecocenter (☎565-7373; www.adventurelanai.com. See Interisland Transportation, p. 267). Painted in a distinctly Jamaican color scheme, Rasta House has character to spare. 3 bedrooms, 6 beds (1 of which is a double), 1 sunken bathroom, and a blue-tile counter with 3 stools in the kitchen. Approx. $60 per person, but prices decrease dramatically if you rent as a group. Mention *Let's Go* for a substantial discount. AmEx/MC/V. ❷

Hale O Lanai, 405 Lanai Ave., at 4th St. (☎247-3637 or 565-6948). A well-furnished 2-bedroom, 2-bath house with full kitchen set on a neatly manicured property just outside the center of town. Hale O Lanai is a great value for a moderately upscale accommodations. Entire house $125-150. ❹

Hotel Lanai, on Lanai Ave., above 8th St. (☎565-7211; fax 565-6450; www.hotellanai.com). The only reasonably-priced hotel on the island, Hotel Lanai is a great value for the service you'll receive. The staff are warm and friendly, and the 10 welcoming rooms all come with pine dressers, immaculate bathrooms, large rugs, and ceiling fans. Local art adorns the walls. Rooms for 1-3 people $98-150. AmEx/MC/V. ❸

McComber's, on Ilima St., 2 blocks south of Dole Park (☎565-6071). It's the big pink house. Intended primarily for the hunting parties that book the place solid on weekends from Feb.-June and Aug.-Oct., this is the most economical option on the island. The 3-bedroom house has no frills but the basics are here: 8 beds, 2 half-baths upstairs, 2 full baths downstairs, and laundry facilities. No phone. Cable TV. Deer cleaning rack out back. $35 per person per night, even if you're renting the place solo. No rentals to groups not travelling together. No credit cards. ❷

Hulopo'e Beach camping, near Manele Bay (see p. 273). For reservations contact Castle & Cook (☎565-7700) or call the park ranger at the beach office (☎565-2345; office open daily 8am-5:30pm). There are 6 official campsites, each with a grill and access to restrooms. The showers that line the beach have pipes that catch the sun, heating the water. There are often groups of locals in semi-permanent campsites on the beach. If you find that the campsites are all booked (a frequent occurrence on summer weekends), try to find a local to sponsor you, which may allow you to camp for free. One-time $10 registration fee, plus an additional $5 per group per night. ❶

🍴 FOOD

The hotel restaurants on Lanai are all exorbitantly expensive. The only exception is **Henry Clay's** ❺, at Hotel Lanai, which serves superb cajun-fusion cuisine and is only marginally out of reach for travelers on a budget. (Appetizers $10-15, entrees $18-36. Open for dinner every day, closed for one variable week in early August.) On Saturday mornings, there's a **swap meet** in Dole Park where locals serve various homemade ethnic dishes and sell knick-knacks.

GROCERY STORES AND MARKETS

Pine Isle Market, on 8th St. (☎565-6488). Equal parts grocery store, hardware store, and drug store, Pine Isle is nonetheless the closest thing to a supermarket on the island. Open M-Sa 8am-7pm.

Richard's Shopping Center, 434 8th St. (☎565-6047). Another grocery store-*cum*-hardware store, with a decent selection of produce and the cheapest ice and coolers in town. Open M-Sa 8:30am-6:30pm.

The Lanai City International Food and Clothing Company, (☎565-6433). As the name implies, it is indeed a warehouse full of food and clothes, leaning toward the food side. Also sells household items, hardware, and hunting/fishing supplies. Open M-F 8am-6pm, Su 8am-1:30pm. AmEx/MC/V.

RESTAURANTS

▥ **Pele's Other Garden,** on 8th St. and Houston St. (☎565-9628). By day, Pele's is a genuine New York deli that serves the best hoagies in the county ($7) on fresh homemade bread. By night, the staff changes the lighting, the tablecloths, and the menu to create a romantic Italian bistro. The bruschetta ($5) is as good as any you'll find in Italy. Pasta dishes $12-19. Reservations recommended. Open M-Sa 9:30am-3pm for lunch, and 5-9pm for dinner. AmEx/MC/V. ❸

▥ **Tanigawa's,** 419 7th St. (☎565-6537). Open for breakfast and lunch, Tanigawa's is where locals have gathered early in the morning to *talk story* for over 52 years. The light, fluffy pancakes ($3.75) are not to be missed, and the burgers and sandwiches ($2.50-4.50) are delicious. Open Th-Tu 6:30am-1pm. ❶

Blue Ginger Cafe, 409 7th St. (☎565-6363). Blue Ginger is Lanai's all-purpose eatery and the best bargain on the island. Two eggs, choice of meat, rice, and toast $5; plate lunches $6-9; and dinner specials $13-15. Known for fresh fish, usually *ono* or mahi mahi. Mexican food on Tu. Open daily 6am-8pm. ❷

Coffee Works, 604 Ilima St., north of Dole Park (☎565-6962). Coffee Works has recently brought its know-how to Lanai after 28 years in business on Oahu. They ship coffee across the country, but you can enjoy yours on the large deck out front. The house special espresso milkshake ($4.50) is worth every penny. Pizza bagels, hot dogs, and other light fare $3-5. Open M-Sa 6am-9pm, Su 7am-5pm. ❶

L A N A I

🎵 ENTERTAINMENT

There isn't much to do on Lanai after dark other than sleep or see a first-run movie at the **Lanai Playhouse,** 467 7th Ave. (☎565-7500. $7, ages 3-12 and seniors $4.50.) The only bar in town is at Hotel Lanai, but it isn't usually the liveliest of scenes. A good way to pass the time is to wander the streets just before sunset, when locals tend their gardens and children play in the streets.

For some daytime excitement, take the highway north of town toward Shipwreck Beach and turn left at the **Lanai Pine Sporting Clays** sign, where you can blast compressed fertilizer discs with a 12-gauge shotgun on a gorgeous sporting clay range. Both car rental agencies provide a voucher for ten free shots, and it's worth taking advantage of the offer if you have the time. (☎559-4600. $85 for 50 clays, $145 for 100. Open daily 9am-2:30pm.)

CENTRAL LANAI

MUNRO TRAIL

To reach the trail from town, take the highway toward Shipwreck Beach. Past the Lodge at Koele, take a right on Cemetary Rd. Veer left after the pavement ends and look for a sign that marks the trailhead. The trail is about 8½ miles long and can take anywhere from 1¼-3hr. to complete, depending on road conditions. Also expect to spend about 30min. making your way from the end of the trail back to the highway.

> The road is generally in good condition, but it can only be navigated in a 4WD vehicle. Be absolutely certain not to attempt the trail if it has rained in the last 24hr.—there are several places where an inopportune skid could send your vehicle over the edge of the road and into a deep ravine. Check with a car rental agency for an update before you head out. Drive slowly, use first gear, and keep your eyes on the road.

If you only have time to do one off-road trek while you're on Lanai, this is by far your best bet. The Munro Trail is a thoroughly enjoyable drive, and the scenery is spectacular. Traveling through forests of ironwood and pine, the road is lined with ferns of all sizes and colors. Much of the trail passes five-alarm views of Maui, Molokai, and Oahu, as well as the former pineapple fields of Lanai far below.

Be certain not to take any of the side roads that veer off from the main road. They are often very muddy because they only exist for water drainage purposes; it should be clear which is the most-traveled road. The only point where you might get confused is after 2 mi. where the road to the left stops after only 50 yards, leading visitors to a **lookout** over the gigantic Maunalei Gulch, the source of the island's drinking water. The road to the right is the trail, and it takes you as close as you can get to **Lana'ihale,** Lanai's highest point (3,368 ft.). After another mile or two, just past the communications tower on the left, is a good view of Ho'okio Gulch, the site of the defeat of native Lanaian warriors by Kalaniopu'u, a powerful chief from the Big Island in 1778.

At the end of the trail, you'll be faced with several options as to which way to go. The road to the right heads back toward the mountain, but it stops at a gated fence after about 1½ mi. The road to the left is the shortest route back to the highway; veer right at the first major fork, proceed through a cattle gate, and continue onto Ho'ike Rd., which connects to the highway at a stop sign and 6 large pine trees. Turn right to head back into town. The road straight ahead eventually meets up with the road on the right, but before it does you'll have a chance to make a sharp left onto a red dirt road. This turnoff is just before some large boulders on the left, where the road you've been traveling on thus far curves right. This red dirt road eventually becomes Hoʻike Rd. If you get lost, be patient, backtrack, and aim for the pine trees that line the highway.

THE SOUTH SIDE

MANELE BAY AND HULOPOʻE BEACH

Dominated by the luxurious Manele Bay Hotel, the sister resort of the Lodge at Koele, **Manele Bay** is home to Lanai's most popular **beach,** only **campground,** and a small harbor where you can catch a ferry to Maui (see **Interisland Transportation,** p. 267). From town, take the highway south. As the road straightens out, you'll be driving through the caldera of an extinct volcano. This area, the **Palawai Basin,** was once the center of the Dole Plantation.

At the end of the highway, the road forks. To the left is **Manele Harbor,** the ferry landing. The harbor was the site of a Hawaiian fishing village during the 18th century, and was the island's principal port until the construction of the commercial harbor at Kaumalapaʻu. To the right is **Hulopoʻe Beach,** the site of the island's best beach for **swimming, snorkeling,** and **sunbathing.** The surf is usually nothing special in the summer, but it sometimes picks up in the winter. The white-sand beach is large enough to never be crowded. Both the beach and the harbor are part of a conservation district which prohibits boat fishing and the removal of any objects, including rocks. Hulopoʻe is also the island's only **campsite,** and the facilities are fabulous. (See **Accommodations and Camping,** p. 269).

From the beach, walk along the bay to the left to reach **Puʻu Pehe Cove.** The cove is full of multi-colored volcanic rock formations and is a good place to watch the sunset. At low tide, the flat shelf on the right side of the cove reveals tide pools teeming with marine life.

LUAHIWA PETROGLYPHS

From town, take the highway toward Manele Bay. After the 7-mile marker, look for the back of a stop sign to the left of the once-paved Hoʻike Rd. After a short mile on this road, make a sharp left at a fencepost where the road rises. Continue along this road until you see a large pipe in the ground, and cross over the pipe and onto the high road. Follow both the road and the pipe about 0.4 mi. to a turnaround; the petroglyphs are on the right.

Lanai's largest collection of petroglyphs is scattered throughout a 4-acre area. The ancient etchings of bird heads, circle patterns, people on horseback, and even the occasional dog are still visible centuries after their initial inscription. Be careful as you scramble around the hill; the footing can be tricky. You don't need a 4WD to get to there, but you do need lots of clearance; a regular car just won't cut it.

KANOLU

Reaching Kanolu is a bit tricky; you'll most definitely need a 4WD vehicle. From town, take the highway toward Kamalapau Harbor. Past the 3-mile marker on the left, you'll see the back of a stop sign and 2 dirt roads, 1 high and 1 low. Take the low road, and reset your odometer just as you leave the highway. After ½ mi., take the red dirt road on the left, which runs parallel to the formerly-paved road that you've been on thus far. 1.9 mi. from the highway, keep your eyes open for a hydrant-like pipe on the left. The pipe sticks vertically out of the ground about 4 ft., and has a wheel-shaped handle at the top. You'll notice a smaller pipe on the right side of the road, also hydrant-like, which may be hidden in some brush. Turn right with the fence on the right side of the road, which stops just before the hydrants and makes a 90° turn. DO NOT go farther if it has rained in the last 24hr. Park and walk the rest of the way if the road becomes impassable. After 2.8 mi., veer right toward the lighthouse. After 4.4 mi., note (and ignore) the sign which claims that you can park to the right of the road. At the end of the road, take the right fork and park near the picnic table underneath a kiawe tree.

Despite the grueling drive to Kanolu, the town is well worth a visit, if only for its historical interest. The site of a small fishing village, Lanai's best-preserved heiau, and the vacation home of Kamehameha the Great, Kanolu also boasts the most ruins and artifacts on the island; archaeologists are frequently seen prowling the lands. **Kanolu Bay** is the southwesternmost point of the island, where currents from the north and east converge.

In Kamehameha's day, Kanolu villagers lived on the right side of the bay and were plagued by flash floods during periods of heavy rain. You can just make out the ruins of Kamehameha's house past the picnic table on the hill on the left. Hike down to the beach and walk across it. At the far side you can walk inland, past the remains of a canoe shed that served as the village shrine to the fishing god, and climb up to the **Halulu Heiau.** Note the square fire pit in the center of the heiau, as well as the well-preserved north and west walls. The entire site is considered holy by the Hawaiian people; do not climb on the walls of the heiau, and don't move or remove any rocks.

Walk toward the ocean for a good view of **Kane'apua Rock,** a large island about 100 yards from shore. With your back to the rock, proceed inland about 25 yards to see some faded **petroglyphs** on a group of large rocks in a quarter-circle. To the left is **Kahekili's Leap,** a 5-foot opening in the cliff wall where Kamehameha's warriors would prove their valor by jumping into the shallow water below. The opening creates a dramatic frame for **Shark Island,** which resembles the dorsal fin of a shark. Peer to the right for a view of **Kolokolo Cave,** where a now-dormant lava tube is believed to have run through the cliffs into the Kanolu village ravine.

KAMALAPA'U HARBOR

Though there isn't much there, the quick trip to Kamalapa'u Harbor is worthwhile simply because it is connected to town by a paved road. Since it is relatively easy to drive every inch of asphalt on the island, you might as well do so. At one time, over a million pineapples a day were sent to canning plants on Oahu via the harbor, but today it is a drab commercial facility operated by an oil company. It is also the landing site for the weekly barge that supplies the island with goods such as cars, furniture, industrial equipment, and wholesale products retailed at grocery and hardware stores. The area is rarely populated after 5pm, and is a good place to watch the sunset.

THE NORTH SIDE

GARDEN OF THE GODS

½ mi. beyond the Kanepuu Preserve; see directions below. The drive requires a 4WD, but the road is usually in decent condition if it hasn't been raining. There are a few places where you might tip your vehicle if you're being careless, but the drive is less challenging than most others on the island.

Keahi Kawelo, or ▨Garden of the Gods, is a vast, desert-like expanse of red earth populated by thousands upon thousands of rock towers. Though some of these are only three stones tall, others are large, intricate structures that have, seemingly impossibly, withstood the elements for ages. These more complex towers were supposedly created by the gods, inspiring locals to follow suit with their own man-made versions. The wind has carved rounded ridges in the terrain, which rises and falls. The winding topography and sheer magnitude of the towers are both surreal and awe-inspiring. The towers are concentrated at the beginning of the garden, but to fully appreciate the splendor of the place you should drive farther. Late afternoon is the best time to visit the garden, as the towers cast long shadows in the early evening and the warm tones of the setting sun complement the colors of the lunar landscape.

KANEPU'U PRESERVE

To reach the Kanepu'u Preserve, take the highway north from town. Just past the Lodge at Koele, turn left onto the dirt road between the tennis courts and the stables. Past the stables, turn right at the intersection with the rock that reads "Garden of the Gods" to the aforementioned road.

A road leading over three sets of cattle grates enters the silvery ironwood and pine forest that comprises the beginning of the preserve. After a short mile on this road, you'll see a sign for a self-guided trail on the right. The hike is very short, and provides information about the rare vegetation in the preserve, including the largest collection of **native Hawaiian dry forest** on the island. The preserve is maintained by the **Nature Conservancy,** 730 Lanai Ave. (☎ 565-7430), and free tours can be arranged upon request.

SHIPWRECK BEACH

To get to Shipwreck Beach, turn left onto a sandy dirt road at the end of the highway. Be careful not to drive into any of the large ruts in the road. Though the road is usually pretty good, do not attempt it in a 2WD vehicle or in the rain. Under no circumstances should you drive on the beach itself; doing so is both illegal and runs the (substantial) risk of your tires digging too deep into the sand to escape.

The drive to Shipwreck Beach is simply beautiful. The short dune grass along Keomuku Rd., the highway north of town, flows along and around hills that wind their way to the sea. This part of the island gets less than a dozen inches of rain per year, and the vegetation is just sparse enough that the bright red dirt of the region peeks through, creating a rough-hewn patchwork of contrasting colors.

The first of the nearby sights is **Federation Camp,** a cluster of fishing shacks built by the island's pineapple plantation workers as vacation homes. A few minutes beyond it is a turnaround with a few picnic tables. Park here and continue walking in the direction you've been driving to reach a cement foundation that once supported a lighthouse. With your back to the sea, walk down the small ramp of the lighthouse foundation for about 100 yards (past a boulder that warns "Do Not Deface,") to reach some well-preserved **petroglyphs.** You can continue to the right through a now-dry creek bed to reach the beach, or back-track and walk down from the lighthouse.

LANAI

SEPULCHRE BY THE SEA According to Hawaiian legend, a local fisherman decided to build his home in a cave in order to prevent other men from laying eyes on his beautiful wife, **Pehe,** for fear that they would covet her. One day, while he was working on the other side of the island, a sudden storm swept his home into the sea, taking his wife with it. Her family recovered the body and brought it back to town. Late that night, the fisherman stole her body and buried it on top of an offshore island (Pu'u Pehe or "Sweetheart's Rock"). Then, overcome with grief, he jumped off the rock to his death. The villagers buried him next to his wife, and if you stand close to the island, you can just make out two grave-like rock formations on its surface.

Once on the beach, walk along the coast toward the shipwreck, which becomes visible almost immediately. Along the way, you'll pass a sign for the **Kaiolohia-Kahue Trail,** which was built in the 19th century by the territorial government to link several small coastal settlements. It has been designated a "demonstration trail" by the Na Ala Hele Trails Access Program, and it should be cleared out for hiking by 2003.

As you continue, keep your eyes open for dozens of piles of sand scattered around holes in the ground. These crab homes, combined with the bizarre array of colors and textures in the surrounding vegetation, give an unearthly feel to the beach. **Sea turtles** have been known to lay eggs on this beach at night. After about 15min. you'll reach the closest point to the **Liberty Ship,** a WWII-era frigate that became stuck on the reef due to navigational error. There are nearly a half-dozen other shipwrecks along the beach, and bits and pieces of them wash up on shore quite frequently. Most of the wrecks are no longer visible, with the exception of the one at **Awula,** 6 mi. beyond the Liberty Ship and accessible via a rough dirt road beyond the Garden of the Gods.

KEOMUKU BEACH AND ENVIRONS

To get to Keomuku Beach from the end of the highway, veer right on a dirt road that runs parallel to the beach. The village is about 5½ mi. down. At the time of writing, the road was in good condition for 3 mi. After that, the road was completely washed out and impassable, forcing traffic to drive along the beach itself. This is neither safe nor legal, since the beach is passable only at low tide, and even then you run a sizeable risk of getting stuck in the deep sand. Also, you will have no way of knowing where to stop to see the sights if you drive on the beach. Check with your rental agency to see if the road has been re-graded before heading out.

The narrow strip of dark sand that runs from the end of Keomuku Rd. southeast to Kahalepalaoa Landing is fit for neither swimming nor sunbathing. The water is shallow and rocky, and the beach is often marred by trash. Until 1900, this part of the island was the most densely populated; now it's empty, save for the occasional fisherman or campsite.

After about 5½ mi. you will reach **Keomuku Village,** a former sugar plantation. The plantation was operated by the Maunalei Sugar Compay, which failed in 1901 when well water used to irrigate the fields turned brackish. The only noteworthy sight is the **Ka Malamalama Church,** which was built by the inhabitants of surrounding villages after the collapse of the island's sugar industry.

Drive slowly as you leave the village; after about a mile you'll see a walking trail on the right. It leads inland to **Kahe'a Heiau,** once the site of human sacrifices, which was partially dismantled by the Maunalei Company to built a railroad. The railroad was used to move sugar to the **Ka'halepalaoa Landing** south of the heiau. The landing is no longer functional, but it has a decent view of Maui and the best beach for sunbathing on this side of the island.

Another 4½ mi. down the road lies **Lopa Beach,** noteworthy only because you must pass it on the way to **Naha,** the site of an ancient fishpond. Naha is nearly 12 mi. from the end of the highway, and probably not worth the trek, though Maui residents sometimes charter boats that drop them at the beach there for the day.

KAHOOLAWE

LAND

At about 45 square miles, Kahoolawe (Kaho'olawe), located 6 mi. southwest of Maui, is the smallest of Hawaii's eight major islands. At its widest and longest points it measures 11 miles by 7 miles. The highest point on Kahoolawe is **Moa'ulanui** (1477 ft.), the caldera of the volcano that created the island. Kahoolawe's sloping northern and western coasts were heavily populated by feral goats and sheep until 1988; overgrazing by these animals destroyed the region's plant cover, causing massive soil erosion. The silt that washed into the ocean as a result of this erosion killed much of the coral there.

HISTORY

Early Hawaiians first inhabited Kahoolawe 1000 years ago, fishing and farming from settlements that spanned the width of the island. Originally named **Kanaloa** or **Kohemalamalama**, after the god of the ocean, Kahoolawe was also a renowned training ground for kahuna, and the island is still home to hundreds of heiaus and shrines.

After the arrival of Westerners 1778, Kahoolawe was inhabited by criminals who had been exiled from Maui. They managed to subsist by raiding settlements on Maui and Lanai. The island's population dwindled until 1858, when R.C. Wyllie, a Scottish resident of Kauai, unsuccessfully tried to start a sheep ranch on Kahoolawe. A second attempt during the early 1870s also failed, due to overgrazing. In 1917, a cattle rancher named **Angus MacPhee** signed a 37-year lease giving him Kahoolawe's land rights for $200 per annum, provided that he improve the island. An investor named Harry Baldwin bought a large interest in the **Kahoolawe Ranch** in 1922, and MacPhee began selling his cattle on Maui for a profit. During his years on the island, MacPhee decreased the goat population to manageable levels and reduced erosion by planting eucalyptus and Australian range grass.

As part of the war effort during WWII, Baldwin and MacPhee gave a small portion of Kahoolawe to the US Army, who turned it into an artillery range, despite the island's fragile archaeological and cultural inheritance. On December 8, 1941, the day after the Japanese attack on Pearl Harbor, the US Navy appropriated the entire island, citing a national emergency, and began using it for bombing practice. After the war, the Navy was supposed to return the island to Baldwin and MacPhee, but no action was taken until the lease ran out in 1954. To maintain control of Kahoolawe, President Eisenhower signed an executive order placing the island under the authority of the Secretary of the Navy. The order stipulated that the island must be restored to habitable condition once it was no longer needed by the military. Nearly every instrument of war used by the US military and its allies since WWII has been dropped, fired, or detonated on Kahoolawe, and the island holds the dubious distinction of being the most bombed island in the Pacific both during and after WWII. Due to the dangers posed by unexploded ammunition on the island and in its surrounding coastal waters, Kahoolawe has been uninhabited since it fell into the hands of the military.

In 1976, Hawaiian residents formed the **Protect Kaho'olawe 'Ohana,** a group dedicated to voicing public opposition to the bombing of Kahoolawe and demanding the return of the island to the Hawaiian people. The 'Ohana staged several occupations of the island, leading to the arrest and conviction of a number of protestors. During the early 1980s, the US offered Kahoolawe to foreign allies for use in bombing exercises, prompting objections from environmental groups in Great Britain, Australia, New Zealand, and Japan. The international media attention generated by the protests eventually led to cancellation of the bombing.

The 'Ohana also filed a lawsuit demanding the return of the island on environmental and religious grounds. The suit was partially settled in 1980, when the federal government signed a consent decree allowing visitors access to the island for cultural, educational, religious, scientific, or archaeological purposes. Under the decree, the 'Ohana have brought over 5000 visitors to Kahoolawe. Several hiking trails have been cleared, and a few religious sites have been rededicated.

In October 1990, President George Bush, Sr. ceased all bombing on the island, and in November of the same year Congress established the **Kahoolawe Island Conveyance Commission** to draft terms for the return of the island to the State of Hawaii. From December 1990 until July 1993, the commission held public hearings and conducted research, eventually outlining some general clean-up measures that would be necessary to make Kahoolawe habitable.

In November 1993, Congress passed a law prohibiting any future military activity on Kahoolawe. The law also appropriated $400 million in federal funds for a ten-year cleanup operation under a special Memorandum of Understanding between the US Navy and the State of Hawaii. That same year, the Hawaii State Legislature established the **Kahoolawe Island Reserve,** declaring the island and the waters within two miles of its coast closed to public access. On May 7, 1994, the island was officially returned to the State of Hawaii, and the governor established a seven-member **Kahoolawe Island Reserve Commission,** which is dedicated to preserving the island's archaeological, historical, and environmental resources for future generations.

TODAY

The goals of the ten-year clean-up plan, which expires in 2003, proved a bit too lofty for the federal government. The Navy had originally intended to clear all surface debris, make the land reasonably safe for human access, re-vegetate the island with native species, clear hiking trails, and construct camping and educational facilities. Unfortunately, the contractors hired by the Navy were held to extremely low standards—only 85% of a particular job had to be completed to qualify the contractor for full payment. As a result, the clean-up has been woefully unsuccessful.

Though much of the island is now reasonably safe for closely controlled visits by the 'Ohana and their guests, visions of true public access remain far-fetched. Unless the clean-up is extended beyond 2003, which seems unlikely, access to the still-contaminated waters around the island will continue to be restricted to fishing boats in the outermost zone on two weekends each month.

VISITING THE ISLAND

If you are set on visiting Kahoolawe, contact the Protect Kaho'olawe 'Ohana (www.kahoolawe.org) to inquire about joining one of their monthly trips. The trips have a religious and cultural focus and are primarily for Hawaiian residents, so don't expect a tour. Oahu's access coordinators are Kim Birnie (☎ 536-8442) and Davianna McGregor (☎ 956-7608). On Maui, contact Bert Sakata (☎ 244-5649).

FURTHER INFORMATION

For general information about the island, contact the **Kahoolawe Island Reserve Commission,** 811 Kolu St. Suite 201 (on Oahu ☎ 243-5020, neighbor islands ☎ 468-4644; fax 243-5885; www.hawaii.gov/kirc). Also try the **US Navy's website** (www.efdpac.navfac.navy.mil/news/kaho/hp1.htm), which has updates about the clean-up process and pictures of bombs being detonated on the island. The various sections about Kahoolawe on the website of the **Bishop Museum,** 1525 Bernice St., Honolulu, may also prove informative (☎ 847-3511; www.bishopmuseum.org). The museum also stocks older books about Kahoolawe in its store.

Most **books** about Kahoolawe are out of print and hard to find. Your best bet is *Kaho'olawe Na Leo o Kanaloa: Chants and Stories of Kaho'olawe.* The book contains stories and chants about the island as well as a collection of photographs. **Inez MacPhee Ashdown,** the daughter of Angus MacPhee, recorded the history of her father's ranch, as well as some stories told to her by local Hawaiians, in a book called *Kaho'olawe,* which has been out of print since 1970. Jay Hartwell's book, *Na Mamo: The Hawaiian People Today,* contains an insightful chapter about Kahoolawe. The more scientifically minded will appreciate J. Gilbert McAllister and Bernice P. Bishop's "Archaeology of Kaho'olawe," a paper published in Vol. 115 of *The Museum Bulletin* in 1933, which was reprinted by the B. Kraus Reprint Company in 1971. The article, also available at the Bishop Museum, includes original accounts of Kahoolawe from before the bombing started.

BIG ISLAND

Let your love affair with the state of Hawaii grow here, on its namesake island, but expect no whirlwind romance—Hawai'i, better known as the Big Island, is vast and varied, and commands both time and attention. The island is 4036 sq. mi. in area and is ever-expanding, thanks to Kilauea's constant eruptions. Geologically the youngest of all her sisters, the Big Island is nonetheless both the largest and one of the most environmentally diverse. Within the island's borders 11 out of 13 climate eco-systems are represented, from the subarctic summits of Mauna Loa and Mauna Kea, to the rainforests of the Hamakua Coast, to the lava fields of the Ka'u desert. To journey through the Big Island is to brush with the rawest forces of nature—earth, sea, and sky. Here, you can almost touch the stars at the planetariums on Saddle Rd., see land birthed at the lava flows of Kilauea, and ride the waves of the mighty Pacific Ocean. Hawai'i's natural beauty is undeniably dazzling, and the essence of Hawai'i thrives in its hidden valleys and striking vistas. The effort required to discover its hidden side only amplifies an appreciation for the many facets of the island, as though you were able to see them as the native Hawaiians who first settled here once did.

The spirit of these Hawaiian pioneers is still strong here, the birthplace of the islands' greatest king, Kamehameha I. The archaeological ruins throughout the island serve as a continual reminder of the accomplishments of this unique culture, and the respect with which the ancients treated the land itself. Spots with great significance to native Hawaiians, such as Ka Lae and Mo'okini Luakini Heiau, are imbued with a spiritual power, what the Hawaiians called *mana*, that is as apparent as the winds that sweep up from the ocean.

Today, the first Hawaiians' spirit of aloha is maintained alongside the island's unique blend of practicality and idealism. Yet, as is always the case in a place with so much to offer, development has reared its ugly head, and seems to contest the values and ideals held by much of the local population. While big resorts and their incumbent infrastructure of golf courses and shopping malls have thus far been limited to the South Kohala Coast, vacation homes and Wal-Marts are spreading from this epicenter at an alarming rate. Some development is inevitable and even necessary on this island, but it awaits to be seen whether Hawaii will be able to grow sustainably. It may be that before long, the predominant green of the island will not be rainforest, but dollar bills, and its black pavement tar instead of lava flows.

HIGHLIGHTS OF BIG ISLAND

SNORKEL among a rainbow of colorful fish in Kealakekua Bay's coral reefs (p. 324).

HIKE to the floor of Waipi'o Valley (p. 336) to a secluded, mile-long beach.

TRAVERSE the Kilauea Iki Crater, which was a lake of lava just forty years ago, in Hawaii Volcanoes National Park (p. 306).

WITNESS the frozen architectural clock downtown Hilo, struck by two tsunamis in 15 years (p. 332).

LIVE YOUR DREAM OF PARADISE at the stunning, 400 ft. Akaka Falls (p. 291).

SEEK INNER PEACE at the Buddhist temple of Nechung Dorje Drayang Ling (p. 330).

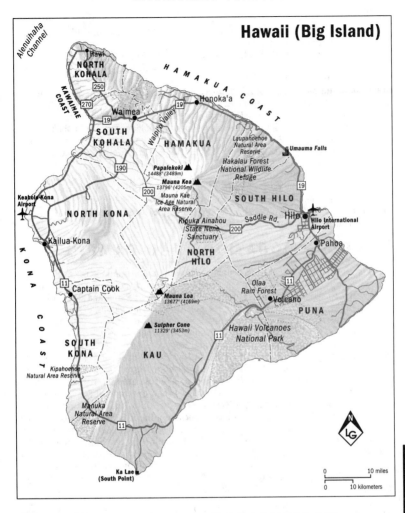

Hawaii (Big Island)

✈ INTERISLAND TRANSPORTATION

Many flights to the Big Island arrive at **Keahole-Kona International Airport,** Keahole Airport Rd. (☎329-2484), 7 mi. north of downtown **Kailua-Kona** off of Queen Ka'ahumanu Hwy. (Rte. 19). Aloha Airlines, All Nippon, American, Continental, Delta, Hawaiian Airlines, Japan, Lufthansa, Northwest, Qantas, and United fly to the mainland and international destinations. **Aloha Airlines** (☎800-367-5250 or 935-5771; www.alohaairlines.com) also has flights to: **Hilo,** Big Island (9:20am); **Honolulu** (14 per day, 6:15am-7:55pm); **Kahului,** Maui (12:20pm); **Lihu'e,** Kauai (10 per day, 6:15am-5:15pm). **Hawaiian Airlines** (☎800-367-5320 or 838-1555; www.hawaii-anair.com) flies to: **Honolulu** (14 per day, 6:23am-8:08pm); **Kahului,** Maui (12:53pm); **Kaunakakai,** Molokai (3:23pm); **Lanai City,** Lanai (3:23pm); **Lihu'e,** Kauai (10 per day,

6:23am-6:13pm). Although **fares** fluctuate considerably, you should never have to pay more than $100 to travel between islands. A $20 **taxi** ride is the only way to get downtown Kailua-Kona from the airport.

Hilo International Airport, Airport Access Rd. (☎934-5801), off of Rte. 11 about ½ mi. south of the intersection of Rte. 11 and Rte. 19 in **Hilo** (see p. 332), is home to 9 gates, helicopter charters out to the volcanoes, Aloha and Hawaiian Airlines for interisland flights, and United Airlines (☎800-241-6522) flights back to the mainland. **Aloha Airlines** flies to: **Honolulu** (45min., 9-11 per day 6:25am-8pm), **Kahului,** Maui (1 per day Su-Th 8:30am, F-Sa 6:55pm), **Lihu'e,** Kauai (8-10 per day 6:25am-5pm). **Hawaiian Airlines** flies to: **Honolulu** (10 per day 6:36am-8:16pm), **Kahului,** Maui (30min., 2 per day 9:33am and 7:01pm), **Lihu'e,** Kauai (2hr., 9 per day 6:36am-6:18pm), and **Molokai** and **Lanai** (1 per day 12:56pm). With interisland coupons, **one-way fares** should not be more than $70. There's a **visitor's booth** by the baggage claim that offers helpful info including maps and brochures (open daily 6am-8pm). An $8-10 **taxi** ride is the only way to get from the airport to downtown Hilo.

Hele-On Bus runs minimalist local bus routes; **car rental** is by far the easiest way to get around the Big Island. For **inter-city and local transportation,** consult the Transportation section for each town

☝ ACCOMMODATIONS AND CAMPING

Permits are required to camp at beach parks and campgrounds across the island. You may apply for permits online at www.hawaii-county.com/parks/parks.htm or by writing to the Hawaii division of the **Department of Parks and Recreation,** 25 Aupuni St., Hilo, HI 96720. (☎961-8311. Open M-F 7:45am-4:30pm. Permits $5, ages 13-17 $2, under 12 $1, per day.) Camping is allowed for up to one week in summer and up to two weeks during the rest of the year per park. The state also oversees rental of **cabins** at Mauna Kea and Kalopa. Reserve permits from the **Division of State Parks** in the Department of Land and Natural Resources, 75 Aupuni St., PO Box 936 Hilo, HI 96720. (☎974-6200. Open 8am-noon. Rates rarely exceed $10 per person.) See **Hawaii Volcanoes National Park** (p. 306) for camping within the park.

Hostels are more prevalent on the Big Island than on some of the other major islands, and **Bed and Breakfasts (B&Bs)** are a relatively affordable option for travelers on a budget. The **Hawaii Island B&B Association, Inc.** is a collection of over 50 B&B owners. Their website (www.stayhawaii.com) lists accommodations by region, complete with photographs. **B&Bs Online** (www.bbonline.com/hi/region4.html) is another good resource, with links to the websites of B&Bs across the island. **Vacation rentals** are another affordable alternative to hotels and resorts for those planning an extended stay on the island. Booking agencies are listed in the accommodations section for Kailua-Kona.

HILO

The devastating tsunamis that struck Hilo in 1946 and 1960 have had a lasting impact on the city. Businesses seeking higher ground abandoned the old-fashioned downtown, which was ravaged by both onslaughts. As a result, Hilo's buildings remain essentially unchanged from its heyday in the first half of the 20th century. Hilo is the metropolis of the Big Island and its county seat. Yet despite being home to more than a quarter of the island's population, the city nonetheless maintains a small-town feel. Hilo is hardly a tourist hotspot, which makes it an ideal place to get a taste of the real Hawaii. The city has a vibrant culture of alternative lifestyles, numerous pan-Pacific stores and restaurants, a colorful farmer's market, and lush botanical gardens and rainforest. Just be sure to keep an eye on the sea—you never know what might be rolling in on the horizon.

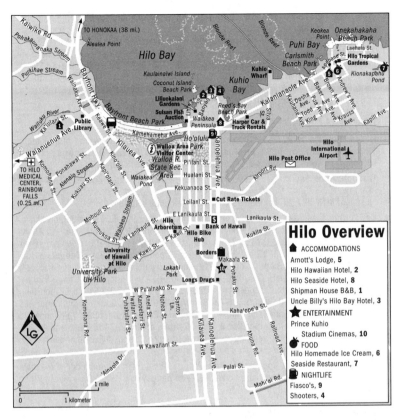

Hilo Overview

🏠 ACCOMMODATIONS
Arnott's Lodge, **5**
Hilo Hawaiian Hotel, **2**
Hilo Seaside Hotel, **8**
Shipman House B&B, **1**
Uncle Billy's Hilo Bay Hotel, **3**
⭐ ENTERTAINMENT
Prince Kuhio
   Stadium Cinemas, **10**
🍴 FOOD
Hilo Homemade Ice Cream, **6**
Seaside Restaurant, **7**
🌙 NIGHTLIFE
Fiasco's, **9**
Shooters, **4**

🔲 ORIENTATION

Hilo lies on the Big Island's east coast, at the intersection of **Rte. 19,** from the Hamakua Coast and Waimea, and **Rte. 11,** which runs from Hawaii Volcanoes National Park. Kailua-Kona is 87 mi. away, across Saddle Rd. There are two distinct portions of Hilo: downtown and the neighborhoods of Waiakea and Pu'ainako. Downtown has been the city's hub for more than a century, occupying the Hawaii County seat and housing a number of museums and restaurants. **Bayfront Hwy.** (Rte. 19) and **Kamehameha Ave.** run parallel along Hilo Bay; Kamehameha serves as downtown's de facto Main St. Farther back from the water **Kilauea Ave.** and **Kino'ole Ave.** are the main arteries that run roughly parallel to the bay. **Waianuenue Ave.** is the major cross street, and eventually becomes Saddle Rd. **Kanoelehua Ave.** (Rte. 11) runs through Waiakea and Pu'ainako, southeast of downtown.

🔲 TRANSPORTATION

INTERCITY TRANSPORTATION

Buses: Hilo is the hub of the **Hele-On bus** (☎961-8744), and it's relatively easier to get around the island from here than from anywhere else. **Mooheau Bus Terminal,** across the street from the corner of Mamo St. and Kamehameha Ave., is the main stop, but there are a number of others in town, including Prince Kuhio Plaza, UH-Hilo, and Kaiko'o Mall. The bus runs to: **Kailua-Kona** (3¼hr., M-Sa 1:10pm, $6) via **Honoka'a** (1½hr., $3.75), **Waimea** (2hr. 10min., $4.50), and **Waikoloa** (2hr. 35min., $5.25); **Ka'u** via **Hawaii Volcanoes National Park** (1hr. 5min., 2:40pm, $2.25), **Pahala** (1¾hr., $3.75), **Na'alehu/Wai'ohinu** (2¼hr., $4.50), and **Ocean View** (2hr. 35min., $5.25); and **Pahoa** (1hr., M-F 2:40 and 4:45pm, $2.25). See **Interisland Transportation** (p. 281) for more transportation and **Hilo International Airport** information.

LOCAL TRANSPORTATION

Buses: Hele-On (☎961-8744), also runs an intra-Hilo bus system that makes stops throughout town, including **Banyan Dr., Prince Kuhio Plaza, Hilo Library,** and **Hilo Medical Center** via **Mooheau Bus Terminal** (M-F 7:05am-4:30pm, 75¢).

Taxis: Ace One Taxi (☎935-8303, open 24hr.) serves Hilo and its environs. **A-1 Bob's Taxi** (☎959-4800 or 963-5470) serves Hilo, Puna, Volcano, and Hamakua. These are just 2 of the many taxi companies in Hilo. $2 initial pick-up fee.

Car Rental: All national chains have offices at the airport (☎934-5801), on Airport Access Rd., off of Rte. 11 about ½ mi. south of the intersection of Rte. 11 and Rte. 19. **Alamo** (☎800-327-9633 or 961-3343). 21+, under-25 surcharge $25 per day. Open daily 6am-8pm. **Avis** (☎800-321-3712 or 935-1290). 25+. Open daily 6am-8pm. **Budget** (☎800-527-7000 or 935-6878 ext. 25 or 26). 21+, under-25 surcharge $20 per day. Open daily 6am-8:30pm. **Dollar** (☎800-800-4000 or 961-6059). 21+, under-25 surcharge $20 per day. Open daily 6am-8:30pm. **Hertz** (☎800-654-3011 or 935-2896). 25+. Open daily 6am-8:30pm. **National** (☎800-227-7368 or 935-0891). 21+, under-25 surcharge $25 per day. Open daily 6am-8pm. **Thrifty** (☎800-367-2277 or 961-6698). 21+, under-25 surcharge $15 per day. **Harper Car & Truck Rentals of Hawaii,** 456 Kalanianaole Ave. (☎969-1478), rents 4WD vehicles as well as economy cars and, unlike other companies, does not restrict travel to the island's major roads. Open daily 6am-8:30pm.

Bike Rental: Hilo Bike Hub, 318 E. Kawili St. (☎961-4452), at the corner of Makaala and East Kawili, offers specialized bikes ($25-45 per day or $120-225 per week). Open M-F 9am-5:30pm, Sa 9am-5pm.

⁊ PRACTICAL INFORMATION

TOURIST AND FINANCIAL SERVICES

Tourist Office: The Hawaii Visitor's Bureau, 250 Keawe St. (☎800-648-2441 or 961-5797; www.bigisland.org), at the corner of Keawe and Haili St., is mainly a marketing agency for the island, but has good maps and brochures as well as a helpful staff.

Budget Travel: Cut Rate Tickets, 688 Kanoelehua Ave. (☎969-1944), at the corner of Kanoelehua and Leilani St., adjacent to the Minit Stop gas station, provides discounted rates on flights. Open M-F 7am-7pm, Sa 9am-5pm, Su 9am-2pm.

Banks: Bank of Hawaii, 417 E. Kawili St. (☎935-9701), at the corner of E. Kawili St. and Kanoelehua Ave. Open M-Th 8:30am-4pm, F 8:30am-6pm. **First Hawaiian Bank,** 1205 Kilauea Ave. (☎969-2211), at the corner of Kilauea and Kekuanaoa. Open M-Th 8:30am-4pm, F 8:30am-6pm, Sa 9am-1pm. Other banks and **24hr. ATMs** are scattered throughout town.

LOCAL SERVICES

Bookstores: Borders, 301 Makaala St. (☎933-1410), in the Waiakea Center. Open Su-Th 9am-9pm, F-Sa 9am-10pm. **Basically Books,** 160 Kamehameha Ave. (☎961-0144), has a ton of Hawaiiana. Open M-F 9am-5pm, Sa 9am-3pm, Su 10am-3pm.

Library: Hilo Public Library, 300 Waianuenue Ave. (☎933-8888), is the place to pick up a visitor's library card ($10) and check your email.

Public Swimming Pools: The Kawamoto Swim Stadium, Hoʻolulu Park (☎961-8698), one block west of Rte. 11 near its intersection with Kamehameha Ave. Open M-F 9-11am, 1:30-3:45pm, and 6-7:15pm; Sa-Su 9-11:45am and 1-3:45pm.

Laundromats: Hilo Quality Washerette, 210 Hoku St. (☎961-6490), near the corner of Kinoʻole, behind 7-Eleven. Wash $1.50-4, Dry 25¢ per 5min. Open daily 6am-10pm.

Equipment Rental: Hilo Surplus Store, 148 Mamo St. (☎935-6398). Open M-Sa 8am-5pm. **Pacific Rent-All,** 1080 Kilauea Ave. (☎935-2974). Open M-Sa 7am-5pm, Su 9am-11am. Both supply tents, sleeping bags, and other camping gear.

Weather Conditions: ☎935-8555.

EMERGENCY AND COMMUNICATIONS

Emergency: ☎911.

Police: Hilo Police Station, 349 Kapiolani St. (☎961-2213), at the corner of Kapiolani Ave. and Kukuau St.

Rape Crisis Hotline: ☎935-0677.

Pharmacy: Long's Drugs, 111 E. Puʻainako St. (☎959-5881), in Prince Kuhio Plaza. Open M-F 8am-10pm, Sa 8am-9pm, Su 8am-7pm.

Medical Services: Hilo Medical Center, 1190 Waianuenue Ave. (☎974-4700).

Internet Access: Beach Dog Rentals and Sales, 62 Kinoʻole St. (☎961-5207), at the corner of Kinoʻole and Waianuenue. Internet access $2 per 20min., $6 per hr. Open M-F 10am-7pm, Sa 10am-2pm.

Post Office: Hilo Main Post Office, 1299 Kekuanaoa St. (☎800-275-8777), on the road to the airport. Open M-F 8am-4:30pm, Sa 8:30am-12:30pm.

Zip Code: 96720.

LOCAL MEDIA AND PUBLICATIONS

Local newspapers are: **West Hawaii Today,** 75-5580 Kuakini Hwy. (☎329-9311), in Kona, which covers the Kona coast; and the **Hawaii Tribune-Herald,** 355 Kinoʻole St. (☎935-6621), in Hilo. Both are published M-F and Su. The three major **tourist magazines** are: *This Week Big Island, Spotlight's Big Island Gold,* and *101 Things to Do on Hawaii: The Big Island,* all of which are free and available just about everywhere. Smaller, less overtly commercial magazines include **Big Island Beach & Activity Guide** and **Coffee Times,** available at most visitor information centers.

There are a number of **radio stations** on the island, but the undisputed king is KAPA (99.1 FM Kona, 100.3 FM Hilo & Kaʻu), which plays all Hawaiian, all the time. **National Public Radio** (NPR) broadcasts out of Hilo at 91.1 FM and can be picked up on the Kona side at 90.7 FM. The Big Island has no television station of its own; Hawaiian news comes from the national affiliates out of Honolulu.

▮ ACCOMMODATIONS

Dolphin Bay Hotel, 333 Iliahi St. (☎935-1466; www.dolphinbayhilo.com). Take Keawe St. over the Wailuku River north of town and make your second left onto Iliahi. Just a short walk from downtown, this meticulously maintained hotel is one of the best accommodations in Hilo. The large, airy rooms have kitchens, and some have their own lanai. Coffee, fresh papaya, and bananas are available in the lobby, and the staff has a wealth of knowledge about the Big Island. Rooms $66-99. ❸

Shipman House Bed & Breakfast, 131 Ka'iulani St. (☎800-627-8447 or 934-8002; bighouse@bigisland.com; www.hilo-hawaii.com). From Rte. 19, take Waianuenue Ave. 5 blocks and turn right on Ka'iulani St. The Victorian-style house was home to a prominent Hilo family and once hosted Jack London. Spacious rooms with porches and towering ceilings beget the classy ambience. Reservations recommended. Check-in 3-6pm. Check-out 10am. Doubles $149-179; each additional guest $25. AmEx/MC/V. ❺

Arnott's Lodge, 98 Apapane Rd. (☎969-7097; info@arnottslodge.com; www.arnottslodge.com). From the end of Rte. 11 by the Hilo waterfront, take a right onto Kalanianaole St. and continue for over 1 mi. to a left on Apapane Rd. This well-run hostel is one of the best spots for backpackers and independent travelers on the island. Oodles of dorm beds, as well as private rooms, Internet access, and full laundry and kitchen facilities. The lodge also **rents bicycles and snorkeling equipment** and runs **tours** for adventurous travelers to Hawaii Volcanoes National Park, Mauna Kea, North Kohala and Hamakua, and South Point and Green Sands Beach ($43-48). Check-out 10am. They have plenty of info on **short-term work** opportunities in the area; work on organic farms in exchange for room and board is the most common arrangement. Tents $9, bunks $17. Single rooms with shared bath $33, doubles $44. Rooms with bath $47-57, 2-bedroom suite (fits 5) $110. DC/MC/V. ❶

Hilo Hawaiian Hotel, 71 Banyan Dr. (☎800-367-5004 or 935-9361; www.castleresorts.com). On Banyan Dr., east of downtown Hilo. Hilo's most luxurious resort hotel is set on the tip of Waiakea Peninsula and features sweeping views of Hilo Bay. Access to beaches, a pool, golf course, and tennis courts. Check-in 3pm. Check-out noon. Rooms $85-240. All major credit cards. ❸

Wild Ginger Inn, 100 Pu'ueo St. (☎800-882-1887 or 935-5556; www.wildgingerinn.com). From downtown Hilo, take Keawe St. over the river; the street becomes Pu'ueo St. Once a ramshackle motel, the Wild Ginger has since been renovated to provide modern-day conveniences including Internet access, cable TV, refrigerators, self-service laundry, and complimentary breakfast. It still maintains its old-school charm with a hot pink exterior and tropical gardens. Continental breakfast included. Check-out 11am. Rooms $45-99. All major credit cards. ❷

Uncle Billy's Hilo Bay Hotel, 87 Banyan Dr. (☎800-367-5102 or 935-0861; resv@unclebilly.com; www.unclebilly.com). On Banyan Dr., east of downtown Hilo. One of the few Hawaiian-owned hotels on the island, Uncle Billy's keeps it real with Hawaiian-themed rooms, A/C, cable TV, fridges, private lanais, and a pool. Kitchenettes available. Check-in 3pm. Check-out noon. Rooms $69-89. All major credit cards. ❸

Hilo Seaside Hotel, 126 Banyan Dr. (☎800-560-5557 or 935-0821; info@sand-seaside.com; www.hiloseaside.com). On Banyan Dr., near the intersection with Kalanianaole Ave. Overlooking a finger of Hilo Bay, but away from the hustle and bustle of most of Banyan Dr., this low-key hotel is a no-hassle place to spend a night. Clean and simple rooms with A/C, ceiling fans, refrigerators, lanais, and a swimming pool. Check-in 3pm. Check-out noon. Rooms $69. All major credit cards. ❸

 FOOD

The amazingly rich and colorful **Hilo Farmers' Market,** on Mamo St. between Kamehameha and Kilauea, kicks off bright and early on W and Sa and runs all day. The **Suisan Fish Auction,** 85 Lihiwai St., near the intersection of Lihiwai and Banyan Dr., is an event worth seeing. Those not planning on opening their own seafood restaurant anytime soon can stop by the retail store next door. (☎935-9349. M-F, bidding starts at 7:30am.) **Island Naturals,** 303 Makaala St., in the Waiakea Center, is the island's best natural food store, with an impressive selection of goods. (☎935-5533. Open M-Sa 8am-8pm, Su 10am-7pm. All major credit cards.)

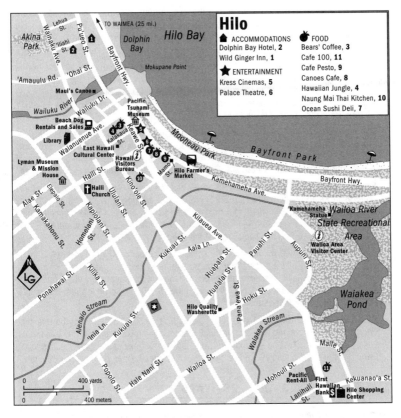

Hilo

⌂ ACCOMMODATIONS
Dolphin Bay Hotel, **2**
Wild Ginger Inn, **1**

★ ENTERTAINMENT
Kress Cinemas, **5**
Palace Theatre, **6**

🍎 FOOD
Bears' Coffee, **3**
Cafe 100, **11**
Cafe Pesto, **9**
Canoes Cafe, **8**
Hawaiian Jungle, **4**
Naung Mai Thai Kitchen, **10**
Ocean Sushi Deli, **7**

Naung Mai Thai Kitchen, 86 Kilauea Ave. (☎934-7540). Near the corner of Kilauea and Mamo St. Everything at this unassuming Thai restaurant has been done with the utmost precision, from the arrangement of the elegant tables to the exquisite food. Spring rolls $7-8. Curries $8-11. BYOB. Open for lunch M-Tu and Th-F 11am-2pm, dinner M-Th 5-8:30pm and F-Sa 5-9pm. No credit cards. ❷

Seaside Restaurant, 1790 Kalanianaole Ave. (☎935-8825), east of downtown Hilo, about 2 mi. from the intersection of Rte. 11 and Kalanianaole Ave. The ponds below the restaurant provide the menu's catches, which are wildly popular among locals. The food isn't fancy, but it is fresh and every entree comes with salad and hot apple pie. Seaside greens ($9), steamed mullet wrapped in *ti* leaves ($18), *Paniolo* prime rib ($22). Open Su, Tu-Th 5-8:30pm and F-Sa 5-9pm. ❹

Ocean Sushi Deli, 239 Keawe St. (☎961-6625), near the corner of Keawe and Haili St. A bustling joint that rolls up lunch for pretty much all of downtown Hilo. The friendly staff is glad to assist sushi novices in navigating the giant selection of fresh fish. *Nigiri* ($2.50-4), *hosomaki* & *temaki* ($1.40-4.50), specialty rolls ($2.50-7.50). Open M-Sa 10am-2pm and 4:30-9pm. MC/V. ❶

Cafe Pesto, 308 Kamehameha Ave. (☎969-6640), near the corner of Kamehameha Ave. and Mamo St. With enormous plate-glass windows that frame the street and the bay beyond, this stylish restaurant is as sophisticated as they come in Hilo. The menu offers a wide selection of Pacific Rim dishes with options ranging from crab cakes and seafood risotto to eclectic salads and designer pizzas. Appetizers $3-13, salads $8-10, entrees $8-28. Open Su-Th 11am-9pm, F-Sa 11am-10pm. All major credit cards. ❸

Hawaiian Jungle, 110 Kalakaua St. (☎934-0700), overlooking Kalakaua Park between Keawe and Kino'ole St. The richly colored wood interior and wide windows make this Mexican and South American restaurant seem as though it would be right at home in the midst of a tropical rainforest. The menu includes Mexican-style *tamales* and *chile rellenos* as well as daily Peruvian specials ($10-17). Live music F-Su. Open Su-Th 11am-9pm, F-Sa 11am-10pm. D/MC/V. ❸

Canoes Cafe, 14 Furneaux Ln. (☎935-4070), near the corner of Furneaux and Kamehameha. This hole-in-the-wall cafe is plastered with canoeing memorabilia. Excellent sandwiches ($6.25) add island flair to old favorites, as well as heaping servings of pizza, pasta, and salads. Open M-Sa 8am-3pm, Su 10am-2:30pm. AmEx/D/MC/V. ❷

Bears' Coffee, 106 Keawe St. (☎935-0708), between Waianuenue and Kalakaua. Bears' brews up hot coffee ($1.50-2.25) for its many adoring fans. Other morning jump starts: granola, fruit, and yogurt ($3.50); waffles ($3.35) or eggs ($3-4). Bears' accommodates late-risers with sandwiches ($4.50) and salads ($4.25-5.25) for lunch. Open M-F 6:30am-4pm, Sa 7am-1pm, Su 7:30am-noon. ❶

Cafe 100, 969 Kilauea Ave (☎935-8683), near the corner of Kilauea and Kekuanao'a St. The birthplace of the *Loco Moco*, and still home to the cheapest eats in town, this roadside drive-in has met the onslaught of fast food chains and healthy diets, and come out unscathed. Most meals $2-4, all items under $7. Open Sa-Th 6:45am-8:30pm, F 6:45am-9pm. No credit cards. ❶

Hilo Homemade Ice Cream, 1477 Kalanianaole St. (☎969-9559), east of the intersection of Kalanianaole and Rte. 11. Dishes out a delicious mixture of milk and local fruits like mango, coconut and passion fruit, cooled below freezing. In essence, it's what would come out if a glacier ever swept over Parker Ranch. Open daily 11am-5pm. ❶

MUSEUMS AND FESTIVALS

PACIFIC TSUNAMI MUSEUM. In a city ravaged by tsunamis twice in 15 years, the diagrams and charts that explain how these enormous walls of water are created become all the more profound. Knowledgeable tour guides provide insightful introductions, and exhibits shed light on recorded tsunamis from around the world. There's also an illuminating video that features the recollections of Hilo tsunami survivors. *(130 Kamehameha Ave., at the corner of Kamehameha and Kalakaua St. ☎935-0926; www.tsunami.org. $5, seniors $4, students $2. Open M-Sa 9am-4pm.)*

LYMAN MUSEUM. Hawaiian history occupies center stage at this fascinating museum. The **Lyman Mission House,** which was built in 1839, is the oldest frame building on the Big Island, and has been restored to represent the lifestyle of missionaries to Hawaii during the mid-19th century. A guided tour takes you through the home, which includes many original furnishings, tools, and household items. Next door is the **Lyman Museum** itself, the galleries of which explore topics such as the formation of the islands, Hawaiian culture from the arrival of the first Polynesian settlers through the waves of international immigrants, and the astronomical observations on the summit of Mauna Kea. It also features changing exhibitions of modern Hawaiian art. *(276 Haili St., at the corner of Haili and Kapiolani St. ☎935-5021; www.lymanmuseum.org. Open M-Sa 9am-4:30pm. $7, seniors $5, family $12.50.)*

PANAEWA RAINFOREST ZOO. Panaewa is the only tropical rainforest zoo in the US, and home to over 75 animal species, including a white Bengal Tiger, Water Buffalo, Aldabra Tortoise, and Pygmy Hippo. *(A few miles south of Hilo on Mamaki St., off of Rte. 11. FOZ@hilozoo.com; www.hilozoo.com. Open daily 9am-4pm. Free.)*

MERRIE MONARCH FESTIVAL. When **King David Kalakaua** ascended the throne in 1883, he took great measures to reassert Hawaiian culture, following half a century of missionary influence. Kalakaua (also known as the **Merrie Monarch** because of his support of dance and music) brought **hula** back into the public sphere by including it in his coronation ceremony. One hundred and sixty years later, the memory of this last Hawaiian king is celebrated by a cultural event held in Hilo the week after Easter. The celebration, which includes a giant parade and other festivities, culminates in a hula competition among dancers from across the islands and both sides of the Pacific. Tickets to the festival go on sale on New Year's Day and sell out quickly. 2003 marks the event's 40th birthday. *(For ticket information, call the Hawaii Naniloa Resort at ☎ 935-9168.)*

🍴 🎵 NIGHTLIFE AND ENTERTAINMENT

Despite being the largest city on the island and a college town to boot, Hilo has a somewhat lackluster nightlife. Catching a movie is often the best option, or if you're up for a little adventure, head up to Mauna Kea to stargaze.

> **Fiasco's,** 200 Kanoelehua Ave. (☎935-7666), at the corner of Rte. 11 and Kuawa St., one block down from Kamehameha Ave. One of the few Hilo hotspots, Fiasco's is a favorite with the college crowd, and has both DJs and live music. Pupus $3-7. Open Tu, Th-Sa 9pm-2am.

> **Shooters,** 121 Banyan Dr. (☎969-7069). A crowd of all ages turns up to get down to the latest hip-hop and house. Happy Hour 3-8pm, drafts $2. Open M-Th 3pm-2am, F-Sa 3pm-3am, Su 6:30pm-2am.

> **Palace Theatre,** 38 Haili St. (☎934-7777), between Kamehameha Ave. and Keawe St. A striking relic from Hilo's glory days, the theater plays host to an art-house film most nights of the week, as well as local and visiting musicians and live theater performances. Movie tickets $6. Most film showings 7:30pm.

> **Kress Cinemas,** 174 Kamehameha Ave. (☎961-3456), on the corner of Kamehameha and Kalakaua St. This old-fashioned theater pays homage to the old-school, showing films a few weeks after they've been released, for back-in-the-day fares ($6).

> **Prince Kuhio Stadium Cinemas,** 111 E. Pu'ainako St. (☎959-4595), in Prince Kuhio Plaza. First-run Hollywood flicks, $7.75.

🏖 BEACHES

Hilo is not known for its beaches, but this has less to do with its weather than with its topography, which is dominated by rocky coastline. The best spots to catch some rays or surf are east of downtown Hilo along Kalanianaole Ave. **Onekahakaha Beach Park,** a little less than 2 mi. northeast of the intersection of Rte. 11 and Kalanianaole Ave., has a sandy-floored pool for relaxed swimming and an appealing lawn for picnics, as well as restrooms and showers. **Richardson Ocean Park,** at the end of Kalanianaole Ave. about 4 mi. east of Hilo, has a bit of black sand masquerading as a beach, and is a popular spot for body boarding as well as snorkeling. Lifeguards, picnic tables, rest rooms, and showers round out the deal.

BIG ISLAND

⚠ OUTDOORS

PARKS

BANYAN DRIVE. The drive runs around the Waiakea Peninsula in a towering, leafy tunnel. While the Banyan trees that form this vaulted ceiling are by no means rare on this side of the island, these trees are noteworthy because many of them were planted in the 1930s by celebrities from all over the world, including Babe Ruth and Franklin Roosevelt. The drive also passes the lovely **Liliuokalani Gardens,** a 30-acre Japanese-style park created to honor Hawaii's Japanese population. The oceanfront park, complete with fish ponds, pagodas and arched bridges, is beautifully maintained and makes a terrific place for a picnic or stroll. *(Banyan Dr. is east of downtown Hilo.)*

WAILOA RIVER STATE RECREATION AREA. Driving between downtown Hilo and the strip malls and developments near Rte. 11, it's a welcome oddity that such a prime piece of realty on the shores of Hilo Bay would be spared simply to give the citizens fields and beaches on which to play. The area had been developed until the 1946 tsunami, which destroyed everything in its path. Residents rebuilt their homes and businesses in the years that followed, only to have them devastated again in 1960. After that time the land was set aside as a park in a concession to the power of the sea, with a memorial dedicated to the victims. *(The park is along Kamehameha Ave. and Bayfront Hwy., between downtown Hilo and Banyan Dr.)*

KALAKAUA PARK. A statue of Hawaii's merrie monarch, David Kalakaua, sits, perhaps in contemplation, with a hula drum and *taro* leaf in hand beneath the park's immense Banyan tree. The park is a splendid bit of green in the midst of sidewalks and streets, and makes for a good resting place on a tour of Hilo. Bordering one edge of the park is the **East Hawaii Cultural Center,** which promotes the arts on the Big Island through many different forums. The exhibition gallery houses the work of many local artists for public enjoyment. *(Park is in downtown Hilo at the corner of Waianuenue Ave. and Kino'ole St. Cultural Center open M-Sa 10am-4pm.)*

WAILUKU RIVER. Just west of downtown Hilo, the Wailuku River comes to meet the ocean from the slopes of Mauna Kea. This powerful piece of nature is just a few minutes away from the restaurants and stores of Kamehameha Ave., allowing nature addicts to get their fix even during a stay in the city. From either of the bridges that cross the river, **Maui's Canoe** is clearly visible in the middle of the current. Legend has it that this unique rock formation was created when the great warrior ran aground as he rushed to save his mother from a watery grave underneath **Rainbow Falls.** The impressive falls lack the pristine appeal they possessed during Maui's time, but are still an inspiring sight, especially framed by hulking Mauna Loa in the distance. *(Falls 2 mi. up Waianuenue Ave.)*

GARDENS

NANI MAU GARDENS. The striking 53-acre garden of exotic flowers, palms and tropical fruits removes any lingering doubts as to why Hawaii is known as the Orchid Isle. *(☎ 959-3500. 421 Makalika St., 3½ mi. south of Hilo Bay off of Rte. 11 toward Volcano. Open daily 8:30am-5pm. $10.)*

HILO TROPICAL GARDENS. Orchids and heliconia flourish with relaxed abundance on this 2-acre plot nestled among tide pools south of Onekahakaha Beach Park. *(☎ 969-9873. 1477 Kalanianaole St., less than 2 mi., northeast of the intersection of Kalanianaole and Rte. 11. Open daily 8:30am-5pm. $6, children $3.)*

⬛ DAYTRIPS FROM HILO

PEPE'EKEO SCENIC DRIVE

Approximately 5 mi. north of Hilo.

The well-marked Pepe'ekeo Scenic Drive branches off Rte. 19 on a journey through lush rainforest and above the pounding surf of the Hamakua Coast before returning to the highway 4 mi. later. The serpentine road crosses over streams on tiny one-lane bridges and winds in and out of ravines laced with passion fruit vines, as well as guava, mango, and African tulip trees.

About 1½ mi. into this adventure, the road leads to the **Hawaii Tropical Botanical Garden,** overlooking Onomea Bay. The garden, which follows the slope of the road down to the sea, is home to over 2000 different species of tropical plant life from around the globe. A well-maintained trail leads visitors through scenery rich with beautiful bromeliads, gingers, heliconias, and orchids. Banyan and monkey pod trees, as well as countless types of palms tower overhead. The combined affect is of a pristine natural paradise, far removed from the dust of city life. The only drawback to this mesmerizing locale is that it comes at a relatively high price. (☎964-5233; www.hawaiigarden.com. Open daily 9am-4pm. $15, under 17 $5, under 5 free. Family pass $35, good for one year.)

Just before the scenic drive returns to the highway, it passes 🏴**What's Shakin' ❶,** 27-999 Mamalahoa Hwy., a modest stand that blends superior smoothies ($4-4.50). Their amazing concoctions—with island-style names such as Papaya Paradise, Mango Tango, and Peanut Bruddah—use no added sugars or ice, only fresh fruit and juice. Entrees ($4-7.50) range from tamales to tempeh burgers. (☎964-3080. Open daily 10am-5pm; June-Aug. 10am-5:30pm. No credit cards.)

AKAKA FALLS STATE PARK

15 mi. north of Hilo, about 4 mi. up the side of Mauna Kea. From Rte. 19, a marked turn-off between the 13- and 14-mile markers leads to Rte. 220 and the falls. Restrooms and picnic tables are adjacent to the parking lot.

The towering Kahuna Falls (400 ft.) and Akaka Falls (442 ft.) make Akaka Falls State Park one of the highlights of the Hamakua Coast. The tiny park is packed with delights, including the awe-inspiring falls and a well-kept walking path. The half-mile paved loop begins at the parking lot, and travels between the two falls, then turns back for a short trek through a vibrant rainforest abloom with orchids and redhead ginger, and filled with mossy Banyan trees, gigantic ferns, and burgeoning stands of bamboo.

HOME AWAY FROM HOME Every summer around Memorial Day, families of native Hawaiian ancestry from Hilo's Keaukaha neighborhood pack tents and camping supplies into their cars, head down the street, and...park for 3 months. In this way, Carlsmith Beach Park is transformed each year from a grassy lawn above Kuhio Bay to a tent city complete with port-a-potties and a social dynamic. Carlsmith park is part of the **Hawaiian Homelands,** and Hawaiians living in its vicinity are given the opportunity to return to their roots and set up camp on the same ground that their ancestors called home a millennium ago. Much has changed since the first arrival of non-Polynesians, with cars now outnumbering canoes and Spam replacing wild boar as a staple food, but the Hawaiian spirit of *aloha* toward the land and each other still remains. In this perennial summer ritual, the embers of appreciation for community and the natural world are stoked simply by spending evenings together under the stars.

BIG ISLAND

HAWAII VOLCANOES NATIONAL PARK

The Hawaiian islands owe their existence to a geological hot spot, which, over the last 5 million years, has periodically spewed forth molten lava from the floor of the Pacific Ocean, creating the chain's magnificent volcanoes. From the alpine desert of Mauna Loa and the rainforest of the windward side of Kilauea to the Ka'u Desert and the lava fields that stretch down to the coast, you can travel a continent's worth of terrain in 20 miles. While the park's roads traverse much of this diverse topography, getting out of the car to explore the rainforest, a'a and pahoehoe flows, pumice summits, and cinder cones on your own is the only way to gain full appreciation of all that Hawaii Volcanoes National Park has to offer.

In 1916, Lorrin Thurston and Dr. Thomas Jaggar convinced President Woodrow Wilson to make the area the United States' 13th national park, despite the fact that Hawaii was not yet a state. Home to **Mauna Loa,** the world's most massive mountain, and **Kilauea,** its most active volcano, Hawaii Volcanoes National Park has more natural wonders within its 377 sq. mi. than almost anyplace on Earth. Rising 18,000 ft. from the ocean floor below the surface of the Pacific, and climbing another 13,677 ft. above sea level, Mauna Loa towers over Mt. Everest and is surpassed only by its neighbor, Mauna Kea (13,796 ft.), in total elevation. In sheer bulk, it is 100 times the size of Washington's Mt. Rainier. Kilauea (4093 ft.) sits in the imposing shadow of Mauna Loa and has been erupting continuously since 1983; the flows have added over 500 acres of new land to the park's coast in the past 10 years. The park is best experienced as a whole, in order to see the amazing number of climatic zones it encompasses within its borders.

AT A GLANCE: HAWAII VOLCANOES NATIONAL PARK

AREA: 218,000 acres.

FEATURES: Kilauea, Mauna Loa, Ka'u Desert, Pu'u Loa Petroglyphs.

HIGHLIGHTS: Hiking over lava flows; walking among the Pu'u Loa petroglyphs; driving past steam vents, pit craters, and lava flows to the summit caldera on Crater Rim Drive.

QUICK FACT: NASA astronauts have trained for lunar landings in the Ka'u Desert, because of terrain's similarity to the moon's surface.

GATEWAY TOWNS: Volcano, 1 mi., see (p. 306). Hilo, 30 mi., see (p. 332).

CAMPING: Camping available free of charge and without reservations at designated campsites (p. 295). Stays limited to 7 days per month and no more than 30 days per year. Registration required for backcountry camping.

FEES & RESERVATIONS: $10 per vehicle; $5 per pedestrian, bicyclist or motorcyclist. No reservations required.

BIG ISLAND

✈ ORIENTATION

The park encompasses a number of distinct geological regions. Of these, the **Southwest Rift Zone** and the **Ka'u Desert** are particularly striking. Resembling charred desolate moonscapes in appearance, they are part of the devastated area that is covered in lava from Kilauea's periodic eruptions. The **East Rift Zone** encompasses the Chain of Craters Road, which stretches south toward the Pu'u Loa Petroglyphs and east to Pu'u O'o. North of this area is **Kilauea,** Crater Rim Dr., and the Kilauea Visitor Center. The **Mauna Loa summit area** is northwest of Kilauea.

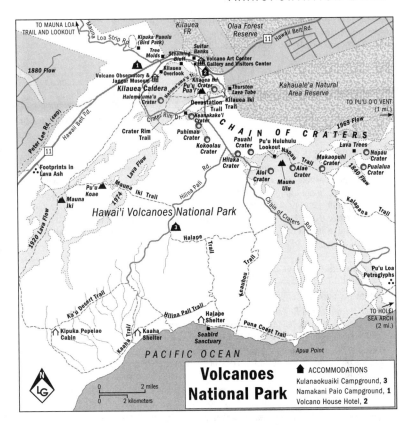

Volcanoes National Park

ACCOMMODATIONS
Kulanaokuaiki Campground, 3
Namakani Paio Campground, 1
Volcano House Hotel, 2

The entrance of the park is off of the **Hawaii Belt Rd.** (Rte. 11), 30 mi. southwest of Hilo and 96 mi. southeast of Kona. The main entrance is north of Kilauea Caldera; a lava flow from Pu'u O'o vent wiped out the Wahaula Visitor Center and a large portion of the coastal road in 1989, closing the southeastern entrance along a continuation of the Kalapana Rd. (Rte. 130). Within the park there are two main roads: the 11-mile **Crater Rim Dr.**, which fittingly circles Kilauea Caldera, and the 40-mile **Chain of Craters Rd.**, which descends the flank of Kilauea toward the coast and abruptly ends where the road meets a bank of lava from a recent flow. **Hilina Pali Rd.** accesses the more remote western portion of the park, while **Mauna Loa Rd.** ascends the mountain and ends at the trailhead of a route to the summit.

⧉ TRANSPORTATION

Volcano (p. 306) is the nearest gateway town, and can satisfy all visitors' basic needs. While a car isn't essential to travel in the park, it is significantly more difficult to see all of the attractions without one. If renting a car is an impossibility, the **Hele-On bus** runs between the park's Visitor Center and Mooheau Bus Terminal in Hilo. (☎961-8744. 2 per day. M-F leaves Volcanoes National Park 8:10am, arrives Hilo 9:20am; leaves Hilo 2:40pm, arrives Volcanoes National Park 3:45pm. $2.25.)

BIG ISLAND

Parking is plentiful, except during eruptions. The vast parking lot at Halemaʻumaʻu Overlook is indicative of the size of the crowds who flock to catch a piece of the action when the volcano blows its top.

⁊ PRACTICAL INFORMATION

Much of the park is **wheelchair-accessible**, including the Devastation Trail, Kilauea Visitor Center, Jaggar Museum, Volcano House Hotel, and Volcano Art Center as well as many pullouts and the pathways to the Steam Vents, Keanakakoʻi, Pauahi Crater, and Muliwai a Pele.

 WHEN TO GO. The park is hospitable at any time of year, and with its distinct regions and nearly 13,000 ft. change in elevation from sea to summit, it has an extremely varied climate. The landscape changes from humid, tree-filled tropics to hot, barren desert to open areas of rock and snow. Visitors to the park should come prepared for variable weather. Temperatures at sea level rarely exceed 90°F, but can fall below freezing toward the summit of Mauna Loa at any time of year. It can be rainy and cool at the highest elevations; the coastal areas are usually warm and dry.

Information: Hawaii Volcanoes National Park, P.O. Box 52, Hawaii National Park, HI 96718-0052. ☎985-6017. www.nps.gov/havo.

Open: The park is open 24hr., 7 days a week.

Fees, Permits, and Regulations: $10 per car or $5 per pedestrian, bicyclist, or motorcyclist; good for 7 days. Year-long Hawaii Volcanoes Pass, $20. Year-long Golden Eagle Passport, good for entrance at parks nationwide, $50.

Driving: The archaic pumps of the Volcano Store (☎967-7210), next to the Volcano post office, still function from 5:30am-7pm daily. There is an Aloha gas station, 19-3972 Old Volcano Rd. (☎967-7555), at Kilauea General Store. Open 6:30am-7:15pm.

Weather: For weather conditions, call ☎961-5532 or 935-8555. Eruption Information is available at ☎985-6000. The park also broadcasts a radio bulletin on AM 530.

Emergency: ☎911. The nearest major medical facility is the **Hilo Medical Center,** 1190 Waianuenue Ave. (☎974-4700).

Facilities: Kilauea Visitor Center (☎985-6017; www.nps.gov/havo) and **Park Headquarters** (☎985-6000), a couple hundred yards beyond the entrance station along the northern arc of Crater Rim Dr., are invaluable resources for exploring the park. Office open daily 7:45am-5pm. **Showers** are available at **Namakani Paio Campground,** about 3 mi. west of the park entrance along Rte. 11. Keys to the showers available from Volcano House for $3. Potable water is scarce in the park—it's a good idea to stock up. **Potable water** is available at the Visitor Center, Jaggar Museum, Thurston Lava Tube, and Namakani Paio Campground. Catchment water that must be treated is available at most backcountry shelters.

Guided hikes and events: The Visitor Center shows a 25-minute introductory film about the park from 9am-4pm daily. The ranger-led **lectures** and **walks** are particularly illuminating. Daily schedule for lectures and walks varies; consult postings on the Ranger Activity bulletin board at the visitor center.

Equipment Outfitters: Hilo Surplus Store, 148 Mamo St. (☎935-6398) in Hilo, sells tents, backpacks, stoves, sleeping bags, and raingear.

Banks and ATMs: There is a **24hr. ATM** in the Volcano House Hotel, across the street from the Visitor Center. The nearest banks are in Hilo: **Bank of Hawaii,** 120 Pauahi St. (☎935-9701) and **First Hawaiian Bank,** 1205 Kilauea Ave. (☎969-2211).

⌘ ACCOMMODATIONS AND CAMPING

Backcountry camping is allowed at designated cabins, shelters, and campgrounds in the southern portion of the park, as well as on the slopes of Mauna Loa, with a free permit available at the Visitor Center on a first-come, first-served basis. Stays are limited to 3 nights per site and to groups of no more than 8 people. There are catchment tanks at most of these sites, but the water must be treated. "Leave no trace" ethics are encouraged, and camping elsewhere in the park is prohibited.

Volcano House Hotel (☎967-7321), along Crater Rim Dr., across from the Visitor Center. The clean, simple rooms are comfortable enough, but with crater views starting at $165, one expects a little more from an establishment set against such a stunning backdrop. Its mediocre restaurant serves buffet-style breakfast ($9.50) and lunch ($12.50), as well as somewhat better a la carte dinners (entrées $14.50-22). Reception 24hr. Check-in 3pm. Check-out noon. Singles and doubles $85-185; each additional person (up to 2) $15. Park entrance fees apply. AmEx/D/MC/V. ❸

Namakani Paio Cabins (☎967-7321), in the Namakani Paio Campground, 3 mi. west of the park entrance along Rte. 11. The spartan cabins, set in wooded surroundings, each contain a double bed, a bunk bed, and little else. Refundable key deposits $12. Linens $20. Reception at Volcano House 24hr. Check-in 3pm. Check-out noon. Singles and doubles $40; each additional person (up to 2) $8. Park entrance fees apply. ❷

Namakani Paio Campground (☎967-7321), 3 mi. west of the park entrance on Rte. 11. In the deep shadows of towering 'ohi'a and eucalyptus trees, this campground is a tranquil place to spend a night after a busy day exploring the volcanoes. There are few designated campsites and availability is on a first-come, first-served basis, but there's generally enough room to set up a tent somewhere. Rest rooms and fireplaces. Stays limited to seven days per year. Free. ❶

Kulanaokuaiki Campground (☎967-7321), off of Hilina Pali Rd. 4 mi. southeast of Chain of Craters Rd. Situated in the midst of the Ka'u Desert, this secluded spot gives a sense of the backcountry without the trek. There's no shade or water and you'll be sleeping on lava, but you can rejoice in the fact that there's probably not another person for miles around. 3 sites with more on the way. Pit-toilets and fireplaces but no drinking water. Stays limited to 7 days per year. Free. ❶

◉ ⌘ SIGHTS AND OUTDOORS

Many of the park's most striking sights are easily accessible from the two main roads: **Crater Rim Drive** and **Chain of Craters Road**.

CRATER RIM DRIVE

The 11-mile loop of Crater Rim Drive encircles Kilauea Caldera as it passes through a diverse cross-section of lava-encrusted landscape, and is excellent for cycling. The drive is best traveled in a counter-clockwise direction, in order to see the ecological transition from the Ka'u Desert and barren lava fields of the Southwest and East Rift Zones to the dense foliage of the windward rainforest.

SULFUR BANKS (0.3 MI.). Can you smell what the Volcano is cooking? At the first stop on the loop, the end of a right turn not far from the Visitor Center, volcanic gases, including carbon dioxide, sulfur dioxide, and hydrogen sulfide—that ubiquitous odor of rotten egg—seep out of this soft spot in the volcanic crust. Sulfur-rich gases deposit crystals on the surrounding rocks as they are released, creating the fluorescent yellow patina that coats the banks.

BIG ISLAND

STEAMING BLUFF/PELE'S SAUNA (0.9 MI.). Down the road, more clouds of gas appear at Pele's Sauna. This towering ledge commands an impressive view of Kilauea Caldera, but the volcanic activity is even closer than it looks—scalding hot lava rock rests just a few feet below the surface. When groundwater seeps down to this level, it is quickly heated to create billows of steam.

SOUTHWEST RIFT ZONE (4.4 MI.). It is evident from the group of deep fractures and gullies here on the southwestern flank of Kilauea that the volcano has been seriously flexing its muscles. The cracks in the crust are caused by the pressure of red-hot magma beneath the volcano's summit. The Southwest Rift Zone extends down to the coast and then beyond to the sea floor.

HALEMA'UMA'U CRATER (5.4 MI.). Pele's immense crater home is a testament to the extreme geological power of the volcano. From the parking lot, it's less than a ½-mile walk to the overlook, where you can peer down into the mouth of the beast. At present, Halema'uma'u is 3000 ft. wide and 280 ft. deep, but it hasn't been that way for long, and may not be in the near future. In 1924, the crater was only 1500 ft. across and almost filled to the brim with a lake of molten lava. The volcano then subsided, or collapsed, and when the dust cleared, the crater had expanded to its current size. The last major eruption of Halema'uma'u occurred in 1967 and created another lava lake, which quickly drained, but the ring around the tub of the high lava mark is still visible about 100 ft. from the top of the rim. The present floor was laid by a small eruption in 1974.

 Halema'uma'u emits strong sulfur fumes—children, pregnant women, and those with heart and/or respiratory problems should avoid the crater.

KEANAKAKO'I CRATER (6.6 MI.). Pit craters such as this one are created when molten material beneath the hardened crust dissipates and the top layer collapses. Keanakako'i means "cave of the adzes," and the crater was essentially a Hawaiian armory until 1877, when fresh lava flows locked its doors forever.

DEVASTATION TRAIL (7.5 MI.). See Hikes (p. 298).

PU'U PUA'I (8.2 MI.). During the 1959 eruption of Kilauea Iki, molten lava fountained to create a spatter cone, burying what had been a portion of Crater Rim Dr. The prevailing winds caused Pu'u Pua'i, or "gushing hill," to form on the southwest side of the vent rather than uniformly around it. What was once an enormous lake of boiling lava has now cooled to become the floor of Kilauea Iki Crater.

THURSTON LAVA TUBE (9.5 MI.). See Hikes (p. 298).

KILAUEA IKI CRATER (9.9 MI.). In November 1959, fountains of lava burst out of the crater wall, flooding Kilauea Iki with a molten lava lake 400 ft. deep. These fountains were so powerful that at times they shot lava as high as 1900 ft.—the greatest height ever recorded. When it was all over, one massive volcano was left standing, 1 mile long, 3000 ft. across, and 380 ft. deep.

CHAIN OF CRATERS ROAD

Be sure to make the necessary preparations before setting out on Chain of Craters Rd., as the whole drive is about 40 miles round-trip from the junction with Crater Rim Dr., and there is neither gas nor water available below the Visitor Center. Chain of Craters is also the park road most likely to be closed due to lava flow or fires, so be sure to check with the Visitor Center about current conditions. All distances are from the junction of Crater Rim Dr. and Chain of Craters Rd.

HILINA PALI RD. (2.2 MI.). Heading into the heart of the Kaʻu Desert, this narrow track is off the beaten path for most park visitors. Those who do make the trek down this 9-mile road are rewarded with a sense of space and solitude that dominates the senses. After passing through colossal flows of barren lava, the road ends in a *pali* that formed when a massive block of this land collapsed into the sea. Kulanaokuaiki Campground and the Mauna Iki trailhead are 4 mi. down the road. The Hilina Pali Overlook is another 5 mi. down, perched a few thousand feet above the Pacific Ocean. The Kaʻu Desert Trail and the Hilina Pali Trail branch out from the overlook (see p. 298).

MAUNA ULU (4.2 MI.). This large shield volcano's powerful eruption between 1969 and 1974 wiped out portions of Chain of Craters Road with massive pahoehoe and aʻa flows. The Puʻu Huluhulu Trail and its extension, the Napau Trail begin at the parking lot. See Hikes (p. 298).

PUʻU LOA PETROGLYPHS (17.1 MI.). While the terrain of Hawaii Volcanoes National Park is in its geological infancy, the land is ancient by human standards and boasts Hawaiian rock art from before the arrival of Western settlers. Some of the most striking examples of these works can be found on the slopes of Puʻu Loa, home to the largest gallery of petroglyphs in Hawaii, with over 15,000 carvings. Puʻu Loa played an important role in early Hawaiian society. Villagers brought the umbilical cord, or *piko*, of each child here and placed it into a hole chiseled into the rock, in the belief that this would assure the child of a long life. This tradition continued until it was suppressed by missionaries in the late 19th century. From the parking lot along Chain of Craters Road, a 2-mile round-trip trail leads to a boardwalk that allows for close examination of the simple yet arresting symbols and figures that tattoo the rock.

HOLEI SEA ARCH (19.6 MI.). The interplay of power between the mighty earth and sea can be witnessed at the imposing Holei Sea Arch. Perched at the boundary between the stark lava flows of the island and the churning waves of the sea, it is a testament to nature's grand architectural plan.

PUʻU Oʻo VENT (20 MI.). Chain of Craters suddenly ends where a blanket of lava sprawls out over the road. The fields of lava that stretch out along the coast from here to Kalapana, in Puna district, have sprung from Puʻu Oʻo vent, Kilauea's east rift eruption, which has been flowing continuously since 1983. The end of the road is the most convenient trailhead for setting out to where some of the world's newest land is being formed. Most often lava from the vent flows underground through established lava tubes to the coast, and rivers of molten lava streaming down the hillside is a rarer sight than some visitors expect.

MAUNA LOA ROAD

This scenic drive starts about 2 mi. west of the park entrance off of Rte. 11. The road climbs 3000 ft. through rainforest to the ◪**Mauna Loa Lookout** (13½ mi. from Rte. 11), a secluded spot perfect for a respite from a day of sightseeing. It provides an interesting perspective on the park and its surroundings. The trail for the hike to the top of Mauna Loa begins at the end of the road (see p. 298). Near the start of the road there is a turn-off for a number of **tree molds,** which are formed when lava engulfs a tree and hardens around it, creating a hollow tube once the tree burns away. A little more than 1 mi. up is **Kipuka Puaulu,** an enclave of native forest that has managed to avoid the torrents of lava that have come tearing down from Mauna Loa over the centuries. This oasis of upland forest is full of koa and ʻohiʻa trees, as well as many other native plants, insects, and birds that have been partially sheltered from invasive foreign species by the surrounding fields of lava. An easy 1.2-mile trail offers a good view of this treasure.

BIG ISLAND

GOING WITH THE FLOW Exploring lava flows requires vigilance and care—the newly formed land is highly unstable and unpredictable. The experience is unparalleled, however, and with the proper precautions should not be missed. Evening is the best time to venture out to see the fiery red of fluid earth; cracks, holes, and other flaws in the flow's crust serve as windows to subsurface activity and an orange glow is visible in many places. Before you set out, be aware of the dangers of lava. Whether the flow is 3hr. from the end of the road or 30min., it pays to heed warnings. Here are a few precautions for viewing lava safely; consult the ranger station or national park service for more information. The Visitor Center provides daily updates on eruptions and will be able to inform you of the nature of present activity.

Stay off of "benches" created by lava flowing into the sea, and don't go near the water! Benches collapse easily, and waves splashing onto molten lava can cause "tephra jets," which are small "explosions" that can scald unsuspecting onlookers.

Stay alert and prepare an escape route when walking down a moving lava flow.

Get ready! Bring water, heavy boots or shoes, a flashlight, a first-aid kit, sunscreen, long pants, a hat, and gloves. Temperatures on a flow can exceed 120°F, and many of the injuries that occur in the park—dehydration, heat exhaustion, and sunstroke—can be avoided by being informed and prepared.

◪ HIKES

The hiking in Hawaii Volcanoes National Park is some of the best on the island, and the 150 mi. of trails are the optimal way to explore the park's diverse environment. There are routes for all skill levels, including everything from easy rainforest dayhikes to intense multi-day trips to the stark terrain of Mauna Loa's summit. Whatever the adventure, some level of preparedness is always required—water, appropriate clothing, and sturdy footwear are essential. The following hikes are just a few highlights along the many miles of splendid trails.

KILAUEA IKI TRAIL. (4 mi., 2-3hr. round-trip. Trailhead: Lava Tube parking lot along Crater Rim Dr. Level: moderate.) Just over 40 years ago, the surface of Kilauea Iki Crater was a boiling lake of molten lava; today, hikers are treated to the experience of walking on what could be termed hell frozen over. This exciting, moderately challenging route—often touted as one of the best dayhikes in the park—passes through lush rainforest, along the still-steaming floor of Kilauea Iki, and by the massive Pu'u Pua'i cinder cone.

DEVASTATION TRAIL. (1 mi., 25min. round-trip. Trailhead: Devastation Trail; ends at Pu'u Pua'i Overlook parking area. Level: easy.) This self-guided trail stretches through a portion of rainforest buried in pumice cinders ejected from Kilauea Iki during the 1959 eruption. The rain of volcanic debris left only a skeleton of what was once a densely forested area. The relative verdure of the trail's surroundings are a testament to the amazing regenerative ability of the ferns, 'ohi'a, ohelo, and non-native plants that grow there.

THURSTON LAVA TUBE. (0.3 mi., 15min. round-trip. Trailhead: Thurston Lava Tube parking area. Level: easy.) In 1913, Lorrin Thurston, a local newspaper man, was the first non-native to discover this tube, and it has been a popular park attraction ever since. Lava tubes are formed when a river of hot lava cools enough so that the outer edges of the flow crust over, but the molten interior continues to move, leaving a tunnel behind. The first portion of the Thurston Tube is lit and provides a interesting perspective on the 'ohi'a forest above, the roots of which dangle

BIG ISLAND

from the ceiling. The trail to the tube then drops into a densely foliated crater, teeming with native birds. Although stairs lead back to the surface after a couple hundred yards, the tube extends another 300 ft., and the intrepid can explore the unmaintained portion of the cavern. A set of stairs leads to the tube's entrance.

HALEMA'UMA'U TRAIL. (7 mi., 6hr. round-trip. Trailhead: Volcano House Hotel. Level: moderate.) The trail traverses the smooth pahoehoe of Kilauea Caldera to Halema'uma'u Crater. From here on the caldera floor, the sheer scale of this enormous hole in the ground becomes all the more apparent, as do the heat of the sun beating down from overhead and the pervasive smell of the volcanic gases boiling up from beneath the crust.

PU'U HULUHULU. (3 mi., 3hr. round-trip. Trailhead: Mauna Ulu parking lot. Level: challenging.) Pu'u Huluhulu extends into the demanding Napau Trail (see below). This shorter trail demonstrates the diverse makeup of the region, passing by pahoehoe and a'a flows, *kipuka* (islands of forest left untouched by the onslaught), and the trail's namesake, Pu'u Huluhulu, a cinder cone that sprouts steam vents and pioneer plants with panache. On clear days, Mauna Loa, Mauna Kea, and Pu'u O'o are visible from its 300 ft. summit.

NAPAU TRAIL. (14 mi., 8-10hr. round-trip. Trailhead: Mauna Ulu parking lot along Chain of Craters Rd. Level: challenging.) Plunging directly into the heart of the action, this demanding route is the only dayhike in the park that requires hikers to register at the Visitor Center. The trail sets out over fairly recent lava flows and past a number of cinder cones and craters toward terrain replete with steaming fumeroles, gaping earthcracks, and other miracles of lava architecture.

HILINA PALI TRAIL. (16 mi., 2 days round-trip. Trailhead: Hilina Pali Overlook. Level: challenging.) In a quick descent to the ocean from Hilina Pali Overlook, the trail drops 2200 ft. in elevation as it crosses the nether regions of the Ka'u desert and Southwest Rift Zone. The daunting ascent back up to civilization encourages hikers to spend a night at the secluded oasis of Halape Beach (shelter and water catchment available).

KA'U DESERT TRAIL. (21 mi. Trailhead: Ka'u Desert Trailhead, along Rte. 11, 10 mi. west of the main park entrance.) Hikes along this trail can be as long as you make them. In its entirety, the route passes over more than 21 mi. of terrain between Crater Rim Drive and Hilina Pali Overlook, but any portion of it provides a good sense of the starkness and solitude that characterize this region of sun and rock. From the trailhead, it's an easy 1-mile walk to see the footprints left in the desert rock after the 1790 eruption of Kilauea. As the story goes, a band of warriors were traveling across the desert back to Ka'u when the volcano erupted, discharging great clouds of gas and ash that suffocated the men, forever cementing their route at the same time.

MAUNA LOA TRAIL. (36.6 mi., 3-4 days round-trip. Trailhead: Mauna Loa Strip Road. Level: challenging.) The steep 7000-foot route changes elevation on an average of 388 ft. per mile. The ascent to the summit of Mauna Loa passes through a moonscape of barren a'a and pahoehoe, creating the sensation of having left the the planet somewhere along the way. Most hikers spend a night in the cabin at Red Hill in order to pace themselves and acclimatize before topping out at Mauna Loa Cabin (13,250 ft.). If you're not blown away by the sheer immensity of Moku'aweoweo Caldera, the year-round snow storms may do the job. The ascent is recommended only for experienced and well-equipped backpackers; backcountry permit required. Those interested in ascending Mauna Loa by less rigorous means can begin at Mauna Loa Weather Observatory, accessible via Saddle Rd. (p. 302).

SOMETHING IN THE AIR Volcanic air pollution has been a problem in Hawaii since Kilauea began erupting in the 1980s; the last major alert was in 1996. The gases that are emitted with the eruptions have periodically combined with air particles to make a thick, destructive haze. The gas emissions can be damaging to breathe, cause or aggravate respiratory problems, and create acid rain. The air pollution caused by sulfur dioxide gas (SO_2) is known as volcanic smog or "vog." The steam plumes that result from hot lava meeting the sea are called "laze"–lava haze. The Hawaiian Volcano Observatory monitors the amount and composition of the emissions and works closely with government and health care professionals to keep residents and visitors informed of potential risks. For more information, contact the US Geological Survey, Hawaiian Volcano Observatory (P.O. Box 51, HVNP, HI 96718. ☎967-7328; http://volcanoes.usgs.gov).

🏛 🅾 MUSEUMS AND FESTIVALS

JAGGAR MUSEUM AND HAWAIIAN VOLCANO OBSERVATORY. The Jaggar Museum, with its excellent exhibits and earth science displays, overlooks Kilauea Caldera in all its glory. The Observatory is closed to the public, but the results of its scientific research are reflected in the museum's exhibits. *(On Crater Rim Dr. Open daily 8:30am-5pm. Admission included in park entrance fee.)*

VOLCANO ART CENTER GALLERY. Volcano Art Center Gallery, adjacent to the Kilauea Visitor Center, is a charming way to cap off a visit to the park. Over 200 local artisans display their work in what was the original Volcano House, with pieces ranging from psychedelic *Raku* pottery to richly grained bowls and figurines carved out of koa and ʻohiʻa, to vibrant paintings of the Hawaiian landscape. *(☎967-7565. Open daily 9am-5pm. AmEx/D/MC/V.)*

SPECIAL EVENTS. On most Tuesday evenings, the park holds lectures and slide presentations by guest speakers on topics ranging from water catchment to vent creation, an event known as **After Dark in the Park.** *(In the Kilauea Visitor Center Auditorium; ask at the Visitor Center for details. Tu 7pm. Free.)* One Saturday in the middle of July, the park plays host to Hawaiian artists and musicians from across the islands in a celebration of Hawaiian heritage during the **Kilauea Cultural Festival.** Hawaiian music and hula, instruction in native crafts and games as well as demonstrations of island traditions are all part of the festivities. *(On the grounds of the Kilauea Military Camp. Admission included in the park entrance fee. Check at the park information desk or online at www.nps.gov/havo for updated information on park activities.)*

VOLCANO

In the 90-odd years since nearby Hawaii Volcanoes National Park opened, the tiny, idyllic village of Volcano seems to have changed very little. Well-maintained traditional plantation homes are surrounded by lush, vibrant gardens, family-run establishments outnumber fast-food chains, and even the casual familiarity of the locals harkens back to another time. Everything about this inviting town makes it an appealing destination, and its disproportionate number of B&Bs provide ample accommodation for those who seek it.

✳ 🅿 ORIENTATION AND PRACTICAL INFORMATION

Business in Volcano centers on the **Old Volcano Hwy.** (Volcano Rd.), which ends just northeast of town. The road runs parallel to **Rte. 11;** these two main thoroughfares are connected by **Haunani Rd.** and **Wright Rd.** A car is the best option for getting to and from Volcano. Alternatively, the **Hele-On** bus runs to Hawaii Volcanoes National Park (p. 306), a one-mile walk away.

The **Volcano Visitor Center,** 19-4084 Volcano Rd., in the Volcano Village Center by Volcano True Value, only occasionally has someone manning the desk. (☎967-8662. Open daily 9am-5pm.) Many stores have **cash machines,** although there is no 24hr. ATM in town. **Volcano Wash and Dry,** is located in the Volcano Village next to Volcano True Value. (Wash $1.75; dry $1.50. Open daily 8am-7pm.) The nearest **police station** is on Old Volcano Rd. in Kea'au. **Email** junkies can get their fix at the **Lava Rock Cafe,** on Old Volcano Hwy. (☎967-8526. $2 per 15 min.; $5 per hr. Open M 7:30am-5pm, Tu-Sa 7:30am-9pm, Su 7:30am-4pm.) Head to the **Volcano Post Office,** 19-4030 Old Volcano Hwy., next to The Volcano Store for snail mail. (☎800-275-8777. Open M-F 7:30am-3:30pm, Sa 11am-noon.) **Zip Code:** 96785.

ACCOMMODATIONS

Volcano Lodging (☎800-908-9764 or 967-8617) and the Volcano Village **website** (www.hawaii-volcano.net/village) are helpful resources for finding local accommodations, as is the Volcano Visitor Center (see above).

Holo Holo Inn, 19-4036 Kalani Honua Rd. (☎967-7950 or 967-8025; holoholo@interpac.net; www.enable.org/holoholo). Coming from the park, make a left onto Old Volcano Hwy. Turn left onto Haunani Rd. just past the Volcano Store and make another left onto Kalani Honua Rd. Yabuki Satoshi, the owner/manager and long-time globetrotter, built this home from the ground up with the hope of creating a inviting spot for international travelers, and Holo Holo Inn is indeed a backpacker's dream. Spotless rooms, laundry facilities, and a spacious kitchen and dining area. Check-in 4pm-9pm. Check-out 11am. Dorm beds $17 (HI-AYH Members $15); doubles $40. No credit cards. ❶

Hale Ohia Cottages, Hale Ohia Rd. (☎800-455-3803 or 967-7986; information@haleohia.com; www.haleohia.com). From the park, toward Hilo on Rte. 11, take a right turn between Haunani Rd. and Wright Rd. This refined, yet relaxed, B&B is the best Volcano has to offer. The tranquil, elegantly furnished rooms are reminiscent of the complex's former incarnation as a summer estate. Check-in 2-5pm. Check-out 11am. Reservations recommended. Rooms $95-130. All major credit cards. ❸

Carson's Volcano Cottages, 6th St. (☎800-845-5282 or 967-7683; carsons@aloha.net; www.carsonscottage.com). From the park toward Hilo on Rte. 11, after the 26 mi. marker, turn right onto Jade Ave., then take another right onto 6th St. If you're aching for some pampering, look no further than this storybook B&B set in the heart of the Volcano rainforest. Many of the ornate rooms and cottages feature luxuries such as wood-burning stoves, goose-down comforters, terrycloth robes, and private hot tubs. Reservations recommended. Rooms $80-165; each additional person $15. All major credit cards. ❸

Kilauea Lodge, Old Volcano Hwy. (☎967-7366; stay@kilauealodge.com; www.kilauealodge.com), between Haunani Rd. and Wright Rd. Nothing about this grand Volcano Village fixture belies its past—the classy establishment was once a YMCA summer camp. Its plush rooms and award-winning restaurant ensure that you'll never be homesick. Breakfast included. Check-in 3pm. Check-out noon. Rooms $125-175; each additional person $15. AmEx/D/MC/V. ❹

My Island B&B Inn, 19-3896 Volcano Rd. (☎967-7216 or 967-7110; myisland@ilhawaii.net; www.myislandinnhawaii.com), on Old Volcano Hwy. between Wright Rd. and Pearl Ave. The Lyman family, the Big Island's first missionaries, built the main house as a summer retreat in 1886. The current owners—the Morse family—lend the inn a home-like feel. Singles $45-60, with bath $70-80; doubles $60-75, with bath $85-125. No credit cards. ❷

Aloha Junction B&B, Old Volcano Hwy. (☎888-967-7286 or 967-7289; relax@bbvolcano.com; www.bbvolcano.com), next to the post office. The lifestyle of sophistication once enjoyed by plantation owners is hard to match. Aloha Junction comes close, however, with uniquely decorated rooms, stellar breakfasts, and a garden hot tub. There's even a tree house bedroom for the young at heart. Full kitchen. Rooms $60-99; each additional person $20. MC/V. ❷

Volcano Inn, 19-3820 Old Volcano Hwy. (☎800-997-2292; 967-7293; volcano@volcanoinn.com; www.volcanoinn.com). Comprised of a number of nearby cottages in addition to the custom-designed home, this B&B is more modern than some of its neighbors. Units feature private baths, phones, refrigerators, and cable TV/VCRs. Stained-glass windows add a finishing touch in many rooms. Singles $75-90, doubles $100-105; additional guests $20. All major credit cards. ❸

🍴 FOOD

A **farmers' market** sets up shop on Sundays from 8:15am to 10:30am at the Cooper Center, near the corner of Old Volcano Hwy. and Wright Rd.

Kilauea Lodge, Old Volcano Hwy. (☎967-7366), in the heart of Volcano between Haunani and Wright Rd. The inviting feel of this posh yet casual restaurant is kindled beside the Fireplace of Friendship, where diners share portions of island-influenced European gourmet classics. Entrees $20-30. Open daily 5:30-9pm. All major credit cards. ❺

Thai Thai Restaurant, 19-4084 Volcano Rd. (☎967-7969), in the Volcano Village Center next to True Value. Hidden behind an unassuming exterior, the interesting juxtaposition of bare boards and crystal chandeliers serves to highlight the quality of the authentic Thai dishes. Massaman Curry $11; Thai Basil Stir Fry $10. Open daily 5-9pm. All major credit cards. ❷

Volcano's Lava Rock Cafe, Old Volcano Hwy. (☎967-8526), next to Kilauea General Store. Favorite fuel includes sweetbread french toast ($4.50) and grilled mahi mahi ($7). **Internet access** available. Open M 7:30am-5pm, Tu-Sa 7:30am-9pm, Su 7:30am-4pm. MC/V. ❶

SADDLE ROAD

Winding its way between the two highest points on the Big Island—**Mauna Kea** to the north and **Mauna Loa** to the south—Saddle Rd. (Rte. 200) is an adventurous journey through a topographical cross-section of Hawaii.

From the Kona Coast, the road first climbs the slopes of Mauna Kea. As the road climbs out of the rolling grasslands of Parker Ranch, the vegetation becomes gradually more sparse. About 19 mi. from the intersection of Rte. 190 and Saddle Rd. lies **Mauna Kea State Recreation Area.** John A. Burns Way, 7 mi. farther on the north side of the highway, leads up Mauna Kea to the **Onizuka Center for International Astronomy.** A graded track continues on to the mountain's summit. Once the road reaches Mauna Loa, there is an abrupt change in landscape. The gradual incline up to the distant summit of Mauna Loa is a mishmash of a'a and pahoehoe fields, punctuated only by a few brave 'ohi'a. A few hundred yards from the turn to the Mauna Kea summit, a rough track heads south to the **Mauna Loa Weather Observatory** on the upper slopes of the mountain. From here, Saddle Rd. begins to drop down toward Hilo in a series of heart-pounding twists and turns. The challenge of driving is increased by the fog—it can be so thick that it's hard to see the road in front of you. The flora is luxuriant and deep, deep green with the addition of all this moisture as the road descends toward the Pacific.

On the Kona side, Saddle Rd. leaves Rte. 190 about 6 mi. south of Waimea and 33 mi. northeast of Kailua-Kona. On the windward side, Waianuenue Ave. splits just above downtown Hilo and forms Kaumana Dr., which becomes Saddle Rd. in the foothills outside of town. Saddle Rd. stretches 54 mi. from end to end.

Be prepared for a rough ride; the highway gets heavy use from tanks and other military vehicles commuting between Kawaihae Harbor and Pohakuloa Military Training Area, located along the lower slopes of both mountains. Almost all rental car companies, except for local **Harper Car and Truck Rentals** (see p. 284), forbid travel on Saddle Rd. While this scares away many visitors, the restriction has little to do with the condition of the road and much more with its distance from towing companies, who charge $300 for any job there. If you're willing to foot the bill in the event of a road emergency, this drive should not be missed. Come well prepared with plenty of gas, water, and warm clothes.

MAUNA KEA

At a towering 13,796 ft., Mauna Kea, or "White Mountain," is taller than many mainland mountains. Yet despite its size, Mauna Kea is known for a less readily apparent feature. The dry, stable air of the summit, as well as the extremely dark sky above it, makes for some of the world's best astronomical viewing conditions.

The Onizuka Center for International Astronomy, located from a turnoff at the 28 mile-marker, educates visitors about the high-tech telescopes located at the summit. John A. Burns Way leads just over 6 miles to the center, climbing almost 3000 ft. and yielding impressive views of the "saddle" between the mountains, Mauna

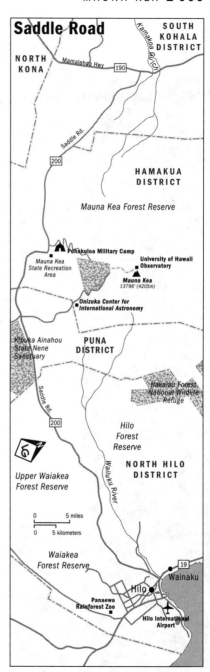

Saddle Road

Loa, and the smaller cinder cones perched on Mauna Kea's slopes. The only real hazard along this section of Saddle Rd. is the free-roaming cattle.

🜨 SIGHTS

MAUNA KEA STATE RECREATION AREA. Located near mile-marker 35, 25 mi. southeast of Waimea and 7 mi. west of the Mauna Kea summit road, this simple park is a good place to base Saddle Rd. explorations. The park has rest rooms, picnic tables, and a pay phone, in addition to a short hike that features great views of Mauna Kea, Hulalai, and Mauna Loa. There are also 7 **cabins** with kitchens, bathrooms, and showers available for rent. *(To reserve a cabin, call the Department of Land and Natural Resources, State Parks Division, 75 Apuni St. ☎ 974-6200. $45 per night.)*

ONIZUKA CENTER FOR INTERNATIONAL ASTRONOMY. Perched on the slopes of Mauna Kea at 9200 ft., this **Visitor Information Center** for the summit telescopes is an invaluable resource. The center is named after **Ellison Onizuka,** an astronaut from the Big Island who died in the 1986 Challenger explosion. A number of exhibits detail the form and function of the summit's 13 telescopes, which range from the dual 390-inch Keck telescopes that allow for binocular-like focus, to Japan's Subaru, which, at 27 ft. in diameter, is the world's largest optical telescope. Displays provide introductions to astronomy and Mauna Kea's natural history.

The center also practices astronomy on a more grass roots level, with nightly **stargazing** sessions. The program begins with an orientation video, which is followed by a discussion of astronomy and Mauna Kea. Then, using several small telescopes (11-16 in.), visitors are able to observe an array of stellar phenomena, including globular clusters, supernova remnants, and white dwarfs. It is crucial to dress warmly; temperatures range from 40 to 50° F during the summer and 25 to 50° F during the winter. If you have your own 4WD vehicle, consider going on one of the Center's **summit tours.** The 4hr. tour includes an orientation video and acclimatization period, caravan ride to the summit, an overview of all the telescopes, as well as a guided visit to one or two of them. *(From Saddle Rd., turn onto John A. Burns Way at the 28-mile marker. The center is a little over 6 mi. down the road. ☎ 961-2180; mkvis@ifa.hawaii.edu; www.ifa.hawaii.edu. Center open M-F 9am-noon, 1-5pm, 6-10pm; Sa-Su 9am-10pm. Free. Coffee, hot chocolate, tea and snacks are available at the center. Stargazing daily 6-10pm. Free. Summit tours Sa-Su 1-5pm. Free. Children under 16 and pregnant women are not allowed on the tours because of high-altitude health hazards.)*

DRIVING TO THE SUMMIT. If you have a 4WD vehicle, you can drive to the top yourself. Visitors are allowed on the summit only from sunrise to sunset as car headlights interfere with the observations after dark. The road to the observatories is well-maintained but unpaved until the last few miles and, because of its fantastically steep grade, is suitable only for 4WD vehicles. **Harper Car and Truck Rental** (see p. 284) rents vehicles suitable for the Mauna Kea ascent. The drive from the Onizuka Center to the summit is 6½ mi. and should take about 30min. Once there, the University of Hawaii telescope and the WM Keck Observatory both have **Visitor Centers.** For all the technological wizardry of the amazing telescopes, however, the sky is amazing even to the naked eye.

The air on the summit has only 60% of the oxygen available at sea level, causing many people to suffer from altitude sickness at the summit. Pregnant women, children, individuals who are overweight or in poor health, and those with a history of heart or respiratory problems are advised not to make the trip.

■ HIKING

MAUNA KEA TRAIL. (6 mi. Trailhead: Onizuka Center. Elevation change: 4500 ft. Level: challenging.) The Mauna Kea Trail climbs from the Onizuka Center to the summit and takes around 4 hours to complete. The path is itself is marked with posts and rock *ahus*, or cairns, and essentially parallels the summit road. Given the altitude and elevation gain, this is an extremely difficult hike, but it provides an intimate view of the mountain's topography, as well as stunning views. Among the unique sights are the eerie landscapes of the Mauna Kea Ice Age Natural Area Reserve. In addition, the trail leads straight to magical Lake Waiau, the third-highest lake in the US, located at 13,020 ft. amidst Mauna Kea's lava fields.

■ TOURS

Paradise Safaris leads nightly tours to the summit for sunset viewing and stargazing. The trips include pick-up at various spots along the Kona and Kohala Coasts, hooded parkas, and a light supper. (☎322-2366. $150.) The knowledgeable guides from **Arnott's Lodge,** 98 Apapane Rd., in Hilo, lead trips from Hilo to Mauna Kea for sunsets and stargazing several times a week. (☎969-7097; info@arnottslodge.com; www.arnottslodge.com. M, W, F departure time seasonally adjusted. $75 for non-lodge guests.) **Mauna Kea Mountain Bikes,** allows you to plunge off the top of Mauna Kea on a 7000 ft. descent to Saddle Rd. They drive you to the top, follow you down, and provide all the equipment you need. (☎888-682-8687 or 883-0130; mtbtour@aol.com; www.BikeHawaii.com. $120.) **Mauna Kea Ski** makes the most of the winter months by providing ski and snowboard tours on the mountain, led by experienced guides. (☎885-4188; www.skihawaii.com. Tours $250-450.)

WAIKI'I MUSIC FESTIVAL Over the second weekend in June each year, a who's-who list of Hawaiian musicians gather at the Waiki'i Ranch Polo Field to revel in two days worth of the Island's best music. The festival, which has been held since 1991, is the largest outdoor Hawaiian cultural event on the Big Island, creating a veritable Hawaiian Woodstock on this spot high on the Saddle Rd., with stars of Hawaiian Music such as Darlene Ahuna, Pati, and Three Plus. In addition to the music, the festival features authentic Hawaiian displays, crafts, food, and hands-on demonstrations. *(Call ☎883-2077 for more information. Tickets $20-25 a day, children under 12 free.)*

BIG ISLAND

MAUNA LOA

Just east of the Mauna Kea turnoff, a serpentine road climbs the Mauna Loa shelf volcano 7 miles to the **Mauna Loa Weather Observatory,** 11,000 ft. above sea level. The drive takes about 45min. and although the road is slowly crumbling, it is passable in any car. The observatory is purely scientific in its objectives and there is no Visitor Center of any kind, so be sure to arrive prepared.

■ HIKING

OBSERVATORY TRAIL. (5½ mi. one-way. Level: challenging. Trailhead: Mauna Loa Weather Observatory. Elevation change: 2500 ft.) The paved road terminates at the observatory and the beginning of the hike to the summit of Mauna Loa or the cabin on the opposite rim of **Moku'aweoweo Caldera.** There is nothing easy about this hike; a good portion of your time is sure to be spent scrambling across the precariously loose rubble of a'a fields and temperatures consistently drop below freezing on the summit. Inclement weather is common here, and picturesque skies are the exception rather than the rule on Mauna Loa. Still, for all the obstacles of the trail, the gaping expanse of the Mauna Loa summit is well worth any hardship suffered along the way. For more information about hiking Mauna Loa see **Hawaii Volcanoes National Park,** p. 306.

PUNA

Puna was the Wild West for hippie-cowboys of the 1960s—and still is for those stuck in the era. Attracted by an ever-expanding frontier of lava flows from Mauna Loa and Kilauea, individuals from all walks of life come here for modern-day prospecting, staking claim to land made inexpensive by the constant threat of lava flows. Yet the agricultural reality of this day and age means that many of these pastoral idealists are more likely to be singing "I Shot the Sheriff" than "Home on the Range." Marijuana cultivation has become such a mainstay over the years that the district is know for its own variety of *pakololo*, Puna Butter. While the region has much to offer when it comes to raw experiences with nature, from the volcanic fireworks of the lava flow in the west to the black sand beaches and thermal springs on the eastern coast, the fiercely independent nature of the environment and the people who live here does not lend itself to haphazard exploration. You're likely to ruffle some feathers or worse if you step on locals' toes (or on their plants). Still, the atmosphere in Puna is changing as viable crops, such as papaya, are being grown on a larger scale, and gentrification has allowed grass to grow even on lava-covered land.

PAHOA

Pahoa's elevated boardwalks and large wooden facades, vestiges of its heyday during the sugar industry boom, still line the town's historic main street, lending the place an Old West feel. Although dreadlocks and tie-dye take precedence over Stetsons and Wranglers, it's hard to make any generalizations about Pahoa—its melange of residents include Hilo professionals, native Hawaiians, and displaced mid-Western farmers eking out a living on Hawaiian land. Pahoa's lack of commercialism is a refreshing change from the rest of Hawaii, and visitors can revel in the fact that there isn't a McDonald's in sight.

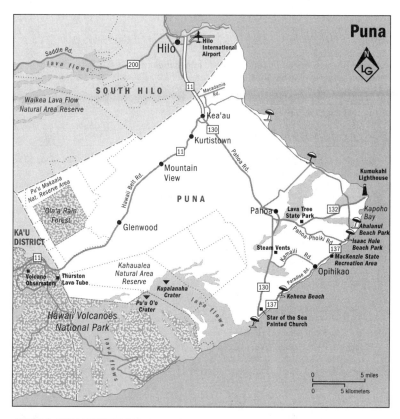

ORIENTATION AND PRACTICAL INFORMATION

Pahoa is located off of **Hwy. 130** (Pahoa Rd.) just west of its intersection with **Hwy. 132** (Pahoa-Kapoho Rd.), a little less than 20 mi. south of Hilo. The town's main drag is **Government Main Rd.,** home to everything from 7-Eleven to Pahoa Natural Groceries.

Pahoa Natural Groceries doubles as the seat of Pahoa's sparse public transportation system; the **Hele-On** bus (☎961-8744) leaves from its doorstep for **Hilo** (1½hr., M-Sa 6:05am, $2.25). **Carl's Taxi** (☎990-RIDE) runs the only local taxi service, in classic London taxi cabs, for $2 per mile.

While there is no official tourist office in Pahoa, **Pahoa Natural Emporium** on Government Main Rd. is a good resource for information. (☎965-6634; open daily 10am-6pm.) Both **Bank of Hawaii** on Government Main Rd. (☎965-9511; open M-Th 8:30am-4pm, F 8:30am-6pm) and **First Hawaiian Bank** on Puna Coastal Pkwy. (☎965-8621; open M-Th 8:30am-4pm, F 8:30am-6pm) have **24hr. ATMs.** Free **Internet access** is available to Hawaii library card holders at **Pahoa Public Library,** 15-3070 Pahoa-Kalapana Rd. adjacent to the school at the intersection of Hwy. 132 and Hwy. 130. (☎965-2171; open M 1-8pm, Tu-Th 10am-5pm, F 9:30am-4:30pm, Sa 9am-noon.) Aloha Outpost, 15-2937 Pahoa Village Rd., behind Big Jake's Island BBQ, offers **Internet access** on brand-new computers. (Open M-F 8am-4pm, Sa 10am-4pm.)

Check out **Suds 'N Duds,** Pahoa Village Center, on the Hilo-side of town, to wash all your hemp clothing. (☎965-8881. Wash $1.25-2; dry 25¢ per 5min. Open daily 7:30am-7:30pm.) There is a **free public swimming pool** behind Pahoa Cash & Carry. (Open daily 1:45-4pm.)

Other local services include: **weather information** at ☎935-8555; a sporadically-manned **police satellite station** on Government Main Rd. across from Pahoa Hardware; **Pahoa Rx Pharmacy,** in the Pahoa Village Center (☎965-7535); and the **Pahoa Post Office,** 15-2859 Puna Rd. (☎800-275-8777. Open M-F 8:30am-4pm, Sa 11am-2pm.) **Zip Code:** 96778.

ACCOMMODATIONS

Kalani Oceanside Retreat, RR2 Box 4500 Pahoa-Beach Rd. (☎800-800-6886 or 965-7828; info@kalani.com; www.kalani.com), on Hwy. 137 along the Puna coast. This oasis of community and creativity is a unique experience, with a little something for everyone. Spectacular oceanfront setting, sumptuous vegetarian cuisine, and a plethora of available classes (yoga, dance, and *watsu*) and educational adventures. Their 1- or 3-month volunteer program provides a unique **short-term work** alternative; see the website for details and application. Reservations recommended. Campsites $20, dorm rooms $60. Rooms with shared bath $135; with private bath $135-240. All major credit cards. ❹

Hale Makamae B&B, 13-3315 Makamae St. (☎965-9090; info@bnb-aloha.com; www.bnb-aloha.com). From Pahoa, head southwest on Hwy. 130. Make a left onto Leilani Ave. after mile-marker 13. After several blocks, make another left on Makamae St. The B&B is at the end of the road on the right. With welcoming hosts, spacious suites, and a secluded setting, staying at this B&B feels more like living in Puna than merely visiting. All rooms have their own entrances and private baths. Doubles $55-85; each additional person $10. MC/V. ❷

Pineapple Park Hostel, 11-3489 Pikake St. (☎877-865-2266 or 968-8170). Heading west on Rte. 11, turn left onto South Kalani Rd. after mile-marker 13. At the T-junction, turn right on Pohala St., and follow it to the end of the pavement before turning left onto Pikake St. Despite distance, Pineapple Park is the best budget accommodation in Puna, and well worth the trip. Features a large kitchen, BBQ, laundry facilities, Internet access, and clean bunks. Be sure to check out the converted sleeper buses out back. Ask about the possibility of trading a bed for a few hours of housekeeping a week. Dorms $20, buses $35, private rooms $40 and up. MC/V. ❶

Pahoa Orchid Inn, Government Main Rd. (☎965-9664; pahoaorchidinn@tourquoise.net; www.pahoaorchidinn.com), upstairs from Luquin's on Government Main Rd. Downtown Pahoa's only accommodation puts on no airs, offering convenience and reasonable prices. Rooms $35-55, with private bath $65. All major credit cards. ❷

FOOD

Pahoa Farmers' Market, held on Sundays from 7am-1pm in the heart of downtown, is a great place to find fresh produce.

Pahoa Natural Groceries, 15-1403 Government Main Rd. (☎965-6263), next to the Pahoa Natural Emporium. This sparkling store is ready to supply all the ingredients for whatever tempeh-tofu-alfalfa sprout concoction you've got in the works, or can nourish you with tasty sandwiches and imported beers if (and when) your culinary skills desert you. Open M-Sa 7:30am-8pm, Su 7:30am-6pm.

Paolo's Bistro, 333 Government Main Rd. (☎965-7033). Simplicity is the name of the game here. The short, straightforward menu, minimal decor, and elementary table settings all serve to highlight the main attraction: the delicious food. Entrees $9-19. Open Tu-Sun 5:30-9pm. MC/V. ❷

Pahoa Fresh Fish, 15-2925 Government Main Rd. (☎965-9898). If you're hankering for something unpretentious and fresh, look no further than this little joint—that's what they do best. Fish & Chips $8; ½ order $5. Open daily 9am-7pm. No credit cards. ❷

Luquin's Mexican Restaurant, Government Main Rd. (☎965-9990), in the heart of downtown. While Mexico may be *muy lejos,* Luquin's manages to evoke memories of that night in Tijuana. Enchiladas to *huevos rancheros*—and everything in between. Entrees $6.50-16.25. Open daily 7am-9pm. All major credit cards. ❷

🔯 SIGHTS

From Pahoa, Highways 132, 135/137, and 130 create a scenic triangle that captures many of Puna's natural wonders.

LAVA TREE STATE PARK. In a staggering synergy of geology and biology, a forest of lava trunks can be seen on the short paved walk from the parking area. These fantastic shapes were formed when a river of lava on its way to the coast ran into a large grouping of 'ohi'a. The trees were large enough that the lava cooled around them to form a crust, rather than tearing them down. *(Heading south on Hwy. 132, giant albizia trees arch over the road, leading to a turnoff to Lava Tree State Park 2 mi. down the road, on the left. The park has restrooms and picnic facilities.)*

KUMUKAHI LIGHTHOUSE. The old lighthouse has been replaced by a new contraption of steel, but you can still see where the flow from a 1960 eruption broke into two, sparing the original structure. Legend holds that days before the eruption, the lighthouse keeper had been visited by an old woman looking for something to eat. He granted her request and when she took her leave, she told him that no harm would come to the lighthouse if he placed mint at its corners. With the flow bearing down on him soon after, he took her advice, and amazingly the flow split. *(After passing fields, Hwy. 132 intersects Hwy. 135. about 6 mi. down the road. Continue straight ahead to the Kumukahi Lighthouse.)*

ALANUIHAHA PARK. Alanuihaha Park is one of the few places on the southeast coast that has protected swimming, and the park is popular among folks from all over Puna. The highlight of the park is a large hot pond, a mixing pot for volcanic hot springs and the incoming tide. *(Just after the 10-mile marker on Hwy. 135. Park open daily 7am-7pm, lifeguard on duty 9:30am-4:45pm.)*

ISAAC HALE BEACH PARK. The Beach Park is the center of all oceanborne activity for Puna and a favorite local camping spot. While the churning waves are only attractive to local surfers, it's an interesting place to get a sense of the way that many Puna folks interact with the natural environment. *(Less than 1 mi. down the road from Alanuihaha, near the junction of Hwy. 135, Hwy. 137, and Pahoa-Pohoiki Rd.)*

MACKENZIE STATE RECREATION AREA. Set on cliffs above the crashing sea in a stand of shady ironwood trees, this area is quiet and secluded—the best place along the coast for visitors to camp. *(A couple of miles down Hwy. 135 from Issac Hale.)*

KEHENA BEACH. Hidden Kehena Beach is one of the island's finest volcanic beaches, and a clothes-optional wonderland of black sand, palm trees, and dolphins. The road (Hwy. 135) abruptly comes to a halt near where the town of Kalapana once stood. There's nothing left now except for acres of the Big Island's newest land and **Verna's Drive-In** (☎965-8234), where you can buy a burger and ice cream, and look out over the flow. *(5½ mi. down the road across from the 19-mile marker.)*

STAR OF THE SEA PAINTED CHURCH. Saved from the 1990 flow that wiped out Kalapana, this amazing piece of Hawaiiana with spectacular paintings and unique stained-glass windows must be seen to be believed. *(Take Hwy. 130 back toward Pahoa from Kehena Beach; the church will be on your left. Open daily 9am-4pm.)*

STEAM VENTS. The steam vents make a perfect natural sauna after a hard day of soaking up rays and frolicking in the warm Hawaiian waters. *(A little way off Hwy. 130, a few miles short of town.)*

KAILUA-KONA

Kailua-Kona, or Kona as it is most popularly known, is the Big Island's tourist capital. The town owes its popularity to one fact: it enjoys more sun day in and day out than anywhere else in the islands. Once the seat of Hawaii's royalty, Kailua-Kona is now a vacation hotbed, with condo after condo hovering over the narrow shoreline. As an inevitable result of this expansion of tourism, larger and larger malls have popped up in the foothills.

■ ORIENTATION

Kailua-Kona lies on the western, leeward coast of the Big Island, almost due west of Hilo, 87 mi. away. **Mamalahoa Hwy.** (Rte. 11), which makes up part of the Hawaii Belt Road, is the main artery from the south. From the north, there are two main roads: **Queen Ka'ahumanu Hwy.** (Rte. 19), the northern extension of Rte. 11 that hugs the coast up into Kohala; and Rte. 190, a portion of the **Hawaii Belt Road** that heads inward to Waimea. Downtown is comprised of relatively few roads. **Ali'i Dr.,** unquestionably the main drag, traces the coastline southward to Keauhou Bay, and houses more Hawaiian shirt stores and restaurants with mai tai specials than you'd care to imagine. **Kuakini Hwy.,** lined with gas stations and shopping malls, parallels Ali'i off the coast. **Palani Rd.** is the town's major cross street and runs into the northern end of Ali'i Dr. The major shopping centers line Rte. 19 and Rte.11.

■ TRANSPORTATION

INTERCITY TRANSPORTATION

Buses: Public transportation around the Big Island is minimal. The sole option for long distances is the **Hele-On Bus** (☎961-8744), which runs from the Lanihau Center on Palani Rd. to **Waimea** and **Hilo** (M-Sa 6:45am, $5.25).

LOCAL TRANSPORTATION

Public Transportation: The **Ali'i Shuttle** (☎775-7121 or 938-1112) runs a route between the Lanihau Center on Palani Rd. and the defunct Kona Surf Resort on Keauhou Bay (45min.; M-Sa 8:30am-7:40pm; $2, $5 per day).

Taxis: Aloha Taxi, ☎329-7779 or 325-5448. **C&C Taxi,** ☎329-6388. **D&E Taxi** (☎329-4279) provides island-wide service. All taxis provide metered service with a $2 initial charge and a rate of $2 per mile. The fixed rate between the airport and town is $20. Taxis run from 6am-10pm.

Car Rental: At the airport. **Alamo Rent a Car,** ☎800-327-9633 or 329-8896; fax 329-2671. Open 5:30am-9:30pm. **Avis Rent a Car,** ☎800-321-3712 or 327-3005; fax 327-3009. 25+. **Budget Car Rental,** ☎800-527-7000 or 329-8511; fax 329-6169.

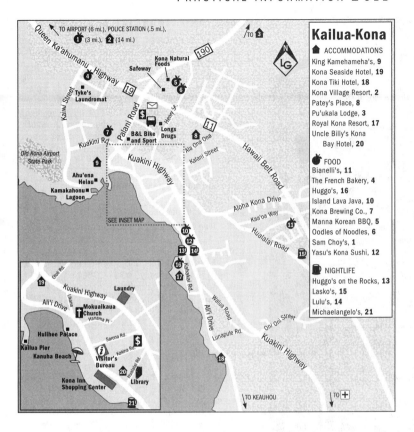

TO AIRPORT (6 mi.), POLICE STATION (.5 mi.),
Queen Ka'ahumanu Highway
1 (3 mi.), 2 (14 mi.)

Kona Natural Foods
Safeway
190

Kaiwi Street
Tyke's Laundromat
19

Palani Road
Henry St.
Longs Drugs
B&L Bike and Sport
7
Kuakini Rd.

Old Kona Airport State Park

Kuakini Highway

Ahu'ena Heiau
Kamakahonu Lagoon
9

SEE INSET MAP

Ala Ona Ona
Kalani Street
11
8

Hawaii Belt Road

Aloha Kona Drive
Kaa'oa Way
Hualalai Road
11

10
12
13
14

16
17

Oloi Rd.
19
Kuakini Highway
Uluna
Ali'i Drive
Laundry

Mokuaikaua Church
Hanama Pl.

Hulihee Palace
Sarona Rd.
Kailua Pier
Kanuha Beach
Kona Inn Shopping Center

i
Visitor's Bureau
20
Kakina Rd.
Hinalea Rd.
Library

Kahakai Rd.

Wailua Road
Ali'i Drive
Lunapule Rd.
Oni Oni Street
Kuakini Highway
18

21

TO KEAUHOU

TO 3
N
LG

Kailua-Kona

▲ ACCOMMODATIONS
King Kamehameha's, **9**
Kona Seaside Hotel, **19**
Kona Tiki Hotel, **18**
Kona Village Resort, **2**
Patey's Place, **8**
Pu'ukala Lodge, **3**
Royal Kona Resort, **17**
Uncle Billy's Kona Bay Hotel, **20**

🍎 FOOD
Bianelli's, **11**
The French Bakery, **4**
Huggo's, **16**
Island Lava Java, **10**
Kona Brewing Co., **7**
Manna Korean BBQ, **5**
Oodles of Noodles, **6**
Sam Choy's, **1**
Yasu's Kona Sushi, **12**

🍸 NIGHTLIFE
Huggo's on the Rocks, **13**
Lasko's, **15**
Lulu's, **14**
Michaelangelo's, **21**

Open daily 5am-9pm. **Dollar Rent a Car,** ☎800-800-4000 or 329-2746; fax 329-4231. **Hertz Rent a Car,** ☎800-654-3011 or 329-3567; fax 329-7430. 25+. **National Car Rental,** ☎800-227-7368 or 327-3755; fax 326-2567. Open daily 5am-9pm. **Thrifty Car Rental,** ☎800-367-2277 or 329-1339; fax 334-1955. Open daily 5:45am-9pm. Unless otherwise noted, all of the above are open daily 5am-9:30pm and rent to those 21+. For deals try **AA Aloha Cars-R-Us,** ☎800-655-7989 or 879-7989.

Bike Rental: B&L Bike & Sports, 75-5699 Kopiko Pl. (☎329-3309), off of Palani Rd. in the center of town, rents bikes from $30 per day to $500 per month. Open M-F 9am-6pm, Sa 9am-5pm, Su 10am-4pm.

🛈 PRACTICAL INFORMATION

As there is no state-run visitor center in Kailua-Kona, numerous time-share centers up and down Ali'i Dr. have filled the gap by hawking various restaurants and activities along with their properties. The nearest non-partisan visitor resource is the **Big Island Visitors Bureau,** 250 Waikola Beach Dr., Ste. B15, in the Kings' Shops at Waikola Beach Resort, 25 mi. north of town off of Queen Ka'ahumanu Hwy. (☎886-1655; fax 886-1652; www.bigisland.org. Open M-F 8am-4:30pm.)

THE BIG SPLURGE

KONA VILLAGE RESORT

Built on the site of an ancient Hawaiian fishing village, the resort has a connection with the past that comes out in nearly every aspect of its character. Each of the thatched roof cottages, or *hale*, that graces the 82-acre property incorporates construction styles and designs from around Polynesia. They are individually decorated with fine artwork and furniture, but the noticeably-absent televisions and telephones are even more striking. Among the luxuries that may be included in packages are snorkeling or kayaking in the protected bay, tennis courts, a fitness center, and three meals a day. The Friday night luau is considered to be among the best on the island. *(Ka'upulehu Dr., 14 mi. north of downtown off Queen Ka'ahumanu Hwy. ☎325-5555 or 800-367-5290; kvr@aloha.net; www.konavillage.com. Reception 24hr. Check-in and check-out times flexible. Reservations required. Double occupancy rooms $495-870, additional adults $193; children ages 6-12 $143, ages 3-5 $38. All major credit cards.)*

TOURIST AND FINANCIAL SERVICES

Tours: Eco-Adventures, King Kamehameha's Kona Beach Hotel (☎329-7116 or 800-949-3483; ecodive@kona.net; www.eco-adventure.com), offers **scuba-diving** adventures for every skill level, including certification courses led by an experienced, professional staff. Expect to pay around $100 for introductory dives. Experienced divers shouldn't miss the night dives, which allow for close encounters with **manta rays.** Travelers with SCUBA instructor certification might start here if searching for short-term work in the area, as Eco-Adventures may be able to place divers with other companies.

Equipment Rental: Snorkel Bob's, 75-5831 Kahakai Rd. (☎329-0770). Snorkel gear rentals $2.50-6.50 per day, $9-39 per week. Open daily 8am-5pm.

Banks: Bank of Hawaii, 75-5595 Palani Rd. (☎326-3900), next to the Lanihau Center **exchanges currency** and offers a healthy selection of all the **ATM** networks. Open M-Th 8:30am-4pm, F 8:30am-6pm. There's also a branch in the **Safeway** (☎326-3966) on Henry St. with extended hours and limited services. Open M-F 10am-7pm, Sa-Su 10am-3pm. Just up the road, **First Hawaiian Bank,** 74-5593 Palani Rd. (☎329-2461), offers similar services. Open M-Th 8:30am-4pm, F 8:30-6pm, Sa 9am-1pm.

LOCAL SERVICES

Bookstore: Protest globalization and browse an extensive selection of Hawaiiana at the **Middle Earth Bookshoppe,** 75-5719 Ali'i Dr. (☎329-2123), in the Kona Plaza Shopping Arcade. Open daily 9am-9pm. If you can't help yourself, **Borders Books, Music & Cafe,** 75-1000 Henry Rd. (☎331-1668), is at the corner of Henry and Rte. 11. Open Su-Th 9am-9pm, F-Sa 9am-10pm.

Library: Kailua-Kona Public Library (☎327-4327), on Hualalai Rd. between Kuakini Hwy. and Ali'i Dr., offers free **Internet access** for Hawaii State Public Library card holders. Open Tu 10am-8pm, W-Th 9am-6pm, F 11am-5pm, Sa 9am-5pm.

Laundromat: Tyke's Laundromat, 74-5483 Kaiwi St. (☎326-1515). Wash $1-3 per load. Dry 25¢ per 7min. Open daily 6:30am-9:30pm.

Weather Conditions: ☎961-5582.

EMERGENCY AND COMMUNICATIONS

Emergency: ☎911.

Police: Kealakehe Station (☎326-4646), on Queen Ka'ahumanu Hwy. about 1 mi. north of town, next to the Kealakehe Transfer Station.

WHAT'S IN A NAME?

Kona or Kailua? The double name suits the dual nature of the Big Island's tourist capital. **Kailua,** as the town was originally called, has had a long history at the center of things. Hawaiian royalty ruled from this portion of the coast before the arrival of *haoles*, and Kailua Bay was later chosen as the spot of the first Western settlement on the island. During the last half of the 19th century the town was the hub of trade for the windward coast; Kailua Pier served as a death row for island cattle that were destined for Honolulu's slaughterhouses.

Today, cruise ships replace the freighters that once graced the bay, just as most of the family-run shops and wooden store fronts of the city's historic downtown have given way to chain stores hawking silk leis and helicopter rides. Like mom-and-pop shops have lost out to chain stores, so Kailua has lost out to Kona. The hyphenated name first came about when Kailua began to vie for inter-island and international limelight, and had to compete with another Kailua on Oahu. **Kona,** which literally means "windward," describes Hawaii's entire western coast, but over the last quarter of a century, as tourism has dwarfed all other industries here, the name has come to be synonymous with the town itself.

Sexual Assault Crisis Line: ☎935-0677

Pharmacy: Long's Drugs, 75-5595 Palani Rd. (☎329-1380), in the Lanihau Center. Open M-Sa 8am-9pm, Su 8am-6pm.

Hospital: Kona Community Hospital, Rte. 11 (☎322-9311), 15 mi. south of Kailua-Kona in Kealakekua.

Internet Access: Island Lava Java, 75-5799 Ali'i Dr. (☎327-2161), in Ali'i Sunset Plaza. $3 per 15min. Open daily 6am-10pm.

Post Office: Kailua-Kona Post Office, 74-5577 Palani Rd. (☎800-275-8777), next to the Lanihau Center. Open M-F 8:30am-4pm, Sa 9am-1:30pm.

Zip Code: 96740.

⛰ ACCOMMODATIONS

CONDOS

Visitors who plan to stay for more than a few days can find a better deal with condos than with the hoards of beach hotels and resorts that line Ali'i Dr.

Hawaii Resort Management, 75-5776 Kuakini Hwy. (☎800-622-5348 or 329-3333; fax 326-4137; kona@konahawaii.com; www.konahawaii.com) in the Kona Islander Inn. Offers condos in a number of complexes, including the oceanfront Kona Magic Sands, Kona Billfisher, and Kona Islander Inn. 3-night minimum stay. Apr.1-Dec. 15 $35-75, weekly $245-495. Dec. 15-Mar. 31 $69-95, weekly $345-695. ❸

Knutson & Associates, 75-6082 Ali'i Dr. (☎800-800-6202 or 329-6311; fax 326-2178; knutson@aloha.net; www.konahawaiirentals.com), in the Casa de Emdeko mall. Offers slightly more upscale options, including the Kona Riviera and Casa de Emdeko. 3-night minimum stay. Apr.1-Dec.15 $85-110, weekly $595-840. Dec. 15-Mar. 31 $95-130/$665-910. ❸

HOTELS

Kona Tiki Hotel, 75-5968 Ali'i Dr. (☎329-1425). Ali'i Dr.'s only small-scale, independently-owned hotel, Kona Tiki offers 15 airy rooms with lanais at a prime oceanfront location. Reservations essential. Reception 7am-7pm. Check-in 3pm. Check-out 11am.

THE BIG SPLURGE

HUGGO'S

The rattan chairs and gleaming wood of Huggo's recall an era in Hawaii when plantations were a way of life and ocean voyages were taken out of necessity rather than choice. It's hard to imagine that they ate as well though. With an impressive wine list and creative bar to go along with fresh catches such as Crab Crusted Ono and Chipolte Mahi Mahi, this is Kona's finest restaurant. *(75-5828 Kahakai Rd. ☎329-1493. Lunch salads and sandwiches $9-14. Appetizers $4.50-12. Entrees $20-46. Open daily 5:30-10pm, M-F 11:30am-2:30pm. All major credit cards.)*

Doubles with queen bed $59; queen and twin $65, with kitchenette $70; each additional guest $8, ages 2-12 $6. No credit cards. ❷

Pu'ukala Lodge, Mamalahoa Hwy. (☎325-1729 or 888-325-1729; Puukala1@aol.com; www.Puukala-lodge.com), 7 mi. from downtown off of Palani Rd. Call for directions. This simple bed and breakfast, located on the lush slopes of Mt. Hualalai, is a world away from the hustle and bustle of downtown. The knowledgeable owners give an insider's perspective on the Big Island. Breakfast included. 2-night minimum stay. Reservations recommended. Doubles $75-110; each additional guest $25. ❸

Kona Seaside Hotel, 75-5646 Palani Rd. (☎329-2455; www.konaseasidehotel.com). This sprawling complex is downtown's best value. The simple rooms feature the conveniences (or necessities, depending on your perspective) of A/C, cable television, mini-fridges and two pools, as well as an excellent location above Ali'i Dr. Reception 24hr. Check-in 3pm. Check-out noon. Doubles start at $64. All major credit cards. ❷

Patey's Place, 75-195 Ala Ona Ona St. (☎326-7018; fax 326-7640; ipatey@gte.net; www.hawaiian-hostels.com). Head south from the corner of Palani Rd. and Kuakini Hwy. Take a left onto Kalani St. at the McDonald's and turn left again onto Alahou St., followed by a right onto Ala Ona Ona St. The town's only hostel caters to a transient backpacker set. The two-building complex is adorned with 24 ocean murals, and provides a kitchen, TV room, washing machines, and Internet ($5 per hr.). They occasionally offer opportunities for **short-term work.** Shared bathrooms. Bedding included. Airport shuttle $10. Reception 8:30am-1:30pm and 4:30-10pm. Check-out 10am. Dorms $20; singles $35; doubles $46, with TV $50. MC/V. ❶

Royal Kona Resort, 75-5822 Ali'i Dr. (☎800-222-5642 or 329-3111; www.HawaiianHotels.com). This large, oceanfront resort just south of downtown dates back to Kona's 1980s tourism boom. The Miami Vice-esque aqua carpets and dark woods of the rooms do little to shrug the association, but the resort's many amenities make it the ritziest accommodation in Kailua-Kona proper. Reception 24hr. Check-in 3pm. Check-out noon. Rooms $89-205. ❸

Uncle Billy's Kona Bay Hotel, 75-5739 Ali'i Drive (☎800-367-5102 or 329-1393). The hotel is a little out of place among the town's resorts and sparkling new chains, and the rooms have seen a lot of wear, but each have a private lanai and all the creature comforts you could want, including mini-fridges, cable TV, central A/C, a pool, and free parking. Reception 24hr. Check-in 3pm. Check-out noon. Rooms start at $69. D/MC/V. ❸

King Kamehameha's Kona Beach Hotel, 75-5660 Palani Rd. (☎329-2911). The King Kamehameha occupies a prime piece of real estate at the northern end of Kailua Bay and Ali'i Dr., ideal for beachfront activities and pool-side lounging. The interior is not quite as inviting, however, despite the mini-fridges and coffee makers. Reception 24hr. Check-in 3pm. Check-out noon. Rates $90-200, depending on view. ❸

◪ FOOD

Do-it-yourselfers can try **Kona Natural Foods,** 75-1027 Henry St., in Crossroads Shopping Center (☎329-2296; open M-Sa 9am-9pm, Su 9am-7pm) or the **Safeway** (☎329-2207; open 24hr.) next door.

▨ **Yasu's Kona Sushi,** 75-5799 Ali'i Dr. (☎326-1696), in the Ali'i Sunset Plaza. Yasu works wonders, providing fresh food and simple satisfaction in a home-away-from-home atmosphere. Combos $8.50-15.50, rolls $4.50-10, sashimi $7.50. Open daily 5-9:30pm; M, W, F-Sa 11:30am-1:30pm. All major credit cards. ❸

Sam Choy's Restaurant, 73-5576 Kauhola St. (☎326-1545), in the Cal-Cam Centre of the new industrial park off of Queen Ka'ahumanu Hwy. north of town. A meal at Sam Choy's is like taking a bite of the Big Island itself—the menu is a compilation of local favorites from the Fried Poke Omelette ($8.50) to the Kaloko Steak ($13). Breakfast $3.50-13. Lunch $5-13. Open M-Sa 6am-2pm, Su 7am-2pm. ❸

Bianelli's, 75-240 Nani Kailua Dr. (☎326-4800), in Pine's Plaza off Hualalai Rd. Uniting the world in aloha love, Bianelli's synthesizes a wealth of international influences. It serves terrific pizzas such as The Greek, The Mexican, and The Pesto ($12-20.40; $3 a slice) and all-you-can-eat pasta ($9.50) on red-checkered table cloths, as well as an international beer list. Open M-F 11am-10pm, Sa 5-10pm. All major credit cards. ❷

Island Lava Java, 75-5799 Ali'i Dr. (☎327-2161), in the Sunset Shopping Center. Everyone from bleary-eyed, tattooed Kona youths to camera-toting, sunburnt tourists turn up for hot beverages ($1.50-4), sandwiches ($6-8), and Lava Java's famous desserts such as Aunty Nene's Chocolate Peanut Butter Delight. **Internet access** ($3 per 15min.). Open daily 6am-10pm. ❶

Oodles of Noodles, 75-1027 Henry St. (☎331-2572), in the Crossroads Shopping Center. Rich woods highlight much of the decor, and almost as much detail seems to have been paid to the presentation of this hip spot as to the excitingly original food. With new takes on old favorites such as pad thai and fettucine alfredo, as well as a large vegan menu, this restaurant is likely to please almost everyone. Open daily 11am-9pm. ❹

The French Bakery, 74-5467 Kaiwi St. (☎326-2688), in the mall near the corner of Queen Ka'ahumanu Hwy and Kaiwi. The gregarious staff bubbles with energy in this hole-in-the-wall bakery. The tastiest pastries (75¢-$1.50) and freshest breads ($1.75-4.25) around, as well as a selection of hearty sandwiches ($3-5). Open M-F 5:30am-3pm, Sa 5:30am-2pm. No credit cards. ❶

Kona Brewing Co., 75-5629 Kuakini Hwy. (☎334-2739), in the North Kona Shopping Center. The wave of micro breweries sweeping the mainland has crashed on the Big Island beaches. Locals have ridden it with typical flare, creating the Kona Brewing Company. This hip restaurant is one of the most popular places in town, with a patio perfect for enjoying a Captain Cook pie (pizzas $8-21), Mauna Loa Spinach Salad (salads $7-10), or suds such as Lavaman Red Ale (pints $4). Open M-Th 11am-9pm, F-Sa 11am-10pm. ❸

Manna Korean BBQ, (☎334-0880) in the Crossroads Shopping Center on Henry St. Korean food in heaping quantities creates quite a bang for your buck. One entree, four sides, and a mountain of rice $5.50-8. Open M-Sa 10am-8:30pm. No credit cards. ❶

BIG ISLAND

LUAUS

Drums of Polynesia Luau (reservations ☎331-1526), at the Royal Kona Resort features a full buffet, open bar and a drum dance performance. M, W, F, Sa evenings. $55.

Island Breeze Luau (reservations ☎326-4969) at King Kamehameha's Kona Beach Hotel, is held on the beach adjacent to Kamalahonu and Ahu'ena—Kamehameha the Great's capital at Kona. $55, children 6-12 $21, under 5 free.

Luau at Kona Village Resort, 14 mi. north of Kona, takes the experience to a another level. The Friday night luau has been a tradition at the resort for over 30 years. It's also the oldest continuously-running luau on the Big Island, featuring Hawaiian foods prepared the traditional way and Polynesian dancing. $76, ages 6-12 $46, under 6 $22.

◎ SIGHTS

HULIHEE PALACE. John Adams Kuakini built the palace of lava rock, coral lime mortar, and timbers of koa and 'ohi'a in 1938 and it remained a favorite retreat of Hawaiian royalty for the remainder of the century. The Daughters of Hawaii now maintain the palace as a museum, which is home to a collection of ancient Hawaiian artifacts such as stone tools, *kapa* and *kapa*-making tools, and wooden storage bowls. Highlights include personal items of the Hawaiian royalty such as javelins and spears belonging to Kamehameha the Great, and Princess Ruth's large koa armchair. *(75-5718 Ali'i Dr. ☎329-1877; hulihee@ilhawaii.net; www.huliheepalace.org. Open M-F 9am-4pm, Sa-Su 10am-4pm. $5, seniors $4, ages 12 and under 50¢.)*

MOKUAIKAUA CHURCH. Constructed in 1837 of the same unique lava rock and 'ohi'a and koa timbers, this is the oldest church in the state. It's also the tallest structure in town; for years fishermen used the 112 ft. steeple for navigation purposes. The church features a model of the *Brig Thaddeus*, the Hawaiian equivalent of the Mayflower. *(At the northern end of Ali'i Dr. ☎329-1589.)*

AHU'ENA HEIAU. Ahu'ena Heiau was the centerpiece of Kamehameha the Great's government from 1813-1819. **Kamehameha,** the only man to unite the Hawaiian archipelago under one ruler, was born on the Kohala coast in the 16th century. After consolidating his authority over the other islands, he returned to Kona to rule (see **History,** p. 13 for more information). He built Ahu'ena Heiau at its present

HARD BODIES Every year, on the third Saturday in October, the streets of Kailua-Kona overflow with chiseled men and women from around the globe. These throngs do not descend upon the town to work on their tans; they're here for the **Ironman Triathlon.** This famous race, the Triathlon World Championship, has almost single-handedly brought triathlons into the world consciousness. Competitors swim 2.4 mi., bike 112 mi., and run a full 26.2 mi. marathon. The drama and excitement of some of the world's greatest athletes pushing themselves to the utmost limits of human endurance are the highlights of each race. Still, the Ironman is not solely about world-class specimens of the human physique—for many who compete in the Ironman, finishing the race before the cheering crowds on Ali'i Dr. is much more important than even approaching the course records. The event is said to bring out the best of Kona, and whether you're here to compete or just to enjoy yourself on a more low-key vacation, be sure to soak in the spirit of exploration and camaraderie that Ironman inspires.

location and dedicated it to Lono, the god of agriculture and prosperity. Ahu'ena Heiau was restored recently, and the grounds, which are open to the public, feature several interpretive displays which provide an insight into Hawaiian culture. The area is one of the most historic sites in Hawaii, and holds great significance for native Hawaiians. (*At the northern end of Kailua Bay, adjacent to King Kamehameha's Kona Beach Hotel.*)

ONIZUKA SPACE CENTER. This small, insightful museum is dedicated to the memory of Ellison S. Onizuka, the first astronaut from Hawaii, who perished aboard the Challenger Space Shuttle in 1986. The center includes a number of exhibits on space travel and the US space program, as well as a piece on Hawaii's role in the space program. (*At the airport, on Keahole Airport Rd.* ☎ *329-3441; www.onizukaspacecenter.org. $3, children $1. Open daily 8:30am-4:30pm.*)

◨ BEACHES

Although Kona's beaches do not compare to those of the rest of the Big Island, there are still a few seaside spots of note. South of town toward Keauhou, **White Sands Beach Park,** north of St. Peter's Catholic Church, is the area's most popular **bodysurfing beach.** Amenities include restrooms, showers, and a volleyball court.

Honokohau Marina, 3 mi. north of town off of Queen Ka'ahumanu Hwy. is home to many charter boats that venture off the coast for deep sea fishing. At the end of each day, they still display their catches just like the old days on Kailua Pier. There are some good secluded beaches just a short walk up or down the coast from the Marina. **Old Kona Airport Beach Park,** north of town at the end of Kuakini Hwy., caters mainly to fishermen and, when the surf's up, local riders. Still, the white sand beach is a great spot to soak up some rays or enjoy a picnic. There are restrooms, showers, picnic tables, soccer and baseball fields, lighted tennis courts, and a gym at the southern end of the park. Even though **Kailua Pier** no longer has the buzz of activity it once did, it still is worth a walk out to the end of the breakwater for a look back on the shore.

◧ NIGHTLIFE

After a long day of scuba-diving and sightseeing, **Wallace Theaters,** Makalapua Center, off of Queen Ka'ahumanu Hwy. next to Kmart, offers welcome respite in state-of-the-art stadium seating. (☎ *327-0444. $7.75, matinee $5.*)

Lulu's, 75-819 Ali'i Dr. (☎331-2633), next to the Coconut Grove Marketplace, is the best place to party in Kona. Pool tables, countless TVs, a huge upstairs lanai and wild theme nights such as "Jamaica Me Crazy" and "Bright Green Pants" featuring $3 Heinekens, make Lulu's the closest thing to a nightclub as you'll find on the Big Island. $5 cover F and Sa. Open daily 11am-2am.

Huggo's on the Rocks, 75-5828 Kahakai Rd. (☎329-1493), at the southern end of Kailua Bay next to the Royal Kona Resort. The drinks aren't cheap (beer $3.50-6), but you're paying for the sky over your head, sand beneath your feet, and the ocean a few yards away. Open daily 11:30am-12:30am.

Lasko's, 75-5819 Kuakini Hwy. (☎331-2558), up the hill from downtown near the intersection of Kuakini and Rte. 11. Out of most tourists' radar, this joint is a great spot to grab drinks and pub grub, and relax Hawaiian-style with the locals til the wee hours of the morning. Karaoke Su-Tu, dancing W-Sa. Open M-F 11am-2am, Sa-Su 2pm-2am.

Michaelangelo's, 75-5770 Ali'i Dr. (☎329-4436), in Waterfront Row. Michaelangelo's morphs from trendy restaurant to hopping dance party most nights after 10pm. The lavender walls and faux trellis are not exactly stylish, but the grooves can't be denied. Happy Hour daily 11am-5pm. Dancing nightly 10pm-2am.

🏃 DAYTRIPS FROM KAILUA-KONA

HOLUALOA

2 mi. south of Kailua-Kona, on Mamalahoa Hwy.

Holualoa is a good half-century away from nearby Kailua-Kona when it comes to lifestyle. Long one of Kona's coffee growing centers, an influx of artists and crafts-people have changed the face of the main street, converting old pool halls and saloons into art galleries and eclectic shops. The most striking example of this transformation is the **Kona Arts Center,** on Mamalahoa Hwy. (Rte. 180), housed in the old coffee mill. This non-profit organization is dedicated to cultural enrichment, offering classes in a number of disciplines including painting, pottery, and fabric design. (Membership $35 per month. Open Tu-Sa 9:30am-2pm.)

Just down the road at the intersection of Hualalai Rd. and Mamalahoa Hwy. is the wonderful **Kimura Lauhala Shop,** which has been weaving and selling *lauhala* hats, baskets, and carrying cases since the 1930s. The simple elegance of these pieces is made all the more appealing by their low price. (☎324-0053. Open M-F 9am-5pm, Sa 9am-4pm.) The town's day-to-day commercial life revolves around **Paul's Place,** a store that has been in the business of selling everything but the kitchen sink for decades. (☎324-4702. Open M-F 7am-8pm, Sa-Su 8am-8pm.)

▨**The Holualoa Inn ❺,** 75-5932 Mamalahoa Hwy. (Rte. 180), is the toast of downtown Holualoa. Perched 1350 ft. up the slope of Mt. Hualalai with a commanding view of the Kona coast, this luxurious inn was once the private home of Honolulu Advertiser Chairman Thurston Twigg-Smith. The rich eucalyptus flooring, rooftop gazebo, brightly-tiled pool, and Hawaiian-style open-air design capture the relaxed spirit of the islands. (☎800-392-1812 or 324-1121; inn@aloha.net; www.konaweb.com/HINN. Breakfast included. Check-in 3pm. Check-out 11am. Reservations recommended. Rooms $165-220; each additional guest $30.)

The hot pink **Inaba's Kona Hotel ❶,** on Mamalahoa Hwy., has been a fixture of downtown Holualoa since 1925. The hotel's inexpensive accommodations keep loyal clientele coming back again and again. (☎324-1155. Check-in and check-out flexible. Singles $20, doubles $26.) Across the street is the funky **Holualoa Cafe ❶,**

76-5901 Mamalahoa Hwy., which serves up steaming cups of 100% Pure Kona coffee ($1.75) and a slew of tasty treats ($2-5) and sandwiches ($7-8) on a shady porch. Books and knick-knacks from around the world are tucked around the comfy lounge. (☎322-2233. Open M-F 6:30am-3pm, Sa 8am-3pm.)

KEAUHOU

Keauhou is 6 mi. south of Kailua-Kona along Ali'i Dr.

The laid-back beachside community of Keauhou sits in on a picturesque strip of sand along the gently arcing curve of Kahaluu Bay. Kahaluu Beach is the site of the best **snorkeling** and swimming in the Kona area, and shelters a healthy helping of waves for surf bums. The beach is part of a state-run park that has restrooms, showers, and picnic tables.

A number of companies sail **snorkeling cruises** from the bay. **Fair Wind,** 78-7130 Kaleiopapa St. (☎800-677-9461 or 322-2788; snorkel@fair-wind.com; www.fairwind.com), is the granddaddy of Kona snorkel cruises, and has an exclusive permit to moor in Kealakekua Bay. They offer an array of tours including the Deluxe Morning Cruise (adults $87; children ages 4-12 $50), the Afternoon Snack Cruise (adults $55; children ages 4-12 $35), and the Afternoon Deluxe Cruise (adults $82; children ages 4-12 $46). All take place on a 60-foot catamaran outfitted for the height of comfort. **Dolphin Discoveries,** 77-116 Queen Kalama Ave., only has one boat, so every adventure is a personalized experience. The husband and wife team are both certified naturalist guides, and will take you to the best snorkeling and dolphin-sighting spots on the island. (☎322-8000; dolphindiscoveries@aloha.net; www. dolphindiscoveries.com. Call for info and pricing.) You can also rent gear at **Kahaluu Bay Beach Rentals,** 78-6685 Ali'i Dr., across the street from Kahaluu Beach. (☎322-4338. Open daily 8:15am-5pm.)

If you're hankering for a meal after a day at the beach, look no farther than the **Royal Thai Cafe ❷,** in the Keauhou Shopping Center on Kamehameha III Rd. No wonder all the Buddhas are smiling in this refined restaurant—anyone surrounded by food this good would have to be happy. (☎322-8424. Curries $9-$14; veggie dishes $8-9. Open daily 11am-10pm. All major credit cards.) Tiny **St. Peter's Catholic Church,** just north of Kahaluu Beach, sits precariously on the water's edge, and almost looks as though it might be swept out to sea by a strong gust. The small quarters and simple decoration focus one's attention on its sole window, behind the altar, which frames an expanse of blue.

KALOKO-HONOKAHAU NATIONAL HISTORICAL PARK

Visitor information is available at the park headquarters, located in the Kaloko Industrial Park. Open M-F 7:30am-4pm. The entrance to the park itself is across Queen Ka'ahumanu Hwy. from the Kona Trade Center in the Kaloko Industrial Park, about 3 mi. north of Kailua-Kona and 3½ mi. south of the airport. Park open daily 8am-3:30pm. There is also access at the northern end of Honokohau Harbor. Free.

Within this 1160-acre coastal park, the two large fishponds of **'Aimakapa** and **Kaloko,** along with a number of fish traps, pens, and a massive seawall, serve to remind visitors of the Hawaiian culture that once flourished along the Kona Coast. Although the area's rough lava fields may appear unsuitable for human habitation, it was once a bustling settlement that maintained elaborate fishponds and raised sweet potatoes, coconuts, chickens, dogs, and pigs. The seawall the Hawaiian settlers constructed here is a fine example of their superior engineering abilities. Hundreds of other archaeological features in the park are remnants of Hawaii's rich cultural history, including *paena wa'a* (canoe landings), *ku'ula* (fishing shrines), and *kahua* (house platforms). Kaloko contains some of the last remaining natural wetlands on the Big Island, which provide habitats for nesting waterbirds such as the endemic **Ae'o** (Hawaiian black-necked stilt) and **'Alae ke'oke'o** (Hawaiian coot), both of which are endangered species.

The park is still under development, and exploration and enjoyment of the area is very much a self-directed endeavor. Only one road directly accesses the park, and a single path, the **Mamalohoa Trail,** or King's Trail, stretches along the coast from Honokohau Harbor in the South to Wawahiwa'a Point in the north, passing both 'Aimakapa and Kaloko Fishpond along the way. There is no potable water and neither overnight camping nor fires are allowed.

SOUTH KONA

On an island such as this, a few miles can make a world of difference. While the hustle and bustle of Kailua-Kona are just up the road from the sleepy coffee town of Honalo, Kealakekua, Captain Cook, and Honaunau precariously straddle the Hawaii Belt Rd. (Rte. 11) on the slopes of Mauna Loa. This series of towns has a funky vibe all its own, and the stretch of coastline is one of the most culturally and ecologically rich on the entire island. Significant pieces of history are protected at Pu'uhonua o Honaunau and Captain Cook Monument, and natural wonders are the main draws to Kealakekua Bay and Miloli'i. In this area, Hawaiians and *haoles* alike recognize the need for preservation, and take steps to ensure that the legacy of conservation continues.

■ ORIENTATION

South Kona's main drag is **Rte. 11** (also known as the **Hawaii Belt Rd.** or **Mamalahoa Hwy.**). Off of this strip, there are a number of roads running east down to the coast, and west, up the mountain. The more significant ones for tourists descend the mountainside to the ocean. These are **Napo'opo'o Rd.,** which runs into **Middle Keei Rd.** and drops to the southern end of Kealakekua Bay and **Rte. 160.** Rte. 160 accesses Puuhonua O Honaunau and eventually leads to the Bay. Honalo and Honaunau are about 8 and 20 mi. south of Kailua-Kona, respectively.

▐ TRANSPORTATION

Driving is the easiest way to get around South Kona. Some travelers hitchhike, but it is potentially very dangerous and *Let's Go* does not recommend it. A number of **taxis** service the area, but they are generally expensive. **Paradise Taxi and Tours** (☎329-1234; open 24hr.; $2 per mile) and **D&E Taxi** (☎329-4279; open 5am-10pm; $2 per mile) are among the multitude of options.

The **Hele-On bus** (☎961-8744) runs from Honaunau, north to Kailua-Kona and west to Hilo. Buses from Honaunau Elementary School to: **Kailua-Kona** (50min., M-Sa 5:55am, $2.25) via Yano Hall in **Captain Cook** (5min., 75¢), Konawaena Schools in **Kealakekua** (15min.), and Ben Franklin in **Kainaliu** (20min.); and from Captain Cook to: **Kailua-Kona** (50min., M-Sa 10:45am and 2:15pm, $2.25). See www.hawaii-county.com for the most up-to-date fares and schedules.

One of the preferred methods of transportation in the area, especially in Kealakekua Bay, is **kayak.** A number of rental companies hawk the crafts along Mamalahoa Hwy. from Kealakekua to Captain Cook. (See Sights and Activities, **Bay Tours** p. 324.)

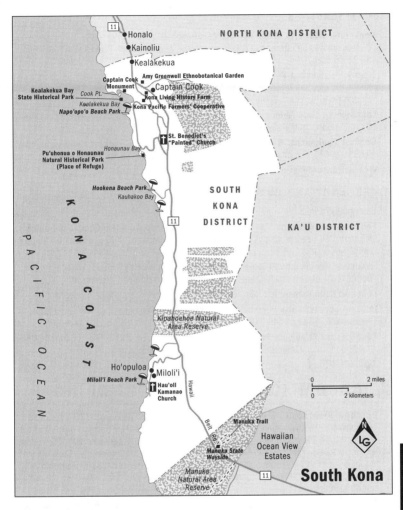

Map legend and labels:

11 Honalo
• Kainoliu
• Kealakekua

NORTH KONA DISTRICT

Captain Cook Monument   Amy Greenwell Ethnobotanical Garden
Kealakekua Bay State Historical Park   Captain Cook
Cook Pt.   Kona Living History Farm
Kealakekua Bay   Kona Pacific Farmers' Cooperative
Napo'opo'o Beach Park

St. Benedict's "Painted" Church

Honaunau Bay
Pu'uhonua o Honaunau Natural Historical Park (Place of Refuge)

Hookena Beach Park
Kauhakoo Bay

SOUTH KONA DISTRICT

KA'U DISTRICT

K O N A   C O A S T

P A C I F I C   O C E A N

Kipahoehoe Natural Area Reserve

Ho'opuloa   • Miloli'i
Miloli'i Beach Park   Hau'oli Kamanao Church

Hawaii

0   2 miles
0   2 kilometers

Belt Rd.

Manuka Trail

Hawaiian Ocean View Estates

Manuka State Wayside

Manuka Natural Area Reserve

11

South Kona

N LG

BIG ISLAND

■ PRACTICAL INFORMATION

TOURIST AND FINANCIAL SERVICES

Tourist Office: The **H.N. Greenwell Store Museum,** 81-6581 Mamalahoa Hwy. (☎323-3222; khs@kona.net; www.konahistorical.org), home of the **Kona Historical Society,** just south of downtown Kealakekua, offers a good range of historical information about the area. Local stores also have a wealth of knowledge for visitors looking to get off the beaten track. Open daily 9am-3pm. Admission $2.

Banks: Bank of Hawaii (☎322-9377), and **First Hawaiian Bank** (☎322-3484), next to each other on Mamalahoa Hwy. in downtown Kealakekua, are both open M-Th 8:30am-4pm and F 8:30am-6pm and have **24hr. ATMs.**

LOCAL SERVICES

Bookstore: Island Books, 79-7360 Mamalahoa Hwy. (☎322-2006), in the Kainaliu Center, shelves an impressive collection of used and rare titles. Open M-Sa 10am-6pm, Su 11am-6pm.

Library: Kealakekua Public Library (☎323-7585), on Mamalahoa Hwy. in downtown Kealakekua, offers **Internet access** to Hawaii Public Library Card Holders. Open M, W, F noon-6pm, Tu 10am-6pm, Th noon-7:30pm, Sa 10am-2pm.

Laundromat: Hale Holoi Laundromat, next to Cap's Drive-In, just north of downtown Captain Cook. Open daily 6am-9pm.

Outdoor Equipment: Hawaii Forest and Trail, 74-5035B Queen Ka'ahumanu Hwy. (☎331-8505). The only one in Kona. Open M-F 8am-5pm, Sa-Su 8am-4:30pm.

Weather Conditions: ☎961-5582.

EMERGENCY AND COMMUNICATIONS

Emergency: ☎911.

Police: A **sub-station** on Mamalahoa Hwy. in the center of Captain Cook is sporadically manned. The nearest district station is just north of downtown Kailua-Kona on Rte. 19 (☎326-4646).

Pharmacy: Kealakekua Pharmacy, 79-7460 Mamalahoa Hwy. (☎322-1639), in Mango Court, south of downtown Kainaliu. Open M-Tu, Th-F 9am-5pm, W 9am-3pm.

Hospital: Kona Community Hospital (☎322-9311), on Haukapila St. in Kealakekua.

Internet access: Kona Mountain Cafe, 81-6637 Mamalahoa Hwy. (☎323-2700), in Kealakekua. $2 per 15min. Open M-F 6:30am-6pm, Sa 7am-5pm, Su 7am-4pm.

Post Office: Kealakekua Post Office, Mamalahoa Hwy. (☎800-275-8777), in the Central Kona Center. Open M-F 9am-4:30pm, Sa 9:30am-12:30pm.

Zip Code: 96750.

▚ ACCOMMODATIONS AND CAMPING

Rainbow Plantation, Mamalahoa Hwy. (☎800-494-2829 or 323-2393; sunshine@aloha.net; www.aloha.net/~konabnb), just north of the Napo'opo'o Rd. turn-off. This splendid B&B is tucked into the mountainside above Kealakekua Bay. The rooms seem to incorporate the surrounding rainforest into their interiors; the "Crow's Nest" room is set in a former coffee shack, and the "Jungle Queen" suite is a converted fishing boat. Doubles $75-95, each additional person $15. 2-night minimum stay. All major credit cards. ❸

Pineapple Park, 81-6363 Mamalahoa Hwy. (☎877-865-2266 or 323-2224; park@aloha.net; www.pineapple-park.com), north of downtown Captain Cook, is a spotless hostel with a great location above Kealakekua Bay. It offers everything a budget traveler could want with a full kitchen, BBQ, high-speed Internet ($10 per hr.), kayaks for rent ($40 per day), and a shuttle to Kealakekua Bay. Breakfast included. They occasionally trade a bed for a few hours of housekeeping a week, or can work out some other form of **short-term work** arrangements. Dorms $20, private rooms $55-75. ❶/❷

Pomaikai "Lucky" Farm B&B, 83-5465 Mamalahoa Hwy. (☎800-325-6427 or 328-2112; nitabnb@kona.net; www.luckyfarm.com), south of Captain Cook between mile-markers 107 and 106. A working macadamia and coffee farm, as well as a B&B, this friendly spot provides a 100% pure Kona taste of Big Island eco-tourism. The converted Coffee Barn recalls life before jumbo jets and vacation packages with bare wood, and high ceilings. Reservations recommended. Rooms $55-65. All major credit cards. ❷

HELL HATH NO FURY As legend goes, there was once a mighty Hawaiian chief named 'Ohi'a, who was much loved by his people. 'Ohi'a was magnificent and strong—one of the best surfers and hula dancers on the island. As true-hearted heroes often do, 'Ohi'a had but one love, a woman named Lehua.

One day 'Ohi'a was catching such serious surf that his entire village came out to watch their chief. 'Ohi'a was riding some huge waves and enjoying himself so much that after one killer tube, he went into a spontaneous hula on the shore. The people were overwhelmed with admiration for their chief.

As the people stared in awe, the most beautiful woman they had ever seen appeared on the beach. She approached 'Ohi'a and told him she could make an even bigger splash—ahem, bigger waves—if he would spend one night with her. 'Ohi'a gazed upon the beautiful woman, and as he did, he caught a spark of fire in her eyes. Before he gave her an answer, he asked her to promise that any agreement they made would not affect his village or his people. The woman agreed to this condition, at which point 'Ohi'a replied to her, "I love only one woman, and that is Lehua, so I will not spend the evening with you." Upon hearing his response, the woman was so overcome with fury that she revealed herself in her true form—the goddess Pele. 'Ohi'a had taken the steps to protect his village and his people, but had failed to protect himself. In her rage, Pele fumed "If I can't have you, than no one shall!" Then and there, before all of his followers, she turned 'Ohi'a into the strong, hardy tree that bears his name.

Soon after, Lehua came down to the beach in search of 'Ohi'a. She asked if anyone had seen her love, and all that the people could do was point her to the tree. Lehua beseeched the gods to change her true love back into his former self, but none were willing to defy the will of Pele. The gods held counsel, and finally agreed that 'Ohi'a and Lehua could spend eternity together, he as the strong, sturdy tree and she as its brilliant red blossom.

Cedar House, Bamboo Rd. (☎328-8829 or 328-1006; cedrhse@aloha.net; www.cedarhouse-hawaii.com). From downtown Captain Cook, turn onto Kiloa Rd. between the post office and the Kealakekua Ranch Center, continue until the T-junction and turn right. Turn left at the next T-junction, and left at the bamboo patch. This elegant B&B is surrounded by the coffee orchards of Captain Cook, high on the mountainside above Kealakekua Bay. Rooms with shared or private bath $65-95. All major credit cards. ❸

Manago Hotel, 82-6155 Mamalahoa Hwy. (☎323-2642; mail@managohotel.com; www.mangagohotel.com), in downtown Captain Cook. The Manago Hotel has been a Captain Cook fixture since 1917, and the rooms probably haven't been renovated much since then. Hotel restaurant open Tu-Su 7am-9am, 11am-2pm, 5-7:30pm. Check-in 1pm. Check-out 11am. Single rooms $25, with private bath $42-47, with Japanese decor $61. D/MC/V. ❷

Hookena Beach County Park, is at a well-marked turn off of Mamalahoa Hwy., 2.6 mi. south of the intersection of Rte. 160 and Mamalahoa Hwy. The park offers the only legal camping in the area. Pitch your tent under swaying palms right on the beach—just keep an eye out for falling coconuts. Free with a permit. ❶

BIG ISLAND

⧉ FOOD

There's a weekly **farmers' market** on Thursdays at **Kona Pacific Farmers Cooperative** (☎328-2411; kpfc@gte.net; www.kpfc.com), on Napo'opo'o/Middle Keei Rd. toward Kealakekua Bay. Follow the pink donkeys.

▨ **Nasturtium Cafe,** 79-7491 Mamalahoa Hwy. (☎322-2193), north of Captain Cook next to Seven Senses. Offering an abundance of fresh foods from *ahi* to zucchini, this tiny cafe is the place for a sit-down lunch in South Kona. Salads ($8-11), and enticing sandwiches ($7-10). Open M-F 11am-2:30pm. All major credit cards. ❷

▨ **Aloha Angel Cafe,** 79-7384 Mamalahoa Hwy. (☎322-3383), in downtown Kainaliu. This hip cafe is situated around the venerable Aloha Theater, and offers the best of outdoor dining on a breezy lanai with views down to the ocean. An eclectic menu features island ingredients. **Aloha Theater** film screenings nightly at 7:30pm ($6). Breakfast and lunch $6-13. Dinner $14-22. Open daily 8am-3pm and 5-9pm. MC/V. ❸

The Coffee Shack, 83-5799 Mamalahoa Hwy. (☎328-9555), south of Captain Cook. Perched over the coastline hundreds of feet below, the great breakfasts, sandwiches, pizzas ($6.50-12) and desserts are almost as amazing as view. Open daily 7am-5pm. D/MC/V. ❷

Billy Bob's Park 'N Pork, 81-6372 Mamalahoa Hwy. (☎323-3371), north of downtown Captain Cook. Heaping helpings of meat and all the fixin's at the southernmost BBQ in the USA fully satisfy any carnal cravings. The Bodacious Meal ($10) satiates a lust for tender meats and mouthwatering sides. Open Th-Tu 5-9pm. MC/V. ❷

Evie's Natural Food, 79-7460 Mamalahoa Hwy. (☎322-0739), in Mango Court south of Kainaliu, is a good spot to stock up for a picnic, or to grab sandwiches at the deli. Evie's also posts a list of **short-term work** opportunities, including farm jobs that trade room and board for labor. Open M-F 8am-7pm, Sa-Su 9am-5pm. MC/V. ❶

Bong Brothers, 84-5229 Mamalahoa Hwy. (☎328-9289), in Honaunau. This little hole-in-the-mountain is the place to cure the munchies with fresh local fruits and vegetables or a scrumptious smoothie ($3.50). Open M-F 9am-6pm, Sa 10am-6pm. ❶

◎ 🎬 SIGHTS AND ACTIVITIES

KEALAKEKUA BAY. The bay and its spectacular coral reef are much the same as they were at the time of Captain Cook's famous arrival over 200 years ago. The area is protected as a **Marine Life Conservation District,** a designation which severely limits fishing in the bay, and prohibits the anchoring of boats in order to preserve the myriad marine life that call the waters home. **Snorkeling** is excellent throughout the well-developed reef that has formed on the shelf between the sheer *pali* and the Ka'awaloa Cove, at the northwestern end of the bay.

The only part of the bay accessible to automobiles and appropriate for the launching of watercraft is Napo'opo'o Beach at the southeastern end in **Kealakekua Bay State Historical Park.** In addition to a launching site, the park has restrooms, picnic tables, some big surf, and **Hikiau Heiau State Monument,** a significant Hawaiian temple. *(To reach the park from Rte. 11, take Napo'opo'o Rd., about 18 mi. south of Kailua-Kona between Kealakekua and Captain Cook. The road winds down the mountainside for a few miles before joining Middle Keei Rd. and continuing on to the bay. The entire journey from highway to shoreline is about 4 mi. The distance from the southeastern to the northwestern shore is about ½ mi., making for an easy kayak or reasonable paddle for able swimmers.)*

BAY TOURS. A number of companies in the area offer **snorkel** cruises to the Kealakekua reef, the best of which are **Fair Wind Cruises,** 78-7130 Kaleiopapa St. (☎800-677-9461 or 322-2788; snorkel@fair-wind.com; www.fair-wind.com) and **Dolphin Discoveries,** 77-116 Queen Kalama Ave. (☎322-8000; dolphindiscoveries@aloha.net; www.dolphindiscoveries.com), both out of **Keauhou Harbor** (see Keauhou p. 319). For those adventurers looking to navigate and explore courtesy of their own two arms, a number of companies up the hill along Mamalahoa Hwy. rent **kayaks** and offer guided excursions. One of the best is **Kona Boys,** 79-7539

FLIPPER, IS THAT YOU? Kealakekua Bay is one of the best spots in Hawaii to see **Spinner dolphins,** who make this crescent of water their personal playground. They are slender dolphins that generally do not exceed 7 ft. in length and have dark grey backs and white stomachs with long, slim snouts. Spinner dolphins travel in groups, or pods, and while they feed in the deep channels offshore, they spend much of their time resting and playing in shallow water. Leaping out of the water to mind-boggling heights and then spinning laterally before splashing down, Spinner dolphins seem to be natural circus performers. With their tremendous leaping ability they are able to rotate as many as 16 times during one flight. They are capable of even more amazing aerial maneuvers like head-over-tail spins when their leap is a series of mid-air somersaults. While there's no schedule for this circus, your best bet for catching a glimpse of these acrobats is in the early morning.

Hawaii Belt Rd., on Mamalahoa Hwy. north of downtown Kealakekua. Kona Boys is the oldest kayak shop in the area, and offers tandem kayaks ($45 per day), singles ($25 per day), and surf or body boards ($10 per day), as well as guided tours and surf lessons ($125 per day) from lifeguard-certified instructors. (☎328-1234 or 322-3600; info@konaboyskayak.com. Open daily 8am-5pm and by appointment.) Another good option is **Aloha Kayak Co.,** 79-7428 Mamalahoa Hwy., in Old Honalo Town, which offers tandems ($150 per week, $40 per day) and singles ($100 per week, $25 per day), guided tours (1½-4hr., $30-65 per person per day) as well as snorkeling equipment, surf- and bodyboards. (☎877-322-1444 or 322-2868; alohakayak@yahoo.com; www.alohakayak.com.)

CAPTAIN COOK TRAIL AND MONUMENT. At the northwestern end of the bay, is the **Captain Cook Monument,** a 27-foot tall pillar erected in Cook's honor by fellow Brits in 1878, 100 years after he set foot on Hawaii. The monument stands near the site where Cook was killed, and has sparked much debate because it is viewed by some native Hawaiians as a testament to Eurocentric myopia and cultural domination. (See **History** p. 12 for more information on Cook's landing.) While a number of ships recreating Cook's voyage have anchored in the bay and left plaques commemorating his "discovery," in all fairness to the Hawaiians, ruins of the ancient village of **Ka'awaloa,** which was founded when Britain was still an uncivilized hinterland of the Roman Empire, are a good deal more interesting to explore. The ruins of the village occupy the flats behind the monument.

To reach the monument by more "pedestrian" means, head to the **Captain Cook Monument Trail.** (4 mi., 2½hr. round-trip. Trailhead: Right-hand side of Napo'opo'o Rd., 200 yards from the intersection of Rte. 11. Level: moderate.) The trail is the first unmarked dirt road on the downhill side of the road, and descends the slope to Ka'awaloa Cove, passing through overgrown sugar cane, exposed lava fields, and finally the dense foliage along the shoreline. The hike loses quite a bit of elevation on the way down, which means a bit of a climb back up. Heading downhill, the trail follows a road for the first few hundred meters before branching off to the left through thick fields of gigantic grasses and wild brush that almost overrun the path. Farther down, the terrain opens up to a'a fields that support a sparse foliage. As the trail approaches the coast, it affords sweeping views of the surrounding countryside. On its final descent, the path drops down into shaded forest along the coast. Bring plenty of water, appropriate footwear and clothing, and, of course, snorkeling gear.

If the sound of the trail appeals to you, but the feel beneath your feet doesn't, check out **King's Trail Rides,** on Mamalahoa Hwy. between Kealakekua and Captain Cook, which offers horseback trail rides down the Captain Cook Monument Trail.

The excursion includes lunch and snorkeling gear, and takes about 4hr., with 2hr. of riding. (*☎323-2388; sales@konacowboy.com; www.konacowboy.com. $95 per person. 9am departure, book 24hr. in advance.*)

FARMS AND GARDENS. The **Amy Greenwell Ethnobotanical Garden,** gives a sense of the close relationship the Hawaiians had with the land before Cook's arrival. Home to native Hawaiian species as well as those brought by Polynesian settlers, this 15-acre garden provides a representative look at the plants and cultivation techniques perfected by the islanders before the arrival of Europeans. (*☎323-3318. On Mamalahoa Hwy., uphill from Captain Cook Monument, just north of downtown Captain Cook. Ages 12 and up $4. Open M-F 8:30am-5pm.*) Tours at the **Kona Pacific Farmers Cooperative** provide insight into the ins and outs of coffee growing. The facility has been processing coffee since 1910 and now handles over 5 million pounds of beans a year. It is the oldest and largest coffee cooperative in the US, and one of the best places to buy 100% pure Kona coffee. They also host a **farmers' market** all day on Thursdays. (*☎328-2411; kpfc@gte.net; www.kpfc.com. On Napo'opo'o/Middle Keei Rd. toward the bay; follow the pink donkeys. Free tours.*) Another way to grab a glimpse of the role of coffee cultivation in Kona is to stop by the **Kona Living History Farm,** which offers guided tours of coffee farm preservation, growth, and processing techniques from the 1920s and 30s. (*☎323-2006 or 323-3222; khs@konahistorical.org; www.konahistorical.org. On Mamalahoa Hwy. in Captain Cook, across from the 110-mile marker. Tours on the hour M-F 9am-1pm. $15, children $10.*)

ST. BENEDICT'S "PAINTED" CHURCH. John Berchman Velge, a Belgian Catholic priest built **St. Benedict's "Painted" Church** between 1899 and 1904. Using ordinary house paints, and some divine inspiration, he created the closest there is to a Gothic cathedral in Hawaii. The vibrant colors of the interior are an eclectic blend of the islands and the Old World, with faux marble columns blossoming into palm trees, an ingeniously constructed vaulted ceiling complete with tropical sky, and walls fashioned after the cathedral in Burgos, Spain. (*Just up the hill from Pu'uhonua o Honaunau. Take Rte. 160 north onto Painted Church Rd., just west of the 1-mile marker, or take Napo'opo'o Rd. and turn onto Middle Keei Rd., then right onto Painted Church Rd.*)

PU'UHONUA O HONAUNAU NATIONAL HISTORICAL PARK

The park entrance is on Rte. 160, 4 mi. downhill from where Rte. 160 leaves Rte. 11 between mileposts 103 and 104. The park can also be reached via a 4-mile, one-way road that runs from Napo'opo'o Beach. There is no public transportation to the park, but you can take the Hele-On Bus (☎961-8744) from Kailua-Kona to the Honaunau stop and walk down (see South Kona transportation, p. 320). The Pu'uhonua o Honaunau Visitor Center has helpful information about the park. Restrooms and water fountains as well. (☎328-2288 or 328-2326; www.nps.gov/puho. Open daily 7:30am-5:30pm.) An orientation talk given at the amphitheater every 30min. from 10-11am and 2-3pm provides a good introduction to the site and its offerings. Park open M-Th 6am-8pm, F-Su 6-11am. $5 per car.

Once the home of Kona's royal chiefs, the rebuilt thatched buildings and skillfully constructed lava rock walls and platforms of Pu'uhonua o Honaunau National Historic Park still evoke the spirit of the ancient Hawaiians. Honaunau Cove's sheltered beach was ideal for canoe landings, and fresh water was always available, making it the natural location for the *ali'i* to establish one of their major residences. The royal residence had no single palace or other dominating structure, but was instead made up of a number of thatched buildings within the coconut palm grove. This area, along with the canoe landing, was open only to *ali'i* and their attendants. All others were prohibited by the *kapu*, or sacred laws, to enter these grounds or in any other way to mar the *mana*, or spiritual power, held by the *ali'i*. It was believed that the breaking of the *kapu* would cause the gods to react violently with lava flows, tsunamis, or earthquakes. (See **Give Me Shelter,** p. 327.)

GIVE ME SHELTER The ancient Hawaiians lived under the rigid structure of a society based on the sacred laws, or **kapu.** The penalty for violating the *kapu* was always death. The *kapu* governed day-to-day life including everything from the interaction of men and women, to the gathering of timber, to the relationship between the royals *(ali'i)* and the commoners. Those who broke the *kapu* were allowed a second chance only if they could make it to the **pu'uhonua** (place of refuge) adjacent to the royal grounds without being killed. To do so, one had to run the gauntlet of warriors who surrounded the *pu'uhonua,* yet no blood could be shed within its walls. If an outlaw were to reach the *pu'uhonua,* a ceremony of absolution was performed by the kahuna, after which the offender could return home safely. Non-combatants in war as well as defeated warriors also sought a haven in the *pu'uhonua.* Hawaiians conducted war in order to exterminate the enemy rather than simply to gain territory, but those unable to fight could find safety in the *pu'uhonua* until the battle was over, after which their allegiance was sworn to the victor. The *pu'uhonua* was deemed a sanctuary because it was the final resting place of the bones of the *ali'i,* and the seat of their *mana.* The newest heiau in Pu'uhonua o Honaunau was dedicated in honor of Keawe, the great-grandfather of Kamehameha I, who possessed such powerful *mana* that it protected the entire *pu'uhonua.*

The area still holds a certain power, and the park provides insight into aspects of ancient Hawaiian life and culture.

There are actually two distinct pieces of Pu'uhonua o Honaunau, the **Royal Grounds** and the *pu'uhonua,* or **Place of Refuge,** separated by a massive stone wall which was built in 1550 and still stands today. The walking tour of the royal grounds and place of refuge, which is laid out for visitors in the park brochure given out at the entrance station, covers the major points of interest within the park. These include: **Keone'ele,** the sandy beach that was the royal canoe landing; **Halau,** a fishing and canoe storage building; **Heleipalala,** the royal fish pond; the **Great Wall,** a physical as well as spiritual demarcation between the royal grounds and the *pu'uhonua;* and **Hale o Keawe,** the reconstructed temple and mausoleum which imparted the place of refuge with great *mana.*

The well-maintained royal grounds and *pu'uhonua* are the park's primary attraction, but **Ki'ilae Village,** a ¾-mile walk from the Visitor Center along the 1871 trail, is also worth exploring for anyone interested in the day-to-day life of the early Hawaiians. You can pick up a comprehensive guide booklet for the village at the Visitor's Center. Highlights of the walk include the **Waiu-O-Hina Lava Tube,** which opens out in the middle of a cliff face overlooking the ocean, and **Keokea Holua,** a slide constructed out of lava rock used by the Hawaiians for *holua,* or sledding. The coast on either side of the park is home to numerous fish as well as the rare **spinner dolphins** (See **Flipper, Is That You?** p. 325). The snorkeling beneath the cliffs and in protective coves is excellent, and the reef just north of the park in Honaunau Cove is a renowned spot for underwater exploration.

KA'U

Tucked away in the southwest corner of the Big Island, the Ka'u district is a mishmash of landscapes, people, and ideas. Full of macadamia nut farms, abandoned sugar cane fields, and verdant pastures, Ka'u is ripe for exploration. From the Hawaiian Ocean View Estates in the black a'a fields of the west coast, to the windswept pastures of Ka Lae, to the little towns of Na'alehu and Pahala and the volcanic playground of the Ka'u Desert and Hawaii Volcanoes National Park, there is

BIG ISLAND

plenty to see. One of the few unifying features of Ka‘u is the unhurried pace at which life goes by. Although Ka‘u is not the place for travelers seeking gourmet dining or sizzling nightlife, those enticed by the region's relatively untamed wilderness and refreshing lack of commercialism will be right at home.

▐ TRANSPORTATION

The only means of transportation in Ka‘u is the **Hele-On bus** (☎961-8744), which runs M-F from Ocean View Center to **Hilo** (2hr. 40min., 6:40am, $5.25) via **Wai‘ohinu/Na‘alehu** (20min., $4.50), and **Pahala Center** (1hr., $3.75).

▒ ORIENTATION

Whatever you want to call it, **Rte. 11, Hawaii Belt Rd.,** or **Mamalahoa Hwy.,** is the undisputed Ka‘u thoroughfare. Ocean View, Wai‘ohinu and Na‘alehu, and Pahala are all located in close proximity to what is the district's only link to the outside world. The only other major route in the area is South Point Rd. which runs the 11 miles between Rte. 11 and Ka Lae.

▐ PRACTICAL INFORMATION

TOURIST AND FINANCIAL SERVICES

Tourist Office: The **Punalu‘u Bake Shop,** Hawaii Belt Rd. (☎929-7343), in downtown Na‘alehu, is the closest thing to a tourist office in Ka‘u. The helpful staff answers your questions and offers a few brochures. Open daily 9am-5pm.

Tours: Down the road in Ocean View, **Kula Kai Caverns** (☎929-7539 or 929-9725; caver@kulakai caverns.com; www.kulakaicaverns.com), leads tours of some of the island's most spectacular lava tubes, which are over a thousand years old. Trips range from a 30-min. introduction ($12) to a full-out spelunking adventure in Maelstrom Cave (3-4hr., $65). All tours are by reservation only; call for details.

Banks/ATM: Video Showplace, Hawaii Belt Rd. (☎929-8436), in Na‘alehu Shopping Center, has an **ATM,** as do some of the other shops in town. Open M-Sa 10am-7pm, Su 11am-7pm. The nearest **bank** with a **24hr. ATM** is **Bank of Hawaii,** (☎928-8356) in Pahala. Open M-Th 8:30am-4pm, F 8:30am-6pm.

LOCAL SERVICES

Library: Na‘alehu Public Library, Hawaii Belt Rd. (☎929-7564), behind the post office, provides **Internet access** to Hawaii State Library card holders. Open M, W, F 12-5pm; T, Th 1-6pm.

Laundromat: Ed's Laundromat (☎929-7157), in the Na‘alehu Shopping Center, serves as a reminder that somewhere out there people still wear collared shirts. Open daily 6:30am-8:30pm.

Weather: ☎961-5582.

EMERGENCY AND COMMUNICATIONS

Emergency: ☎911.

Police: Ka‘u District Police Station (☎939-2520), is east of town on Hawaii Belt Rd.

Hospital: Ka‘u Hospital (☎928-8331), in Pahala, provides basic medical services. The nearest **pharmacies** are on the roads to Kona or Hilo.

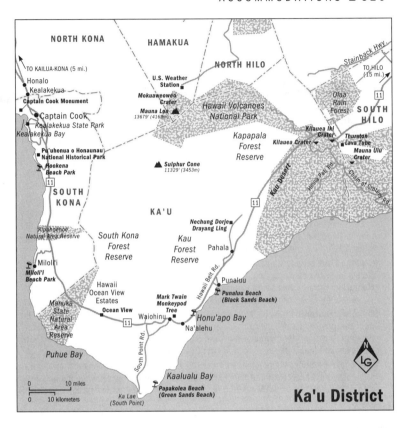

Ka'u District

Telephones: There's a **pay phone** across the street from the post office in downtown Na'alehu.

Post Office: Na'alehu Post Office, 95-5663 Mamalahoa Hwy. (☎800-275-8777) Open M-F 7:45am-4:15pm, Sa 10:15-11:15am.

Zip Code: 96772.

■ ACCOMMODATIONS

There aren't many options for accommodations in this region; the best are in the tiny town of Wai'ohinu.

■ **Margo's Corner,** Wakea Ave. (☎929-9614). From Wong Yuen Store in Wai'ohinu, take Kama'oa Rd. up the hill and make a left onto Wakea Ave. Keep a look out for the rainbow flag and the sign on the corner of Wakea and Kaikane Loop. Two beautifully-crafted suites pamper guests with luxuries such as a sauna and massage table. Guests on a budget may also set up a tent in the front garden. Owner Margo cooks up delectable meals. Breakfast and dinner included. On-site natural food store. Reservations appreciated. Suites $75-115; camping $25. No credit cards. ❶/❷

Shirakawa Motel, Mamalahoa Hwy. (☎929-7562), across from Wong Yuen Store in Wai'ohinu. The southernmost motel in the US is about as cheap as you can get on this island. While the simple rooms are nothing special, they're clean, and provide a terrific place to bed down en route between Kona and Hilo. Roll-away beds $10, child-sized $8. Singles $30, doubles $35; with kitchenette $42, with full kitchen $50. ❷

Macadamia Meadows, Kama'oa Rd. (☎929-8097; kaleena@aloha.net). Turn onto Kama'oa Rd. next to Wong Yuen Store and head up the hill. It'll be about ½ mi. up on the left. While the 8-acre working macadamia nut farm may be its most compelling attraction, there are plenty of amenities for guests at this lovely Japanese-style cedar home, including a tennis court, swimming pool, and BBQ. Many rooms include refrigerators, microwaves, and cable TV. Rooms $65-125. All major credit cards. ❸

⬡ FOOD

🔲 **The Desert Rose Cafe,** Hawaii Belt Rd. (☎939-7673), in Pohue Plaza in Ocean View. On the outside, this unassuming diner blends into the a'a desert that is Hawaii Ocean View Estates, but inside, the delicious food puts this place head-and-shoulders above the rest. Dishing out some of the best food in Ka'u ($5.75-11.25) with lots of daily specials, this joint is not to be missed. Open M-Th 7am-7pm, F-Su 7am-8pm. ❷

Na'alehu Fruit Stand, Mamalahoa Hwy. (☎929-9009), in the eastern end of downtown Na'alehu. With everything from local fruit and vegetables to Haagen-Dazs ice cream and Nantucket Nectars, this stand is worth a stop to fuel South Point adventures. Open M-Th 9am-6pm, F-Sa 9am-7pm, Su 9am-5pm. ❶

Shaka Restaurant, 95-5763 Mamalahoa Hwy. (☎929-7404), in downtown Na'alehu near the post office. Na'alehu may not have much to offer when it comes to culinary delights, but this friendly restaurant with a relaxed island flair serves up a variety of home-cooked meals at reasonable prices. Open Tu-Su 10am-9pm. MC/V. ❷

Punalu'u Bake Shop, Mamalahoa Hwy. (☎929-7343), in Na'alehu center. Their famous sweetbread is baked here and shipped around the island, so get it while it's hot. They also serve plate lunches ($6-7) and ice cream on a shady garden patio. Open daily 9am-5pm. ❶

⬡ SIGHTS

MANUKA STATE WAYSIDE. This turn-off amid the dense forests and crumbling lava fields of **Manuka State Natural Area Reserve** is an ideal spot to cast off the tourist chains of resort packages, rental car agreements, and fresh sunburn in favor of the natural calm of the island. The 2-mile **Manuka Loop Trail** runs through 8 acres of land that was set aside in the mid-1930s for 48 species of native Hawaiian flora and 150 other species from around the Pacific. The park is also a quiet locale for a lunch or rest stop with bathrooms and shaded picnic tables. *(Between the 81- and 82-mile markers on the Hawaii Belt Rd.)*

NECHUNG DORJE DRAYANG LING. This **Buddhist temple** and retreat center in the hills northeast of Pahala is an ideal example of the Ka'u's other-worldly essence. Once a Japanese *Nichiren* Mission, the temple was established by Nechung Rinpoche in 1973 as a non-sectarian center for the dissemination of Buddhist teachings, and is worth even just a short visit. The entire complex is richly colored in traditional Tibetan style and beautifully maintained. The Dalai Lama visited the temple in 1980 and again in 1994, giving a public talk to a crowd of several thousand people. Immaculate grounds, punctuated with towering eucalyptus, palm trees, and bamboo as well as a number of magnificent pea-

MILOLIʻI Tucked 5 mi. below Rte. 11, between the 88- and 89-mile markers, in the no-man's-land of lava fields and dense forest between the Kona coast and the rolling pastures of Kaʻu is the town of Miloliʻi. It is one of the Big Island's last true fishing villages and a vestige from another era. Although a traditional lifestyle based in and around the sea holds sway here, the town itself is anything but traditional, with 4X4s and SUVs parked in the shadow of satellite dishes atop newly constructed homes. The torturous drive down to the town provides panoramic views of the titanic lava flow that devastated the area in 1926, and there is still so little vegetation in the black fields that the lava seems freshly cooled. At the end of the road is **Miloliʻi Beach Park** along with the tiny **Hauʻoli Kamanaʻo Church.** The park offers restrooms and a sheltered picnic area as well as camping, and there is some good **snorkeling** along the rough shoreline. At the end of the day, the church, with its cool yellow exterior and red tin roof, mirrors the island's beautiful sunsets.

cocks, add to the sense of serenity. Individual visitors interested in quiet introspection and rest are welcome to stay for a minimum of 2 nights. *(From Rte. 11 take the turn-off to Pahala, 12 mi. northeast of Naʻalehu and 22 mi. southwest of Volcano. Take the first right onto Pikake St. and follow the paved road 4 mi. The temple will be on the right. ☎928-8539; nechung@aloha.net; www.nechung.org. Dorms $35, singles $50, doubles $70.)*

KA LAE/SOUTH POINT

The 11-mile road that rolls down from the Hawaii Belt Rd. (between the 69- and 70-mile markers, 6 mi. west of Waiʻohinu) to South Point is like a runway to another world. Dense rainforest gives way to pastures full of grazing cattle and the astonishing spectacle of the **Kamaʻoa Wind Farm.** Some of the enormous windmills here have lost their blades and look like fallen soldiers, but others continue to whip around at a considerable clip. Below these giants are windswept fields that stretch down to the azure sea. Rental car companies don't permit their cars to drive this road because (they say) they worry that drivers, swept away by the expansive views, will drive straight off the road. In actuality, the companies just don't want to have to shoulder the expense of dealing with cars anywhere off the island's main roads, and therefore prohibit travel to South Point. The road, which eventually becomes a single lane, poses no major difficulties.

🜚 SIGHTS

KA LAE NATIONAL HISTORIC LANDMARK DISTRICT. Near the coast, the road enters the 710-acre Ka Lae National Historic Landmark District. It eventually forks, and the right-hand route heads down to a red-earth parking lot and 30-foot cliffs. The left-hand track leads to the Ka Lae Information Center where there's parking for those setting out on the hike to Green Sands Beach. *(Office open daily 9am-6pm. Parking $5.)*

KA LAE BEACH. Ka Lae is a spectacular spot—as the convergence of currents from the windward and leeward sides of the beach create some pretty intense surf. A number of ladders and platforms on the cliff's edge adjacent to the parking lot enable fishermen and their catches to get up from the boats moored below, and double as a perfect venue for cliff jumping.

SOUTH POINT. "The Point" itself is a couple of minutes beyond the parking lot at the extremity of the island. This piece of land is thought to be the spot of the

Polynesians' first landing in the Hawaiian Islands, and has been an important location throughout Hawaiian history as both the site of Kalalea Heiau, which still stands today, and because of its abundance of fish.

◤ BEACHES

GREEN SANDS BEACH. From the Ka Lae Visitor Information Center, Green Sands Beach, or **Papakolea**, is a 3-mile, hour-long jaunt along the coast. If you can handle the walk, Green Sands should not be missed. Be sure to get directions, as the trail is not marked. The beach is not the verdant green of the surrounding windswept pasture, but more of a drab olive, thanks to the aptly named olivine. Regardless of its color, the solitude and stunning beauty of the spot will knock you over—if the ripping winds and crashing waves don't do it first. Surrounded by towering lava rock cliffs shaped by the ravages of wind and water, the narrow strip of sand resembles a vestige of a primordial Eden, somehow overlooked by all those who have explored this coast before. Come early enough in the day and you'll likely have the place to yourself. The surf here, which is generally bigger than at most other beaches on the island, makes for excellent body surfing. Be sure to bring plenty of water and appropriate footwear as the walk back may seem even longer after a couple of hours basking in the sun.

PUNALU'U BLACK SAND BEACH. Eight miles northeast of Na'alehu and a little less than 5 mi. south of Pahala along Rte. 11 lies Punalu'u Beach, the island's largest **black sand beach** and home to a large population of **hawksbill turtles.** Unfortunately, this combination of attractions has made Punalu'u very popular, especially with the tour buses that perpetually circle the island. It's rare that the area is not packed with visitors. Still, Punalu'u is a nice place to take a dip or **snorkel** around the rocks that serve as the primary feeding grounds for the turtles. You can sometimes spot them from the shore or from underneath the coconut palms that shade the sparkling sand. Just south of the beach itself are county park facilities, including protected picnic areas, restrooms, showers, and campsites.

HAMAKUA COAST

The drive along the Hawaii Belt Rd. (Rte. 19), between Hilo and Waimea, features some of the most spectacular tropical scenery on the island. Waterfalls peek around each bend in the highway, and rainbows of brilliant blossoms dot the mountainside. Although Hamakua was once the sugar cane gold mine of the Big Island, not a single plantation remains today. Nothing has filled the void left by the former sugar industry, and the region is one of the few places on the island where extensive expansion has not been the prevailing trend. Unlike much of the Big Island, the Hamakua Coast still has stretches of land that are inaccessible by car. Between Pololu Valley and Waipi'o Valley, a dozen miles of virgin shoreline can only be reached via ocean-going vessels or legs strong enough to hike up and down the *palis*. Small communities now occupy the intriguing historic shells of what were once bigger, bustling towns, but no one seems to mind the downsizing. Natural wonders dominate the landscape, which is punctuated by oases of civilization whose inhabitants are happy with life just the way it is.

HONOKA'A

For much of the 19th and 20th centuries, Honoka'a occupied a lofty position in the Big Island's sugar cane industry. Set atop rich volcanic soil on Mauna Kea's wet

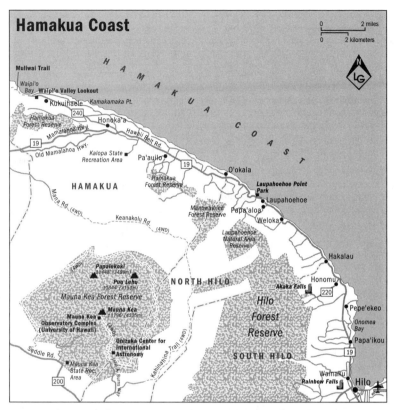

Hamakua Coast

0   2 miles
0   2 kilometers

Muliwai Trail

Waipi'o Bay   Waipi'o Valley Lookout

Kukuihaele   Kamakamaka Pt.

240

Hamakua Forest Reserve

Mamalahoa Hwy.

Honoka'a

Hawaii Belt Rd.

19

Old Mamalahoa Hwy.

Kalopa State Recreation Area   Pa'auilo

19

HAMAKUA

Hamakua Forest Reserve

O'okala

Laupahoehoe Point Park

Laupahoehoe

Manowaiolee Forest Reserve   Papa'aloa

Mana Rd. (4WD)

Keanakolu Rd. (4WD)

Weloka

Laupahoehoe Natural Area Reserve

Hakalau

Papalekoki 11148' (3489m)

Puu Lehu 10844' (3153m)

NORTH HILO

Honomu

Akaka Falls

220

Mauna Kea Forest Reserve

Mauna Kea 13796' (4205m)

Hilo Forest Reserve

Pepe'ekeo

Onomea Bay

Mauna Kea Observatory Complex (University of Hawaii)

Onizuka Center for International Astronomy

Papa'ikou

Kahinahina Trail (4WD)

SOUTH HILO

19

Saddle Rd.

Mauna Kea State Rec. Area

200

Burns Way

Wainaku

Rainbow Falls

Hilo

windward coast, the town proved a perfect match for the flourishing commercial enterprise. The sugar industry eventually waned, however, and Honoka'a's last mill closed in the mid-1990s. Honoka'a has rallied in its stead, forging a future on its own terms. The circa-1920 store fronts of the town's main drag still house a hardware store and a five-and-dime, but recently, funky art galleries, eclectic antique shops, and daring restaurants have sprung up among them. The range of establishments within the town's small borders reveals the diverse nature of Honoka'a's residents as well.

■ ▐ ORIENTATION AND TRANSPORTATION

Honoka'a sits along **Rte. 240,** just off of Rte. 19, about 40 miles northwest of Hilo and 15 miles east of Waimea. **Waipi'o Valley** is 9 miles northwest of town, at the end of Rte. 240. Life in Honoka'a centers on **Mamane St.** (Rte. 240), which is home to almost all of the town's businesses; a handful more lie along the highway up the hill. From Waimea, **Plumeria St.** leaves Rte. 19 and drops down through Honoka'a, meeting Mamane St. in the center of town.

Honoka'a is on the main route between Hilo and Kona, and receives more traffic from the **Hele-On bus** than any other small town on the island. Buses run from the high school to **Hilo** (1¼hr.; M-Sa 5:50, 8:30am, 3:15, 5:10, 5:25pm; $3.75) and **Kona** (1¾hr., 2:40pm, $4.50) via **Waimea** (40min., 75¢) from the Dairy Queen on Rte. 19.

🔻 PRACTICAL INFORMATION

Despite the presence of two tourist information centers in Honoka'a, travelers will be hard pressed to rustle up some useful information. The **Honoka'a Visitor Center,** adjacent to Tex Drive-In along Rte. 19, is more of a gift shop than anything else. However, it is staffed and there are a few brochures. (☎775-0598 or 966-5416; www.hawaii-culture.com. Open daily 9am-5pm.) In town, the **Hamakua Heritage Center and Visitor Information** is little more than a shack filled with flyers for local (and not-so-local) tourist attractions. No one seems to man this office, which means it has the one bonus of being open 24hr.

Honoka'a has several more helpful services. Both **Bank of Hawaii** (☎775-7218) and **First Hawaiian Bank** (☎775-7276) have **24hr. ATMs.** The banks are located on Mamane St. and are open M-Th 8:30am-4pm and F 8:30am-6pm. The **Honoka'a Public Library,** 45-3380 Mamane St., offers **Internet access** to those with a Hawaii Public Library card. (☎775-8881. Open M, Th 11am-7pm; Tu-W 9am-5pm; and F 9am-3pm.) Laundry facilities are available at **Washerette,** on Kike St., near the corner of Kike and Mamane St. (☎987-7731. Open daily 6am-9pm.) The **Honoka'a Swimming Pool,** on Mamane St., next to the high school, is open to the public. (☎775-0650. Open mid-afternoons M-F.) For **weather information,** call ☎961-5582. For **emergencies,** call ☎911 or the **police** mini-station (☎775-7533) on Mamane St. **Liu's Pharmacy,** 45-3551A Mamane St., across from the bank, is well-stocked. (☎775-0496 or 775-9974. Open M-F 8am-6pm, Sa 9am-1:30pm.) The **post office** is at 45-490 Lehua St., on the corner of Lehua and Mamane St. (☎800-275-8777. Open M-F 9am-4pm, Sa 8:15-9:45am.) **Zip Code:** 96727.

🔻 ACCOMMODATIONS AND CAMPING

Hotel Honoka'a Club, Mamane St. (☎800-808-0678 or 775-0678; www.hotel-hono.com). You can't miss this rambling establishment, built in 1908 as a club for plantation managers. With the death of the sugar industry, the building was transformed into a hotel, though the clean, eccentrically decorated rooms are reminiscent of an earlier era. Breakfast included. Linens not provided. Reception 7:30am-1pm and 4-8pm. Check-out noon. Dorms $15, economy rooms $35-55. Two-bedroom suites $80. All major credit cards. ❶

Waipio Wayside, off of Hwy. 240 (☎800-833-8849 or 775-0275; wayside@bigisland.net), on the way toward Waipio Valley, a few miles west of downtown Honoka'a. Formerly a plantation house, this secluded inn boasts incredible views of the Pacific Ocean. Each bedroom is individually decorated and comfortable, but the gazebo and various decks are the best places to soak up the soothing tropical atmosphere. Breakfast included. Rooms $95-155. All major credit cards. ❸

Kalopa Forest State Park and Recreation Area, located off of Rte. 19, about 1 mi. south of the intersection of Rte. 19 and Rte. 240. Camping is available on a first-come, first-served basis. Reserve cabins in advance by calling ☎974-6200, or speak to the caretaker stationed at the park entrance. Cabins include access to the recreation hall and kitchen. Bedding provided. Check-in 2pm. Check-out 10am. Camping free. Cabins $55-175. ❷

🔻 🔻 FOOD AND ENTERTAINMENT

Taro Junction Natural Foods, Mamane St. (☎775-9477). Holding its own against chain convenience stores, this natural food store stocks the basic nuts and grains. Open M-F 10am-5:30pm, Sa 9am-5pm.

Jolene's Kau Kau Korner Restaurant, (☎775-9498) at the corner of Mamane St. and Plumeria St. A friendly local joint serving down-home grub, including mahi mahi and teriyaki-you-name-it. If you want authentic Hawaiian favorites, this the place to stop. Plate lunches and dinners $6.50-7.75. Open M, W, F 10am-8pm; Tu, Th 10am-4pm. ❶

Simply Natural, Mamane St. (☎775-0119). Unique dishes such as *taro*-banana pancakes ($3.50) augment a menu of reliable stand-bys, including tempeh sandwiches and garden burgers ($6). The juxtaposition of rainbow ceiling fans and checkerboard linoleum floors make for a fresh take on typical diner decor. Open M-Sa 9am-4pm. ❶

Mamane Street Bakery, Mamane St. (☎775-7498). Freshly baked bread and pastries (75¢-$4) are perfect for a picnic. Open Sa-W 6:30am-5pm, Th-F 6:30am-6pm. ❶

Tex Drive-In, 45-690 Pakalana St. (☎775-0598), above downtown Honoka'a, just off of Rte. 19. Drawing a sizable crowd with local specialties (*loco moco* $3.55; *bento* $5) and quality burgers ($3-5), this straightforward joint does fast-food well. Pick up their famous *malasadas* (80¢) in the morning, when they're fresh. Open daily 6am-9pm. ❶

Cafe Il Mondo, 45-3626A Mamane St. (☎775-7711). Walking into this cozy cafe, you get the distinct impression that the folks behind the counter are doing what they love. Customers reap the benefit of their passion for pizza; the food is excellent. Slices ($2-2.50), calzones ($8), pizzas ($8-18.25). Open M-Sa 11am-8pm. ❶

Honoka'a People's Theater, on Mamane St. (☎775-0000). The theater has been painstakingly restored over the last decade, and now shows a wide range of movies, from arthouse films to Hollywood blockbusters. $6, seniors $4, under 12 $3.

⚠ OUTDOORS

KALOPA FOREST STATE PARK AND RECREATION AREA. This 615-acre reserve has been protected since 1903, but much of the surrounding land has been all but destroyed by sugar cane production. The park includes 100 acres of virgin Hawaiian rainforest situated between heights of 2000 and 3500 ft. The land receives approximately 90 in. of precipitation a year. An easy 0.7-mile loop, the Native Forest Nature Trail, passes through the heart of the 'ohi'a rain forest. There are a number of other trails within the greater forest reserve area, including the Gulch Rim Trail, which skirts Kalopa Gulch and Hanaipoe Gulch. There are group cabins, a campground, and a picnic area (see Accommodations and Camping, p. 334) all of which are available for public use. *(Located off of Rte. 19, about 1 mile south of the intersection of Rte. 19 and Rte. 240.)*

LAUPAHOEHOE POINT Early in the morning on April 1, 1946, the children of the village of Laupahoehoe ("leaf of smooth lava") were greeted at school by a peculiar sight. Their school, which was set at the tip of a finger of land jutting into the Pacific, normally overlooked turbulent waves crashing against the lava shoreline. That day, however, the nooks and crannies of the rough black headland, usually covered by water, were dry. Students and teachers ventured down to the shore to investigate the phenomenon. Minutes later, a massive tsunami crashed down upon them. The entire school was wiped away, and 20 children and 4 teachers were killed.

Today, the point is home to a well-maintained beach park with a monument dedicated to those lost in the disaster. Facilities include restrooms, showers, picnic tables, and campsites, as well as volleyball and basketball courts. The point is about halfway between Hilo and Honoka'a, 1 mile off of Hwy. 19, at the end of a marked turn.

WAIPI'O VALLEY

The massive valley, which is a mile wide at its mouth and extends 6 miles back from the coast, inspires awe in even the most jaded traveler. Walled in on either side by 2000-foot high *pali*, Waipi'o Valley is a world unto itself. The wide, twisting **Waipi'o Stream** channels fresh water from the Kohala Mountains to the sea. This natural irrigation nourishes an abundance of fruit trees, which are ripe for the picking. Lush *taro* patches dot the landscape, and the tree branches sink under the weight of avocados, bananas, coconuts, mango, guava, and passion fruit. With a stunning gray-sand beach that stretches between the warm surf of the Hamakua Coast, canopied rainforest, striking waterfalls, and myriad vistas, the valley has a little bit of everything.

Before the arrival of Captain Cook in 1778, between 4000 and 10,000 native Hawaiians had established their own private Eden in the crevices of Waipi'o Valley. The largest of the seven valleys on the windward side of the Kohala Mountains, the Waipi'o Valley was once the political and religious center of Big Island. 'Umi, the first ruler to unite the people of the Big Island, systematically laid out *taro* fields in Waipi'o in the 16th century. The bounty from the valley's fields could feed the entire island during times of need. The valley began to attract non-Hawaiians, particularly the Chinese, a few hundred years later. The immigrants took advantage of the fertile climate to farm small plots, and by the end of the century, the valley boasted schools, churches, and restaurants, in addition to a post office, jail, and hotel. The **tsunami** of 1946 wiped out almost all of the valley's homes and infrastructure, forcing many inhabitants to move to higher, safer ground. Today, the valley is home to no more than 100 residents, and much of the cultivated land has been reclaimed by the rainforest. For those willing to explore it, the spirit and bounty of the land remains untarnished.

■ ORIENTATION

Waipi'o Valley sits at the end of **Rte. 240,** about 8 miles west of Honoka'a. The state highway terminates at the parking area for the **Waipi'o Valley Lookout,** but a very steep paved road (25% grade), passable only by vehicles with 4WD, takes visitors down the mile-long descent to the valley floor. Park here to hike down.

■ CAMPING

Camping is free for up to 4 nights at 4 sites, located underneath the trees on the eastern side of Waipi'o Stream. Permits are available from the **Bishop Estate,** 78-6831 Ali'i Dr., in Keauhou Shopping Center, which owns 60% of the land in the valley and manages it with the intent of preserving Hawaiian heritage. (☎322-5300. Open M-F 7:30am-4:30pm.)

■ HIKING

The easiest way to "explore" the valley is with your eyes, from the **Waipi'o Valley Lookout** at the end of Rte. 240, at the top of the eastern *pali* (900 ft. above the valley floor). Across the valley, on the opposite *pali*, you can see the switchback trail that climbs over to **Waimanu Valley** on the opposite side of the ridge. The views from the lookout are more expansive than any you'll see once you head down into the valley itself, but you're cheating yourself if you stop here. From the lookout, an intimidatingly steep (but relatively short) paved road plunges to the valley's floor. This road doesn't present any difficulties for 4WD vehicles on the way down, but you'll have difficulty getting back without one. All rented 4WD vehicles are prohibited from traveling anywhere below the valley rim, so walking becomes the best—and only—option. The hike down is a brief 30min., but can be a little slippery when wet. The hike back up should take about 45min. and, counter-intuitively, it is somewhat easier because you're more in control. Bring plenty of water, as there are no facilities on the valley floor.

At the base of the *pali*, the road forks and the left branch heads back into the interior of the valley while the right continues down to the beach. A left turn yields views of the shimmering **Hi'ilawe Falls** (1200 ft.), Hawaii's highest single-drop waterfall. It's possible to hike to the base of Hi'ilawe in about 1½hr., but it requires bushwhacking through all sorts of rainforest thicket. Adventurers need also exhibit sensitivity; "*kapu*" and "No Trespassing" signs line the way.

Turning right at the fork takes you on a muddy, 10-minute walk to the matchless **Waipi'o Beach.** Looming *pali* dramatically border the sandy expanse, which is bombarded by the aggressive Pacific surf. Up and down the jagged coast, waterfalls tumble down steep cliffs before splashing onto the lava boulders of the shoreline. Despite a strong riptide and rough waves, the beach is popular with surfers. Waipi'o Stream cleaves the beach in two, on its way to the ocean, and the western bank is much less popular than the more accessible eastern shore. Be careful when crossing the stream—the current is stronger than it looks and the stream is deeper in some places than in others.

From the beach, you can see the impressive **Kalauahine Falls** sparkling off the *pali* to the east. There's a rough trail along fairly loose lava rock that runs from the intersection of the cliffs and the ocean to the foot of the falls. At the western end of the beach, a switchback trail leads up the *pali* and over to Waimanu Valley. Waipio's neighboring valley is about 10 miles away, but the trek up the valley wall to a series of secluded pools and a glittering waterfall makes a good day hike. If you plan on going any farther, make sure to come well-prepared with appropriate water, food, and rain gear, as well as a **backcountry camping permit** from the **Division of Forestry and Wildlife,** 19 E. Kawili (☎974-4221) in Hilo. Like Waipi'o, Waimanu Valley once had a sizeable Hawaiian settlement, which has since been abandoned. Waimanu Valley is protected as a National Estuarine Research Reserve because it is one of the few remaining unaltered Hawaiian freshwater ecosystems.

⬛ TOURS

If you've been down to the valley floor and are interested in seeing things from another perspective, there are a number of outfits that offer tours along the Waipi'o rim including **Waipi'o Ridge Stables** (☎775-1007), **Mountain Biking Waipi'o Valley** (☎775-9393), **Kukui ATV & Adventures** (☎775-1701), and **Waipi'o Rim Backroad Adventures** (☎775-1122). While these tours, as well as the ones listed below, are an interesting way to see the valley, they are not the only options. Waipi'o's waterfalls and beach are off-limits to tours.

Waipi'o Valley Shuttle (☎ 775-7121), embellishes the natural beauty of the valley with educational tidbits. The tour features views of Hi'ilawe Falls and *taro* patches, and knowledgeable guides narrate tales of Hawaiian history and legends in the background. The 1½hr. tours leave from Waipi'o Valley Artworks, in Kukuihaele. M-Sa 9, 11am, 1, and 3pm. Reservations recommended. $40, ages 10 and under $20.

Waipi'o Na'alapa Stables (☎ 775-0419; naalapa@ilhawaii.net), offers 2½hr. horseback adventures in the valley. Experienced guides lead the rides through the rainforest to spectacular waterfalls and vistas. Trips begin at Waipi'o Valley Artworks in Kukuihaele. M-Sa 9:30am and 1pm. Reservations required. $75.

Waipiʻo on Horseback (☎ 775-7291), specializes in leisurely excursions that highlight waterfalls and one of Waipiʻo's largest *taro* farms. Meet at the Last Chance Store in Kukuihaele for a drive to the valley floor. M-Sa 9:30am and 1:30pm. Reserve 24hr. in advance. $75.

Waipiʻo Valley Wagon Tours (☎ 775-9518), explore the *taro* fields, lush tropical foliage, and majestic waterfalls of the valley from the cushioned seats of a mule-drawn covered wagon. The 1½hr. tours depart from the Last Chance Store in Kukuihaele. M-Sa 9:30, 11:30am, 1:30, and 3:30pm. Reservations required. $40, children $20.

WAIMEA

Known locally as Kamuela, Waimea centers on Parker Ranch, its pride and joy. The ranch was named for its founder, John Palmer Parker, and is the largest privately-owned cattle ranch in the US. In the early 19th century, Parker, a Massachusetts-born sailor, garnered Kamehameha I's favor by taming the longhorns that ran rampant on the Big Island. He was rewarded with a small parcel of land on the slopes of Mauna Loa. In the decades that followed, Parker hired experienced cattlemen (*paniolos*) from Mexico, and gradually increased his holdings. In 1847, he established the Parker Ranch. Today, the ranch encompasses over 225,000 acres and has 35,000 head of cattle.

Despite Waimea's Stetson stylings, it is merely a ritzy vacation haven masquerading as a small working community. The Parker Ranch is omnipresent, with its name emblazoned everywhere from fairgrounds to museums, although it employs only 11 full-time *paniolos* and about 50 other workers. Look no further than the Western-façade Starbucks at the Parker Ranch Center to discover what lies below Waimea's surface. Chic restaurants and couture boutiques are more common than feed stores and tack shops, and price doesn't seem to be a concern here.

Waimea is nonetheless worth a visit for its history and culture. All the money flowing through the town has the benefit of attracting a plethora of colorful events, such as the Waikiʻi Music Festival and the July 4th Horse Races and Rodeo. In addition, Waimea is uniquely situated between the wet Hamakua Coast and the dry Kohala Coast, making misty rainbows a common sight.

■ ORIENTATION

Waimea is set smack dab in the middle of everything, 54 mi. northwest of Hilo and 40 mi. from Kailua-Kona. In the center of town, **Rte. 190** (Hawaii Belt Rd.) from Kona intersects with **Hwy. 19** (Kawaihae Rd.). Two miles west of downtown Waimea, on the road to Kawaihae, **Kohala Mountain Rd.** (Hwy. 250) splits off toward Hawi. **Mamalahoa Hwy.** and **Kawaihae Rd.,** branching east and west respectively, are the two main commercial strips.

■ TRANSPORTATION

Flights: Waimea-Kohala Airport (☎ 885-4520), off of Rte. 190, a little more than 1 mi. south of Waimea center. **Pacific Wings Airlines** (☎ 888-575-4546 or 887-2104; www.pacificwings.com) runs flights to **Honolulu** (W-M 8am) and **Kahului,** Maui (W-M 6:10pm). Both cost approximately $120.

Bus: The **Hele-On bus** (☎ 961-8744) runs through Waimea with some consistency. Daily trips to **Hilo** from both Ace Hardware (1¼hr.; 2:55, 4:55, and 5pm; $4.50) and the Parker Ranch Center (1hr. 40min., M-Sa 8:05am, $4.50), as well as to **Kailua-Kona** from the Parker Ranch Center (1¾hr., M-Sa 3:20pm, $3).

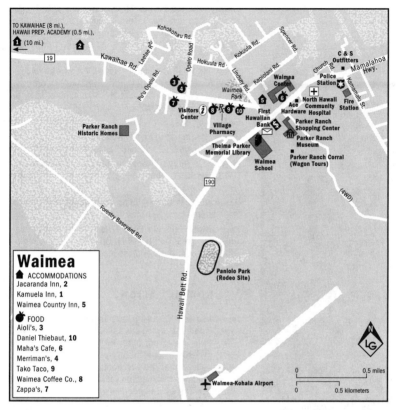

Waimea

▲ ACCOMMODATIONS
Jacaranda Inn, **2**
Kamuela Inn, **1**
Waimea Country Inn, **5**

🍖 FOOD
Aioli's, **3**
Daniel Thiebaut, **10**
Maha's Cafe, **6**
Merriman's, **4**
Tako Taco, **9**
Waimea Coffee Co., **8**
Zappa's, **7**

Taxis: Several taxi companies serve the Waimea area, including **Alpha Star Taxi** (☎885-4771) and **Elsa Taxi** (☎887-6446). Both have flexible hours and charge the standard island rate of $2 per mile.

Bike and Equipment Rentals: C&S Outfitters, 64-1066 Mamalahoa Hwy. (☎885-5005), at the corner of Hwy. 19 and Kamamalu St. Full suspension bikes $30 per day, $130 per week. Kayaks (Nov.-Apr.) $30-45 per day, $120-160 per week. Open M-Sa 9am-5pm. **Mauna Kea Mountain Bikes** (☎888-682-8687 or 883-0130; mtb-tour@aol.com; www.BikeHawaii.com), offers rentals as well as mountain bike excursions. Rentals $30 per day, $130 per week. See **Tours,** p. 341.

🛈 PRACTICAL INFORMATION

Tourist Office: Waimea Visitor Center, 65-1291 Kawaihae Rd. (☎885-6707; www.northhawaii.net or www.kamuela.com). The most helpful Visitor Center on the island, with information to spare and an informed staff. Open M-F 8:30am-3:30pm.

Banks: Bank of Hawaii, 67-1191 Mamalahoa Hwy. (☎885-7995). Open M-Th 8:30am-4pm and F 8:30am-6pm. **First Hawaiian Bank** (☎885-7991), in front of the Parker Ranch Center at the corner of Mamalahoa Hwy. and Kawaihae Rd. Open M-Th 8:30am-4pm, F 8:30am-6pm, and Sa 9am-1pm. Both have **24hr. ATMs.**

THE BIG SPLURGE

IN DANIEL'S KITCHEN

The classy Daniel Thiebaut restaurant, located in the painstakingly restored **Chock In Store,** is about as sophisticated as the Big Island gets. The intriguing fusion of French and Asian cuisine results in delicious entrees such as wok-fried sea scallops with Asian-style risotto. Lunch $7-15. Dinner $18-39. *(65-1259 Kawaihae Rd. ☎887-2200, west of downtown on Hwy. 19. Reservations recommended. Open for lunch M-F 11:30am-1:30pm, dinner nightly 5:30-9pm. All major credit cards.)*

Library: Thelma Parker Memorial Library, 67-1209 Mamalahoa Hwy. has **Internet access** for those with a Hawaii Public Library card (three-month card $10). Open M-Tu, Th 9am-4:30pm; W noon-7:30pm; F-Sa 9am-1pm.

Swimming Pool: The pool at **Hawaii Preparatory Academy,** 65-1692 Kohala Mt. Rd. (☎881-4028), on Hwy. 250., is open for public use M-F 6-7am, noon-1pm, 5-6pm and Su 1-4pm. $2.

Emergency: ☎911.

Police: Waimea Police Station (☎887-3080), at the corner of Kamamalu St. and Mamalahoa Hwy.

Pharmacy: Village Pharmacy, 65-1267 Kawaihae Rd. (☎885-4824). Open M-F 8:30am-5:30pm and Sa 8:30am-2pm.

Hospital: North Hawaii Community Hospital, 67-1125 Mamalahoa Hwy. (☎885-4444).

Post Office: Kamuela Post Office, 67-1197 Mamalahoa Hwy. (☎800-275-8777). Open M-F 8am-4:30pm, Sa 9am-noon. Don't address mail to Waimea.

Zip Code: 96743.

▗ ACCOMMODATIONS

Jacaranda Inn, 65-1444 Kawaihae Rd. (☎885-8813; tji@ilhawaii.net; www.jacarandainn.com), along Hwy. 19 a little over 1 mi. outside of downtown Waimea. Built in 1897, this rambling plantation-style estate eventually came into the hands of Lawrence Rockefeller and has housed both Jackie Kennedy and Henry Kissinger. The estate-turned-inn retains its original elegance, and each of the eight suites features eclectic furnishings and detailed luxury. Breakfast included. Check-in 3-6pm. Check-out 11am. Reservations recommended. Rooms $95-350. All major credit cards. ❸

Kamuela Inn, 65-1300 Kawaihae Rd. (☎800-555-8968 or 885-4243; aminn@aloha.net; www.hawaii-bnb.com/kamuela.html), along Hwy. 19 west of Waimea Center. The inn is Waimea's best value, with clean, spacious rooms. The tasteful up-country motif is a far cry from the generic decor of most of the island's basic hotels. Continental breakfast included. Check-in 3pm. Check-out noon. Standard $59, deluxe $72; Suites with kitchenette (fits 3-4) $89-99. All major credit cards. ❷

Waimea Country Inn, 65-1210 Lindsey Rd. (☎800-367-5004 or 885-6711; www.castleresorts.com), off of Kawaihae Rd. just west of Waimea center. The spotless rooms are made all the more appealing by refined Hawaiian accents. The rooms on the second floor have tall, exposed ceilings, and are particularly spacious. Check-in 3pm. Check-out noon. Reception 7am-11pm. Rooms $93-118. All major credit cards. ❸

FOOD

For a break from restaurant dining, pick up fresh ingredients at the **Homestead Farmers' Market**, at the State of Hawaii Department of Homelands, a couple miles east of town on Hwy. 19 (Sa 7am-noon).

Aioli's (☎885-6325), in Opelo Plaza on Kawaihae Rd., a little less than 1 mi. west of Waimea center. With unadorned bamboo furniture and funky local artwork on the walls, this simple bistro is short on pretension and long on quality. The innovative offerings include house special garlic soup, famous *liliko'i* cheesecake, and roasted rack of lamb and spinach, *roquefort,* and walnut stuffed pasta (entrees $14-23). Reservations recommended. Open Tu 11am-4pm, W-Th 11am-8pm, F-Sa 11am-9pm, Su 8am-2pm. D/MC/V. ❹

Merriman's (☎885-6822), on Kawaihae Rd. next to Aioli's. Specializing in cutting edge Hawaiian regional cuisine, Merriman's uses fresh Big Island products to create inventive, delectable dishes. Lunch $6-11, dinner $19-33. Reservations suggested. Open for lunch M-F 11:30am-1:30pm, dinner nightly 5:30-9pm. All major credit cards. ❺

Maha's Cafe, One Waimea Center (☎885-0693), off of Mamalahoa Hwy. in downtown Waimea. Set in the historic Spencer House, the restaurant is named after one of the queens of Hawaiian home cooking, Harriet-Ann Namahaokalani Schutte Kraan ("Maha"). Island-style edibles, such as *Lalamilo* Veggie and Tutu's Tuna Sandwiches, are made with fresh local ingredients. Breakfast $2.75-5.25, lunch $6.25-10.75. Open Th-M 8am-4:30pm. All major credit cards. ❷

Tako Taco, 65-1271 Kawaihae Rd. (☎887-1717), on Hwy. 19 west of the town center. A little shack straight out of Baja beach, this taqueria is the place to pick up tasty Mexican eats for cheap. Burritos $4.25-8.50, tacos $3.50-8.50, salads $6.50-8.50. Open M-Sa 11am-8pm. MC/V. ❶

Zappa's, 65-1210 Kawaihae Rd. (☎885-1511), behind the Opelo Corner gas station. Zappa's tosses up Waimea's best pizzas, and dishes out solid grinders and pasta. Take-out available. Pizzas $9-22, grinders $7, pasta $8-9. Open daily 6:30am-1:30pm and W-M 4:30pm-8pm. D/MC/V. ❷

Waimea Coffee Co. (☎885-4472), in Parker Sq. on Kawaihae Rd. The best place to grab a cup of joe ($1.50). Open M-F 7am-5pm, Sa 8am-4pm. ❶

TOURS

Parker Ranch Wagon Tours (☎800-262-7290 or 885-7655), in Parker Ranch Corral, next to the Parker Ranch Visitor Center. Explore a small portion of Parker Ranch with a knowledgeable guide, in the comfort of a covered *paniolo* wagon. Hourly Tu-Sa 10am-2pm. Tours $15, ages 12 and under $12.

Mauna Kea Mountain Bikes (☎888-682-8687 or 883-0130; mtbtour@aol.com; www.BikeHawaii.com), offers mountain bike tours around Waimea. Tours range from beginner to advanced, and one even drops off the summit of Mauna Kea. Bike included. Reserve 24hr. in advance. Tours $50-120. See **Rentals**, p. 339.

Hawaii Forest and Trail, 74-5035 B Queen Ka'ahumanu Hwy. in Kailua-Kona (☎800-464-1993 or 331-8505; info@hawaii-forest.com; www.hawaii-forest.com), next to the Chevron station between downtown Kailua-Kona and the airport. Expert guides enhance the adventures, many of which have cultural and historical themes. Half-day $95, children $85; full-day $145/$105.

FROM THE ROAD

THE BOYS OF SUMMER

I arrived at the Parker Ranch's Paniolo Park for the 40th annual July 4th Horse Races and Rodeo to see that the stands are packed, as expected. However, the audience was about as strange a rodeo crowd as I could imagine. Rather than Stetsons rising above a forest of denim, I saw tie-dyed tees, plumeria leis, Hawaiian shirts, and baseball caps. I picked out a spot in the colorful crowd and took my seat above the race track and arena. All the riders racing are panio-los from one of the island's many ranches, but the ones who really stand out are the wranglers from Parker Ranch. All day, they had been cleaning up in both the races and rodeo competitions, showing a degree of poise their colleagues couldn't seem to match. In the last event of the morning, the relay race, I placed my bet on the boys from Waimea—$10 on Parker Ranch. The riders took their positions, and with the wave of a couple flags, they were off. They were neck and neck at the first pass until the Parker Ranch jockey pulled out. On the inside turn, the other rider clawed the distance back. At the next pass, it was unclear who was ahead, and as the cowboys pounded around the final turn, the other rider edged in front. But with a burst of speed, the Parker Ranch rider pulled out all the stops, finishing first by a nose. I went to collect my cash, and was dismayed to learn that one of my boys from Parker Ranch had dropped the baton on the first leg, disqualifying the team. No worries—I'm sure the Parker panio-los will be back in the saddle shortly.

-Bryden Sweeney-Taylor

 SIGHTS

PARKER RANCH MUSEUM. For all the Parker Ranch hype in Waimea, the museum dedicated to the history of this ranch is surprisingly low-key. A small exhibit hall explores a bit of early Hawaiian history before focusing on the ranch's owners—from John Palmer Parker in the early 1800s to sixth-generation Parker, Richard Smart, who died in 1992. Most of the displays are visual and a 25min. video detailing the ranch's history provides useful background informa-tion. *(67-1185 Mamalahoa Hwy., in the Parker Ranch Center. ☎885-7655; info@parkerranch.com; www.parkerranch.com. Open daily 9am-5pm. $6, seniors $5, children $4.50.)*

PARKER RANCH HISTORIC HOMES. These exquis-itely maintained homes illustrate two different eras in the history of Parker Ranch. **Mana Hale** is the New England-style wooden saltbox that served as John Palmer Parker's home during his first years as a rancher. Its appealing simplicity is highlighted by the gleaming koa floorboards that were transported here from the home's original location, about 12 mi. out-side of Waimea on the slopes of Mauna Kea. **Puopelu,** Richard Smart's ranch estate, was built in 1862. Over the course of the following century, nearly 8000 sq. ft. were added to building. The towering ceilings and light-filled rooms make the home an excellent show-case for Smart's French Impressionist and Chinese art collection. *(On Rte. 190, 1 mi. south of town on the road to Kona. ☎885-5433. $8.50, seniors $7.50, children $6. Open M-Sa 10am-5pm. Admission to both the museum and historic homes $12, children $9.50.)*

KAHILU THEATRE. This state-of-the-art theater, founded by Richard Smart in 1981, is the Big Island's premier performance venue. From fall to spring, the theater plays host to a wide range of global artists, such as Bela Fleck and The Flecktones and the Aspen Santa Fe Ballet. It also welcomes local per-formers and productions on a regular basis and screens art-house films throughout the year. *(67-1186 Lindsey Rd., behind the Parker Ranch Center. ☎885-6868 or 887-6368 for movie info; boxoffice@kahilutheatre.org; www.kahilutheatre.org. Tickets for major events $28-45.)*

NORTH KOHALA

On the way to North Kohala, Hwy. 250 winds along the spine of the Kohala Mountains, twisting and turn-ing past some of the Big Island's most breathtaking scenery. The visual odyssey includes extended views of Mt. Hualalai and the South Kohala Coast, as well as Maui's Haleakala in the distance.

Located at the tip of an outcropping, North Kohala is removed from the rest of Big Island both literally and figuratively. Kohala Mountain, Hawaii's oldest volcano, presides over the area's endless pastures, towering 5480 ft. at its highest point. Unlike the stark black fields that cover much of the Big Island, North Kohala has rich red soil that nourishes the luxuriant flora of the region. The mountain's eastern side is marked by deep valleys carved out of lava rock foundations, which are found nowhere else on the island. Within these valleys, powerful waterfalls plunge through dense masses of native forest and wild horses run rampant.

The people of North Kohala are as unique as the terrain, mainly folks who came looking to avoid anything and everything mainstream. Weathered ranchers, aging hippies, former yuppies, and down-home locals all live side-by-side in a community happily removed from the rest of the Big Island.

HAWI AND KAPA'AU

Off the beaten path, the vibrant towns of Hawi and Kapa'au (also referred to as Kohala) revel in their nonconformity. Each town is lined with intriguing stores, fresh galleries, and innovative restaurants, and residents have taken advantage of their distance from the rest of the Big Island to create a culture of their own.

■❊⬅ ORIENTATION AND TRANSPORTATION

Hawi is located at the intersection of **Rte. 250** (Kohala Mountain Rd.) and **Rte. 270,** 19 mi. north of Kawaihae and 20 mi. northwest of Waimea. This stretch of Rte. 270 is also known as **Akoni Pule Hwy.** and functions as the town's main drag. It continues east from Hawi for close to 7 mi., passing through Kapa'au after 2 mi.

North Kohala is the one district of the island through which the Hawaii Belt Road does not run. The **Hele-On** bus has daily routes running from downtown Kapa'au to **Hawi** and six resorts in **South Kohala,** the last of which is the Hilton Waikoloa. (☎961-8744. 6:20am 75¢ per bus ticket, three bus tickets required to travel anywhere besides Hawi.)

🛈 PRACTICAL INFORMATION

The **North Kohala Civic Center,** in downtown Kapa'au, was once the Kohala Courthouse but now serves as the area's Visitor Center, and is staffed by helpful senior citizens. (Open M-F 10am-4pm.) The **Bank of Hawaii,** on Akoni Pule Hwy. in downtown Kapa'au, has a **24hr. ATM.** (☎889-6217. Open M-Th 8:30am-4pm, F 8:30-6pm.) The **Kohala Book Shop,** 54-3885 Akoni Pule Hwy., in downtown Kapa'au, is one of

---

> ## THE ONCE AND FUTURE KING About 2 mi. east of
> Kapa'au, along Hwy. 270 to Pololu Valley, just above a narrow bridge, a huge boulder sits on the side of the road. The lump of lava rock would be indistinguishable from any other, if not for the "HVB Warrior" sign posted next to it.
>
> Legend holds that Kamehameha demonstrated the potency of his *mana*—and validated his claim to rule over all the islands—by carrying this rock over his head up from the beach below. The impossibility of this feat is slightly tempered by other myths, which maintain that Kamehameha stood between 6 ft. 8 in. and 7 ft. 4 in. tall.
>
> The rock is said to have rested in this spot until workers widening the road attempted to move it to another location. They managed to lift the rock off the ground in preparation for its transport, but it immediately tumbled back into its familiar resting place.

IN RECENT NEWS

CLICK IT OR TICKET

Recent studies have shown that 68% of car accident fatalities in Hawaii occur solely because passengers were not buckled up. In light of these findings, the Hawaii Department of Transportation and local police departments have teamed up to enforce seat belt use. Citations begin at $100 and can be even higher if children are not buckled up as well. While people are still allowed to drive pretty much anything, from a go-kart to a Monster truck wherever they want, seat belts are a matter of life and death for those patrolling the highways and byways. During the first week of the campaign, eagle-eyed cops nabbed over 2800 offenders.

the island's best book stores. (☎889-6400. Open Tu-Sa 11am-5pm, closed for Sept.) The **Bond Memorial Public Library,** on Akoni Pule Hwy. in downtown Kapa'au, offers **Internet access** to Hawaii State Public Library card holders. (☎889-6729. Open M noon-8pm, Tu-Th 9am-5pm, F 9am-1pm.) The **North Kohala District Police Station** (☎889-6540) is in Kapa'au, behind the Kamehameha statue and North Kohala Civic Center. **Kamehameha Pharmacy** is at 54-3877 Akoni Pule Hwy., in downtown Kapa'au. (☎889-6161. Open M-F 9am-12:30pm and 1:30-5pm.) **Kohala Hospital** (☎889-6211), is east of downtown Kapa'au, off of Hwy. 270. **Kohala Computer Center,** on Akoni Pule Hwy. in downtown Hawi, has **Internet access.** ($3 per 15min., $10 per hr. Open M-F 10am-5pm.) **Hawi Post Office,** 55-515 Hawi Rd., sits near the corner of Rte. 250 and 270. (☎800-275-8777. Open M-F 8:30am-noon and 12:30-4pm, Sa 9am-10am.) **Zip Code:** 96719. **Kapa'au Post Office,** 54-396 Union Mill Rd., is a smaller office. (☎889-6766. Open M-F 7:30am-4pm, Sa 9-10:30am). **Zip Code:** 96755.

ACCOMMODATIONS

Privacy and comfort can be had at **Kohala Country Adventures Guest House ❸,** ¼ mi. above Kapa'au on the road between the Bank of Hawaii and the statue of Kamehameha. Set on 11 acres of farmland, this cozy B&B offers spectacular views of the surrounding countryside. The spotless rooms include refrigerators and kitchen access, and luxurious west-facing decks that are perfect for sunset-watching. (☎866-892-2484 or 889-5663; getaway@pixi.com; www.kcadventures.com. Reservations recommended. Check-in 3pm. Rooms $70-135. No credit cards.) If you need a little more space, **Kohala's Guest House ❷,** about 3 mi. east of Kapa'au on the road to Keokea Beach, rents whole homes with 1, 2, or 3 bedrooms. (☎889-5606; svendsen@gte.net; http://home1.gte.net/svendsen/index.htm. $49-125. No credit cards.) **Kohola Village Inn ❶,** 55-514 Hawi Rd., is right in the middle of downtown Hawi, at the corner of Rte. 250 and 270. With basic accommodations at basic prices, it's the most convenient place to spend a night. (☎889-0419. Check-in 4:30pm. Check-out noon. Rooms $55-59, suite $72. MC/V.)

FOOD

For the self-sufficient, **Kohala Health Foods,** on Akoni Pule Hwy. in Hawi, is a great place to stock up. (☎889-0277. Open M-F 10am-6pm, Su 11am-4pm.)

Bamboo, Akoni Pule Hwy. (☎889-5555), in downtown Hawi. Locals from all over flock to this Jimmy Buffet-inspired restaurant for favorites such as *Pua'a A Opai* (pork tenderloin and black tiger shrimp nestled on papaya salad) and the original passion fruit margarita. Open Tu-Sa 11:30am-2:30pm and 6-9pm, Su 11am-2pm. DC/MC/V. ❸

Jen's Kohala Cafe (☎889-0099), on Akoni Pule Hwy. in Kapa'au. Serving up Hawaiian favorites and Thai spice (entrees $8.25-9.50), Jen's has aloha to spare. Snag a tasty salad ($7.50), sandwich ($5.50-6), or ice cream ($2). Open M-F 10am-5pm, Sa-Su 10am-3:30pm. Thai dinner Sa-Su 4:30-8:30pm. MC/V. ❷

Nanbu Courtyard Cafe, 54-3885 Akoni Pule Hwy. (☎889-5546), in Kapa'a. Sophistication in the form of gourmet coffees ($1.50-3) and sandwiches ($5-7.25). Open M-F 6:30am-4pm, Sa 8am-4pm. MC/V. ❶

Hula La's Mexican Kitchen (☎889-5668), Kohala Trade Center in Hawi. A basic walk-in *taqueria* with satisfying burritos ($6.50-7.50). Open M-F 10am-9pm, Sa-Su 9am-9pm. No credit cards. ❶

Kohala Coffee Mill (☎889-5577), Akoni Pule Hwy. in Hawi. Heaping scoops of sensational Tropical Dreams Hawaiian Ice Cream ($2-4), as well as standard smoothies ($3.75), and a wide selection of teas and coffees ($1.75-3). ❶

⚐ TOURS

If you're looking to ride the range *paniolo*-style, there are a number of operations available to assist you. **Dahana Ranch,** Kohala Mountain Rd., between Hawi and Waimea, offers 1½-hour "Ranch Rides" across their wide-open pastures. On 2½-hour "Range Station Rides," visitors get their hands dirty helping wranglers guide cows between grazing areas. (☎885-0057; www.dahanaranch.com. Ranch Ride $55; Range Station Ride $100, lunch included.) **Kohala Na'alapa Stables,** Kohala Ranch, arranges rides within the historic Kahua Ranch on the top of Kohala Mountain. (☎889-0022; naalapa@ithawaii.net. 1½-hour ride daily 1:30pm $55, 2½-hour ride daily 9am $75.) **Horseback Rides Through Paniolo Adventures,** Mile 13.2 Kohala Mountain Rd., explores some of the 11,000 acres of another working cattle ranch in Kohala Mountain. The outfit specializes in authentic range experiences, providing every rider with leather chaps, cowboys hats, and boots. (☎889-5354; stable@panioloadventures.com. For groups of 3 or more: 1½-hour ride $63; 2½-hour $89; 4-hour $130.)

Flum'ln Da Ditch, 55-519 Hawi Rd., above the intersection of Hwy. 250 and 270 in Hawi, offers something entirely different—kayak rides through the old sugar cane flumes of Kohala. (☎889-6922; res@flumindaditch.com; www.flumindaditch.com. Cruises daily 8:15am and 12:15pm. $89, children $68.)

KOHALA DITCH The Kohala Ditch was completed in 1906 as a monument to labor-intensive engineering. Sugar cane planter **John Hind's** pet project, the ditch was designed to bring water from the valleys of east Kohala to the fields around Hawi and Kapa'a. **Samuel Parker** of Parker Ranch financed the venture and Japanese immigrant laborers provided the manpower. These workers were paid poorly for the risks they took and a number of workers died over the course of the ditch's construction. The completed ditch is a maze of flumes, tunnels, and channels that transport water over more than 22 miles. Despite the decline of the sugar cane industry, the ditch is still used in the operation of area ranches and farms today. To get up close and personal with it, try one of the **Flum 'In Da Ditch excursions** (p. 103).

BIG ISLAND

FROM THE ROAD

A DATE WITH A KING

Turning off the highway, I roll down a one-lane strip of pavement toward the sea. I am soon met by a chainlink fence and a narrow airstrip. A red dirt track to the left, full of puddles from the recent rain, stretches along the coast. No problem with the first major puddle, as the wheels spin efficiently through the water. The track, however, is heavily rutted in some places, and I worry about dragging the rented vehicle's undercarriage across the rough lava rocks as I slowly bump my way along. In an attempt to avoid getting the car stuck on the hummock of grass in the middle of the road, I heavily favor the embankments on either side. At one point, looking at the sky out of my right window and the ground out of my left, I feel as though I am on some sick roller coaster. I then dodge a minefield of fuel-tank puncturing rocks strategically placed across the road. To my left, I can see the outline of the massive Mo'okini Luakini Heiau, beyond which lies Kamehameha's Birthplace, my destination. A huge puddle appears on the road in front of me, and stepping on the accelerator, I tackle the last of my obstacles. Into the mud I drop and a wave of rich brown water crashes down on my windshield, spraying through my wide open windows and covering everything in a fine coating of mud. I continue to plow forward and flip on my windshield wipers. When I can see in front of me again, I am back on dry land, appropriately baptized in the earth for a visit to Kamehameha.

-Bryden Sweeney-Taylor

NORTH KOHALA SIGHTS

LAPAKAHI STATE HISTORICAL PARK

The park located just off Hwy. 270, nearly 14 mi. north of Kawaihae. There is no running water so be sure to bring your own, as well as sunscreen. Open daily 8am-4pm. Free.

Sometime in the 14th century, Hawaiian fishermen founded a village on the isolated northern Kohala Coast. The site was inhabited for over 500 years, and today, the area lies within the protected Lapakahi State Historical Park.

Settlers most likely chose this location because its coral and lava rock shoreline offered one of the few safe canoe landing spots on the Kohala coast. Despite the area's current dry and inhospitable appearance, water was more abundant at the time of the early Hawaiians. Villagers were able to grow crops and had a steady stream of drinking water. Eventually, some of the first villagers moved up into the wetter Kohala Mountains, where they could farm more extensively. These upland farmers traded with the coastal fishermen in an arrangement they called *ahupua'a.* In the 19th century, however, Lapakahi's water table dropped. Coupled with drastic changes that were sweeping the island due to the arrival of non-Hawaiians, the villagers found that their method of subsistence was no longer feasible. Most of the area's inhabitants, some descendants of the original settlers, left in search of vacant, more fertile land.

Much of the abandoned village still remains. A one-mile trail circles the area, passing along crumbling foundations, burial platforms, and canoe sheds. Relics of everyday life (salt pans, konane boards, and fish shrines) are still present. The small coral beach provides access to crystal-clear waters that are part of a marine life conservation district and perfect for **snorkeling.** A number of native trees, which once played an integral part in the village's irrigation system, now simply add a little green to the otherwise barren spot.

MO'OKINI LUAKINI HEIAU AND KAMEHAMEHA'S BIRTHPLACE

To reach the heiau, turn makai at mile-marker 20 on Rte. 270, about a mile west of Hawi, and continue nearly 2 mi. to Upolu Airport. From the airport, drive down the rutted dirt track (not recommended for vehicles with low clearance) that traces the coast for about 1½ mi. to a fork in the road; the heiau is on the hill to the left. Kamehameha's birthplace is another ¼ mi. down the right-hand fork, just up from the coast. For more information about visiting the heiau call ☎ 591-1170 or 591-1142.

IF YOU BUILD IT... In 1790, while Kamehameha was consolidating his power by invading Maui, Lanai and Molokai, he learned that his cousin and chief adversary, **Keoua Kuahu'ula**, was invading his territory on the Big Island. Despite his successes on the other islands, Kamehameha was uncertain how best to deal with Kuahu'ula, who was preventing him from uniting all of the islands. He sent his aunt to seek advice from the prophet **Kapoukahi**, who revealed that Kamehameha would reign over the entire chain of Hawaiian islands only if he were to build a large temple dedicated to Kuka'ilimoku atop Pu'ukohola.

Upon his return to Hawaii, Kamehameha immediately set to work on the heiau, following the strict guidelines of the prophecy. Kapoukahi served as the royal architect to ensure that not a stone was misplaced, and thousands of men spent nearly a year working on the massive complex. Since the entire heiau was built out of water-worn lava rock, it is believed that the stones were passed from Pololu Valley in a human chain some 20 miles long.

The heiau was finished in the summer of 1791. Kamehameha invited Kuahu'ula to the dedication ceremony. When Kuahu'ula arrived on the beach below Pu'ukohola, there was a scuffle that left Kamehameha's cousin and most of his followers dead. Kuahu'ula's body was then taken to the heiau and offered as the dedicatory sacrifice to the god Ku.

Kuahu'ula's death marked the end of serious opposition to Kamehameha on the Big Island, and Kapoukahi's prophecy soon came true. By 1810, Kamehameha was able, through conquest and treaties, to extend his rule throughout the Hawaiian Islands.

This ancient heiau is one of Hawaii's oldest and largest historic sites, and among its most sacred. In 1963, Mo'okini Luakini was designated the first **National Historic Landmark** in Hawaii. According to oral history, the heiau was built in AD 480 and expanded to its present size (roughly 250 ft. by 125 ft.) in AD 1000. The 30-foot walls, which were constructed without mortar, are made of water-worn basalt stones that are said to have been passed along a human chain spanning 14 miles. Tradition holds that High Priest **Kuamo'o Mo'okini** directed the construction of the heiau and dedicated it to the god Ku. The Mo'okini family was designated the site's *kahuna nui* (guardian-priests). The sacred spot was reserved exclusively for *ali'i* who fasted, prayed, and offered human sacrifices to the gods here. Since the heiau's dedication, one Mo'okini family member in each generation has been instructed in temple rituals and traditions.

Surrounded on all sides by rolling grasslands and perched atop a small bluff, the heiau has an air of solitude and serenity. A few hundred yards down the coast from the heiau there is a large, double-walled enclosure reputed to be the site of **Kamehameha's birth** in 1758. While the low walls and simple design are uninspiring, the grounds are immaculately maintained and the site is regarded as sacred. Although the legendary king was born here, these were not Kamehameha's childhood stomping grounds. Soon after his birth, Kamehameha was spirited away to Waipi'o Valley for his own safety.

POLOLU VALLEY

Rte. 270 ends abruptly at the western rim of Pololu Valley, about 6 mi. from Hawi.

Pololu Valley is a densely foliated incision cut deep in the surrounding mountains, much of which is protected as a forest reserve. The valley was once home to *taro* farmers, but now it is frequented mainly by visitors looking to catch a glimpse of Big Island's wilder side.

BIG ISLAND

The **Pololu Valley Trail** departs from the parking lot at the end of the road and drops quickly down the slope to the valley's gray-sand beach. From top to bottom, the gently sloping trail should take about 20min. Near the beach, the valley becomes so densely vegetated that a machete is almost a necessary exploration tool. Nevertheless, the cows and horses who inhabit the valley manage to make their way to and fro without much difficulty. In theory, the trail climbs the *pali* at the far end of the valley, reaching the ridge before dropping down into the even wilder and more remote terrain of **Honokanenui.** This journey is probably better suited to wild animals than humans.

SOUTH KOHALA

Despite the relative enormity of the Big Island, the vast majority of its tourist industry is concentrated in a 10-mile stretch of shoreline on the Kohala Coast. With three major resort areas featuring hotels, condos, and every amenity imaginable, Hawaii's "Gold Coast" is to the rich what toy stores are to the young.

The beauty of South Kohala is that you need not be Gucci-clad and thick-walleted to partake in the pleasures of the region. What brought the resorts and the ancient Hawaiians here in the first place is the phenomenal weather, even by tropical standards. The South Kohala coast enjoys some of Hawaii's sunniest weather and the resorts take meticulous care of the beach areas. Best of all, because all Hawaiian shorelines are public, even travelers on shoestring budgets can live it up on the sands of the most exclusive resort beach—just don't forget a bag lunch.

MAUNA KEA RESORT

Off of Hwy. 19. Kauna'oa Beach is open to the public via the Mauna Kea Beach Hotel, where parking spaces have been set aside for visitors.

This state-of-the-art resort was the brainchild of Laurance Rockefeller, who set his plan into motion in 1960. At the time, it was unlike anything else in the world, and today the resort encompasses two luxury hotels located just yards from world-famous **Kauna'oa Beach** (Mauna Kea Beach). Kauna'oa is a stunning crescent of pristine sand that slopes gradually out into the bay. It is excellent for swimming and snorkeling. Within the resort, there are 6 restaurants and lounges, including the swanky **Batik,** two 18-hole golf courses, and 13 tennis courts. It also boasts an incredible collection of artwork, with over 1600 pieces from across the Pacific.

The opulent **Mauna Kea Beach Hotel ❺,** 62-100 Mauna Kea Beach Dr., was the first resort constructed on the Big Island, and it set the standard for the multitudes that succeeded it. Although it is approaching its 40th birthday, the entire complex recently underwent a multi-million dollar restoration and still maintains the highest standards of quality, with elegant yet simple rooms. A beachfront **luau,** complete with *kalua* pig and Hawaiian song and dance, completes the package. (☎800-882-6060 or 882-7222; www.MaunaKeaBeachHotel.com. Luau Tu 5:45pm. $72, children $36. Reservations recommended. Check-in 3pm. Check-out noon. Rooms $360-1400. All major credit cards.)

The newest component of Mauna Kea Resort, the **Hapuna Beach Prince Hotel ❻,** 62-100 Kauna'oa Dr., was built during the early 1990s. It sits perched above Hapuna Beach and features an open design that creates a relaxed yet luxurious feel. Each of the hotel's 350 rooms feature an ocean view and a private lanai. (☎800-882-6060 or 880-1111; www.HapunaBeachPrinceHotel.com. Reservations recommended. Check-in 3pm. Check-out noon. Rooms $360-595, suites $1200-7000. All major credit cards.)

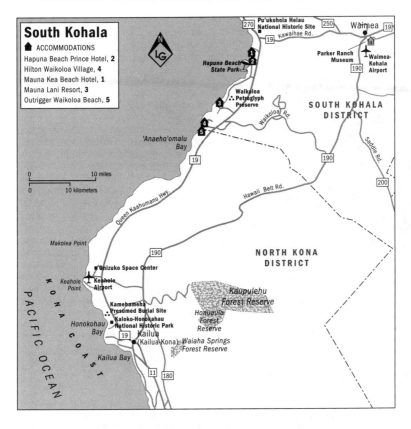

South Kohala

▲ ACCOMMODATIONS

Hapuna Beach Prince Hotel, **2**
Hilton Waikoloa Village, **4**
Mauna Kea Beach Hotel, **1**
Mauna Lani Resort, **3**
Outrigger Waikoloa Beach, **5**

WAIKOLOA BEACH RESORT AND PETROGLYPHS

From the Kona airport, take Queen Ka'ahumanu Hwy. north to Waikoloa Beach Dr. Turn left into the resort.

The Disney World of the Kohala Coast, this impressive resort houses a glittering collection of hotels, condos, stores, and beaches. Darling, anyone who is anyone knows that this is *the* place to go on the Big Island. The resort's mall, **King's Shops,** is open to the public and has upper-echelon stores of the Louis Vuitton variety. The adjacent **'Anaeho'omalu Beach** (see below) is touted as the Big Island's nicest strip of sand.

Within the Waikoloa complex, **Hilton Waikoloa Village ❺** is its own little upscale playground. There are 1200 rooms, 7 restaurants, 2 golf courses, 8 tennis courts, a multi-million dollar art collection, and a 4-acre swimming and snorkeling lagoon complete with **DolphinQuest,** an interactive dolphin-guest program. All are linked by miles of pathways, an air-conditioned tram, and mahogany boats that navigate the complex's narrow waterways. The entire grounds are open to visitors. (425 Waikoloa Beach Dr. ☎900-221-2424 or 886-1234; www.hiltonwaikoloavillage.com. Legends of the Pacific luau on F $60, ages 5-12 $27. Check-in 3pm. Check-out noon. Rooms $189-620. Suites $950-5530. All major credit cards.)

BIG ISLAND

Up the road from the Hilton, the **Outrigger Waikoloa Beach** ❺ is eclipsed by its flashy neighbor more often than not. However, this hotel offers a quieter resort experience with all the large scale attractions just a short walk away. (69-275 Waikoloa Beach Dr. ☎800-922-5533 or 866-6789; owb.reservations@outrigger.com; www.outrigger.com. Check-in 3pm. Check-out noon. Rooms $315-535. Suites $965-3100. All major credit cards.)

For a change from glitzy resort life, visit the **Waikoloa Petroglyph Preserve**, a small field of ancient carvings. The location, tucked behind the King's Shops and flanked on one side by a new condo development and by a golf course on the other, is less than inspiring. In spite of this, the petroglyphs are worth a look, if only to break the monotony of shops and restaurants. Humans, canoes, and other aspects of early Hawaiian life appear among the varied designs, although some of the names and letter reflect the influence of non-Hawaiians. The shadows of early morning and late afternoon make for the best viewing conditions. (Park in the King's Shops lot and follow the signs along the short walk to a section of the King's Trail that passes through the carvings. Open 24hr.)

'ANAEHO'OMALU BEACH

To reach the beach, make the turn for the Waikoloa Beach Resort between mile-markers 76 and 77, 8 mi. south of Kawaihae and 25 mi. north of Kailua-Kona. The beach parking lot is the first left turn on the road across from the King's Shops.

Waikoloa Beach Resort sits on a white-sand beach that stretches south toward Kona along a picturesque bay. Known to locals as "A Beach," 'Anaeho'omalu's consistently calm waters and sandy bottom make it one of the most popular swimming spots around. It also offers some of the island's best **windsurfing** and **snorkeling**. *'Anaeho'omalu* translates to "protected mullet" and descends from ancient Hawaii when the bodies of water between the large coconut grove and the beach were royal fish ponds stocked with mullet. Only the *ali'i*, however, were allowed to enjoy the fish from the ponds.

The beach is part of a state park, and has showers, toilets, and drinking water at the southern end of the crescent. The northern end of the beach sits in front of the Outrigger Waikoloa Beach hotel and has perks such as chin-up bars and a volleyball net. **Ocean Sports,** a beach hut in front of the hotel, arranges all sorts of aquatic activities in the area—from snorkeling for a few dollars to chartering glass bottom boats for considerably more. (☎886-6666. Open daily 8am-5pm.)

Camping is also allowed within the park with a permit. Heading south along the coast, there are a number of secluded spots where you can sleep right on the beach. (Contact the Department of Land and Natural Resources, State Parks Division, 75 Apuni St. ☎974-6200. Permits are $5 per day.)

MAUNA LANI RESORT

68-1400 Mauna Lani Dr. 19 mi. north of the Kona airport, off of Hwy. 19. ☎367-2323.

Nestled between Waikoloa's over-the-top exuberance and Mauna Kea's choice beachfront location, Mauna Lani is relatively low-key. Its hotels are every bit as luxurious as those that line rest of the coast, but Mauna Lani places more emphasis on Hawaiian culture than it does on its restaurants and spas. The land around Mauna Lani is redolent with historical and cultural significance, with ancient fish ponds, settlement remains, and an extensive collection of petroglyphs.

PU'UKOHOLA HEIAU NATIONAL HISTORIC SITE

The park is located 10 mi. west of Waimea and 34 mi. north of Kailua-Kona along Rte. 270 near the intersection of Hwy. 19 and 270. The park and its visitor center (☎882-7218; www.nps.gov/puhe) are open daily 7:30am-4pm. Free admission. The self-guided walking tour of the sites begins at the Visitor Center, where an orientation film is shown.

With the construction of modern eyesores such as the highway and Kawaihae Harbor nearby, Pu'ukohola Heiau ("Temple on the Hill of the Whale") has been stripped of some of its original natural splendor. Nevertheless, it retains a commanding position on the coastline and holds immense historical and cultural significance. The heiau was one of the last sites constructed before outside influences encroached on traditional Hawaiian culture. According to legend, it also played a key role in Kamehameha's ascendancy (see **If You Build It**, p. 347).

The first site along the walking path is the sprawling Pu'ukohola Heiau, built by Kamehameha in the late 18th century. The temple measures 224 ft. by 100 ft. with 16- to 20-foot high walls. The temple platform is now bare, but during Kamehameha's time it was covered with ceremonial structures. A little farther down the hillside, between Pu'ukohola Heiau and the ocean, is **Mailekini Heiau**, an older structure thought to have been built for warlike or agricultural purposes. This heiau is nearly the size of Pu'ukohola, but its construction is considerably inferior. **Hale o**

gone up, and unless they were well endowed by their parents, they're struggling to make enough money working at low-paying jobs to get by. Both groups really have to take some time to understand where one another is coming from if there's to be harmony. The easy way of course is for the locals to say, "Well we need the tourists for their dollars, but otherwise f**k 'em." And the easy way for the tourist is for them to say "Well, we need the locals for their cleaning of toilets, but otherwise step on them." Locals cannot help but feel overwhelmed by the increasing presence of tourists who move here and stay here and take up the space that would otherwise be for their children. It would be nice to reserve these islands for the locals. I've tended the land, and through farming and hiking, have a relationship with the land to where I basically feel local, and my kids were raised here. But I try to bear in mind that I need to retain my status as a guest, and that I and my children can move away and find other places to live. To the extent that I have a choice, it's better for me to continue being a guest rather than to see myself as entitled in some way.

Kapuni Heiau, submerged just offshore, was dedicated to the shark gods. Although this temple was initially built above the high-water mark, it has been underwater since the 1950s. On the beach below Pu'ukohola and Mailekini lies **Pelekane,** the royal courtyard of Kawaihae. Kamehameha II prepared to take the throne here following the death of his father. Across Rte. 270 and off the self-guided walking trail in the far corner of the park, is the site of **John Young's homestead.** Young, a British sailor stranded on Hawaii in 1790, became a trusted military adviser to Kamehameha as well as his trading agent. His European-style house was built using basalt and a mortar composed of sand, burnt coral, *poi*, and hair.

The park is one of the few places on the Big Island that officially celebrates **La Hae Hawaii,** or Hawaiian Flag Day, every July 31. In addition, **Establishment Day** (Aug. 17) is also honored with a Hawaiian cultural festival, held on the weekend in August closest to the 17th.

KAUAI

As the oldest and northernmost of the major islands, Kauai (Kaua'i) stands apart in the Hawaiian chain. Hawaiian spirit flourishes among the island's 56,000 residents, and locals are fiercely proud of both their heritage and Kauai's relative lack of commercial development. Aptly nicknamed "The Garden Isle," Kauai's plentiful rains nurse the verdant land, and support local agriculture. Kauai's rainforest jungle is best described as primordial (*Jurassic Park* was filmed here, after all), but markers of the island's 6 million weathered years are apparent in its impressive geological features. Kauai's miles of sandy shoreline testify to the land's relative age, and mark the border between the shimmering blue of the Pacific and the green land of the interior. The cliffs of the Na Pali Coast, the island's deep valleys, and the jagged Waimea Canyon were all carved by millennia of running rainfall—the northeast slope of Waialeale Mountain is the wettest spot on earth, receiving 450 inches of rain annually.

Kauai's peaceful solitude, as well as the abundant opportunities to get back to nature that are readily available in the island's untamed landscape, once attracted a healthy hippie culture. Though their particular presence has since diminished somewhat, Kauai still draws a more rugged, individualistic type of traveler than Maui or Oahu. Of the visitors who come here to blaze their own paths through "real Hawaii," many are drawn to the hiker's paradise of the Na Pali Coast, and its grueling Kalalau Trail. Opportunities for exploration are endless, whether you wish to lose yourself on the island's trails, basking on its beaches, or to immerse yourself in the aloha spirit on Kauai, a paradise within Paradise.

HIGHLIGHTS OF KAUAI

INDUCE VERTIGO on the trails and overlooks of the Waimea Canyon, the Grand Canyon of the Pacific (p. 402).

GO ONE-ON-ONE WITH SEA TURTLES in the waters of PK's Beach, one of the many beautiful beaches near Poi'pu (p. 392).

SPY on rare birds, spinner dolphins, monk seals, and humpback whales at the Kilauea National Wildlife Reserve (p. 374).

TAME the Kalalau Trail, the hard-core hiker's mecca on the Na Pali Coast (p. 386).

✈ INTERISLAND TRANSPORTATION

All commercial flights fly into **Lihu'e Airport (LIH)**. Direct flights to Kauai from the mainland are rare, and most passengers connect in Honolulu. However, **American Airlines** (☎800-433-7300; www.aa.com) has daily non-stop service to Kauai from Los Angeles, and **United Airlines** (☎800-241-6522; www.ual.com) flies daily from Los Angeles and San Francisco. **Aloha Airlines** (☎800-367-5250; www.alohaair.com) flies to: **Hilo**, Big Island (2hr., 8 per day 6:30am-5pm); **Honolulu**, Oahu (30min., 17 per day 6:30am-8:30pm); and **Kona**, Big Island (2hr., 10-12 per day 6:30am-6pm). **Hawaiian Airlines** (☎800-367-5320; www.hawaiianair.com) flies to: **Hilo**, Big Island (2hr., 10 per day 6:30am-4:30pm); **Honolulu**, Oahu (30min., 16-20 per day 6:30am-8:15pm); **Kahului**, Maui (1½hr., 26-32 per day 6:30am-6:45pm); **Kona**, Big Island

Kauai

(2hr., 14-17 per day 6:30am-5pm); **Lanai City**, Lanai (3hr., 2-4 per day 2:37pm and 3:07pm); and **Molokai** (1½hr., 1-2 per day 2:37pm and 3:07pm). Flights to Kauai begin at around $100 round-trip.

The Kauai Bus runs 7 routes around the island, but the easiest and most convenient way to get around Kauai is by **car**. For **inter-city** and **local transportation**, consult the **Transportation** section for each town.

CAMPING

Camping in Kauai can be an easy way to save on travel expenses, and oftentimes the view from the sand more than makes up for the lack of amenities. There are a number of state and county parks on the island that allow camping with a permit, though they require that campers have tents. The various county parks are closed on certain days of the week and, unless otherwise noted, campers are limited to 7 nights at each campsite. Some state parks also have **cabins** available for rent. If you plan on camping in Kauai, it's a good idea to rent a **car** with a lockable compartment for your gear. Be prepared for **mosquitoes, sun,** and **rain.** You might want to bring a **stove** for cooking and boiling water. Each type of park in Kauai issues its own **permits.**

County parks (☎241-6660; www.kauaigov.org/parks.htm) require a permit, which is good for a maximum of 7 consecutive nights. Limit 60 days in a year-long period. Permits $3 per night, free for Hawaii residents and those under 18, if accompanied by an adult. Contact Dept. of Public Works, **Division of Parks and Recreation,** 4444 Rice St., Lihu'e, Kauai 96766. Permits are issued M-F 8am-4pm.

State parks (☎274-3444; www.state.hi.us/dlnr/dsp/dsp.html) including Koke'e ($5 per person, per night; cabins are rented through **Koke'e Lodge,** see p. 403) and Polihale ($5 per person, per night) require permits, good for 5 days. Na Pali Coast ($10 per person, per night) has a 3-day limit at Miloli'i and a 5-day limit along the Kalalau Trail. Contact the **Division of State Parks,** 3060 Eiwa St., #306, Lihu'e, Kauai 96766.

Forest reserves (☎274-3433), including Kawaikoi (3-night limit), Sugi Grove (3-night limit), and Waimea Canyon (4-night limit) require permits. Permits can be obtained free of charge at the **Forestry and Wildlife office,** 3060 Eiwa St., Room 306, Lihu'e, Kauai 96766. Permits are issued M-F 8am-4pm.

EAST SHORE

Anchored by Lihu'e, Kauai's county seat, the eastern shore is the center of government and commerce for the island. Most of Kauai's population is concentrated here, as evidenced by the multitude of restaurants and shopping centers. Drop your bags and buy your groceries here, but seek the true down-home island lifestyle elsewhere. The area just north of Lihu'e, also known as the Coconut Coast, was once the home of *ali'i,* and now provides a cross-section of Kauai's offerings from heiaus to boating adventures on the Wailua River.

LIHU'E

Welcome to the Big City. Home to the island's only Wal-Mart, and the official headquarters of Kauai County, dusty Lihu'e sees plenty of tourist traffic. Everyone comes, but, despite a number of notable historic attractions and a decent beach, few stay the night. Originally a plantation town that housed workers from the sprawling Grove Farm, Lihu'e has yet to grow into its important new role, and

KAUAI

Lihu'e Region

🏠 ACCOMMODATIONS
Garden Island Inn, **1**
The Kauai Inn, **2**

(map of the Lihu'e region showing roads including Maalo Rd. (583), Kuhio Hwy., Hoohana St. (56), Hipa Rd., Hehi Rd., Hanama'ulu Stream, Hanama'ulu Beach Park, Ahukini Landing, Hanama'ulu Bay, PACIFIC OCEAN, Ahukini Rd. (570), LIHU'E, Hoomana Rd., Hardy St., Nawiliwili Stream, Kaumuali'i Hwy. (50), TO PUHI (0.3 mi.), Pikake St. (51), Rice St., Kapule Hwy., Lihue Airport, Kalepa St. (58), Nawiliwili Rd., Puali Stream, NIUMALU, Lala Rd., Niumalu Rd., Hulemalu Rd., Kalapaki Beach, Nawiliwili Beach Park, Nawiliwili Bay, Ninini Point)

those expecting cosmopolitan sophistication will be gravely disappointed. For travelers on a budget, however, Lihu'e's central location and affordable hotels brighten up an otherwise dull town.

🔲 ORIENTATION

Lihu'e is shaped like a big "V," with **Rice St.** and downtown forming the right side, **Nawiliwili Rd.** forming the left side, and **Nawiliwili Harbor** creating the base. Most budget accommodations are located downtown, while the central waterfront holds mid-range hotels and Kalapaki Beach. From the beach, Nawiliwili Rd. runs northwest to Kauai's largest shopping center, **Kukui Grove**.

⬛ TRANSPORTATION

Flights: Lihu'e Airport, 3901 Mokulele Loop (☎246-1440 or 246-1448), 2 mi. east of town. **Aloha Airlines** (☎245-3691; www.alohaair.com) and **Hawaiian Airlines** (☎800-882-8811; www.hawaiianair.com) connect Kauai to the other Hawaiian islands with flights departing approximately every hr. from 6am-6pm. Direct flights to Kauai from the mainland are rare, and most passengers connect in Honolulu. However, **American Airlines** (☎800-433-7300; www.aa.com) has daily non-stop service to Kauai from Los

Downtown Lihu'e

Map labels:
- Wilcox Memorial Hospital
- Isenberg Park
- Eha St.
- Eono St.
- Efima St.
- 56
- Wal-Mart
- Ehiku St.
- Oxford St.
- TO ✈ (1.5 mi.)
- Hilo Hattie's
- Ahukini Rd. 570
- Fujii St.
- Hiraoka St.
- Jenes St.
- Nakamura St.
- Inoue St.
- Poinciana St.
- Kuhio Hwy.
- Akahi St.
- Efua St.
- Umi St.
- Uluhui St.
- Alohi St.
- Palai St.
- Keli St.
- Hoomana Rd.
- Old Lutheran Church
- Nawiliwili Stream
- Big Save Market
- State Building
- Library
- Lihu'e Civic Center
- Hardy St.
- Kaana St.
- Puaole St.
- Kaumuali'i Hwy.
- Rice St.
- Kauai Museum
- Courthouse
- Lihu'e Park
- Matae St.
- TO KILOHANA (1 mi.)
- Lihu'e Sugar Mill
- Kele St.
- Wa'a Rd.
- Visitor's Bureau
- 50
- Hala Rd.
- Wehe St.
- Nawiliwili Rd.
- Kukui Grove St.
- Haleko Rd.
- Pua Loke St.
- Rice Shopping Center
- Kalena Park
- Malama
- 51
- Heala St.
- Ho'olako St.
- Halau St.
- Kapule Hwy.
- Vidinha Memorial Stadium
- 51
- Old Nawiliwili Rd.
- Sam's Place
- Pikake St.
- Aukoi St.
- Kanani St.
- Hill St.
- Aheane St.
- Rice St.
- Kapena St.
- Oni Ohi St.
- Aukele St.
- Peleke St.
- Haoa St.
- Kukui Grove Shopping Center
- Nawiliwili Rd.
- Palaumahu St.
- Grove Farm Homestead Museum
- Mokoi St.
- 58
- TO NAWILIWILI HARBOR
- 0 — 500 yards
- 0 — 500 meters

▲ ACCOMMODATIONS
Motel Lani, 5
Tip Top Motel, 1

🍴 FOOD
Deli and Bread Connection, 9
Hamura Saimin Stand and Halo Halo Shave Ice, 6
Kalapaki Beach Hut, 11
Kauai Bakery and Cinnamons, 9
Nueva España, 12
Okazu Hale, 8
Oki Diner and Bakery, 2
Vim 'n Vigor, 3

★ NIGHTLIFE & ENTERTAINMENT
Duke's Canoe Club Barefoot Bar, 10
Kukui Grove Cinemas, 7
Lihu'e Bowling Center, 4
Nawiliwili Tavern, 13
Rob's Good Times Grill, 4

Angeles, and **United Airlines** (☎800-241-6522; www.ual.com) flies daily from Los Angeles and San Francisco.

Buses: The Kauai Bus (☎241-6410) runs 7 bus routes around the island, offering infrequent (every 1-3hr.) but affordable transportation between Kauai's communities. Carryons are limited to 9x14x22 inches, and oversized backpacks and suitcases are prohibited. Besides the regularly scheduled stops, riders can request on-call pickup at a number of locations. Stop by the Lihu'e Civic Center for a schedule. $1.50, seniors over 60 and ages 7-18 75¢, children 6 and under free; frequent rider monthly pass $15.

Taxis: Cab rides are a costly luxury on Kauai. Fares begin with an initial $2 fee and increase $2 for each subsequent mile. Some companies tack on an additional 25¢ per bag or $5 per surfboard. Most will provide vans upon request. The following companies offer service throughout the island: **Akiko's Taxi** (☎822-7588), **Brian's Taxi** (☎245-6533), **City Cab** (☎245-3227), **North Shore Cab** (☎826-6189), and **South Shore Cab** (☎742-1525).

Car Rental: For the less image-conscious traveler, ◪ **Rent-a-Wreck** (☎821-9582), in Harbor Mall, offers used cars and SUVs, as well as a few new rentals, at a considerable savings. Rates vary with age of car and length of rental, and discounts may be negotiated with the very friendly management. Open M-F 8am-6pm, Sa 8am-5pm. In addition, **Alamo** (☎800-327-9633 or 246-0645), **Avis** (☎800-831-8000 or 245-3512), **Budget**

IN RECENT NEWS

FROG WARS

An incessant pest since the 1900s when it immigrated from Puerto Rico, the Coqui frog is the target of Operation: Eradication, a massive campaign to destroy the antagonistic amphibians once and for all. With the help of federal funding, local officials have completed weapons testing and are now working on strategy.

The Coqui frogs, so named for the distinctive "co-KEE" sound of their call, begin screeching just before sunset, and don't stop until sunrise. A single frog can keep a work-weary Hawaiian awake for hours, and the creatures can be as concentrated as 8000 per acre. Tormented victims of these menaces have been known to pay neighborhood children as much as $5 per captured frog, but this hand-to-frog combat is woefully inefficient. The frogs are also ravaging the environment; capable of consuming 46,000 creatures per acre, they threaten the indigenous food chain.

In early 2000, a concentrated caffeine spray and a lime-infused water bomb were deemed effective methods of elimination. By October 2002, nearly $200,000 federal dollars will have been invested in the frog war. Local officials expect that number to reach $2 million in 2003, and to surpass $10 million by 2007. The first island scheduled for purging is Kauai (which has the smallest frog population), followed by Oahu, then Molokai, and finally the Big Island. The goal is merely to contain the frogs on the Big Island, as the pests are so prevalent that eradication is beyond the powers of even the federal government.

(☎800-527-7000 or 245-1901), **Dollar** (☎800-800-4000 or 245-3651), **Hertz** (☎800-654-3131 or 245-3356), **National** (☎800-227-7368 or 245-5636), and **Thrifty** (☎800-847-4389 or 246-6252) are all located at the airport, and charge similar rates. Travel agents, package deals and AAA can usually get you a discount.

🛈 PRACTICAL INFORMATION

TOURIST AND FINANCIAL SERVICES

Tourist Office: Kauai Visitor's Bureau, 4334 Rice St. #101 (☎245-3971; fax 246-9235; www.kauaivisitorsbureau.com), in the Watamull Plaza building, has good maps and the usual collection of brochures.

Banks: Bank of Hawaii, 4455 Rice St. (☎246-6761) and **First Hawaiian Bank,** 4423 Rice St. (☎245-3388) flank the post office, and have many other branches throughout the island, including one in Kukui Grove. Both have **24hr. ATM** access and are open M-Th 8:30am-4pm, Sa 9am-1pm.

Camping and Hiking Permits: The County of Kauai Dept. of Public Works, **Division of Parks and Recreation,** 4444 Rice St. #150 (☎241-6660), on the 1st floor of the Lihu'e Civic Center Mo'ikeha Building, issues camping permits for the seven **county campgrounds.** For more information about a specific campground, please see the appropriate listing. Permits issued M-F 7:45am-4:30pm. Back country permits for Kauai's **state parks** are issued by the State of Hawaii Department of Natural Resources, **Division of State Parks,** 3060 Eiwa St. Room 306 (☎247-3444). Permits issued M-F 8am-3:30pm. The **Division of Forestry and Wildlife** (☎274-3433), in the same office but with a different door, has fancy topographical maps, mountain biking information, and guides to Kauai's flora and fauna. This side of the office issues camping permits for Kauai's **Forest Reserve camping areas** at Kawaikoi, Sugi Grove, and Waimea Canyon. Permits, maps, guides and advice dispensed M-F 7:45am-4:30pm.

LOCAL SERVICES

Bookstore: Border's Books Music & Cafe, 4303 Nawiliwili Rd. (☎246-0862), carries a large selection of maps and other publications about Hawaii. Open M-Th 9am-10pm, F-Sa 9am-11pm, Su 9am-8pm. Cafe open M-Th 7:30am-10pm, F 7:30am-11pm, Sa 8am-11pm, Su 8am-8pm.

Library: 4344 Hardy St. (☎241-3222). Visitor cards cost $10 and provide full privileges, including book and video borrowing and **Internet access,** for 3 months at all of Hawaii's public libraries. Open M, W 10am-8pm; Tu, Th 9am-5pm; F 10am-5pm, Sa 9am-1pm.

Laundromat: Lihu'e Laundromat, in Rice Shopping Center. Wash 25¢, dry $1.50, detergent 50¢ Open 24hr.

Weather Forecast: ☎245-6001.

Marine Forecast: ☎245-3564.

EMERGENCY AND COMMUNICATIONS

Emergency: ☎911.

Police: 3060 Umi St. (☎241-6711).

Hospital: Wilcox Memorial Hospital, 3420 Kuhio Hwy. (☎245-1100).

Internet Access: Sam's Place, 4303 Nawiliwili Rd. #107 (☎245-7332), in Kukui Grove Shopping Center, has nine computers with DSL ($2 for 10min., $1 each additional 10min.). The cafe serves Ben and Jerry's ice cream ($2.50 per scoop), pastries and coffees (from $1.25). Black and white printing 50¢ a page, domestic **faxes** $2 a page. Open M-Th 6am-10pm, F 6am-9pm, Sa 6am-8pm, Su 9am-5pm.

Post Office: 4441 Rice St. (☎800-275-8777). Open M-F 8am-4pm, Sa 9am-1pm.

Zip Code: 96766.

▚ ACCOMMODATIONS

Those looking for luxury and spectacular surroundings will likely accelerate their rental cars right out of Lihu'e, but the town's central location and the relative abundance of affordable accommodations make it a good choice for the budget traveler. Although the **Kauai Marriott,** fronting Kalapaki Beach, has a nice golf course and pretty views, its location within the drab town of Lihu'e makes other resorts shine in comparison.

▨ **The Kauai Inn,** 2430 Halemalu Rd. (☎245-9000; info@kauaiinn.com), just past Nawiliwili Harbor on the left. Beautifully landscaped grounds, tropical flowers, and lush banana trees surround a pool and pleasant courtyard. This family-owned hotel's deluxe rooms—with soft carpeting, private lanais, king-size (or 2 double) beds, refrigerators, microwaves, and modern baths—are Lihu'e's best deal. Complimentary continental breakfast served on the outdoor patio. Laundry on-site. Reception 8am-9pm. Deluxe rooms $69. ❸

Garden Island Inn, 3445 Wilcox Rd. (☎245-7227; fax 245-7603; http://planet-hawaii.com/g-i-inn), across from Anchor Cove Shopping Center. Fresh flowers and an ocean view are standard in every gently aging room, and the cheerful staff provide frank opinions of local restaurants and attractions. The great location, next to the Harbor Mall and within walking distance of Kalapaki Beach, becomes a little loud at night. Reception 8am-9pm. Ground floor rooms with TV, ceiling fan, and kitchenette $75; second floor rooms with A/C and ocean-view lanai $85. ❸

Tip Top Motel & Cafe, 3173 Akahi St. (☎245-2333; fax 246-8988; tiptop@aloha.net). European backpackers mingle with local businessmen at tidy Tip Top. Family-run for 85 years, the motel's central location and reliable rooms keep visitors coming back. Downstairs, the **Tip Top Cafe** boasts a loyal local following, and the delicious scent of macadamia and banana pancakes ($4.50) fills the air every morning. The gray vinyl booths and pleasant atmosphere also make a nice setting for an affordable lunch (nothing over $7). Reception M 7:30am-3pm, Tu-Su 6:30am-3pm and 5:30-9pm; after-hours check-in at the bar. Cafe open Tu-Su 6:30am-2pm. Spartan doubles $45, tax included. ❷

Motel Lani, 4240 Rice St. (☎245-2965). Lots of plants and a friendly staff brighten up the dull cinder block building. Six basic rooms have beds, bathrooms, tiny refrigerators, and A/C. Three larger rooms feature TVs. 2-night minimum stay. Reception 6:30am-9:30pm. Rooms $34, larger rooms $52. ❷

THE BIG SPLURGE

A PACIFIC CAFE

The comfortable and pleasant dining room of Pacific Cafe will quickly wipe away all memories of the surrounding shopping center. Although the food is definitely upscale, the waitstaff and atmosphere are casual and relaxed. Executive chef Jean-Marie Josselin has been praised in the pages of *Bon Appetit* and won a number of culinary awards for his fusion of French techniques, local produce, and Asian flavors. Two daily tasting menus feature three courses of fish ($42) or vegetarian cuisine ($32) and dessert, with an optional wine pairing for $16. The a la carte menu is heavy on fish (lemongrass macadamia nut crusted *ahi* with vanilla basil coconut vinaigrette and crispy shrimp $23.25), but also includes a number of meat entrees (wood-fired "Mongolian-style" rack of lamb with baby *bok choy*, *soba* noodle cake, and Chinese black bean Maui onion Cabernet sauce $25). Appetizers feature local ingredients incorporated in creative ways (seared *kalua* pork *gyoza* with papaya salsa, sweet Thai chiles, and *beurre blanc* $8.50). Children can order off a separate menu with more basic flavors (boneless grilled chicken with stir-fry veggies and garlic mashed potatoes $9) at kid-size prices. (☎822-0013, *in Kauai Village. Reservations recommended. Open 5:30-10pm.*)

☐ FOOD

Lihu'e plays host to an unbelievable assortment of restaurants, and a good meal awaits around every corner. Sandwiches, *saimin*, and local food dominate and will more than satisfy your tummy. Those looking for something a little fancier are best off saving their dollars for a splurge in scenic Po'ipu or Princeville. There is a **Big Save Market** behind the Kauai Museum at the corner of Hardy and Eiwa. (☎245-6571. Open daily 7am-11pm.) **Star Market,** in Kukui Grove Shopping Center, carries all the necessities as well. (☎245-7777. Open daily 6am-11pm.) Lihu'e holds two **Sunshine Markets,** one on Mondays at 3pm in Kukui Grove Shopping Center and another on Fridays at 3pm in the lot behind Vidinha Stadium.

Okazu Hale, 4100 Rice St. #6 (☎245-6554), in the turquoise strip mall behind Ace Hardware. Just steps off the tourist path, Okazu Hale serves yummy Japanese meals to a lively local clientele. Lunch and dinner served with miso soup, rice and tossed salad (teriyaki chicken $6; veggie tempura $6.50). Vegetarians will rejoice over the stir frys, rice bowls, and ramen. Open M-Sa 11am-2pm and 5-9pm. ❶

Kauai Bakery and Cinnamons (☎246-4765), in Kukui Grove Shopping Center. Eager customers crowd one side of the long counter, while bakers shape massive amounts of dough on the other. Hidden within the unassuming storefront are divine baked goods, including donuts, pastries, and custom birthday cakes ($22 and up). Don't miss the incredibly moist banana bread ($1 per slice), or the perfect apple turnovers ($1.35). Most of the good stuff sells out by noon. Open M-Th and Sa 7am-7pm, F 7am-9pm, Su 7am-6pm. ❶

Kalapaki Beach Hut, 3474 Rice St. (☎246-6330), across from Harbor Mall. Order at one window and grab a seat at the counter while you wait. Juicy burgers, tons of toppings (try the Aloha Classic—teriyaki glaze, pineapple and cheese; $5.60), and a prime location make the Beach Hut a popular lunchtime destination. Most people take their burgers to go, but the upstairs tables offer a decent view of the ocean (which is only somewhat diminished by the dusty parking lot below). *Keiki* (kids) meals with burger, fries and drink $4; veggie tempeh burger $5. Open daily 7am-7pm. ❶

Oki Diner and Bakery, 3125 Kuhio Hwy (☎245-5899), a yellow building just east of Rice St. on the *mauka* side of the highway. A comfortable diner complete with jukebox, covered patio, and picture menu, Oki serves "award-winning" hotcakes 21hr. a day. Burgers, sandwiches, and local cuisine round out the menu, with most entrees available in regular or "mini" sizes. For a break from sandwiches, order an *Oki bento* box to go ($3.75; served 7am-noon). Open daily 6am-3am. ❶

Nueva España (☎ 632-0513), in Anchor Cove Shopping Center. All but a few tables rim the spacious patio overlooking Nawiliwili Bay, and the pleasant setting makes the hearty Mexican breakfasts (*huevos rancheros* $6.50) even more delicious. Vegetarians will be pleased with the array of meatless dishes, ranging from taco salad to *chiles rellenos*. Lunch and dinner entrees $8-14.50. Open daily 8am-9pm. ❷

Deli and Bread Connection (☎ 245-7115), next to Macy's in Kukui Grove Shopping Center. The "famous" sweet bread, endless variety, and reasonable prices make the wait worthwhile. A number of vegetarian selections (local avocado sandwich $5) and fresh daily soups complement the menu of standard (B.L.T. $4) and unique ("crimp" or crab and shrimp $5) options. MC/V. ❶

Vim 'n Vigor (☎ 245-9053), in Rice Shopping Center. Lihu'e's only health food store stocks the usual assortment of grains, soy products, dried fruits, and vitamins. Prepared sandwiches (avocado and veggie $3.59) and salads (complete with fork and napkin; $2.50) are perfect for a healthy picnic. Open M-Sa 7:45am-5pm. ❶

Hamura Saimin Stand and **Halo Halo Shave Ice,** 2956 Kress St. (☎ 245-3271), at Halenani. Local teens and savvy travelers slurp bowls of *saimin* at a winding, orange counter. Brusque service and zero vegetarian options, but it's one of the cheapest meals in town. *Saimin* from $3.50. Open M-Th 10am-11pm, F-Sa 10am-1am, Su 10am-9:30pm. Pretty good shave ice served M-F 10am-4pm. ❶

🔍 SIGHTS

Well before the advent of Wal-Mart, Lihu'e cemented its role as the center of commercial life on Kauai. The town's location alongside Nawiliwili Harbor, the island's main port, supported the grand old sugar plantations that shaped Kauai's history. Today, a number of historic sights allow visitors to relive the island's golden age.

GROVE FARM HOMESTEAD MUSEUM. Those who reserve well in advance can enjoy an intimate and informative 2hr. walking tour of the residence of **George "G.N." Wilcox,** Kauai's first and greatest sugar baron. The tour begins in G.N.'s office, with a brief biography of the hard-working man who funded his Yale education by gathering *guano.* Continuing through the estate, the tour stops in the spartan cottage G.N. called home, as well as the spectacular main house that he gave to his brother Sam and his family of seven. Gleaming 'ohi'a wood floors, a grand koa staircase, beautiful paintings, and vast collections of books and Hawaiiana are just a few of the well-preserved furnishings. The tour also includes visits to the kitchen—where a tasty surprise awaits—a plantation cottage, and a very nicely furnished guest house that puts G.N.'s own humble cottage to shame. A devout Christian, G.N. preferred to spend his hard-earned dollars helping others, and, among other good deeds, he donated both the land and the finances for Nawiliwili Harbor. The grounds surrounding the house feature tropical gardens, lush orchards, and acres of pastures. (*Northbound on Nawiliwili, turn right at the small sign onto a private dirt road about 1.3 mi. past the harbor. ☎ 245-3202. Tours M, W, Th at 10am and 1pm. Reservations required. $5, children 12 and under $3.*)

KILOHANA. Built in 1935 by G. N. Wilcox's youngest nephew, **Gaylord Parke Wilcox,** and his wife, Ethel, Kilohana was once the grandest and most expensive home on Kauai. Today, the 16,000 sq. ft. Tudor-style mansion's eight bedrooms, and accompanying bathrooms, have been converted into retail shops featuring local art, jewelry, and collectibles. Much of the furniture and artwork remaining in the house dates to the 1930s, when the Wilcoxes ordered a house-full of furnishings from Gump's in San Francisco, a high-class specialty store. Unlike other historical

KAUAI

homes, Kilohana welcomes guests to sit on the furniture and truly experience the house. Take a seat on the couch in the curtained nook at the rear of the living room—where Gaylord conducted his private business—and you'll feel almost as if you've stepped back into Kauai's golden age. Guests are also free to wander around the 35 acres of flowering gardens, historic cottages and the working farm that surround the main house.

Those who would like to learn more about Kilohana's history can do so either at the historic high tea, or on a Clydesdale horse-drawn carriage tour of the grounds. **Gaylord's Restaurant,** whose tables line the original lanai, provides a peaceful setting for an outdoor lunch. *(1.4 mi. west of Lihu'e on the mauka side of Hwy. 50. ☎ 245-5608. 20min. carriage rides daily 11am-6pm; $10, children 12 and under $5. 1hr. sugar cane wagon rides M-Tu and Th-F at 11am and 2pm; $24, children 12 and under $12; reservations required. High tea M and Sa 2pm; $29.50; reservations required. Gaylord's Restaurant open for lunch M-Sa 11am-3pm, dinner daily 5-9pm, brunch Su 9:30am-3pm. Reservations requested. Luau Kilohana Tu, Th 5pm. $58, over 55 and teenagers 13-18 $54, children 5-12 $30, under 5 free. Luau includes mai tai pour, activities and exhibitions, imu ceremony, dinner and entertainment. House and galleries open M-Sa 9:30am-9:30pm, Su 9:30am-5pm. Free admission.)*

KILOHANA GALLERIES. The galleries within the Kilohana house are worth a look, if only for the innovative ways in which the owners have interpreted their space. Housed in the Wilcoxes' library, the **Country Store** displays Hawaiian crafts on the original library shelves. Upstairs, the patio in **Sea Reflections** served as Ethel's private sewing room, and the shop has cleverly utilized the bathroom to display its ocean-themed merchandise. Across the hall, the asymmetric room now occupied by **Grande's Gems** was once the bedroom of the Wilcoxes' two children. While exploring the second floor, keep your eyes open for the ghost of Ethel Wilcox—many of Kilohana's visitors have reported passing her in the halls. *(See above for directions. Free admission to the galleries.)*

KAUAI MUSEUM. Small, but overflowing with information, the Kauai Museum provides an introduction to everything you ever wanted to know about the island—and a nice place to spend a rainy afternoon. A self-guided tour of the museum begins in the smaller Rice building with an aerial video that shows an overview of the island. Comprehensive displays illustrating Kauai and Niihau's geologic origins and ecology combine with others featuring the islands' history. The main building, Wilcox, houses rotating displays and exhibits of local art, including a small gallery of contemporary photography. *(4428 Rice St. at Eiwa. ☎ 245-6931. Guided tours M-Th 10am. Open M-F 9am-3pm, Sa 10am-2pm. $5, over 65 $4, students $3, children 6-12 $1, under 6 free.)*

ALEKOKO (MENEHUNE) FISHPOND OVERLOOK. According to legend, the **menehune** (p. 23) were a race of mischievous, pot-bellied elf-like creatures who lived in the forest and were famed for completing complicated building projects overnight. Many years ago, a Hawaiian king asked the menehune to build him a fishpond, and they happily complied. Thousands of menehune formed a long line stretching to the west and passed lava rock from Kalaheo all the way back to Lihu'e where others skillfully shaped the walls of the pond. Despite their efforts, the menehune were unable to complete the seaward wall, and, as the sun began to rise, they hurriedly washed their hands (scratched and bleeding from the rough lava rock) in the pond before disappearing into the woods. *Alekoko* ("rippling blood") provided the ancient Hawaiian royalty with fish—their primary source of protein. *'Ama'ama* (striped mullet) and *awa* (milk fish) continue to thrive in the pond today, laying their eggs amidst the tangled roots of mangroves that have taken hold along the walls. Unfortunately, although beneficial to the fish, the roots of the invasive mangroves are causing irreparable harm to the rock walls.

The lush, undeveloped wetlands and fertile hills and valleys to the west form part of the **Huleia National Wildlife Refuge,** established in 1973 to protect the habitats of endangered endemic waterbirds, including Hawaii's largest population of *koloa* ducks. Traditionally used for the cultivation of wetland crops such as *taro* and rice, the refuge now houses 18 species of waterbirds in its 238 acres. Movie buffs may recognize the river valley as the site of Indy's heart-pounding, rope-swinging escape in one of the opening scenes of *Raiders of the Lost Ark.* Unfortunately, the refuge is closed to the public. *(From Nawiliwili Rd., drive ½ mi. up Hulemalu to a small lookout on the left.)*

NININI LIGHTHOUSE. A good place from which to spot humpback whales, the 86-foot Ninini Lighthouse also offers a fantastic, if incredibly windy, view of the ocean and Nawiliwili Bay. At Ninini Point, a lone picnic table welcomes those who are able to enjoy their meals despite the wind, and if you're lucky, an attendant may be on site to escort visitors to the top. The drive to the lighthouse is slow but passable—when dry—for even the wimpiest rental cars. *(Turn right at the small yellow "shoreline access" sign about ½ mi. up Hwy. 51 from the intersection with Rice St. Drive past the gatehouse and keep left at the fork. The access road runs alongside a fence separating the golf courses to the west from the airport to the east; at the end, a small dirt parking lot provides easy access to the lighthouse.)*

LIHU'E LUTHERAN CHURCH. Hawaii's oldest Lutheran church was founded by a congregation of German immigrants in 1883. Having suffered extensive damage from Hurricane Iwa in 1982, the church was rebuilt according to the original plans. The diminutive cream-colored building conceals a beautiful interior, laid out in the "old upside-down ship style" that recalls the immigrants' six-month sea voyage to reach the islands. Just as the deck of a ship slopes to shed rainwater, the floor of the church bows upward in the center. The ceiling mimics the curvature of a hull, and the ships' original oil lamps have been wired with electricity. *(4602 Hoomana Rd. Drive about ¼ mi. up Hoomana Rd. from Hwy. 56 and the church will be on your right. ☎ 245-2145. Services Su 8 and 10:30am)*

⚑ BEACHES AND FALLS

KALAPAKI BEACH. A surprisingly pretty beach considering its overgrown commercial surroundings, Kalapaki entices beachgoers with a ¼ mi. of fine white sand. The surrounding bay creates gentle waves perfect for swimming and other shoreside activities. Unfortunately, you may have to jostle with abandoned catamarans, volleyball nets, and Marriott guests with beach chairs for an empty spot of gradually sloping beach. To the west of the beach, **Nawiliwili Beach Park** has picnic tables and grass galore for a more peaceful oceanfront meal. *(Public parking is available on the far east side of the Marriott or in the Nawiliwili Beach Park lot behind Anchor Cove.)*

WAILUA FALLS. Ancient Hawaiian *ali'i* (chiefs) dove from the cliffs overlooking the pool to prove their courage. Today, the only thing tumbling down the cliffs are two stunning streams of water. Legend aside, classic television fans may recognize the sight from the opening scenes of *Fantasy Island.* The southern fork of the **Wailua River** creates this natural wonder, and the appearance of the falls varies with rain and the river's flow. Come early to avoid the crowds and enjoy the morning sunlight sparkling on the falls. *(From Lihu'e, drive one mile east on Hwy. 56 and turn left at Hwy. 583 (Ma'alo Rd.). Four winding miles later you will find yourself at the top of the falls amidst families with video cameras and tour buses aplenty. An unofficial "trail" leads to the bottom of the falls from a dirt turnout ½ mi. before the view point. Only expert hikers should attempt the steep and slippery descent.)*

HANAMA'ULU BEACH PARK. Two miles east of Lihu'e, in the dusty town of Hanama'ulu, there are prime beachfront campsites. Hanama'ulu Beach is narrow and crescent-shaped with fine sand but somewhat silty waters. Gentle swells of cloudy water wash right up to the tents and picnic tables lining the shore. Full facilities including grills, trash cans, showers, a pavilion, a grassy park, and a prime oceanfront location, welcome mostly local campers. For more information, see **Camping**, p. 327. *(Two miles east of Lihu'e on Hwy. 56. Take a right on Hanama'ulu Rd., and another right on Hehi Rd.)*

■ ♪ NIGHTLIFE AND ENTERTAINMENT

Unassuming as it may appear, Lihu'e is the place to be after dark; nightlife here is as thick as it gets in Kauai. The ubiquitous free hula show takes place every Saturday at **Kukui's Restaurant** at 6:30pm.

Lihu'e Bowling Center (☎245-5263), in the Rice Shopping Center. 28 lanes, video games, and a diner (local pupus and meals, $2-5.50) provide entertainment enough, but things get even more exciting with "Rock 'n Glow" bowling on weekends. $3.25 per game, children and seniors $2.35, students $2.60; shoe rental $1.50. "Rock 'n Glow" F-Sa 9pm-11:30pm, $10. Open M-Th 9am-11pm, F-Sa 9am-11:30pm, Su noon-10pm.

Kukui Grove Cinemas, 4368 Kukui Grove (☎245-5055). Kauai's biggest movie theater has 4 screens showing current films. Adults $6.50, children 12 and under $3.50. Bargain matinees (first show on Sa and Su) $3.50. Shows M-Th from 6-9pm, F 4-9pm, Sa-Su 1:30-10pm.

Rob's Good Times Grill (☎246-0311), in Rice Shopping Center. Happy Hour draws familiar *pau hana* (literally "quit work time") faces to this casual neighborhood bar. Rob and his wife, Lolly, pour drinks and mingle with customers who kick back in intimate booths or battle it out on the foosball table. Pool tables, tons of TVs, and the only dance floor in town keep things going until closing time. Enjoy local pupus (sliced hot dog with onions $5) and typical bar food (jalapeño poppers $6) while bobbing to Top 40 hits. M and Tu karaoke 6pm-2am, W country line dancing 8pm-11pm and dance party 11pm-close, F-Su dance music 9pm-2am. Happy Hour daily 2-6pm (draft and domestic beers $2.75). Open daily 2pm-2am.

Duke's Canoe Club Barefoot Bar, 3610 Rice St. (☎246-9599), at the west end of Kalapaki Beach. Literally on the beach, Duke's serves island pupus (from $3) and drinks (mai tai $5.75) to sunburnt beachgoers. Although the ambiance may seem a little contrived—wooden tables are shielded by grass umbrellas and servers wear aloha shirts—the stunning view can't be beat. Taco Tuesdays 4-6pm, $2 draft beer and $2 fish tacos; Tropical Fridays 4-6pm, $4 tropical drinks. Live music Th 4-6pm, F 4-6pm and 9-11pm. Open daily 11am-11:30pm.

Nawiliwili Tavern, 3488 Paena Loop (☎245-1781), in the old Hotel Kuboyama next to Kalapaki Beach Hut. Neon beer signs, darts, billiards, shuffleboard, and lots of beer welcome a mixed crowd. The back room boasts Kauai's largest karaoke collection, where you can practice before putting your skills on display during the Friday night contests. Locally brewed Keoki on tap ($3). Happy hour daily 2-6pm (all drinks 50¢ off). Food service 5pm-midnight. Open daily 2pm-2am.

WAILUA

The Tahitian pioneers who first settled Hawaii landed in Wailua, where "two waters become one." The spot, at the meeting of the north and south forks of the great Wailua River, became the center of the Tahitians' new society. Long the preferred home of the Hawaiian *ali'i*, Wailua and its surrounding lands have always been Kauai's most prestigious—and most popular—address.

ACCOMMODATIONS

Wailua is home to a number of mid-range hotels and small B&Bs, most of which advertise on the Internet. One particularly choice option is the 200-room **Kauai Sands ❸**, 420 Papaloa Rd., part of a Hawaiian family-owned chain that also operates on Maui and the Big Island. The efficiently run hotel features super-clean rooms with two double or one king-sized bed, fans, cable TVs, mini-fridges, and private lanais. The oceanfront grounds also include two swimming pools, a laundry room, exercise facilities, and a restaurant. (☎822-4951 or 800-560-5553; fax 822-0978. Rack rates $98-130, but promotional rates, ranging from $65-104, are almost always available. Each additional person $12.)

🍴 FOOD

Wailua Shopping Plaza and Kinipopo Shopping Village, across the highway from one another between the 6- and 7-mile markers, both feature a number of shops and restaurants.

Caffe Coco, 369 Kuhio Hwy. (☎822-7990), at the back of a parking lot on the *makai* side of the highway just past Kinipopo Shopping Village. A bistro with both indoor and garden seating, Caffe Coco features an outstanding variety of tasty dishes for vegetarians and carnivores alike. Platters combine salads, rice, and other sides with entrees such as black sesame ahi ($18), Pacific-rim tofu ($18), and slow-roasted pork ($16). BYOB with a $5 corkage fee. Open Tu-Su 4-9pm. ❸

Korean Bar-B-Q Restaurant, 356 Kuhio Hwy. (☎823-6744), in Kinipopo Shopping Village. A local favorite, this small restaurant offers a tasty alternative for lunch on the go. For those unfamiliar with *katsu* and *bibim-bob*, a helpful picture menu hangs over the counter. Plate lunches (teriyaki beef and BBQ chicken combo $6.50) include rice and macaroni salad, as well as veggies. Open M, W-Su 10am-9pm; Tu 4:30-9pm. ❶

Kintaro, 370 Kuhio Hwy. (☎822-3341), opposite Caffe Coco. The upscale dining room serves Kauai's best Japanese cuisine. Most menu options are complete dinner combinations served with miso soup, rice, and tea (soba noodles, salmon, and beef teriyaki $17). Unadventurous diners can order one of a few Western dishes, such as charbroiled filet mignon with fresh vegetables ($20). Reservations recommended. Open M-Sa 5:30-9:30pm. ❹

🎵 ENTERTAINMENT

Wailua rivals Lihu'e as the center of Kauai's modest nightlife. The small dance floor at patio-style **Tradewinds,** in the Coconut Marketplace, fills up with giddy locals and sunburned tourists on weekend nights. Arcade games, a jukebox, satellite sports, and dart boards entertain the less rhythmically-inclined. Although Tradewinds has no kitchen of its own, guests are welcome to order from the menu of any other restaurant in the shopping center. (☎822-1621. Happy Hour 4-6pm daily; mai tais $4.25, domestic beers $2.50. W night DJ, local bands F-Sa at 9:30pm. Open daily 10am-2am.) The Coconut Marketplace also offers family-friendly entertainment with a **free hula show** nightly at 5pm. The **Coconut Marketplace Cinema** shows new releases. (Daily 1:30-9:30pm. $6.50, seniors and children under 12 $3.50, matinees $4.)

🎭**Smith's Tropical Paradise** (see **Wailua River State Park,** below) hosts the island's most spectacular luau. Gates open at 5pm, and guests are welcome to tour the gardens on foot or by tram ($1). Following an *imu* ceremony, cocktails and music

THE LOCAL STORY

EYE TO EYE WITH INIKI

Mainland transplant Joyce Jenney runs historical tours at Kilohana. She shared her story in July 2002.

Q: Why did you move to Kauai?
A: I taught for my whole career in Minnesota. I did love teaching; I hated the cold. I hadn't been here very long when we had a major hurricane in 1992, it was called Iniki. I came from the Midwest so I wasn't really afraid at all. I just thought you taped the windows. That wasn't the way the hurricane was at all—it was devastating. The winds were 230 miles an hour when the wind gauges broke. I was renting at that time because I'd only been here a short while and that was on the second floor of a four-story condo and the very first gust shattered all the doors and windows. I realized we shouldn't be there, but it was far too late to go anywhere. We took the single mattress, and we went into the shower stall. It was shaking and the things above us were sliding; I knew that the roof was gone. If it came down we'd be dead so we were praying a great deal. We were in there I think about six hours because the hurricane hit us, lingered over us about three hours, then turned, and the eye hit us on the way back. When we came out, I could not believe the damage. It looked like a nuclear bomb had exploded. The earth is red, so everything looked very burned and red. No one had a roof anymore. There were no trees; the big palm trees were ripped out of the ground. There were no stoplights left, there were no telephone poles left.

accompany a buffet dinner, after which the festivities move to the lagoon amphitheater. A troupe of 25 dancers and entertainers performs in a fantastic show highlighting the many cultures of Hawaii. (Luau M, W, and F 5pm. $56, ages 7-13 $29, ages 3-6 $19. Show only $15; ages 13 and under $18.)

🏞 PARKS

WAILUA RIVER STATE PARK. The unifying link between all of the area's attractions is the majestic **Wailua River,** which flows 21 mi. from its source atop Mt. Wai'ale'ale to the northern end of Lydgate Park. Separated into two branches for much of its path, the river forms one dominating waterway as it descends to sea level, mixing with salty ocean water to form a brackish environment that supports healthy populations of fish.

During the time of the *ali'i,* the Wailua River basin was the home of the royal chiefs, who claimed this area for its sandy beaches, easy canoe landings, fertile fields, and fresh and salt water resources. Known as the King's Highway, in honor of Kauai's last king, Kamehameha, the river is accompanied by a line of heiaus, paralleling the water's path from mountain to ocean. Six of the heiaus that form this sacred path can be seen today, while the seventh sits atop the wild summit of Wai'ale'ale. Nearly all of the sights listed below fall within the rather confusing boundaries of the thousand-acre Wailua River State Park, which encompasses the Wailua River, Wailua (see p. 364) and Opaeka'a Falls, Kuamo'o Rd., Fern Grotto, and Lydgate Park.

Although dominated by tourist-filled riverboats, the Wailua River is also a favorite of kayakers who put in on the north bank. Turn left on Kuamo'o Rd. and take the second left into Wailua River State Park. The trip to Fern Grotto and a small waterfall on the north fork is about 5 mi. round-trip and takes 2½hr., including stops. A convenient place to rent kayaks is **Wailua Kayak and Canoe,** located next to the Smith's Tropical Paradise shack on the north bank. From here, the river is a short walk away. All rentals come with a map, dry bag, and brief orientation for first-time kayakers. (☎821-1188. Single kayak $25 per day; double $50 per day. Open daily 8am-5pm.)

LYDGATE STATE PARK. A popular beach park, Lydgate's long, grassy lawn is dotted with picnic tables. A few shade trees provide refuge along the modest sands that front two wonderful saltwater pools. Artificial lava rock walls enclose the large pools that shelter swimmers from the unpredictable surf and create a paradise for beginning snorkelers. The larger pool is deep enough for those looking to showcase their strokes, while the shallower adjoining pool is appropriate for younger *keiki*. Restrooms, showers, a lifeguard stand, and a large pictorial fish finder back the pool-front beach at the northern end of the park. On the other side of the parking lot, **Kamalani Playground** welcomes waterwary children. The sprawling wood playground presents an endless source of amusement for kids of all ages, and the pretty mosaic benches are a nice place to catch your breath.

Hikina A Ka La ("rising of the sun"), at the extreme northern end of the park, is the first of seven heiaus connecting ocean to mountain. The stacked rock walls form a large rectangle, within which the kahunas celebrated the dawning of each new day with prayers and chants. At one end of the heiau was **Hauola,** the City of Refuge, where criminals could go to find sanctuary from punishment. Untouchable within its boundaries, the criminals could stay until purified of their wrongdoings by a kahuna. Behind the sanctuary, near the mouth of the river, the sand hides a number of boulders that bear etched petroglyphs. *(Turn right onto Leho Dr. at the Lydgate State Park sign after the 5-mile marker. A right turn on Nalu Rd. leads to the parking lot.)*

FERN GROTTO. Once a temple for the worship of Lono, the Hawaiian god of the harvest, the famed cave now welcomes tourists by the boatload, and brides and grooms by the dozens. A small waterfall creates an iridescent curtain of water at the base of the cave, which hosts an average of four to ten weddings per week. Although still an appealing example of natural beauty, the Fern Grotto of years past has recently become less than spectacular. In order to facilitate photo-happy tourists, the state cut down a large number of ancient trees; unable to adapt to the increased sunlight, the beautiful ferns that used to cover the entire cave have been reduced to sparse, dangling bits. The only way to reach the grotto is by river. Two companies, **Wai'ale'ale Boat Tours** (☎ 822-4908) and **Smith's** (see below), cruise the two plus miles from the Wailua Marina, alternating every half hour on the half hour. *(The marina is located on the southern bank of the Wailua River, down a paved road just south of the river crossing.)*

SMITH'S TROPICAL PARADISE. Descended from a whaler who came to Kauai on an early boat, the Smith family has helped to introduce visitors to the beauty and culture of the island for three generations. The one-and-a-half hour covered **boat tours** to

There were boards through cars—it was incredible. We cried when we came out—I think it was relief that we were alive. The fourth floor of the building was completely gone when we came out.

Q: What happened after?

A: The trees and shrubs came back very quickly. It was the economy that we could not get recovering because five of our biggest hotels went into bankruptcy. All our people worked for the hotels. The hurricane is something I would not want to do often but, at the same time I think it's like any serious illness or accident in your family. You get your priorities in line very, very quickly, and you're just thankful to be alive. [The hurricane] forced change and banded people together too. Everyone helped each other. The Red Cross said it was very different than it was in Florida [with Hurricane Andrew]. In Florida, they had Red Cross workers to come in and fix it for them. Here on the island of Kauai, people helped each other. They rolled up their sleeves and started to work. There was a lot of looting in Florida, but here we didn't have that, people didn't do that.

Q: Did [Iniki] make you question your decision to stay here?

A: Not at all. I had always thought that I belonged here. I wanted to stay immediately, the very first time I visited. I went home reluctantly, came back about eight times, always wanting to stay. The hurricane—no. My family called and said "Come home right now" but I never considered that. I think being here and being part of the recovery increased my love for the island.

Fern Grotto include a 30-minute stop at the cave, with a guided walk up the trail and some history. A group of musicians serenades each group from below, taking advantage of the grotto's perfect acoustics to sing the *Hawaiian Wedding Song*. Hula dancers and a Hawaiian band entertain passengers on the outbound cruise; the return trip features local stories and legends.

A 30-acre tropical garden, west of the marina, is divided into themed areas featuring rainforest plants, a flower garden, fruit trees, a fish-filled lagoon, a Polynesian village, and more. The gardens also play host to Kauai's most authentic luau (see **Entertainment,** p. 365) three nights a week. *(174 Wailua Rd., past the marina.* ☎ *821-6895; fax 822-4520; smiths@aloha.net. 1½hr. boat cruise $15, children $7.50. Tours sail daily from 9am-4pm. Self-guided walking tour of gardens $5.25. Open daily 8:30am-4pm.)*

KUAMOʻO RD. (HWY. 580)

Running along the northern bank of the river from the famous Coco Palms Resort, where Elvis tied the knot in *Blue Hawaii,* past Opaekaʻa Falls, the highway follows the course of the historic King's Path, along which the *aliʻi* walked from one religious site to another. The following sights all lie along the road.

THE BELLSTONE. Whenever a newborn's *piko* was found intact, the kahuna would lead a parade of other kahunas and members of the *aliʻi* up the King's Path to the bellstone, a large rock that, when struck with another stone, emitted a loud ringing sound to announce the birth of a new chief. *(Just past Poliahu, heading downhill on Kuamoʻo Rd., take the dirt road next to the Falling Rocks sign on the right. The Bellstone lies in a pile of rocks down a dirt trail and 30 yards past the guardrail.)*

POLIAHU HEIAU. Some believe Poliahu, a large heiau overlooking the river, was built by the mystical menehune who shaped the rock walls out of stones carried up from the river below. Religious ceremonies took place here until the abolition of the Hawaiian religion in 1819. *(On the opposite side of the road, downhill from the Opaekaʻa Falls overlook.)*

OPAEKAʻA FALLS. A tall waterfall flowing in a number of broad streams to a pretty pool below, Opaekaʻa Falls is a popular scenic viewpoint. *(The viewpoint is located a short walk west from a parking lot 1½ mi. up Kuamoʻo Rd. on the right.)*

WAIPOULI

Infamous for horrendous traffic, the short stretch of highway running north from Wailua to Kapaʻa is lined with shopping centers that afford some of the island's best prices. The constant flow of cars provides ample customers for Waipouli's many restaurants, which rival the ritzier North and South Shore establishments.

◪ **PRACTICAL INFORMATION.** A small **Waldenbooks** in Kauai Village Shopping Center carries Hawaiiana and an adequate selection of other reading materials. (☎822-7749. Open M-Sa 8am-9pm, Su 8am-5pm.) The most affordable groceries on the island line the shelves of ◪**Safeway Food and Drug,** 831 Kuhio Hwy., also in Kauai Village. Take a few extra minutes and apply for a "Safeway Club Card" to conserve a lot more cash. (☎822-2464. Open 24hr.) Those with piles of dirty clothes will love the triple-load washers and dryers at the **Kapaʻa Laundry Center,** 1105J Kuhio Hwy., in Kapaʻa Shopping Center. (☎823-3113. Coin-operated standard wash $1.50, dry 25¢. Drop-off service also available, $10 minimum. Drop-off M-F 7:30am-4:30pm. Open daily 7:30am-9:30pm.) The Kapaʻa **post office,** 1101 Kuhio Hwy., is tucked away at the back of Kapaʻa Shopping Center behind the laundry. (☎800-275-8777. Open M-F 8am-4pm, Sa 9am-2pm.) **Zip Code:** 96746.

FOOD. Waipouli's extensive shopping centers house a wide variety of dining options. **Papaya's ❶**, 831 Kuhio Hwy., in Kauai Village Shopping Center, is a whole foods market selling fresh fruits and veggies. There is also a popular deli counter (veggie stir fry $6; sandwiches $5) that caters to a loyal lunchtime clientele. (☎823-0190. Open M-Sa 9am-8pm. Food served until 7pm.) **King and I Thai Cuisine ❷**, 901 Kuhio Hwy., in Waipouli Plaza, has a long menu of reasonably priced meals ($7-10) and a whole section of vegetarian dishes. (☎822-1642. Dinner served daily 4:30-9pm.) Just north of Waipouli Plaza, on the *mauka* side of the road, **Coconuts ❸** has a funky, modern dining room and an affordable menu. Locals and tourists leave with bellies full of good food and wallets only slightly dented. The menu includes organic green salads ($5.50), crispy chicken with mac & cheese, onion rings, and veggies ($14), seafood paella ($18), and usually one vegetarian pasta dish. (☎823-8777. Dinner served M-Sa 4-10pm.)

NIGHTLIFE. Inflatable footballs and *papier-maché* Kahlua bottles dangle from the ceiling at **Lizard Lounge Bar & Grill** in Waipouli Town Center. Talkative regulars down good draft beers in the cozy booths, along the bar, or hanging around the pool tables and juke box. The kitchen cooks up a number of entrees to satisfy late-night munchies. (☎821-2205. Food served until 1am. Happy Hour daily 2-6pm. BBQ ribs $14; pesto sea scallops $18; draft beer $3. Open daily 10:30am-2am.)

SIGHTS. The *ali'i* who inhabited the Wailua River basin marked the boundaries of their home, *Wailua Nui Hoano* (sacred Wailua area), with the Pacific Ocean to the east, and an imaginary line, running from the Sleeping Giant on the north bank to Mount Kapu on the south bank, to the west. **Mount Kapu** ("forbidden") has a legend of its own. In ancient times, the Wailua area was home to Kauai's grandest heiaus. Jealous of the sacred idols kept at Poliahu on the King's Path, the residents of the South Shore sent a brother and a sister to Wailua to steal the idols away. They failed in their mission and never returned home, disappearing somewhere along the way. The mountain was so named to remind others of the pair's evil ways.

LEGENDS OF THE TALL Nounou Mountain, better known as the **Sleeping Giant**, stretches from Wailua to Kapa'a. Long ago, in the time of the *ali'i*, a man was fishing on the Wailua River, and he caught a strange-looking fish with bright red eyes. The mystical fish spoke and begged for its life, and the kind man allowed it to live. Upon hearing the good news, the fish transformed into a large and still-growing man, who went to live with the fisherman, but soon ate all of the family's food. The huge man continued to eat until he had exhausted the village's supplies, yet his hunger was still not satiated. Terrified, a local kahuna fed the giant bundles of bananas to make him drowsy, and led him to a faraway hill where a young girl played a magic song that lulled him to sleep. He sleeps above the river valley to this day, and locals still caution against young women singing or playing music near the mountain, for fear that the wrong song might awaken the giant from his trance. Another legend describes the giant not as a greedy outsider, but a friendly neighbor who helped the townsfolk to build a great heiau. Having celebrated the completion of the temple with a little too much wine and food, the giant fell asleep on his back for a nap that became eternal.

If you are having difficulty making out the features of the giant, look up toward the highest peak of the mountain, and, from left to right, you will see his forehead, then the bump of his eyebrows, his long flat nose, his slightly open mouth, and his broad chest. *(The best view of the Giant is from a viewpoint on the* mauka *side of the highway between the 7- and 8-mile markers, across the street from the Chevron station.)*

KAUAI

KAPA'A

Settled as a plantation town in the late 1800s, Kapa'a followed sugar with rice, and a group of Chinese merchants and mill owners funded much of the town's development. While the rest of the country suffered during the Great Depression, Kapa'a became a center of commerce, thriving as a cannery for locally produced pineapple. Home to a large number of the island's residents, and conveniently located next to the shopping centers of Waipouli, Kapa'a continues to thrive today. The historic wooden buildings that formed the original downtown have been restored twice, following extensive damage during both Hurricanes Iwa and Iniki; they now house health-conscious restaurants and retail shops galore.

■ ⚑ ORIENTATION AND PRACTICAL INFORMATION

Downtown Kapa'a occupies a few blocks of highway just north of the 8-mile marker. While tourists generally stick to the coast, the residents of Kauai's most populous town make their homes farther inland.

Bank of Hawaii, 1407 Kuhio Hwy. (☎822-3471), on the *mauka* side of the highway at the northern end of downtown, and **First Hawaiian Bank,** 1366 Kuhio Hwy. (☎822-4966), *makai* in the center of town, are both open M-Th 8:30am-4pm and F 8:30am-6pm. Each bank also has a **24hr. ATM.** The well-stocked shelves of **Kapa'a Public Library,** 1464 Kuhio Hwy. (☎821-4422), are available for browsing M, W, F 9am-5pm and Tu, Th noon-8pm. Four computers provide **Internet access** to library card holders. Card-less travelers can surf the web at **Aloha Dude Internet Hut,** 1387 Kuhio Hwy (☎822-3833), next to Olympic Cafe. (DSL connection $3 per 15min. $5 minimum. Printing 25¢ per page, faxes $2 for the first page, $1 each additional page. Open M-Sa 9am-7pm.)

⚑ ACCOMMODATIONS

The lodgings listed below are located within a few blocks of downtown Kapa'a.

◪ **Kapa'a Beach House,** 1552 Kuhio Hwy. (☎822-3313), *makai* on the way out of town. A relaxed, family-run hostel, the rambling Beach House features a shared outdoor kitchen with a long picnic table, a comfortable patio-style common area with TV, VCR, stereo, and cushy couches, a washing machine and clotheslines, and a fantastic view of the Pacific from the rooftop shower. Spacious dorms, featuring extra-long full bunks with curtains and mirrored walls (a holdover from the building's days as a chiropractic gym), open up to oceanfront patios. Linens provided. Bunks $23 single or $35 couple. Private rooms, with 4 beds and shared bath $50 for two; each additional person $5. ❶

Hotel Coral Reef, 1516 Kuhio Hwy. (☎800-843-4659 or 822-4481; fax 822-7705; www.hotelcoralreef.com), *makai* past the library at the northern end of town. Pretty tile floors, small refrigerators, fans, cable TVs, and ocean views make the phone-less, basic rooms a good value. Reception daily 7am-9pm. Oceanview rooms from $59, oceanfront rooms with sliding glass doors and private lanais from $89, two-room suites from $79; each additional person $10. ❷

Kauai International Hostel, 4532 Lehua St. (☎823-6142; www.hostels.com/kauaihostel), one block *mauka* of downtown. Steps from downtown Kapa'a, the International hostel hosts a predominantly European clientele of backpackers. Facilities include a shared kitchen and laundry room, cable TV, and an outdoor pool table. The staff sometimes organizes sightseeing or hiking daytrips around the island. Dorms $20, double private room $50. ❶

KAUAI

FOOD

Hungry visitors will not be disappointed by downtown Kapa'a's numerous restaurants. For a quick snack of baked goods and fresh fruit, or to stock up on local produce, stop at the weekly **Sunny Side Farmer's Market,** 1345 Kuhio Hwy., *mauka* at the southern end of downtown. (☎822-0494. W 3pm.)

Killer Juice Bar, 1586 Kuhio Hwy. (☎821-1905), at Kou Rd. under many green umbrellas, sells fresh local fruits and veggies, including cold coconuts ($1.50) and freshly baked organic bread. Creative sandwich combinations include a chevre cucumber nori wrap ($5), marinated tofu or chicken ($4.50 or $6), and turkey avocado tomato ($6). Fresh juices, frozen fruit frosties, and smoothies round out a healthy meal. $20 minimum for credit. Open daily 8:30am-7pm. ●

Ono Family Restaurant, 1292 Kuhio Hwy. (☎822-1710), *makai* at the southern end of downtown. Cozy wooden booths dominate the homey dining room, and super-nice waitresses welcome diners like family. Breakfast features lots of egg dishes, including a whole page of omelettes (mushroom, cheese, and avocado $8). Fruit smoothies $4; tropical hotcakes with bananas, macadamia nuts, and coconut $7. The midday menu is packed with sandwiches, burgers, veggie items, and local favorites (Portuguese-style pork $8; *saimin* $4). Breakfast served daily 7am-1pm; lunch 11am-2pm. ❷

Olympic Cafe, 1387 Kuhio Hwy. (☎822-5825), *mauka* in the center of town. Huge windows and open doors welcome the sun into the bright yellow dining room, and provide diners with nonstop people-watching fun. The extensive menu will please a whole family of picky eaters from meat lovers (chili burger with seasoned waffle fries $8), to fish fans (*ahi* burrito $11), to staunch vegans (tofu salad $9). Open daily 6am-3pm. ❷

Java Kai, 1384 Kuhio Hwy. (☎823-6887), the big green building in the center of town. Good coffee drinks, including lots of cold, blended concoctions of caffeine sweetness. Cushy armchairs and popular magazines make it a pleasant place to sit. Free refills on mango iced tea and lemonade "for here." 16- or 20-oz. smoothies from $4.50; big muffins and yummy aloha bars $2. Open M-Sa 6am-7pm, Su 6am-1pm. ●

Poppy's Natural Foods Market, 1495 Kuhio Hwy. (☎823-9373), *mauka* in the yellow 2-story building. Run by two yoga instructors from Santa Cruz, Poppy's sells a small selection of natural foods and some prepared (mostly) vegan items (apple pie $3). A counter in back whips up a small menu of vegetarian and vegan sandwiches (avocado and tofu $5; fakin' bacon BLT $5), salads, and smoothies. Open Tu-Su noon-8pm. ●

BEACHES

Those tired of fighting traffic on the way to North Shore beaches happily swim and sunbathe along Kapa'a's continuous stretch of sandy beach. Fronting the ocean just south of downtown, **Waipouli Beach Park** (better known as **Baby Beach**), on Moana Kai Rd., boasts fine golden sand and a long stone breakwater running north from the end of Makaha Rd., which forms a shallow pool at the southern end of the beach. A shower and good-sized parking lot lie farther north. On the other side of the canal, **Kapa'a Beach Park** parallels downtown Kapa'a. The long, very narrow beach is popular with kitesurfers, who usually stick to the southern end. Restrooms, a soccer field, and a big parking lot back the sandy shore. Farther north, those who prefer chlorine to salt can get wet at **Smokey Louie Gonsalves Jr. Swimming Pool,** a public oceanfront pool at the end of Kou St., past Killer Juice Bar. (Open M, Th-F and Su 1-4:30pm; Tu and Sa 10am-4:30pm.)

KAPA'A TO KILAUEA SCENIC DRIVE

1 KEALIA BEACH. At the 10-mile marker, the entire long, golden-sand beach is visible from the highway, and a dirt parking lot at the northern end, past a lifeguard stand and a port-a-potty, provides access to the most sheltered part of the beach. Swimmers and less experienced wave-riders are advised to stay within the protective breakwater and watch as seasoned boogie boarders and surfers battle the giant waves.

2 DONKEY BEACH. Half a mile past the 11-mile marker, a short paved road leads to a small parking lot. From here, the beach is a 10-minute walk down a well-marked path through picturesque privately owned fields. The path is gradual and pleasant, and at the bottom, a long crescent of rock-edged golden sand awaits. Trees provide a bit of shade; for sunbathers, the chirping birds and the empty fields backing the beach make for a pleasant tanning spot. The waves come fast and furious here, and the incredibly strong breaks challenge even experienced surfers.

3 ANAHOLA. A sleepy little community inhabited mostly by native Hawaiians, Anahola's major tourist attraction is **Duane's Ono-Char Burger ❶,** on the *makai* side of the highway just south of the 14-mile marker.

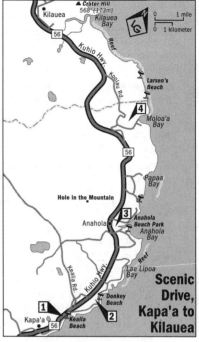

Scenic Drive, Kapa'a to Kilauea

TIME: 20min.

DISTANCE: 10 mi.

SEASON: year-round

Concrete tables topped with umbrellas provide a shady place to eat or to endure the sometimes frustratingly long wait. A huge variety of toppings complement the famous ¼ lb. burgers (plain "ono" burger $4; "local boy" with teriyaki sauce, cheddar cheese, and pineapple $5.65); wash it down with creamy milkshakes for $3. (☎822-9181. Open M-Sa 10am-6pm, Su 11am-6pm.) Immediately after the 14-mile marker, the first Aliomanu Rd. leads to the northern half of **Anahola Beach Park.** Most residents favor the more protected waters of the southern end, accessible from Anahola Rd. between the 13- and 14-mile markers, but the uncrowded golden sands and picnic tables here set the stage for a tranquil afternoon.

4 KO'OLAU RD. A narrow country road lined with flowering trees and wide green fields, Ko'olau also leads to two of the area's prettiest beaches. Crescent-shaped **Moloa'a Beach** hides behind a wall of secluded homes and vacation rentals. To get there, turn right on the first Ko'olau Rd., just before the 17-mile marker, and take another right onto Moloa'a Rd. Park at the end of the road on the left, and walk down to the beach. Walk to the right, to the southern end, where the daunting waves that greeted you give way to gentle aquamarine swells. This part of the beach also boasts fine sand that makes for a pleasant stroll along the shore. Back on the highway, the northern end of Ko'olau Rd. meets the highway just before the 20-mile marker. One mile south, a dirt road heads seaward to a small parking area and short trail to **Larsen's Beach,** a stretch of nearly deserted sands protected by a long reef. **Snorkelers** will enjoy the exceptionally clear waters during the calm summer months—at other times, a strong rip current can make the waters unsafe.

HOLE IN THE MOUNTAIN Past mile 15 on the way to Kilauea, look inland for the once very impressive but now rather diminutive hole in the mountain. Following a rockslide in the early 1980s, the famous landmark nearly disappeared. Legend explains the creation of the hole as the work of a warrior who threw a large spear with so much force that it went right through the mountain. Another legend claims the hole served as a peephole for mountain dwellers to look out at Anahola.

NORTH SHORE

The northern, windward side is the wettest and most lush part of an island already known for its heavy rainfall and verdant landscape. The region is the island amplified, and both locals and wealthy mainland refugees revel in its glory. All are searching for paradise in its fertile valleys, at the base of spectacular cliffs, or somewhere along the seven one-lane wooden bridges that meander between Hanalei and Haena.

KILAUEA

Sprawling pastures, organic farms, and grassy bluffs shape peaceful Kilauea. While many of the island's former plantation towns have moved away from farming and toward tourism, this small North Shore community shuns cheesy commercialism. Known for its picturesque lighthouse and seabird refuge, Kilauea is home to a motley collection of people from all walks of life. Native Hawaiian families, wandering surfers, dreadlocked hippies, and wealthy refugees from the mainland live in harmony in this eclectic town.

■ ORIENTATION

Kilauea Rd. meets **Hwy. 56** about ½ mi. north of the 23-mile marker, and heads northeast to Kilauea Point. The **Kong Lung Center,** on Kilauea Rd. at Keneke Rd., a few blocks from the highway, has restaurants, shops, and a movie theater. The town also boasts the only highway gas station between Kapa'a and Princeville—**Shell,** on the right as you turn off the highway into Kilauea. (Open M-Sa 6am-7pm, Su 6am-2pm.) Next door to the Shell, the **Menehune Food Mart** has a Bankoh (Bank of Hawaii **ATM**) that is open daily 5:30am-9pm.

■ FOOD

Kilauea's few restaurants feature fresh ingredients grown in the surrounding lush valleys. Those who prefer to cook for themselves can stock up on organic herbs and all sorts of good stuff at the weekly **Sunshine Market** (Th 4:30pm), in the parking lot next to Kilauea Farmers' Market.

■ **Banana Joe's** (☎828-1092). Look for the yellow sign on the *mauka* side of the highway, just north of town. Island produce, juices, and homemade granola line the counters of this friendly fruit stand. A pineapple frostie ($2.50), made from freshly frozen fruit, is the perfect refreshment after a long, hot drive on the highway. Open daily 9am-6pm. ●

Kilauea Bakery and Pau Hana Pizza (☎828-2020), in Kong Lung Center. Decadent cakes, cookies, and brownies will satisfy any sweet tooth, and a wide selection of coffees and teas wash down the tasty baked goods. For lunch, the ovens turn out delicious

North Shore Kauai

pizzas, topped with good-for-you extras such as tofurella, spinach and local fish, as well as traditional meats (Italian sausage and smoked ham). Open daily 6:30am-9pm. ❶

Kilauea Farmers' Market (☎828-1512). A small grocery in Kong Lung Center next to the movie theater. Local organic vegetables share shelf space with gourmet foods and basic ingredients. The deli counter in back whips up hearty sandwiches (avocado veggie $6.50; fresh island fish $7), homemade soups, and salads. Open M-Sa 8:30am-8:30pm, Su 8:30am-8pm. Deli open daily until 3pm. ❶

🅖 🎵 SIGHTS AND ENTERTAINMENT

Kilauea's green bluffs shelter a wildlife refuge and secluded beach; the surrounding land is dotted with farms both small and large. In addition, the quiet town is home to one of Kauai's few cinemas. The **Kilauea Theater** (☎828-0438), next to the Farmers' Market, has one screen that plays independent and big-budget films daily, usually around 5 and 8pm.

KILAUEA POINT NATIONAL WILDLIFE RESERVE. The focal point of the reserve is the historic **Kilauea lighthouse,** built in 1913 to guide commercial boats on their journey to the Orient. The lighthouse still features a giant clamshell lens and an unbeatable view of the frothing blue ocean, despite being decommissioned in 1976. The old communications building alongside the light has a historical display, a video, and reference books about the refuge's habitats and residents. A **Visitor Center** just past the entrance features an ecological diorama, and sells a variety of books and souvenirs. Endangered **nene** wander around, while a variety of seabirds soar overhead and perch on the protected bluffs. The most easily identifiable of the species are the bright, red-footed **boobies,** who build their nests in the trees. **Great frigate birds** fish the offshore waters year-round, while laysan **albatross** can be found from December to July. From March to October, red- and white-tailed **tropic-birds** swoop grandly over the water, coming to rest on **Moku'ae'ae Rock.** After breeding in the north, Pacific **golden plovers** winter in Kauai, while wedge-tailed shearwaters favor the island during the spring. As it's the northernmost point in

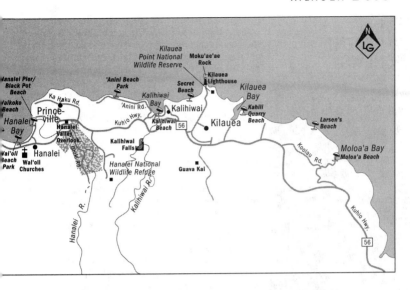

the main Hawaiian islands, you can also catch a glimpse of **spinner dolphins, monk seals, sea turtles,** or migrating **humpback whales** here in the winter. Free one-hour guided **hikes** to the top of Crater Hill afford even more amazing views. *(At the end of Kilauea Rd. ☎828-0168; www.kilaueapoint.com. Hikes M-Th 10am. Reservations required. Refuge open daily 10am-4pm. $3 admission.)*

GUAVA KAI. Fans of the sweet, pink fruit will enjoy a stop at Guava Kai, a plantation and agronomical engineering center dedicated to perfecting guava production. The **Visitor Center** stocks guava products galore, sells souvenirs, and shows a video illustrating the life of a plantation-grown guava. A few displays detailing the cultivation process are located next to a small table laden with all sorts of guava-flavored sauces and spreads, as well as a dispenser of guava juice, free for tasting. Harvested by hand, the plantation's guava trees have been engineered to produce a year-round harvest—as opposed to biannual wild trees—that is maintained by cyclical fertilization and pruning, as well as simulated seasonal conditions. The resulting fruits are shipped to nationwide distributors. A short nature walk features tropical flowers and a picturesque pond. A small snack shop adjacent to the Visitor Center serves guava floats and other chilly treats, plus heartier items such as *saimin* ($2.50) and beef burritos. *(On Kuawa Rd., which runs* mauka *from the highway just south of the 23-mile marker. ☎828-6121. Open daily 9am-5pm. Free.)*

◢ BEACHES AND FALLS

Other than **Kahili Quarry Beach,** most of the area's best beaches lie within the boundaries of Kalihiwai. The town's winding mountain roads hide spectacular beaches and towering waterfalls. **Kalihiwai Rd.,** once a U-shaped loop bridging the Kalihiwai River, was split by a tsunami that destroyed the bridge in the 1950s. The two branches of the road now meet at the base of **Kalihiwai Bay,** on the sandy shores of **Kalihiwai Beach.**

KAHILI QUARRY BEACH. Along with seabirds and guavas, Kilauea also boasts a broad beach. Tucked away on a dirt road, Kahili Quarry Beach is perfect for a

IN RECENT NEWS

FIGHT FOR YOUR RIGHTS

Hawaii Democratic Sens. Daniel Akaka and Dan Inouye are at the forefront of a movement lobbying the federal government to allow Native Hawaiians the same rights as other indigenous people. Their bill would see the formation of Native Hawaiian governing bodies, similar to those of American Indian tribes. The senators, with their supporters, argue that it only fair that Native Hawaiians have the same rights and privileges as other indigenous people, namely American Indians and Alaska Natives. The cause has picked up momentum, especially with admittance of a white student to traditionally all-Native Hawaiian Kamehameha School. Major American Indian and Alaska Native groups, along with Hawaiians, have traveled to Washington to plea their case in forums, meetings, and roundtable discussions. Currently, Republicans have stalled the bill in both the House and the Senate. Critics of the measure argue that it give Hawaiians a preferred status in Hawaii. Negotiations are ongoing.

peaceful afternoon. The fine golden sands slope into a sharp foreshore toward the right. The left side of the beach has more protection and safer swimming, although the mouth of the Kilauea stream sometimes creates cloudy water and unpredictable currents. The quarry is usually pretty empty, save for a few surfers. *(Accessible from Wailapa Rd., which runs seaward from the highway between the 21- and 22-mile markers. After 0.4 mi., follow a dirt road downhill to the left, and park at the end. The beach is a very short stroll to the right or a quick walk to the left.)*

■ **SECRET BEACH.** Officially Kauapea Beach, this formerly hidden spot has outgrown its mysterious nickname, and the small parking area can no longer accommodate the shiny rental cars lined up along the road. Despite its discovery, Secret Beach is still a true gem. A vast expanse of superfine golden sand sprinkled with lava rocks, the beach features big surfing waves and beautiful views of Kilauea Point and the surrounding bluffs. From the bottom of the trail, the glistening sands stretch far to the right, where a sheltered cove and more gently sloping shore provide safer swimming. *(From Hwy. 56 northbound, turn right on the first Kalihiwai Rd., just before the 24-mile marker, and right again at the first dirt road. Park alongside all of the other cars and follow a well-marked trail for 10 steep minutes down to the beach.)*

KALIHIWAI BEACH. Boogie boarders and surfers come to play in the waves off the shore, while local families favor Kalihiwai for weekend picnics. A wide crescent of soft golden sand, the beach continues to the west on the other side of the lava-rock lined river mouth. *(Take the 1st Kalihiway Rd. to the end and park under the trees facing the beach.)*

KALIHIWAI FALLS. For a quick glance at the tall, cascading waters of Kalihiwai Falls, look *mauka* from the bridge over the Kalihiwai River, just north of the 25-mile marker. A more extended—but not necessarily more relaxed—view can be had from the bridge itself. Park in the dirt turnout just before the bridge, and walk out to the center, being careful to avoid the lines of cars flying around the curve.

'ANINI BEACH PARK. The golden sands of 'Anini Beach line the coast for nearly two miles. A long reef fringes the narrow sand beach, creating a wide, shallow lagoon of crystal clear water. Swimmers frolic at the eastern end of the beach, while local boat owners, surfers, and windsurfers occupy the waters to their left. County **campgrounds,** complete with spacious beachfront sites and full facilities, are available (see

Camping, p. 355). The lawn backing the county park features pavilions and picnic tables aplenty. Beyond the campground, local fishermen wade into the lagoon in pursuit of dinner. The flat shore and incredibly calm waters make 'Anini one of Kauai's safest swimming beaches, and the warm lagoon provides the perfect windsurfer's paradise.

Shallow turquoise waters and the warm offshore breeze invite young and old alike to try their hand at sailing boards. A veteran windsurfer with 17 years of teaching experience, Celeste at **Windsurf Kauai** takes small groups (up to six) out on the lagoon. A 3hr. introductory lesson, open to competent swimmers ages 5 and up, includes an hour on a land simulator before the remaining two on the water. Those who catch the windsurfing bug can take a second lesson that focuses on advanced skills and qualifies students for certification. Rentals and surfing lessons also available. *(To reach the beach, head makai on Kalihiwai Rd., between the 25- and 26-mile markers, and turn left on 'Anini Rd., which runs the length of the beach. Windsurf Kauai ☎ 828-6838; windsurfkauai@aol.com. 3hr. lesson, including all equipment $75.)*

PRINCEVILLE

Robert Crichton ("R.C.") Wyllie, a visiting merchant who caught the attention of King Kamehameha III, served as the king's Minister of Foreign Affairs for more than two decades. Settling on Kauai's North Shore, the grandly ambitious Wyllie began buying up large parcels of land on which to build a posh and splendid manor like those in his native Scotland. Wyllie was absolutely devoted to the royal family and planned to bequeath his lands to Prince Albert, the charming infant son of Kamehameha IV and Princeville's namesake. Sadly, Albert died at the age of four, followed within a year by Wyllie himself, whose estate, though divided and sold, retains its royal name to this day. Modern Princeville is a meticulously planned resort community where golf courses, condominiums, and the island's most luxurious hotel make up for the town's overall lack of personality.

■✚ ⁊ ORIENTATION AND PRACTICAL INFORMATION

Located 28 mi. north of Lihu'e on Hwy. 56, Princeville's manicured lawns and oceanfront accommodations attract affluent golf club-swinging travelers with fat wallets and expensive tastes. The lack of affordable accommodations and food, and the super expensive gas—the Princeville Center Chevron has the last pumps on the North Shore—will drive more budget-minded travelers south to Kapa'a for beds and north to Hanalei for meals.

Princeville Center, situated at the 28-mile marker, offers numerous real estate offices, and all of the following. **Bank of Hawaii** (☎ 826-6551) is next to the post office and **First Hawaiian Bank,** 4280 Kuhio Hwy. (☎ 826-1560) is at the eastern end of the shopping center. (Both open M-Th 8:30am-4pm, F 8:30am-6pm with **24hr. ATMs.**) The **Princeville Public Library,** 4343 Emmalani Dr., is across the street. (☎ 826-4310. Open Tu, Th-Sa 9am-5pm; W noon-8pm.) Email junkies can surf the web at **Akamai.** (☎ 826-1042. **Internet access** $2 minimum for 10 minutes, 20¢ each additional minute. Open M-F 10am-5pm.) Princeville's **post office,** 4280 Kuhio Hwy., mails coconuts and more. (☎ 828-1721. Open M-F 10:30am-3:30pm, Sa 10:30am-12:30pm.) **Zip Code:** 96722.

⌂ ACCOMMODATIONS

Built into a bluff at the eastern end of Hanalei Bay, the glorious **Princeville Hotel** ❺ boasts expansive views and decadent luxury. The crown jewel of the resort community, the hotel's floors are a series of tiers that maximize its stunning vis-

---

PIKO-BOO! Long ago, in the time of the *ali'i*, the common people lived high up in the hills, far away from the sacred area bounded by the ocean and an imaginary line from Nounou Mountain (See **Legends of the Tall,** p. 369) on the north bank to Mount Kapu on the south. The only commoners allowed to cross this boundary were pregnant women who walked the King's Path to Holoholoku, where they offered their sons to the *ali'i*. A kahuna met expectant mothers at the heiau, where they remained until they were ready to give birth. When the time came, the women were laid out on Pohaku Hoo Hanau, the **birthstone.** After giving birth, mothers left their sons in the care of the kahuna and retraced their steps up the hill. The kahuna would then take the *piko* (umbilical cord) of the newborn, wrap it in cloth, and place it in the crack of a big rock called Pohaku Piko. If the cord disappeared (was eaten by a rat) within a 4-day period, the child was proved a rat-like thief and executed, but if the kahuna returned to find the cord intact, a new chief of the *ali'i* was born. *(Up Kuamo'o Rd. on the left.)*

---

tas. The ninth floor lobby sits atop the bluff, and the first floor opens out to a swimming pool and Pu'u Poa Beach. Although most travelers blanch at the thought of $405 garden view rooms, the Princeville Hotel's restaurants, luau, spa, and fantastically posh lobby provide non-hotel guests with affordable opportunities to taste the good life. The floor-to-ceiling lobby windows offer unmatched views of aquamarine Hanalei Bay and a verdant backdrop of cliffs, cascading waterfalls, and Bali Hai. All of the guest rooms and suites feature tasteful and comfortable furnishings that match the hotel's opulence. (5520 Ka Haku Rd., at the end of the road. ☎ 800-325-3589 or 826-9644; fax 826-1166; www.princeville.com. Rooms $405-4500.)

◘ FOOD

Within the resort, three restaurants and a posh cocktail lounge serve a variety of casual and haute cuisine to meet a range of tastes and budgets. A more affordable option is **Foodland,** a market featuring an extensive deli (sandwiches $4) that sells fried chicken and deli counter pasta salads. (☎ 826-9880. Open daily 6am-11pm.)

The Beach Restaurant, located poolside above the sparkling bay water, serves standard lunchtime fare. Sandwiches with chips (turkey, avocado, and bacon $14), hot dogs ($10) and salads (grilled chicken Caesar $15) taste even better at the swim-up bar. Open daily 11am-sunset. ❸

Cafe Hanalei, the hotel's main dining room, features *al fresco* dining on a pleasant terrace overlooking the bay, tall waterfalls and majestic Bali Hai. Serves continental cuisine with an Asian flair and fresh island ingredients. Breakfast selections include french toast with macadamia nuts ($9) and Eggs Benedict ($12). Salads and sandwiches ($12-18) dominate the lunch menu, which also offers a few seafood specialties (*unagi* platter $19). Dinner is a bit pricier (Pacific Rim-inspired seafood and steak entrees $22-35). Sunday brunch buffet ($35, children ages 3-12 $2 per each year of age), Friday night seafood buffet ($45, children $2.50 per year). Reservations recommended for dinner. Open for lunch 11am-2:30pm, dinner 5:30-9:30pm. ❹

The Living Room, with plush couches and a relaxed ambience, provides a wonderful setting for high tea or a few drinks. An outdoor lanai overlooks the bay and makes for an excellent place to watch the sun set over the Na Pali cliffs. High tea daily 3-5pm. Sushi bar, pupus and desserts daily 5-9:30pm. Demonstrations of traditional Hawaiian hula and chant Su and Th at 6:30pm. Live music nightly 7-11pm. Beverage service nightly until midnight. Dinner served nightly 6-10pm. ❹

La Cascata, specializing in upscale Mediterranean and Italian cuisine, is worth the splurge. Named for the towering waterfalls that dominate its view, the restaurant is accessed through a set of antique gates that transport diners to an Italian coastal village with pretty murals and hanging ivy. Entrees $24-34. Three-course meal $50. Reservations recommended. Dinner served nightly 6:30-10pm. ❺

🐚 BEACHES

Princeville's bluff-top location affords excellent views of Hanalei Bay and tall waterfalls, but sharp drops mean steep (and sometimes slippery) descents to the resort's secluded beaches. All resort beaches are open to the public.

QUEEN'S BATH. A deep lava rock pool carved by Mother Nature, Queen's Bath is a unique swimming and snorkeling spot. Waves splash ocean water over the black rock walls, and a small inlet allows fish and saltwater to circulate through the pool. High tides and heavy winter surf sometimes obscure it, but during the summer Queen's Bath attracts droves of locals and tourists alike. Adventurous swimmers leap off the rocks above the water while their more mellow friends are content to float in the clear, turquoise waves and enjoy their bath. *(From Ka Haku Rd., turn right on Punahele, which curves to the right to form a loop with Kapiolani. Just past the base of the loop, a trail leads down toward the ocean. A small waterfall flows to the right of the trail, which ends 5min. from the road at a wide lava rock shelf. Turn left and walk across the rocks for another 5min. to Queen's Bath.)*

HIDEAWAYS. Also known as **Pali Ke Kua Beach,** Hideaways is a beautiful—albeit short—stretch of coarse gold sand with amazingly clear water and exceptional snorkeling. Although swimming is usually considered safe here, winter sometimes brings high surf and unpredictable tides. *(For both Hideaways and Pu'u Poa, park in the tiny public lot wedged between the Princeville Hotel lot and the Pu'u Poa condos. From there, Hideaways is 10min. down the narrow trail that runs between the lot and the tennis court. Wet weather can make the walk slippery and even dangerous; use caution.)*

PU'U POA BEACH. Fronting the Princeville Hotel and extending south into Hanalei Bay, Pu'u Poa is the resort's longest beach. A broad stretch of sand slopes gently to shallow and transparent water, and a long fringe reef protects a wide swath of tranquil water, where even the littlest *keiki* can safely swim and snorkel the afternoon away. *(Accessible from a marked path that begins to the left of the Princeville Hotel's gatehouse and leads down to the beach. Use caution on the walk down.)*

HANALEI

Situated in a deep, green valley surrounded by sheer cliffs and towering waterfalls, Hanalei's natural splendor is matched by its welcoming, laid-back vibe. Within the diverse community, local *taro* farmers rub elbows with affluent mainland refugees, and everyone flocks to the colorful downtown shopping centers to socialize. The name Hanalei translates to "crescent-shaped bay" or "lei valley," and indeed, stunning rainbows often hang like leis in the rain-soaked sky. Pristine Hanalei Bay makes a wonderful backdrop for photographs and romantic moments; its sparkling shore also served as the inspiration for *Peter, Paul and Mary's* classic song about a dragon named Puff who lived by the sea.

✈ 🏨 ORIENTATION AND PRACTICAL INFORMATION

Hanalei lies just a few miles west of Princeville's manicured lawns and sprawling condominium complexes. Two retail centers, brimming with enticing restaurants

KAUAI

and shops, face each other across the highway in the center of town. *Mauka*, **Hanalei Center** features a pleasant lawn dotted with stands and picnic tables. Across the way, **Ching Young Center** has restrooms, payphones, plus a mermaid cut-out to stick your head through.

At the western end of Ching Young, **Big Save** sells groceries and has an **ATM**. (☎826-6652. Open daily 7am-9pm.) Hanalei's **post office**, 5226 Kuhio Hwy., is immediately west of Ching Young Center. (☎800-275-8777. Open M-F 9am-4pm, Sa 10am-noon.) **Zip Code:** 96714.

Hanalei town has most of the North Shore's **equipment rental** and activity shops. **Pedal 'n Paddle,** in Ching Young Center, rents a quality selection of kayaks ($15-35 per day, $60-140 per week), snorkel gear ($5 per day, $20 per week; children $3/ $10), boogie boards ($5 per day, $20 per week), and bikes ($10 per day, $40 per week), in addition to selling camping gear and other outdoor paraphernalia. (☎826-9069; www.pedalnpaddle.com. Open daily 9am-6pm.) On the *makai* side of the highway on the way into town, **Kayak Kauai** has an even bigger selection of gear at slightly higher prices, and also offers tours (see **Tours**, p. 380). **Hanalei Surf Company** (☎826-9000), in Hanalei Center, stocks rash guards and stylish beach wear and rents snorkel gear, boogie boards, and surfboards at reasonable prices.

◻ FOOD

Nearly all of the North Shore's restaurants are located along the highway in Hanalei, and serve local and global cuisine in comfortable, and usually intimate, surroundings. For a healthy snack or wholesome groceries, visit the small, family-run **Hanalei Natural Foods,** in Ching Young Center. (☎826-6841. Open daily 8am-7pm.) Their mobile **Aloha Juice Bar ❶,** parked in the lot, blends smoothies and fresh organic juices (from $3.50) and sells prepared sandwiches. (Open daily 9am-6pm.)

Village Snack and Bakery (☎826-6841), in Ching Young Center. The heavenly aroma of fresh-baked pies and delectable pastries makes up for the minimal ambience. Breakfast features typical dishes (2 eggs and toast $2.75, *loco moco* $6). Plate lunches make a hearty lunch ($6). Breakfast until 11am. Open daily 6am-6pm. ❶

Neide's Salsa and Samba (☎826-1851), in Hanalei Center. Enjoy spicy Mexican *antojitos* or authentic Brazilian cuisine in the casual yet sophisticated dining room, or relax on the wooden lanai. Locals rave about the house special *muqueca* (fresh catch with coconut sauce, shrimp, and Brazilian rice; market price). Most of the Mexican entrees can be made vegetarian. Fish tacos $12, nachos grande $9, huevos rancheros $9. Open daily 11:30am-2:30pm and 5-9pm. ❸

Java Kai (☎826-6717), in Hanalei Center. Savor fabulous aloha bars (made with shortbread, coconut, macadamia nuts, and chocolate) in the plush armchairs. Early birds can enjoy a sweet Kauai waffle (topped with banana, papaya, macadamia nuts, and whipped cream $7) or a fruit-filled papaya boat on the lanai. Breakfast until 11am. Open daily 6:30am-6:30pm. ❶

Tropical Taco (☎827-8226), in the long green building past Kayak Kauai. A Hanalei institution, this former food truck has moved indoors to accommodate the lunchtime rush for its homemade corn tortillas and beer-battered fish burritos ($6.75). Huge beef taco $6.75, veggie burrito $5.50. Open M-Th and Sa 11am-7pm, F 11am-3pm. ❶

Hanalei Mixed Plate (☎826-7888), in Ching Young Center. Locals and tourists alike queue up for big portions of hearty local food. Plate lunches include entrees such as *shoyu* ginger chicken, *kalua* pork, and veggie stir-fry (1 entree $6, 2 entrees $7, 3 entrees $8). Less ambitious eaters can munch on salads, sandwiches, and burgers (tempeh burger $6.50; cheeseburger $6). Open M-Sa 11:30am-8:30pm. ❶

LEGENDARY LOVE A common sight throughout the islands, the delicate blossoms of the native *hau* tree, a type of hibiscus, bloom a brilliant yellow in the morning, then turn deep orange by afternoon and bright red the next day before falling from the tree. Besides beautifying gardens, the trees provide myriad other services: fish net floats are built from smaller branches, bigger, stronger branches are used as outriggers for canoes, and the tough bark is shaped into rope or hula skirts. The legend of the *hau* tree comes from the Wailua area, where many years ago a man named Hi-Hi-Aka-La-La-Hau fell in love with Poliahu, the goddess of a sacred heiau. Failing in his quest to win her love by scaling a massive cliff overnight, the man was turned into a tree that grew twisting in every direction. One day, a terrible storm uprooted the tree, carrying it all the way up to Mt. Wai'ale'ale, where the tree continued to grow until an even more violent storm tore it to pieces and washed the tree down through Kauai's five rivers to the ocean, and farther to the other islands where the pieces took root and grew into many, many *hau* trees. The *hau* tree's magical origins are apparent in its round leaves which feature a central ridge, or Mt. Wai'ale'ale, and five rivers (from left to right the Waimea, Hanapepe, Wailua, Kealia, and Hanalei Rivers) flowing outward to the ocean.

Zelo's Beach House (☎826-9700), at Aku Rd. next to Ching Young Center. With more than a hint of cheesy Hawaiian kitsch, Zelo's whimsical dining room belies its serious food. Loyal patrons and hungry visitors line the bamboo bar to enjoy Kauai's most extensive beer list while waiting patiently for patio tables. Burgers (bacon cheddar $9.25, veggie $8.50) dominate the lunch menu. Dinner ranges from smoked tofu salad ($9) to varied seafood and steak dishes (tenderloin $24, *wok*-charred mahi mahi $22), and all-you-can-eat spaghetti ($10). Pricey nightly specials feature fresh island fish. Happy Hour 3:30-5:30pm. Open daily 11am-3:30pm and 5:30-10pm. ❸

Bubba's (☎826-7839), in Hanalei Center. A fun-loving burger shack that flips patty after patty of "88% fat-free, fresh ground Kauai beef." *Keiki* can chomp on baby burgers, while dad polishes off ½ lb. Big Bubba's. Diners can also choose from fish ($5.25), chicken ($5.75), or tempeh ($5.25) patties. Open daily 10:30am-8pm. ❶

◉ SIGHTS

HANALEI NATIONAL WILDLIFE REFUGE. Many years ago, ancient Hawaiians settled the valleys of Hanalei, cultivating *taro* in the fertile wetlands. Today, part of that tradition is preserved in the refuge, visible from a highway **overlook** slightly west and *mauka* of the Princeville Shopping Center. The small turnout provides a bird's-eye view of the patchwork ponds and fields that cover the valley floor, as well as the meandering Hanalei River. Although most of the reserve is closed to visitors, narrow **Ohiki Rd.** runs through the valley for a couple of miles. Established to protect the endangered populations of native waterbirds, including the gallinule, coot, *koloa* duck, and black-necked stilt, the refuge also hosts migrant birds who winter in the warm valley. Through a partnership with the refuge, local Hawaiian farmers work the *taro* ponds on a rotating cycle. Early growth ponds make nourishing feeding sites for the resident waterbirds, while later growth ponds provide protection from inclement weather and would-be predators. The man-made *taro* ponds also serve as the birds' primary nesting area, sheltering delicate eggs from human and animal interference. (*To reach Ohiki Rd., turn left immediately after the Hanalei Bridge at the entrance to the valley. A grassy parking area, 0.7 mi. down Ohiki Rd. on the left, provides access to a short trail that leads to an overlook.*)

KAUAI

WAI'OLI CHURCHES. Missionaries discovered Kauai in the 19th century and established one of their earliest congregations in Hanalei. Today, the bright green **Wai'oli Hui'ia Church** attracts visitors and a loyal congregation to Sunday worship. The American gothic-style church was built in 1912 to accommodate the growing community. Beautiful stained-glass windows line the walls, and a small bell tower still houses the congregation's original bell, brought from Boston in 1843. Just west of the green church, the **Original Wai'oli Church,** completed in 1941, now serves as a mission hall. The **Wai'oli Mission House Museum,** behind the church, was built by the Reverend William Alexander in 1837, but it is best known as the home of **Abner and Lucy Wilcox,** of Kauai's illustrious Wilcox family. One of the first Western-style homes constructed on the island, the frame house was shipped in parts from Boston. Although the Alexanders had hoped to evoke their native New England, the house features distinctly Hawaiian features, such as a large lanai and wide sloping roof to accommodate the North Shore's frequent downpours. *(The Wai'oli Hui'ia Church is across from the 3-mile marker. ☎ 826-6253. Services Su 10am. Museum ☎ 245-3202. Open Tu, Th, and Sa 9am-3pm. Free.)*

◪ BEACHES

Postcard-pretty **Hanalei Bay** attracts beachgoers by the dozens with its soft, sandy shores. Swimming is usually considered safe during the summer, but tides from the surrounding ocean sometimes sneak into the wide bay, creating fabulous winter surf and unpredictable sea conditions. From June to August, novice surfers learn to ride the baby swells that gently graze the shallow shoreline, but in winter experienced wave riders paddle all the way out to the mouth of the bay in search of the perfect wave.

BLACK POT BEACH. A pleasant place for an evening picnic, Black Pot has a lawn with full facilities, and a sturdy pier that juts out into the bay. While the picnic tables and pier provide great **sunset views,** the beach itself is nothing special. Named for the communal cooking pot used by campers, the flat beach blends into the sandy parking lot and slopes very gradually into slightly cloudy water. For information on camping at Black Pot, see **Camping,** p. 355. *(From the highway, turn makai on Aku Rd., next to Zelo's. Take a right where Aku ends at Weke Rd. and continue to the parking area at the end of the road.)*

HANALEI PAVILION BEACH PARK. Shady trees and wooden benches dot the wide lawn, and a huge pavilion shelters a few picnic tables. *Keiki* play in the gentle waves that break right along the sandy shore and young boogie boarders try their luck in the surf as a lifeguard looks on. *(From Aku Rd., turn right on Weke. The parking area will soon appear on the left. Restrooms and showers are located alongside the pavilion.)*

WAI'OLI BEACH PARK. Nicknamed "Pinetrees" by the local surfers who rest beneath the shade of the tall ironwoods, Wai'oli is a long, wide stretch of beach that forms the bottom of Hanalei Bay. Less crowded than Hanalei Pavilion, the eastern end of Wai'oli Beach features similar rolling waves. The western half is more exposed to ocean currents and consequently more popular with surf and kiteboard instructors. Constant summertime swells provide the perfect learning environment, but winter surf here is strictly for the experienced. Volleyball nets toward the western end offer water-free fun, and a lifeguard stand, restroom, and shower are located at the eastern end of the beach. *(From Aku Rd., turn left on Weke and then right down He'e, Ama'ama, or Anae Rd. to small dirt parking areas.)*

WAIKOKO BEACH. Narrower than other Hanalei Bay beaches, Waikoko is visible from the highway between the 4- and 5-mile markers. The near-shore waters are a little too shallow for swimming, but local fishermen and in-the-know snorkelers find the calm, reef-protected beach perfect for their purposes. Farther west of town, Waikoko's ribbon of fine sand provides a nice place to sit and admire the scenery. *(Park anywhere along the road after the 4-mile marker and walk down to the beach. One access is halfway between the 4- and 5-mile markers, where a short, steep trail leads down to the beach from a turn-out just before the "15 mph" sign.)*

TOURS

Kayak Kauai offers kayaking and hiking tours (including a 17-mile ocean kayak trip along the Na Pali Coast $165), as well as surfing lessons ($40). Wannabe surfers looking for the best value and most personal attention should call ▣**Learn to Surf.** Run by a local family, most lessons are given by the very friendly, very knowledgeable, and very tall Cliff, who will meet students at whichever beach has the best surf that day. (☎826-7612. 90min. lessons for up to two people $35; three or more students $30.) In Ching Young Center, **(H.S.C.) Backdoor** has surfing lessons with Australian pro Russell Lewis. (☎826-1900. 2hr. lesson, daily 10am and 1pm, $50. Open daily during summer 8am-9:30pm, in winter 8am-9pm.)

HAENA

Cruising through on their way to golden beaches and snorkeling nirvanas, few visitors venture into the heart of Haena proper. Completely devoid of commercial establishments, Haena is less a town than a small residential community comprised of narrow roads and fancy beachfront homes.

ORIENTATION AND PRACTICAL INFORMATION

Leaving Hanalei, **Rte. 560** ascends parallel to the western shore of Hanalei Bay before dropping into the miniscule town of **Wainiha** and following the coast through Haena to **Ke'e Beach.**

The only place to buy drinks, snacks, or sunblock west of Hanalei is the **Wainiha General Store,** on the left after the Wainiha Bridge. (☎826-6251. Open daily from 9:30 or 10:30am-7:30pm.) The tiny **Bradda Lou's Sandwich Shack ❶** next door makes tasty sandwiches which are great for beach picnics. (Veggie wrap $7, *kalua* pork sandwich $6.75, build-your-own sandwich $6.50. Open daily 10am-2pm.)

ACCOMMODATIONS AND CAMPING

A number of deluxe beachfront vacation rentals line the narrow streets of Haena, and those with cash to burn can enjoy the opulence. A quick online search or a call to a rental agent will turn up many appealing, though pricey, options. Less affluent travelers needn't despair—Haena is also home to the North Shore's only budget accommodation. **YMCA Camp Naue ❶,** right by the 8-mile marker at the western end of Alealea Rd., welcomes guests to their bunkhouse and grassy campsites. (☎826-6419. No linens. Bunks $12, tents $10 per person.)

SIGHTS

There are a few other natural wonders in Haena that merit your attention, besides the wide stretches of stunning beach.

KAUAI

LIMAHULI GARDEN. The final link in Kauai's trio of **National Tropical Botanical Gardens** (see p. 391), **Limahuli Garden** features a comprehensive collection of native plants as well as traditional rock-wall **terraces,** used for *taro* farming, that date back over 700 years. Nestled in the foothills of the Na Pali cliffs, the garden's primary goals are educating the public and reestablishing native plants among more aggressive introduced flora. Limahuli's focus on conservation complements the themes of art and science advocated by its sister gardens, the Allerton and McBryde Gardens in the Lawai Valley. A sometimes steep and uneven trail meanders through the terraces and climbs up a bluff to a perch with outstanding views of the soft green mountains and bright blue ocean. (☎826-1053. *Mauka between the 9- and 10-mile markers. Open Tu-F and Su from 9:30am, last entry at 4pm. Guided tours by reservation only $15. Self-guided tours, including guidebook filled with history and legend, $10.*)

MANINIHOLO DRY CAVE. Across the highway, facing Haena Beach Park, Maniniholo Dry Cave is a large crevice carved out of the soaring rock walls. A sojourn into the interior of the cave can be a little dank, but adventurous visitors may encounter local artisans selling their wares inside. In the 1950s, a tsunami closed up much of what was once a huge cave. Lore attributes the origin of the cave to a tribe of menehune led by a fisherman named Maniniholo who dug into the rock in order to capture an evil spirit that had been stealing their catches.

WET CAVES. Just west of the dry cave lies the boundary of **Haena State Park,** which encompasses Ke'e Beach and the legendary wet caves. Scientists estimate that the caves were formed 4000 years ago, during an earlier geological period that was marked by a higher sea level. Native Hawaiians disagree, crediting the fire goddess Pele with creating the two water-filled caverns. Scouring the islands for a hot, dry home to suit her needs, **Pele** came across the North Shore of Kauai but quickly left when her subterranean explorations yielded water. Linked to the ocean below ground, the level of the two freshwater caves fluctuates with the tide, and divers sometimes explore the upper cave, **Waiakapala'e.** The upper cave is said to be home to a water-loving lizard goddess, and the graying water of the cavern supposedly reflects her aging hair. The even murkier **Waikanaloa** cave is a short distance down the road. (*A grassy parking lot on the makai side of the highway provides access to the short trail and left-forking gravel path that lead to the cave. Farther up the highway, just before the Ke'e parking lot, is Waikanaloa.*)

MAKANA. The towering green peak that dominates North Shore vistas is known to the world as **Bali Hai.** The name comes from the landmass' famous appearance in the musical *South Pacific*, but the mountain's true name is Makana ("gift"). Anchoring the northern end of the Na Pali cliffs, Makana has long been respected by the Hawaiian people. In ancient Hawaii, the soaring summit hosted sacred fire-throwing ceremonies (*'oahi*) that honored visiting *ali'i* or marked special occasions such as the graduation of hula students at Ka-ulu-a-Paoa (see **Ke'e Beach,** p. 385). Trained fire-throwers would ascend the mountain carrying narrow logs of *papala* and *hau*. As the moon rose and darkness descended, they lit their makeshift spears and hurled them out over the ocean. Buoyant trade winds held the flaming logs aloft, carrying them far, far out to sea, and the fiery arcs stretching from Makana Mountain to the ocean were visible for miles around.

▶ BEACHES

Haena's beaches are strikingly beautiful—from the stark black lava rocks of Kahalahala to the lush cliffs of Ke'e. Despite their soft sands and endless winter surf, the beaches of Hanalei Bay pale in comparison to the series of glorious golden beauties that pave the shoreline to the west.

KAHALAHALA BEACH. Picture-perfect lava rocks border either end of this short, wide beach, one of which makes a dramatic diving platform above the amazingly clear water. Glistening gold sand meets sparkling aquamarine waters in a feast for the eyes. Visitors who want to do more than just look will revel in Kahalahala's calm summertime waters. Unfortunately, powerful winter tides can turn the tranquil beach into a dangerous spot. Popular with locals and visitors, Kahalahala is crowded by Kauai standards, but there is typically enough sand for all who make the trek. *(Leaving Hanalei, the highway takes a U-curve toward the sea before the 5-mile marker. Long turnouts lined with parked cars hug the base of the curve, and a short marked trail leads down to the beach from the 2nd turnout.)*

LUMAHAI BEACH. By far the widest beach on Kauai, stunning Lumahai graces many a photo album. Unfortunately, this golden, sandy paradise also plays host to the unpredictable forces of Pacific tradewinds. Devastating surf and powerful currents make swimming here **unsafe** year-round, and the ocean has claimed more than one human victim. Sunbathers and fans of *South Pacific* frequent the picturesque beach, and families with *keiki* sometimes take a dip in the stream along the western end. Although it may appear calm, the clear stream is subject to the occasional flash flood from neighboring waterfalls or ocean tides, and swimming is not advised. *(An opening in the trees leads to a dirt parking lot ¾ mi. after the 5-mile marker.)*

KEPUHI BEACH. This long ribbon of sand hugs the shoreline, hidden from the highway behind a series of residential roads. Few visitors ever encounter Kepuhi, and even locals tend to pass it over in favor of Tunnels in the west. Crazed snorkelers battle for tight parking spots up the road, while Kepuhi's long reef is all but ignored. Although it is not quite as protected as its neighbor, the sloping beach provides good snorkeling during calm surf, but currents sometimes penetrate the breaks in the reef. Local surfers and kiteboarders frequent the western end of the beach during the summer. *(Access from either end of Alamoo Rd. From the hwy., turn right on One-one Rd. between the 7- and 8-mile markers right after Hanalei Colony Resort; take a left on Alealea and then a right on Alamoo.)*

TUNNELS (MAKUA) BEACH. A wide horseshoe reef encloses the fine, and sometimes scalding hot, sand of the North Shore's most popular **snorkel** and **shore dive** locale. On calm summer days, Tunnels' crystalline waters and intricate reef outshine the competition. Despite its fame for complex underwater topography, the beach's name actually describes its characteristic curving winter surf break. Trees back the long sandy beach, providing much-appreciated shade, and limited parking translates into plenty of space for snorkelers. A lifeguard sits at the western end, which also affords fabulous views of the surrounding mountains. There are no facilities, but Haena Beach Park is just a ten-minute stroll to the west. *(Access is via two unmarked dirt roads. The first is ½ mi. west of the 8-mile marker, just before a "Weight Limit 10 Tons" sign, and the second is ¼ mi. farther.)*

HAENA BEACH PARK. Popular with the Winnebago set and backpacker-types on their way to the Kalalau Trail, Haena boasts a huge lawn and full facilities. A lifeguard keeps watch over the lovely, yet completely unprotected beach. Haena is known for being **dangerous for swimmers.** *(Two parking areas are located right on the highway just before the 9-mile marker and across from Maniniholo Dry Cave.)*

KE'E BEACH. At the end of the road, Ke'e features soft sand, brilliant blue water, and towering cliffs. Kalalau dayhikers (see **Kalalau Trail,** p. 386), beachgoers and cave explorers share the sprawling parking lot, which forks right to restrooms and payphones. During the summer months, experienced snorkelers can explore the area just outside of the reef, where an amazing variety of fish swim alongside sea turtles. The sandy shore stretches east to Haena Beach, but most visitors stick

KAUAI

to the area just west of the parking lot. Here, a jumble of lava rocks leads around the bend to stunning views of the Na Pali cliffs—and a very popular spot for sunset photographers. Another trail heads uphill from the western end of the beach to the remains of **Ka-ulu-a-Paoa,** an ancient heiau where the island's best hula students were trained in the ancient art of dance and chant. *(At the end of the highway.)*

NA PALI COAST

Comprised of 15 rugged miles of jagged cliffs and pristine coastline, the Na Pali Coast stretches from Ke'e Beach (p. 385) in the north to Polihale State Park (p. 407) in the south. There is no way to drive through this part of Kauai; visitors can journey either by foot or by boat. Those who do gain access to the coast's hidden treasures will encounter steep lava rock walls, lush green valleys, secluded sandy beaches, and cascading waterfalls.

The steep Na Pali ("the cliffs") tower up to 4000 ft. above the aquamarine ocean; at one time, however, the terrain sloped gradually from the ancient volcanic dome to the sea. This change in topography is the result of millions of years of constant thrashing by wind and waves. Powerful winter surf gradually wore away at the aging volcanic rock, eroding its foundations and causing massive landslides. Slowly, the coast's prominent cliffs and narrow canyons were formed. Simultaneously, streams of water flowing down from the peak of Mt. Wai'ale'ale carved out Na Pali's valleys. As they continued on to the sea, the streams formed the curtain of narrow waterfalls that stretches along the coast.

The five large valleys strung between Kalalau and Miloli'i are fertile agricultural lands that once sustained hundreds of inhabitants. Reliable water flow provided easy irrigation for *taro lo'is,* where the valley communities cultivated their staple food. Native fishermen reaped abundant catches in the waters offshore, and the moist, rich soil proved perfect for cultivating Polynesian crops such as banana, sweet potato, coconut, and breadfruit. Today, these trees continue to flourish alongside the more recently introduced mango, passion fruit, guava, and Java plums that have all but conquered the ancient rock terraces. The simple life of farming and fishing was standard in the Na Pali valleys for hundreds of years, until the beginning of the 20th century, when many residents began to abandon their remote settlements for the flourishing towns of Waimea and Hanalei. By the 1920s, the splendid coast's only inhabitants were grazing herds of cattle. Cows dominated the valleys for nearly 50 years, until a sudden wave of camping hippies took over in the late 1960s. Unhappy with this turn of events, the state worked to control the burgeoning tent cities and protect the wild coast from sanitary disaster. Beginning with the Kalalau Valley, the establishment of the Na Pali Coast State Park has strictly regulated human access and allowed the coastline to regain most of its natural splendor.

KALALAU TRAIL

Long ago, a series of trails stretched all the way from Polihale to Haena, but hundreds of years of winds and waves have erased the fragile dirt paths, and now only the ▨Kalalau Trail remains. Originally cleared by Hawaiian traders who traveled the coast by canoe and on foot, the trail was widened in 1860 to allow for the transport of coffee, oranges and cattle from Na Pali's valleys to markets in Hanalei.

Today, adventurers from around the globe come to Kauai to experience the unique beauty of the Na Pali Cliffs and the challenge of the Kalalau Trail. **Permits** are required for dayhiking and camping beyond **Hanakapi'ai Beach,** and backpackers hoping to enjoy the trail during summer months are advised to mail their permit applications a full year in advance (see **Camping,** p. 355). Despite its immense popularity, the trail's conditions can be surprisingly poor at times. The brittle volcanic rock path is greatly eroded in places, and footing can be uncertain. Frequent rainstorms can turn the dirt trails into slippery mud and flood the streams. Remote camping areas are crowded but rarely maintained, and sanitation problems have prompted recent closures.

The Kalalau Trail travels 11 miles southwest along the Na Pali Coast, from a trailhead in the **Ke'e Beach** parking lot to Kalalau Valley. Although crowded during the day, Ke'e's remote location makes leaving rental cars there unsafe, and hikers are advised to make alternative arrangements or park at **Haena Beach Park** one mile to the east. Strong hikers can finish the 22-mile round-trip hike in two days, but most allow up to five so as to enjoy the stunning vistas and pristine beaches along the way. Dipping in and out of countless cliffs and valleys, the strenuous trail also fords a number of streams and crosses sometimes frighteningly narrow oceanside ledges before reaching Kalalau Beach. Unstable terrain and the grueling ascents and descents make sturdy, comfortable hiking boots a must.

FOLLOW THE RULES Although 22 mi. may sound like a cakewalk to experienced backpackers, the unique conditions of the Kalalau Trail merit caution and respect.

1. **Treat all water** before drinking, no matter how pure it may appear. Thanks to the feral goats and other land species that inhabit the valleys, there is **leptosirosis** in Na Pali's streams.
2. Slather on the **sunscreen** and bring a wide-brimmed **hat.** Most visitors to the islands are unaccustomed to the direct sunlight of the tropics, which, combined with the dry heat of the West Shore, results in sunburns and heat exhaustion.
3. Wear strong **hiking boots.** Precipitous drop-offs and narrow ledges look cool from afar, but walking on the sometimes-muddy scree can be frightening.
4. Avoid crossing **streams** that are flowing too quickly or swollen above knee-level. Haste can be dangerous; instead wait for the water level to go down or look for a safer crossing.
5. During the summer, carefully observe **ocean conditions** before heading in for a dip. Powerful undertows and fast-moving longshore currents make winter swimming treacherous.
6. If you notice a sharp drop in sea level, immediately **climb** to higher ground, as low-lying valleys are at risk for flash **floods** during tsunamis (tidal waves caused by underwater volcanic eruptions).
7. Na Pali Coast State Park is open to goat **hunters** during the summer months; keep out of their way and protect the fragile environment by staying on the trail.
8. Practice **leave-no-trace camping** and pack out everything that you pack in.

🔧 HIKES

KE'E BEACH TO HANAKAPI'AI BEACH. (2 mi. Trailhead: Ke'e Beach parking lot. Level: moderate.) The hike from Ke'e Beach to Hanakapi'ai is the section of the trail least likely to induce vertigo. A popular dayhike for both visitors and locals, traffic on the trail can be downright congested during the summer, especially along the first mile and at Hanakapi'ai Beach. The first mile climbs steadily uphill, affording panoramic views of Ke'e and the verdant cliffs. Less ambitious hikers can walk a short but strenuous half-mile and enjoy the view. About three-quarters of the way to Hanakapi'ai, a striped pole marks the elevation below which hikers would be in danger during a tsunami. A wide, glorious stretch of sand in summer, Hanakapi'ai all but disappears during the winter. Totally exposed to the forces of the ocean, it is Kauai's most dangerous beach. Powerful longshore currents from the north can drag helpless victims along the coast for six miles before reaching the next beach. More than half of the bodies of drowning victims at Hanakapi'ai have never been recovered. Although the beach can be calm and inviting in summer, swimmers are cautioned to evaluate ocean conditions before jumping in.

HANAKAPI'AI FALLS. (2 mi. Trailhead: Hanakapi'ai Beach. Level: challenging.) Many dayhikers combine this spur trail with the hike from Ke'e, making a tiring 6hr. round-trip. From Hanakapi'ai Beach, allow three hours to hike in and enjoy the waterfall. The first half of the trail is moderately easy, crossing rock-wall *taro lo'is*, and passing under mango trees, coffee plants, and the remains of an old coffee mill once operated by *haole* planters. A number of the stream crossings can be intimidating for those used to better-maintained trails, and the last bit of the hike stumbles through rocks and fallen trees. Weary hikers are rewarded with a tall, picturesque waterfall cascading into a wide pool. Falling rocks can be a problem here, and swimming is not recommended.

HANAKAPI'AI BEACH TO HANAKOA VALLEY. (4 mi. Trailhead: Hanakapi'ai Valley. Level: challenging.) A grueling ascent out of Hanakapi'ai Valley toughens hikers for the hardest part of the trail: an endless series of steep switchbacks that leads 800 ft. uphill. This segment of the trail passes through **Hono-o-na-pali Natural Reserve,** which encompasses two valleys brimming with native lowland forest greenery. Exhausted hikers can sleep under the stars on the well-preserved terraces of hanging **Hanakoa Valley** before pressing on to the end of the trail.

HANAKOA FALLS. (1 mi. Trailhead: Hanalapi'ai Valley. Level: moderate.) Many tired hikers forego this short sidetrip, but the tall waterfall and peaceful solitude away from the hordes of dayhikers at Hanakapi'ai make the trip worthwhile.

HANAKOA VALLEY TO KALALAU BEACH. (5 mi. Trailhead: Hanakoa Valley. Level: moderate.) After ascending the ridge out of Hanakoa Valley, the conditions of the trail seem to change instantly. The lush lowland valleys and abundant trees are replaced by arid terrain. The dry heat of the West Shore and the lack of tree cover make this segment of the trail very sweaty, but spectacular views of the surrounding cliffs and coast make up for the discomfort. From Hanakoa to Kalalau, the trail weaves in and out of steep gullies and traverses some very narrow ledges on the *makai* side. Wading across **Kalalau Stream** brings hikers to the gorgeous beach at trail's end, where luscious fruit trees have overgrown the ancient terraces.

KALALAU VALLEY. (4 mi. Trailhead: Hanakoa Valley. Level: easy.) This spur trail takes only 2hr. and ends with a refreshing dip in a stream-fed pool. The trail passes through a series of agricultural terraces and guava groves to Kalalau Valley.

WEST OF KALALAU

From Kalalau Valley south to Polihale, the cliffs of the Na Pali Coast are too steep and fragile for hikers. Those who wish to explore this part of the coast must do so by boat, and there are a number of **ocean tour operators** that advertise all over the island. More adventurous travelers can tour the coast by kayak, either alone or as part of a guided trip; **Kayak Kauai** (see p. 380) leads 14hr. sea kayak tours of the coast that include transportation back from Polihale. Most kayakers travel the coast only one way—launching at Ke'e, following the currents from north to south, and making their final landing at Polihale. Those planning to go it alone should check weather forecasts before departing, as a slackening of the dominant tradewinds or strong Kona winds can make paddling more than difficult.

By sea, the nearly 1½hr. hike to **Hanakapi'ai Beach** from Ke'e becomes a quick five-minute paddle, but because the beach is so popular with dayhikers, boat landings are prohibited. Cruising past the trail-accessible section of the shoreline, boaters and kayakers arrive at Honopu, the second of five major valleys stretching from **Kalalau** in the northeast to Miloli'i in the southwest. Although the hanging valley of Honopu lies far above ocean travelers, its scenic beach, divided by an arch, makes a for a pretty photograph. Continuing west for ¼ mi., **Awa'awapuhi Valley** winds through a deep canyon 3000 ft. below the sheer, green cliffs. A strenuous trail in **Koke'e State Park** ends at a steep ridge overlooking this same valley (see p. 403). Nine miles west of Ke'e Beach, the beach at **Nu'alolo** is sheltered by a wide reef, so landing there is much easier than along the exposed coast. It is another 11 mi. from Ke'e to Miloli'i, where a reef provides safe landing at the very secluded beach. For information about camping at Miloli'i, see p. 355. A few more miles of plunging cliffs and amazingly clear water separate the Na Pali Coast from **Polihale State Park** (p. 407), where, exhausted from rowing and dizzy from the stunning views, tired kayakers can crash on the beach.

Not surprisingly, most visitors to Kauai forego the kayaks and view the Na Pali Coast from the relative comfort of power **catamarans** that cruise the waters daily. Countless tour operators leave from the West Shore, and a few from the North, most offering half-day **snorkeling** and **sight-seeing** trips twice daily.

SOUTH SHORE

The southern shore of Kauai draws the greatest concentration of the island's tourists with a luxuriant garland of sandy beaches. The laid-back shoreline fronts the calmest water of the island year-round, and is the only recommendable place to swim in winter. Recently named "America's #1 Beach" by Steve "Dr. Beach" Leatherman, Po'ipu takes its throngs of adoring fans in stride, and nearby Koloa still harbors a small-town ambience amidst the growing presence of tourism.

PO'IPU

The southernmost town on Kauai, Po'ipu is known for its sunny skies and white sand beaches. Huge resorts and pricey restaurants hover above clear aquamarine waves and sandy shores, where families and honeymooners dedicate their days to the pursuit of the perfect tan. Sea turtles and dozens of colorful fish also favor the warm southern waters, which offer excellent opportunities for snorkeling and scuba diving. The town itself is overshadowed by the stunning coast—downtown Po'ipu is no more than a shopping center facing a wall of condominiums and vacation rentals that line the beaches.

■ ORIENTATION

From Lihu'e, Hwy. 50 runs 7 mi. to Hwy. 520. The highway turns into the **Tree Tunnel,** where a mile-long "tunnel" of eucalyptus trees leads travelers south toward Po'ipu and Koloa. The boundaries between the two towns can be tricky especially along the coast, so for simplicity's sake, all of the sights and beaches lining the ocean are hereby located in Po'ipu. Five miles after leaving Hwy. 50, Hwy. 520 passes Po'ipu Plaza and forks left to **Po'ipu Rd.,** where most of the area's resorts and condominiums are concentrated, and right to **Lawa'i Rd.** and **Spouting Horn.**

KAUAI

🔋 PRACTICAL INFORMATION

Composed primarily of resorts and beaches, Po'ipu does not offer a full complement of services. However, nearby Koloa can supply anything that Po'ipu lacks. A small branch of **Bank of Hawaii**, 2360 Kiahuna Plantation Dr., in Po'ipu Shopping Village, has a **24hr. ATM**. (☎742-6800. Open M-Th 8:30am-4pm, F 8:30am-6pm.) **Kukuiula Store,** 2827 Po'ipu Rd., in Po'ipu Plaza, is the town's biggest grocery store. (☎742-1601. Open M-F 8am-8:30pm, Sa-Su 8am-6:30pm.)

■**Kauai Nature Tours,** 1770 Pe'e Rd., is at the top of the hill. Geologist Chuck and his son, Rob, lead small group adventures to some of Kauai's most fascinating natural wonders. Tours range in difficulty, from easy coast walks along Maha'ulepu to strenuous day treks of the Na Pali Coast, Waimea Canyon, and Sleeping Giant. Full-day hikes include lunch, water, and snacks. (☎888-233-8365 or 742-8305; www.kauainaturetours.com. Tours $82-97, children 5-12 $49-64.) For conveniently located and fairly priced **snorkel and beach gear,** visit **Nukumoi Surf Company,** on Ho'one Rd. across from Brennecke's Beach. (☎742-8019. Snorkel sets or boogie boards $5 per day or $15 per week. Open daily 8am-8pm.) **Outfitters Kauai,** 2827A Po'ipu Rd., in Po'ipu Plaza, rents **kayaks** (singles $40 per day, doubles $50 per day) and **bikes** ($20-45 per day). They also offer a variety of active **tours** including a downhill bicycle ride from the rim of Waimea Canyon and a one-day sea kayak along the Na Pali Coast. (☎888-742-9887 or 742-9667; www.outfitterskauai.com. Tours $80-165, children under 14 permitted on certain tours for a reduced rate. Open daily 9am-5pm, phone lines until 9pm.)

🍴 FOOD

Eating out can be a costly habit in touristy Po'ipu, but there are enough little sandwich shops and cheap burrito stands to satisfy your tummy without breaking the bank. High-end restaurants abound, as well as glossy magazine advertisements for them. If you're in the mood for a splurge, choosing can be difficult. However, the two more upscale establishments listed below stand out for their outstanding food and relaxing atmospheres.

■ **Beach House Restaurant,** 5022 Lawa'i Rd. (☎742-1424), next to Lawa'i Beach. Endless views and the best location on the South Shore keep this casually elegant beachfront restaurant packed. Tables are well-spaced both inside the open windows and on the pretty patio. The sophisticated menu blends international flavors with local seafood and vegetables. Seared crab-stuffed pork medallions with Okinawan sweet potato mash $24; fish nachos with refried black Thai rice, roasted Hawaiian corn and chili salsa, and mango *chipotle* sauce $10. The limited vegetarian options are not quite as spectacular. Reservations strongly recommended. Lounge open daily 5-10pm. Dinner served nightly 5:30-10pm, low season 6-10pm. ❹

Shipwreck Subs and Ice Cream (☎742-7467), in Po'ipu Shopping Village. This little stand is a popular place for a quick lunch and the shaded shopping center plaza supplies a comfortable place to enjoy a break from the midday sun. Great subs with lots of veggie toppings come in 6- or 13-inch sizes (6-inch 1-meat $5.50; veggie $4.50). Creamy Tropical Dreams ice cream, made on the Big Island, $2.40 a scoop. Shave ice $2. Open M-Sa 10am-9pm, Su 10am-7pm. ❶

Taqueria Nortenos, 2827A Po'ipu Rd. (☎742-7222), a literal hole-in-the-wall in Po'ipu Plaza. Burritos are a bit soggy, but a little drip only slightly dampens the extraordinarily affordable prices. Burritos with meat $3.75, veggie $3. Open M, Th-Su 11am-10pm. ❶

Roy's Po'ipu Bar and Grill (☎742-5000), in Po'ipu Shopping Village. Hawaii's celebrity chef, Roy Yamaguchi, has attracted a loyal following with his "Hawaiian-fusion" cuisine.

KAUAI

Classy granite tables, tropical-themed paintings, and fresh flowers on every table complement the airy interior. An ever-changing menu features fresh island fish (lemongrass-crusted *ono* with fresh Thai mango vinaigrette $27) and plenty of red meat (Parmesan-crusted lamb shank $21), as well as dim sum-style appetizers, fresh local salads, and *imu*-baked pizzas. Reservations recommended. Dinner daily 5:30-9:30pm. ❺

🔆 SIGHTS

Many visitors to Po'ipu never venture beyond the manicured lawns and sparkling pools of their resort hotels, but it's worth a quick drive to the west along **Lawai Rd.** for this trio of outdoor activities.

NATIONAL TROPICAL BOTANICAL GARDEN (NTBG). A verdant valley sheltered by steep cliffs, **Lawa'i Valley** holds two of the NTBG's five gardens (a third is located near Haena). The tram ride to the two gardens winds along a private road, stopping at a high coastal vista of pristine (and private) Lawai Kai Beach. Dedicated to science, the **McBryde Garden** is divided into four short walking tours, featuring native Hawaiian plants, palm trees, food and spice plants, and canoe plants. A self-guided tour of the mile-long loop that links the four walks crosses picturesque bridges and open fields and winds through narrow flower-lined trails. Flitting butterflies, wild chickens, ripe guavas, and croaking frogs may well be your only company. The only way to see the **Allerton Garden,** the more aesthetic of the two, is on a guided walking tour. Volunteer naturalists share their knowledge and admiration of the stunning garden, laid out by Robert Allerton in a series of outdoor "rooms." Divided by walls of trees, carpeted with grass, and covered by umbrella-like monkeypod trees, the rooms feature sculptures, fountains, and a brilliant array of tropical plants. A cutting garden full of heliconia, ginger, and other flowers blooms year round, and coffee, bananas, mangoes, chocolate, and breadfruit hang in the trees. Children and movie fans will appreciate a stop at the three towering Moreton Bay fig trees that hid a giant cracked eggshell in *Jurassic Park*. The tour ends at the Allerton Family home on Lawai Kai, where a cottage once inhabited by Queen Emma faces a pretty beach frequented by egg-laying sea turtles. *(4425 Lawa'i Rd., 2 mi. west of the fork. ☎ 742-2623; www.ntbg.org. Trams depart from the Visitor Center to the gardens every hour on the half-hour. McBryde Garden self-guided tours daily 9:30am-2:30pm; $15. Allerton Garden 2½hr. guided tours M-Sa at 9, 10am, 1 and 2pm; reservations required; $30. Visitor Center open daily 8:30am-5pm. Free.)*

SPOUTING HORN BEACH PARK. Beneath the securely fenced viewing area, a thin shelf of lava rock extends outward from the coast. Waves breaking over the shelf move water into the narrow spaces between the rocks, forcing a giant plume of water to spout skyward to the delight and applause of camera-toting onlookers. A few mini-spouts surround the large central plume, while another opening in the lava contributes the "horn" by spouting only air. The overlook provides a pretty view of Kukuiula Harbor to the east, and a small lawn dotted with picnic tables welcomes those who wish to stay a while. Most visitors simply snap a few photographs before lingering over the row of outdoor gift shops near the restrooms. *(On the makai side of Lawai Rd., west of the National Tropical Botanical Garden Visitor Center.)*

PRINCE KUHIO PARK. A pleasant but largely empty grassy space, the park, and a small monument in the center, honor Prince Kuhio, Hawaii's first delegate to the United States Congress. A large pavilion with picnic tables, grills, and a bathroom occupy the northeastern corner; the rock terraces at the western end shelter a terraced rock heiau. *(Mauka side of Lawai Rd., about a mile after the fork.)*

♫ ENTERTAINMENT

Pub crawlers and dancing queens may be disappointed with Po'ipu's rather mellow evening scene, and those looking for a late night should catch the next shuttle to Honolulu. After a long day at the beach, most travelers are happy just to slather on aloe and crawl into bed. If you must have a drink, **The Point** at the Sheraton offers fantastic vistas of Po'ipu Beach to the east and the setting sun to the west. The opulent **Stevenson's Library** at the Hyatt features a koa wood bar, pool and chess tables, and a pleasant terrace. The Hyatt also hosts the South Shore's only luau, the **Drums of Paradise Luau.** (☎ 742-1234. Open bar. Reservations recommended one week in advance. Su and Th at 6pm. $65, young adults 13-20 $50, children 6-12 $32.50, under 5 free. Show only $38, young adults and children $18, under 5 free.)

⌘ BEACHES

Recently recognized as "America's #1 Beach" by Steve "Dr. Beach" Leatherman, sunny Po'ipu Beach and the host of neighboring coves that line Kauai's southern coast boast excellent snorkeling, safe swimming, crystal-clear waters, and spectacular sea cliffs. The beaches below are listed from west-to-east, and all lie on or just off Lawai Rd. or Po'ipu Rd.

LAWA'I BEACH. Its proximity to nearby condos, as well as the occasional monk seal sighting, make this diminutive stretch of sand and rocks a daytime hotspot. Boogie boarders ride the inshore waves, while experienced surfers favor the crashing swells behind the Beach House. Swimming is usually safe, and snorkelers troll the shallow waters just west of the restaurant. High tides obscure nearly all of the sand, but the pleasant lawn around the Beach House provides a consistent and comfortable cushion for sunbathers and a great view of Kauai's famous sunsets. (On Lawai Rd., about 1 mi. west of the fork and next to the Beach House Restaurant.)

PK'S. A teensy patch of sand, PK's is surrounded by rocks that do their best to make entry difficult. Early risers can take advantage of relatively calm waters for excellent snorkeling and private time with the big sea turtles that thrive in the often intimidating waves. PK's is also an excellent—and uncrowded—place for non-snorkelers to catch a glimpse of turtles bobbing with the tide. (On Lawai Rd. across from Prince Kuhio Park.)

BABY BEACH. Hidden behind Hoona Rd., a narrow ribbon of fine sand fronts a calm, shallow pool protected by a wall of black lava rocks. Away from shore, the sand soon gives way to rock, and full-sized beachgoers will have to squat rather than swim—this one is definitely for the *keiki*. (On Hoona Rd. The best access is about a 2min. walk east from PK's to a marked beach access—look for the red handrail just past a big brown stone house.)

KOLOA LANDING. Once the largest port on Kauai, Koloa Landing is now the South Shore's premier scuba diving spot. Local dive shops, including **Fathom Five** (see **Koloa,** p. 394), often bring entry-level shore divers here, and the waters can get downright crowded. An old boat ramp provides very easy access to the slightly cloudy near-shore water that clears up away from land. A handful of snorkelers can usually be found kicking about the western end of the rocky inlet. (Down a one-lane road from Ho'onani Rd. From Lawai Rd. eastbound, turn right on Ho'onani and park in the dirt clearing half a block up on the right. Additional parking can be found down the access road to the left, but space is limited.)

PO'IPU/KIAHUNA BEACH. Running from the Sheraton to the Kiahuna Plantation Resort, this long crescent beach is backed by a neat row of tall, swaying palms. Those seeking solitude should continue east to Maha'ulepu, but if you thrive on activity, wedge your towel into an available spot of sand and join the throngs of young boogie boarders eagerly greeting every oncoming wave. *(On Ho'onani Rd. The first of two public parking lots sits just west of the entrance to the Sheraton; another more crowded lot is at the eastern end of the road.)*

■ **PO'IPU BEACH PARK.** Extensive facilities, including picnic tables, showers, restrooms, a large grassy lawn, playgrounds for young *keiki*, and a lifeguard station, attract a diverse crowd to Po'ipu's most popular beach. A strip of sand runs seaward from the center of the beach, joining it to Nukumoi Point slightly offshore. At low tide, sunbathers looking for a little privacy can walk all the way out to the point, but high tide submerges the pathway. Swimming is safe on both sides of the point, especially to the east; snorkelers prefer the shallow area just west of the point. Sand space is at a premium, and late arrivals will probably be relegated to the western end, where the beach narrows and the gently lapping waves get a bit bigger. *(Access from the southern end, at Hoowili Rd. From eastbound Po'ipu Rd., turn right at the "Po'ipu Beach" sign a few blocks past Po'ipu Shopping Village. Two large parking lots lie at the end of the road directly across from the beach.)*

BRENNECKE'S BEACH. A small, semi-protected patch of sand bordered by rocks, Brennecke's is best known for its tantalizingly large, yet still safe, boogie-boarding and bodysurfing waves. The rocky shore and breaking waves also host a population of friendly sea turtles. *(From Po'ipu Beach Park (see above), walk east to the end of the grassy area and Brennecke's will be right in front of you.)*

SHIPWRECK BEACH (KEONILOA BAY). Po'ipu's widest beach fronts the grand Hyatt Regency. Surprisingly few hotel guests venture into this beautiful—but slightly windy—natural beach, preferring the artificial sand-ringed pools and comfy lounge chairs behind the hedge. Makawehi Point, the striking cliff to the east, recently made its Hollywood debut as a diving platform for Harrison Ford in *6 Days/7 Nights*. Big waves break offshore, making for safe swimming near the beach and good surfing toward the east. *(Turn right on Ainako from Po'ipu Rd. immediately after the Hyatt. A big parking lot is located right behind the sand.)*

■ **MAHA'ULEPU BEACHES.** These three pretty—and relatively deserted—beaches offer peaceful sunbathing, occasionally safe swimming, pole-fishing galore, and a wonderful place for beach-walking. From west to east, the first stop on the road is **Gillin's Beach**, a long, narrow stretch of sand that runs east into Kawailoa Bay. Although backed by trees and grass, there is little shade to be found, and the waves here can get choppy. For calmer waters, either drive or walk along the coast to **Kawailoa Bay**, a pleasant half-crescent of white sand most often visited by picnicking locals. The rocky outcroppings just east of the bay are a popular pole-fishing spot. The area also boasts a few shady trees and some of Maha'ulepu's best swimming. The last in the trio is deserted **Ha'ula Beach**, which lies past a few other sandy coves and at the end of a 15-minute walk. Although the waves are almost always too rough for swimming, the empty sands provide a private moment far from the crowds of Po'ipu. A few picnic tables and a grill are hidden behind a dune at the back of the beach. A local stable sometimes runs horseback-riding tours to a "secret" beach, and their comings and goings are quite evident from the amount of horse excrement along the path. All three of these beaches are located on privately owned land, so please respect the natural surroundings and refrain from giving the owners any reason to suspend access. *(Con-*

KAUAI

tinue down Po'ipu Rd. as it turns into dirt past the Hyatt, and turn right 1.6 mi. later at the dead end. Another 0.3 mi. later, you will arrive at a guard house, and 0.3 mi. after that, the parking area for **Gillin's Beach.** *The beach is a short walk down any of the overgrown access trails from the lot, or to the right of the lot. To reach* **Kawailoa Bay,** *turn left out of the parking area and drive until the road runs alongside the ocean. A small parking area on the right is marked by a line of boulders. For* **Ha'ula,** *keep going until the road turns left at a pair of wide metal poles, and park in the turn-around to the left. Walk from the poles toward the ocean and head east along the coast. After 5min., you will reach a fence; go through the opening and walk along the lithified sand cliffs, following the coastline for 10min. to Ha'ula Beach. Open 7:30am-7pm.)*

KOLOA

Hawaii's oldest sugar plantation town has undergone quite a facelift to keep up with neighboring Po'ipu's constant influx of tourists. Historic buildings that once housed barber shops and bathhouses have been spruced up and filled with souvenirs and beachwear, and a charming raised wooden boardwalk now runs along the main street. Underneath its tourist-coated exterior, however, Koloa retains a comfortable small-town feel and a strong sense of pride in its past.

■ ▪ ORIENTATION AND PRACTICAL INFORMATION

Koloa is located about 10 mi. southwest of Lihu'e—7 mi. west on Hwy. 50 and 3 mi. down Hwy. 520. Most of the town's commercial establishments center on **Old Koloa Town,** at the intersection of Po'ipu Rd. and Koloa Rd., a couple of miles north of the coast.

First Hawaiian Bank, 3506 Waikomo Rd., at the eastern end of town, has a **24hr. ATM.** (☎742-1642. Open M-Th 8am-4pm, F 8:30am-6pm.) The **Koloa Public and School Library,** on the west side of Po'ipu Rd. about ½ mi. south of the Chevron station, offers cardholders high-speed **Internet access,** and a huge video collection. (☎742-8455. Open M-Tu and Th-F 8:30am-5pm, W noon-8pm.) Those without library cards can check their **email** at the **Koloa Country Store.** (Internet access $5 minimum charge for 30min., $2 for each additional 10min. Printing 75¢ per page. Open M-Sa 8am-8pm, Su 9am-5pm.) Parking is at a premium in front of **Big Save Market,** on Koloa Rd. next to the bank. (☎742-1614. Open daily 7am-11pm.) Koloa's weekly **Sunshine Market** is held Mondays at noon at the Koloa Ball Park, north of downtown. An open-air **laundromat** behind Big Save has bench-seating and lots of machines. (Wash $1.25, dry 25¢.) The **post office,** 5485 Koloa Rd., sits across from Big Save. (☎800-275-8777. Open M-F 9am-4pm, Sa 9-11am. **Zip Code:** 96756.

The knowledgeable folk at **Fathom Five Divers,** 3450 Po'ipu Rd. (☎742-6991; fax 742-9791; www.fathomfive.com), behind the Chevron station, offer scuba diving and snorkel rental as well as a variety of boat and shore dives. Shore dives head out from Koloa Landing on the South Shore or Tunnels Beach in the north, while boats depart from Kukuiula Harbor. (Open M-Sa 7am-5pm, Su 10:30am-4:30pm. After hours call for availability and weather conditions. Two-tank shore dive $80, boat dive $100, certification courses for ages 10 and up $395-495.) For bargain basement snorkel gear, check out **Snorkel Bob's,** 3236 Po'ipu Rd., on the east side of Po'ipu Rd. just north of the library. An island-wide chain, Snorkel Bob's boasts free inter-island and 24hr. rentals. (☎742-2206. Snorkel sets from $2.50 per day or $9 per week. Boogie boards $6.50 per day or $26 per week. Open daily 8am-5pm.)

ACCOMMODATIONS

Most of the South Shore's accommodations are in Koloa. Countless condominium developments and a few resort hotels line Lawai Rd. and Po'ipu Rd., and a quick online search will uncover a multitude of options. Visitors wishing to save a few hundred dollars a night may want to focus their searches on privately owned and listed condos or vacation homes. Numerous cottages and inns also offer a good value and a homey feel.

Koloa Landing Cottages, 2704B Ho'onani Rd. (☎800-779-8773 or 742-1470; www.koloa-landing.com), on the left, just south of Lawai Rd. Five colorful cottages, ranging from studios to a 2-bedroom house, all boast full kitchens and lanais. Another 2-bedroom "budget" house near the center of Koloa town, as well as a 3-bedroom house and 1-bedroom ocean-view cottage near Brennecke's, round out the offerings. Units are cheerful, airy, and clean, and the friendly owners do their best to make you feel at home. Discounts may be negotiated for longer stays. Units $70-150. Rates do not include taxes or cleaning fees ($20-60 extra). ❸

Garden Isle Cottages, 2660 Puuholo Rd. (☎800-742-6711 or 742-6717; www.ocean-cottages.com), just south of Lawai Rd. Four luxurious and tasteful oceanfront 1-bedroom cottages, each with a private lanai overlooking a rocky cove and the ocean beyond. 2-night minimum stay. High season $164, low season $143; plus tax. 10% discount for stays of a week or more. ❺

Strawberry Guava Bed and Breakfast (☎332-7790), in Lawai. From Hwy. 50 westbound, turn right onto Kua Rd. After 0.8 mi., turn right up an unmarked steep hill and drive 0.2 mi. to the third driveway on the right. Turn in and bear right at the "The Sullivans" sign at the fork. Small and out-of-the-way, Strawberry Guava's biggest perk is its super-low price tag. Ask for the suite with mountain views—the other looks out at a yard and purple bougainvillea. Breakfast included. $65-75 per night. No credit cards, but personal checks are accepted. ❸

FOOD

A variety of restaurants inhabit the historic buildings of downtown Koloa, catering to a wide range of tastes and wallets.

Sueoka Snack Shop, 5392 Koloa Rd. (☎742-1112), behind Sueoka Store. Lots of choices, quick service, and rock bottom prices make this little stand a local favorite. Hamburgers $1.20, *saimin* $1.75, plate lunches $3.65-4.50. Cash only. Open M-Sa 9am-3pm, Su 9:30am-3pm. ❶

Dali Deli, 5492 Koloa Rd. (☎742-8824), across from the post office. A comfortable and modern cafe, Dali Deli provides a relaxing setting for your morning cappuccino. The limited breakfast menu includes bagelwiches ($6), and a tasty breakfast burrito ($7). Lunch features hot and cold sandwiches ranging from tuna salad ($5.75) to cheese steak ($8) and even portobello mushroom ($8.75). Open M-Sa 8am-3pm. ❶

Lappert's Ice Cream (☎742-1272), in the middle of downtown, is a bright ice cream parlor with tons of flavors and lots of icy goodness. Made right here in Kauai, many of the options feature island flavors. A coffee and espresso bar, plus plenty of baked goods, make for a tasty breakfast. Ice cream $3 per scoop. Open daily 6am-10pm. ❶

Tomkats Grille, 5402 Koloa Rd. (☎742-8887). Although the "kat" theme gets a little tiresome, this breezy patio-style restaurant boasts a big menu and tasty food. Nibblers include crab-stuffed mushrooms ($7.50) and jalapeño poppers ($6.25). Entrees feature fish, steak, and sandwiches ($6.25-25.50), with vegetarian options limited to salad or a Garden Burger ($7.25). "Kitten" meals $3.50-4. Happy Hour daily 3-6pm; mai tais $4, beer $2. Restaurant open daily 11am-10pm. Bar until 12:30am. ❸

👁 SIGHTS

Koloa ("long cane") was established in 1834 as a commercial center for the plantation community. Home to a sugar plantation and the major sea port of Koloa Landing, the town soon developed into a hub of activity. Throughout the 19th century,
oranges, sweet potatoes, and sugar left Koloa Landing for California. Ever proud
of its key role in Hawaii's history, Koloa markets itself as Old Koloa Town. A **History Center,** next to the Country Store, presents a life-size diorama of plantation
life, including a Japanese bathhouse, photographs of the landing and the plantation, and cardboard cutouts of workers. Interpretive plaques accompany the displays. Across the street, at the corner of Koloa Rd. and Hwy. 520, a grassy field
immortalizes the plantation tradition. Koloa's **Sugar Monument** features a circular
concrete sculpture that represents a mill stone opened to show seven bronze figures, each signifying one of the main ethnic groups—Hawaiian, Puerto Rican, Chinese, Korean, Japanese, Filipino, and Portuguese—who played a role in Hawaii's
history. A plaque facing the monument describes an eighth figure as well, a Cauca-
sian overseer on horseback, whose image was omitted at the last minute in
response to heavy criticism. The accompanying plaques will teach you more about
the sugar industry than you ever desired to know. The stone chimney at the western edge of the field was salvaged from the remains of a mill boiling house, and the
messy stand of tangled and half-dried plants to the south was once a display of 14
types of sugar cane each with a now-faded sign.

WEST SHORE

A ride into the legendary sunsets of America's westernmost frontier passes
through rugged scenery and small towns, along a continuum of sand that stretches
from Waimea to Polihale. Though the region maintains the sense of a small-town
community, authenticity is tempered to some degree by the inevitable appearance
of vacation rentals and extravagant houses on hillsides overlooking the ocean. The
towns of the West Shore serve as gateways to the grand parks farther north—
Waimea Canyon State Park, Koke'e State Park and Polihale State Park. According
to Hawaiian myth, the souls of the dead followed the path of the sun west, departing the world in a blaze of glory in the famed sunsets at Polihale.

KALAHEO

A quiet one-light town, Kalaheo doesn't offer much in the way of tourist attractions. However, a handful of superb restaurants and a couple of solid accommodations make the town worth a stop.

🔳🔁 ORIENTATION AND PRACTICAL INFORMATION. Kalaheo is located 11
mi. west of Lihu'e on Hwy. 50. Nearly all of the establishments listed below line the
highway, and directions assume westbound travel. The **post office,** 4489 Papalina
Rd. (☎800-275-8777), behind Kalaheo Coffee Company, is open M-F 8am-4pm, Sa
8-10am. **Zip Code:** 96741.

🔳 ACCOMMODATIONS. Kalaheo has two excellent accommodations for the
traveler on a budget. To get to 🔳**Classic Vacation Cottages ❷,** 2687 Onu Place
(☎332-9201; fax 332-7645; clascot@hawaiian.net), turn right on Puuwai Rd. just
after entering Kalaheo and stay to the right. Onu Place will be on the left. The 12
units are all unique and range from studios to a 4-bedroom house; some of the studios have kitchenettes, the larger units all have full kitchens. The friendly owners,
Chris and Sandy, live on-site and have stocked a garage full of beach and picnic
gear, sporting equipment (including bikes, tennis racquets, and golf clubs), and

West Kauai

more. Charcoal grills, a 6-person Jacuzzi, and free use of the Kiahuna Tennis Club facilities round out the fun. Free laundry on-site. Studios from $45; cottages and houses $75-$100. Discounts can be negotiated for longer stays. Another good value is the **Kalaheo Inn ❷**, 4444 Papalina Rd. (☎888-332-6023 or 332-6023; fax 332-5242; www.kalaheoinn.com). Turn left at the stoplight; the inn will be one block up on the left. Plain but sparkling clean, rooms are arranged in tidy rows. Two-night minimum stay. Units range from $55-125; 10% discount for month-long stays.

◘ FOOD. Outstanding Italian food, a friendly coffee shop, juicy hamburgers, and the island's best pizza make Kalaheo the hidden gem of Kauai dining. **Kalaheo Coffee Company & Cafe ❶**, on the *makai* side of the highway just past Papalina, is a popular local meeting spot. Breakfast features egg dishes (from $5), a great burrito ($7), and a mouth-watering selection of baked goods. Hearty sandwiches dominate the lunch menu (grilled cajun tofu and eggplant with roasted bell peppers $7), and taste even better with a foaming cup of chai. (☎332-5858. Open M-F 6am-3pm, Sa 6:30am-3pm, Su 6:30am-2pm.) *Kama'aina* rave about **Brick Oven Pizza ❷**, on the *mauka* side of the highway just after you enter town. Although the red-and-white checkered table cloths and wood-beam ceilings make for a pleasant dining experience, the 10% charge tacked on for table service makes take-out more appealing. (☎332-8561. 15-inch cheese pizza $18.35. Open Tu-Su 11am-10pm.) More Italian cuisine can be found across the highway at **Pomodoro ❹**, on the 2nd floor of Rainbow Plaza. The house specialties, including veal sauteed in marsala sauce with fresh mushrooms ($20) and eggplant parmesan ($18), have a loyal local following. (☎332-5945. Open daily 5:30-10pm.) For big burgers ($4-6) and yummy pies (slices $3.50; whole pies $9-15), head north to **Camp House Grill ❶,** across from Kalaheo Coffee Co. The endless menu also includes a zillion breakfast plates, soups, salads, and more. (☎332-9755. Open daily 6:30am-9pm.)

◙ **SIGHTS.** Just west of Kalaheo, Hwy. 540 runs south from Hwy. 50 to **Kauai Coffee.** The oceanfront fields, encompassing thousands of acres, were once prolific producers of sugar and macadamia nuts. However, adverse weather conditions prompted the switch to coffee about a decade ago. The gift shop stocks a comprehensive array of the company's products, as well as an array of coffee-drinking accessories. A covered lanai divides the shop from a "museum" that honors the long Hawaiian tradition of coffee cultivation. The displays include original stovetop coffee roasters as well as early MJB and Folger's tins—both brews contained primarily Hawaiian coffee. (Open daily 9am-5pm. Free.) A short drive west of Kalaheo, at the 14-mile marker, a dirt turnout leads to **Hanapepe Valley Lookout.** High above the lush green valley, the vista would be even more amazing if not for the abundance of tangled sugar cane and other overgrowth that prevent a clear look down into the valley.

KALAHEO TO WAIMEA

'ELE'ELE

A residential community situated along the western shore of the Hanapepe River, across from the 16-mile marker, 'Ele'ele contains a noteworthy sight and a surprisingly comprehensive cluster of businesses. The **'Ele'ele Shopping Center** houses fast food outlets, a Big Save, a branch of First Hawaiian Bank, a laundromat, and a small post office. Two popular restaurants cater to locals and Waimea Canyon-bound tourists. ◙**Toi's Thai Kitchen ❷,** features a huge menu of delicious entrees, all served with papaya salad, a choice of rice, and dessert (house specialty Toi's Temptation $11-17). Those wary of new flavors can order an "American plate" (honey dip chicken with french fries, tossed salad, and dessert $10) and miss out on all the fun. (☎335-3111. Dinner served nightly 5:30-9:30pm. Karaoke F-Sa 10pm-1:30am.) At the far end of the shopping center, **Grinds Cafe and Espresso ❶** offers a basic menu of baked goods ($1.25), pizza (15-inch cheese $12.50; slice $2), and breakfast all day (from $5.75). Dinner is still affordable (mahi mahi $7.50; chili and rice $4.50), but slightly more sophisticated. (☎335-6027. Open daily 5:30am-9pm.)

Continuing south from the 'Ele'ele Shopping Center, Waialo Rd. forks right to Port Allen and left to the very unique sands of **Glass Beach.** From Waialo, turn left on Aka Ula and right onto the dirt road. Glass Beach is just below, before the road turns left. Named for its once-famed shores, made up of millions of sea glass particles washed ashore from fishing boats and auto parts, Glass Beach has deteriorated over the years. A decade ago, the black lava rocks, green cliffs, and crashing blue surf highlighted the sparkling multi-hued beauty of the beach. Today, the beach still shines, but mostly clear or brown, against its industrial backdrop of oil silos. Once a hidden gem, Glass Beach's "discovery" led to its downfall—each visitor, dazzled by the glistening shore, pocketed a tiny handful of its beauty.

HANAPEPE

The "biggest little town" on Kauai, Hanapepe entices visitors with art galleries, gourmet vegetarian cuisine, and a unique bridge. Less than ¼ mi. past the 'Ele'ele Shopping Center, a few signs on the right side of the highway mark the turn for Hanapepe Rd. The horseshoe-shaped downtown is lined with storefronts featuring

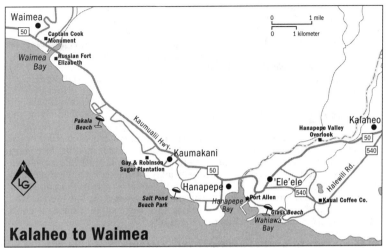

Kalaheo to Waimea

the works of local painters, artisans, and designers. Erratic hours sometimes frustrate would-be gallery browsers, and true art-lovers would be best off visiting the town on Friday evenings—each week a different gallery hosts special events to celebrate **Art Night** from 6-9pm. A darling of earth-crunchy food connoisseurs island-wide, the **Hanapepe Cafe ❸**, 3830 Hanapepe Rd., satiates veggie-craving tummies with healthy breakfasts (tofu scrambler $9.75), lunches (grilled vegetable sandwich $9), salads (from $6), and flavorful pastas (southwestern lasagne $18.75) from its entirely vegetarian menu. (☎335-5011. Open Tu-Sa for breakfast 9-11am and lunch 11am-2pm. Dinner served F 6-9pm.)

A rather unsteady, but thrilling, view of the hills and fields surrounding the town can be had from the middle of Hanapepe's **swinging footbridge.** A sign near the central curve of Hanapepe Rd. points the way. Just west of Hanapepe, a left turn past the 17-mile marker onto Lele Rd. leads south to one of Kauai's best-kept secrets. *Kama'aina* of all ages and walks of life treasure **Salt Pond Beach Park** for its wide curving bay and soft sands. Only the gentlest of swells make their way over the rocky bar that encloses the warm and uncrowded waters. On the eastern end of the beach, a grassy field welcomes campers. For more information on camping, see **Camping Permits,** p. 358.

KAUMAKANI TO MAKAWELI

Most drivers cruise right by the small dirt roads that lead into the sugar plantation towns of Kaumakani and Makaweli, and the Robinson family probably prefers it this way. The close-knit plantation community of Makaweli, which boasts more than a few emigrants from mysterious Niihau, wards away tourists with a number of "Private Property" signs. The sugar cane fields that dominate this stretch of highway belong to **Gay and Robinson,** the only operating family-run sugar plantation left on the islands. The **Visitor Center,** on Kaumakani Ave., has displays of sugar history and plantation life, illustrating everything from processing to field operations to community in the 1930s. Tours of the field and factory run from the Visitor Center. (Take a left turn off westbound Hwy. 50 right after the 19-mile marker. ☎335-2824. Tour reservations recommended. 2hr. tour M-F at 9am and 1pm. $30, children 7-15 $21. Children under age 7 are not allowed on the factory portion of the tour. Wear closed-toe shoes and clothes that can get dirty. Open M-F 8am-4pm.)

KAUAI

One of three forts established on Kauai during the early 19th century, the remnants of Russian **Fort Elizabeth** are reminders of the brief cooperation between Russia and King Kaumualii. The long-abandoned fort, named after the czarina at the time and constructed under the direction of Georg Schaeffer, is just a pile of rubble. An overgrown, confusing path winds its way through the ruins, and an information board near the parking lot provides a brief history and (sometimes) guide maps. A dirt road continues out of the parking lot to a cleared dirt area with a decent view of the muddy and unspectacular mouth of the Waimea River.

WAIMEA

Once an important agricultural port, Waimea was the first stop for many visitors to Hawaii, including Christian missionaries, Russian emissaries, and the legendary Captain Cook. The historic wooden buildings that line Waimea Rd. downtown date back to the town's colorful past. Nowadays, Waimea's dusty streets and swinging doors call forth images of spaghetti Westerns with high-noon showdowns. There's no shortage of genuine hospitality, however; the few tourists who lounge over a picnic in Hofgaard Park or take in a movie at the fabulous Waimea Theater are warmly welcomed into the community.

■ **ORIENTATION AND PRACTICAL INFORMATION.** The biggest town on the West Shore, Waimea lies 23 mi. west of Lihu'e on **Hwy. 50.** After crossing the Waimea River just beyond Fort Elizabeth, the highway runs through the center of town. Most services and restaurants lie right along the highway or on Waimea Rd.

The stately **First Hawaiian Bank,** 4525 Panako Rd., has a **24hr. ATM.** (☎338-1611. Open M-Th 8:30am-4pm, F 8:30am-6pm.) **Waimea Library,** 9750 Kaumualii Hwy., is a good place to catch up on the news or surf the **Internet.** (☎338-6848. Open M and W noon-8pm, Tu and Th 9am-5pm, F 10am-5pm.) Wash the red dirt out of your shorts at **Wishy Washy Laundry Center,** on Waimea Rd., across from the monument. (Wash $1, dry 50¢. Open 24hr.) Other services include: the **police** (☎338-1831), on the *mauka* side of the highway, across Menehune Rd. from Big Save; the **West Kauai Medical Center,** 4643 Waimea Canyon Dr. (☎338-9431); and the **post office,** 9911 Waimea Rd. (☎800-275-8777. Open M-F 8:30am-4pm, Sa 8:30-10:30am.) **Zip Code:** 96796.

▐ **ACCOMMODATIONS AND CAMPING.** Originally built to house sugar plantation workers at the beginning of the 20th century, the **Waimea Plantation Cottages** ❹, 9400 Kaumualii Hwy #367 (☎800-922-7866 or 338-1625; fax 338-2338; www.waimea-plantation.com), have been restored and filled with modern amenities. Each comfortable cottage has its own lanai overlooking either the spacious palm-dotted grounds or the ocean. The windy dark-sand beach and murky waters make for poor swimming, but the oceanfront pool is a pleasant place for a dip. Units range from studios with kitchenettes ($130-145) to the very luxe 5-bedroom manager's estate ($515-575). **Campsites** are available in Lucy Wright Beach Park (see **Sights,** p. 401).

◘ **FOOD.** Compared to the limited offerings of other West Shore towns, Waimea is a diner's paradise. Stock up for a big day of hiking at ▧**Ishihara Market** ❶, 9894 Kaumualii Hwy., *makai* and across from the Cook Monument. Everything—from plate lunches ($6-6.50) and sushi ($3) to sandwiches ($4) and salads ($3)—is available at the extensive deli. (☎338-1751. Open M-F 6am-8:30pm, Sa-Su 7am-8:30pm.) ▧**Jo-Jo's Shave Ice** ❶, on the *makai* side of the highway, across from the high school, has been crowned the best shave ice ($2) on Kauai. Choose from a whopping 60 flavors for your ultra-fine ice. (Open daily 10am-6pm.) Locals rave about

Waimea

⌂ ACCOMMODATIONS
Waimea Plantation Cottages, **1**

🍎 FOOD
Ishihara Market, **6**
Jo-Jo's Shave Ice, **4**
Waimea Brewing Co., **2**
Waimea Deli & Bakery, **5**

★ ENTERTAINMENT
Waimea Theatre, **3**

TO WAIMEA CANYON STATE PARK

Waimea Canyon Dr.

Gay Rd.

0 — 200 yards
0 — 200 meters

TO KEKAHA (2 mi.)

Keolewa St.

Haina Rd.

Nele Rd.

Oiol Rd.

Waimea Canyon Dr.

Maule Rd.

Oma Rd.

Haina Rd.

Waimea Athletic Field

West Kauai Medical Center

50

Huakai Rd.

Waena Rd.

Makaihaiki Rd.

Tsuchiya Rd.

Waimea High School

Kanu Rd.

Nima Rd.

Menehune Rd.

Ape Pl.

Alawai Rd.

Waimea River

Ola Rd.

Big Save

Maile Rd.

Laau Rd.

Moana Rd.

Waimea Rd.

First Hawaiian Bank

Pokole Rd.

Kahakai Rd.

Lucy Wright Beach Park

50

Kaumualii Hwy.

Captain Cook Landing National Historic Landmark and Hofgaard Park

Russian Fort Elizabeth State Historic Park

TO HANAPEPE (6 mi.)

Kaumualii Hwy.

the delicious sandwiches served at the 🍽**Waimea Deli and Bakery ❶,** 9875 Waimea Rd. Gourmet made-to-order sandwiches feature mahi mahi or *ahi* ($6.50), *kalua* pork ($5.50), or a homemade *taro* burger ($5) served on just-baked sweetbread. Fresh juices and baked goodies full of local fruits are perfect complements to lunch or breakfast. (☎338-1950. Take-out only. Open Th-Tu 6:30am-4pm.) Adjacent to Waimea Plantation Cottages, **Waimea Brewing Company ❸,** the westernmost brewery in the US, serves good food at big prices. The casual menu features hearty sandwiches (*ahi poke* wrap $10.50; ½ lb. burger $8.50) and standard pupus (onion rings $7). Entrees (penne with Portuguese sausage and grilled chicken $17; strip steak $20) appeal to the truly carnivorous. (Open Su-Th 11am-9pm, F-Sa 11am-11pm.) A teensy pizzeria with big ambitions, **Pacific Pizza and Deli ❶,** 9852 Kaumualii Hwy., bakes up creative combinations, such as the *Hapa Haole* (pesto, sun-dried tomatoes, mushrooms, zucchini, olives, and Canadian bacon), for a predominantly local clientele. Calzones, wraps, and deli sandwiches ($5.25) round out the menu. (☎338-1020. Open daily 11am-9pm.)

🎬 🎭 SIGHTS AND ENTERTAINMENT. Two sites commemorate **Captain James Cook,** the British explorer who discovered the Hawaiian islands and who first landed at Waimea in 1778. The triangle of grass that separates Waimea Rd. from the highway is **Hofgaard Park,** a monument to the captain. Scattered trash cans and pic-

KAUAI

THE LOCAL STORY

DOCTOR CHUCK

Geoscientist Chuck Blay became interested in drowning patterns after he moved to Kauai in 1995. He researched all Kauai drownings since 1970, comparing certain factors and variables. In July 2002, Blay spoke about his project and conclusions.

Q: Is there a typical victim?
A: Absolutely. When I gave the talk, I had my son take a picture of me, on the shoreline with a University of Washington t-shirt on, with my snorkel in hand, and a big smile. The typical profile is the middle-aged white guy from the mainland, just like me. Over 75% of the people who drown are visitors. Nine out of 10 are men, and the median age is around 40-45. I would say the main reason for people drowning here is ignorance. They're not aware of the invisible forces in the ocean, the currents that you just can't see.

Q: Despite all the signs?
A: Well, the signs are ridiculous. They have the same sign at the most dangerous beach as they do at the safest beach, so they're generic. But see, that's part of our litigious society. In order for the legislature to say that the state is immune to prosecution if somebody gets in trouble and drowns, they have to put up a sign. Therefore [people] are duly warned; if they get in trouble, it's their problem, not the state's. What I would like to see are billboard signs at each of the most dangerous beaches that say exactly what it is that's dangerous there, how many people have drowned...

Q: Wouldn't that scare people from going in the water?

nic tables surround the central statue that presides over Waimea traffic. At the southern end of Alawai Rd., a small dirt parking lot faces the mouth of the Waimea River and a solitary boulder directly to the south, in **Lucy Wright Beach Park.** A small plaque (now decorated with graffiti) that is embedded in the unceremoniously-placed rock memorializes Capt. Cook's landing spot. In addition to the landing, the park has a baseball field, as well as a grassy area available to campers, complete with showers, restrooms, picnic tables and a pavilion. The "beach" consists of a small stretch of brownish-gray sand and cloudy waters.

Long before Captain Cook's arrival, the menehune constructed their own monuments in Waimea. Along the western bank of the Waimea River, 1.3 mi. north of the highway, a narrow ditch runs along the left side of the road. Many years ago, Hawaii's legendary little people dug this ditch to divert the flow of the river, and it still functions to this day. Much of the ancient **Menehune Ditch** has been obscured by road construction and development, but sections of the rock wall are still visible. Right before the **swinging bridge** that crosses the river, a plaque honors the menehune and their miraculous building skills.

Originally housed in an Art Deco building that boasted the first electric marquee on Kauai, the restored ▨**Waimea Theater,** 9691 Kaumualii Hwy., is still a local landmark. The large screen and modern sound system do not detract from the cozy charm of the "loge"—two rows of roomy rattan armchairs that put standard movie theater seats to shame. (☎338-0282 for show times. $6; students, seniors over 55, and military $5; children 5-12 $3. Films Tu-Su at 7:30pm.)

WAIMEA CANYON STATE PARK

Brilliant red cliffs plunge into a lush green valley, carved by streams and faults millions of years ago. Soaring birds, fragrant flowers, and the constant buzz of tourist-laden helicopters complete the scene. Waimea Canyon State Park, situated in the desolate area between north and west, encompasses forests, trails, and amazing vistas—all surrounding the awesome splendor of the deep canyon.

⊙ LOOKOUTS

From central Waimea, Waimea Canyon Dr. slowly winds its way up to the rim of the canyon, joining the much more relaxed—but not nearly as scenic— Koke'e Rd. after 8 glorious miles. Every one of the road's turns affords a view of the ocean, the valleys, or the canyon itself. About ½ mi. past the 10-mile marker, a huge parking lot welcomes tour buses and families galore to the Waimea Canyon Lookout. A commanding and expansive view of the colorful canyon lies just beyond the green railing. Back on the road, the next official lookout is Pu'u Hinahina, between the 13- and 14-mile markers. A short path, heading away from the restrooms, leads to a Niihau viewpoint; on clear days, the 18-mile-long island and accompanying little Lehua are pretty impressive.

■ HIKES AND TRAILS

On the right side of Waimea Canyon Dr., about 0.7 mi. past the 8-mile marker, a sign points the way toward two very different hiking experiences. Just before the trailhead, a small dirt turnout on the left provides a few convenient parking spaces. A scramble up the steep slope to the top of the embankment reveals decent views of the canyon, as well as signs that guide you to the right. From here, the **Iliau Nature Loop** is a short 10- to 20-minute stroll along a wide dirt trail. Situated high above the populated coasts, Waimea Canyon supports a healthy population of indigenous and endemic plants, many of which are described in signs along the trail. A few minutes into the Iliau Loop, another sign directs hard-core hikers to the right, down a trail that quickly narrows and descends more than 2000 ft. down the western edge of the canyon. After 2½ mi. of wobbling knees, the **Kukui Trail** ends at a river and campground. Those who haven't planned ahead and brought camping gear must simply turn around and climb the grueling miles back up the canyon.

KOKE'E STATE PARK

Continuing up the road, past the 14-mile marker, Waimea Canyon State Park gives way to Koke'e State Park. The cool upland forests of Koke'e present a marked contrast to the lush valleys below, and temperatures here are often 10-15 degrees cooler than at sea level. With thermometers hovering around 60 degrees, the sprawling trails of Koke'e present spectacular—and comfortable—hiking adventures. Although most of the park's 45 miles of trails feature stunning vistas and peaceful forests, Koke'e also boasts the muddy, but fascinating, **Alaka'i Swamp.**

■ PRACTICAL INFORMATION

For trail information and advice, head to the **Koke'e Natural History Museum** (☎ 335-9975; www.aloha.net/kokee), on the left after the 15-mile marker. Inter-

A: Maybe it would. For example, you go to Hanakapi'ai. In that area, there had been 24 drownings in 27 years—14 bodies never recovered. Nineteen in the winter, 5 in the summer. If you put up a sign that emphasized this...I think that would be more effective than "Swim at your own risk."

Q: Did you find any strange patterns?
A: Well, the main thing that saved lives on Kauai in terms of drownings have been two hurricanes. Fewer people came, so fewer people were possible to drown.

Q: What is the relative danger of drowning here as opposed to the other islands?
A: Actually there are more drownings on the other islands, but Kauai is much higher for visitors drowning. The state spends tons of money to promote tourism here, but they do relatively little to keep people safe. You get this local attitude, "Ah, another stupid *haole* drowned on the North Shore."

Q: If people get in trouble what should they do?
A: The correct response is to stay calm, and breathe. I always tell people before they go in the water to use the ten-minute rule. Sit on the beach and watch the water for ten minutes, because within ten minutes you're going to see the biggest waves and the smallest waves, because every few minutes you get a swell coming in. Every wave is not big because the waves travel in sets; you have to be aware of that. The biggest hazard is ignorance.

esting and comprehensive displays present general information about Kauai's ecology and geology. At times quite graphic (using stuffed heads), the exhibits illustrate the hunting, fishing, and hiking opportunities in the park. They also provide an overview of the indigenous birds and plants that call the park home. Historical photographs give a glimpse of the park as it appeared to early explorers, and a fascinating one-room display details the destruction wrought by Hurricane Iniki, as well as the park's slow but encouraging recovery. Short guides to popular trails, maps, and a variety of gift items are available for sale. (Open daily 9am-4pm.)

Next door, the **Koke'e Lodge** stocks gifts and snacks, and maintains **public restrooms.** A super-friendly **window ❶** at the back sells tasty and filling food that can be eaten at the inside tables. Although crowded at lunch time, the lodge's long windows provide a pleasant setting for a casual meal. The breakfast menu includes quiche ($6.75), hot cornbread ($3), and fruit ($3.25). Lunch features sandwiches ($6) on yummy 12-grain bread, hot dogs ($3), meaty or vegetarian chili ($6.25), and plenty of alcohol for those celebrating the completion of a tough hike. (Food served 9am-3:30pm.)

▨ CABINS AND CAMPING

The lodge acts as the rental office for the 12 wooden cabins located just to the south. The cabins, ranging from studios to 2-bedrooms, come equipped with kitchens, hot showers, linens, and wood-burning stoves. There is a maximum stay of 5 days. Reservations recommended 2-4 months in advance, one year for holiday weekends. For reservations or more information, write or call Koke'e Lodge, P.O. Box 819, Waimea, HI 96796 (☎335-6061). **Cabins ❷** range from $35 to $45. On the other side of the museum, the Koke'e campground is made up of a series of spacious, grassy sites laid out along a curving dirt road. Facilities include restrooms, drinking water, and picnic tables. Two forest reserve campgrounds, **Kawaikoi** and **Sugi Grove,** are located farther east, along the 4WD-only Mohihi-Camp 10 Rd. For information on obtaining a permit see **Camping,** p. 355.

YWCA Camp Sloggett ❶ (☎335-6060 or 245-5959 for groups) is located down a marked, uneven dirt road opposite the lodge and has affordable indoor accommodations. Large groups sometimes take over the camp, which includes a lodge that can sleep 10, a bunkhouse, and tent-camping sites. At other times, however, the long bunkhouse, lined with rows of metal twin bunks and anchored at either end by a private studio with kitchen, makes a decent hostel. Two bathrooms are provided for guests; tent camping facilities are limited to showers. A caretaker lives on-site and welcomes phone calls or walk-ins until 8pm. Bunks are $20 and tents are $10 per person per night. Rates are negotiable for groups or weekday stays.

◎ LOOKOUTS

While the Waimea Canyon Dr. viewpoints look inland, over a dramatic stream-formed canyon, the Koke'e lookouts turn the other way, providing expansive views of the wild **Na Pali Coast** and its endless valleys. Although cooler temperatures may be welcome while hiking, the 4000 ft. elevation and chilly winds of the two Na Pali lookouts can get uncomfortable. Across from the 18-mile marker, the **Kalalau Lookout** presents a postcard-perfect view of the **Kalalau Valley** and the beginning of the rugged Na Pali coastline. Many travelers stow their cameras and turn around here, to their own loss. Another less popular (but equally stunning) vista awaits at the end of the road. Free of massive tour buses and chatty guides, the **Pu'u o Kila Lookout** boasts a magnificent view of the sloping green cliffs and valleys as well as the bright blue ocean beyond. Unfortunately, perhaps due to the lighter tourist traffic, a growing wall of shrubbery encroaches on the sights. A sign to the east points toward Mt. Wai'ale'ale, and Pu'u o Kila also serves as the starting point for trails into the Alaka'i Swamp.

🗺 HIKING

Over 40 miles of trails criss-cross the park, from short forest walks through groves of Methley plums to heart-pounding balancing acts across narrow, rocky ridges. Unfortunately for budget travelers in economy cars, many of Koke'e's trails are accessible only by 4WD. However, a more than adequate selection of both tame and exciting trails lies within walking distance of the road.

Near the 14-mile marker, a dirt road leads to the right. Park officials consider **Halemanu Rd.** suitable for **4WD vehicles** only, and even locals with big trucks and big tires have gotten stuck in the ruts. That said, during the best of conditions, the road is passable for regular cars. Most visitors leave their vehicles at the good-sized dirt parking area opposite Halemanu Rd. and walk the 0.8 mi. to the trailheads of a number of canyon-view trails.

Another option is to take advantage of the park's **Wonderwalks.** Led by park employees or local naturalists, these guided hikes are informative and accessible. State vehicles transport the 4WD-less to otherwise unreachable trailheads, while knowledgeable leaders lead hikers through a wide range of hikes. (Call ☎ 335-9975 or stop by the museum for a schedule. Reservations are recommended, some hikes have limited capacities. All Wonderwalks leave at 12:30pm from Koke'e Museum.)

> Anyone hiking in the park should carry sufficient water; although streams and falls do cross a few trails, feral pigs and goats make leptosirosis, a bacteria that can sneak right through most water filters, a constant concern. Hikers should also avoid attempting the trails during wet and rainy weather, when the condition and stability of dirt trails may greatly deteriorate. The faint of heart should be aware; many of the canyon and Na Pali view hikes include extremely steep drops and, occasionally, frighteningly narrow ledges.

🥾**CANYON TRAIL.** (1.7 mi., 2½-3hr. round-trip. Trailhead: the end of Halemanu Rd., past the trailhead for the Cliff Trail. Level: moderate.) Deservedly Koke'e Park's most popular hike, the Canyon Trail skirts the edges of the Waimea Canyon, revealing breathtaking views at every corner. After guiding travelers through verdant native forest brimming with koa trees and blackberry bushes, the trail passes over an old sugar plantation ditch. A quick climb out of the forest leads to a broad ridge with an exhilarating view of the valley below. From here, the trail descends to Waipo'o Falls. Most hikers turn back at this point; continue on, and you can escape some of the crowds. To the left, a short spur takes adventurers to a small swimming hole that is only safe when water is running. More breathtaking views await atop Kumuwela Ridge.

CLIFF TRAIL. (0.9 mi., 1hr. round-trip from parking lot. Trailhead: parking lot across from Halemanu Rd. Level: moderate.) Halemanu Rd. winds its way to the trailheads, passing through koa and 'ohia trees, fragrant *Kahili* ginger, and other flowering plants. At the end of the road, a short turnoff leads to the very brief (0.1 mi.) Cliff Trail. Perfect for hikers with limited time, the Cliff Trail delivers gorgeous views for minimal exertion. The trail ends at an overlook with an expansive view of the Waimea Canyon. The return trip includes a 400-foot climb that, along with the sometimes unstable rocky road, makes for a slightly challenging hike.

NU'ALOLO-NU'ALOLO CLIFF/AWA'AWAPUHI LOOP. (10.3 mi., about 6-7hr. round-trip. Trailheads: Nu'alolo trailhead, 100 yards south of the lodge road; 'Awa'awapuhi trailhead, just past the 17-mile marker, on the left. Level: very challenging.) The Nu'alolo-Awa'awapuhi Loop is the combination of two hikes, both of which are difficult in their own regard. Together, they form a grueling trek best suited for masochistic adventurers. If you choose to tackle the loop, start early on a sunny day—wet weather will make the already-scary cliff truly terrifying. The **Nu'alolo Trail** gradually descends 4 mi., through dry upland forests dominated by towering koa trees and flowering shrubs. After 3.2 mi., a junction on the left connects to the **Nu'alolo Cliff Trail,** which tip-toes precariously along a ridge atop the Nu'alolo Valley. Before heading toward the cliff, continue along the Nu'alolo Trail for another 0.4 mi. to a stunning vista. However, do not attempt either the trail to the vista or the cliff walk during rainy weather; they are not safe. The Nu'alolo Cliff Trail traverses stretches of bare cliffs with wide open views, ventures into the lush green forest and happens upon an exposed ridge with picnic tables, and a stream crossing. A valley later, an unexpected little waterfall emerges from mossy rocks. At the **Awa'awapuhi junction,** turn right to return to the road, or take a short 10-minute walk to the left, where yet another amazing vista awaits. Take a minute to enjoy your moment on the cliff before starting the 3-mile, 1700-foot gradual climb back up to the highway.

PU'U KA 'OHELO-BERRY FLATS LOOP. (2 mi., 1hr. round-trip. Trailhead: ½ mi. down the Mohihi-Camp 10 Rd. Level: easy.) Although Mohihi-Camp 10 Rd. is classified as 4WD-only, the beginning segment that leads to the trailhead is generally passable. This pleasant hike wanders through a forest shadowed by tall koa trees and lacy ferns. The constant struggle between indigenous and introduced plants is evident—flowering honeysuckle, beautiful but destructively invasive, lines the path and the far end of the loop is dominated by Japanese *sugi* pines and California redwoods, which have prevented native plants from taking root.

KALUAPUHI TRAIL. (2 mi., 1hr. round-trip. Trailhead: An overgrown grassy slope with room for one car to park on the right side of the road, a little less than ¼ mi. past the Awa'awapuhi trailhead, on the left. Level: easy to moderate.) Due to the elusive trailhead, you may very well have the path to yourself. The well-maintained trail travels inland, through native upland forest, ending just past the **Kalalau Lookout.** With a change in elevation of only 120 ft., the peaceful stroll can be enjoyed by all, especially families with children. Native Hawaiian flora and fauna prevail here; indigenous birds swoop down from above the forest canopy of 'ohia, and strawberry guava grows in abundance. At the T-intersection in the grove, take the left fork—the right fork leads to a dead-end hunting trail. The trail ends in a orchard of Methley plums, which are harvested by locals in early summer.

PIHEA TRAIL TO ALAKA'I SWAMP TRAIL. (4 mi., 3-4hr. round-trip. Trailhead: to the right of the Pu'u o Kila Lookout, at the end of Waimea Canyon Dr. Level: challenging.) The first section of the Pihea Trail features sweeping views of the Na Pali cliffs and valleys. Hovering around 4000 ft., this stretch weaves beneath 'ohia trees that form a leafy roof overhead and attract a steady stream of native birds. After 1 mi., a steep offshoot leads to the pleasant, but not amazing, **Pihea Vista,** and the main trail turns into a rustic wooden boardwalk. After another mile, the **Alaka'i junction** bridges joins the path with the **Alaka'i Swamp Trail;** turn left to continue. A striking contrast to the Pihea Trail, this path meanders for two miles through muddy bogs and mossy vegetation, which are havens for endemic birds and plants. After the taxing journey, hikers emerge at the Kilohana Lookout, with its amazing (though usually cloudy) view of the North Shore.

KEKAHA

Once a sugar town where everything centered around the big (and now rusting), mill, modern-day Kekaha functions mainly as a gateway to **Koke'e State Park** (see p. 403). Tour buses regularly roll through the town, but few ever stop to enjoy the miles of wide, uncrowded beach where locals gather around grills on lazy Sunday afternoons.

⛝ PRACTICAL INFORMATION. The westernmost town in the United States, Kekaha lies 26 miles west of Lihu'e on Hwy. 50. **Kekaha Rd.** branches left from the highway between the 24- and 25-mile markers and runs 2 miles west to **Waimea Canyon Plaza** at the base of Koke'e Rd. The plaza features a couple of standard tourist shops stocked with aloha shirts and beach towels, as well as the last place to fill your tummy—or your picnic basket—before heading north to Koke'e or west to Polihale.

☐ FOOD. The **Menehune Food Mart ❶** has a good selection of the basics plus Icees, prepared sandwiches ($3), and other plastic wrapped goodies. (☎ 237-1335. Open daily 5am-8pm.) Both Obsessions Cafe ❶ and the Waimea Canyon Snack Shop ❶ sell sandwiches ($3.75-6), salads, and ice cream ($2.75 per scoop) to fuel you up for a day outside. Obsessions (☎ 337-2224) is open daily 8:30am-6pm; Snack Shop (☎ 337-9227), daily 8am-4:30pm.

⛵ BEACHES. Across Kekaha Rd. from the Plaza, the sprawling **Faye Park,** complete with track, baseball fields, tennis courts, basketball court, playground, picnic tables, pavilion, and grills, has hosted many a neighborhood barbecue. There are restrooms behind the pavilion and an outdoor shower at the other end of the park (right on the highway facing the beach). Every Saturday morning at 9am, a Sunshine Market sets up shop next to the tennis courts. Kekaha's main attraction, the glistening white **Kekaha Beach Park,** runs alongside the town before winding north for 15 uninterrupted miles all the way to **Polihale.** Like other West Side beaches, pretty Kekaha hides strong rip currents, and swimmers should be aware of surf conditions before entering the water. Families with young *keiki* favor the eastern end of the beach, where a small, reef-fringed pool (just east of the church) creates safer waters.

FLYING FEATHERS
Every summer, droves of eager bird-watchers fly to Kauai to catch a glimpse of the island's tropical birds. While the binocular-slinging experts tread muddy swamp trails and search through isolated forest, even the most apathetic couch potato will have ample opportunities to photograph Kauai's most notorious flying species: the **domestic chicken.** Introduced by early European sailors who carried hens for food, these *gallus domesticus* now run rampant—from the mountain valleys of Koke'e to the busy roads of Kapa'a. Like their counterparts on the other islands, Kauai's chickens grew up in pens, but the annihilating force of Hurricane Iniki destroyed cages across the island. Kauai is free of predators, most notably the vile mongoose that were introduced to the other islands in the 1880s to keep rats out of the sugar fields. As a result, the colorful chickens breed frighteningly fast and entice many a newly-arrived traveler into a taking a few photographs of them. While freedom has brought cheer to the chickens, the constant crowing of wild roosters reveling in their morning routine sparks quite a bit of grumbling from their human neighbors.

KAUAI

◪ OUTDOORS. Outside of Kekaha, **Polihale State Park** is worth a trip. Hwy. 50 ends five miles out of Kekaha; following the signs to Polihale, veer right at the fork and turn left onto the first dirt road. While trucks full of local teenagers careen merrily down miles of potholes, bumps, and rocks to the park, visitors in modest rental cars may have a more difficult—but definitely worthwhile—ride. Ease off the gas, avoid braking suddenly, and shift into low gear as you navigate your way through the cane fields. Five miles later, you will arrive at the campgrounds, complete with restrooms, showers, drinking water, and pavilions. For more information, see **Camping** p. 355. Those without a permit can save themselves a few thousand bumps by turning left at the big monkeypod tree 3.4 mi. up the road (1½ mi. before the campground). Beginning at the small parking area, Polihale's famous dunes give way to three miles of wide white sand and crystal clear waters. If you've got shoes, put them on, as constant exposure to the scorching West Side sun makes the pretty sand feel as hot as fiery coals. A safe swimming area, known as **Queen's Pond,** is a quick stroll to the north. At the northern end of the beach, past the campsites, an ancient **heiau** is nestled at the base of Polihale Cliff. According to legend, the souls of the ancient dead used the cliff as a departure point, floating away from the earth and into the glorious setting sun. The world-famous **Polihale sunset** is best seen from this end, where the blazing orange sun sinks below crashing waves, and the forbidden isle of **Niihau** sits 20 mi. offshore, providing a perfect backdrop for a romantic picnic.

NIIHAU

LAND

Niihau (Ni'ihau) lies 18 miles southwest of Kauai and is the westernmost of Hawaii's eight major islands. Only 70 square miles in area, Niihau has a flat, arid landscape. While Mt. Waialeale on neighboring Kauai is the rainiest spot on earth, Niihau's average rainfall is a mere 12 inches per year. Because it lacks the lush tropical vegetation that characterizes the other islands, Niihau, with its grassy lowland topography, is particularly well-suited for grazing by the herds of animals that today outnumber people on the island.

HISTORY

Niihau was never conquered during **Kamehameha I's** campaign to unite all of the Hawaiian islands under one rule in the late 1700s. Rather, it joined the kingdom of its own volition in 1810.

In 1863, **Eliza Sinclair,** a Scottish widow turned New Zealand farmer, moved to Honolulu, where **King Kamehameha V** offered to sell her a parcel of land on Oahu stretching from Honolulu Hale to Diamond Head for $10,000. (Not a bad deal, considering this area is some of the most lucrative real estate in the world today.) Sinclair did not think this land was suitable for farming, however, and instead spent her $10,000 to purchase the entire island of Niihau, along with all of its inhabitants. Sinclair established the **Niihau Ranch** on the island, where she raised cattle and other livestock, enlisting the island's residents and her own family as employees. After her death in 1892, Sinclair's grandson, **Aubrey Robinson,** took over the ranch.

The island is highly isolated and uninvited visitors have been forbidden on Niihau since its purchase in the 19th century—hence its nickname, **"The Forbidden Isle."** One memorable intruder, a Japanese pilot, crash landed on the island after the attack on Pearl Harbor in 1941. After a week spent sporadically dispensing machine gun fire from the wreckage of his plane, the pilot was eventually subdued by Niihau native **Benehakaka Kanahele.** Kanahele received the Congressional Medal of Honor for his bravery.

The island is famous for the handstrung **shell leis** that native women have produced for hundreds of

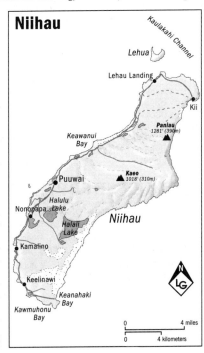

years. Tiny *Laiki, Kehelelani,* and *Momi* seashells wash up on Niihau during certain seasons of the year, and they are then collected and strung into intricate necklaces. **Captain James Cook** returned from his first expedition to Hawaii with one of these leis, which is now the property of the British Museum. Many of these beautiful necklaces have become treasured heirlooms in Hawaiian families, and can fetch 4 figures in antique shops throughout Hawaii.

TODAY

Niihau is still owned by the Robinson family, and today Eliza Sinclair's great-great-grandsons, **Keith and Bruce Robinson,** manage the ranch. Nowadays the island is home to about 250 people (all employed by the ranch in some capacity), 2000 head of cattle, 3000 wild turkeys, and 12,000 sheep.

There is no electric power on the island, with the exception of that produced by the occasional privately-owned generator. There are also no telephones and no paved roads. There is one school on the island, which provides instruction up to grade 8. Students who wish to pursue a high school education commute to schools on Kauai or Oahu.

Hawaiian is the primary language spoken on Niihau, and residents of the island are known for their insularity and staunch opposition to Western ways of life. In addition to the widespread rejection of modern conveniences that would allow for greater contact with the outside world, Niihau was the only island that voted against Hawaiian statehood in 1959.

Although uninvited visitors are prohibited, residents are free to come and go as they choose. However, the inhabitants, including the Robinson family, are highly committed to preserving traditional Hawaiian culture, and therefore most choose to stay on the island, rejecting the pull of the commercialism that governs life throughout much of Hawaii.

VISITING THE ISLAND

Technically, nobody is allowed to visit Niihau unless they are invited by a resident. However, **helicopter tours** are permitted on the island, which are run by **Niihau Helicopters.** Flights leave M-Sa morning from Port Allen Field on Kauai. An afternoon flight is occasionally run when there is sufficient demand. Trips include an aerial tour of the island, half a day at a secluded beach, and lunch. Reservations are required, and tours are often booked months in advance. (P.O. Box 690370, Makaweli, HI 96769. ☎877-441-3500 or 335-3500. www.hawaiian.net/~niihauisland/heli.html. $280 per person; group and charter rates available.)

FURTHER INFORMATION

Niihau: The Last Hawaiian Island, by Ruth M. Tabrah. This book is based on the author's experiences in Niihau, and is a good source for general information about the island.

Niihau Incident, by Allan Beekman. An account of the Japanese fighter pilot who landed on Niihau in 1941 and terrorized the island's residents.

A Chronicle and Flora of Niihau, by Juliet Rice Wichman. An illustrated volume documenting wildlife on Niihau.

NORTHWESTERN HAWAIIAN ISLANDS

LAND

The Northwestern Hawaiian Islands are an archipelago of reefs, small islands, and coral atolls that stretch for 1000 miles across the Pacific from 150 miles northwest of Kauai. The land areas of the expanse constitute a federal wildlife refuge which is administered by the US Fish and Wildlife Service. The islands and their surrounding waters constitute the **Northwest Hawaiian Islands Coral Reef Ecosystem Reserve,** which is the largest protected area in the US, covering 131,800 sq. mi. (3.5 million acres). The unique and fragile **ecosystems** of the Northwest Hawaiian Islands contain over 70 percent of the coral reefs located in US waters, as well as 7000 marine species, half of which are endemic (unique to the island chain). Among the threatened and **endangered species** that reside there are: the Hawaiian monk seal, loggerhead turtle, hawkbill turtle, leatherback sea turtle, and the green sea turtle.

About 1400 total monk seals reside in the islands, with the largest breeding colony located on **French Frigate Shoals,** an atoll in the chain. **Nihoa Island** is the first island in the chain, as well as the largest, at 170 acres in area. Next is **Necker Island** (Mokumanamana Island), the top of a giant shield volcano that is also the oldest-known active volcano in the chain. Numerous heiaus on the island indicate that it was once inhabited, or at least frequented, by ancient mariners. **French Frigate Shoals** (Mokupapapa Island), **Gardner Pinnacles** (Puhahonu, named for their resemblance to turtles coming up for air), and **Marco Reef** (Nakukakala, meaning "surf that arrives in combers") follow in the chain. Nearby **Laysan Island** (Kauo, meaning either the yolk or white of an egg) is a large atoll which somewhat resembles a cracked egg, and is notable for the salty lagoon at its center, as well as the large number of birds that nest on the island. Beyond it lies **Pearl and Hermes Atoll,** called Holoikauaua by the ancient Hawaiians. The name means "dog-like animal that swims in the water," the name also given to the Hawaiian monk seal. **Kure Atoll** (Kanemiloha'i, named for Pele's brother) is the most distant island, but before it lie the **Midway Islands** (Pihemnau, meaning "the loud din of birds"), the best-known group in the island chain. Midway includes an atoll and a few small islands, including Sand Island and Green Island.

HISTORY OF THE ISLANDS

There exists evidence of human presence on the islands from ancient times, and it is known that King Kalakaua had a wooden house built on distant Kure Atoll in 1885 and stocked it with provisions for anyone who became stranded on the island. US acquisition of the islands in 1867 led to more permanent activity, at Midway in particular. In 1903, part of the trans-Pacific cable was laid on the island and residents came to Midway to manage the station. **Midway** was made a national defense area in 1941 and served as a US Naval Base through World War II. One of the most decisive battles of World War II's Pacific theater occurred at Midway Islands in June of 1942. The **Battle of Midway** was a victory for US forces which turned the tide of war in their favor against the Japanese. (See History: World War II, p. 17). Midway continued to serve as a naval base until 1996 when the area was deemed a **National Wildlife Refuge** by the US Fish and Wildlife Service and was opened for ecotourism.

NW ISLANDS

Northwestern Hawaiian Islands

Kure Atoll

Midway Atoll

Pearl and Hermes Atoll

0 ⊢ 200 miles
0 ⊢ 200 kilometers

Laysan Island

Lisianski Island

Marco Reef

Kure Atoll

Sand Island
Green Island

Midway Atoll

Sand Island
Gooney Spit Is.
Eastern Island

Gardner Pinnacles

0 ⊢ 100 yds
0 ⊢ 100 m

Pearl and Hermes Atoll

North Is.
Little North Is.
Sand Is.
Bird Is.
Southeast Is.
Grass Is.
Kittery Is.
Seal Is.

Marco Reef

Laysan Island

PACIFIC OCEAN

180 175 W 170 W 165 W 160 W 155 W

28 N 25 N Tropic of Cancer 22 N 19 N

Kure Midway Pearl and Hermes Lisianski Laysan Marco Reef Gardner Pinnacles French Frigate Shoals Necker Nihoa Kauai Oahu Maui Hawaii

French Frigate Shoals

Tern Is. Trig Is. Skate Is. Whale Is. Mullet Is. Round Is. Nea Is. Shark Is. East Is. Le Pérouse Pinnacle Gin Is. Little Gin Is. Disappearing Is.

Scale for all detail maps
except Gardner Pinnacles:
0 ⊢ 1 mile
0 ⊢ 1 kilometer

Nihoa Island

Adams Bay

Necker Island

Shark Bay

Lisianski Island

PACIFIC OCEAN

25 N Tropic of Cancer

Kauai Niihau Nihoa Necker Island Nihoa Island Gardner Pinnacles French Frigate Shoals

160 W 165 W 170 W

TODAY

Over the past decade, federal officials have hemmed and hawed over the fate of the Northwestern Hawaiian Islands. There are a number of administrative organizations for the islands and their surroundings, some of which overlap in jurisdiction. In 1992, the Midway Islands officially relinquished their military role when the Department of Defense shut down the Midway Naval Air Facility. It is now a federal refuge under the management of Midway Phoenix Corp. Most of the dry land within the Northwestern Hawaiian region is part of a **national wildlife refuge,** while the state controls everything within three miles from the beaches.

President Clinton established the islands as a coral reef ecosystem in 2000, with an aim to protect and conserve the area. This further restricted the area, and the problems of administration were made even more complicated by recent moves by the state of Hawaii and the federal government. In January 2002, Hawaii proposed new, tighter access regulations. In addition to controlling the waters surrounding the islands, under the new rules, the state would forbid any entry without a permit. Simultaneously, the federal government is attempting to upgrade the islands from reserve status to a **national marine sanctuary.** Their efforts have been thwarted by bureaucratic red tape; the Coast Guard, National Marine Fisheries, and the Department of Land and Natural Resources are only a few of the agencies with some modicum of control over the region. If the projected change were to occur, the islands would fall under the National Ocean Service and join the 13 present national marine sanctuaries. There is ongoing debate concerning both proposals.

Until 2002, the Midway Islands housed a resort for **ecotourism.** However, the Midway Phoenix Corporation shut down all operations in March 2002, citing a lack of profit. This move has jeopardized the Coast Guard refueling base and an emergency commercial landing spot situated there. However, the Fish and Wildlife services haven't given up hope; they are looking to establish a temporary arrangement with another organization.

FURTHER INFORMATION

Isles of Refuge: Wildlife and History of the Northwestern Hawaiian Islands, by Mark J. Rauzon. An account of the biology and history of the islands, complete with high-quality photographs and artwork.

Midway, by Hugh Bicheno. Complete with illustrations and maps, this account focuses on why the Japanese strategy failed during the battle of Midway.

Midway: The Battle That Doomed Japan, by Mitsuo Fuchida, Masatake Okumiya, Thomas B. Buell, and Kenji Kawakami. Told from the Japanese perspective, this version of the battle presents first-hand accounts from two naval aviators who give their insights as to why Japan lost at Midway.

Miracle at Midway, by Gordon William Prange, Donald M. Goldstein, and Katherine V. Dillon. Featuring eyewitness accounts from both sides, this narrative describes the battle of Midway in vivid detail, and how American military strategy led to a turning point in the Pacific war.

NW ISLANDS

RIDE THE WAVE
Surfing in Hawaii

Known as the "sport of kings," surfing was born and bred in Hawaii. *Aliʻi,* or Hawaiian royalty, perfected the sport in the 1700s, and King Kamehameha could often be seen riding waves alongside his favorite wife, Queen Kaʻahumanu. In the early 1900s, Duke Kahanamoku reigned the surf scene. He and his group of Waikiki Beachboys helped turn the sport into a national trend with their surfing skill and striking looks.

As surfing's popularity swelled, so did its associated adrenaline levels. The popular slogan "Eddie Would Go," often seen on t-shirts and bumper stickers, refers to the legendary moves of Eddie Aikau on Oahu's North Shore in the early 1970s. Eddie would go where no other big-wave rider dared, swimming out in 60-foot surf, risking life and limb for the thrill of the tube. The extreme sport of tow-in surfing, though no less dangerous, has since replaced the perils of paddling through pounding waves. Jet skis tow surfers from calm, onshore harbors to beyond the break, just in time for the intrepid individual to drop in for a monster set. Maui's world-renowned Peahi Bay (p. 237)—also nicknamed "Jaws" for its all-consuming waves—was home to the first annual Tow-In World Championship, held in January 2002, as well as the site of the unforgettable sequence in the latest Bond movie, *Die Another Day,* in which three camouflaged stunt men (all from Hawaii) are dropped from a helicopter into the surf below.

Today, surfing is one of the world's most popular sports and has developed into a thriving industry. Movies, fashion, and music have cemented surfing's place in pop culture. New technology now allows designers to tailor boards to unique surf conditions, so that surfers own not just one but an entire fleet of different models. Shapers such as Dick Brewer of Kauai and Maui's Rod Ole and Jeff Timpone are the elite artists of the surfing design world.

Surfing is also the second-fastest growing sport among women. While Queen Kaʻahumanu may have paved the way for her gender, the past 50 years have witnessed the most rapid rise in the number of surfing kahunesses. Changes in board construction have made surfboards easier for women to carry and maneuver. In 1959, the first Gidget movie was released, promoting the image of female surfers. Women finally made their way into the professional circuit with the founding of the Women's Pro Surfing Association in 1979 (though their winnings are still less than half that of professional male surfers). The best evidence for the growing popularity among women comes from *Surfer Magazine*; world pro Lisa Andersen was featured on its cover in 1995 with the line, "Lisa Andersen surfs better than you." Now, surf schools such as Surf Diva in California and Maui Surfer Girls in Maui cater primarily to women, while retailers like Girl in the Curl and Chicks with Sticks have also gained popularity. Movies have become the latest focal point for the rapidly spreading craze among *wahine* of all ages. The movie *Blue Crush,* shot on location in Oahu and released in 2002, re-introduced surfer girls to the big screen for the first time in a half-century. On any given day, women make up a solid percentage of those catching waves, dropping in, carving out their own place in this colorful pastime. *Imua!*

Maren Lau was a Researcher-Writer in Hawaii for Let's Go: California & Hawaii 1997. *She now lives in Maui and attends business school.*

INVISIBLE FOOTPRINTS
Sustainable Travel in a Dying World

Faced with harsh demands created by modern travelers, natural wonders and cultural landscapes are being irreparably damaged. Even conscientious tourists are inadvertently wreaking havoc on local traditions. By 2020, more than one billion people are expected to travel to another country, more than double the number today. Increasingly, globetrotters are seeking out "biodiversity hot spots" that cover just 2% of the earth's land surface, but encompass over half of its biodiversity. By 1999, tourism to developing countries had risen to 38% of all travel, an astounding increase from 3% in 1950.

There are a number of ways to minimize the impact travelers have. One of the most important ways is by practicing "sustainable travel," a philosophy quickly gaining popularity. Sustainable travel is a most meaningful way to tour the globe; it emphasizes environmentally safe and culturally active travel. Its proponents are on-the-road philanthropists, preserving their experiences for future travelers.

Sustainable travel and ecotourism have long been on the rise in Hawaii. In July 2001, a survey conducted by the University of Hawaii's Travel Industry Management School investigated the growing concern for the preservation of Hawaii's resources among residents, environmentalists, and tourists. The school has also participated in sustainable travel think tanks, the most recent of which occurred in April 2002.

There are many other Hawaiian organizations and establishments that actively work to promote sustainable travel and ecotourism. For example, the Ka'anapali Beach Hotel in Maui trains its personnel extensively to share with its guests a respect for the native culture of indigenous islanders. For its efforts in keeping the language and customs alive, Ka'anapali was designated Hawaii's Most Hawaiian Hotel by the Waiaha Foundation, a non-profit organization dedicated to the health of the island's culture. There are also numerous tour operators who pride themselves on educating visitors on Hawaiian culture and heritage. A list of some of these "alternative" guides is available online (www.travelwithachallenge.com/Hawaii_Operators.htm).

Other day-to-day ways to be a responsible traveler include conserving energy wherever possible, whether it means riding a bicycle instead of taking a bus, being more conscientious about recycling, or taking a shorter shower in the morning. For those who seek more active involvement, Earthwatch International, Operation Crossroads Africa, and Habitat for Humanity offer fulfilling volunteer opportunities. The publication, *Invest Yourself: The Catalogue Of Volunteer Opportunities*, published by the Commission on Voluntary Service and Action (☎718-638-8487), is an excellent reference guide of such organizations.

For more information on being a conscientious traveler, ample resources are available on the Internet. The Hawaii Ecotourism Association has a comprehensive website with links, news articles, and more (www.hawaiiecotourism.org). Alternative Hawaii, the "Hawaii Ecotourism Site," identifies Hawaii's "special places" (accommodations and sights) on the major Hawaiian islands (www.alternative-hawaii.com). Malama Hawaii is a partnership of multiple organizations that promotes Hawaii's heritage (www.malama-hawaii.org). More general information is available at www.sustainabletravel.org.

This can become a powerful grassroots movement, but travelers need to spread the word. Recommending services to friends and colleagues upon returning home is an easy way to reward exemplary sustainable enterprises. Introduce your world back home to local causes and charities that you found on your travels.

Michael Seltzer is the Director of Business Enterprises for Sustainable Travel (BEST). BEST supports travel that helps communities preserve natural and cultural resources and create sustainable livelihoods. Visit www.sustainabletravel.org for listings of community-based travel experiences, innovative travel companies and internships.

FLORAL HAWAII

Visitors to Hawaii are greeted with plumeria leis when they arrive at the airport. The roads they travel are lined with guava and coconut, ripe for the plucking. The balmy Hawaiian evenings are scented with the fragrance of ginger. All of these plants are typically associated with Hawaii's bountiful paradise, yet none are native. Hawaii's flora was introduced by travelers—Polynesian or otherwise—who passed through the "crossroads of the Pacific."

Within a land mass totaling just 6500 sq. mi., there exist more than 10,000 native plant and animal species found nowhere else, that make up some of the world's most diverse ecosystems. Yet more than one-third of Hawaii's native flora and fauna is on the U.S. Endangered Species list, and already two-thirds of the state's native forest has been lost. Most Hawaiian flora remain unfamiliar to visitors, though each has a prominent place in Hawaiian heritage.

Hawaiians incorporated plants into many of their daily practices. The root of the *'awa* plant, known for its sedative properties, was often used in Hawaiian medicines and brewed as a potent ceremonial beverage. *'Akia* berries were crushed into a paste and thrown into ponds to stun fish temporarily. Coastal *wiliwili* trees provided light lumber for surfboards and fishnet floats. The prized koa wood is still used for making furniture, canoes, paddles and spears.

Native plants are also an integral part of Hawaiian lore. For example, the *naupaka* plant grows in both mountain and coastal varieties. Legend has it that two lovers, upon angering the gods, were separated and transformed into the *naupaka* plant, one located on the mountain and the other on the coast. Each of the plant's flowers is missing half of its petals, and needs the other to be complete. *Pa'u-o-Hi'iaka*, a groundcover vine, tells the story of Hi'iaka, sister of the volcano goddess Pele. One day, Pele left her baby sister on the seashore as she frolicked in the surf. As the sun blazed, Hi'iaka grew increasingly hot and uncomfortable. Onlooking gods took pity on the babe and covered her with vines to protect her from the heat. *Pa'u-o-Hi'iaka*, or "the skirt of Hi'iaka," can be seen along island beaches.

Today, tremendous efforts are being made to restore and conserve native flora. More endemic species are being incorporated into residential landscapes, and many nonprofit groups have organized to encourage the growth of greenery in public spaces. Community courses provide instruction on native gardening, and nurseries are beginning to specialize in these endemic resources.

Still, some of the best spots to view endemic flora are on Hawaii's protected slopes, including Haleakala National Park on Maui and Volcanoes National Park on the Big Island. The mystifying results of centuries of metamorphosis can still be experienced firsthand there, despite the threats facing the islands' natural splendor. In these havens, bogs house miniature rainforests; native silversword blooms once in its fifty-year life span, then dies; and Pele's hair grows long and silver.

Maren Lau was a Researcher-Writer in Hawaii for Let's Go: California & Hawaii 1997. She lives in Hawaii and attends business school.

GLOSSARY

COMMON HAWAIIAN WORDS AND PHRASES

WORDS		
'aina	eye-nah	land, earth
aikane	aye-kah-nee	friend
ala	al-lah	road
alelo	ah-lay-low	tongue, language
ali'i	ah-lee-ee	Hawaiian chiefs, royalty
aloha	ah-low-ha	love, hello, goodbye
aole	ah-oh-lay	no
halau	hah-lau	school
hale	hah-lay	house
haole	how-lay	caucasians
hapa	hah-pah	half, part
hauoli	how-oh-lee	happiness
heiau	hey-ee-au	temple
hoaloha	ho-ah-low-hah	friend
honi	ho-nee	to kiss
hui	hoo-ee	club, association, or group
hula	hoo-lah	Hawaiian dance
i'amaka	ee-ah-ma-kah	raw fish
imu	ee-moo	underground oven
inu	ee-new	to drink
kahuna	ha-hoo-na	priest
kalua	kah-loo-ah	to bake underground
kane	kah-nay	man
kapa	kah-pah	tapa, bark cloth
kapu	kah-poo	keep out
kaukau	kow-kow	food
keiki	kay-kee	child
ki	kee	plant in daily activities, also an ancient symbol of power
kiawe	kee-ah-way	common Hawaiian lumber tree
koa	ko-ah	valuable endemic Hawaiian lumber tree
kokua	ko-koo-ah	help, aid, relief
koloa	ko-low-ah	Hawaiian duck
kumu	koo-moo	teacher, tutor
kupuna	koo-poo-nah	grandparent, ancestor
lahui	la-hoo-ee	nation, race, tribe
lanai	lah-nye	porch

WORDS		
lei	lay	garland, wreath of flowers
lomi lomi	low-me low-me	massage
lua	loo-ah	restroom
luau	loo-ow	Hawaiian feast
mahalo	mah-hah-low	thank you
ma'ika'i	mah-ee-kah-ee	good, fine
makai	mah-kye	in the direction of the sea
makaainana	mah-kah-ay-nah-nah	common people
makua	mah-koo-ah	parent, parent generation
malama	mah-lah-mah	to take care of, attend to
malihini	mah-lee-hee-nee	stranger, foreigner
mauka	mah-ow-kah	inland, in the direction of the uplands
mele	meh-leh	a song, chant, or poem
menehune	meh-neh-hoo-neh	legendary race of little people
muumuu	moo-moo	loose gown, dress
nalu	nah-loo	wave, surf
nani	nah-nee	beautiful
nui	noo-ee	big
ohana	oh-hah-nah	family
'ohia lehua	oh-hee-ah leh-hoo-ah	native Hawaiian plant
ola	oh-lah	life, health
'olapa	oh-lah-pah	dancer
'olelo	oh-leh-loh	language, speech, word
ono	oh-no	delicious
pali	pah-lee	cliff
paniolo	pah-nee-oh-low	Hawaiian cowboy
pakololo	pah-kow-low-low	marijuana
pau	pow	finished
pilikia	pee-lee-kee-ah	trouble of any kind
pule	poo-leh	prayer or incantation
pupu	poo-poo	hors d'oeuvre
pupule	poo-poo-lay	crazy
ukelele	oo-keh-leh-leh	"jumping flea," Hawaiian instrument
waha	wah-hah	mouth, speech
wahine	wah-hee-nay	woman, girl, female
wai	why	water, liquid or liquor
wiki wiki	wee-kee-wee-kee	fast, speedy, to hurry
PHRASES		
aloha'aina	ah-low-hah eye-nah	love of the land
aloha ahiahi	ah-low-hah ah-hee-ah-hee	Good evening
aloha kakahiaka	ah-low-hah kah-kah-hee-ah-kah	Good morning
aloha kakou	ah-low-hah kah-koo	Greetings, everybody
'a'ole pilikia	ah-o-lay pee-lee-kee-ah	no problem, no trouble

PHRASES		
kamaʻaina	kah-mah-ay-nah	"child of the soil," native-born or long-time resident
kanaka maoli	kah-nah-kah mah-oh-lee	full-blooded hawaiian person
kipa mai	kee-pah mah-ee	You're welcome
mahalo nui loa	mah-ha-low new-ee low-ah	Thank you very much
maʻi kaʻi	mah-ee kah-ee	I am fine.
ʻolelo noʻeau	oh-lay-low no-ee-ah-oo	proverb, wise saying
owai kau inoa	oh-why kah-oo ee-no-ah	What is your name?
pehea ʻoe	pay-hay-ah oh-ay	How are you?
pau hana	pow hah-nah	end of the work day
ua kaumaha au	oo-ah cow-mah-hah ow	I am sorry

LOCAL FOODS AND DISHES

adobo: pork or chicken in a vinegar and garlic sauce
ʻahi: yellowfin tuna
arare: crisp rice crackers seasoned with soy sauce
azuki: sweetened red or black beans
butterfish: black cod
crack seed: popular snack of preserved fruits mixed with salt, sugar, and seasonings
dim sum: Chinese brunch of appetizer-size portions of food (often dumplings) dispensed from carts
halakahiki: pineapple
haupia: coconut pudding
heʻi: papaya
huli huli chicken: chicken barbequed on spits over an open grill
lau lau: meat and fish wrapped in leaves (usually taro or ti) and then baked or steamed
li hing mui: dried seasoned plum, a type of crack seed
lilikoʻi: passion fruit
limu: edible seaweed
loco moco: a fried egg on top of a hamburger, served over rice and smothered in gravy
lomi salmon: sushi-type salmon mixed with Maui onion, and seasoned
kalua pig: barbequed pork, cooked whole in an imu
katsu: pork or chicken deep-fried and served with a soy-based dipping sauce
kim chee: heavily seasoned pickled vegetables
kona coffee: coffee from beans grown in the upcountry Kona District of the Big Island
kulolo: dessert made of baked taro root mixed with coconut milk and honey or sugar
mahi mahi: dolphin fish
malassadas: sweet Portuguese doughnuts
mochi: balls of cooked, pounded sweet rice
musubi: rice ball wrapped in dried seaweed
niu: coconut
nori: dried, compressed seaweed
onaga: red snapper
ono: similar to mackerel or tuna
opae: shrimp
opakapaka: pink snapper
opihi: limpet (a shellfish delicacy)
plate lunch: two scoops white rice, macaroni salad, and a local-style meat or seafood entree
poi: paste-like food made of pounded taro root
poke: appetizer consisting of cubed raw fish, marinated and served with raw seaweed
puna goat cheese: rich creamy cheese from organically-raised goats in the Puna District of the Big Island, used in many regional cuisine dishes

saimin: Japanese noodle soup
shave ice: shaved ice topped with syrup, lighter and flakier than a snow cone
shoyu: Japanese word for soy sauce
spam: spiced ham in a can
tako: octapus
'ulu: breadfruit
wasabi: green, Japanese-style horseradish

LOCAL SPEAK

Auntie: respectful address for a female elder
an den: "What's up?" or expression of boredom
ass why: "That's the reason"
any hine: anything
bang 'em: to cause a collision
boo: pronoun, equivalent to man, guy etc...
brah: friend, bro
braddah: brother
broke da mout: delicious
buggah: a chap or a fellow
charge it: to assail a problem or obstacle (ex: a formidable wave)
chicken skin: goose bumps
choke: many, a large amount
choke cars: traffic
cockaroach: to steal
cruise/cruisin': to take it easy
da cute: how precious!
da kine: the kind (versatile pidgin phrase, can mean almost anything)
foa: used instead of "to"
grind: to eat
grinds: good food
hana hou: once more, again
Hele on: "Let's go"
Howzit?: condensation of the greeting, "How is it going?"
kay den: all right
Like beef?: equivalent of asking someone if they want to fight
moke: very large local (derogatory)
no can: unable to
shoots: ok ("Why not?")
slippah: flip-flop sandals, slippers
shaka: greeting in the form of a hand gesture ("Hang loose")
sistah: sister
stink eye: dirty look, sideward glance
talk stink: say something bad about somebody, gossip
talk story: chit chat, casual conversation
titah: brutish local woman, female moke (derogatory)
Uncle: respectful address for a male elder
whaddsdascoops: What's the scoop? What's going on?
wassamattayou: What's the matter with you?

WHO WE ARE

A NEW LET'S GO FOR 2003

With a sleeker look and innovative new content, we have revamped the entire series to reflect more than ever the needs and interests of the independent traveler. Here are just some of the improvements you will notice when traveling with the new *Let's Go*.

MORE PRICE OPTIONS

Still the best resource for budget travelers, *Let's Go* recognizes that everyone needs the occassional indulgence. Our "Big Splurges" indicate establishments that are actually worth those extra pennies (pulas, pesos, or pounds), and price-level symbols (❶ ❷ ❸ ❹ ❺) allow you to quickly determine whether an accommodation or restaurant will break the bank. We may have diversified, but we'll never lose our budget focus—"Hidden Deals" reveal the best-kept travel secrets.

BEYOND THE TOURIST EXPERIENCE

Our Alternatives to Tourism chapter offers ideas on immersing yourself in a new community through study, work, or volunteering.

AN INSIDER'S PERSPECTIVE

As always, every item is written and researched by our on-site writers. This year we have highlighted more viewpoints to help you gain an even more thorough understanding of the places you are visiting.

IN RECENT NEWS. *Let's Go* correspondents around the globe report back on current regional issues that may affect you as a traveler.

CONTRIBUTING WRITERS. Respected scholars and former *Let's Go* writers discuss topics on society and culture, going into greater depth than the usual guidebook summary.

THE LOCAL STORY. From the Parisian monk toting a cell phone to the Russian *babushka* confronting capitalism, *Let's Go* shares its revealing conversations with local personalities—a unique glimpse of what matters to real people.

FROM THE ROAD. Always helpful and sometimes downright hilarious, our researchers share useful insights on the typical (and atypical) travel experience.

SLIMMER SIZE

Don't be fooled by our new, smaller size. *Let's Go* is still packed with invaluable travel advice, but now it's easier to carry with a more compact design.

FORTY-THREE YEARS OF WISDOM

For over four decades *Let's Go* has provided the most up-to-date information on the hippest cafes, the most pristine beaches, and the best routes from border to border. It all started in 1960 when a few well-traveled students at Harvard University handed out a 20-page mimeographed pamphlet of their tips on budget travel to passengers on student charter flights to Europe. From humble beginnings, *Let's Go* has grown to cover six continents and *Let's Go: Europe* still reigns as the world's best-selling travel guide. This year we've beefed up our coverage of Latin America with *Let's Go: Costa Rica* and *Let's Go: Chile;* on the other side of the globe, we've added *Let's Go: Thailand* and *Let's Go: Hawaii.* Our new guides bring the total number of titles to 61, each infused with the spirit of adventure that travelers around the world have come to count on.

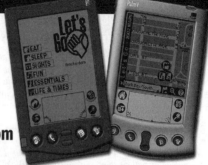

INDEX

Members SAVE More

Join the Student Advantage® Membership Program to save hundreds of dollars a year on food, clothing, travel and more! Members enjoy ongoing, exclusive savings at more than 15,000 locations around campus, online, and throughout the U.S.A. Here are just a few:

U·S AIRWAYS

Member-only discounts and
bonus Dividend Miles®

Foot Locker.

$10 OFF purchases of $50 or more
(some exclusions may apply)

Booking fee waived

15% OFF walk-up fares

Plus, receive the **Student Advantage Bonus Savings Book** with over
$200 in additional savings from J.Crew, Timberland®,
Student Advantage Tech Store and more!

JOIN TODAY!

Go to studentadvantage.com or call 1.877.2JOINSA and reference promotion code LET88P9001.
This code entitles you to special Membership pricing.

1-year Membership: $15.00*   (SAVE $5)

4-year Membership: $50.00*   (SAVE $10)

*Plus $2.50 shipping and handling for 1-year Membership and $5.00 for 4-year Membership.
Student Advantage® is a registered trademark and product of Student Advantage, Inc.

studentadvantage.com

Book your air, hotel, and transportation all in one place.

MAP INDEX

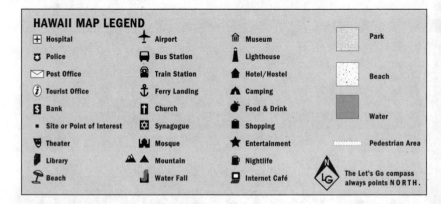

HAWAII MAP LEGEND

✚ Hospital	✈ Airport	🏛 Museum
🚓 Police	🚌 Bus Station	🗼 Lighthouse
✉ Post Office	🚂 Train Station	⚓ Hotel/Hostel
ⓘ Tourist Office	⚓ Ferry Landing	⛺ Camping
$ Bank	🏫 Church	🍎 Food & Drink
■ Site or Point of Interest	✡ Synagogue	🛍 Shopping
🎭 Theater	☪ Mosque	★ Entertainment
📖 Library	▲▲ Mountain	🍷 Nightlife
🏖 Beach	🌊 Water Fall	💻 Internet Café

Park

Beach

Water

Pedestrian Area

The Let's Go compass always points N O R T H.